Conduct and Oppositional Defiant Disorders

Epidemiology, Risk Factors, and Treatment

Conduct and Oppositional Defiant Disorders

Epidemiology, Risk Factors, and Treatment

WITHDRAWN

Edited by

CECILIA A. ESSAU
Westfälische Wilhelms–Universität Münster

2003

LAWRENCE ERLBAUM ASSOCIATES, PUBLISHERS
Mahwah, New Jersey   London

Lawrence Erlbaum Associates, Inc., Publishers
10 Industrial Avenue
Mahwah, New Jersey 07430

Cover design by Kathryn Houghtaling Lacey

Library of Congress Cataloging-in-Publication Data

Conduct and oppositional defiant disorders : epidemiology, risk factors, and treatment /
   Edited by Cecilia A. Essau.
      p. cm.
   Includes bibliographical references and index.
   ISBN 0-8058-4061-3 (cloth : alk. paper)
      1.   Conduct disorders in children. 2. Conduct disorders in adolescence. 3. Oppositional
Defiant disorder in children. 4. Oppositional defiant disorder in adolescence. I. Essau,
Cecilia.

RJ506.C65C65 2003
618.92'89—dc21

                                                                        2003040829

Books published by Lawrence Erlbaum Associates are printed on acid-free paper,
and their bindings are chosen for strength and durability.

Printed in the United States of America
10   9   8   7   6   5   4   3   2   1

Contents

PART IV: OUTSTANDING ISSUES

Preface

There is probably no other child and adolescent psychopathology that has attracted more attention than conduct disorder (CD) and oppositional defiant disorder (ODD). There are a number of reasons for the attention devoted to these disorders, their risk factors, and sequelae. First, they are among the most common disorders in children and adolescents in the general population. They also represent the most common reasons for referral to children's mental health or counseling services. Second, the scope of impairment in children with CD is great; including impaired educational achievement, poor social relationships, and involvement with the legal system. Third, CD and ODD are not only chronic, but also tend to increase risk for developing comorbid disorders such as depressive and substance use disorders. Fourth, CD also entails costs for the society, both monetarily and socially. The monetary cost of CD is enormous with figures in the hundreds of millions: Children with this disorder are involved in multiple systems such as the mental health, juvenile justice, special education, and social services. The social costs include the "impaired" and unsafe learning environments in schools as a result of behaviors of children with CD. The quality of life for the victims of children's antisocial and aggressive acts and for those who live in high-crime neighborhoods is greatly reduced.

The frequency, chronicity, associated cost, and the debilitating consequences of CD and ODD has resulted in an explosion of studies conducted to identify risk factors and gold standards for the prevention and treatment of these disorders. Consequently, the literature has been accumulating at a fast and exciting pace. In the 14 chapters to follow, contributors provide state of the art, comprehensive reviews and analyses of almost all aspects CD and ODD.

The contributors have been carefully selected. They are the world's leading experts in their respective areas. Organized into four parts, the volume begins with a general overview of CD and ODD. Part I summarizes classification and assessment, epidemiology and comorbidity, as well as course and outcome. Part II examines factors that put children and adolescents at risk—familial/genetic, and neuropsychological and neuroendocrine. Part III presents numerous empirically supported approaches to prevention and cognitive-behavioral and pharmacological treatment of CD. An epilogue reviews progress and unresolved issues and suggests needs for future research.

The wealth of information about the definition, prevalence, comorbidity, course, risk factors, prevention, and treatment of CD will make this volume a valuable reference for both the novice and the expert and to both the clinicians and the researchers. I hope this volume will not only serve to illustrate our current knowledge of CD and ODD but may well stimulate further researcher toward improving our understanding of these disorders.

I acknowledge the efforts of the contributors, whose expertise and dedication to the project have been outstanding. It has been a great honor for me to work with such an outstanding group of scholars. Without them, a comprehensive coverage of the various topics would not have been easily achieved. Additionally, I acknowledge the support and patience of the staff at Lawrence Erlbaum Associates.

—*Cecilia A. Essau*

GENERAL ISSUES

1

Classification and Assessment

Bryan R. Loney
Elizabeth N. Lima
Florida State University

Youth antisocial behavior has increased steadily over the past several decades despite improvements in the identification and treatment of the most severe offenders (Silverthorn & Frick, 1999; Snyder & Sickmund, 1995; Wilson, 2000). Recent school shootings have been highly publicized and sensationalized events that do not capture the more dominant undercurrent of youth antisocial activity. The Office of Juvenile Justice and Delinquency Prevention has published data from the past 2 decades that highlight this disturbing trend. From 1983 to 1992, the juvenile violent crime rate increased 100% with an almost identical increase in the number of boys and girls seen in court for suspected delinquent activity (see Silverthorn & Frick, 1999; Snyder & Sickmund, 1995). The most recent Office of Juvenile Justice and Delinquency Prevention data indicate an 83% increase in female criminal cases and a 39% increase in male criminal cases during the period of 1988 to 1997 (Wilson, 2000). Youth antisocial behavior is increasing and at a high cost to society in such forms as property destruction, treatment needs of the victim(s) and perpetrator, and general legal and institutional expenses.

This chapter focuses on the classification and assessment of conduct disorders (CDs), and we are indebted to the earlier discussions of researchers who have made significant contributions in this area (e.g., Achenbach, 1995; Achenbach & Edelbrock, 1978; Frick, 1998; Kazdin, 1995; Kolko, 1994; Loeber, Burke, Lahey, Winters, & Zera, 2000; McMahon, 1994; and Quay, 1972, 1979, 1986, 1999). The label of CDs is intended to include the negative, argumentative, and defiant behaviors characteristic of oppositional defiant disorder (ODD), as well as the aggressive and rule-violating behaviors characteristic of a CD diagnosis. In this chapter, ODD is viewed as a mild variant of CD, and general reference to CD is intended to include the variety of behaviors in both ODD and CD diagnoses. A system of classification provides rules for placing individuals in distinct groups or diagnostic categories. In child psychopathology, a primary goal of classification is the documentation of patterns of behavior that are unique in terms of etiology, developmental course, outcome, associated variables, and effective treatments (Kazdin, 1995). What follows is a discussion of the most prominent approaches to classifying CD. These can be divided into two models referred to as the *multivariate* and *medical models*. Common threads in these approaches are discussed. However, the inherent imperfections of any one classification system are also addressed. As Millon (1991) noted, "In fields such as . . . psychopathology, classifications are, in considerable measure, splendid fictions, compelling notions, or austere formulas devised to give coherence to their inherently imprecise subjects" (p. 246). Millon further stated that "Prevailing frameworks must continue to be challenged, and imaginative alternatives encouraged" (p. 259).

MULTIVARIATE MODEL

The multivariate approach to classifying CD is a bottom-up approach that attempts to determine covarying symptom patterns or syndromes through the use of multivariate statistical techniques (e.g., factor and cluster analysis). This approach is relatively atheoretical; however, it is not theory free, as researchers must decide what behaviors to assess and enter into analyses. Quay (1986) summarized the results of multivariate studies dating back to the seminal work of Hewitt and Jenkins (1946) who conducted an early empirical investigation employing both statistical techniques and clinical interpretation to arrive at two CD dimensions labeled *unsocialized aggressive* and *socialized delinquent*.

Consistent throughout the multivariate investigations is the presence of separate dimensions for overt (or confrontive) and covert (or concealed) behavior. Loeber and Schmaling (1985) conducted a meta-analysis of 22 studies that employed factor or cluster analysis. They used a multidimensional scaling approach to summarize the findings from these studies and to determine if CD is best represented by one or multiple dimensions. Their results indicate the presence of two dimensions: an overt dimension characterized by behaviors such as fighting, temper tantrums and arguing, and a covert dimension characterized by behaviors such as stealing, substance use, and fire setting. Quay (1986) simultaneously conducted a qualitative review of 61 factor analyses spanning approximately 40 years. The results of his investigation support the presence of two similar CD dimensions that he labeled *undersocialized aggressive* and *socialized aggressive*. These dimensions roughly map onto the overt–covert distinction. The undersocialized dimension is characterized by symptoms such as fighting, defiance, and temper tantrums, and the socialized dimension is characterized by group stealing, truancy, and loyalty to a delinquent peer group.

The distinction between overt and covert conduct problems was further confirmed by a second generation multivariate study conducted by Achenbach, Conners, Quay, Verhulst, and Howell (1989), who conducted a large cross-national investigation of 8,194 American and Dutch clinic-referred children between the ages of 6 and 16. Their intent was to assess the robustness of earlier dimensions across age, gender, method variance (i.e., different rating scales), and cultural setting. Parent rating scale data were obtained using two of the most widely used broadband measures, the Child Behavior Checklist (Achenbach & Edelbrock, 1983) and the ACQ Behavior Checklist (Achenbach, Conners, & Quay, 1983). Consistent with previous research, Achenbach et al. (1989) found robust support for two CD dimensions labeled *aggressive* and *delinquent* that were very similar to the overt–covert and undersocialized–socialized distinctions of prior investigations. The aggressive or overt dimension contains a blend of ODD and aggressive CD symptoms listed in the fourth edition of the *Diagnostic and Statistical Manual of Mental Disorders* (4th ed. [*DSM–IV*]; American Psychiatric Association, 1994). In contrast, the delinquent or covert dimension is more uniquely associated with nonaggressive CD symptoms such as status (e.g., truancy) and property offenses (e.g., vandalism; see Frick, 1998; Loeber et al., 2000).

Frick et al. (1993) recently conducted a meta-analysis of over 60 factor analyses representing 28,401 children and adolescents. Using multidimensional scaling analyses, Frick et al. (1993) found support for an overt–covert dimension relatively consistent with earlier research. However, there was also indication of a separate destructive–nondestructive dimension that, when crossed with the overt–covert dimension, produced four CD groupings: overt-destructive (e.g., aggressive behavior), overt-nondestructive (e.g., oppositional and argumentative behavior), covert-destructive (e.g., property violations), and covert-nondestructive (e.g., status offenses). Frick and Ellis (1999) later noted that this division of CD is more consistent with legal classification systems and recent research suggesting the presence of multiple CD subtypes with unique correlates.

The studies discussed so far have focused on the dimensional nature of broadly defined CD. Another approach has been to focus specifically on the dimensional nature of aggressive behavior. For example, there is a developing literature on the distinction between reactive and proactive aggression (Atkins & Stoff, 1993; Brown, Atkins, Obsborne, & Milnamow, 1996; Dodge &

Coie, 1987). The former is hostile and retaliatory and is associated with a tendency to misinterpret social cues and attribute hostile intent to ambiguous or neutral social feedback (Dodge & Coie, 1987). Proactive aggression is premeditated or instrumental in nature and involves a deliberate attempt to manipulate others for personal gain (Crick & Dodge, 1996; Dodge & Coie, 1987; Frick & Ellis, 1999). Factor analytic investigations have generally substantiated a distinction between reactive and proactive behavior (Brown et al., 1996). However, Frick and Ellis (1999) indicated that there is an asymmetrical relation between the dimensions that could limit their usefulness in classifying CD. There are children exhibiting elevated levels of reactive aggression in the absence of concurrent proactive aggression. However, children exhibiting elevated proactive aggression are usually elevated in reactive behavior (Brown et al., 1996). Research has suggested that proactive aggression is more predictive of later antisocial behavior than reactive aggression (Vitaro, Gendreau, Tremblay, & Oligny, 1998). However, the independence of these dimensions from one another and from the general covert–overt distinction is in need of further study (Frick & Ellis, 1999; Loeber et al., 2000).

Loeber et al. (2000) described other categories or distinctions that could assist in refining current multivariate models such as the distinction between aggression that is impulsive versus nonimpulsive, predatory versus affective, and indirect versus direct (see also Vitiello & Stoff, 1997). Björkqvist and colleagues (Björkqvist, Lagerspetz, & Kaukiainen, 1992; Lagerspetz, Björkqvist, & Peltonen, 1988) developed the indirect versus direct distinction which is similar to a newer area of research suggesting an important distinction between relational and physical aggression (Crick, 1996; Crick & Grotpeter, 1995). Research on indirect versus direct and relational versus physical aggression is particularly important as it pertains to a growing interest in gender differences in CD. Historically, CD has been viewed as a predominately male disorder (Webster-Stratton, 1996; Zocolillo, 1993). For this reason, research on CD has often excluded female participants.

Confusion regarding the nature and development of severe female antisocial behavior is partly attributable to an overreliance on gender-biased symptoms (Webster-Stratton, 1996; Zahn-Waxler, 1993; Zocolillo, 1993). Current conceptualizations of CD emphasize physical aggression that overshadows the more indirect, covert, and interpersonal antisocial behavior that is clinically relevant and more prevalent in females. Crick and her colleagues (Crick, 1996, 1997; Crick & Grotpeter, 1995; Werner & Crick, 1999) have developed a program of research focused on expanding current conceptualizations of CD to include deliberate attempts to manipulate or control the relationships of others (i.e., relational aggression). Initial factor analytic investigations support the presence of a distinct relational aggression dimension (Crick & Grotpeter, 1995) that includes the spreading of rumors and the exclusion of others from desired peer groups and activities. Research has suggested that relational aggression symptoms are as predictive of impairments in emotional, behavioral, and peer functioning as traditional CD symptoms (Crick, 1997; Crick, Casas, & Mosher, 1997).

MEDICAL MODEL

The medical model is a top down approach that attempts to define qualitatively distinct diagnostic categories and symptoms based initially on the assumption of an underlying disease process with a specific etiology (Hinshaw, 1987; Kamphaus & Frick, 2002; Kazdin, 1995). There is an assumption of a clear break between normal and abnormal functioning based on variables such as the number, severity, persistence, and impairment of symptoms (Kazdin, 1995). Early medical models were particularly influenced by psychoanalytic theory; however, more recent models have attempted to employ an atheoretical approach to symptom assessment akin to the multivariate model (Kamphaus & Frick, 2002). This review highlights the *DSM–IV* that is promulgated by the American Psychiatric Association and is the officially sanctioned diagnostic system used in the United States. A discussion of similarities and differences with the *International Classification of Diseases* (10th ed. [*ICD–10*]; World Health Organization [WHO], 1992) follows, as the *ICD–10* is the official classification system of the WHO, which has well over 100 member nations (Thangavelu & Martin, 1995). Our review focuses on the past 2 decades including the *DSM–III* (3rd ed.; American Psychiatric Association, 1980), *DSM–III–R* (3rd ed., rev.; American Psychiatric Association, 1987), and *DSM–IV* to address current trends and to make recommendations for future diagnostic systems. Of note, the *DSM–IV* was recently revised to incorporate new research on the diagnostic categories without any substantive change to diagnoses or diagnostic criteria. Therefore, the current discussion of the *DSM–IV* pertains to the recent text revision (TR), the *DSM–IV–TR* (American Psychiatric Association, 2000).

The *DSM–III* was introduced in 1980 and represented a substantive increase in the number of childhood diagnoses, symptom lists, and disorder descriptions from two pages in the *DSM–II* (2nd ed.; American Psychiatric Association, 1968) to over 65 pages in the *DSM–III* (Kazdin, 1995). The *DSM–III* diagnosis of oppositional disorder (OD) contains negative, argumentative, and mild CD symptoms that do not violate major social norms or the rights of others. The CD diagnosis encompasses two subtypes, undersocialized–socialized and aggressive–nonaggressive, which can be crossed to form four separate diagnostic categories (e.g., undersocialized-aggressive, undersocialized-nonaggressive, etc.). In contrast to OD, the CD symptoms represent more severe behavioral transgressions that violate the rights of others or major societal norms. The designation of undersocialized is based on whether there is evidence of affective and interpersonal impairments resulting in sufficient difficulty initiating and sustaining social attachments.

Research attempting to substantiate the CD categories, particularly the undersocialized–socialized distinction, has found that undersocialized CD is characterized by more aggressive behavior, more sensation seeking, poorer institutional adjustment, poorer response to treatment, and more probation violations than socialized CD (see Frick, 1998; Frick & Ellis, 1999; Quay, 1979, 1986). Furthermore, there is evidence that undersocialized CD is uniquely related to a lower resting heart rate, low levels of serotonin, and decreased reactivity of the sympathetic branch of the autonomic nervous system (Frick & Ellis, 1999; Lahey, Loeber, Quay, Frick, & Grimm, 1992; Quay, 1987; Rogeness, Hernandez, Macedo, & Mitchell, 1982). Interestingly, these correlates are similar to the associated variables found for adults and children characterized by elevated levels of emotional detachment in psychopathy. However, despite studies validating the distinction, definitional confusion and related reliability concerns resulted in the removal of the undersocialized–socialized distinction in revisions of the *DSM* (Frick & Ellis, 1999).

DSM–III–R and DSM–IV

Table 1.1 depicts the change in select *DSM–III* subtypes across subsequent revisions of the manual along with a list of current ODD and CD symptoms contained in the *DSM–IV*. The arrows included in the table refer to proposed overlap between subtypes in the *DSM–III, DSM–III–R*, and *DSM–IV*. The *DSM–III–R* bears many similarities to its predecessor. The primary change was an attempt to develop a more explicit format for capturing the undersocialized–socialized distinction of the *DSM–III* (Frick & Ellis, 1999). The two subtypes of the *DSM–III* were supplanted with three CD subtypes: the group type, the solitary aggressive type, and a residual category referred to as the *undifferentiated type*. An emphasis was placed on the social context of CD in an attempt to capture the most observable properties of the undersocialized–socialized distinction. The new diagnostic labels were based on research suggesting that most children exhibiting socialized (or group) CD display primarily nonaggressive CD symptoms, whereas most children exhibiting undersocialized (or solitary) CD display primarily aggressive CD symptoms (Frick, 1998; Hinshaw, Lahey, & Hart, 1993). Kolko (1994) likened the group type to the *DSM–III* socialized-nonaggressive type and the solitary aggressive type to the *DSM–III* undersocialized-aggressive type.

Specific changes to the CD diagnosis included significant expansion and refinement of diagnostic criteria, a three-symptom diagnostic threshold as opposed to a two-symptom threshold in the *DSM–III*, and the removal of se-

TABLE 1.1

Changes to the *Diagnostic and Statistical Manual of Mental Disorders* (DSM)
Nomenclature and Current ODD/CD Criteria

1980 DSM–III	*1987* DSM–III–R	*1994* DSM–IV
1. Undersocialized-aggressive Aggressive and rule-violating behavior accompanied by emotional detachment in the form of minimal peer loyalty and deficient empathy and affection for others	⇒ Solitary-aggressive Aggressive and rule-violating behavior that is primarily initiated by an individual and not a delinquent peer group	⇒ Childhood-onset CD Aggressive and rule-violation behavior with one symptom present before the age of 10
Diagnostic criteria: One out of 2 symptoms of aggression including physical violence against persons *and* no more than 1 out of 5 signs of emotional connection such as friendships that have lasted over 6 months	Diagnostic criteria: Three out of 13 aggressive and/or rule-violating behaviors including stealing, lying, physical fighting, and vandalism; symptoms have been present for at least 6 months	Diagnostic criteria: Three out of 15 aggressive and/or rule-violating behaviors including bullying, fire-setting, lying to obtain goods or favors, and truancy; symptoms have occurred in the past 12 months with at least one symptom occurring in the past 6 months
2. Socialized-nonaggressive Aggressive and rule-violating behavior committed primarily in a group context by a child with evidence of social attachment	⇒ Group Aggressive and rule-violating behavior committed primarily in a group context	⇒ Adolescent-onset CD Aggressive and/or rule-violating behavior with no symptoms present before the age of 10
Diagnostic criteria: One out of 2 aggression symptoms including physical violence against persons *and* more than 1 out of 5 signs of emotional connection such as friendships that have lasted over 6 months	Diagnostic criteria: Three out of 13 aggressive and/or rule-violating behaviors including stealing, lying, physical fighting, and vandalism; symptoms have been present for at least 6 months	Diagnostic criteria: Three out of 15 aggressive and/or rule-violating behaviors including bullying, fire-setting, lying to obtain goods or favors, and truancy; symptoms have occurred in past 12 months
3. Atypical Residual diagnostic category	⇒ Undifferentiated Residual diagnostic category	⇒ Disruptive behavior, NOS Residual diagnostic category

(Continued)

TABLE 1.1
(Continued)

DSM–IV ODD	DSM–IV CD	
1. Often loses temper	1. Often bullies, threatens, or intimidates others	9. Has deliberately destroyed others' property
2. Often argues with adults	2. Often initiates physical fights	10. Has broken into someone else's house, building, car
3. Often actively defies or refuses to comply with adults' requests or rules	3. Has used a weapon that can cause serious physical harm to others	11. Often lies to obtain goods or favors or to avoid obligations
4. Often deliberately annoys people	4. Has been physically cruel to people	12. Has stolen items of nontrivial value without confronting a victim
5. Often blames others for his or her mistakes	5. Has been physically cruel to animals	13. Often stays out at night despite parental prohibitions
6. Is often touchy or easily annoyed	6. Has stolen while confronting a victim	14. Has run away from home overnight at least twice while living in parental or parental surrogate home
7. Is often angry and resentful	7. Has forced someone into sexual activity	15. Is often truant from school
8. Is often spiteful or vindictive	8. Has deliberately engaged in fire setting with the intention of causing serious damage	

Note. ODD = oppositional defiant disorder; CD = conduct disorder; NOS = not otherwise specified.

lect symptoms such as "bullies" that exhibited poor discriminant validity with respect to CD diagnoses (Loeber, Lahey, & Thomas, 1991). Additionally, the *DSM–III–R* collapsed multiple symptom lists representative of each of the subtypes into one 13-item list containing more specific criteria. Subsequently, Lahey et al. (1990) provided structured interview data on clinic-referred children indicating a drop in the prevalence rate of CD based on the *DSM–III–R* formulation with a concurrent increase in criterion validity (e.g., association with school suspensions). Lahey et al. (1994) found that a three-symptom threshold provided an optimal level of reliability while maximizing the association with impairment criteria (e.g., police contacts).

Changes to the OD diagnosis included a revised label (i.e., ODD), a larger symptom list, a five-symptom diagnostic threshold as opposed to a two-symptom threshold in the *DSM–III*, and the provision of a normative comparison statement. A diagnosis was only to be provided if the behavior appeared exaggerated relative to children of the same mental level (Quay, 1999). The ODD diagnosis was also based on five out of nine symptoms rather than two out of five symptoms in the *DSM–III*. Lahey et al. (1994) provided data suggesting a similar drop in prevalence and increased association with impairment criterion. Select criteria were removed (i.e., "violation of minor rules" and "stubbornness") based on a comparison with normative data and an inability to discriminate between CD categories. Additionally, a provision was added that a child meeting criteria for a CD diagnosis could not be diagnosed with ODD.

Although the *DSM–III–R* represented a significant step forward in the blending of the medical and empirical models of classification, the evaluation of the *DSM–III–R* criteria was to a large extent based on post hoc analyses designed to validate a classification system that was already in use (Loeber et al., 2000; Shaffer et al., 1989). This changed dramatically with the development and introduction of the *DSM–IV*. The development process of the *DSM–IV* included the formation of several expert committees supervising 150 literature reviews, 40 data reanalyses, and 12 field trials (Essau, Feehan, & Ustun, 1997; Lahey et al., 1994; Thangavelu & Martin, 1995). Research was a guiding force behind the revision process with the work groups carrying more responsibility than in the formation of prior manuals (Volkmar & Schwab-Stone, 1996).

The *DSM–IV* ODD and CD diagnoses retained the hierarchical nature introduced in the *DSM–III–R* with a diagnosis of CD precluding a separate ODD diagnosis. In addition, the symptom lists are quite similar with more modest revision of criteria than in prior revisions. For example, the ODD diagnosis removed one previous criterion (i.e., "often swears and uses obscene language") and shifted the diagnostic threshold from five out of nine symptoms to four out of eight symptoms. This new symptom threshold was based on field trial data suggesting that a 4-symptom diagnosis maximized agreement with clinician diagnosis and impairment criterion (Lahey et al., 1994). The biggest change was an emphasis on the developmental trajectory of CD symptoms based on age of onset (American Psychiatric Association, 1994; Frick & Loney, 1999; Moffitt, 1993a, 1993b).

DSM–IV CD contains a childhood-onset subtype and an adolescent-onset subtype derived from a number of prnospective longitudinal investigations suggesting that similar behavioral presentations that vary primarily in age of onset are characterized by different underlying risk factors and causal mechanisms (see Dilalla & Gottesman, 1989; Loeber et al., 2000; McMahon, 1994; Moffitt, 1993a). For example, research conducted by Moffitt and colleagues (Moffitt, 1993a; Moffitt, Caspi, Dickson, Silva, & Stanton, 1996) indicated that childhood-onset conduct problems are unique in terms of the severity and persistence of behavioral difficulties and the association with various child and familial risk factors including significant attention-deficit/hyperactivity disorder (ADHD) symptoms, verbal intellectual impairments, heightened parenting difficulties, and psychopathic traits. Despite the shift in emphasis away from level of socialization or peer relatedness, the early-onset category is quite similar to the earlier *undersocialized* label in terms of symptoms and associated variables (Quay, 1999).

ICD–10 (WHO, 1992)

In contrast to the *DSM*, the *ICD* is broadly focused on medical and mental health concerns. The first edition to contain mental health diagnoses was the *ICD–6* (WHO, 1948), with the *ICD–10* being introduced by the WHO in 1992. Thangavelu and Martin (1995) provided a thorough review of the similarities and differences between the *DSM* and *ICD* resulting in the statement that the two manuals are different dialects and not different languages. Both have employed a multiaxial framework to produce categorical diagnoses using a polythetic approach to symptom assessment. Both systems have also based changes on expert committees and field trial data and cover almost identical symptom content for the child disruptive behavior disorders. However, Volkmar and Schwab-Stone (1996) suggested that the *DSM* places a heavier emphasis on symptom reification that has the potential to produce less parsimonious diagnostic decisions. This is evident in the *ICD*'s provision for comorbid diagnostic categories.

Table 1.2 contains an outline of CD categories covered by the *ICD* along with representative symptom content. The *ICD–10* provides one diagnosis for children exhibiting prominent symptoms of both ADHD and CD labeled *hyperkinetic conduct disorder* that takes the place of two separate diagnoses in the *DSM–IV*. This distinction is supported by recent research suggesting that children exhibiting prominent symptoms of ADHD and CD are characterized by an earlier age of onset of conduct problems (Moffitt, 1990; Walker, Lahey, Hynd, & Frame, 1987) and a greater variety and severity of antisocial offending (Frick & Loney, 1999; Hinshaw, 1994; Loeber et al., 2000) than CD children without an ADHD diagnosis. The *ICD–10* also contains other comorbid categories such as depressive conduct disorder and mixed disorder of conduct and emotions.

The *ICD–10* also varies from the *DSM–IV* with respect to its treatment of ODD. The *ICD* is firm in its view of ODD as a mild variant of CD that is a subtype of CD rather than a separate diagnosis (Kaplan & Sadock, 1998). The symptom lists for ODD and CD are collapsed but differentiated with respect to level of severity. There is one 23-item list that contains the same symptoms in the 8-item ODD and 15-item CD of the *DSM*. The *ICD–10* shares the same symptom diagnostic thresholds and views a CD diagnosis as preemptive of an ODD diagnosis. Finally, the *ICD–10* differs with respect to the CD subtypes because it has retained the undersocialized versus socialized CD distinction. The *ICD–10* has labeled these categories *unsocialized* and *socialized* and argued that this distinction has obtained the greatest support from empirical investigation of youth conduct problems (WHO, 1992). The distinction is based primarily on level of peer connectedness in antisocial activity similar to the *DSM–III* classification approach.

TABLE 1.2
ICD–10 CDs and Related Diagnostic Categories

Subtypes	Comorbid Diagnostic Categories

1. ODD
  Analogous to *DSM–IV* ODD and viewed as a mild form of CD; characterized by negative, argumentative, and defiant behaviors such as arguing with adults
2. Unsocialized CD
  Analogous to *DSM–IV* CD with the additional criterion of a lack of connection with peers and/or an absence of lasting friendships
3. Socialized CD
  Analogous to *DSM–IV* CD with the additional criterion of evidence of normal connection with peers
4. CD confined to the family context
  CD in which the individual's disturbance occurs only in the family environment
5. CD unspecified
  Individual meets criteria for CD, but specific subtype cannot be established
	1. Hyperkinetic CD
	  Individual meets diagnostic criteria for ADHD and CD
	2. Depressive CD
	  Individual meets diagnostic criteria for CD and one of the mood disorders
	3. Mixed disorders of conduct and emotions
	  Individual meets criteria for *CD* and an additional neurotic, stress-related, somatoform disorder in the *ICD–10*
	Specifiers
	1. Age of onset
	  Childhood onset = at least one CD symptom occurs before age 10
	  Adolescent onset = No CD symptom occurs before age 10
	2. Severity level
	  Mild
	  Moderate
	  Severe

Note. ICD–10 = International Classification of Diseases (10th ed.); ODD = oppositional defiant disorder; CD = conduct disorder; *DSM–IV = Diagnostic and Statistical Manual of Mental Disorders* (4th ed.); ADHD = attention deficit hyperactivity disorder.

CONSIDERATIONS FOR FUTURE DIAGNOSTIC SYSTEMS

One issue that will need to be addressed in future revisions of the *DSM* and *ICD* is the limited focus on principles of developmental psychopathology. The *DSM–IV* is to be commended for its emphasis on developmental trajectories represented largely by age-of-onset distinctions. However, current ODD and CD symptom criteria are limited with respect to addressing age-specific behavioral manifestations and changes in behavioral topography across time (i.e., heterotypic continuity; Garber, 1984; Kamphaus & Frick, 2002; Kazdin, 1995; McMahon, 1994). Achenbach (1995) argued that the top-down approach of current categorical systems is based on minimal data particularly with respect to the discriminant utility of symptoms between genders and within more specified age ranges. Kazdin (1995) similarly argued that the CD criteria are "delineated in a fixed way so that they are applied equally across the full period of childhood and adolescence. Yet perhaps symptoms required to meet the diagnosis should vary with age and sex" (pp. 25–26). An important first step is to continue to address the robustness of current diagnoses and subtypes across gender and finer age distinctions. For example, the applicability of many CD symptoms and symptom threshold levels for infants and young children is in need of further investigation (McMahon, 1994; Shaffer et al., 1989).

The *DSM* and *ICD* recognize two broad developmental trajectories to CD, but recent research has suggested further division of the childhood-onset category (Frick, 1998; Hogan, 1999). Moffitt et al. (1996) found that approximately 50% of children with childhood-onset CD do not persist in their antisocial behavior into adolescence. This has led researchers to consider the unique qualities of the persistent early-onset CD children. Lynam (1996, 1998) has proposed that comorbid ADHD symptoms differentiate the most severe behavioral presentations. However, Frick and colleagues (Barry et al., 2000; Frick, 1998; Frick et al., in press) have argued that the presence of a callous and unemotional interpersonal style (e.g., superficial charm, shallow emotions, and lack of guilt) is associated with a more severe pattern of antisocial and aggressive behavior, a reward dominant response style, and impairments in the processing of fearful and aversive stimuli (Blair, 1999; Frick, 1998; Frick, Lilienfeld, Ellis, Loney, & Silverthorn, 1999; Loney, Frick, Clements, Ellis, & Kerlin, in press). Based on these findings, Frick (1998) proposed a division of the childhood-onset subtype into separate callous-unemotional and impulsive conduct problems groups.

Research on female antisocial behavior is currently attempting to address the applicability of developmental models derived largely from male samples. Based on an extensive review of the female antisocial behavior research literature, Silverthorn and Frick (1999) argued that female CD presentations are more homogeneous in age of onset, severity of behavior, and risk factors than male CD presentations. Female CD is described as similar to the adolescent-onset trajectory in timing but similar to the childhood-onset trajectory in terms of severity of behavior and correlates with established child, parenting, and familial risk factors. This model was recently challenged by Moffitt and Caspi (2001) who presented preliminary data supporting the childhood- versus adolescent-onset model in a female sample. Addressing indirect and relational aggression symptoms will likely assist in bringing clarity to this issue. Current research has suggested that boys and girls are similar in rates of preadolescent aggression when collapsing across relational and physical aggression categories (see Crick, 1997). Future research will need to address the utility of expanding *DSM–IV* and *ICD–10* symptom sets to include relational aggression items.

Researchers must also continue to address the independence of ODD and CD. Support for separate diagnoses rests primarily on the developmental asymmetry between ODD and CD. Research has suggested that most children who meet criteria for CD prior to puberty will also meet criteria for an earlier diagnosis of ODD. However, approximately 75% of children who meet criteria for a diagnosis of ODD do not progress to a diagnosis of CD during the next 3 years. Furthermore, there is a significant number of children that develop CD during adolescence without indication of a prior diagnosis of ODD (Lahey et al., 1992, 1994). Despite this developmental asymmetry between the disorders, the *ICD–10* takes a stance that is more consistent with the bulk of research in this area. The greatest support for ODD as a subtype of CD comes from research demonstrating that ODD and CD are associated with the same quality but different quantity of associated variables. For example, Loeber, Green, Lahey, and Stouthamer-Loeber (1991) found that both ODD and CD demonstrate significant relations to family adversity, history of antisocial behavior, socioeconomic status, and parental antisocial behavior. Further support for viewing ODD as a mild variant of CD is documented in the previously reviewed investigations suggesting that ODD and mild CD symptoms tend to cluster together in factor analytic investigations. These findings support the framework espoused in the *ICD–10*. However, the similarities between the *ICD–10* and *DSM–IV* should not be understated. Both respect the hierarchical nature of ODD and CD, viewing a diagnosis of CD as precluding an ODD diagnosis. The treatment of diagnostic comorbidities is a more complicated manner. Further research is needed to substantiate the incremental validity of comorbid diagnoses, particularly diagnoses with an apparent lack of research investigation such as CD confined to the family context (Quay, 1999).

The *DSM* and *ICD* both indicate the importance of an age-of-onset specifier to the CD diagnosis. A principal strength of the age-of-onset variable is the potential ability to capture many aspects of the prior undersocialized–socialized distinction using a more explicit and reliable criterion of age (Frick & Ellis, 1999). Unfortunately, there is research that has suggested the need for caution in interpreting parent and child report of age of onset. Angold, Erkanli, Costello, and Rutter (1996) assessed the reliability and precision of parent and child report of conduct problems using a structured interview administered to 87 clinic-referred children and adolescents ages 8 to 18. Participants were administered a structured interview on two occasions separated by a mean interval of 5 days. Surprisingly, only 42% of child age-of-onset responses and 60% of parent age-of-onset responses to the two interviews fell within 1 year of one another. Additionally, many symptoms were reported to be present on one but not both interviews. These results suggest that parents and children are similarly unreliable in their reporting of age-of-onset information.

Given these concerns and the potential for further subtyping of the early-onset CD category, future revisions should consider the utility of symptom lists designed to more reliably and validly assess the interpersonal and affective features of the undersocialized category. Frick and Hare (2001) developed a multi-informant measure that has been used to uniquely predict chil-

TABLE 1.3
A Comparison of Undersocialized CD and APSD Callous-Unemotional Items

DSM–III *Criteria for Undersocialized CD*	*Callous-Unemotional Scale From the APSD*
1. Has one or more peer-group friendships that have lasted over six months	1. Is concerned about the feelings of others
2. Extends himself or herself for others even when no immediate advantage is likely	2. Feels bad or guilty
3. Apparently feels guilt or remorse when such a reaction is appropriate (not just when caught in difficulty)	3. Is concerned about schoolwork
4. Avoids blaming or informing on companions	4. Keeps promises
5. Shares concern for the welfare of friends or companions	5. Does not show emotions
	6. Keeps the same friends

Note. CD = conduct disorder; APSD = Antisocial Process Screening Device. CD characterized by no more than one indicator of the five signs of attachment listed. DSM-III criteria for undersocialized CD were reprinted with permission from the *Diagnostic and Statistical Manual of Mental Disorders, Third Edition*. Text revision. Copyright © 1980 American Psyciatric Association. The Antisocial Process Screening Device items were reproduced with permission, copyright 2001. Multi-Health Systems Inc. All rights reserved. In the USA, P.O. Box 950, North Tonawanda, NY 14120-0950, 1-800-456-3003. In Canada, 3770 Victoria Park Ave., Toronto, ON M2H 3M6, 1-800-268-6011. Internationally, +1-416-492-3343. Author names: Paul J. K. Frick, Ph.D and Robert D. Hare, Ph.D.

dren exhibiting cognitive–emotional, behavioral, and family dysfunction similar to severe adult antisocial offenders (Frick, 1998; Loney, Frick, Ellis, & McCoy, 1998). This measure taps a callous and unemotional interpersonal style in a more explicit and reliable fashion than prior attempts to capture similar qualities using descriptive statements associated with the *undersocialized* label. See Table 1.3 for a side-by-side comparison of the *DSM–III* undersocialized CD category and the Antisocial Process Screening Device (APSD; Frick & Hare, 2001) callous-unemotional items. Research on the APSD requires replication in increasingly diverse samples; however, it would be useful to consider whether items contained on this scale could serve as an additional measure to be considered in subtyping the early-onset category. If the distinction between impulsive and callous-unemotional CD is justified by future research efforts, it is conceivable to imagine qualifiers related to both ADHD and callous-unemotional traits in future diagnostic manuals.

ASSESSMENT OF CHILD CONDUCT DISORDERS

Diagnoses such as CD are frequently criticized as being overused. The use of a well-constructed assessment battery employing both categorical and dimensional measures of behavioral functioning assists in minimizing these concerns. Kazdin (1995) suggested that no assessment measure is "free of some source of bias, artifact, or judgment" (p. 47). This sentiment is reflected in the current focus on developing multimethod and multi-informant assessment batteries that assess CD across time and situation. There is substantial variety to the assessment batteries that are employed in mental health and medical care offices. Time and staff constraints can lead to the use of minimal measures (e.g., one or two rating scales) and a brief unstructured interview. This approach is not supported by the broader assessment literature and has the potential to distort symptom patterns, to miss important associated features and comorbid conditions, and to heighten rates of false-positive and negative diagnoses.

The core of a multimethod, multi-informant assessment for CD contains an interview, rating scale, and potentially observation data obtained from parent, child, and teacher (Altepeter & Korger, 1999; Craig & Pepler, 1997; Essau et al., 1997; Frauenglass & Routh, 1999; Kamphaus & Frick, 2002). The use of a multimethod, multi-informant battery assumes that no one measure is perfect and that multiple measures allow for a more reliable assessment of symptom content areas akin to a latent variable in structural equation modeling (Altepeter & Korger, 1999). This approach is also based on the assumption that there is a significant amount of situational variability to child behavior as a result of differing levels of structure, task demands, learning history, and related contextual parameters such as the quality and quantity of adult supervision (Achenbach, McConaughy, & Howell, 1987; Altepeter & Korger, 1999; Frick, 1998). The multi-informant component makes an implicit assumption that there may be informant-specific areas of knowledge. For example, children and adolescents are particularly important informants for their own covert antisocial behavior (e.g., theft and substance abuse; Angold & Costello, 1996; Hart, Lahey, Loeber, & Hanson, 1994; Loeber, Green, Lahey, & Stouthamer-Loeber, 1989).

Multimethod Categories

We highlight methods and example instruments but do not provide the detailed review of assessment instruments contained in sources such as Kazdin (1995), Essau et al. (1987), and Kamphaus and Frick (2002). Different measures have unique strengths with respect to documenting relevant diagnostic information including the presence, severity, duration, and impairment of CD symptoms. What follows is a brief discussion of relevant method categories for assessing CD. Table 1.4 provides an example assessment battery along with information on the strengths and weaknesses of select CD measures.

The Interview. The unstructured interview is the oldest and most widely used assessment measure to tap CD. The unstructured interview allows maximum flexibility to address the needs of the individual who is be-

TABLE 1.4
Components of a CD Assessment

Method	Instrument	Unique Contribution	Limitations
Unstructured interview	Not applicable	Rapport building and initial exploration of assessment targets	Unsystematic and unreliable
Structured interview	Diagnostic Interview Schedule for Children (version IV) (Shaffer, Fisher, Lucas, Dulcan, & Schwab-Stone, 2000)	Reliable and comprehensive in tapping *DSM* and *ICD* symptom content; documentation of symptom parameters including onset, duration, and impairment	Time consuming and lacking normative data
Omnibus and single-domain rating scales	Behavior Assessment System for Children (Reynolds & Kamphaus, 1992)	Normative comparisons allowing for determination of severity; efficiency in tapping target symptoms and associated conditions; facilitation of multi-informant comparisons	Lack of onset, duration, and impairment information; less symptom overlap with *DSM* and *ICD* than structured interview
Behavioral observation	Dyadic Parent–Child Interaction Coding System (Forster, Eyberg, & Burns, 1990)	Direct assessment of behaviors with no reporter biases; in-depth investigation of causal and maintenance factors that adds idiographic properties to the assessment and informs treatment	Conduct problems are often of low frequency and covert in nature; reactivity of child to being observed may produce atypical behavior
Sociometric measure	Peer nomination technique (Strauss, Lahey, Frick, Frame, & Hynd, 1988)	Expand the multi-informant battery to include unique peer report; provision of valuable information on the important associated variable of peer functioning	Classroom disruption and time demands on teacher informant; absence of normative data

Note. DSM = Diagnostic and Statistical Manual of Mental Disorders; ICD = International Classification of Diseases.

ing assessed. However, the lack of structure allows for unsystematic biases to be introduced into each interview (Loney & Frick, in press; McClellan & Werry, 2000). The unstructured interview assists with the establishment of rapport and provides an initial exploration of the presenting complaints. However, it is unreliable and may not provide a valid assessment of CD. In contrast, structured interview schedules were developed to provide more explicit and reliable guidelines for assessing child and adult psychopathology. Loney and Frick (in press) reviewed nine of the most widely used and investigated measures that all contain specific questions pertaining to CD. All of the interviews provide a set of core questions with follow-up questions to address relevant parameters such as frequency, duration, age of onset, and impairment. The unique strength of the structured interview in assessing CD is the direct overlap with *DSM–IV* and *ICD–10* criteria and the documentation of symptom parameters (e.g., duration and impairment) that are lacking on most other measures of CD.

The Diagnostic Interview Schedule for Children (DISC; Shaffer, Fisher, Lucas, Dulcan, & Schwab-Stone, 2000) is perhaps the most widely used and validated structured interview for the assessment of CD and other child diagnostic categories. The current version of the DISC, the DISC–IV (Shaffer et al., 2000), is unique in the provision of an experimental teacher version that was designed to assess externalizing and internalizing symptoms most likely to occur in the school environment. Although the DISC–IV and related diagnostic interviews assist in increasing the reliability and comprehensiveness of symptom assessment, these interviews are often criticized for being overly comprehensive, time consuming (60–120 min to administer), and for lacking normative data.

The Rating Scale. There are a wide variety of pencil-and-paper measures with well-established psychometric properties for the assessment of CD (see Altepeter & Korger, 1999; Essau et al., 1997; Kamphaus & Frick, 2002). The unique strength of the rating scale is the provision of age-normative data that can be used to document the severity of CD presentations and to build further support for the impairment criterion. Rating scales vary in terms of the number of items, symptom content (e.g., overlap with the *DSM* and *ICD*), response format (e.g., true–false or Likert type), and scoring method. Frick (1998) reviewed a number of commonalities that capture the importance of these scales in an assessment of CD. First, these scales provide an efficient and standardized method of obtaining information on a wide variety of CD subtypes and related conditions from multiple informants. It is important in any assessment of CD to assess for frequently co-occurring difficulties such as ADHD, anxiety, depression, peer difficulties, academic difficulties, and family dysfunction (e.g., parenting dysfunction and parental psychopathology). Rating scales provide an easy and time efficient manner of broadening an assessment of CD to tap the target symptoms and related areas of dysfunction. Second, many rating scales have been standardized on large numbers of children and adolescents to provide age normative data (e.g., T scores and percentiles). Finally, many rating scales contain parent, child, and teacher versions that allow for the investigation of informant agreement in terms of specific symptoms and the overall level of reported behavioral dysfunction.

Rating scales can be divided into broadband (or omnibus) and narrowband (or single-domain) categories. The former include measures that tap CD as well as multiple other symptom categories and areas of adaptive functioning such as relations with peers, teachers, and family members. One prominent broadband measure used in the assessment of CD is the Behavior Assessment System for Children (BASC; Reynolds & Kamphaus, 1992). The BASC is a multi-informant rating (i.e., parent, child, and teacher) scale that produces separate age-normative scale scores for conduct problems and aggressive behavior that are roughly analogous to the covert and overt categories described in the discussion of multivariate models. In addition, the BASC contains scales for related areas of clinical dysfunction (e.g., anxiety, depression, and ADHD) and adaptive behavior (e.g., study skills, relationships with parents, self-esteem). Please see Kamphaus and Frick (2002) for examples of additional broadband rating scales and a discussion of narrow-band measures (e.g., Eyberg Child Behavior Inventory; Eyberg, 1974), including a comparison of symptom content and psychometric properties.

The Observation. Behavioral observations can vary in level of structure from a basic narrative description of a child's behavior in the classroom to a detailed account of the frequency of various CD symptoms conducted in accordance with a standardized coding system. The unique strengths of a behavioral observation are the absence of reporter biases, the documentation of specific treatment targets, and an enhanced view of symptom parameters including relevant causal and maintenance factors. A prominent criticism of medical models of classification is the failure to inform treatment decisions. The behavioral observation addresses this limitation by providing idiographic information that can guide and assist in monitoring the treatment process. Two of the prominent omnibus rating scales, the BASC and the Childhood Behavior Checklist (CBCL; Achenbach, 1991), contain companion observation schedules that provide detailed instruction for coding classroom or group interactions. Both measures involve a brief observation followed by the completion of a checklist measure containing a wide variety of behavioral indicators (Achenbach, 1986; Reynolds & Kamphaus, 1992). The clinician records each of the behaviors that occurred during the observation period. The CBCL requires multiple 10-min observations followed by Likert-type ratings of 96 target behaviors, whereas the

BASC bases similar ratings on one 15-min observation divided into 30 observation periods using a momentary time-sampling procedure (Frick, 1998; Reynolds & Kamphaus, 1992).

Although the structured observation offers an opportunity to observe behavior in a more natural setting, there are a number of factors that may limit its usefulness in assessing CD. For example, many CD symptoms occur with low frequency and are covert in nature. Coding systems designed to assess typical school behavior may miss these behaviors. Additionally, the observation can produce reactivity on the part of the observed child who may be cognizant of being observed and respond in an atypical fashion. Although these factors limit the usefulness of the observation schedule for assessing CD, the ability to observe the child's behavior in a natural environment is a valuable component of a comprehensive assessment. If a school-based observation is not conducted, it could prove useful to conduct a standardized observation of parent–child interaction given that parent–child interaction difficulties are a primary referral concern and a primary treatment target. Observing the parent and child during unstructured and structured play activities allows for a dynamic and detailed assessment of communication patterns such as the parent's use of attending, praise, and commands, and the child's compliance and responsiveness to parental structure (Patterson, DeBaryshe, & Ramsey, 1989). The Dyadic Parent–Child Interaction Coding System (DPICS; Eyberg & Robinson, 1983; Forster, Eyberg, & Burns, 1990) provides a highly detailed and structured coding system for observing a brief 15-min parent–child interaction. The DPICS assesses treatment relevant parent–child interactions during three 5-min scenarios: a child directed play period, a parent directed play period, and a parent directed clean-up period. This type of assessment is particularly useful to employ throughout the treatment process to monitor treatment gains (Frick & Loney, 2000).

Additional Measures. Although interview, rating scale, and observation information will provide a thorough assessment of CD symptoms, there are additional measures that should be considered to tap associated features and socioemotional functioning. First, consideration should be given to the use of a sociometric measure that provides valuable information on classmates' perceptions. There are a variety of sociometric formats. However, a basic peer nomination approach can be used in which teachers ask all of their students to write down the three children that they "like the most," "like the least," "fight the most," "are the meanest," and so forth (see Strauss, Lahey, Frick, Frame, & Hynd, 1988). These prompts can be adjusted to fit the particular needs of the assessment. However, one important variable that is often extracted from this assessment approach is a social preference score calculated by subtracting the number of liked-least ratings from the number of liked-most ratings. The direction and degree of this score indicates whether a child is generally viewed as popular, rejected, neglected, controversial, or average (see Hughes, 1990).

In addition to peer nomination, an assessment of CD symptoms may also benefit from a review of institutional and school records. Measures such as police contacts, school attendance, grades, suspensions, and expulsions could augment parent and teacher report and provide a more comprehensive assessment of relevant conduct problem behavior. Report cards can provide important academic information and contain teacher comments that might provide clues to classroom behavior across a lengthy time period. Despite the potential benefits of these measures, Kazdin (1995) indicated that these measures may also underestimate antisocial behavior given that many relevant behaviors are not included in records and may go undetected.

Multi-Informant Issues

The use of multiple methods to assess CD is critical given the lack of a gold standard or single preeminent assessment device and the unique information provided by different methods (Achenbach et al., 1987; Essau et al., 1997). Reliance on a single informant can similarly produce a limited and potentially distorted picture of behavioral functioning (Frick, 1998; Loeber et al., 2000; Rowe & Kandel, 1997). The multi-informant recommendation is based on the notion that different informants have unique and valid perspectives on the child's behavior given their access to different samples of behavior in potentially different settings (e.g., school, home, playground, etc.; Achenbach, 1995; Rowe & Kandel, 1997; Loeber et al., 2000).

Achenbach et al. (1987) addressed the importance of multiple informants by conducting a meta-analysis of 269 samples contained in 119 studies assessing the relation between parent, teacher, child, and other report of emotional and behavioral difficulties in children ages $1\frac{1}{2}$ to 19 years. They found a strong relation between the reports of adults who have observed children in similar situations (average $r = .60$) such as two parents and a much lower correlation between the reports of adults observing children in different situations (average $r = .28$) such as a parent and teacher. This latter correlation was quite similar to the average correlation between children and all adult informants ($r = .22$). This study supports the importance of multiple informants rather than casting doubt on the reliability of any one informant. With respect to CD, assessors are generally concerned about false negatives (or underreporting of problem behaviors) rather than false positives (Kamphaus & Frick, 2002; Loeber et al., 1989). Sampling from different informant categories increases the likelihood of documenting behaviors that may be undetected or not reported by any one informant.

However, several recent investigations have challenged the notion that different informants provide unique but useful information in the assessment of CD. For example, Loeber and colleagues (Hart et al., 1994; Loeber et al., 1989, 1991) have suggested that clinic-referred children ages 7 to 12 are not a vital source of information for ODD symptoms. These researchers used an analysis of conditional probabilities to assess the likelihood of a child endorsing an ODD symptom if the same symptom was endorsed on either parent or teacher report. The findings indicate that the probability of children endorsing ODD symptoms that were endorsed by another adult informant was much lower than the reverse. Piacentini, Cohen, and Cohen (1992) stated that these findings suggest that children provide little unique information in the assessment of ODD symptoms. In contrast, Loeber et al. (1989) found that children do provide useful and unique information regarding CD symptoms with conditional probabilities suggesting that approximately 50% of child and parent information is unique to the informant. This is similar to findings for teacher report supporting the usefulness of parent, teacher, and child report of CD symptoms.

One prominent limitation of current classification systems is the failure to inform assessment decisions including optimal informants for symptom content areas. Although this is definitely the case for CD, it is important to note that child report of ODD symptoms was not used in the *DSM–IV* disruptive behavior disorder field trials given minimal evidence for the validity of this information (Lahey et al., 1994). This decision was a factor of the conditional probabilities discussed previously, as well as follow-up investigations suggesting that clinic-referred children significantly underreport ODD symptoms relative to parent and teacher ratings (Loeber et al., 1991) and child-reported ODD symptoms bear little relation to relevant impairment criteria such as police contacts and school suspensions (Hart et al., 1994). Both of these findings have led to current recommendations to focus on parent and teacher report in the assessment of ODD. In contrast, most investigations indicate that children provide unique and valid information on CD symptoms. For example, Angold and Costello (1996) stressed the importance of child-reported CD in predicting impairment criteria and CD diagnosis 1 year later. Loeber et al. (2000) further indicated that a particular strength of child-reported CD symptoms is the documentation of covert behaviors (e.g., vandalism, theft, and substance use) that often go undetected by adult informants.

Kamphaus and Frick (2002) suggested that the reliability of child report is questionable before age 9 for the majority of symptom content areas. This is consistent with the results of Edelbrock, Costello, Dulcan, Conover, and Kala (1986) who documented a sharp increase in the reliability of child report of externalizing and internalizing symptoms after age 9 for clinic-referred children. They found a notable increase for the report of aggressive CD symptoms in older children. Future studies will need to investigate the robustness of informant findings for ODD and CD across the adolescent age range.

FINAL RECOMMENDATIONS

Faced with the variety of information that can be obtained in a multi-method, multi-informant assessment battery, it can be difficult to combine this information and arrive at a diagnostic impression. Achenbach (1995) noted that the "assessment of children's behavioral and emotional problems requires systematic procedures for gathering and aggregating data from multiple sources, both to optimize our criteria for disorders and to evaluate individual cases according to the defining criteria" (p. 262). Frick (1998) described a useful multistep strategy for pulling together assessment information into a comprehensive and cohesive description of behavioral functioning. An assessment of child psychopathology should attempt to

1. Document all significant pieces of assessment information (e.g., elevations on rating scales and diagnostic interviews).
2. Attempt to pinpoint commonalities across method and informant that portray a consistent pattern of behavioral dysfunction.
3. Attempt to explain any discrepancies through investigating for such factors as the situational specificity of symptoms and potential rater biases.

Clinical impression often plays a prominent role in the diagnosis of CD. For example, a diagnosis is sometimes given when there is indication of subthreshold symptomatology on interview and rating scale measures. Bird, Gould, and Staghezza (1992) stated that diagnostic decisions are influenced by a number of "tangible and intangible variables, such as the clinician's theoretical orientation and his or her level of training and years of experience, differences in socioeconomic class between the clinician and the family being assessed, age and cognitive level of the child, the clinician's personal psychopathology, intuition, and plain common sense" (p. 78).

Piacentini et al. (1992) conducted an investigation that attempted to address the merits of different methods of combining informant information. These researchers compared a best estimates (i.e., either-or) procedure employing equal weighting of informant information to various complex schemes in which there is differential weighting of symptoms by informant category. The best estimates procedure counts a symptom as present if it is endorsed by the parent, teacher, or child. The researchers reported data from multiple investigations suggesting that a simple either-or scheme performs as well as more complex schemes in terms of the sensitivity and specificity of diagnostic decisions, as well as agreement with clinician ratings.

In the assessment of ODD and CD symptoms, current research suggests that a simple combination of parent, teacher, and child information is a good starting point or default rule for combining informant information. This is particularly the case with children 9 years and older and with CD symptoms. However, on a case-by-case basis, the clinician may have access to information that cautions against the reliability and validity of a given informant's information (Piacentini et al., 1992). For example, a parent report may be viewed with caution given evidence of parental stress and depression symptoms that have been associated with a lowered threshold for symptom reporting including inflated rates of behavior problems (Fergusson, Lynskey, & Horwood, 1993; Querido, Eyberg, & Boggs, 2001). Similarly, there may be practical benefits of exaggerated symptom reports such as school placement and classroom modification that could unknowingly compromise the integrity of responding.

Given that the tendency of clinic-referred youth is to underreport rather than to overreport symptoms, the either-or scheme should function equally well across ODD and CD symptom categories. Structured interview and checklist information can be combined using an either-or strategy and can be compared with rating scale data to delineate relevant symptom parameters such as intensity and impairment. This information can be augmented with behavioral observation and unstructured interview data to expand on and individualize the assessment information and to guide treatment decisions.

SUMMARY

Current classification and assessment approaches for CD are based on over 50 years of theory and research. Recent years have witnessed the blending of multivariate and medical approaches to classifying CD. This has resulted in diagnoses with enhanced psychometric properties and greater sensitivity to issues of diagnostic heterogeneity and developmental psychopathology. The medical model is the zeitgeist of the mental health community. However, categorical diagnoses, symptoms, and symptom thresholds are increasingly based on multivariate investigations to minimize the role of theoretical presuppositions in distorting actual symptom patterns. The multivariate model has substantially impacted the view of ODD as a mild variant of CD and has also been influential in documenting new CD dimensions. Relational aggression and callous-unemotional symptoms have been addressed and appear to have the greatest potential for impacting future symptom content of the *DSM* and *ICD*.

A multimethod, multi-informant assessment battery is essential to document the presence, severity, duration, and impairment of CD symptoms necessary for diagnostic decisions. Different types of measures contribute unique information to the assessment. For example, structured interviews provide detailed information on symptom parameters, whereas rating scales provide unique age normative data on the severity of CD symptoms and various associated variables (e.g., parenting behavior). The inclusion of multiple informants addresses the situational specificity of CD symptoms and maximizes the possibility of detecting low base-rate and underreported behaviors. Current research suggests that children are a unique and valuable source of information with regard to CD but not ODD symptoms. Information from parents, teachers, and children can be combined using a best estimates procedure. However, on a case-by-case basis, differential weighting of informant information may be necessary.

Classification and assessment are dynamic and interactive processes. The development of new assessment techniques such as measures of callous and unemotional traits is a necessary component of expanding the classification of CD. These refinements could, in turn, greatly improve the sensitivity of future classification, assessment, and treatment efforts. The goal of any classification system is to balance comprehensiveness with parsimony. This balance has not been reached with the *DSM–IV* or *ICD–10* perspectives on CD. A primary criticism of current classification approaches is the failure to inform treatment intervention. Diagnostic heterogeneity will always exist, but a reduction in this heterogeneity is essential to developing more effective treatment interventions for severe CD.

REFERENCES

Achenbach, T. M. (1986). *Child behavior checklist-direct observation form* (rev. ed.). Burlington: University of Vermont.

Achenbach, T. M. (1991). *Manual for the Child Behavior Checklist/4-18 and 1991 profile.* Burlington: University of Vermont, Department of Psychiatry.

Achenbach, T. M. (1995). Empirically based assessment and taxonomy: Applications to clinical research. *Psychological Assessment, 7,* 261–274.

Achenbach, T. M., Conners, C. K., & Quay, H. C. (1983). *The ACQ behavior checklist.* Burlington: University of Vermont Department of Psychiatry.

Achenbach, T. M., Conners, C. K., Quay, H. C., Verhulst, F. C., & Howell, C. T. (1989). Replication of empirically derived syndromes as a basis for taxonomy of child/adolescent psychopathology. *Journal of Abnormal Child Psychology, 17,* 299–323.

Achenbach, T. M., & Edelbrock, C. (1978). The classification of child psychopathology: A review and analysis of empirical efforts. *Psychological Bulletin, 85,* 1275–1307.

Achenbach, T. M., & Edelbrock, C. (1983). *Manual for the child behavior checklist and revised child behavior profile.* Burlington: University of Vermont Department of Psychiatry.

Achenbach, T. M., McConaughy, S. H., & Howell, C. T. (1987). Child/adolescent behavioral and emotional problems: Implications of cross-informant correlations for situational specificity. *Psychological Bulletin, 101,* 213–232.

Altepeter, T. S., & Korger, J. N. (1999). Disruptive behavior: Oppositional defiant disorder and conduct disorder. In S. D. Netherton & D. Holmes (Eds.), *Child and adolescent psychological disorders: A comprehensive textbook* (pp. 118–138). New York: Oxford University Press.

American Psychiatric Association. (1968). *The diagnostic and statistical manual of mental disorders* (2nd ed.). Washington, DC: Author.

American Psychiatric Association. (1980). *The diagnostic and statistical manual of mental disorders* (3rd ed.). Washington, DC: Author.

American Psychiatric Association. (1987). *The diagnostic and statistical manual of mental disorders* (3rd ed., rev.). Washington, DC: Author.

American Psychiatric Association. (1994). *The diagnostic and statistical manual of mental disorders* (4th ed.). Washington, DC: Author.

American Psychiatric Association. (2000). *The diagnostic and statistical manual of mental disorders: DSM–IV–TR* (text rev.). Washington, DC: Author.

Angold, A., & Costello, E. J. (1996). Toward establishing an empirical basis for the diagnosis of oppositional defiant disorder. *Journal of the American Academy of Child and Adolescent Psychiatry, 35,* 1205–1212.

Angold, A., Erkanli, A., Costello, E. J., & Rutter, M. (1996). Precision, reliability and accuracy in dating symptom onsets in child and adolescent psychopathology. *Journal of Child Psychology & Psychiatry, 37,* 657–664.

Atkins, M. S., & Stoff, D. M. (1993). Instrumental and hostile aggression in childhood disruptive behavior disorders. *Journal of Abnormal Child Psychology, 21,* 165–178.

Barry, C. T., Frick, P. J., DeShazo, T. M., McCoy, M. G., Ellis, M., & Loney, B. R. (2000). The importance of callous-unemotional traits for extending the concept of psychopathy to children. *Journal of Abnormal Psychology, 109,* 335–340.

Bird, H. R., Gould, M. S., & Staghezza, B. (1992). Aggregating data from multiple informants in child psychiatry epidemiological research. *Journal of the American Academy of Child and Adolescent Psychiatry, 31,* 78–85.

Björkqvist, K., Lagerspetz, K. M. J., & Kaukiainen, A. (1992). Do girls manipulate and boys fight? Developmental trends in regard to direct and indirect aggression. *Aggressive Behavior, 18,* 117–127.

Blair, R. J. R. (1999). Responsiveness to distress cues in the child with psychopathic tendencies. *Personality and Individual Differences, 27,* 135–145.

Brown, K., Atkins, M. S., Osborne, M. L., & Milnamow, M. (1996). A revised teacher rating scale for reactive and proactive aggression. *Journal of Abnormal Child Psychology, 24,* 473–479.

Craig, W. M., & Pepler, D. J. (1997). Conduct and oppositional defiant disorders. In C. A. Essau & F. Peterman (Eds.), *Developmental psychopathology: Epidemiology, diagnosis, and treatment* (pp. 97–139). Amsterdam: Harwood Academic.

Crick, N. R. (1996). The role of overt aggression, relational aggression, and prosocial behavior in the prediction of children's future social adjustment. *Child Development, 67,* 2317–2327.

Crick, N. R. (1997). Engagement in gender normative versus nonnormative forms of aggression: Links to social-psychological adjustment. *Developmental Psychology, 33,* 610–617.

Crick, N. R., Casas, J. F., & Mosher, M. (1997). Relational and overt aggression in preschool. *Developmental Psychology, 33,* 579–588.

Crick, N. R., & Dodge, K. A. (1996). Social information-processing mechanisms in reactive and proactive aggression. *Child Development, 67,* 993–1002.

Crick, N. R., & Grotpeter, J. K. (1995). Relational aggression, gender, and social-psychological adjustment. *Child Development, 66,* 710–722.

Dilalla, L. F., & Gottesman, I. I. (1989). Heterogeneity of causes for delinquency and criminality: Lifespan perspectives. *Development and Psychopathology, 1,* 339–349.

Dodge, K. A., & Coie, J. D. (1987). Social-information-processing factors in reactive and proactive aggression in children's peer groups. *Journal of Personality and Social Psychology, 53,* 1146–1158.

Edelbrock, C., Costello, A. J., Dulcan, M. K., Conover, N. C., & Kala, R. (1986). Parent–child agreement on child psychiatric symptoms assessed via structured interview. *Journal of Child Psychology & Psychiatry & Allied Disciplines, 27*, 181–190.

Essau, C. A., Feehan, M., & Ustun, B. (1997). Classification and assessment strategies. In C. A. Essau & F. Peterman (Eds.), *Developmental psychopathology: Epidemiology, diagnosis, and treatment* (pp. 19–62). Amsterdam: Harwood.

Eyberg, S. M. (1974). *Eyberg child behavior inventory*. Gainseville: University of Florida.

Eyberg, S. M., & Robinson, E. A. (1983). Dyadic parent–child interaction coding system: A manual. *Psychological Documents, 13*, Ms. No. 2582.

Fergusson, D. M., Lynskey, M. T., & Horwood, L. J. (1993). The effect of maternal depression on maternal ratings of child behavior. *Journal of Abnormal Child Psychology, 21*, 245–269.

Forster, A. A., Eyberg, S. M., & Burns, G. L. (1990). Assessing the verbal behavior of conduct problem children during mother–child interactions: A preliminary investigation. *Child and Family Behavior Therapy, 12*, 13–22.

Frauenglass, S., & Routh, D. K. (1999). Assessment of disruptive behavior disorders: Dimensional and categorical approaches. In H. C. Quay & A. E. Hogan (Eds.), *Handbook of disruptive behavior disorders* (pp. 49–71). New York: Kluwer Academic/Plenum.

Frick, P. J. (1998). *Conduct disorders and severe antisocial behavior*. New York: Plenum.

Frick, P. J., Cornell, A. H., Bodin, D., Dane, H. A., Barry, C. T., & Loney, B. R. (in press). Callous-unemotional traits and developmental pathways to severe conduct problems. *Developmental Psychology*.

Frick, P. J., & Ellis, M. (1999). Callous-unemotional traits and subtypes of conduct disorder. *Clinical Child and Family Psychology Review, 2*, 149–168.

Frick, P. J., & Hare, R. D. (2001). *The antisocial process screening device*. Toronto, Ontario, Canada: Multi-Health Systems.

Frick, P. J., Lahey, B. B., Loeber, R., Tannenbaum, L. E., Van Horn, Y., Christ, M. A. G., Hart, E. A., & Hanson, K. (1993). Oppositional defiant disorder and conduct disorder: A meta-analytic review of factor analyses and cross-validation in a clinic sample. *Clinical Psychology Review, 13*, 319–340.

Frick, P. J., Lilienfeld, S. O., Ellis, M., Loney, B., & Silverthorn, P. (1999). The association between anxiety and psychopathy dimensions in children. *Journal of Abnormal Child Psychology, 27*, 383–392.

Frick, P., & Loney, B. (1999). Outcomes of oppositional defiant disorder and conduct disorder. In H. C. Quay & A. E. Hogan (Eds.), *Handbook of disruptive behavior disorders* (pp. 507–524). New York: Kluwer Academic/Plenum Publishers.

Frick, P. J., & Loney, B. R. (2000). The use of laboratory and performance-based measures in the assessment of children and adolescents with conduct disorders. *Journal of Clinical Child Psychology, 29*, 540–554.

Garber, J. (1984). Classification of childhood psychopathology: A developmental perspective. *Child Development, 55*, 30–48.

Hart, E. L., Lahey, B. B., Loeber, R., & Hanson, K. S. (1994). Criterion validity of informants in the diagnosis of disruptive behavior disorders in children: A preliminary study. *Journal of Consulting and Clinical Psychology, 62*, 410–414.

Hewitt, L. E., & Jenkins, R. L. (1946). *Fundamental patterns of maladjustment, the dynamics of their origin*. Springfield: State of Illinois.

Hinshaw, S. P. (1987). On the distinction between attentional deficits/hyperactivity and conduct problems/aggression in child psychopathology. *Psychological Bulletin, 101*, 443–463.

Hinshaw, S. P. (1994). Conduct disorder in childhood: Conceptualization, diagnosis, comorbidity, and risk status for antisocial functioning in adulthood. In D. C. Fowles, P. Sutker, & S. H. Goodman (Eds.), *Progress in experimental personality and psychopathology research* (pp. 3–44). New York: Springer.

Hinshaw, S. P., Lahey, B. B., & Hart, E. L. (1993). Issues of taxonomy and comorbidity in the development of conduct disorder. *Development and Psychopathology, 5*, 31–49.

Hogan, A. E. (1999). Cognitive functioning in children with oppositional defiant disorder and conduct disorder. In H. C. Quay & A. E. Hogan (Eds.), *Handbook of disruptive behavior disorders* (pp. 317–335). New York: Kluwer Academic/Plenum Publishers.

Hughes, J. (1990). Assessment of social skills: Sociometric and behavioral approaches. In C. R. Reynolds & R. W. Kamphaus (Eds.), *Handbook of psychological and educational assessment of children: Personality, behavior, and context* (pp. 423–444). New York: Guilford.

Kamphaus, R. W., & Frick, P. J. (2002). *Clinical assessment of child and adolescent personality and behavior (2nd edition)*. Boston: Allyn & Bacon.

Kaplan, H. I., & Sadock, B. J. (1998). *Kaplan and Sadock's synopsis of psychiatry: Behavioral sciences/clinical psychiatry* (8th ed.). Baltimore: Williams & Wilkins.

Kazdin, A. E. (1995). *Conduct disorders in childhood and adolescence* (2nd ed.). Thousand Oaks, CA: Sage.

Kolko, D. J. (1994). Conduct disorder. In M. Hersen & R. T. Ammerman (Eds.), *Handbook of aggressive and destructive behavior in psychiatric patients* (pp. 363–394). New York: Plenum.

Lagerspetz, K. M. J., Björkqvist, K., & Peltonen, T. (1988). Is indirect aggression typical of females? Gender differences in aggressiveness in 11- to 12-year-old children. *Aggressive Behavior, 14*, 403–414.

Lahey, B. B., Applegate, B., Barkley, R. A., Garfinkel, B., McBurnett, K., Kerdyck, L., Greehill, L., Hynd, G. W., Frick, P. J., Newcorn, J., Biederman, J., Ollendick, T., Hart, E. L., Perez, D., Waldman, I., & Shaffer, D. (1994). DSM–IV field trials for oppositional defiant disorder and conduct disorder in children and adolescents. *American Journal of Psychiatry, 151*, 1163–1171.

Lahey, B. B., Loeber, R., Quay, H. C., Frick, P. J., & Grimm, J. (1992). Oppositional defiant and conduct disorders: Issues to be resolved for DSM–IV. *Journal of the American Academy of Child and Adolescent Psychiatry, 31*, 539–546.

Lahey, B. B., Loeber, R., Stouthamer-Loeber, M., Christ, M. A. G., Green, S., Russo, M. F., Frick, P. J., & Dulcan, M. (1990). Comparison of DSM–III and DSM–III–R diagnoses for prepubertal children: Changes in prevalence and validity. *Journal of the American Academy of Child and Adolescent Psychiatry, 29*, 620–626.

Loeber, R., Burke, J. D., Lahey, B. B., Winters, A., & Zera, M. (2000). Oppositional defiant and conduct disorder: A review of the past 10 years, Part I. *Journal of the American Academy of Child and Adolescent Psychiatry, 39*, 1468–1484.

Loeber, R., Green, S. M., Lahey, B. B., & Stouthamer-Loeber, M. (1989). Optimal informants on childhood disruptive behaviors. *Development and Psychopathology, 1*, 317–337.

Loeber, R., Green, S. M., Lahey, B. B., & Stouthamer-Loeber, M. (1991). Differences and similarities between children, mothers, and teachers as informants on disruptive behavior. *Journal of Abnormal Child Psychology, 19*, 75–95.

Loeber, R., Lahey, B. B., & Thomas, C. (1991). Diagnostic conundrum of oppositional defiant disorder and conduct disorder. *Journal of Abnormal Psychology, 100*, 379–390.

Loeber, R., & Schmaling, K. B. (1985). The utility of differentiating between mixed and pure forms of antisocial child behavior. *Journal of Abnormal Child Psychology, 13*, 315–336.

Loney, B. R., & Frick, P. J. (in press). The structured diagnostic interview for children and adolescents: A comparison of current interview formats. In C. R. Reynolds & R. W. Kamphaus (Eds.), *Handbook of psychological and educational assessment of children*.

Loney, B. R., Frick, P. J., Clements, C., Ellis, M., & Kerlin, K. (in press). Callous-unemotional traits, impulsivity, and emotional processing in antisocial adolescents. *Journal of Clinical Child and Adolescent Psychology*.

Loney, B. R., Frick, P. J., Ellis, M., & McCoy, M. G. (1998). Intelligence, callous-unemotional traits, and antisocial behavior. *Journal of Psychopathology and Behavioral Assessment, 20*, 231–247.

Lynam, D. R. (1996). The early identification of chronic offenders: Who is the fledgling psychopath? *Psychological Bulletin, 120*, 209–234.

Lynam, D. R. (1998). Early identification of the fledgling psychopath: Locating the psychopathic child in the current nomenclature. *Journal of Abnormal Psychology, 107*, 566–575.

McClellan, J., & Werry, J. S. (2000). Introduction to special section: Research psychiatric diagnostic interviews for children and adolescents. *Journal of the American Academy of Child and Adolescent Psychiatry, 39*, 19–27.

McMahon, R. J. (1994). Diagnosis, assessment, and treatment of externalizing problems in children: The role of longitudinal data. *Journal of Consulting and Clinical Psychology, 62*, 901–917.

Millon, T. (1991). Classification in psychopathology: Rationale, alternatives, and standards. *Journal of Abnormal Psychology, 100*, 245–261.

Moffitt, T. E. (1990). Juvenile delinquency and attention deficit disorder: Boys' developmental trajectories from age 3 to age 15. *Child Development, 61*, 893–910.

Moffitt, T. E. (1993a). Adolescent-limited and life-course-persistent antisocial behavior: A developmental taxonomy. *Psychological Review, 100*, 674–701.

Moffitt, T. E. (1993b). The neuropsychology of conduct disorder. *Development and Psychopathology, 5*, 135–151.

Moffitt, T. E., & Caspi, A. (2001). Childhood predictors differentiate life-course persistent and adolescence-limited antisocial pathways among males and females. *Development and Psychopathology, 13*, 355–375.

Moffitt, T. E., Caspi, A., Dickson, N., Silva, P., & Stanton, W. (1996). Childhood-onset versus adolescent-onset antisocial conduct problems in males: Natural history from ages 3 to 18 years. *Development and Psychopathology, 8*, 399–424.

Patterson, G. R., DeBaryshe, B. D., & Ramsey, E. (1989). A developmental perspective on antisocial behavior. *American Psychologist, 44*, 329–335.

Piacentini, J. C., Cohen, P., & Cohen, J. (1992). Combining discrepant diagnostic information from multiple sources: Are complex algorithms better than simple ones? *Journal of Abnormal Child Psychology, 20*, 51–63.

Quay, H. C. (1972). Patterns of aggression, withdrawal, and immaturity. In H. C. Quay & J. S. Werry (Eds.), *Psychopathological disorders of childhood* (pp. 1–29). New York: Wiley.

Quay, H. C. (1979). Classification. In H. C. Quay & J. S. Werry (Eds.), *Psychopathological disorders of childhood* (pp. 1–42). New York: Wiley.

Quay, H. C. (1986). Classification. In H. C. Quay & J. S. Werry (Eds.), *Psychopathological disorders of childhood* (3rd ed., pp. 1–42). New York: Wiley.

Quay, H. C. (1987). Patterns of delinquent behavior. In H. C. Quay (Ed.), *Handbook of juvenile delinquency* (pp. 118–138). New York: Wiley.

Quay, H. C. (1999). Classification of the disruptive behavior disorders. In H. C. Quay & A. E. Hogan (Eds.), *Handbook of disruptive behavior disorders* (pp. 3–21). New York: Kluwer Academic/Plenum Publishers.

Querido, J. G., Eyberg, S. M., & Boggs, S. R. (2001). Revisiting the accuracy hypothesis in families of young children with conduct problems. *Journal of Clinical Child Psychology, 30*, 253–261.

Reynolds, C. R., & Kamphaus, R. W. (1992). *Behavior assessment system for children (BASC).* Circle Pines, MN: American Guidance Service.

Rogeness, G. A., Hernandez, J. M., Macedo, C. A., & Mitchell, E. L. (1982). Biochemical differences in children with conduct disorder socialized and undersocialized. *American Journal of Psychiatry, 139*, 307–311.

Rowe, D. C., & Kandel, D. (1997). In the eye of the beholder? Parental ratings of externalizing and internalizing symptoms. *Journal of Abnormal Child Psychology, 25*, 265–275.

Shaffer, D., Campbell, M., Cantwell, D., Bradley, S., Carlson, G., Cohen, D., Denckla, M., Frances, A., Garfinkel, B., Klein, R., Pincus, H., Spitzer, R. L., Volkmar, F., & Widiger, T. (1989). Child and adolescent psychiatric disorders in DSM–IV: Issues facing the work group. *Journal of the American Academy of Child and Adolescent Psychiatry, 28*, 830–835.

Shaffer, D., Fisher, P., Lucas, C. P., Dulcan, M. K., & Schwab-Stone, M. E. (2000). NIMH diagnostic interview schedule for children version IV (NIMH DISC–IV): Description, differences from previous versions, and reliability of some common diagnoses. *Journal of the American Academy of Child and Adolescent Psychiatry, 39*, 28–38.

Silverthorn, P., & Frick, P. J. (1999). Developmental pathways to antisocial behavior: The delayed-onset pathway in girls. *Development and Psychopathology, 11*, 101–126.

Snyder, H. N., & Sickmund, M. (1995). *Juvenile offenders and victims: A national report.* Washington, DC: Office of Juvenile Justice and Delinquency Prevention.

Strauss, C. C., Lahey, B. B., Frick, P. J., Frame, C. L., & Hynd, G. W. (1988). Peer social status of children with anxiety disorders. *Journal of Consulting and Clinical Psychology, 56*, 137–141.

Thangavelu, R., & Martin, R. L. (1995). ICD–10 and DSM–IV: Depiction of the diagnostic elephant. *Psychiatric Annals, 25*, 20–28.

Vitaro, F., Gendreau, P. L., Tremblay, R. E., & Oligny, P. (1998). Reactive and proactive aggression differentially predict later conduct problems. *Journal of Child Psychology & Psychiatry, 39*, 377–385.

Vitiello, B., & Stoff, D. M. (1997). Subtypes of aggression and their relevance to child psychiatry. *Journal of the American Academy of Child & Adolescent Psychiatry, 36*, 307–315.

Volkmar, F. R., & Schwab-Stone, M. (1996). Annotation: Childhood disorders in DSM–IV. *Journal of Child Psychology and Psychiatry and Allied Disciplines, 37*, 779–784.

Walker, J. L., Lahey, B. B., Hynd, G. W., & Frame, C. L. (1987). Comparison of specific patterns of antisocial behavior in children with conduct disorder with and without coexisting hyperactivity. *Journal of Consulting and Clinical Psychology, 55*, 910–913.

Webster-Stratton, C. (1996). Early-onset conduct problems: Does gender make a difference? *Journal of Consulting and Clinical Psychology, 64*, 540–551.

Werner, N. E., & Crick, N. R. (1999). Relational aggression and social-psychological adjustment in a college sample. *Journal of Abnormal Psychology, 108*, 615–623.

Wilson, J. J. (2000). *OJJDP fact sheet: Detention in delinquency cases, 1988–1997.* Washington, DC: Office of Juvenile Justice and Delinquency Prevention.

World Health Organization. (1948). *International classification of diseases* (6th ed.). Geneva, Switzerland: Author.

World Health Organization. (1992). *International classification of diseases* (10th ed.). Geneva, Switzerland: Author.

Zahn-Waxler, C. (1993). Warriors and worriers: Gender and psychopathology. *Development and Psychopathology, 5*, 79–89.

Zoccolillo, M. (1993). Gender and the development of conduct disorder. *Development and Psychopathology, 5*, 65–78.

2

Epidemiology and Comorbidity

Cecilia A. Essau

Westfälische Wilhelms-Universität, Münster, Germany

One of the main advantages of epidemiological research using samples from the general population is the ability to produce findings of greater generalizability than studies of clinical samples. Data from clinical settings are generally unrepresentative of individuals with conduct disorder (CD) and oppositional defiant disorder (ODD) or other psychiatric disorders because of bias in service attendance through restrictions in evaluating, access, and selection processes in terms of help-seeking behavior, symptoms, and chronicity (Essau, Petermann, & Feehan, 1997). Samples from the community and clinical settings may also differ in the risk factors, comorbidity, natural history, and response to treatment of their CD and ODD. An additional problem with using clinical samples is that children's referrals to clinical settings may be related to parental characteristics such as tolerance level, stress, and the presence of psychopathology (Shepherd, Oppenheim, & Mitchell, 1971). The finding that most children in the community with significant problems do not receive adequate help (Essau, 2002; McGee, Feehan, & Williams, 1995) also underscores the importance of epidemiological studies. For these reasons, numerous epidemiological studies on CD and ODD have been conducted in recent years. This chapter reviews these studies with an emphasis on the prevalence and comorbidity of CD and ODD in children and adolescents. Data from clinical studies is also reviewed, as they could contribute to our understanding of the etiological mechanisms in CD/ODD.

METHODOLOGICAL ISSUES

Much progress has been obtained in epidemiological studies of children and adolescents in recent years. This progress is strongly influenced by the following related developments in adult psychiatric epidemiology (Essau, 2002; Wittchen & Essau, 1993):

1. Greater specificity of diagnostics of psychiatric disorders that permits the operationalization of specific diagnostic decisions instead of broad, unspecific decisions about "caseness."

2. The development of highly structured diagnostic instruments that reduce the observer, information, and criteria variance and allow comparison of results across studies. Due to their structured nature, such instruments can be administered by trained lay interviewers, which leads to the reduction of costs when compared to using clinicians as interviewers.

3. The use of a lifetime approach to estimate the prevalence of CD/ODD enables the determination of the occurrence, clustering, and sequence of syndromes and disorders over the person's life span.

4. The systematic integration of information from different informants (e.g., parent, teacher, clinician, and child; Verhulst, 1995).

Despite these recent developments, there are some inconsistencies across studies that should be taken into consideration in interpreting data on the epidemiology and the comorbidity of CD/ODD. One of the major difficulties in interpreting the prevalence rates is related to the frequent changes in the definition of CD and ODD (see chap. 1, this volume). Oppositional disorder was first introduced as a diagnostic category in 1980 (*Diagnostic and Statistical Manual of Mental Disorders*, 3rd ed. [*DSM–III*]; American Psychiatric Association, 1980), with the addition of ODD in 1987 (*DSM–III–R* [3rd ed. rev.]; American Psychiatric Association, 1987) and its modification in 1994 (*DSM–IV* [4th ed.]; American Psychiatric Association, 1994). The definition of CD was made significantly more stringent in *DSM–III–R* with additional modifications in *DSM–IV*. Furthermore, estimates of prevalence of CD/ODD are highly dependent on the definitional criteria used. Even if the same diagnostic criteria is used, studies differ in their definition of whether a disorder is present. For example, in the Dunedin Multidisciplinary Health and Developmental Study (Anderson, Williams, McGee, & Silva, 1987), prevalence estimates were obtained by combining information about the child's mental health as provided by the parents, children, and teachers. A disorder was considered to be present when *DSM–III* criteria diagnoses were provided by more than one informant.

Another factor that contributed to variations in the prevalence rates of CD/ODD is the inclusion of an impairment criterion. For instance, in a Dutch survey (Verhulst, van der Ende, Ferdinand, & Kasius, 1997), a 5-point Global Maladjustment Severity scale based on clinical judgment was combined with *DSM–III* criteria to establish whether a disorder was present. In the Ontario Child Health Study (OCHS; Boyle et al., 1987) clinical judgment and a statistical strategy of balancing false positives and negatives was used to determine whether a disorder was present. In a New York study (Velez, Johnson, & Cohen, 1989), the presence of a disorder was determined by using a combination of *DSM–III–R* criteria and a Severity scale. In a Puerto Rican study (Bird et al., 1988), the presence or absence of a disorder was determined by combining *DSM–III* criteria based on parents' and children's report and adaptive functioning based on Children's Global Assessment Scale cutoff scores. In the Quebec Child Mental Health Survey (Bergeron, Valla, & Breton, 1992), an impairment index was further categorized into three levels: at least one problem at home, at school, or with other children; one problem at home, at school, or with other children; and problems at home, at school, and with other children. The extent to which the inclusion of impairment influences the prevalence rate is inconsistent. Some authors (Shaffer et al., 1996) found the inclusion of impairment on CD and ODD to have a negligible effect. In Bird et al.'s (1988) study, the inclusion of impairment reduced prevalence rates of ODD and also other disorders such as separation anxiety disorder, attention deficit disorder, adjustment disorder, functional enuresis, and simple phobia. In a study by Romano, Tremblay, and Vitaro (2001), the inclusion of functional impairment criterion had a greater effect on reducing the prevalence of internalizing disorders (e.g., anxiety and depression) than on externalizing disorders such as CD and ODD. It has been argued that internalizing disorders are not intrinsically as impairing as externalizing disorders. That is, anxiety-disordered youth can function reasonably in various life domains compared to youth with CD. It has furthermore been argued that impairment resulting from internalizing disorders is not as observable or as easy to measure as externalizing-related impairment (Romano et al., 2001).

Differences in the prevalence rates also contributed to the type (e.g., adolescents, teacher, parents) and gender of the informants from whom the information needed to diagnose the presence of CD/ODD was obtained. Among the disorders examined, the greatest differences between prevalence based on parents' and adolescents' report were found for CD (Fergusson, Horwood, & Lynskey, 1993; Verhulst et al., 1997). In most studies, adolescents' report resulted in significantly higher prevalence than parents' report. Thus, parents may be unaware of their children's antisocial activities, whereas a high proportion of the adolescents are willing to report these activities. Studies also vary in the way in which information from different sources (parents, teachers, and children) are combined; this in turn influences the prevalence of CD and ODD. For example, in the study by Fergusson et al. (1993), higher prevalence of CD was obtained when the optimal informant, as compared to the latent-class method, was used. In the study by Webster-Stratton (1996), male and female informants differed in their reporting of the children's behavior. Specifically, mothers perceived boys as having more externalizing problems than girls, and fathers perceived girls as having more internalizing problems than boys. Teachers reported boys as being more hostile–aggressive and more hyperactive than girls. In contrast to this discrepancy, in home observations of parent–child interactions, girls and boys were observed as having the same levels of externalizing behaviors and verbal deviance (yelling, swearing, arguing); moreover, girls were as noncompliant to parental requests as boys and no more or less affectionate (physical warmth). These findings suggest that the gender of the parent and teacher lead to different interpretations of the child's behavior, depending on their gender. That is, fathers were more tolerant of physical aggression in boys, and they were aware of girls' internalizing behavior that mothers and teachers did not report as problematic. Boys' higher levels of physical negative aggression make them more visible (and more disruptive in the classroom) than girls, whereas girls' high levels of a nonaggressive conduct problems (CP) (i.e., noncompliance and verbal bullying) were noticeable by parents and teachers.

Prevalence of CD and ODD also vary according to the time frames, ranging from current to lifetime. Because lifetime prevalence covers the life span of the individual, the lifetime rates will be higher than current prevalence.

Given these methodological differences across studies, it is not surprising to find variation in the prevalence of CD/ODD.

PREVALENCE OF CD/ODD

Since the seminal first large-scale epidemiological survey by Rutter and his colleagues in the late 1960s (Graham & Rutter, 1973; Rutter, Tizard, & Whitmore, 1970), several studies have been conducted on children and adolescents with the aim of establishing the prevalence of CD and ODD and other disorders. In the study by Rutter et al. (1970), parents and teachers of all of the 10- to 11-year-old children who lived on the Isle of Wight completed a set of questionnaires about the child's emotional and behavioral problems. Children at high risk for psychiatric disorders were selected for a more detailed assessment. Psychiatrists and other clinicians were used as interviewers to make psychiatric diagnoses. Similar methods have been used in

Norway (Vikan, 1985), Germany (Esser, Schmidt, & Woerner, 1990), and Australia (Connell, Irvine, & Rodney, 1982). However, having clinicians as interviewers in large-scale surveys can be expensive. Furthermore, clinicians may differ in the information they ask due to experience, personality, and professional training. This may lead to information variability and lack of reliability. To overcome these problems, standardized diagnostic interviews were developed in the 1980s that could be used by trained lay interviewers. This method has been used in various U.S. studies and in studies conducted in New Zealand, Holland, Switzerland, and Germany. In some other studies (e.g., Boyle et al., 1987), questionnaires completed by parents, children, and teachers were used to derive the diagnostic-like syndromes as reflected in the symptom structure of *DSM* CD/ODD.

Table 2.1 and Table 2.2 summarize recent large-scale epidemiological surveys that provide information on the prevalence and comorbidity of CD and ODD, respectively. Most of these community surveys have relied on the two-stage design, namely, on the use of screening and diagnostic instruments and the use of the multiple-informant approach. Overall, estimates of the prevalence of CD among children and adolescents range widely, from less than 1% to nearly 9%. ODD was less common, with a prevalence of 2%. The 1-year prevalence of CD, adjusted for impairment in life functioning, help seeking, or police contact was 5.5% (Feehan, McGee, Nada-Raja, & Williams, 1994). The prevalence of CD and ODD in clinical settings was much higher. For example, in one clinical study (Arredondo & Butler, 1994), 26% of inpatient adolescents met criteria for CD and 12% met criteria for ODD.

As mentioned earlier, one of the factors that contributed to differences in the prevalences of CD/ODD is the type of informant who gave information about the child's behavior or problem. The prevalence based on report by parents was lower than that based on report by adolescents (Bergeron et al., 1992; Fergusson et al., 1993; Verhulst et al., 1997). As shown by Verhulst et al., the greatest discrepancies between prevalences based on information from parent versus youth was found for CD. As presented in Table 2.1, the 6-month prevalence for CD based on parents' report was 5.6% compared to 1.2% based on adolescent report. A similar result was reported by Romano et al. (2001) in that mothers reported higher rates of CD/ODD than adolescents themselves. That is, when considering the symptom criteria only, the 6-month prevalence of CD/ODD based on adolescent's report was 6.3% versus 3.5% based on mothers' report. However, this difference disappeared when the criteria for the presence of CD/ODD was based on *DSM–III–R* criteria plus impairment. That is, the rate of CD based on adolescents' report was 4.2% compared to 3.3% based on mothers' report.

Changes in diagnostic criteria can also produce variations in prevalence. A comparison of *DSM–III* and *DSM–III–R* diagnoses on the same sample showed that between *DSM–III* and *DSM–III–R*, the rate was reduced by 44%

TABLE 2.1
Prevalence of CD in Major Epidemiological Studies

Authors	Instruments/ Criteria	Age (years)	Prevalence (%) Total	Boys	Girls
Kashani et al. (1987)	DICA; *DSM–III–R*	14–16		C = 9.3	C = 8.0
McGee et al. (1990)	DISC; *DSM–III*	11	agg = 1.6 no-agg = 5.7		
Feehan, McGee, Nada-Raja, and Williams (1994)	DISC; *DSM–III*	15		C = 2.6	C = 0.8
Bergeron, Valla, and Breton (1992)	DISC; *DSM–III–R*	6–11, 12–14	C = 1.5 C = 1.4		
Fergusson, Horwood, and Lynskey (1993)	Rating scale; *DSM–III–R*	15	C = 3.2 P = 3.3	C = 5.1 P = 1.8	C = 1.8 P = 3.3
Cohen et al. (1993)	DISC; *DSM–III–R*	10–13, 14–16, 17–20		C = 16.0 C = 15.8 C = 9.5	C = 3.8 C = 9.2 C = 7.1
Lewinsohn, Hops, Roberts, Seeley, and Andrew (1993)[a]	K-SADS; *DSM–III–R*	14–18	C = 3.22	C = 4.9	C = 3.2
Fombonne (1994)[b]	Rating scale; *ICD–9*	8–11		P = 9.3	P = 3.2
Jensen et al. (1995)	DISC; *DSM–III–R*	6–17	C = 0.0 P = 1.9		
Costello et al. (1996)[c]	CAPA; *DSM–III–R*	9, 11, 13	3.32	5.43	1.13
Verhulst, van der Ende, Ferdinand, and Kasius (1997)	DISC; *DSM–III–R*	13–18	C = 5.6 P = 1.2		
Romano, Tremblay, and Vitario (2001)	DISC; *DSM–III–R*	14–17	C = 6.3 C + I = 4.2 P = 3.4 P + I = 3.3	C = 9.1 C + I = 5.5 P = 3.6 P + I = 3.6	C = 3.6 C + I = 2.9 P = 3.3 P + I = 3.0

Note. CD = conduct disorder; DICA = Diagnostic Interview for Children and Adolescents (Reich & Welner, 1988); *DSM–III–R = Diagnostic and Statistical Manual of Mental Disorders* (3rd ed., rev.; American Psychiatric Association, 1987); C = child report; DISC = Diagnostic Interview Schedule (Costello et al., 1987); *DSM–III* = 3rd ed. (American Psychiatric Association, 1980); agg = CD aggressive; no-agg = CD nonaggressive; P = parent report; K-SADS = Schedule for Affective Disorders and Schizophrenia for School-age Children (Puig-Antich & Chambers, 1978); *ICD–9 = International Classification of Diseases* (9th ed.); CAPA = Child and Adolescent Psychiatric Assessment (Angold & Costello, 1995); I = impairment.

[a]Lifetime prevalence. [b]3-month prevalence (the rates include mixed disorders and hyperkinetic disorders). [c]3-month prevalence.

38

TABLE 2.2
Prevalence of ODD in Major Epidemiological Studies

Authors	Instruments/ Criteria	Age (years)	Prevalence (%)		
			Total	Boys	Girls
Kashani et al. (1987)	DICA; *DSM–III–R*	14–16		C = 9.3	C = 8.0
McGee et al. (1990)	DISC; *DSM–III*	1511	C = 1.7		
Feehan, McGee, Nada-Raja, and Williams (1994)	DISC; *DSM–III*			C = 3.6	C = 2.1
Bergeron, Valla, and Breton (1992)	DISC; *DSM–III–R*	6–11 12–14	C = 2.9 P = 1.5 C + I = 0.0 P + I = 1.5		
Fergusson, Horwood, and Lynsky (1993)	Rating scale; *DSM–III–R*	15	C = 5.1 P = 1.8		
Cohen et al. (1993)	DISC; *DSM–III–R*	10–13 14–16 17–20		C = 14.2 C = 15.4 C = 12.2	C = 10.4 C = 15.6 C = 12.5
Lewinsohn, Hops, Roberts, Seeley, and Andrew (1993)[a]	K-SADS; *DSM–III–R*	14–18	C = 2.46		
Fombonne (1994)[b]	Rating scale	8–11		C = 9.3	C = 3.2
Jensen et al. (1995)	DISC; *DSM–III–R*	6–17	C = 0.5 P = 4.9		
Costello et al. (1996)[c]	CAPA; *DSM–III–R*	9, 11, 13	2.75	3.16	2.33
Verhulst et al. (1997)	DISC; *DSM–III–R*	13–18	P = 0.6 C = 0.7 C/P = 1.3		

Note. ODD = oppositional defiant disorder; DICA = Diagnostic Interview for Children and Adolescents (Reich & Welner, 1988); *DSM–III–R = Diagnostic and Statistical Manual of Mental Disorders* (3rd ed., rev.; American Psychiatric Association, 1987); C = child report; DISC = Diagnostic Interview Schedule (Costello et al., 1987); *DSM–III* = 3rd ed. (American Psychiatric Association, 1980); P = parent report; I = impairment; K-SADS = Schedule for Affective Disorders and Schizophrenia for School-age Children (Puig-Antich & Chambers, 1978); CAPA = Child and Adolescent Psychiatric Assessment (Angold & Costello, 1995).

[a]Lifetime prevalence. [b]3-month prevalence (the rates include mixed disorders and hyperkinetic disorders). [c]3-month prevalence.

and 25% in CD and ODD, respectively (Boyle et al., 1996; Lahey et al., 1990). In a study by Costello and Angold (1998), the prevalence of *DSM–IV* CD was slightly lower than that of *DSM–III–R*. The rates of ODD differed only slightly between *DSM–III–R* and *DSM–IV* (Costello & Angold, 1998).

The impact of impairment on the prevalence of CD/ODD have been inconsistent. In most studies (e.g., Bergeron et al., 1992; Bird et al., 1988), the inclusion of impairment had a considerable impact in reducing the rates of ODD, with the exception of Romano et al.'s (2001) study. In Romano et al., the inclusion of an impairment criterion did not have a significant impact on CD/ODD prevalence rates. That is, based on a child's report, the prevalence of CD that used only the symptom criteria was 6.3%, and the rate of CD based on symptoms criteria plus impairment was 4.2%. A lesser difference in rates of CD/ODD could be observed when the mother was used as an informant. Specifically, the rate of CD/ODD with symptom criteria was 3.4%, and the rate with symptom plus impairment criteria was 3.3%. This finding was interpreted as suggesting that most adolescents who meet symptom criteria for CD/ODD also experienced a high level of associated impaired functioning. Differences in the definition of *impairment* could have also contributed to these findings.

The way in which information from different sources (parents, teachers, and children) is combined also influenced the prevalence rates. For example, in the study by Fergusson et al. (1993), when maternal and child reports were combined using the optimal informant, the prevalence obtained was 10.8%; by latent-class method it was 8.1%. Based on an optimal informant, the prevalence found for boys was 12.2% and for girls 9.5%. By using latent class, the rate for boys was 8.6% and for girls 7.5%.

Variations in the prevalence rates may also arise from the type of settings from which the children and adolescents were recruited. In a recent study by Garland et al. (2001), the highest past year prevalence of CD was found among adolescents from Public School Services for Youth with Serious Emotional Disturbance (34.3%), followed by those from the Alcohol and Drug services (32.1%), Juvenile Justice (29.9%), mental health services (28.1%), and child welfare service (16.1%). ODD had the highest past year prevalence among adolescents who were recruited from school (22.6%) and from mental health service (20.2%) (Garland et al., 2001). As with the CD, ODD was the least common in the child welfare services at 13.5%.

CD/ODD and Gender and Age

In almost all studies, significantly more boys than girls met the diagnosis of CD during preadolescence (Lewinsohn, Hops, Roberts, Seeley, & Andrews, 1993; Robins & Price, 1991; Romano et al., 2001; Verhulst et al., 1997; see review by Loeber, Keenan, Russo, Green, Lahey, & Thomas, 1998). Indeed, Robins (1991) noted that "the most stable of all observations is the high rate of conduct disorder in boys as compared to girls" (p. 205). This gender difference, however, diminishes from studies of preadolescent children to adolescents (McGee, Feehan, Williams, & Anderson, 1992; Zoccolillo, 1993). For example, the prevalence of CD among 13-year-old German children were 6% and 5% for boys and girls, respectively (Esser et al., 1990). McGee et al. (1990) also reported the prevalence of CD being 7.2% and 7.4% for 15-year-old boys and girls, respectively. In the study by Cohen et al. (1993), there was a significant gender difference in the shapes of the prevalence curves. For boys, the highest prevalence was in the youngest group and declined over the ages of 10 to 20. Among girls, there was an increase in prevalence to a peak age of 16 followed by a sharp decline. ODD showed the same prevalence and age pattern for boys and girls, with low levels in the 10- and 11-year-olds rising to high levels among 13- to 16-year-olds and a sharp decline thereafter (Cohen et al., 1993).

The finding that the frequency of CD increased for girls by adolescence but not for boys may be explained in three ways (Cohen et al., 1993). First, CD may have developed later in girls than in boys. Furthermore, in girls the peak for CD appeared 2 or 3 years after menarche and was more related to social than hormonal changes (Cohen et al., 1993). Third, physical aggression seems to be more common among boys during age groups, whereas indirect aggression may be dependent on maturation and on the existence of a social network. That is, indirect aggression appears more often among girls but is not fully developed at the age of 8. Because girls develop verbal skills quicker than boys, they may have developed indirect aggressive strategies earlier than boys, as boys develop verbal skills much later in life. It could be that the prevalence ratio from preschool to adolescence is due to the fact that the early behavior symptoms are different for girls than boys; that is, girls are less overtly aggressive.

Symptoms of CD/ODD and CD-Related Behavior

Numerous studies have examined the prevalence of CD/ODD symptoms using self-report questionnaires. The most commonly used questionnaires are the Child Behavior Checklist (CBCL; Achenbach, 1991a) and the OCHS scales (Boyle et al., 1993). By using the OCHS scales, the most commonly reported CD symptom among German adolescents was that of "lying or cheating," reported by 41.4% of the adolescents (Essau, Petermann, & Ernst-Goergens, 1995). In the Canadian sample (Boyle et al., 1993), the most common symptoms were "cruelty, bullying, or meanness to others" (Table 2.3), reported by about half of the children and adolescents (53.3%). For ODD, the German adolescents reported using swearing or obscene language at a higher frequency than the Canadian adolescents (Table 2.4). Comparison of findings across these two studies showed only a few minor differences between German and Canadian adolescents in the frequency of CD/ODD symptoms (Tables 2.3 and 2.4).

To overcome the subjective and vague rating (e.g., *never, occasionally, often,* and *very often*) for the assessment of CD/ODD symptoms, Burns et al. (2001) suggested the use of rating procedures based on frequency counts for a specific time interval. By using their newly developed 7-point rating scale, the average occurrence for ODD symptoms in 12- to 19-year-olds based on parent rating was 3.47 and for CD symptoms it was 1.37. The CD symptoms with the highest means of occurrence were lying, followed by

TABLE 2.3

Frequencies of Conduct Disorder Symptoms
(Percent With a Positive Response) Based on *DSM–III–R* Criteria

Symptoms	Essau, Petermann, and Ernst-Goergens (1995)[a] Self-Report	Boyle et al. (1993)[b]		
		Self-Report	Parent Report	Teacher Report
Sets fires	7.5	5.0	1.8	0.4
Physically attacks people	20.5	11.0	6.9	7.1
Runs away from home	1.4	4.8	2.4	N/A
Lying or cheating	41.4	42.6	32.7	12.8
Truancy, skips school	24.7	20.0	14.3	11.9
Has broken into someone else's house, building, or car	2.3	2.5	1.1	N/A
Steals at home	8.5	9.2	9.2	N/A
Steals outside the home	8.4	7.2	6.1	N/A
Cruel to animals	8.8	6.1	2.8	1.3
Uses weapons when fighting	5.1	8.4	2.5	1.6
Cruelty, bullying, or meanness to others	14.9	53.3	31.1	19.0
Vandalism	7.4	7.5	2.2	5.0

Note. DSM–III–R = Diagnostic and Statistical Manual of Mental Disorders (3rd ed., rev.; American Psychiatric Association, 1987); N/A = not available.

[a]Adolescents are 11- to 19-year-olds. From Essau et al. (1995). © 1995 by S. Karger GmbH. Adapted with permission. [b]Adolescents are 12- to 16-year-olds. From Boyle et al. (1993). © 1993 by Blackwell Publishing Ltd. Reprinted with permission.

TABLE 2.4

Frequencies of Oppositional Disorder Symptoms
(Percent With a Positive Response) Based on *DSM–III–R* Criteria

Symptoms	Essau, Petermann, and Ernst-Goergens (1995)[a] Self-Report	Boyle et al. (1993)[b]		
		Self-Report	Parent Report	Teacher Report
Does things that annoy others	60.3	62.1	54.0	27.6
Angry and resentful	55.8	31.2	34.4	23.7
Temper tantrums or hot temper	37.7	53.9	41.3	16.1
Argues a lot with adults	76.3	55.8	53.1	19.7
Defiant, talks back to adults (staff)	83.2	63.2	48.8	17.0
Easily annoyed by others	55.3	73.7	55.7	26.9
Gets back at people	44.2	55.4	23.2	14.9
Swearing or obscene language	94.4	69.8	38.5	16.2
Blames others for own mistakes	39.5	37.6	48.3	25.4

Note. DSM–III–R = Diagnostic and Statistical Manual of Mental Disorders (3rd ed., rev.; American Psychiatric Association, 1987).

[a]Adolescents are 11- to 19-year-olds. From Essau et al. (1995). © 1995 by S. Karger GmbH. Adapted with permission. [b]Adolescents are 12- to 16-year-olds. From Boyle et al. (1993). © 1993 by Blackwell Publishing Ltd. Reprinted with permission.

fighting, destruction, and cruelty to others. For ODD symptoms, the symptoms with the highest mean of occurrence included irritation, anger, annoyance, and temper. These behaviors also occurred more than once per day.

The CBCL (Achenbach, 1991a) has been used in numerous studies to measure internalizing and externalizing problems in children and adolescents. The most frequently reported externalizing problems were that of aggressive and delinquent behavior, especially in younger boys compared to older boys or girls (Steinhausen, Winkler-Metzke, Meier, & Kannenberg, 1997). In a Russian study by Slobodskaya (1999), boys scored higher than girls on the Delinquent Behavior scale for self-ratings and teachers' ratings. Teachers also rated boys higher than girls on externalizing problems. Slobodskaya's finding also showed teachers' ratings for girls' delinquent behavior to be significantly higher than U.S. ratings.

Information on CD-related behavior in U.S. children and adolescents has been provided by the 1997 National Longitudinal Survey of Youth (Modi, 2000, cited in Synder & Sickmund, 1999). In this study, 9,000 adolescents across the United States were asked to report whether they had been involved in various types of deviant and delinquent behavior; 28% of the youths indicated having had purposely destroyed property, 8% had stolen something worth over $50.00, 10% had carried a handgun, 11% had run away from home, and 5% had belonged to a gang. All of these activities were more common in boys than in girls and they generally increased with age.

Gender, Age and CD Symptoms

Symptoms of CD generally show significant gender and age effects. In Essau et al. (1995), symptoms related to direct aggressive behavior showed a general decrease in frequency with age, whereas symptoms related to truancy and theft increased with age; one symptom (i.e., lying or cheating) seemed to hold constant across the age groups. Boys and older adolescents had higher number of symptoms for CD. Specifically, there was a linear decrease in the mean number of symptoms with age in boys, whereas the reverse was observed in girls. This was attributed to a higher number of nonaggressive symptoms reported by older girls. In the Dunedin study (McGee et al., 1992), the clearest increase from age 11 to age 15 was related to symptoms labeled *nonaggressive*. By contrast, the aggressive type showed no increase in prevalence over time and was a disorder primarily of boys; aggressive behavior such as the use of weapons, threatening others, setting fires, and damaging property showed little increase across the adolescent years.

The number and type of CD symptoms differed across age groups. As reported in several studies, certain types of nonaggressive behavior (e.g., serious theft, fraud; Loeber et al., 1998) and certain covert conduct problems increased from childhood through adolescence (Loeber & Stouthamer-Loeber, 1998). In a recent study by Lambert, Wahler, Andrade, and Bickman (2001), the most commonly endorsed criteria among children were related to child-level misbehavior such as lying, running away, and theft without confrontation, whereas adolescents more often exhibited adult misbehavior such as forced sexual activity and theft with confrontation. The number of symptoms of CD decreased with age in boys but increased with age in girls (Essau et al., 1995). This increase was related to higher rate of "indirect" types of aggressive behavior (e.g., lying).

Prevalence of CD-Related Behavior Based on Institutional Records

Information on CD-related behavior is also available from institutional records such as contact with the police or arrest records. However, the extent to which a behavior is defined as *criminal* depends on legislation concerning the age of criminal responsibility, which varies from one country to another and even within countries. This makes international or even national comparisons difficult (Rutter, Giller, & Hagell, 1998). Another problem with institutional records is the fact that most antisocial and delinquent acts are not recorded. As reported by Empey (1982), 9 of 10 illegal acts are not detected or not acted on officially. The 2000 British Crime Survey (cited in Stationery Office, 2000) suggested that less than half of all offenses are reported to the police; of these, less than one fourth are recorded. Furthermore, many adolescents who are reported to the authorities are not arrested, and if they are arrested, it is generally for certain delinquencies (Rutter et al., 1998). Therefore, official records may underestimate the occurrence of antisocial behaviors due to discretionary recording of the act on some archival record. Nevertheless, institutional records may represent socially significant measures of the impact of the problem. They also show social trends and facilitate decision making in terms of allocating resources and services for a particular problem (Kadzin, 1995).

The international trends in juvenile crime based on official statistics have been summarized by Rutter et al. (1998) and by Smith (1995) as follows:

1. Of all the reported or detected crimes, about one third were by juveniles.
2. Most crime is theft related. A small proportion of the crime is related to violence. For example, in the United Kingdom about 10% of the juvenile crime in 1995 was violence related.
3. The highest age of offending is in the late teens.
4. More males than females are detected to commit crime.
5. More than one third of offenders committed at least one violent crime.

In addition to these, official statistics in various countries have also indicated the high prevalence of CD-related behavior in children and adolescents (Smith, 1995). For example, data from the German Federal Criminal Department showed a steady increase in the number of child and adolescent criminal suspects from 1993 and 2000 (Bundeskriminalamt, 2000). Of all the indictable offenses in the year 2000, 6.4% were committed by children under 14 years, 12.9% by adolescents 14 to 18 years, and 10.8% by young adults aged 18 to 21 years. Most common offenses reported for children (under 14 years) among boys were fire setting (19.5%) and damaging objects (12.3%), and in girls these were stealing (5.1%) and fire setting (3.4%). Among adolescents, the most common antisocial behavior was damaging objects (56.8%), stealing (33.6%), and cheating (10.9%).

According to the Youth Lifestyles Survey conducted in the United Kingdom (East & Campbell, 1999), there was a 14% increase in the proportion of 14- to 17-year-old boys admitting an offense between 1992 to 1993 and 1998 to 1999; no such significant increase could be noted for girls. According to their 1998 to 1999 survey, 47% of the 12- to 30-year-olds admitted committing an offense sometime in their lives (57% male and 37% female). The average age at which offending began was 13½ years for boys and 14 years for girls. Shoplifting and criminal damage were the most frequent offenses among girls under 15 years, and for boys, the offenses were related to their involvement in fights, in buying stolen goods, "other theft," and criminal damage.

In the United States, reports on CD-related behavior are available from the Federal Bureau of Investigation and the National Report. For example, the Federal Bureau of Investigation's Supplemental Homicide Report indicated that about 1,400 of the persons murdered in the United States in 1997 were determined by law enforcement to involve adolescent offenders (Snyder & Sickmund, 1999). Victims of juvenile offenders are more likely to be acquaintances (56%) than strangers (34%). Male juvenile homicide offenders usually used a firearm, whereas female offenders generally used a knife or other means to kill (e.g., hands or feet, strangulation, drowning, or fire). According to the 1999 National Report, in the United States there has been a 35% increase in juvenile arrests (e.g., for robbery, aggravated assault for weapons, drugs, and curfew violations) between 1988 and 1997.

Official statistics on juvenile crime in Australia have been reported for the state of Queensland (Ogilvie, Lynch, & Bell, 2000). As reported in most industrialized countries, there has been an increase of juvenile crime over the last 20 years. Most offenses were related to less serious types of property crime and shoplifting (especially among girls). The monetary cost related to criminal youth has been extremely high. According to Potas, Vining, and Wilson's report in 1990, the cost of crime by youth was estimated to be $1.5 billion per year; this included $610 million in direct costs and $800 million in costs for the criminal justice system. The annual cost for detaining juveniles was estimated at $70 million.

Psychosocial Impairment and Services Utilization

In most studies, children with CD and ODD were impaired in many life domains. These include poor social relationships, significant conflict with parents and teachers, involvement with legal systems, and high emotional distress. Romano et al. (2001) found that among the disorders examined, the most impairment arose from oppositional and conduct symptoms (71.8%) followed by anxiety symptoms (22.9%). In a study by Lambert et al. (2001), children with CD showed the worst problem and impairment scores in comparison with 11 other common diagnoses. These children not only had significantly worse scores on measures of acting out but also on measures of internalizing disorders such as being more withdrawn and having more somatic problems, more problems with anxiety and depression, and more social problems. Among Japanese secondary school children, the presence of CD was strongly associated with school failure (Morita, Suzuki, Suzuki, & Kamoshita, 1993). By using data from seven community studies, Costello, Messer, Bird, Cohen, and Reinherz (1998) examined the impact of impairment on youth psychiatric functioning to estimate the prevalence of youth serious emotional disturbance (i.e., the presence of a psychiatric diagnosis and significant functional impairment). The median prevalence of serious emotional disturbance with global impairment was highest for conduct and/or oppositional disorders (2.5%) followed by anxiety disorders (1.9%). In addition to these "personal costs," CD has tremendous monetary and social costs. For example, according to Lambert et al.'s (2001) study, the cost of treatment based on total dollar cost from billing records was much greater for children with CD than those without (M = $21,000 vs. $8,000, respectively) and the duration was longer (M = 8.1 months vs. 7.1, respectively).

In Verhulst et al.'s (1997) study, 26% of children with CPs, attention deficit, or substance abuse sought professional help. However, the association between CD and service utilization seemed to be moderated by gender. That is, among girls, significant correlations were found between CD and frequency of doctor visits and frequency of meeting with a friend (Essau et al., 1995). The finding of the positive correlation between CD and the frequency of meeting with a friend is of interest. As proposed by Björkqvist, Lagerspetz, and Kaukiainen (1992), girls generally formed tighter groups or cliques, and they were likely to facilitate indirect aggression toward a third person. Girls are also known to mature faster verbally than boys, which in turn may facilitate the use of indirect means of aggression because increasing verbal skills are needed for the manipulations in question.

COMORBIDITY

One of the most consistent findings in childhood and adolescent psychopathology is the high rate of co-occurrence of disorders. As reported by Anderson et al. (1987), 55% of children with a diagnosable condition have two or more additional disorders. With respect to CD, comorbidity is the rule rather than the exception. For example, in a study by Lambert et al. (2001), the average number of primary diagnoses among CD children was 2.2 compared to 1.3 diagnoses in children without CD; one fourth of the children with CD had three or more *DSM–III–R* diagnoses. In a Dutch study (Verhulst et al., 1997), CD–ODD frequently occurred in combination with two or more other psychiatric disorders. CD in youth most frequently occurs with attention deficit hyperactivity disorder (ADHD), as well as with depression, anxiety, and substance use disorders.

The specific rates of comorbidity cannot be strictly compared across studies because of methodological differences in informants, assessment procedure (e.g., clinical judgment, diagnostic instruments), sample size, diagnostic criteria, age range, and gender composition (Nottelmann & Jensen, 1999). The extend to which diagnoses are made by clinicians or derived from computer algorithms also determines the comorbidity rates. Bird, Gould, and Staghezza (1993) found higher comorbidity rates when the diagnoses were made by computer algorithm than when they were derived at clinically. The low level of agreement is unclear. It has been suggested that clinicians generally assign the more severe or the more clinically relevant diagnoses and obviate those that are less relevant over the threshold of caseness. Algorithms cannot be expected to distinguish between the diagnoses of greater or lesser clinical significance (Bird et al., 1993). As such, the algorithm diagnoses may reflect the true pattern of comorbidity better than the clinical diagnoses because algorithms are less prone to that type of bias. Comorbidity rate is also effected by the level of impairment, with higher level of impairment being related to higher comorbidity rates.

The way in which this level of agreement between parents' and childs' report is dealt with also seems to influence comorbidity. For example, Bird et al. (1993) found higher comorbidity rates based on diagnoses using parent report compared to diagnoses based on child data, whereas Jensen et al. (1996) noted greater comorbidity based on combined versus single informant diagnoses. Another methodological issue is connected with the sampling bias in which persons with two or more disorders are more likely to be hospitalized or treated. As such, the clinic samples are generally comprised of individuals with comorbid disorders. This phenomenon arises because the chances of being referred to mental health services is higher for children and adolescents with a comorbid disorder than for those with only CD or ODD.

Comorbidity of CD and ODD

About 90% of the clinically referred children diagnosed with CD also meet the criteria for ODD (Faraone, Biederman, Keenan, & Tsuang, 1991; Loeber, 1988; Walker et al., 1991). Among those with both disorders, ODD generally occurs before CD. Studies have also reported that a subset of children with ODD generally advance to CD. These findings have led to the postulation (Lahey & Loeber, 1994) that ODD is a precursor of CD.

Comorbidity of CD/ODD and ADHD

ADHD is one of the most common concomitants to CD (Fergusson et al., 1993) with as many as three fourths of children with CD reporting the presence of ADHD as well. Unlike CD, ODD is not significantly associated with ADHD; 27% of ODD adolescents had a comorbid diagnosis of ADHD (Arredondo & Butler, 1994). In most of the cases, ADHD preceded the development of CP. In fact, impulsivity or hyperactivity components of ADHD are often considered to be the "motor" responsible for the development of early-onset CP, especially in boys (Loeber & Keenan, 1994; White et al., 1994). According to some authors (e.g., Loeber, 1990) ADHD may act as a catalyst for CD by contributing to the persistence of CPs and by leading to an escalation in an overt pathway to disruptive behavior.

Children with both CD and ADHD have more negative outcomes compared to those with CD only. That is, they had more physical aggression, a greater range and persistence of antisocial activity, more severe academic underachievement, and higher rates of peer rejection (Farrington, Loeber, & Van Kammen, 1990; Hinshaw, Lahey, & Hart, 1993; McGee et al., 1992). The presence of comorbid ADHD also predicts an earlier onset of CD (Hinshaw et al., 1993).

Comorbidity of CD/ODD and Depressive Disorders

CD is also frequently associated with depressive disorders. In epidemiological and clinical studies, comorbidity between CD/ODD and depressive disorders occurred at a rate greater than expected by chance (see review by Nottelmann & Jensen, 1999). In the days when masked depression was a popular concept, CPs were considered as one of the most frequent masks of depression (Cytryn & McKnew, 1972). In this view, children do not express depression directly with depressive symptoms but in behaviors that mask the underlying depressive feelings. "Depressive equivalents" commonly noted in depressed children and adolescents include temper tantrums, boredom, restlessness, hypochrondriasis, truancy, disobedience, self-destructive behavior, delinquency, school phobias, learning disabilities, hyperactivity, aggressive behavior and psychosomatic illness (Toolan, 1962).

Support for the masked depression hypothesis comes from early studies that showed that about 20% of adolescent delinquents were diagnosed with depression (Kashani, Ray, & Carlson, 1984). However, others have raised concern about a link between these disorders given the broad conditions under which aggression and dysphoric feelings may occur (Puig-Antich, 1982).

Mood disorders that most frequently co-occur with CD are major depression (33%), followed by bipolar disorder (25%), dysthymia (9%), and affective psychosis (5%; Arredondo & Butler, 1994). In contrast to the high comorbidity rates between CD and depression, the co-occurrence of ODD and depression exists less frequently. In Arredondo and Butler (1994), only 27% of the adolescents with ODD (compared to 76% with CD) met the diagnosis of mood disorder. Of these, 4% met criteria for bipolar disorder, 19% met criteria for major depression, and 4% met criteria for dysthymia. There were no cases of psychotic depression in adolescents diagnosed with ODD (Arredondo & Butler, 1994).

In attempting to explain the association between CD/ODD and depression, it has been suggested that (a) depression precipitates acting out behavior; (b) CD and its associated impairment may lead to demoralization and dysphoria; and (c) CD and depression have similar underlying psychological, familial, or psychobiological factors (Hinshaw & Anderson, 1996). Finally, the so-called dual failure model has also been used to explain comorbid conduct and depressive conditions (Patterson & Capaldi, 1991). According to this model, antisocial behavior increases risk for depression due to interference with social skill acquisition. Social deficits in antisocial boys may be further amplified by high levels of interpersonal conflict with peers, teachers, and parents, which leads to rejection. School failure and difficulties in developing friendships may then lead to depressed mood. Thus, some youth with CPs may be at increased risk for developing depressive problems. Depressive symptoms (e.g., irritability, emotional liability) may interact with defiant, aggressive, and impulsive rule-breaking behaviors that characterize conduct difficulties, which may intensify problem behaviors including increased substance use.

In most clinical (e.g., Biederman, Faraone, Mick, & Lelon, 1995; Goodyer, Herbert, Secher, & Pearson, 1997) and community studies (e.g., Lewinsohn, Clarke, Seeley, & Rohde, 1994), CD/ODD generally precedes rather than follows the development of depression. For example, Biederman et al. (1995) reported the age at onset for CD and ODD was about 6 to 7 years, compared to about 8 years for major depressive disorder (MDD). Among hospitalized girls with CD and MDD, the first symptom of CD occurred at 8.2 years old, and that of MDD at 13.5 years (Zoccolillo & Rogers, 1991). By contrast, Kovacs, Paulauskas, Gatsonis, and Richards (1988), who followed their sample of 8- to 13-year-olds, found that CD was more likely to follow than precede depression. Specifically, more depressed children with comorbid CD developed depressive disorders prior to CD (56%) rather than CD prior to depressive disorders (25%). The onset of depression in children with co-morbid CD (M = 12.2 years) was 2 years later than in depressed children without a CD diagnosis (M = 10.8 years).

The co-occurrence of CD and depression is associated with impairment in various life domains. For example, in the study by Lewinsohn, Rohde, and Seeley (1995), adolescents with both depression and CD were more likely at follow-up than adolescents without CD to have received treatment for any disorder, to have poor global functioning, and to have academic problems. Among clinical samples, adolescents with CD and depression were significantly more likely to have run away, had police or juvenile court contacts, and had school suspension than those without CD; the presence of comorbid CD did not influence the course of MDD, the length of the index episode, or the length of the interval between index episode and the subse-quent depressive episode (Kovacs et al., 1988). In the study by Harrington, Fudge, Rutter, Pickles, and Hill (1990), depressed children with CD had worse outcomes than depressed children without CPs. About 18 years later, outcome for the depressed group comorbid with CD was similar to that of the nondepressed CD group in that they had a high rate of criminality, and a higher rate of antisocial personality disorder, alcohol abuse, and depend-ence than depressed children without CPs. The depressed group with CD had lower risk for adult MDD than depressed children without CPs. The ad-olescents in the MDD + CD group showed similar outcomes with that of ado-lescents with CD; poorer global functioning, more academic problems, and more involvement in criminal behavior is likely to be worse than for MDD without comorbid CD.

Children with comorbid depression and CDs were significantly less com-petent than depressed children (Renouf, Kovacs, & Mukerji, 1997). The find-ings also suggest that social impairment associated with comorbid depres-sion and CD is mostly due to the CD; CD has a more severe and longer term impact on children's social competence than does depression. However, the presence of both disorders (comorbidity) predicted greater impairment in social competence than the presence of only one disorder. The co-occurrence of CD and depression is associated with increased risk of sui-cidal behavior (Shaffi, Carrigan, Whittinghill, & Derrick, 1985).

Comorbidity of CD/ODD and Anxiety Disorders

The other group of disorders that commonly co-occur with CD are the anxi-ety disorders, especially in girls (Loeber & Keenan, 1994). The interplay be-tween these two disorders is complex. Boys with CD alone compared to prepubertal boys with CD and anxiety disorder had significantly less ag-gressive behavior (e.g., bullying) and were less likely to be nominated by classmates for fighting (Lahey & Loeber, 1994; Walker et al., 1991). However, no group differences were found for the covert, nonaggressive symptoms of CD (e.g., lying). Using data from a Developmental Trends Study, Lahey and McBurnett (1992) found that although boys with comorbid CD and anxiety disorders showed less aggression during the first 2 years (when they were 9.5 and 10.5 years of age, respectively) than did the CD only group, the comorbid group showed more aggression during the 3rd and 4th years (when they were 11.5 and 12.5 years of age, respectively). Among CD-only boys, physical aggression was high during the first 2 years, however, it decreased with increasing age. In the CD/anxiety-disorder group, serious aggression increased over the previously mentioned 4 years until it surpassed the level of the CD-only group. Across all 4 years, anxiety was unrelated to the development of nonaggressive (covert) CD behaviors.

Comorbidity of CD/ODD and Substance Use Disorders

Substance use disorders are also frequent co-occurrence of CD/ODD (Arredondo & Butler, 1994; Feehan et al., 1994). The association between substance use disorders and CD/ODD has often been explained using the Jessor and Jessor's (1977) problem behavior theory. Within this framework, different problem behaviors are viewed as part of a broader deviance pattern that reflects a single, underlying syndrome and includes various types of norm-violating behaviors. For example, in the study by Miller-Johnson, Lochman, Coie, Terry, and Hyman (1998), children and adolescents who displayed high levels of conduct problems during early adolescence were at risk for increased levels of substance use from sixth through tenth grades; similar trends were also found for tobacco, alcohol, and marijuana use.

Although not all youth who use substance have a history of CD, the preexisting CD constitutes a significant risk factor for substance use (Hawkins, Catalano, & Miller, 1992), particularly in girls (Loeber & Keenan, 1994). In addition, concurrent substance use may increase the risk of more serious delinquent behavior (Loeber & Keenan, 1994).

Categorical Approach. In examining the comorbidity rates and comorbidity patterns, almost all studies have used the categorical approach, with the exception of a study by Yang, Chen, and Soon (2001). In this study, the rates and patterns of comorbidity between behavioral syndromes in adolescents were examined based on reports by parents and teachers using the CBCL and Teacher's Report Form (TRF; Achenbach, 1991b), respectively. High comorbidity rates between adolescent behavioral syndromes existed in both parents' and teachers' report. The highest comorbidity rate was found for delinquent behavior and aggressive behavior; the odds ratios based on the CBCL was 35.7 and based on the TRF it was 41.4. The comorbidity rates between attention problems and aggression were much higher based on the CBCL than on the TRF, being 27.6 and 10.8, respectively. In both the CBCL and the TRF, the comorbidity between anxiety/depression and aggression, as well as between anxiety/depression and delinquency were quite low. Overall, the high comorbidity between delinquent behavior and aggressive behavior in the Yang et al. study replicated the findings of studies that used a categorical approach.

Meaning of Comorbidity

Despite the pervasiveness of comorbidity between CD/ODD and other psychiatric disorders, the meaning of comorbidity for psychopathology and classification issues remains unclear. Current debate about the possible cause of comorbidity has centered around four main issues: classification, developmental process, methodology, and etiology. The first is the area of classification, such as the issue on the appropriateness of diagnostic boundaries or artificial subdivision of syndromes. Some of the debate related to classification issues include the overlap of symptoms (Angold & Costello, 1993; Nottelmann & Jensen, 1999). A related issue is the presence of assessment bias, which may include a large degree of symptoms that overlap between different diagnostic categories or the application of diagnostic hierarchies that may mask an association between disorders (Widiger & Ford-Black, 1994).

Comorbidity has also been considered as part of the developmental processes in children and adolescents (Nottelmann & Jensen, 1999). It has been argued that psychopathology may present differently at different stages of development, and the transition from one developmental stage to the next may suggest the existence of comorbidity. For example, underlying psychopathology may manifest differently at successive stages of development, but during transition from one developmental stage to the next developmental stage may show the existence of comorbidity. Rutter (1994) argued that the core of every disorder is a struggle for adaptation, but the way in which the phenotype is expressed depends on environmental conditions and person–environment interactions. The former suggests that an index disorder causes or predisposes the development of subsequent disorders. In order words, the presence of one disorder is the prerequisite condition for the development of the other. Comorbidity may also arise from the nonspecific nature of symptoms of disorders, which are quite diffuse in their expression. As shown by findings from the Dunedin study (Anderson & McGee, 1994), disorders tend to become increasingly distinct with age, with broad separations between internalizing and externalizing disorders by the age of 15 years.

Another explanation is related to the etiology of disorders. As argued by Merikangas (1989), the co-occurrence of disorders could be etiologic in that one disorder causes the second disorder (i.e., causal association), or that the two disorders are manifestations of the same underlying etiologic factors (i.e., common etiology), or that it may reflect different stages of the same disease.

Methodological biases include treatment or sampling bias (also known as "Berkson's bias") in which persons with two or more disorders have a greater chance to be hospitalized or treated. As such, the clinical samples are generally comprised of individuals with comorbid disorders. This phenomenon arises because the chances of being referred to mental health services is higher for adolescents with a comorbid disorder than for those with only anxiety disorder. Data from clinical samples may also be problematic due to factors affecting the referral process such as the presence of parental psychopathology or externalizing disorders (Essau, 2002).

Regardless of this controversy, comorbidity is often associated with a negative course and outcome of CD/ODD. It would be of interest to examine the extend to which comorbidity may change the clinical course of the disorder by affecting the time of detection, prognosis, and treatment selection.

CONCLUSION

The purpose of this chapter was to review findings from epidemiological studies on the prevalence and comorbidity of CD and ODD. CD and ODD are common disorders affecting a significant number of children and adolescents in the general population. Comorbidity is a common feature of CD presentations. CD most frequently co-occurs with ADHD, as well as with depression, anxiety, and substance use disorders. Longitudinal studies are needed to enhance our understanding of comorbidity. Such studies should contribute to (a) solving the issue of diagnostic specificity by exploring the temporal sequence of these disorders; (b) establishing differences and similarities of characteristics of youth with comorbid versus noncomorbid CD/ODD; and (c) examining the impact of comorbid disorders in the natural history of CD/ODD. Epidemiological studies provide a powerful tool for investigating the nature and associated features (e.g., comorbidity and risk factors) of CD/ODD. Due to the complex nature of these disorders, future studies need to use developmental, epidemiological, and longitudinal approaches to answer some of the outstanding issues related to CD and ODD.

REFERENCES

Achenbach, T. M. (1991a). *Manual for the Child Behavior Checklist/4–18 and 1991 profile*. Burlington: University of Vermont Department of Psychiatry.

Achenbach, T. M. (1991b). *Manual for the Teacher's Report Form and 1991 profile*. Burlington: University of Vermont Department of Psychiatry.

American Psychiatric Association. (1980). *Diagnostic and statistical manual of mental disorders* (3rd ed.). Washington, DC: Author.

American Psychiatric Association. (1987). *Diagnostic and statistical manual of mental disorders* (3rd ed., rev.). Washington, DC: Author.

American Psychiatric Association. (1994). *Diagnostic and statistical manual of mental disorders* (4th ed.). Washington, DC: Author.

Anderson, J. C., & McGee, R. (1994). Comorbidity of depression in children and adolescents. In W. M. Reynolds & H. F. Johnston (Eds.), *Handbook of depression in children and adolescents* (pp. 581–601). New York: Plenum Press.

Anderson, J. C., Williams, S., McGee, R., & Silva, P. A. (1987). DSM–III disorders in preadolescent children. Prevalence in a large sample from the general population. *Archives of General Psychiatry, 44*, 69–76.

Angold, A., & Costello, E. J. (1993). Depressive comorbidity in children and adolescents: Empirical, theoretical, and methodological issues. *American Journal of Psychiatry, 150*, 1779–1791.

Angold, A., & Costello, E. J. (1995). A test-retest study of child-reported symptoms and diagnoses using the Child and Adolescent Psychiatric Assessment (CAPA). *Psychological Medicine, 25*, 755–762.

Arredondo, D. E., & Butler, S. F. (1994). Affective comorbidity in psychiatrically hospitalized adolescents with conduct disorder or oppositional defiant disorder: Should conduct disorder be treated with mood stabilizers? *Journal of Child and Adolescent Psychopharmacology, 4*, 151–158.

Bergeron, L., Valla, J. P., & Breton, J. J. (1992). Pilot study for the Quebec Child Mental Health Survey: Part I. Measurement of prevalence estimates among six to 14 year olds. *Canadian Journal of Psychiatry, 37*, 374–380.

Biederman, J., Faraone, S., Mick, E., & Lelon, E. (1995). Psychiatric comorbidity among referred juveniles with major depression: Fact or artifact? *Journal of the American Academy of Child and Adolescent Psychiatry, 34*, 579–590.

Bird, H., Canino, G., Rubio-Stipec, M., Gould, M. S., Ribera, J., Sesman, M., Woodbury, M., Huertas-Goldman, S., Pagan, A., Sanchez-Lacay, A., & Moscoso, M. (1988). Estimates of the prevalence of childhood maladjustment in a community survey in Puerto Rico. *Archives of General Psychiatry, 45*, 1120–1126.

Bird, H. R., Gould, M. S., & Staghezza, B. M. (1993). Patterns of diagnostic comorbidity in a community sample of children aged 9 through 16 years. *Journal of the American Academy of Child and Adolescent Psychiatry, 32*, 361–368.

Björkqvist, K., Lagerspetz, K. M., & Kaukiainen, A. (1992). Do girls manipulate and boys fight? Developmental trends in regard to direct and indirect aggression. *Aggressive Behavior, 18*, 117–127.

Boyle, M. H., Offord, D. R., Hofman, H. G., Catlin, G. P., Byles, J. A., Cadman, D. T., Crawford, J. W., Links, P. S., Rae-Grant, N. I., & Szatmari, P. (1987). Ontario Child Health Study: I. Methodology. *Archives of General Psychiatry, 44*, 826–831.

Boyle, M. H., Offord, D. R., Racine, Y., Fleming, J. E., Szatmari, P., & Sanford, M. (1993). Evaluation of the revised Ontario Child Health Study scales. *Journal of Child Psychology and Psychiatry, 34*, 189–213.

Boyle, M. H., Offord, D. R., Racine, Y., Szatmari, P., Fleming, J., & Sanford, M. (1996). Identifying thresholds for classifying psychiatric disorder: Issues and prospects. *Journal of the American Academy of Child and Adolescent Psychiatry, 35*, 1440–1448.

Bundeskriminalamt. (2000). *Polizeiliche Kriminalstatistik 2000—Bundesrepublik Deutschland*. Wiesbaden, Germany: Bundeskriminalamt. Retrieved Jan. 2002 http://www.bka.de/pks/pks2000

Burns, G. L., Walsh, J. A., Patterson, D. R., Holte, C. S., Sommers-Flanagan, R., & Parker, C. M. (2001). Attention deficit and disruptive behavior disorder symptoms. *European Journal of Psychological Assessment, 17*, 25–35.

Cohen, P., Cohen, J., Kasen, S., Velez, C. N., Hartmark, C., Johnson, J., Rojas, M., Brook, J., & Streuning, E. L. (1993). An epidemiological study of disorders in late childhood and adolescence: I. Age- and gender-specific prevalence. *Journal Child Psychology and Psychiatry, 34,* 851–866.

Connell, H. M., Irvine, L., & Rodney, J. (1982). Psychiatric disorder in Queensland primary school children. *Australian Pediatrics Journal, 18,* 177–180.

Costello, A. J., Edelbrock, C., Dulcan, M. K., Kalas, R., & Klaric, S. (1987). *The Diagnostic Interview Schedule for Children (DISC).* Pittsburgh: University of Pittsburgh.

Costello, E. J., & Angold, A. (1998). *Three-month prevalence of disruptive disorders by age and sex.* Unpublished data. Durham, NC: Department of Psychiatry, Duke University.

Costello, E. J., Angold, A., Burns, B. J., Stangl, D., Tweed, D. L., & Erkanli, A. (1996). The Great Smoky Mountains Study of youth: Goals, designs, methods, and the prevalence of DSM–III–R disorders. *Archives of General Psychiatry, 53,* 1129–1136.

Costello, E. J., Messer, S. C., Bird, H. R., Cohen, P., & Reinherz, H. Z. (1998). The prevalence of serious emotional disturbance: A re-analysis of community studies. *Journal of Child and Family Studies, 7,* 411–432.

Cytryn, L., & McKnew, D. H. (1972). Proposed classification of childhood depression. *American Journal of Psychiatry, 129,* 149–155.

East, K., & Campbell, S. (1999). *Aspects of crime: Young offenders 1999.* Retrieved Jan. 2002 http://www.homeoffice.gov.uk/rds/youthjustice1.html

Empey, L. T. (1982). *American delinquency: Its meaning and construction.* Homewood, IL: Dorsey.

Essau, C. A. (2002). *Depression bei Kindern und Jugendlichen* [Depression in children and adolescents]. München, Germany: Ernst Reinhardt Verlag.

Essau, C. A., Petermann, F., & Ernst-Goergens, B. (1995). Aggressives Verhalten im Jugendalter [Aggressive behavior in adolescence]. *Verhaltenstherapie, 4,* 226–230.

Essau, C. A., Petermann, F., & Feehan, M. (1997). Research methods and designs. In C. A. Essau & F. Petermann (Eds.), *Developmental psychopathology: Epidemiology, diagnostics and treatment* (pp. 63–95). London: Harwood.

Esser, G., Schmidt, M. H., & Woerner, W. (1990). Epidemiology and course of psychiatric disorders in school-age children—Results of a longitudinal study. *Journal of Child Psychology and Psychiatry, 31,* 243–263.

Faraone, S. V., Biederman, J., Keenan, K., & Tsuang, M. T. (1991). Separation of DSM–III attention deficit disorder and conduct disorder: Evidence from a family genetic study of American child psychiatric patients. *Psychological Medicine, 21,* 109–121.

Farrington, D. P., Loeber, R., & Van Kammen, W. B. (1990). Long-term criminal outcomes of hyperactivity-impulsivity-attention deficit and conduct problems in childhood. In L. N. Robins & M. Rutter (Eds.), *Straight and devious pathways to adulthood* (pp. 62–81). New York: Cambridge University Press.

Feehan, M., McGee, R., Nada-Raja, S., & Williams, S. M. (1994). DSM–III–R disorders in New Zealand 18-year-olds. *Australian and New Zealand Journal of Psychiatry, 28,* 87–99.

Fergusson, D. M., Horwood, L. J., & Lynskey, M. T. (1993). Prevalence and comorbidity of DSM–III–R diagnoses in a birth cohort of 15 year olds. *Journal of the American Academy of Child and Adolescent Psychiatry, 32,* 1127–1134.

Garland, A. F., Hough, R. L., McCabe, K. M., Yeh, M., Wood, P. A., & Aarons, G. A. (2001). Prevalence of psychiatric disorders in youths across five sectors of care. *Journal of the American Academy of Child and Adolescent Psychiatry, 40,* 409–418.

Goodyer, I., Herbert, J., Secher, S., & Pearson, J. (1997). Short term outcome of major depression: I. Comorbidity and severity at presentation as predictors of persistent disorder. *Journal of the American Academy of Child and Adolescent Psychiatry, 36,* 179–187.

Graham, P., & Rutter, M. (1973). Psychiatric disorders in the young adolescent: A follow-up study. *Proceedings of the Royal Society of Medicine, 66,* 1226–1229.

Harrington, R., Fudge, H., Rutter, M., Pickles, A., & Hill, J. (1990). Adult outcomes of childhood and adolescent depression: I. Psychiatric status. *Archives of General Psychiatry, 47*, 465–473.

Hawkins, J. D., Catalano, R. F., & Miller, Y. (1992). Risk and protective factors for alcohol and other drug problems in adolescence and early adulthood: Implications for substance abuse prevention. *Psychological Bulletin, 112*, 64–105.

Hinshaw, S. P., & Anderson, C. A. (1996). Conduct and oppositional defiant disorders. In E. J. Mash & R. A. Barkley (Eds.), *Child psychopathology* (pp. 113–149). New York: Guilford.

Hinshaw, S. P., Lahey, B., & Hart, L. (1993). Issues of taxonomy and comorbidity in the development of conduct disorder. *Development and Psychopathology, 5*, 31–49.

Jensen, P. S., Watanabe, H., Richters, J., Cortes, R., Roper, M., & Liu, S. (1995). Prevalence of mental disorder in military children and adolescents: Findings from a two-stage community survey. *Journal of the American Academy of Child and Adolescent Psychiatry, 34*, 1514–1524.

Jensen, P. S., Watanabe, H. K., Richters, J. E., Roper, M., Hibbs, E., Salzberg, & Liu, S. (1996). Scales, diagnoses, and child psychopathology. II. Comparing the CBCL and the DISC against external validators. *Journal of Abnormal Child Psychology, 24*, 151–168.

Jessor, R., & Jessor, S. L. (1977). *Problem behavior and psychosocial development: A longitudinal study of youth.* New York: Academic.

Kashani, J. H., Carlson, G. A., Beck, N. C., Hoeper, E. W., Corcoran, C. M., McAllister, J. A., Fallahi, C., Rosenberg, T. K., & Reid, J. C. (1987). Depression, depressive symptoms, and depressed mood among a community sample of adolescents. *American Journal of Psychiatry, 144*, 931–934.

Kashani, J. H., Ray, J. S., & Carlson, G. A. (1984). Depression and depressive-like states in preschool children in a child development unit. *American Journal of Psychiatry, 141*, 1397–1402.

Kazdin, A. E. (1995). Conduct disorder. In F. C. Verhulst & H. M. Koot (Eds.), *Epidemiology of child and adolescent psychopathology* (pp. 258–290). Oxford, England: Oxford University Press.

Kovacs, M., Paulauskas, S. L., Gatsonis, C., & Richards, C. (1988). Depressive disorders in childhood: III. Longitudinal study of comorbidity with and risk for conduct disorders. *Journal of Affective Disorders, 15*, 205–217.

Lahey, B. B., & Loeber, R. (1994). Framework for a developmental model of oppositional defiant disorder and conduct disorder. In D. K. Routh (Ed.), *Disruptive behavior disorders in childhood* (pp. 139–180). New York: Plenum.

Lahey, B. B., Loeber, R., Stouthamer-Loeber, M., Christ, M. A. G., Green, S. M., Russo, M. F., Frick, P. J., & Dulcan, M. (1990). Comparison of DMS–III and DSM–III–R diagnoses for prepubertal children: Changes in prevalence and validity. *Journal of the American Academy of Child and Adolescent Psychiatry, 29*, 620–626.

Lahey, B. B., & McBurnett, K. (1992, February). Behavioral and biological correlates of aggressive conduct disorder: Temporal stability. In D. Routh (Chair), *The psychobiology of disruptive disorders in children. In tribute to Herbert Quay.* Symposium conducted at the annual meeting of the Society for Research in Child and Adolescent Psychopathology, Sarasota, FL.

Lambert, E. W., Wahler, R. G., Andrade, R. A., & Bickman, L. (2001). Looking for the disorder in conduct disorder. *Journal of Abnormal Psychology, 110*, 110–123.

Lewinsohn, P. M., Clarke, G. N., Seeley, J. R., & Rohde, P. (1994). Major depression in community adolescents: Age of onset, episode duration, and time to recurrence. *Journal of the American Academy of Child and Adolescent Psychiatry, 33*, 809–819.

Lewinsohn, P. M., Hops, H., Roberts, R. E., Seeley, J. R., & Andrews, J. A. (1993). Adolescent psychopathology: I. Prevalence and incidence of depression and other DSM–III–R disorders in high school students. *Journal of Abnormal Psychology, 102*, 133–144.

Lewinsohn, P. M., Rohde, P., & Seeley, J. R. (1995). Adolescent psychopathology: III. The clinical consequences of comorbidity. *Journal of the American Academy of Child and Adolescent Psychiatry, 34*, 510–519.

Loeber, R. (1988). The natural histories of juvenile conduct problems, substance use and delinquency: Evidence for developmental progressions. In B. B. Lahey & A. E. Kazdin (Eds.), *Advances in clinical child psychology* (Vol. 11, pp. 73–124). New York: Plenum.

Loeber, R. (1990). Development and risk factors of juvenile antisocial behavior and delinquency. *Clinical Psychology Review, 10,* 1–41.

Loeber, R., & Keenan, K. (1994). Interaction between conduct disorder and its comorbid conditions: Effects of age and gender. *Clinical Psychology Review, 14,* 497–523.

Loeber, R., Keenan, K., Russo, M. F., Green, S. M., Lahey, B. B., & Thomas, C. (1998). Secondary data analyses for DSM–IV on the symptoms of oppositional defiant disorder and conduct disorder. In T. A. Widiger, A. J. Frances, H. J. Pincus, R. Roth, M. B. First, W. Davis, & M. Kline (Eds.), *DSM–IV Sourcebook* (Vol. 4, pp. 465–490). Washington, DC: American Psychiatric Press.

Loeber, R., & Stouthamer-Loeber, M. (1998). Development of juvenile aggression and violence. Some common misconceptions and controversies. *American Psychologist, 53,* 242–259.

McGee, R., Feehan, M., & Williams, S. (1995). Long-term follow-up of a birth cohort. In F. C. Verhulst & H. M. Koot (Eds.), *Epidemiology of child and adolescent psychopathology* (pp. 366–384). Oxford, England: Oxford University Press.

McGee, R., Feehan, M., Williams, S., & Anderson, J. (1992). DSM–III disorders from age 11 to age 15 years. *Journal of the American Academy of Child and Adolescent Psychiatry, 31,* 50–59.

McGee, R., Feehan, M., Williams, S., Partridge, F., Silva, A., & Kelly, J. (1990). DSM–III disorders in a large sample of adolescents. *Journal of the American Academy of Child and Adolescence Psychiatry, 29,* 611–619.

Merikangas, K. R. (1989). Comorbidity for anxiety and depression: Review of family and genetic studies. In J. D. Maser & C. R. Cloninger (Eds.), *Comorbidity of mood and anxiety disorders* (pp. 331–348). Washington, DC: American Psychiatric Press.

Miller-Johnson, S., Lochman, J. E., Coie, J. D., Terry, R., & Hyman, C. (1998). Comorbidity of conduct disorder and depressive problems at sixth grade: Substance use outcomes across adolescence. *Journal of Abnormal Child Psychology, 26,* 221–232.

Modi, M. (2000). *"NLSY97."* Summaries of surveys measuring well-being. Retrieved http://www. wws.princeton.edu/~kling/surveys/NLSY97.html

Morita, H., Suzuki, M., Suzuki, S., & Kamoshita, S. (1993). Psychiatric disorders in Japanese secondary school children. *Journal of Child Psychology and Psychiatry, 34,* 317–332.

Nottelmann, E. D., & Jensen, P. S. (1999). Comorbidity of depressive disorders in children and adolescents: Rates, temporal sequencing, course and outcome. In C. A. Essau & F. Petermann (Eds.), *Depressive disorders in children and adolescents: Epidemiology, risk factors, and treatment* (pp. 137–191). Northvale, NJ: Jason Aronson.

Ogilvie, E., Lynch, M., & Bell, S. (2000). *Gender and official statistics: The juvenile justice system in Queensland, 1998–99.* Canberra, Australian Capital Territory, Australia: Australian Institute of Criminology. Retrieved July 2002 http://www.aic.gov.au/publications/tandi162.html

Patterson, G. R., & Capaldi, D. M. (1991). Antisocial parents: Unskilled and vulnerable. In P. A. Cowan & E. M. Hetherington (Eds.), *Family transitions* (pp. 195–218). Hillsdale, NJ: Lawrence Erlbaum Associates.

Potas, I., Vining, A., & Wilson, P. R. (1990). *Young people and crime: Costs and prevention.* Canberra, Australian Capital Territory, Australia: Australian Institute of Criminology.

Puig-Antich, J. (1982). Major depression and conduct disorder in prepuberty. *Journal of the American Academy of Child Psychiatry, 21,* 118–128.

Puig-Antich, J., & Chambers, W. (1978). *The Schedule for Affective Disorders and Schizophrenia for school-aged children.* New York: State Psychiatric Institute, New York.

Reich, W., & Welner, Z. (1988). *Diagnostic Interview for Children and Adolescents (DICA).* St. Louis, MO: Department of Psychiatry, Washington University.

Renouf, A. G., Kovacs, M., & Mukerji, P. (1997). Relationship of depressive, conduct, and comorbid disorders and social functioning in childhood. *Journal of the American Academy of Child and Adolescent Psychiatry, 36,* 998–1004.

Robins, L. N. (1991). Conduct disorder. *Journal of Child Psychology and Psychiatry, 32,* 193–212.

Robins, L. N., & Price, R. K. (1991). Adult disorders predicted by childhood conduct problems: Results from the NIMH Epidemiologic Catchment Area project. *Psychiatry, 54*, 116–132.

Romano, E., Tremblay, R. E., & Vitaro, F. (2001). Prevalence of psychiatric diagnoses and the role of perceived impairment: Findings from an adolescent community sample. *Journal of Child Psychology and Psychiatry, 42*, 451–461.

Rutter, M. (1994). Comorbidity: Meanings and mechanisms. *Clinical Psychology: Science and Practice, 1*, 100–103.

Rutter, M., Giller, H., & Hagell, A. (1998). *Antisocial behavior by young people.* Cambridge, England: Cambridge University Press.

Rutter, M., Tizard, J., & Whitmore, K. (1970). *Education, health and behavior.* London: Longmans.

Shaffer, D., Fisher, P., Dulcan, M. K., Davies, M., Piacentini, P., Schwab-Stone, M. E., Lahey, B. B., Bourdon, K., Jensen, P. S., Bird, H. R., Canino, G., & Regier, D. A. (1996). The NIMH Diagnostic Interview Schedule for Children Version 2.3 (DISC-2.3): Description, acceptability, prevalence rates, and performance in the MECA Study. *Journal of the American Academy of Child and Adolescent Psychiatry, 35*, 865–877.

Shaffer, D., Gould, M. S., Brasic, J., Ambrosini, P., Fisher, P., Bird, H., & Aluwahlia, S. (1983). A children's global assessment scale (CGAS). *Archives of General Psychiatry, 40*, 1228–1231.

Shaffi, N., Carrigan, S., Whittinghill, J. R., & Derrick, A. (1985). Psychological autopsy of completed suicide of children and adolescents. *American Journal of Psychiatry, 142*, 1061–1064.

Shepherd, M., Oppenheim, B., & Mitchell, S. (1971). *Childhood behaviour and mental health.* London: University of London Press.

Slobodskaya, H. R. (1999). Competence, emotional and behavioral problems in Russian adolescents. *European Child and Adolescent Psychiatry, 8*, 173–180.

Smith, D. J. (1995). Youth crime and conduct disorders: Trends, patterns and causal explanations. In M. Rutter & D. J. Smith (Eds.), *Psychosocial disorders in young people: Time trends and their causes* (pp. 389–489). Chichester, England: Wiley.

Snyder, H. N., & Sickmund, M. (1999). *Juvenile offenders and victims: 1999 National reports.* Retrieved Jan. 2002 http://www.ncjrs.org/html/ojjdp/nationalreport99

Stationery Office. (2000). *Criminal statistics: England and Wales 1999.* Retrieved Jan. 2002 http://archive.offical-documents.co.uk/document/CM50/5001/5001.htm

Steinhausen, H.-C., Winkler-Metzke, C., Meier, M., & Kannenberg, R. (1997). Behavioral and emotional problems reported by parents for ages 6 to 17 in a Swiss epidemiological study. *European Child and Adolescent Psychiatry, 6*, 136–141.

Toolan, J. M. (1962). Depression in children and adolescence. *American Journal of Orthopsychiatry, 32*, 404–414.

Velez, C. N., Johnson, J., & Cohen, P. (1989). A longitudinal analysis of selected risk factors for childhood psychopathology. *Journal of the American Academy of Child and Adolescent Psychiatry, 28*, 851–864.

Verhulst, F. C. (1995). The epidemiology of child and adolescent psychopathology: Strengths and limitations. In F. C. Verhulst & H. M. Koot (Eds.), *Epidemiology of child and adolescent psychopathology* (pp. 1–21). Oxford, England: Oxford University Press.

Verhulst, F. C., van der Ende, J., Ferdinand, R. F., & Kasius, M. C. (1997). The prevalence of DSM–III–R diagnoses in a National sample of Dutch adolescents. *Archives of General Psychiatry, 54*, 329–336.

Vikan, A. (1985). Psychiatric epidemiology in a sample of 1,510 ten-year-old children: I. Prevalence. *Journal of Child Psychology and Psychiatry, 26*, 55–75.

Walker, J. L., Lahey, B. B., Russo, M. F., Christ, M. A., McBurnett, K., Loeber, R., Stouthamer-Loeber, M., & Green, S. M. (1991). Anxiety, inhibition, and conduct disorder in children: I. Relations to social impairment. *Journal of the American Academy of Child and Adolescent Psychiatry, 30*, 187–191.

Webster-Stratton, C. (1996). Early-onset conduct problems: Does gender make a difference? *Journal of Consulting and Clinical Psychology, 64*, 540–551.

White, J. L., Moffitt, T. E., Caspi, A., Bartusen, D., Needles, D., & Stouthamer-Loeber, M. (1994). Measuring impulsivity and examining its relation to delinquency. *Journal of Abnormal Psychology, 103,* 192–205.

Widiger, T. A., & Ford-Black, M. M. (1994). Diagnoses and disorders. *Clinical Psychology: Science and Practice, 1,* 84–87.

Wittchen, H.-U., & Essau, C. A. (1993). Epidemiology of anxiety disorders. In P. J. Wilner (Ed.), *Psychiatry* (pp. 1–25). Philadelphia: J. B. Lippincott Company.

Yang, H.-J., Chen, W. J., & Soon, W.-S. (2001). Rates and patterns of comorbidity of adolescent behavioral syndromes as reported by parents and teachers in a Taiwanese nonreferred sample. *Journal of the American Academy of Child and Adolescent Psychiatry, 40,* 1045–1052.

Zoccolillo, M. (1993). Gender and the development of conduct disorder. *Development and Psychopathology, 5,* 65–78.

Zoccolillo, M., & Rogers, K. (1991). Characteristics and outcome of hospitalized adolescent girls with conduct disorder. *Journal of American Academy of Child and Adolescent Psychiatry, 30,* 973–981.

3

Course and Outcomes

Jeffrey D. Burke
Western Psychiatric Institute and Clinic

Rolf Loeber
University of Pittsburgh

Benjamin B. Lahey
University of Chicago

Oppositional Defiant Disorder (ODD) and Conduct Disorder (CD) continue to be the predominant juvenile disorders seen in mental health and community clinics (Frick, 1998; Kazdin, 1995) and are of great concern because of their high degree of impairment (Lahey, Loeber, Quay, Frick, & Grimm, 1997), potential for persistence over time, and association with negative outcomes. Research in recent years has provided a good deal of clarity regarding the course of antisocial behavior from childhood through adulthood. Clearly, much remains to be addressed, from the relevance and prognostic utility of nonsymptomatic early childhood precursors to alternative outcomes in adulthood for those who do not progress to Antisocial Personality Disorder (APD). In this chapter, we discuss the course of ODD and CD (referred to jointly as disruptive behavior disorders [DBD]), including their stability, subtypes with prognostic utility, conditions that are associated with the progression of ODD and CD, and the development from ODD to CD. We review evidence for symptom-driven alternative models of the development of early antisocial and disruptive behavior. We discuss outcomes associated with CD, including APD, as well as violence, substance use, and persisting antisocial behavior not captured by the APD diagnosis. Finally, we present a life-span model of early disruptive behavior to APD. Throughout this review, we highlight available research demonstrating gender differences and similarities. Most theories of DBD are based on data from males and probably apply only in part to females, given differences in patterns of risk factors between the genders (Pakiz, Reinherz, & Giaconia, 1997).

The review summarizes a vast body of empirical findings and, in addition, selectively draws from major reviews and books. Among the general reviews, mention should be made of the work by Hinshaw (1994), Kolko (1994), Lahey, Waldman, and McBurnett (1999), Loeber (1990), and Tolan and Loeber (1993). Readers are also referred to monographs on DBD by Kazdin (1995); Frick (1998); Loeber, Farrington, Stouthamer-Loeber, and Van Kammen (1998); and Patterson, Reid, and Dishion (1992); and edited collections of papers on disruptive behaviors (Hill & Maughan, 2000; Pepler & Rubin, 1991; Routh, 1994; Rutter, Giller, & Hagell, 1998; Sholevar, 1995; Stoff, Breiling, & Maser, 1997). In addition, increasing attention has been drawn to DBD in girls, with reviews by Goodman and Kohlsdorf (1994); Keenan, Loeber, and Green (1998); Loeber, Lahey, and Thomas (1991); Loeber and Keenan (1994); Silverthorn and Frick (1999); and Zoccolillo (1993).

COURSE OF ODD AND CD SYMPTOMS
AND DIAGNOSES

The essential features of ODD are a recurrent pattern of negativistic, defiant, disobedient, and hostile behavior toward authority figures, which leads to impairment, whereas the essential features of CD are a repetitive and persistent pattern of behavior in which the basic rights of others and major age-appropriate societal norms or rules are violated (American Psychiatric Association, 1994). The basic developmental model expressed in the *Diagnostic and Statistical Manual of Mental Disorders* (4th ed. [*DSM–IV*]; American Psychiatric Association, 1994) is that ODD and CD are not transient but relatively stable disorders and that ODD can be a precursor to CD, which in turn can be a precursor to APD.

Because of their similarity, considerable dialogue has taken place regarding the degree to which ODD and CD can be distinguished from one another. The majority of empirical evidence supports a distinction between ODD and CD (Cohen & Flory, 1998; Fergusson, Horwood, & Lynskey, 1994; Frick et al., 1993), as well as distinctions between Attention Deficit Hyperactivity Disorder (ADHD) and both ODD (Waldman & Lilienfeld, 1991) and CD (Hinshaw, 1994). On the other hand, the model expressed in the *International Classification of Diseases* (10th rev. [*ICD–10*]; World Health Organization, 1992) does not distinguish as sharply between ODD and CD. A diagnosis for CD in the *ICD–10* system would be given for three of a set of symptoms essentially the same as *DSM–IV*. However, a diagnosis of ODD could include symptoms of both *DSM–IV* ODD and CD, provided no more than two CD symptoms are present.

Extensive reviews regarding issues of the stability of ODD and CD and their symptoms, including aggression, have been conducted by Caspi and Moffitt (1995), Loeber (1991), and Maughan and Rutter (1998). Starting with Robins (1966), persistence of diagnosis has been reported at 50% of children continuing to qualify for the disorder (or serious behavior problems; Campbell, 1991; Lahey et al., 1995). In the Ontario Child Health Study (OCHS; Offord et al., 1992), 44% of children initially assessed with CD persisted with CD at follow-up 4 years later. Lahey et al. (1995) found higher persistence in a clinic-referred sample of boys, with 88% of the CD boys meeting criteria again at least once in the next 3 years. Cumulative stability of CD is much higher and clinically more relevant than year-to-year stability.

Although less well examined, the stability of disruptive behaviors tends to be as high or higher for females than males. Tremblay et al. (1992) showed that aggression and later delinquency were equally highly correlated in boys and girls (product–moment correlations .76 and .79, respectively). The temporal stability of an aggression factor (Verhulst & van der Ende, 1991) was consistently higher for girls than boys in four measurements between ages 4 to 5 and 10 to 12 years. Cote, Zoccolillo, Tremblay, Nagin, and Vitaro (2001) identified four developmental trajectories for disruptive behaviors among girls between the ages of 6 and 15 years. The authors found evidence of stability of disruptive behavior among the four groups and found evidence that there is an early onset pathway to CD among girls. Thus, despite a lower prevalence of disruptive behavior in girls than boys, once such behavior becomes apparent in girls it remains at least as stable as in boys.

FACTORS INFLUENCING THE COURSE OF ODD AND CD

Within the diagnoses of ODD and CD, there has been much interest in developing useful subtypes, primarily of CD. This has been a matter of great concern because of the need to differentiate among those youth who are likely to persist in disruptive behavior, those who will escalate to serious levels of such behavior, and those who are likely to outgrow or to desist from the behavior. The *DSM–IV* (American Psychiatric Association, 1994) discusses subtyping of CD based on age of onset and refers to use of the number and intensity of symptoms as clinical indicators of severity. Evidence supporting the prognostic utility of other factors such as aggression, the presence of early APD symptoms, and the effects of comorbid psychopathology on the course of DBD has accrued over the past decade.

Severity Levels of Symptoms

DSM–IV makes a distinction among different severity levels of symptoms of ODD and CD, but such distinctions are not often referred to in the psychiatric literature (but see Lahey & Loeber, 1994; Loeber, Keenan, et al., 1998). In contrast, delinquency studies have demonstrated the high predictive utility of severity scaling of various forms of delinquent acts (e.g., Farrington, Loeber, Stouthamer-Loeber, Van Kammen, & Schmidt, 1996; Loeber, Farrington, et al., 1998). Evidence suggests that the severity of symptoms influences the course of the disorder. Cohen, Cohen, and Brook (1993) found high persistence from late childhood to adolescence for severe ODD and CD (odds ratio (OR) = 8.3 and 13.9, respectively) and lower persistence for mild or moderate ODD or CD (OR = 3.2 and 6.0 for ODD, respectively; 3.1 and 7.8 for CD, respectively). Regarding individual symptoms, Cohen and Flory (1998) found that the singular symptoms of cruelty to people and weapon use best predicted subsequent diagnosis of CD.

The age and gender atypicality of symptoms are prognostic of later outcome. Frick, Lahey, et al. (1994) in cross-sectional analyses found that in younger children (below age 13) the symptoms of cruelty, running away, and breaking into a building were most predictive of CD. Additionally, they found that for girls fighting and cruel behavior were atypical symptoms and were most predictive of CD. Unfortunately, there are not yet age-normative and gender-specific tables to judge the relative deviance of particular disruptive behaviors.

Early Versus Late Onset

DSM–IV (American Psychiatric Association, 1994) subtypes based on the age of onset (age 10 or earlier vs. 11 and older) of first CD symptoms have been supported by a consensus of research findings for boys (Moffitt, 1993; Robins, Tipp, & McEvoy, 1991; Tolan & Thomas, 1995), and their validity has been confirmed by Lahey et al. (1998) in two large studies. Pertinent to the course of the CD, early onset is suggestive of persistent CD (Moffit, Caspi, Dickson, Silva, & Stanton, 1996). Further, age of onset of CD is significantly related to the number of aggressive behaviors (Lahey et al., 1998); boys who meet criteria for CD with an age of onset of less than 10 years are 8.7 times more likely to show at least one aggressive symptom than are youth who qualify for CD at a later age (Lahey et al., 1998).

However, it is important not to oversimplify an early age of onset of CD as a marker of psychopathology. Several studies (Fergusson, Horwood, &

Lynskey, 1996; Lahey, Loeber, Burke, & Rathouz, 2002; Moffitt et al., 1996; Nagin & Tremblay, 1999) have identified groups of boys noted for the early demonstration of high levels of disruptive behaviors who desisted in such behavior through adolescence.

Age of onset has been criticized because it is based on a single measurement (the presence or absence of a symptom before a certain age; Loeber & Stouthamer-Loeber, 1998), because of the unreliability of recall of age of onset (Angold, Erkanli, Costello, & Rutter, 1996), and because it lacks empirical, prognostic support for girls.

Evidence that the average onset of CD is earlier for boys than for girls is not uniform across studies (Lahey et al., 1998). Retrospective studies including female adolescents indicate the presence of two groups: an early-onset group and a group with late onset, emerging during adolescence (Zoccolillo, 1993). Prospectively, Cote et al. (2001) found evidence supporting an early-onset group with a high level trajectory of disruptive behavior. However, other reviewers conclude that late onset is the only type of CD for girls (Silverthorn & Frick, 1999). It remains to be tested whether the early–later onset distinction is important for the prognosis of CD in girls (Moffitt, 1993; T. E. Moffitt, personal communication, January 1996), but it appears relevant for the severity of later delinquency (Loeber & Farrington, 2001). Factors such as ADHD (see discussion following) have been demonstrated to influence the course of CD by hastening its onset.

Overt Versus Covert Disruptive Behavior

There is substantial evidence for a subtyping of CD according to the distinction between overt (confrontational, such as fighting) and covert (concealing, such as theft) disruptive behaviors (Fergusson et al., 1994; Frick et al., 1993; Loeber & Schmaling, 1985). Biederman, Mick, Faraone, and Burback (2001), in a sample of ADHD boys, found that the number of covert symptoms of CD distinguished between those who persisted and those who desisted in their CD over a 4-year period. Specifically, persisting CD was noted by the stability of covert CD symptoms compared to a decline in such symptoms in desisting CD. The authors found that the number of overt symptoms did not distinguish between those who persisted and those who desisted in their CD over a 4-year period (Biederman et al., 2001).

Aggression

However, the presence of aggression within the symptomatology of ODD or CD suggests a more severe course. Several reviews have attested to the importance of aggression and physical fighting in the development of ODD and CD (Coie & Dodge, 1998; Loeber & Farrington, 1998; Loeber & Stouthamer-Loeber, 1998; Vitiello & Stoff, 1997). Aggression in a proportion of boys emerges early in life and is usually accompanied by ODD symptoms (Loeber, Green, Lahey, & Kalb, 1998).

Although physical fighting by preschool-age boys is common (Loeber & Hay, 1994, 1997), some boys stand out by their persistent fighting. Even those who desist in fighting may be at risk for later delinquency (Haapasalo & Tremblay, 1994), but it is the group of stable fighters that appears at highest risk for other disruptive behaviors (Loeber, Tremblay, Gagnon, & Charlebois, 1989; Tremblay et al., 1991). In a prospective study by Loeber (1998), of all possible symptoms of CD, only physical fighting together with the diagnosis of ODD were the best predictors of the onset of CD. Biederman et al. (2001) found that the Aggression subscale of the Child Behavior Checklist measured at baseline (prior to age 8) was a good predictor of whether a boy would persist or desist in CD through adolescence (Achenbach, 1991).

Not all physical fighting, however, appears equally relevant for the development of CD. Subclassifications of aggression have been proposed, such as impulsive versus nonimpulsive, predatory versus affective, hostile versus instrumental, and, for clinical groups, impulsive-hostile-affective aggression versus predominantly controlled-instrumental-predatory aggression (Vitiello & Stoff, 1997). The demonstration of proactive aggression (in contrast to reactive aggression) may be an indicator of later maladjustment (Dodge, 1991) and has been found to predict CD symptoms in boys (Vitaro, Gendreau, Tremblay, & Oligny, 1998). The degree to which these different dimensions will further the understanding of the course of CD remains to be seen. It is believed that the emotional component of aggression is important because a high degree of anger is associated with rumination, the maintenance of grudges, and desire for revenge. For example, Pelham et al. (in press) found that children with comorbid ADHD and ODD/CD held a grudge longer than other children.

Early Antisocial Personality Features

The most serious young adult outcomes of DBD are APD and psychopathy, and these outcomes are reviewed following. However, researchers have investigated whether emerging antisocial personality features may be identified in adolescence. *Psychopathy*, as defined by Cleckley (1976) and by Hare, Hart, and Harpur (1991) includes two dimensions. One dimension includes the personality traits of egocentricity, callousness, and manipulativeness. The second dimension is more similar to APD, encompassing impulsivity, irresponsibility, and antisocial behavior (Cleckley, 1976; Hare et al., 1991).

Under *DSM–IV* rules, APD cannot be diagnosed until age 18 (American Psychiatric Association, 1994). However, there is emerging evidence that psychopathic characteristics emerge during childhood (Frick, O'Brien, Wootton, & McBurnett, 1994) and that these characteristics are associated with antisocial behavior prior to adulthood. Christian, Frick, Hill, Tyler, and Frazer (1997) found that referred CD children who showed callous and unemotional symptoms and conduct problems compared to those with conduct problems only displayed a higher variety of conduct problems and more police contacts. Loeber, Green, and Lahey (in press) scored boys on psychopathic characteristics and found that between ages 7 and 12, 69.1% of CD boys already displayed three or more APD symptoms compared to 38.5% of the boys without CD. Lynam (1997) reported that childhood psychopathy predicted serious, stable antisocial behavior in adolescence over and above other known predictors.

Although a subclassification of CD boys on the basis of APD symptoms appears plausible, it remains to be seen how such classification relates to others mentioned previously (although it is likely that they overlap with early-onset CD cases) and what the effect of such symptoms might be on the course and outcome of CD. Further caution is suggested by Edens, Skeem, Cruise, and Cauffman (2001) who reviewed evidence supporting a link between early features of psychopathy and aggression in juveniles but a lack of evidence of the prediction from early psychopathy to antisocial outcomes in young adulthood. Edens et al. (2001) caution against mistaking transitory elements of adolescent development with enduring personality features.

SIGNIFICANCE OF EARLY AND LATER COMORBID PSYCHOPATHOLOGY

The importance of studying target disorders in the context of comorbid disorders has been highlighted in several reviews (Caron & Rutter, 1991; Loeber & Keenan, 1994; Nottlemann & Jensen, 1995). Several comorbid conditions of ODD and CD may occur already early, such as ADHD, and somewhat later, such as anxiety disorders and depression. In adulthood, there is ample evidence that APD often co-occurs with other disorders (Newman et al., 1996) such as depression (Harrington, Fudge, Rutter, Pickles, & Hill, 1991), alcoholism (e.g., Lewis & Bucholz, 1991; Shubert, Wolf, Patterson, Grande, & Pendleton, 1988), and drug abuse (Brooner, Herbst, Schmidt, Bigelow, & Costa, 1993; Robins & Przybeck, 1985; Shubert et al., 1988). In addition, Lahey, Loeber, Burke, Rathouz, and McBurnett (2001) found corresponding improvement in comorbid ODD, anxiety, and depression among boys whose CD improved from childhood to adolescence. We briefly review the state of knowledge of comorbidities of CD and discuss their relevance for the course and outcomes of DBD.

ADHD. CD boys with ADHD have a poorer course and outcome than CD boys without ADHD (Hinshaw, 1994; Satterfield & Schell, 1997). Indeed, several authors have concluded that there are at least two important subtypes of ADHD children: those with and without CD (Jensen, Martin, & Cantwell, 1997; Satterfield & Schell, 1997). The distinction may be important because longitudinal research indicates that the presence of ADHD is predictive of an early onset of CD in clinic-referred boys (Loeber, Green, Keenan, & Lahey, 1995). The most consistent finding across studies is that youths with ADHD and comorbid CD (or antisocial behavior defined in other ways) have an earlier age of onset of DBD symptoms than youths with CD alone (Moffitt, 1990; Walker, Lahey, Hynd, & Frame, 1987). For example, in 92% of referred ADHD boys who developed CD, the onset of CD occurred prior to age 12 (Biederman et al., 1996; Hinshaw, Lahey, & Hart, 1993). Hinshaw et al. (1993), in reviewing the literature, concluded that children with CD and comorbid ADHD have an earlier age of onset of CD, exhibit more physical aggression, and exhibit more persistent CD than other children with CD. There has been very little investigation of ODD comorbid with ADHD (but see Campbell, 1991). However, it seems plausible that the presence of ADHD among ODD children is a marker for the early onset of CD symptoms. Some support for this notion comes from Nagin and Tremblay (1999) who found high levels of chronic hyperactive behavior through childhood and adolescence to be a far smaller risk for juvenile delinquency than high levels of aggression or oppositionality.

Our own analyses on a clinic-referred sample of boys in the Developmental Trends Study (Loeber, Green, Lahey, Frick, & McBurnett, 2000) show that once the presence of ODD is taken into account, ADHD by itself does not increase the likelihood that a child will meet criteria for CD. On the other hand, ADHD is associated with an early onset of CD. Therefore, we hypothesize that ADHD is not a precursor to APD by itself, but ADHD indirectly increases the likelihood of APD by influencing the age of onset, the degree of aggression, and the persistence of CD. Thus, in our life-span developmental model of APD (see Figs. 3.1 and 3.2), only children with ADHD who also exhibited comorbid ODD will develop CD in childhood (Lahey et al., 1997), with a subset of the children with CD later developing APD. Thus, we hypothesize a heterotypic developmental continuity (changing manifestations of the same disorder) in ODD, CD, and APD, but we see a role for ADHD in influencing the developmental progression from less serious to more serious manifestations of CD.

Anxiety. There is a growing literature that suggests that the interplay of CD and anxiety disorders is important and complex. On one hand, several epidemiologic studies indicate that prepubertal children with anxiety disorders who do not have CD are at a reduced risk for later conduct problems in adolescence (Graham & Rutter, 1973; Rutter, Tizard, & Whitmore, 1970).

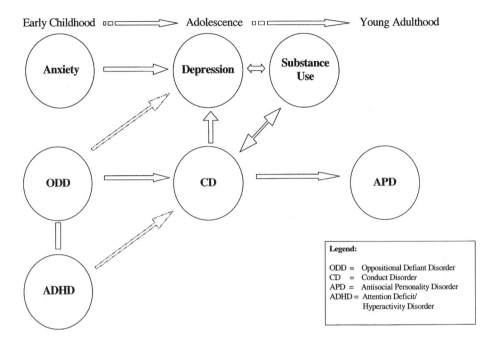

FIG. 3.1. Developmental sequences between disruptive behavior disorders and comorbid conditions. The dotted arrow from ADHD to CD indicates a relation in which ADHD serves to hasten the onset and worsen the severity of CD but only in the presence of ODD. The dotted arrow from ODD to depression indicates a hypothesized contribution of ODD symptoms to depression. From "Oppositional Defiant and Conduct Disorder: A Review of the Past 10 Years, Part 1," by R. Loeber, J. D. Burke, B. B. Lahey, A. Winters, and M. Zera, 2000. *Journal of the American Academy of Child and Adolescent Psychiatry, 39,* p. 1480. Copyright © 2000 by Lippincott Williams & Williams. Reprinted with permission.

On the other hand, a substantial body of evidence suggests that CD and anxiety disorders are comorbid at substantially higher than chance rates during childhood and adolescence (Loeber & Keenan, 1994; Zoccolillo, 1992). Similarly, men in the Epidemiologic Catchment Area study with APD were 2.0 to 5.3 times more likely to exhibit anxiety disorders, especially at higher levels of severity of antisocial behavior (Robins et al., 1991). Paradoxically, then, childhood anxiety disorders seem to protect against future antisocial behavior when they occur alone, but youth who do develop CD (and adults with APD) are at an increased risk for comorbid anxiety disorder.

It has been well established that psychopaths have lower levels of anxiety than nonpsychopaths (e.g., Fowles, 1980; Hare, 1970; Lykken, 1957). Examination of the startle reflex, which is an indicator of anxiety, shows that psychopaths do not show the expected potentiation of the startle reflex that normally occurs during the presentation of aversive cues such as un-

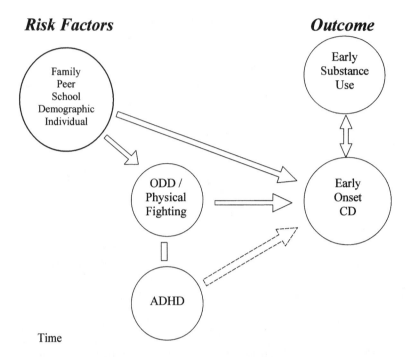

FIG. 3.2. ODD = oppositional defiant disorder; CD = conduct disorder; and ADHD = attention deficit hyperactivity disorder. Schematic configuration of early risk factors to explain ODD and CD. We assume reciprocal relations between child disruptive disorders and family, peer, and school risk factors. The dotted arrow depicts the influence of ADHD on the age of onset of CD rather than a unique causal contribution to the onset of CD. From "Findings on Disruptive Behavior Disorders from the First Decade of the Developmental Trends Study," by R. Loeber, S. M. Green, B. B. Lahey, P. J. Frick, and K. McBurnett, 2000, *Clinical Child and Family Psychology Review, 3*, p. 55. Copyright © 2000 by Plenum Publishing Corporation. Adapted with permission.

pleasant photographs or punishment clues (Patrick, 1994). How early in life this aspect of the startle response can be measured reliably as a predictor of adult APD remains to be established.

Depression. Investigations of the relation between CD and depressive symptomatology show that the two often co-occur; studies of their temporal relation, however, have produced controversial results (Capaldi, 1992; Holmes & Robins, 1987; Kovacs, Paulauskas, Gatsonis, & Richards, 1988). Biederman et al. (2001) found that CD that persisted over time was associated with a higher risk for depression than temporary CD, whereas Lahey et al. (2001) found that worsening and improvement in CD corresponded with worsening or improvement in comorbid depression symptomatology.

In studies of comorbid depression and CD that have examined the relative contributions of each individual disorder to poor outcomes, CD has been identified as the greater risk factor (Bardone et al., 1998; Renouf, Kovacs, & Mukerji, 1997). Bardone et al. (1998) found that CD, rather than depression, was a stronger predictor of poor outcomes including medical problems, self-reported overall health, lower body mass index, alcohol or marijuana dependence (or both), tobacco dependence, daily smoking, more lifetime sexual partners, sexually transmitted disease, and early pregnancy. Depression predicted only adult tobacco dependence and more medical problems. Renouf et al. (1997) found that the social dysfunction associated with comorbid depression and CD was primarily a function of CD rather than depression and that the impact of depression on social competence is temporary and lessens with the remission of depression.

Several points regarding the relation between these disorders raise important questions about the impact of depression on the course and outcomes of CD and highlight the need for further investigation of their comorbidity. First, it is possible that CD is a precursor to depression in some children and not others (Capaldi, 1992; Holmes & Robins, 1987). Second, the course of both CD and depression may be different when they co-occur; indeed, a diagnostic category of depressive CD has been proposed (Puig-Antich et al., 1989) and is included in the *ICD–10* (World Health Organization, 1992). Third, it has been suggested that some proportion of late-onset, nonaggressive CD is actually secondary to depression and distinct from other CD (Masten, 1988; Puig-Antich, 1982). Fourth, both CD and depression have been linked to substance abuse (Buydens-Branchey, Branchey, & Noumair, 1989) and suicide (Shaffer, 1974; Shaffi, Carrigan, Whittinghill, & Derrick, 1985), particularly when they co-occur.

Substance Use. Concurrent and longitudinal studies have shown that the more serious the substance use the higher the likelihood that individuals engage in serious forms of delinquency and antisocial behavior (Bukstein, Brent, & Kraminer, 1989; Clark, Parker, & Lynch, 1999; Loeber, 1988b; White, 1997). Whitmore et al. (1997) found that for men by not for women the severity of substance use was positively associated with the severity of CD.

The course of CD may be influenced by substance use. Boys with CD begin using psychoactive substances at an earlier age, and their use of illegal substances may increase the risk for progression to APD (Modestin, Matutat, & Würmle, 2001). Furthermore, Biederman et al. (2001) found that a persistent course of CD, in contrast to a desisting course, was associated with greater drug and alcohol dependence and greater cigarette smoking among a sample of ADHD boys.

If drug involvement and antisocial behavior are intertwined, does this also mean that a decrease in drug use is followed by a decrease in antisocial behavior? There is evidence for this in interview studies of narcotic addicts. When individuals began using hard drugs less frequently, their criminal involvement also decreased (Ball, Shaffer, & Nurco, 1983; Nurco, Shaffer, Ball, & Kinlock, 1984). This is not surprising in light of the decreased need to obtain funds to purchase the drugs. Longitudinal analyses on juveniles (Van Kammen & Loeber, 1994) also showed that discontinuation of illegal drug use (or drug selling) was associated with a decrease in delinquent activities. The extent to which a decrease in antisocial behavior is associated with a subsequent decrease in drug involvement is not clear from the available studies. Thus, substance use is probably an important influence in the worsening and improvement of conduct problems, but further evidence is needed to clarify the directions of effect.

Developmental Sequences Among DBD and Comorbid Conditions.
Whereas ODD and CD appear to place children and adolescents at risk for a large number of disorders, there appears to be a modal sequence in the onset of comorbid conditions to DBD. Figure 3.1 provides a visual depiction of a hypothesized sequence of the development in males of DBD and comorbid conditions that may apply to many youth. ODD may often be a precursor to CD, which is thought to be a precursor to APD. In clinical samples, ADHD is a commonly comorbid condition with ODD and CD but is hypothesized not to affect the course of CD without prior ODD (Lahey et al., 2000). Its onset more typically co-occurs early, before the age of 7. Anxiety and depression are less likely in childhood and tend to emerge concurrently and interactively with CD, with anxiety often preceding depression in onset. Substance abuse tends to develop concurrently and recursively with CD (see review by Le Blanc & Loeber, 1998). It is likely that the manifestation of APD, particularly the expression of violence, is aggravated by the proximal consumption of substances such as alcohol. These developmental trends may differ between the genders, given findings of differing risk of depression, for example, between girls and boys.

In summary, aside from onset and severity as mentioned in *DSM–IV*, factors of age and gender atypicality of symptoms, the presence of aggression, the distinction between overt and covert conduct problems, the presence of early APD or psychopathy-related symptoms, and the influence of comorbid Axis I psychopathology all appear to be of importance to the course of ODD and CD.

RESEARCH ON THE PROGRESSION OF DISRUPTIVE BEHAVIOR DISORDERS

Development From ODD to CD

Some researchers maintain that ODD is a relatively benign disorder with good prognosis (see review by Loeber et al., 1991). Others perceive the two disorders to be hierarchically related (Lahey et al., 1997) with only a proportion of ODD cases progressing to CD (Cohen & Flory, 1998; Loeber et al., 1991). For example, Cohen and Flory (1998), using longitudinal data from the Upper New York Study, found that the risk of the onset of CD was four times higher in ODD cases than in children without prior ODD or CD. Additionally, Nagin and Tremblay (1999) found that chronic oppositionality was a precursor to covert antisocial behavior. As children mature, there are major shifts in the manifestations of disruptive behavior they display, which reflect continuity rather than stability. The most deviant children at one age represent the most deviant at a later age, even though absolute levels of deviance might vary over time (Farrington, 1997).

It is unclear to what extent ODD constitutes a stepping stone to CD in girls. If late onset of CD is more common in girls than boys, it is plausible that a proportion of girls with late onset do not show a history of ODD and that for girls there are alternative pathways to CD (Silverthorn & Frick, 1999). Moreover, it is unclear whether specific CD symptoms in girls, such as lying, usually precede the emergence of more serious behaviors such as stealing.

Models of Developmental Sequences in Symptoms

It can be argued that ODD and CD are syndromes too broad for developmental research aimed at describing the developmental course of disruptive behavior. Instead, it may be useful to examine developmental sequences among DBD symptoms, as well as nonsymptomatic precursors to disruptive behavior in early childhood because they may illuminate essential components of the disorders as well.

Longitudinal research has increasingly clarified the orderly unfolding of DBD symptoms with age (Kelley, Loeber, Keenan, & DeLamatre, 1997; Loeber, DeLamatre, Keenan, & Zhang, 1998; Loeber, Keenan, & Zhang, 1997; Loeber, Keenan, Lahey, Green, & Thomas, 1993). In general, the onset of less serious symptoms tend to precede the onset of moderately serious symptoms, which in turn tend to precede the onset of serious symptoms. Lahey and Loeber (1994) presented a model of three levels of DBD according to developmental sequence of the onset of symptoms and the severity of the symptoms: modified ODD, intermediate CD, and advanced CD. Evidence for the model was presented in Loeber, Keenan, Lahey, Green, and Thomas (1993) and Russo, Loeber, Lahey, and Keenan (1994), and Loeber (1998). However, despite longitudinal data supporting the model of hierarchical multiple levels of DBD, it did not find favor with the *DSM–IV* committee, and in the final version of *DSM–IV* severity indicators of DBD were considerably watered down.

Loeber and colleagues (Kelley et al., 1997; Loeber et al., 1993, Loeber et al., 1997; Loeber et al., in press) investigated developmental pathways to serious conduct and delinquent problem behavior. The data best fitted three pathways: (a) an overt pathway, starting with minor aggression, followed by physical fighting, and followed in turn by violence; (b) a covert pathway prior to age 15, consisting of a sequence of minor covert behaviors, followed by property damage (firesetting or vandalism) and moderate to serious forms of delinquency; and, (c) an authority conflict pathway prior to age 12, consisting of a sequence of stubborn behavior, defiance, and authority avoidance (truancy, running away, staying out late at night). Children can be on more than one pathway at the same time. The pathways have been replicated in several other samples of males (Tolan & Gorman-Smith, 1998). Further, Elliott (1994) and Le Blanc (1997) have found similar evidence for developmental sequences toward violence.

Each of the three pathways are thought to represent different developmental tasks (Loeber & Stouthamer-Loeber, 1998). The overt pathway represents aggression as opposed to positive problem solving; the covert pathway represents lying, vandalism, and theft versus honesty and respect for property; the authority conflict pathway represents conflict with and avoidance of authority figures versus respect for authority figures. This conceptualization implies that if a juvenile achieves one developmental task (such as honesty), he or she will not necessarily achieve another developmental task. Alternatively, youth may fail to achieve several of these developmental tasks. Thus, pathways in disruptive behavior can be conceptualized as different lines of development, with some boys advancing on several pathways at the same time. This is advantageous in that the pathway model can help to account for multiproblem boys. Further studies on girls should include gender-specific manifestations of DBD.

Much of the work on developmental pathways did not extend into the preschool period. However, recent research has clarified that aggressive behavior in the first years of life is very common (e.g., Nagin & Tremblay, 1999) and decreases subsequently in most children. What is less clear is the extent to which escalation in the severity of aggression in mid to late childhood and in adolescence primarily represents children who never outgrew preschool aggression, children who temporarily ceased their aggression, or children who started aggression de novo.

Nonsymptomatic Precursors in Early Childhood

It is clear that a proportion of youth who eventually qualified for DBD already showed nonsymptomatic problem behavior other than ODD symptoms in the preschool years. Two factors, temperament and attachment, have been hypothesized to be related to the continuity of early problem behavior. Temperamental problems, which have long been associated with the development of internalizing disorders, have been introduced as a precursor to behavior problems (Cole & Zahn-Waxler, 1992). Cole and Zahn-Waxler argued that dysregulated temperament facilitates the progression from early disruptive problems to CD. In addition, distinguishing between types of temperamental difficulties such as dysregulated temperament and inhibited temperament may help define early stages in the developmental trajectories of disruptive and internalizing disorders, respectively. However, there is still no agreement among investigators which temperamental dimension is most relevant for the development of DBD and its subtypes—either early or later—or overt or covert disruptive behaviors.

Moral Development as a Cognitive Component of DBD

A large number of studies reviewed by Smetana (1990) and Turiel (1998) indicate that conduct-problem youth, on average, function at a lower level of sociomoral development than non-conduct-problem youth. It is probable that children's failure on developmental tasks (referred to previously) leading to their progress on disruptive behavior pathways is related to delays in sociomoral reasoning. However, it remains to be determined whether sociomoral reasoning is a causal influence on behavior or is an epiphenomenon of the putative core processes involved in DBD. Furthermore, that such sociocognitive developmental delays are already taking place at a very early age (e.g., the preschool period) is probable but remains to be substantiated.

Importance of the Developmental Context

Forehand and Wierson (1993) stressed the importance of understanding the development of DBD in the context of children's growth, development, and maturation. The key is to understand how DBD symptoms reflect individuals' adaptive and maladaptive responses to developmental tasks and challenges and that these tasks and challenges differ for different stages in the life course. Further, it is important to understand DBD as a function of developmental transition between life stages, such as from infancy to early childhood when cognitions develop and emotions are often labile and shallow, or from early childhood to middle childhood when moral reasoning becomes more an issue (Forehand & Wierson, 1993).

OUTCOMES OF CD

APD. Foremost among the outcomes that have been associated with ODD and CD is APD, in large measure because of the definition of APD itself. The *DSM–IV* (American Psychiatric Association, 1994) diagnostic criteria for APD, presented in Table 3.1, suggests the underlying hypothesis that a de-

TABLE 3.1
DSM–IV Definition of Antisocial Personality Disorder

A. Current age at least 18
B. Pervasive disregard for and violation of the rights of others indicated by 3 of the following:
   1. Failure to conform to social norms with respect to lawful behavior
   2. Impulsivity or failure to plan ahead
   3. Reckless disregard for safety of self or others
   4. Irresponsibility indicated by repeated failure to sustain consistent work behavior or honor financial obligations
   5. Deceitfulness
   6. Irritability and aggressiveness
   7. Lack of remorse
C. Conduct Disorder with an age of onset before 15 years

Note. Reprinted with permission from the *Diagnostic and Statistical Manual of Mental Disorders, Fourth Edition.* Text revision. Copyright © 1994 American Psychiatric Association.

velopmental relation exists between CD and APD. *DSM–IV* criteria for APD describe a pattern of irresponsible and antisocial behavior that is engaged in without remorse and require that the individual has demonstrated three criteria for CD during childhood. The decision to include a requirement of childhood conduct problems in the definition of APD was influenced by Robins' (1978) conclusion that "adult antisocial behavior virtually *requires* childhood antisocial behavior" (p. 611). In four samples available at that time, she found that 65% to 82% of highly antisocial adults displayed high levels of antisocial behavior as children or adolescents. It is possible that *DSM–IV*'s additional criterion of CD in childhood or adolescence has prematurely discouraged the investigation of CD (and other disruptive behaviors) as childhood precursors to APD and has not addressed methodological limitations of the use of retrospective reports. Not until the late 1990s did prospective longitudinal data become available using more valid prospectively collected information and including a wider range of potential risk factors.

Prevalence of APD in Males. As a primary outcome of CD, it is crucial to identify the prevalence of APD. According to the Epidemiologic Catchment Area Study (ECA), the lifetime prevalence of *DSM–III* (American Psychiatric Association, 1980) APD is 4.5% for men (Robins et al., 1991). In a representative sample of the United States, the lifetime prevalence of APD among 15- to 54-year-olds was similarly found to be 5.8% for males (Kessler et al., 1994). A survey of a large representative sample in Edmonton, Canada, found lifetime prevalence rates for *DSM–III* APD of 8.7% for males in the 18–24 year age range (Swanson, Bland, & Newman, 1994). Unfortunately, no data from population-based samples are available on the prevalence of the *DSM–IV* definition of APD, as such data could shed light on the impact of *DSM–IV* changes in the requirement of childhood conduct problems. In

summary, given the relatively low prevalence of APD in general populations, the etiology of APD can best be studied either in longitudinal studies
of very large community samples or in longitudinal studies of high-risk individuals such as clinic-referred boys with disruptive behavior disorders.

Findings on the Development From CD to APD. Whereas there are
multiple poor outcomes of CD in adulthood (see following), the importance
of CD in predicting APD has been investigated in several studies. Robins'
(1978) summary showed that only about a third of the youth with CD later
developed APD. The percentage was somewhat higher (40%) in an English
sample of boys who had been reared away from home (Zoccolillo, Pickles,
Quinton, & Rutter, 1992). Rey, Morris-Yates, Singh, Andrews, and Stewart
(1995) assessed 145 clinic-referred adolescents (mean age 13.7 years) using
unstructured clinical interviews and reassessed them as young adults
(mean age 19.6 years) using a structured interview for personality disorders. Adolescents with CD were significantly more likely to meet criteria for
APD at follow-up than adolescents without CD (OR = 4.6). Myers, Stewart,
and Brown (1998) studied 53 female and 84 male adolescents (mean age 15.9
years) who met criteria for *DSM–III–R* (American Psychiatric Association,
1987) CD according to a structured interview and were receiving inpatient alcohol and drug abuse treatment at the time of the first assessment. Four
years later, 71% of male adolescents met criteria for *DSM–III–R* APD at a mean
age of 20.0 years based on structured interviews. Bardone, Moffit, Caspi, and
Dickson (1996) provided unique data on the development of APD in women.
The authors followed up a sample of 15-year-old girls at age 21 and found elevated APD symptom counts for those who had CD at age 15 compared to
groups of depressed and control girls. However, only 3 of the total sample of
470 women met criteria for APD (although 37 girls had CD at age 15).

Lahey and Loeber (1994) calculated the relative risk of APD in individuals with and without childhood CD from five independent studies (Harrington et al., 1991; Robins, 1966; Robins & Ratcliff, 1979; Robins et al., 1991;
Zoccolillo et al., 1992). The relative risks ranged from 3.2 to 18.0, and when
combined in meta-analytic fashion across differing definitions of disorder
and design, but weighting for sample size, the overall estimate of relative
risk was 16.8 for the prediction of CD from APD. Specifically, 1.7% of individuals without a history of CD were given the diagnosis of APD in adulthood
across studies compared to 28.5% of individuals with a history of childhood
CD. This very high relative risk for predicting APD from childhood CD is
consistent with the *DSM–IV* view that few individuals will meet adult criteria
for APD without exhibiting at least three symptoms of CD in childhood. A
lack of adequate available studies prevents us from identifying risks for
APD in girls across studies. Zoccolillo et al. (1992) did provide some evidence that the risk for APD among girls with CD was similar to that of boys.

Limitations of the Literature Regarding the Progression
From CD to Adult APD

Several previous studies relating childhood CD to adult APD used samples of adults identified through records of clinics they attended as youths and consisted of single interviews conducted during adulthood (e.g., Robins, 1966). Most of these follow-back studies were limited by methodological shortcomings typical of the era in which they were conducted, such as use of existing records and retrospective bias. For these reasons, we focus on prospective studies.

Much of the available literature, although providing useful preliminary data on the relation between childhood CD and adult APD, are limited by a number of methodological and practical shortcomings. These include a follow-up to only age 20 or 21, which may not capture the development of APD through the many transitions of early adulthood. Furthermore, studies that rely on only one child assessment of CD and one adult assessment of APD very likely underestimate the association between CD and APD. APD has not been adequately studied to ensure consistency over multiple measurements. Data regarding CD throughout adolescence suggest that the cumulative stability of CD is relatively high, but the fluctuation from year to year indicates that a single measurement may not be reliable, and this may be true for APD as well. Any error of measurement or true temporal instability over time in either CD or APD tends to underestimate the strength of association. For this reason, studies that employ multiple assessments in childhood and adulthood are needed.

The currently available literature on the development from early DBD to APD comes from studies that used a wide range of definitions of both childhood conduct problems and antisocial outcomes, some of which are very different from current definitions. This is important, as even small differences in diagnostic criteria can produce large differences in findings (Lahey et al., 1990). Many studies also began with youths who were either already adolescents or with youths with a broad range of ages. To best understand the developmental sequences, it is important to begin such longitudinal studies at a young age.

Potential Importance of Adult CD

Two factors warrant the consideration of CD during adulthood as a developmental outcome of CD in addition to APD. There is no reason why the diagnosis of CD could not be given to an adult, as *DSM–IV* allows the diagnosis of CD in persons 18 years or older who do not meet criteria for APD. CD in adulthood is virtually never studied, however, perhaps because of the untested assumption that all adults who still meet criteria for CD will also meet criteria for APD. A second reason for proposing to study adult CD is the rate of APD among adults with a history of CD. Although the previous studies reviewed suggest that many youths with CD during childhood or adolescence later met criteria for APD as adults, many do not. Averaged across the studies reviewed previously, it appears that only about 50% of youths with CD will meet criteria for APD in adulthood. What is the outcome of the other half of the adults who had CD as youths? It is possible that a substantial proportion of these youths continue to meet criteria for CD although they do not meet criteria for APD? Finally, a proportion of boys with CD in childhood recover by adulthood and no longer qualify for APD or CD.

Other Adverse Outcomes of Childhood CD

CD has several other adverse outcomes in adulthood. Robins (1966) found that 69% of adults who had serious conduct problems in childhood or adolescence but did not develop APD still suffered from a wide range of social dysfunction in adulthood (see also Robins & Price, 1991). Other studies have similarly found very poor adjustment among most adults who had exhibited CD during childhood, whether they met criteria for APD. Zoccolillo et al. (1992) traced children raised in group foster homes and found that only 13% of the children with CD exhibited adequate social functioning in adult life. Harrington et al. (1991) found that 60% of clinic-referred youths with CD had been convicted of a crime by age 30 compared to 10% of youths with depression in childhood. Bardone et al. (1996) reported outcomes of girls with CD at age 15, compared to healthy controls, which included increased likelihood of depressive disorders, anxiety disorders, substance use, dropping out of school, early pregnancy and child bearing, and violent victimization at the hands of a partner.

Capaldi and Stoolmiller (1999) used data from the prospective Oregon Youth Study to show that childhood conduct problems among boys strongly predicted a wide range of adjustment problems at ages 18 to 20 years, including dropping out of school, unemployment, driver's license suspensions, causing unwanted pregnancies, problems with peers and parents, low self-esteem, and substance abuse. Farrington (1995) found juvenile delinquency to be associated with increased hospital treatment for both injuries and illnesses, and a follow-back study of 12,000 Swedish children found that indicators of early conduct problems in school or child guidance records were associated with a three-fold increase in mortality by age 30 (Kratzer & Hodgins, 1997). Elander, Rutter, Simonoff, and Pickles (2000) identified a group of late onset criminal offenders (those who were never convicted of an offense before the age of 22). This group had a higher mean number of childhood CD symptoms than a group of never-convicted participants and did not differ in the number of childhood CD symptoms from groups with convictions only before age 22 or with convictions before and after age 22. Thus, CD in childhood often is associated with a variety of undesirable outcomes, of which APD is among the most serious.

Among a group of men with opioid dependence in adulthood, Modestin et al. (2001) found that 66 percent of those with borderline personality disorder in adulthood retrospectively had CD in childhood. CD with comorbid ADHD was also related to earlier onset of substance use than those without CD and ADHD, as well as a higher number of accidents while intoxicated. CD was related to greater frequency of violation of drug laws and more frequent loss of romantic partner due to substance use than those with ADHD or without either disorder (Modestin et al., 2001). Finally, Dowson, Sussams, Grounds, and Taylor (2001), in a retrospective study, found that the symptoms of CD were highly specific to APD and were, on the whole, not related to each of the other personality disorders defined in *DSM–III–R*. The authors also found that the relations between CD symptoms and APD was weaker for women than for men.

Psychopathy

In contrast to the *DSM* tradition, Hare and his colleagues (Hare et al., 1990, 1991; Harpur, Hare, & Hakstian, 1989) have argued that the construct of APD should be replaced by a two-dimensional construct of psychopathy that is based on the description provided by Cleckley (1976; see Early Antisocial Personality Features section previously). The *ICD–10* (World Health Organization, 1992) definition of dissocial personality disorder is more similar to the construct of psychopathy than *DSM–IV* APD. Because longitudinal data will improve our understanding of both APD and psychopathy (and their relation to one another), prospective studies of the origins of APD should measure adult outcomes in terms of both APD and psychopathic characteristics. Although highly related to criminality and violence, psychopathy has received scant prospective study as an outcome of CD (see Edens et al., 2001). However, several retrospective studies have found psychopathy to be associated with a history of CD in both men and women (Dowson et al., 2001; Vitelli, 1998).

Potential Mediators in the Progression From CD to APD

Knowledge about factors associated with the progression from CD to APD is severely restricted because of the scarcity of prospective longitudinal studies with APD as an outcome. We briefly summarize the available findings.

81

Intelligence and Education. Robins et al. (1991) found that individuals who had one or more indicators of low intellectual ability were at increased risk of APD, but only among non-Hispanic Whites and not among other groups. These findings are generally consistent with the large literature that indicates that childhood CD and adult criminal behavior are most common among individuals with lower intelligence, particularly verbal intelligence (Lahey, Miller, Gordon, & Riley, 1999).

Family Factors and Parenting. Two studies demonstrated that adults with APD are more likely to have highly antisocial parents (Robins, 1966; Robins & Ratcliff, 1979). Little is known about the relation of parenting during childhood to the development of APD in adulthood. Robins (1966) reported, however, a protective effect of strict or adequate discipline for later sociopathy, even for children with antisocial fathers. On the other hand, childhood abuse is a significant correlate of APD in males, even when demographic characteristics and criminal history are controlled (Luntz & Widom, 1994).

Demographic Factors. Although there are race or ethnic differences in rates of incarceration, Robins et al. (1991) found similar rates of APD among non-Hispanic Whites, Hispanics, and African Americans in the ECA Study. Luntz and Widom (1994) similarly found no race or ethnic differences in APD. Parental education and occupation are related to the prevalence of sociopathy, but these socioeconomic variables add nothing to the prediction of sociopathy among children with high numbers of conduct problems (Robins, 1978). Robins et al. (1991) also found that APD was more prevalent in urban than rural areas, but the urban–rural difference was found only among non-Hispanic whites.

Some Key Issues. It appears likely that not all children who meet criteria for CD will later meet criteria for APD in adulthood. It is of great importance, therefore, to ask which variables distinguish between children with CD who will later meet criteria for APD and those who will not. One likely factor is the relative severity of childhood CD. Robins and Ratcliff (1979) found that higher numbers of childhood conduct problems before age 15 predicted greater adult antisocial behaviors. Similar findings for Hare's psychopathy construct (Hare et al., 1991) have been reported by Rogers, Johansen, Chang, and Salekin (1997) in a sample of adolescent offenders. Myers et al. (1998) also found that three variables predicted which adolescents with CD would later meet criteria for APD: number of CD behaviors, age of onset of CD before 10 years, and number of substances abused. Further, in an adult sample, Vitelli (1997) reported that an earlier age of first arrest was associated with increased likelihood of APD. Little is known at present about other predictors of APD among youth with CD. This is a critical shortcoming in our current knowledge that must be addressed. In summary, several factors in the individual, the family, and community setting appear to be associated with APD. These correlates are largely the same as those known for CD (Lahey, Waldman, et al., 1999; Robins, 1978; Stouthamer-Loeber et al., 1993), suggesting a continuum of influences that may take place over decades. However, firmer conclusions about patterns of risk factors leading to later APD are severely restricted by the lack of predictive studies covering a wide range of potential risk and protective factors.

LIFESPAN DEVELOPMENTAL MODEL OF APD

Based on our own research, as well as the findings summarized previously, we proposed a life span developmental model of the origins of chronic antisocial behavior and personality. Sroufe (1997) posited that changing manifestations of problem behavior over the course of development result from successive transactions of developing persons with their changing social environments (see also Loeber, 1991). As such, roles for person variables, developmental variables, and environmental variables are specified in the model, as are dynamic interactions among these classes of variables. The age of onset of CD is a key element of our model for two reasons: early-onset CD is much more likely to persist into adulthood as APD or adult CD, and the causal influences on CD vary with its age of onset (Loeber, 1988a; Moffitt, 1993). Because much more is known about CD in boys than girls, this model may be applicable only to boys.

Our life-span developmental model focuses on developmental progressions from early childhood through adolescence for ODD (especially with physical fighting) and CD and is schematically represented in Fig. 3.2 (based on Lahey & Loeber, 1994; Lahey, Waldman, et al., 1999; Loeber, Keenan, Lahey, Green, & Thomas, 1993). Risk factors influence which youth make the transition from ODD to CD. The risk factors are situated in several domains: the family (e.g., young motherhood, antisocial parents, poor child rearing practices), peer group (association with deviant peers), school (e.g., low grades), demographics (e.g., family size, socioeconomic status, ethnicity), and individual risk factors (see following). We assume reciprocal relations between child disruptive disorders and risk factors within the family, peer group, and school. Among children with ADHD, the age of onset of CD appears to be earlier than children without ADHD. We postulate a reciprocal influence between CD and substance use.

As an illustration of specific relations within the model (not shown in Fig. 3.2), we propose that individual risk factors such as low intelligence and three dimensions of temperament that emerge early in life (higher oppositionality, lower harm avoidance, and higher callousness) constitute a predisposition to antisocial behavior. During childhood, these factors increase antisocial propensity primarily by evoking maladaptive transactions with parents, siblings, and teachers. Genetic factors (not shown in Fig. 3.2) are thought not to influence antisocial behavior directly but do so indirectly by influencing both the predisposing traits and the youth's exposure to, and selection of, social environments. Predisposed children who experience ineffective or abusive parenting and other adverse social interactions (Patterson et al., 1992) are more likely to develop CD. In the absence of maladaptive parenting and social interactions, predisposed children are unlikely to develop CD. However, due to gene–environment covariance, children with greater predisposition are more liable to encounter environments (both passively and actively) that foster antisocial behavior. In particular, children who are predisposed to CD are more likely to be raised by ineffective (and often abusive) parents with histories of antisocial behavior, psychopathology, and substance abuse. Additional social influences on the development of CD probably lie in the neighborhood and school environments. At this point, much more is known about risk factors for the onset of CD than for its persistence into adulthood. Early findings suggest that some risk factors for the onset of CD also predict its persistence (Lahey et al., 1995). Specifically, the persistence of CD appears to be predicted in childhood by the severity of CD, child's low intelligence, parental antisocial behavior, and parental supervision.

The risk–outcome constellation shown in Fig. 3.2 is part of a larger schema of influences occurring from adolescence to early adulthood (see Fig. 3.3). In a minority of youth, the sequella of ODD and CD are APD and violence. Personality traits and early psychopathic features modulate the relation between earlier risk factors and transitions from ODD through CD to APD. In addition, APD is reciprocally related to substance abuse and dependence. Finally, anxiety and depression are primarily related to substance use and dependence rather than to APD.

CONCLUSION

The course of disruptive behavior as exists within the diagnostic framework of the DSM–IV suggests that early disruptive behavior problems reflected in ODD serve as a precursor to CD. Persistence of CD into adulthood increases the probability of APD. Although it is clear that oppositional behavior and covert delinquent behavior are distinct syndromes, it is not yet clear whether aggression should be considered to be part of ODD, part of CD (aggressive and covert CD behaviors), or distinct from both ODD and covert CD. ODD, CD, and later APD are hierarchically and developmentally related. Broad

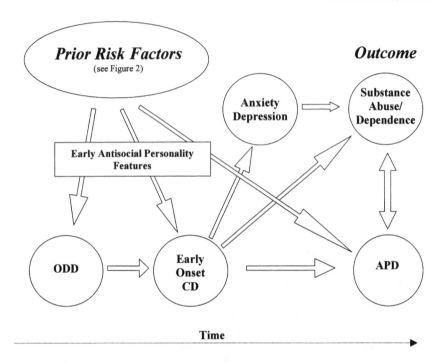

FIG. 3.3. ODD = oppositional defiant disorder; CD = conduct disorder; and APD = antisocial personality disorder. Schematic configuration of later risk factors to explain progression to APD. From "Findings on Disruptive Behavior Disorders from the First Decade of the Developmental Trends Study," by R. Loeber, S. M. Green, B. B. Lahey, P. J. Frick, and K. McBurnett, 2000, *Clinical Child and Family Psychology Review, 3,* p. 56. Copyright © 2000 by Plenum Publishing Corporation. Adapted with permission.

pathways between the disorders, and more specific symptomatic and conceptual pathways, have been tentatively identified and appear to have demonstrated utility. Subtypes and factors intrinsic to CD have been related to the course and prognosis of the disorder, including early onset, severity, overt versus covert symptoms, and the presence of aggression. Several conditions, including ADHD, depression, anxiety, and substance use are associated with CD, and when present influence the course and outcomes of the disorder. However, much remains to be addressed regarding the nature of these comorbid conditions, including whether the relations are recursive, whether one or the other disorder tends to play an activating or inhibitory role, and how their comorbidity influences outcomes.

Issues remain concerning the early demonstration of disruptive behavior. Early indicators of later disruptive behavior may not be captured by ODD. This is especially true for girls, for whom the behavioral criteria of ODD and CD may not accurately describe the nature of the antisocial behavior some girls display. Additionally, constructs of early childhood such as temperament have not been adequately defined by distinct behavior referents. This makes difficult the task of distinguishing between early signs of ODD and indicators of temperament.

Issues also remain regarding the transitions from CD to APD or to other conditions. Few studies have prospectively examined the developmental precursors to APD, adult violence, and other personality disorders. Especially perplexing is the status of roughly one half to two thirds of the CD cases that do not develop to APD. Do they persist with adult CD, or do they remit in their antisocial behavior? This crucial question involves the identification of distinguishing antecedent factors. The answer plausibly lies in a combination of childhood behavior, family characteristics, and peer and school factors. Ordinarily however, explanations based on earlier factors are modest in strength. This is especially true when considering an outcome like APD, which is somewhat unstable in adulthood, with some males qualifying for the diagnosis one year but not in the next. This means that studies with repeated assessments of APD are needed to optimize the accurate measurement of this outcome. Finally, substance use is often associated with APD in adulthood and is proximally related to violence and other antisocial behaviors. The role substance abuse plays in fostering the persistence of antisocial behavior from late adolescence to adulthood must be better understood.

ACKNOWLEDGMENTS

This chapter was supported in part by NIMH Grants MH 42529 and MH 50778 and incorporates work from a review article (Loeber, Burke, Lahey, Winters, & Zera, 2000) published in the *Journal of the American Academy of Child and Adolescent Psychiatry*.

REFERENCES

Achenbach, T. M. (1991). *Manual for the Child Behavior Checklist/4–18 and 1991 Profile.* Burlington, VT: University of Vermont Department of Psychiatry.

American Psychiatric Association. (1980). *Diagnostic and statistical manual of mental disorders* (3rd ed.). Washington, DC: Author.

American Psychiatric Association. (1987). *Diagnostic and statistical manual of mental disorders* (3rd ed., rev.). Washington, DC: Author.

American Psychiatric Association. (1994). *Diagnostic and statistical manual of mental disorders* (4th ed.). Washington, DC: Author.

Angold, A., Erkanli, A., Costello, E. J., & Rutter, M. (1996). Precision, reliability and accuracy in the dating of symptom onsets in child and adolescent psychopathology. *Journal of Child Psychology and Psychiatry, 37*, 657–663.

Ball, J. C., Shaffer, J. W., & Nurco, D. (1983). Day to day criminality of heroin addicts in Baltimore—A study in the continuity of offense rates. *Drug and Alcohol Dependence, 12,* 119–142.

Bardone, A. M., Moffitt, T., Caspi, A., & Dickson, N. (1996). Adult mental health and social outcomes of adolescent girls with depression and conduct disorder. *Development and Psychopathology, 8,* 811–829.

Bardone, A. M., Moffitt, T. E., Caspi, A., Dickson, N., Stanton, W. R., & Silva, P. A. (1998). Adult physical health outcomes of adolescent girls with conduct disorder, depression, and anxiety. *Journal of the American Academy of Child and Adolescent Psychiatry, 37,* 6.

Biederman, J., Faraone, S. V., Milberger, S., Jetton, J. G., Chen, L., Mick, E., Greene, R. W., & Russell, R. L. (1996). Is childhood oppositional defiant disorder a precursor to adolescent conduct disorder? Findings from a four-year follow-up of children with ADHD. *Journal of the American Academy of Child and Adolescent Psychiatry, 35,* 1193–1204.

Biederman, J., Mick, E., Faraone, S. V., & Burback, M. (2001). Patterns of remission and symptom decline in conduct disorder: A four-year prospective study of an ADHD sample. *Journal of the American Academy of Child and Adolescent Psychiatry, 40,* 290–298.

Brooner, R. K., Herbst, J. H., Schmidt, C. W., Bigelow, G. E., & Costa, P. T. (1993). Antisocial personality disorder among drug abusers—Relations to other personality diagnoses and the 5-factor model of personality. *Journal of Nervous and Mental Disease, 181,* 313–324.

Bukstein, O. G., Brent, D. A., & Kraminer, Y. (1989). Comorbidity of substance abuse and other psychiatric disorders in adolescents. *American Journal of Psychiatry, 146,* 1131–1141.

Buydens-Branchey, L., Branchey, M. H., & Noumair, D. (1989). Age of alcoholism onset: I. Relationship to psychopathology. *Archives of General Psychiatry, 46,* 225–230.

Campbell, S. B. (1991). Longitudinal studies of active and aggressive preschoolers: Individual differences in early behavior and outcome. In D. Cicchetti & S. L. Toth (Eds.), *Rochester Symposium on Developmental Psychopathology* (pp. 57–90). Hillsdale, NJ: Lawrence Erlbaum Associates, Inc.

Capaldi, D. M. (1992). The co-occurrence of conduct problems and depressive symptoms in early adolescent boys: II. A 2-year follow-up at Grade 8. *Development and Psychopathology, 4,* 125–144.

Capaldi, D. M., & Stoolmiller, M. (1999). Co-occurrence of conduct problems and depressive symptoms in early adolescent boys: III. Prediction to young adult adjustment. *Development and Psychopathology, 11,* 59–84.

Caron, C., & Rutter, M. (1991). Comorbidity in child psychopathology: Concepts, issues and research strategies. *Journal of Child Psychology and Psychiatry, 32,* 1063–1080.

Caspi, A., & Moffitt, T. E. (1995). The continuity of maladaptive behavior: From description to understanding in the study of antisocial behavior. In D. Cicchetti & D. J. Cohen (Eds.), *Developmental Psychopathology* (Vol. 2, pp. 472–511). New York: Wiley.

Christian, R. E., Frick, P. J., Hill, N. L., Tyler, L., & Frazer, D. R. (1997). Psychopathy and conduct problems in children: II. Implications for subtyping children with conduct problems. *Journal of the American Academy of Child and Adolescent Psychiatry, 36,* 233–241.

Clark, D. B., Parker, A. M., & Lynch, K. G. (1999). Psychopathology and substance-related problems during early adolescence: A survival analysis. *Journal of Clinical Child Psychology, 28,* 333–341.

Cleckley, H. (1976). *The mask of sanity* (5th ed.). St Louis, MO: Mosby.

Cohen, P., Cohen, J., & Brook, J. (1993). An epidemiological study of disorder in late childhood and adolescence: II. Persistence of disorders. *Journal of Child Psychology and Psychiatry, 34,* 869–877.

Cohen, P., & Flory, M. (1998). Issues in the disruptive behavior disorders: Attention deficit disorder without hyperactivity and the differential validity of oppositional defiant and conduct disorders. In T. Widiger, A. J. Frances, H. J. Pincus, R. Roth, M. B. First, W. Davis, & M. Kline (Eds.), *DSM–IV Sourcebook* (Vol. 4, pp. 455–463). Washington, DC: American Psychiatric Press.

Coie, J. D., & Dodge, K. A. (1998). Aggression and antisocial behavior. In W. Damon & N. Eisenberg (Eds.), *Handbook of child psychology: Social, emotional and personality development* (Vol. 3, pp. 779–862). New York: Wiley.

Cole, P. M., & Zahn-Waxler, C. (1992). Emotional dysregulation in disruptive behavior disorders. In D. Cicchetti & S. L. Toth (Eds.), *Developmental perspectives in depression* (pp. 173–209). Rochester, NY: University of Rochester Press.

Cote, S., Zoccolillo, M., Tremblay, R. E., Nagin, D., & Vitaro, F. (2001). Predicting girls' conduct disorder in adolescence from childhood trajectories of disruptive behaviors. *Journal of the American Academy of Child and Adolescent Psychiatry, 40,* 678–684.

Dodge, K. (1991). The structure and function of reactive and proactive aggression. In D. J. Pepler & K. H. Rubin (Eds.), *The development and treatment of childhood aggression* (pp. 201–218). Hillsdale, NJ: Lawrence Erlbaum Associates, Inc.

Dowson, J. H., Sussams, P., Grounds, A. T., & Taylor, J. C. (2001). Associations of past conduct disorder with personality disorders in "non-psychotic" psychiatric inpatients. *European Psychiatry, 16,* 49–56.

Edens, J. F., Skeem, J. L., Cruise, K. R., & Cauffman, E. (2001). Assessment of "juvenile psychopathy" and its association with violence: A critical review. *Behavioral Sciences and the Law, 19,* 53–80.

Elander, J., Rutter, M., Simonoff, E., & Pickles, A. (2000). Explanations for apparent late onset criminality in a high-risk sample of children followed up in adult life. *British Journal of Criminology, 40,* 497–509.

Elliott, D. S. (1994). Serious violent offenders: Onset, developmental course, and termination— The American Society of Criminology 1993 Presidential Address. *Criminology, 32,* 1–21.

Farrington, D. P. (1995). The development of offending and antisocial behaviour from childhood: Key findings from the Cambridge study in delinquent development. *Journal of Child Psychology and Psychiatry, 36,* 929–964.

Farrington, D. P. (1997). A critical analysis of research on the development of antisocial behavior from birth to adulthood. In D. M. Stoff, J. Breiling, & J. D. Maser (Eds.), *Handbook of antisocial behavior* (pp. 234–240). New York: Wiley.

Farrington, D. P., Loeber, R., Stouthamer-Loeber, M., Van Kammen, W. B., & Schmidt, L. (1996). Self-reported delinquency and a combined delinquency seriousness scale based on boys, mothers, and teachers: Concurrent and predictive validity for African-Americans and Caucasians. *Criminology 34,* 501–525.

Fergusson, D. M., Horwood, L. J., & Lynskey, M. T. (1994). Structure of DSM–III–R criteria for disruptive childhood behaviors: Confirmatory factor models. *Journal of the American Academy of Child and Adolescent Psychiatry, 33,* 1145–1157.

Fergusson, D. M., Horwood, L. J., & Lynskey, M. T. (1996). Childhood sexual abuse and psychiatric disorder in young adulthood: II. Psychiatric outcomes of childhood sexual abuse. *Journal of the American Academy of Child and Adolescent Psychiatry, 35,* 1365–1374.

Forehand, R., & Wierson, M. (1993). The role of developmental factors in planning behavioral interventions for children: Disruptive behavior as an example. *Behavior Therapy, 24,* 117–141.

Fowles, D. C. (1980). The three arousal model: Implications of Gray's two-factor learning theory for heart rate, electrodermal activity, and psychopathy. *Psychophysiology, 17,* 87–104.

Frick, P. J. (1998). *Conduct disorders and severe antisocial behavior.* New York: Plenum.

Frick, P. J., Lahey, B. B., Applegate, B., Kerdyck, L., Ollendick, T., Hynd, G. W., Garfinkel, B., Greenhill, L., Biederman, J., Barkley, R. A., McBurnett, K., Newcorn, J., & Waldman, I. (1994). DSM–IV field trials for the disruptive behavior disorders: Symptom utility estimates. *Journal of the American Academy of Child and Adolescent Psychiatry, 33,* 529–539.

Frick, P. J., Lahey, B. B., Loeber, R., Tannenbaum, L., Van Horn, Y., Christ, M. A. G., Hart, E. A., & Hanson, K. (1993). Oppositional defiant disorder and conduct disorder: A meta-analytic review of factor analyses and cross-validation in a clinical sample. *Clinical Psychological Review, 13,* 319–340.

Frick, P. J., O'Brien, B. S., Wootton, J. M., & McBurnett, K. (1994). Psychopathy and conduct problems in children. *Journal of Abnormal Psychology, 103,* 700–707.

Goodman, S. H., & Kohlsdorf, B. (1994). The developmental psychopathology of conduct problems: Gender issues. In D. C. Fowels (Ed.), *Progress in experimental personality and psychopathology research* (pp. 121–161). New York: Springer.

Graham, P., & Rutter, M. (1973). Psychiatric disorders in the young adolescent: A follow-up study. *Proceedings of the Royal Society of Medicine, 66,* 1226–1229.

Haapasalo, J., & Tremblay, R. E. (1994). Physically aggressive boys from ages 6 to 12: Family background, parenting behavior, and prediction of delinquency. *Journal of Consulting and Clinical Psychology, 62,* 1044–1052.

Hare, R. D. (1970). *Psychopathy: Theory and research.* New York: Wiley.

Hare, R. D., Harpur, T. J., Hakstian, A. R., Forth, A. E., Hart, S. D., & Newman, J. P. (1990). The revised Psychopathy Checklist: Reliability and factor structure. *Psychological Assessment: A Journal of Consulting and Clinical Psychology, 2,* 338–341.

Hare, R. D., Hart, S. D., & Harpur, T. J. (1991). Psychopathy and the DSM–IV criteria for antisocial personality disorder. *Journal of Abnormal Psychology, 100,* 391–398.

Harpur, T. J., Hare, R. D., & Hakstian, A. R. (1989). Two-factor conceptualization of psychopathy: Construct validity and assessment implications. *Psychological Assessment: A Journal of Consulting and Clinical Psychology, 1,* 6–17.

Harrington, R., Fudge, H., Rutter, M., Pickles, A., & Hill, J. (1991). Adult outcomes of childhood and adolescent depression: II. Links with antisocial disorders. *Journal of the American Academy of Child and Adolescent Psychiatry, 30,* 434–439.

Hill, J., & Maughan, B. (Eds.). (2000). *Conduct disorders in childhood and adolescence.* Cambridge, England: Cambridge University Press.

Hinshaw, S. (1994). Conduct disorder in childhood: Conceptualization, diagnosis, comorbidity, and risk status for antisocial functioning in adulthood. In D. C. Fowles, P. Sutker, & S. H. Goodman (Eds.), *Progress in experimental personality and psychopathology research* (pp. 3–44). New York: Springer.

Hinshaw, S., Lahey, B. B., & Hart, E. (1993). Issues of taxonomy and comorbidity in the development of conduct disorder. *Development and Psychopathology, 5,* 31–49.

Holmes, S. J., & Robins, L. N. (1987). The influence of childhood disciplinary experience on the development of alcoholism and depression. *Journal of Child Psychology and Psychiatry, 28,* 399–415.

Jensen, P. S., Martin, D., & Cantwell, D. P. (1997). Comorbidity in ADHD: Implications for research, practice, and DSM–IV. *Journal of the American Academy of Child and Adolescent Psychiatry, 36,* 1065–1079.

Kazdin, A. E. (Ed.). (1995). *Conduct disorders in childhood and adolescence* (2nd ed.). Thousand Oaks, CA: Sage.

Keenan, K., Loeber, R., & Green, S. (1998). *A review of sex differences and similarities in conduct disorder.* Manuscript submitted for publication.

Kelley, B. T., Loeber, R., Keenan, K., & DeLamatre, M. (1997). *Developmental pathways in boys' disruptive and delinquent behavior.* Washington, DC: Office of Juvenile Justice and Delinquency Prevention, U.S. Department of Justice.

Kessler, R. C., McGonagle, K. A., Zhao, S., Nelson, C. B., Hughes, M., Eshelman, S., Wittchen, H.-U., & Kendler, K. S. (1994). Lifetime and 12-month prevalence of DSM–III–R psychiatric disorders in the United States: Results from the National Comorbidity Survey. *Archives of General Psychiatry, 51,* 8–19.

Kolko, D. J. (1994). Conduct disorder. In M. Hersen, R. T. Ammerman, & L. Sisson (Eds.), *Handbook of aggressive and destructive behavior in psychiatric patients* (pp. 363–393). New York: Plenum.

Kovacs, M., Paulauskas, S., Gatsonis, C., & Richards, C. (1988). Depressive disorders in childhood. *Journal of Affective Disorders, 15,* 205–217.

Kratzer, L., & Hodgins, S. (1997). Adult outcomes of child conduct problems: A cohort study. *Journal of Abnormal Psychology, 25,* 65–81.

Lahey, B. B., & Loeber, R. (1994). Framework for a developmental model of oppositional defiant disorder and conduct disorder. In D. K. Routh (Ed.), *Disruptive behavior disorders in childhood* (pp. 139–180). New York: Plenum.

Lahey, B. B., Loeber, R., Burke, J. D., & Rathouz, P. (2002). Adolescent outcomes of childhood conduct disorder among clinic-referred boys: Predictors of improvement. *Journal of Abnormal Child Psychology, 30,* 333–348.

Lahey, B. B., Loeber, R., Burke, J. D., Rathouz, P., & McBurnett, K. (2001). *Waxing and waning in concert: Dynamic comorbidity of conduct disorder with oppositional and emotional problems over seven years among clinic-referred boys.* Manuscript submitted for publication.

Lahey, B. B., Loeber, R., Hart, E. L., Frick, P. J., Applegate, B., Zhang, Q., Green, S. M., & Russo, M. F. (1995). Four-year longitudinal study of conduct disorder in boys: Patterns and predictors of persistence. *Journal of Abnormal Psychology, 104,* 83–93.

Lahey, B. B., Loeber, R., Quay, H. C., Applegate, B., Shaffer, D., Waldman, I., Hart, E. K., McBurnett, K., Frick, P. J., Jensen, P. S., Dulcan, M., Canino, G., & Bird, H. (1998). Validity of DSM–IV subtypes of conduct disorder based on age of onset. *Journal of the American Academy of Child and Adolescent Psychiatry, 37,* 435–442.

Lahey, B. B., Loeber, R., Quay, H. C., Frick, P. J., & Grimm, J. (1997). Oppositional defiant disorder and conduct disorder. In T. A. Widiger, A. J. Frances, H. A. Pincus, R. Ross, M. B. First, & W. Davis (Eds.), *DSM–IV sourcebook* (Vol. 3, pp. 189–209). Washington DC: American Psychiatric Association.

Lahey, B. B., Loeber, R., Stouthamer-Loeber, M., Christ, M. A. G., Green, S. M., Russo, M. F., Frick, P. J., & Dulcan, M. (1990). Comparison of DMS–III and DSM–III–R diagnoses for prepubertal children: Changes in prevalence and validity. *Journal of the American Academy of Child and Adolescent Psychiatry, 29,* 620–626.

Lahey, B. B., Miller, T. L., Gordon, R. A., & Riley, A. W. (1999). Developmental epidemiology of the disruptive behavior disorders. In H. C. Quay & A. Hogan (Eds.), *Handbook of the disruptive behavior disorders* (pp. 23–48). New York: Plenum.

Lahey, B. B., Schwab-Stone, M., Goodman, S. H., Waldman, I. D., Canino, G., Rathouz, P. J., Miller, T. L., Dennis, K. D., Bird, H., & Jensen, P. S. (2000). Age and gender differences in oppositional behavior and conduct problems: A cross-sectional household study of middle childhood and adolescence. *Journal of Abnormal Psychology, 109,* 488–503.

Lahey, B. B., Waldman, I. D., & McBurnett, K. (1999). The development of antisocial behavior: An integrative causal model. *Journal of Child Psychology and Psychiatry, 40,* 669–682.

Le Blanc, M. (1997). Identification of potential juvenile offenders. *European Journal on Criminal Policy and Research, 5,* 9–32.

Le Blanc, M., & Loeber, R. (1998). Developmental criminology updated. In M. Tonry (Ed.), *Crime and justice: A review of research* (Vol. 23, pp. 115–197). Chicago: The University of Chicago Press.

Lewis, C. E., & Bucholz, K. K. (1991). Alcoholism, antisocial behavior and family history. *British Journal of Addiction, 86,* 177–194.

Loeber, R. (1988a). Behavioral precursors and accelerators of delinquency. In W. Buikhuisen & S. A. Mednick (Eds.), *Explaining criminal behavior* (pp. 51–67). Leiden, Netherlands: Brill.

Loeber, R. (1988b). Natural histories of conduct problems, delinquency, and associated substance use. Evidence for developmental progressions. In B. B. Lahey & A. E. Kazdin (Eds.), *Advances in clinical child psychology* (Vol. 11, pp. 73–124). New York: Plenum.

Loeber, R. (1990). Development and risk factors of juvenile antisocial behavior and delinquency. *Clinical Psychology Review, 10,* 1–41.

Loeber, R. (1991). Antisocial behavior: More enduring than changeable? *Journal of the American Academy of Child and Adolescent Psychiatry, 31,* 393–397.

Loeber, R., Burke, J. D., Lahey, B. B., Winters, A., & Zera, M. (2000). Oppositional defiant and conduct disorder: A review of the past 10 years, Part I. *Journal of the American Academy of Child and Adolescent Psychiatry, 39,* 1468–1484.

Loeber, R., DeLamatre, M., Keenan, K., & Zhang, Q. (1998). A prospective replication of developmental pathways in disruptive and delinquent behavior. In R. Cairns, L. Bergman, & J. Kagan (Eds.), *Methods and models for studying the individual* (pp. 185–215). Thousands Oaks, CA: Sage.

Loeber, R., & Farrington, D. P. (Eds.). (1998). *Serious and violent juvenile offenders: Risk factors and successful interventions.* Thousand Oaks, CA: Sage.

Loeber, R., & Farrington, D. P. (Eds.). (2001). *Child delinquents: Development, intervention and service needs.* Thousand Oaks, CA: Sage.

Loeber, R., Farrington, D. P., Stouthamer-Loeber, M., & Van Kammen, W. B. (Eds.). (1998). *Antisocial behavior and mental health problems: Explanatory factors in childhood and adolescence.* Mahwah, NJ: Lawrence Erlbaum Associates, Inc.

Loeber, R., Green, S. M., Keenan, K., & Lahey, B. B. (1995). Which boys will fare worse? Early predictors of the onset of conduct disorder in a six year longitudinal study. *Journal of the American Academy of Child and Adolescent Psychiatry, 34,* 499–509.

Loeber, R., Green, S. M., & Lahey, B. B. (in press). Risk factors for antisocial personality. In J. Coid & D. P. Farrington (Eds.), *Primary prevention of adult antisocial personality.* Cambridge, England: Cambridge University Press.

Loeber, R., Green, S. M., Lahey, B. B., Frick, P. J., & McBurnett, K. (2000). Findings on disruptive behavior disorders from the first decade of the Developmental Trends Studies. *Clinical Child and Family Psychology Review, 3,* 37–60.

Loeber, R., Green, S. M., Lahey, B. B., & Kalb, L. (2000). Physical fighting in childhood as a risk factor for later mental health problems. *American Academy of Child Adolescent Psychiatry, 39,* 421–428.

Loeber, R., & Hay, D. F. (1994). Developmental approaches to aggression and conduct problems. In M. Rutter & D. F. Hay (Eds.), *Development through life: A handbook for clinicians* (pp. 488–515). London: Blackwell.

Loeber, R., & Hay, D. F. (1997). Key issues in the development of aggressive and violence from childhood to early adulthood. *Annual Review of Psychology, 48,* 371–410.

Loeber, R., & Keenan, K. (1994). The interaction between conduct disorder and its comorbid conditions: Effects of age and gender. *Clinical Psychology Review, 14,* 497–523.

Loeber, R., Keenan, K., Lahey, B. B., Green, S. M., & Thomas, C. (1993). Evidence for developmentally based diagnoses of oppositional defiant disorder and conduct disorder. *Journal of Abnormal Child Psychology, 21,* 377–410.

Loeber, R., Keenan, K., Russo, M. F., Green, S. M., Lahey, B. B., & Thomas, C. (1998). Secondary data analyses for DSM–IV on the symptoms of oppositional defiant disorder and conduct disorder. In T. A. Widiger, A. J. Frances, H. J. Pincus, R. Roth, M. B. First, W. Davis, & M. Kline (Eds.), *DSM–IV sourcebook* (Vol. 4, pp. 465–490). Washington, DC: American Psychiatric Press.

Loeber, R., Keenan, K., & Zhang, Q. (1997). Boys' experimentation and persistence in developmental pathways toward serious delinquency. *Journal of Child and Family Studies, 6,* 321–357.

Loeber, R., Lahey, B. B., & Thomas, C. (1991). Diagnostic conundrum of oppositional defiant disorder and conduct disorder. *Journal of Abnormal Psychology, 100,* 379–390.

Loeber, R., & Schmaling, K. (1985). Empirical evidence for overt and covert patterns of antisocial conduct problems. *Journal of Abnormal Child Psychology, 13,* 337–352.

Loeber, R., & Stouthamer-Loeber, M. (1998). Development of juvenile aggression and violence. Some common misconceptions and controversies. *American Psychologist, 53,* 242–259.

Loeber, R., Tremblay, R. E., Gagnon, C., & Charlebois, P. (1989). Continuity and desistance in disruptive boys' early fighting in school. *Development and Psychopathology, 1,* 39–50.

Luntz, B. K., & Widom, C. S. (1994). Antisocial personality disorder in abused and neglected children grown up. *American Journal of Psychiatry, 151,* 670–674.

Lykken, D. T. (1957). A study of anxiety in the sociopathic personality. *Journal of Abnormal and Clinical Psychology, 55,* 6–10.

Lynam, D. R. (1997). Pursuing the psychopath: Capturing the fledgling psychopath in a nomological net. *Journal of Abnormal Psychology, 106,* 425–438.

Masten, A. S. (1988). Toward a developmental psychopathology of early adolescence. In M. D. Levine & E. R. McArney (Eds.), *Early adolescent transitions* (pp. 261–278). Lexington, MA: Heath.

Maughan, B., & Rutter, M. (1998). Continuities and discontinuities in antisocial behavior from childhood to adult life. In T. H. Ollendick & R. J. Prinz (Eds.), *Advances in clinical child psychology* (Vol. 20, pp. 1–47). New York: Plenum.

Modestin, J., Matutat, B., & Würmle, O. (2001). Antecedents of opioid dependence and personality disorder: Attention-deficit/hyperactivity disorder and conduct disorder. *European Archives of Clinical Neuroscience, 251,* 42–47.

Moffitt, T. E. (1990). Juvenile delinquency and attention deficit disorder: Boys' developmental trajectories from age 13 to age 15. *Child Development, 61,* 893–910.

Moffitt, T. E. (1993). Adolescence-limited and life-cycle-persistent antisocial behavior: A developmental taxonomy. *Psychology Review, 100,* 674–701.

Moffitt, T. E., Caspi, A., Dickson, N., Silva, P., & Stanton, W. (1996). Childhood-onset versus adolescent-onset antisocial conduct problems in males: Natural history from ages 3 to 18 years. *Development and Psychopathology, 8,* 399–424.

Myers, M. G., Stewart, D. G., & Brown, S. A. (1998). Progression from conduct disorder to antisocial personality disorder following treatment to adolescent substance abuse. *American Journal of Psychiatry, 155,* 479–485.

Nagin, D., & Tremblay, R. E. (1999). Trajectories of boys' physical aggression, opposition, and hyperactivity on the path to physically violent and nonviolent juvenile delinquency. *Child Development, 70,* 1181–1196.

Newman, D. L., Moffitt, T. E., Caspi, A., Magdolm, L., Silva, P. A., & Stanton, W. R. (1996). Psychiatric disorder in a birth cohort of young adults: Prevalence, comorbidity, clinical significance, and new case incidence from ages 11 to 21. *Journal of Consulting and Clinical Psychology, 64,* 552–562.

Nottelmann, E. D., & Jensen, P. S. (1995). Comorbidity of disorders in children and adolescents: Developmental perspectives. *Advances in Clinical Child Psychology, 17,* 109–155.

Nurco, D. N., Shaffer, J. W., Ball, J. C., & Kinlock, T. W. (1984). Trends in the commission of crime among narcotic addicts over successive periods of addiction and nonaddiction. *American Journal of Drug and Alcohol Abuse, 10,* 481–489.

Offord, D. R., Boyle, M. H., Racine, Y. A., Fleming, J. E., Cadman, D. T., Blum, H. M., Byrne, C., Links, P. S., Lipman, E. L., MacMillan, H. L., Grant, N. I. R., Sandford, M. N., Szatmari, P., Thomas, H., & Woodward, C. A. (1992). Outcome, prognosis, and risk in a longitudinal follow-up study. *Journal of the American Academy of Child and Adolescent Psychiatry, 31,* 916–922.

Pakiz, B., Reinherz, H. Z., & Giaconia, R. M. (1997). Early risk factors for serious antisocial behavior at age 21: A longitudinal community study. *American Journal of Orthopsychiatry, 67,* 92–101.

Patrick, C. J. (1994). Emotion and psychopathy: Startling new insights. *Psychophysiology, 31,* 319–330.

Patterson, G. R., Reid, J. B., & Dishion, T. J. (1992). *Antisocial boys.* Eugene, OR: Castalia.

Pelham, W. E., Waschbusch, D. A., Greiner, A. R., Jennings, J. R., Tarter, R. E., & Moss, H. B. (in press). Reactive aggression in boys with disruptive behavior disorders: Behavior, psychology, and affect. *Developmental Psychology.*

Pepler, D. J., & Rubin, K. H. (Eds.). (1991). *The development and treatment of childhood aggression.* Hillsdale, NJ: Lawrence Erlbaum Associates, Inc.

Puig-Antich, J. (1982). Major depression and conduct disorder in prepuberty. *Journal of the American Academy of Child Psychiatry, 21,* 118–128.

Puig-Antich, J., Goetz, D., Davies, M., Kaplan, T., Davies, S., Ostow, L., Asnis, L., Twomey, J., Iyengae, S., & Ryan, N. (1989). A controlled family history study of prepubertal major depressive disorder. *Archives of General Psychiatry, 46*, 406–418.

Renouf, A. G., Kovacs, M., & Mukerji, P. (1997). Relationship of depressive conduct, and comorbid disorders and social functioning in childhood. *Journal of the American Academy of Child and Adolescent Psychiatry, 36*, 998–1004.

Rey, J. M., Morris-Yates, A., Singh, M., Andrews, G., & Stewart, G. W. (1995). Continuities between psychiatric disorders in adolescents and personality disorders in young adults. *American Journal of Psychiatry, 152*, 895–900.

Robins, L. N. (1966). *Deviant children grown up: A sociological and psychiatric study of sociopathic personality.* Baltimore: Williams & Wilkins.

Robins, L. N. (1978). Study childhood predictors of adult antisocial behavior: Replication from longitudinal studies. *Psychological Medicine, 8*, 611–622.

Robins, L. N., & Price, R. K. (1991). Adult disorders predicted by childhood conduct problems: Results from the NIMH Epidemiologic Catchment Area project. *Psychiatry: Journal for the Study of Interpersonal Processes, 54*, 116–132.

Robins, L. N., & Przybeck, T. R. (1985). Age of onset of drug use as a factor in drug and other disorders. In C. Jones & R. Battjes (Eds.), *Etiology of drug abuse: Implications for prevention* (National Institute on Drug Abuse Research Monograph No. 56). 178–192. US: US Department of Health and Human Services.

Robins, L. N., & Ratcliff, K. S. (1979). Risk factors in the continuation childhood antisocial behavior into adulthood. *International Journal of Mental Health, 7*, 96–116.

Robins, L. N., Tipp, J., & McEvoy, L. (1991). Antisocial personality. In L. N. Robins & D. A. Regier (Eds.), *Psychiatric disorders in America* (pp. 258–290). New York: Free Press.

Rogers, R., Johansen, J., Chang, J. J., & Salekin, R. T. (1997). Predictors of adolescent psychopathy: Oppositional and conduct-disordered symptoms. *Journal of the American Academy of Psychiatry and Law, 25*, 261–271.

Routh, D. K. (Ed.). (1994). *Disruptive behavior disorders in childhood.* New York: Plenum.

Russo, M. F., Loeber, R., Lahey, B. B., & Keenan, K. (1994). Oppositional defiant and conduct disorders: Validation of the DSM–III–R and an alternative option. *Journal of Clinical Child Psychology, 23*, 56–68.

Rutter, M., Giller, H., & Hagell, A. (1998). *Antisocial behaviour in young people.* Cambridge, England: Cambridge University Press.

Rutter, M., Tizard, J., & Whitmore, K. (1970). *Education, health and behavior.* New York: Wiley.

Satterfield, J. H., & Schell, A. (1997). A prospective study of hyperactive boys with conduct problems and normal boys adolescent and adult criminality. *Journal of the American Academy of Child and Adolescent Psychiatry, 36*, 1726–1735.

Shaffer, D. (1974). Suicide in childhood and early adolescence. *Journal of Child Psychology and Psychiatry, 15*, 275–291.

Shaffi, N., Carrigan, S., Whittinghill, J. R., & Derrick, A. (1985). Psychological autopsy of completed suicide of children and adolescents. *American Journal of Psychiatry, 142*, 1061–1064.

Sholevar, G. P. (1995). *Conduct disorders in children and adolescents.* Washington, DC: American Psychiatric Press.

Shubert, D. S. P., Wolf, A. W., Patterson, M. B., Grande, T. P., & Pendleton, L. (1988). A statistical evaluation of the literature regarding the associations among alcoholism, drug abuse, and antisocial personality disorder. *International Journal of the Addictions, 23*, 797–808.

Silverthorn, P., & Frick, P. J. (1999). Developmental pathways to antisocial behavior: The delayed-onset pathway in girls. *Development and Psychopathology, 11*, 101–126.

Smetana, J. G. (1990). Morality and conduct disorders. In M. Lewis & S. M. Miller (Eds.), *Handbook of developmental psychopathology* (pp. 157–179). New York: Plenum.

Sroufe, L. A. (1997). Psychopathology as an outcome of development. *Development and Psychopathology, 9*, 251–268.

Stoff, D. M., Breiling, J., & Maser, J. D. (1997). *Handbook of antisocial behavior.* New York: Wiley.

Stouthamer-Loeber, M., Loeber, R., Farrington, D. P., Zhang, Q., Van Kammen, W. B., & Maguin, E. (1993). The double edge of protective and risk factors for delinquency: Interrelations and developmental patterns. *Development and Psychopathology, 5,* 683–701.

Swanson, M. C., Bland, R. C., & Newman, S. C. (1994). Antisocial personality disorders. *Acta Psychiatrica Scandinavica, 89,* 63–70.

Tolan, P. H., & Gorman-Smith, D. (1998). Development of serious and violent offending careers. In R. Loeber & D. P. Farrington (Eds.), *Serious and violent juvenile offenders: Risk factors and successful intervention* (pp. 68–87). Thousands Oaks, CA: Sage.

Tolan, P. H., & Loeber, R. (1993). Antisocial behavior. In P. Tolan & V. Cohler (Eds.), *Handbook of clinical research and practice with adolescents* (pp. 307–331). New York: Wiley.

Tolan, P. H., & Thomas, P. (1995). The implications of age of onset for delinquency risk II: Longitudinal data. *Journal of Abnormal Child Psychology, 23,* 157–181.

Tremblay, R. E., Loeber, R., Gagnon, C., Charlebois, P., Larivée, S., & Le Blanc, M. (1991). Disruptive boys with stable and unstable high fighting behavior patterns during junior elementary school. *Journal of Abnormal Child Psychology, 19,* 285–300.

Tremblay, R. E., Masse, B., Perron, D., Le Blanc, M., Schwartzman, A. E., & Ledingham, J. E. (1992). Early disruptive behavior, poor school achievement delinquent behavior, and delinquent personality: Longitudinal analyses. *Journal of Consulting and Clinical Psychology, 60,* 64–72.

Turiel, E. (1998). The development of morality. In W. Damon (Ed.), *Handbook of child psychology—Social, emotional, and personality development* (5th ed., Vol. 3, pp. 863–932). New York: Wiley.

Van Kammen, W. B., & Loeber, R. (1994). Are fluctuations in delinquent activities related to the onset and offset in juvenile illegal drug use and drug dealing? *Journal of Drug Issues, 24,* 9–24.

Verhulst, F. C., & van der Ende, J. (1991). Four year follow-up of teacher-reported problem behaviours. *Psychological Medicine, 21,* 965–977.

Vitaro, F., Gendreau, P. L., Tremblay, R. E., & Oligny, P. (1998). Reactive and proactive aggression differentially predict later conduct problems. *Journal of Child Psychology and Psychiatry, 39,* 377–385.

Vitelli, R. (1997). Comparison of early and late start models of delinquency in adult offenders. *International Journal of Offender Therapy and Comparative Criminology, 41,* 351–357.

Vitelli, R. (1998). Childhood disruptive behavior disorders and adult psychopathy. *American Journal of Forensic Psychology, 16,* 29–37.

Vitiello, B., & Stoff, D. M. (1997). Subtypes of aggression and their relevance to child psychiatry. *Journal of the American Academy of Child and Adolescent Psychiatry, 36,* 307–315.

Waldman, I. D., & Lilienfeld, S. O. (1991). Diagnostic efficiency of symptoms for oppositional defiant disorder and attention-deficit hyperactivity disorder. *Journal Consulting and Clinical Psychology, 59,* 732–738.

Walker, J. L., Lahey, B. B., Hynd, G. W., & Frame, C. L. (1987). Comparison of specific patterns of antisocial behavior in children with conduct disorder with or without coexisting hyperactivity. *Journal of Consulting and Clinical Psychology, 55,* 910–913.

White, H. R. (1997). Longitudinal perspective on alcohol use and aggression during adolescence. In M. Galanter (Ed.), *Recent developments in alcoholism* (Vol. 13, pp. 81–103). New York: Plenum.

Whitmore, E. A., Mikulich, S. K., Thompson, L. L., Riggs, P. D., Aarons, G. A., & Crowley, T. J. (1997). Influences on adolescent substance dependence: Conduct disorder, depression, attention deficit hyperactivity disorder, and gender. *Drug and Alcohol Dependence, 47,* 87–97.

World Health Organization. (1992). *The ICD-10 classification of mental and behavioural disorders: Clinical descriptions and diagnostic guidelines.* Geneva, Switzerland: World Health Organization.

Zoccolillo, M. (1992). Co-occurrence of conduct disorder and its adult outcomes with depressive and anxiety disorders: A review. *Journal of the American Academy of Child and Adolescent Psychiatry, 31,* 547–556.

Zoccolillo, M. (1993). Gender and the development of conduct disorder. *Development and Psychopathology, 5*, 65–97.

Zoccolillo, M., Pickles, A., Quinton, D., & Rutter, M. (1992). The outcome of conduct disorder: Implications for defining adult personality disorder and conduct disorder. *Psychological Medicine, 22*, 971–986.

RISK FACTORS

4

Individual and Psychosocial Risk Factors

Heather K. Alvarez
Thomas H. Ollendick
Virginia Polytechnic Institute and State University

The identification of individual and psychosocial risk factors of conduct disorder (CD) and oppositional defiant disorder (ODD) has prompted considerable scientific inquiry in recent years. Given the value in understanding and preventing the development of these complex forms of psychopathology, such pursuit is understandable. Efforts to predict and prevent the deleterious effects associated with conduct problems[1] in youth have uncovered an array of early physiological features, behavioral patterns, and environmental situations that seem to precede the onset of CD and ODD.

Although the identification of specific risk factors is useful in describing the precursors of CD and ODD, this task falls short of predicting the actual onset and course of these disorders. This is largely because of the heterogeneity observed in individuals who eventually become diagnosed with conduct problems, in terms of both current presentation and developmental course (Frick, 1998a). Indeed, knowing what characteristics or events precede the onset of CD or ODD does not adequately explain the mecha-

---

[1]Both CD and ODD are often grouped together and referred to as conduct disorders. However, as we discuss later, the overlap between CD and ODD is not perfect. Although the majority of youth with CD have developmental histories of ODD, over two thirds of children with ODD do not develop or progress into CD (Greene & Doyle, 1999; Hinshaw, Lahey, & Hart, 1993). For purposes of this chapter, when overlap between the disorders is evident (e.g., children are referred to only as aggressive), we refer to these children as having conduct problems; however, when distinctions are clear and one or the other disorder is specifically referred to, we retain the labels of CD and ODD, respectively, to refer to these children.

nisms by which these risk factors lead to the development of the disorders. To account for this limitation, investigators are increasingly incorporating a developmental psychopathology framework to address the full array of features associated with these disorders (cf. Toth & Cicchetti, 1999).

It is widely recognized that behavior problems are expressed in a multitude of forms and in a breadth of environmental and interpersonal contexts across the life span. Further, social and parental expectations change as a child develops more sophisticated communication skills, self-regulation, social relations, and coping strategies. For a majority of individuals, conduct problems are short lived, minor in severity, and associated with concurrent developmental tasks and changes, as well as familial, social, and cultural expectations. Adolescents, for instance, are faced with dramatic hormonal fluctuations, increased independence and mobility, as well as greater expectations for academic and financial productivity. Not surprisingly, for most individuals the behavioral problems associated with this age group often subside once tasks are accomplished (e.g., high school diploma, job security) and physiological changes wane (Siegel & Scovill, 2000). It is likely that the developmentally based explanatory tools used in understanding the "normal" rise and fall of behavior problems will also serve to inform the progression of the most severe disruptions of behavior.

Greater emphasis is, in fact, being placed on the organization of specific problem behaviors in the context of salient developmental issues including age-appropriate competencies and adaptation. As such, the role of isolated risk factors and causal pathways in the development of behavior disorders are considered within a transactional context involving the growing child and his or her environment (Lease & Ollendick, 2000; Toth & Cicchetti, 1999). Thus, resultant diagnosis of any one disorder could be considered the product of interwoven maladaptive or inadequate social, emotional, or cognitive competencies that impede adaptation to the psychosocial system at a particular developmental level (for a detailed description, see Lerner, Hess, & Nitz, 1990). This definition reflects the inextricably bound nature of individual and environmental factors involved in the emergence of behavior disorders. Furthermore, given relations among risk factors, there exist a countless number of trajectories through which systems of risk factors lead to CD and/or ODD. The identification and discussion of any single risk factor should therefore account for its role in a larger, dynamic pattern of risk and resiliency. However, as Frick (1998b) noted, few studies to date evaluate the interaction of more than one factor in the development of CDs.

In light of this trend emphasizing more integrated, developmentally relevant approaches to the study and prediction of CD and ODD, the following discussion of individual and psychosocial risk factors not only details the nature of the risk factor but also elucidates the system or context in which the factor develops, co-occurs with other characteristics, and potentially influences the emergence of the disorders. In particular, in this chapter we discuss the role of various dispositional factors, sociodemographic characteristics, behavioral patterns, and interpersonal influences that are implicated in the development of conduct problems.

DISPOSITIONAL RISK FACTORS

Temperamental Features

Difficult Temperament. Difficult temperament, first evident during infancy, is a frequently identified risk factor in the later development of conduct problems. Difficult temperament often includes such elements as emotional lability, restlessness, negativism, and short attention span. Although difficult to specifically operationalize, this constellation of behaviors has consistently predicted later behavior problems across independent investigations (Keenan, Loeber, & Green, 1999). For instance, Caspi, Henry, McGee, Moffitt, and Silva (1995) found that both boys and girls identified as having difficult temperament at 3 years of age were significantly more likely to be diagnosed with CD at age 15. Similarly, recent findings from the Bloomington Longitudinal Study (Olson, Bates, Sandy, & Lanthier, 2000) suggest that early difficult temperament reported by a child's mother is associated with later maternal and self-ratings of externalizing behavior problems into late adolescence.

One likely pathway by which difficult temperament leads to conduct problems involves the parenting strategies and overall attitudes directed toward a child with these characteristics. Children with difficult temperament may be more difficult to discipline, soothe, and engage in interpersonal interaction. As such, they may be more likely to be the target of increased parental anger and problematic parenting practices (Caspi, Elder, & Herbener, 1990).

Reward Dominance. Psychobiological models, closely linked with notions of temperament, have also been useful in the understanding of risk factors for conduct behavior problems (O'Brien & Frick, 1996). In particular, Gray (1970) suggested that behavioral patterns are associated with two independent subsystems of the brain, the Behavioral Inhibition System (BIS) and Behavioral Activation System (BAS). The BIS inhibits behavior in the context of novel stimuli, innate fear stimuli, and signals of nonreward or punishment. Alternatively, the BAS activates or energizes behavior in these contexts. Applications of this theory to the study of conduct problems and antisocial behavior suggest that antisocial individuals have an unbalanced system in which the BAS system is in ascendance and dominates ongoing behavior. In this unbalanced system, behavior is dependent on rewards rather than the avoidance of punishment. As a result, it is hypothesized that these individuals develop patterns of behavior with less consideration to social norms and consequences. Support for this idea comes from numerous studies testing reward dominance paradigms with children (e.g., O'Brien, Frick, & Lyman, 1994).

The presence of a reward-dominant behavioral style in children with conduct problems provides a possible explanation for the symptom patterns evidenced, at least in some children. Antisocial children are often involved in risky, socially deviant activities that lead to hazardous or harmful outcomes. Despite the consequences of their actions, a certain subset of children continue to engage in such behaviors, becoming involved in greater risk and harm as time passes. Without appropriate consideration of consequences, these children anticipate less need to inhibit their actions to avoid adverse consequences. It is interesting that the subset of children who evidence this behavioral style is largely confined to those who also display callous and unemotional (CU) traits (O'Brien & Frick, 1996).

CU Traits.   A subset of children who develop conduct problems may be identified by the earlier onset of a different subset of temperamental-like traits related to the concept of psychopathy. CU traits found in youth consist of lacking sympathy and helpfulness, selfishness, diminished guilt, reduced need for social affiliation and approval, and dampened emotional expression (Frick, O'Brien, Wootton, & McBurnett, 1994; Lahey, Waldman, & McBurnett, 1999). These traits may account for those children less affected by changes or problems in the social environment in their development of conduct problems and later antisocial behavior (Wootton, Frick, Shelton, & Silverthorn, 1997). CU traits are suggestive not only of the onset of conduct problems but also the increased severity and chronicity of these behavioral patterns once they are developed. For instance, children identified with CU traits tend to exhibit a greater number and variety of CD symptoms (Frick, 1998a). Specifically, these individuals express more covert antisocial behavior and property destruction than those children who do not have CU traits, regardless of CD status (Christian, Frick, Hill, Tyler, & Frazer, 1997).

Although the pathway from which conduct problems develop is less clear than the description of the CU traits associated with these disorders, two possible hypotheses have been proposed by Frick and colleagues (Frick, 1998a; Frick et al., 1994). First, many children with CU traits also evidence lower behavioral inhibition, as manifested by increased thrill and adventure seeking and low fearfulness and low autonomic reactivity on skin conductance measures (Frick et al., 1994). Lower behavioral inhibition, as noted earlier, is related to increased dependence on rewards and decreased attention to punishments or consequences. This may help to explain why children with CU traits are less influenced and affected by the painful reactions and experiences of others as a function of their behavior. Second, in addition to the role of underlying physiological processes, it is possible that interactions among parents and children both sharing CU features lead to the development of CDs (Frick, 1998a). In this case, the ability for a parent to provide adequate social modeling, responsiveness to a child's emotional needs, and appropriate discipline strategies may be impeded by his or her own subset of psychopathic features. As a result, a child with existing difficulties would not likely receive the parenting necessary to counter the development of antisocial behaviors.

Decreased Cortisol Levels

Cortisol is a hormone produced by the adrenal cortex during times of stress. Low salivary cortisol levels, both at resting state and in response to stress, have been found in both boys and girls with CD symptomatology (McBurnett, Lahey, Rathouz, & Loeber, 2000). In-depth investigation by Loeber, Green, Lahey, Frick, and McBurnett (2000), as part of the Developmental Trends Study, reveals that this association is most strong for aggressive symptoms. Both self- and peer-report measures of aggression support these findings.

Cortisol has been associated with both underlying physiological processes as well as external influences that may be implicated in its production. In their study of anxiety and CD symptomatology, McBurnett et al. (1991) found that children with CD only had significantly lower levels of salivary cortisol compared to those with comorbid CD and anxiety disorder (see also chap. 7, this volume). As such, salivary cortisol may serve as a marker for the BAS and BIS system interchange (as described previously) in the manifestation of dysfunctional behavioral patterns such as conduct problems. Alternatively, reductions in cortisol production can result from environmental stressors during prenatal and early childhood development (Loeber et al., 2000). It is important to note, however, that whereas this physiological factor may provide a sound marker for later conduct problems, it is not a sufficient predictor of a CD without consideration of other interacting individual and psychosocial factors (Schulz, Halperin, Newcorn, Sharma, & Gabriel, 1997), a conclusion consistent with the developmental psychopathology perspective.

Intellectual Deficits and Academic Underachievement

Low intellectual ability is commonly identified as a risk factor for the development of conduct problems. Youth with conduct problems, on the whole, have a slightly lower IQ than the general population, especially in the measurement of verbal intelligence (Loeber, Green, Keenan, & Lahey, 1995; Moffitt, 1993; T. H. Ollendick, 1979). In fact, this pattern is still evident when controlling for social class (Rutter, Giller, & Hagell, 1998). Although the process by which or through which intellectual deficits contribute to the onset of conduct problems is unclear, a number of possible mechanisms have been hypothesized (cf. Greene & Doyle, 1999; Moffitt, 1993). First, intellectual deficits could negatively affect a child's range of responses to perceived or actual threats or provocation. Second, verbal intellectual deficits could impair the development of important self-regulation strategies that would enable a child to delay gratification, modulate affective reactions, or anticipate consequences. Third, lower intelligence may interfere with the generalization of learning across different contexts. In this case, internalization and application of overarching social norms or moral expectations across interpersonal relationships may be inhibited. Fourth, these deficits may hinder positive social experiences with parents and other adult figures. For instance, poorly developed communication skills may interfere with parents' attempts to socialize their child, which may lead to increased frustration and negativity directed toward the child. As a result, children with low intelligence may also be limited in their formation of social bonds with important models of prosocial behavior. The association between intellectual deficits and conduct problems is most apparent in those individuals who show an earlier onset of conduct problems in the absence of psychopathic traits (Frick, 1998a).

Low intelligence alone, however, does not fully account for the academic problems experienced by children with conduct problems. Academic underachievement in which academic performance is below that which is predicted by one's intellectual level is also found in a greater percentage of children with conduct problems (D. G. Ollendick & Ollendick, 1976). Indeed, between 11% and 61% of children with conduct problems have a significant learning disability (Hinshaw, 1992). Hinshaw (1992) recognized two possible developmental pathways from which academic underachievement may lead to conduct problems. First, attention deficit hyperactivity disorder (ADHD) in early childhood may lead to both academic problems as well as conduct problems in early to middle childhood. Alternatively, in those children who do not evidence conduct problems before adolescence, academic underachievement may lead to conduct problems in the absence of ADHD. Thus, the role of academic underachievement must be considered in the context of other developing behavioral patterns. Further, given the delayed-onset pathway of CD in girls, it is not surprising to find less consistent support exists for the predictive utility of learning disabilities for behavioral problems in girls (Smart, Sanson, & Prior, 1996).

Social Cognition

To fully appreciate the complex manner in which social cognitive mechanisms lead to conduct problems, it is necessary to consider both the social information processing pathway as well as the ways in which this pathway can be lead astray. As reviewed by Dodge (1993), there exists a linear set of steps in which social information is processed. These steps include encoding relevant aspects of a social stimulus, storing meaningful interpretations of the stimulus, accessing one or more behavioral and affective responses, evaluating the response in terms of moral acceptability or anticipated outcomes, and enacting the response. Several theories contend that deficits and distortions at any one of these steps may independently contribute both to the development of conduct problems and to the differentiation of triggers and types of conduct problems (e.g., Dodge & Frame, 1982; Short & Simeonsson, 1986). Clearly, the actual pattern of symptoms depends on a multiplicity of interacting factors in this process.

At least two cognitive processing distortions have been implicated in the development of conduct problems. First, research shows that children with conduct problems, and particularly those with aggressive characteristics, tend to selectively attend to or misperceive hostile cues in social interactions (Dodge & Frame, 1982). Often, when faced with a negative circumstance, these children perceive intentional threat or provocation in others, even in situations where others' acts are characterized as ambiguous or even benign (Crick & Dodge, 1996). As a result, these children may be more likely to reinforce, maintain, or exacerbate their conduct problems (e.g., retaliatory aggression) through this ongoing distortion of their social environment. Indeed, Dodge (1980) reported that a child will react with an aggressive response 70% of the time after a hostile attribution is made compared to 25% of the time following a benign attribution. Second, children with conduct problems may also misperceive their own behavior. Specifically, these children tend to not only minimize the harmful and dysfunctional nature of their actions but also overvalue rewards associated with these actions (Crick & Dodge, 1996). One limitation to this work, however, is that participants in these experiments have been predominantly male. Although recent investigations are focusing specifically on the development of social distortions in female participants, it is still unclear whether factors like oversensitivity to social hostility and rejection leads to conduct problems in girls (Keenan et al., 1999).

Youth with conduct problems also tend to evidence more deficient social cognition whereby insufficient cognitive processing occurs in situations in which it is required. For instance, Dodge and Frame (1982) found that aggressive children are less able to attend to relevant social cues when interacting with peers. As a result, they may overlook important facial expressions, body gestures, or verbal cues that may change or alter the meaning or tone of a social interaction. Additionally, children with conduct problems seem to lack organized nonaggressive problem-solving skills in response to a conflict or frustration, including generating and selecting among alternative prosocial solutions, as well as the ability to enact more appropriate solutions once and if they are accessed (Asarnow & Callan, 1985).

SOCIODEMOGRAPHIC RISK FACTORS

Gender

Although gender differences are alluded to within the context of other individual risk factors, it is clear that gender itself may be an important risk factor in the onset of conduct problems. From preschool age on, young boys tend to engage in significantly more aggressive and nonaggressive antisocial behavior than girls (Keenan & Shaw, 1997). This trend is also apparent in more serious manifestations of conduct problems. As it is currently defined in the *Diagnostic and Statistical Manual of Mental Disorders* (4th ed. [*DSM–IV*]; American Psychiatric Association, 1994), the prevalence of CD and ODD is greater for males than for females. Further, severity ratings of CD symptomology are significantly higher for males, particularly those involving physical harm to others (Lahey et al., 2000). It is important to note, however, that this distinction in prevalence is less apparent by mid-adolescence (American Psychiatric Association, 1994). For example, Olson et al. (2000) found no relation between gender and either maternal or self-reports of externalizing problems when adolescents were assessed at 17 years of age.

A number of hypotheses have been generated to explain the gender specificity observed in the onset and phenomenology of these disorders. For example, a recent review of the literature (Keenan et al., 1999) suggests that young girls score higher on ratings of empathy, as well as guilt and rumination about breaking rules and hurting others. These early factors may temporarily protect girls from engaging in early-onset antisocial behavior. However, girls' guilt about aggressive behavior seems to decline with age (Keenan et al., 1999), perhaps helping to explain the decreasing gender distinction in conduct problems in adolescence. As such, an interaction between gender and age also warrants consideration. Additionally, there seem to be gender differences in the development of communication skills such that girls may be more skilled at social interaction at an earlier age than boys (see Keenan & Shaw, 1997). As a result, adult figures, including parents as well as peers, may find it easier to socialize with girls than boys of the same age. In this case, perhaps the very group that most needs modeling and practice of appropriate social interactions is that which receives the least. There has also been much speculation regarding the role of gender-specific hormone levels (e.g., testosterone) in the onset of conduct problems, but findings are inconsistent (Steiner et al., 1997). Finally, the development of conduct problems may be related to the interaction between gender and parental responses to behavior problems. Evidence suggests that parents may respond differently to temperamental traits and antisocial behaviors exhibited by girls versus boys (Keenan & Shaw, 1997). Thus, it is also possible that both girls and boys have similar initial developmental trajectories in the development of conduct problems, but differential parental responses directly influence risk for diagnosis.

Despite recent advances, as most earlier investigations have focused solely on the study of male participants, data regarding gender differences in CD and ODD are relatively sparse. Additionally, debate exists as to the appropriateness of the current diagnostic nosology in these disorders. For instance, girls and boys tend to vary on the specific types of antisocial behavior exhibited. Girls tend to engage in more relational aggression and nonphysical antisocial behavior, whereas boys fit better into the mold of the standard *DSM* diagnosis, including overt physical features and delinquency. However, both boys and girls are clearly engaging in problematic social deviance and on follow-up may meet criteria for CD or ODD. Thus, there is still much to discover about the role of gender in the risk for, as well as the emergence and expression of, conduct problems.

Socioeconomic Status (SES)

Low SES is also a risk factor in the emergence of conduct problems. In one study (Loeber et al., 1995), low SES was found in almost 60% of families of children with CDs as opposed to 23.8% of families with non-CD children. However, the exact nature of the association between conduct problems and SES remains a source of considerable debate. Researchers have found a direct relation with SES and specific CD symptoms such as aggression (Loeber et al., 2000). Further, Lahey et al. (1995) suggested that SES is more reflective of other factors that give rise to conduct problems than it is a causal pathway in itself. In fact, they found that low SES was related only to transient forms of antisocial behavior in the absence of other risk factors. As Frick (1998b) acknowledged, it is difficult to specifically identify which factors in a child's social ecology are related to the development of conduct problems. Children from families with low income may have increased likelihood of exposure to high-crime neighborhoods, delinquent peers, parental stress and maladjustment, and reduced community and academic support. In many cases, SES may serve as a risk factor for both parental dysfunction and child conduct problems, or, alternatively, as a consequence of parental dysfunction and a correlate of conduct problems. Additionally, Frick (1998b) asserted that wide variations found inside the same impoverished neighborhoods provide further evidence for the importance of other environmental and individual risk factors that exist within this context.

Further complicating this relation, evidence supports that the risk for conduct problems associated with low SES may be more or less evident depending on the informant source of the report regarding the child. As Olson et al. (2000) noted, although family SES was unrelated to maternal reports of externalizing behavior in adolescents, it was moderately predictive of self-reported aggression by the adolescents themselves.

Ethnicity

Although rates of conduct problems differ as a function of ethnicity, the developmental course of these problematic behavioral patterns seems consistent across many ethnic groups (Barrera, Biglan, Ary, & Li, 2001). Thus, it is likely that ethnicity, much like SES, serves as a risk factor to the degree that it suggests elevations in other related risk factors. The role of ethnicity in the emergence of conduct problems is important then in identifying which individuals may be exposed to adversity that in turn may lead to problematic outcomes.

Age

It is widely recognized that the age at which conduct problems or antisocial behavior emerge critically influences the developmental course and phenomenology of conduct problems. In fact, this factor has formed the basis for a division in diagnostic subtypes of CD. The onset of conduct problems during early childhood of greater severity or persistence than what would be considered normative (i.e., "the terrible twos") is related to longstanding disorders and antisocial behavior into adulthood (Frick, 1998b). The early age of onset is usually related to a system of transacting individual and family environment risk factors that take place early in life and prevent the child from developing the social skills and self-regulation required to prevent the onset of conduct problems (Moffitt, 1993).

A second diagnostic subtype is based on those individuals who display non-normative patterns of conduct problems and antisocial behavior but only during adolescence. Although this developmental period is associated with general increases in rebelliousness and status offenses (e.g., alcohol use, truancy), conduct problems are evident in a small subset of adolescents who show more extreme or persistent forms of behavior problems. As we discuss in later sections, the development of conduct problems in adolescence may be related more to proximal risk factors that also emerge during this age period rather than chronological age per se. For instance, by adolescence there is a need for youth to interact with a greater number of authority figures, make decisions regarding academic and vocational goals, and transition from the family of origin to a more independent lifestyle (Steiner et al., 1997).

BEHAVIORAL PATTERNS

Aggression

The link between early aggression and later onset of conduct problems is well established (see Vitaro, Gendreau, Tremblay, & Oligny, 1998). In particular, physical aggression is considered one of the best predictors of a CD diagnosis (Loeber et al., 1995). Despite the tendency for aggression to decline with age in the general population, there is an age-related increase in the frequency and severity of aggressive behavior in a subset of youths who subsequently develop conduct problems. This developmental course is characterized by the replacement of minor forms of aggression (e.g., bullying) with new, more serious aggressive behaviors (e.g., mugging), as well as a shift in other aggressive behaviors to a more serious form of the same behavior (e.g., from fighting to using weapons in fights; Lahey, Goodman, et al., 1999).

Recent efforts inspired by Dodge's (1980) large-scale studies of aggressive boys have suggested a distinction in aggression based on two primary subtypes: reactive and proactive aggression. The first subtype, reactive aggression (i.e., hostile, affective), is characterized by a maladaptive defensive response following perceived or actual threat or provocation. This form of aggression is related to underlying deficits in affective modulation, social cognition, and impulse control (Vitiello & Stoff, 1997). A second subtype, proactive aggression (i.e., instrumental, predatory), is recognized as a pattern of unprovoked, instrumental, and goal-oriented aggressive actions. Proactive aggression differs from its counterpart on a wide variety of dimensions related to social, affective, and cognitive functioning (see Greene & Doyle, 1999). Given this distinction, early forms of aggression may differentially predict specific emerging symptom patterns of conduct problems. For instance, Vitaro et al. (1998) found that proactive aggression but not reactive aggression predicted later antisocial, delinquent behavior.

The risk associated with aggression also likely depends on the context of associated dysfunctional characteristics or consequences. In a recent large-scale prospective study of precursors to male criminality, children most at risk for later delinquency exhibited aggression in addition to norm-breaking behavior (e.g., disruptive classroom behavior, truancy, substance use) and poor school performance (Hamalainen & Pulkkinen, 1996). Importantly, the increase in risk is not isolated to the interaction of risk factors. For instance, whereas anxiety is considered a protective factor against the expression of milder forms of CD symptoms (T. H. Ollendick, Seligman, & Butcher, 1999), highly aggressive children with concurrent anxiety are at increased risk for conduct problems (Serbin, Peters, McAffer, & Schwartzman, 1991).

Impulsivity and ADHD

The role of ADHD in the development of conduct problems is widely debated in the field despite numerous efforts to elucidate the nature of this relation. Specifically, a high rate of comorbidity between the disruptive behavior disorders is well recognized such that the proportion of children with ADHD ranges from 65% to 90% in samples of children with conduct problems (Frick, 1998b). Additionally, it is known that children with ADHD tend to display more severe and persistent conduct problems (Farrington, Loeber, & van Kammen, 1990). However, data supporting the status of ADHD as a risk factor per se for the onset of conduct problems is less consistent. Early prospective studies report a greater likelihood of children with an ADHD diagnosis to meet criteria for CD after age 16 than those who do not receive such a diagnosis (e.g., Gittleman, Mannuzza, Shenker, & Bonagura, 1985). Moffitt and Silva (1988) also found that almost 60% of children with an earlier diagnosis of ADHD had become delinquent by age 13. Although this suggests that ADHD may be predictive of later conduct problems, critics note that these studies did not consider the role of early oppositional behavior (including ODD) in this developmental pathway.

The complexity in identifying a predictive relation is likely related to the multidimensional nature of ADHD in which one or more diagnostic features including impaired impulse control, hyperactivity, and inattention may be present. As such, it is possible that particular executive skill deficits associated with ADHD rather than the disorder itself are most predictive of the onset of CD. Recent researchers support this contention, showing that impulsivity but not hyperactivity is predictive of later conduct problems. Children who have difficulty evaluating and anticipating consequences, applying learning obtained from past experiences, and adjusting to the needs of a specific social situation are more likely to exhibit and maintain behavioral problems (Holmes, Slaughter, & Kashani, 2001). In fact, according to a study conducted by Tremblay, Pihl, Vitaro, and Dobkin (1994), impulsivity rated in kindergarten was the strongest predictor of the onset of stable, highly delinquent behavior at age 13. Alternatively, structural equation models evaluating the contributions of hyperactivity and parenting problems suggest that hyperactivity alone does not predict such behavioral outcomes (Patterson, DeGarmo, & Knutson, 2000).

Oppositionality

Considerable discussion has surrounded the nature of the relation between ODD and CD (Greene & Doyle, 1999). ODD is classified as a recurrent pattern of negativistic, defiant, disobedient, and hostile behavior toward authority figures, whereas a CD diagnosis involves more serious violation of the basic rights of others or major age-appropriate social norms or rules (American Psychiatric Association, 1994).

Although considered independent diagnoses, researchers recognize the continuity between CD and ODD such that the onset of ODD often occurs in the context of earlier forms of oppositional and defiant behavior, whereas the onset of CD emerges subsequently to an existing ODD diagnosis. Specifically, Loeber et al. (1995) found that 80% of boys who developed CD had a previous diagnosis of ODD at least 1 year earlier. The developmental sequence of these disorders then suggests a developmental and hierarchical pattern of behavioral problems of less severity that precedes more serious forms of aggression and delinquency, at least for some youth.

However, continuity between the disorders is not bidirectional such that over two thirds of children with ODD are not subsequently diagnosed with CD (Greene & Doyle, 1999; Hinshaw et al., 1993). Thus, the pathway by which early forms of oppositionality lead to the emergence of less severe forms of conduct problems (i.e., ODD) and to the development of more severe manifestations (i.e., CD) is multifaceted. For example, oppositionality may contribute to impaired interpersonal relationships, often starting in the home and then spanning to school and other community settings. Early oppositionality is also associated with increased peer rejection and decreased opportunity for classroom learning (Fergusson & Horwood, 1996; Lewin, Davis, & Hops, 1999). In addition to the impairment caused by the symptoms themselves, the patterns of oppositional behavior are highly relevant in the prediction of later delinquency. Studies show that higher frequency and variety of early oppositional behavior, as well as the presence of problem behavior in multiple settings, increases a child's risk for later deviant outcomes (Biederman, Mick, Faraone, & Burback, 2001; Loeber, 1990). Thus, not only the specific behaviors but also the presentation of these behaviors is important in maintaining this cycle of escalating and transforming antisocial behavior. Further, as Loeber (1991) commented, antisocial behaviors tend to be enduring, and once established these behaviors are often resilient to attempts at behavioral change.

INTERPERSONAL INFLUENCES

Although individual risk factors largely contribute to the development of conduct problems, these patterns of behavior do not occur outside an ever-changing social context. Indeed, given the nature of the symptoms, the severity of conduct problems is often evaluated more in terms of impairment within various social settings (i.e., community, school, home) rather than distress experienced within or by the child. Thus, influences from a child's social environment are critical in the onset, persistence, or desistance of conduct problems. The family environment, including relationships with parents, siblings, and other family members or caregivers is clearly meaningful in the early development of interpersonal skills, self-regulation, and moral understanding (Frick, 1998b). Of additional import are the peer affiliations that may serve to initiate, reinforce, and maintain conduct problems. Longitudinal studies show that poor peer relationships in early and middle childhood predict social maladaption (including delinquency) in later childhood and adolescence (T. H. Ollendick, Weist, Borden, & Greene, 1992; Rutter et al., 1998). However, the nature of this influence is admittedly complex. As Fergusson and Horwood (1996) recognized, peer affiliations tend to be reciprocally related to an individual's offending behavior. One's behavior may both influence the nature of peer affiliations and be influenced by these affiliations. For example, as a result of children's aggressive behavior, they may be rejected by their prosocial peers and at the same time accepted by another group of more socially deviant peers engaging in similar behaviors. Both aspects of this reciprocity are considered risk factors in the development of conduct problems.

Peer Rejection

Peer rejection is one important facet in the emergence and persistence of conduct problems. However, the context in which peer rejection occurs tends to involve a complex pattern of individual and environmental risk factors that may precede and/or co-occur with the rejection. For instance, risk for antisocial outcomes is found to be greatest for those aggressive children who are also experiencing peer rejection (Farrington et al., 1990). Peer rejection interestingly predicts later antisocial behavior and delinquency, even when taking into account initial levels of aggression (Rutter et al., 1998). Additional risk factors including academic failure and poor parental monitoring, when combined with peer rejection, are also predictors of poorer social outcomes (including involvement with antisocial peers; Dishion, Patterson, Stoolmiller, & Skinner, 1991). These results suggest that peer rejection alone may be a powerful risk factor for conduct problems but even more so in the presence of other risk factors.

The pathway by which peer rejection leads to conduct problems over and above the influence of other individual and environmental risk factors is not well known. Rejection from one's prosocial peers, which is often evident as early as preschool (Mandel, 1997), may impede the development of many necessary social skills that would normally be practiced and modeled in this peer group throughout the school-age years. Though less likely, it is also possible that the stress associated with peer isolation and rejection places a child at greater risk for many forms of psychopathology, including depression, ODD, and CD (Rutter et al., 1998).

Affiliation with Deviant Peer Groups

The association between a child's antisocial behavior and that of his or her peer group has been established both for boys and girls (Keenan, Loeber, Zhang, Stouthamer-Loeber, & Van Kammen, 1995). Although it remains unclear whether the association with a deviant peer group actually leads to conduct problems per se, it is clear that this environment nurtures the development and persistence of antisocial patterns of behavior such as substance abuse that could contribute to a greater risk for conduct problems (Keenan et al., 1999; Mandel, 1997). In particular, children with antisocial behavior tend to have fewer prosocial friends and instead attract more friends who engage in similar, antisocial behavior. As Lahey, Waldman, et al. (1999) hypothesized, these children may teach and encourage new antisocial behaviors among each other, thus contributing to development of well-established, disordered patterns of conduct problems. Further, continued participation in antisocial activities may be a source of prestige, companionship, and endorsement within a deviant peer group (Rutter et al., 1998). This reinforcement likely encourages the patterns of behavior indicative of a conduct problem.

Peer Influences and Moderating Factors

The risk for conduct problems associated with peer influences may be moderated by sociodemographic risk factors including age and gender. It is suggested, for example, that peer relationships may be more influential in the emergence of conduct problems during adolescence (Fergusson, Lynskey, & Horwood, 1996). It is during this developmental period that peer influences generally tend to take precedence over parenting influences (Rutter et al., 1998). Specifically, relationships between adolescent peers begin to include more active involvement, sharing of feelings and ideas, and less supervision of activities by adult figures. In addition, there is an overall increase in defiant and antisocial behavior during this time such that greater support for behavior associated with conduct problems may exist. Without resistance or rejection from certain peer groups, an increase in the persistence and/or severity of the symptom patterns is likely.

The role of peer influences may also be gender specific. There is evidence to suggest that girls are at greater risk for negative effects on their behavioral and emotional functioning as a result of peer problems given their high social orientation (Keenan et al., 1999). For instance, as girls tend to perceive more stress in relation to peer problems, peer rejection may have a stronger negative influence. Further, given differential gender role expectations, girls who exhibit aggression may be more likely to be rejected by their peers than boys who are aggressive.

SUMMARY

Individual and psychosocial risk factors of conduct problems represent a complex subset of characteristics and circumstances that are associated with the clinical diagnosis of CD or ODD. Although we present these risk factors separately in this chapter to provide a more parsimonious overview of the literature, this depiction is not intended to represent the multiply determined nature of conduct problems in which a combination of individual characteristics and environmental stressors interact and transact throughout the developmental course. Furthermore, as noted by Rutter and Casaer (1991), it is the accumulation of these interacting risk factors that leads to conduct problems such that no single factor in isolation is a sufficient, nor for that matter necessary, predictor. As noted in this chapter, the predictive value of individual risk factors, sociodemographic characteristics, and behavioral patterns increases in the context of various psychosocial stressors in the home, school, and community.

Of additional importance is the changing nature and strength of risk factors during the course of a child's growth and development. As with many childhood disorders, risk factors associated with CD and ODD may change as a child spends more time with his or her peer group outside the home, strengthens physically, and develops cognitively and physiologically (e.g., puberty). Each change in an individual presents new opportunities for positive or negative change.

The complex nature of conduct problems greatly impacts both the assessment and treatment of this disorder. First, in developing an effective treatment, it is useful to develop causal models of the presenting symptom pattern. This is particularly important for conduct problems given the large number of possible causal pathways leading to the same diagnosis. Consequently, the identification of critical factors associated with conduct problems requires assessment strategies that can effectively yield such information. Unfortunately, given the nature of symptoms associated with conduct problems, a complete picture of a child also requires multiple informants. It is often the case that much antisocial behavior will occur outside of the home environment, either in the school or community setting, particularly by adolescence. Adding into this mix, the requirements of corporate medicine and managed care further complicate the modes of addressing already complicated behavioral patterns. Children with conduct problems often present with a complex system of risk and causal factors, many of which necessitate identification and some form of intervention to ameliorate a disorder (Brestan & Eyberg, 1998). This is difficult, at best, given current guidelines and standards of practice.

Finally, there exist many limitations in the empirical study of risk factors associated with conduct problems, which would hopefully help to inform the clinical approaches with youths evincing such symptomatology. Despite the increase in longitudinal studies comparing children with and without behavioral problems (e.g., Lahey et al., 1995), these efforts are often limited by particular sociodemographic factors such as gender, age, and ethnicity. It is important to note, however, that similar pathways from which risk factors interact in the development of conduct problems are found across cultures (e.g., Ruchkin, Koposov, Eisemann, & Hagglof, 2001). Further, the control or manipulation of clinical risk factors is often impractical or even unethical. For instance, the removal of a child from his or her home or school for purposes of prevention of onset of disorder may be unjustifiable, even if it serves to help us understand the onset and course of these disorders. Of course, under certain circumstances such removal might be quite justified and pose few if any ethical problems. Despite these limitations, recent theoretical and empirical work have furthered our understanding of specific risk factors associated with conduct problems as well as the intriguing patterns and interrelations that exist among these risk factors. Although much remains to be learned, good progress has been made.

REFERENCES

American Psychiatric Association. (1994). *The diagnostic and statistical manual of mental disorders* (4th ed.). Washington, DC: Author.

Asarnow, J., & Callan, J. (1985). Boys with peer adjustment problems: Social cognitive processes. *Journal of Consulting and Clinical Psychology, 53,* 80–87.

Barrera, M., Jr., Biglan, A., Ary, D., & Li, F. (2001). Replication of a problem behavior model with American Indian, Hispanic, and Caucasian youth. *Journal of Early Adolescence, 21,* 133–157.

Biederman, J., Mick, E., Faraone, S. V., & Burback, M. (2001). Patterns of remission and symptom decline in conduct disorder: A four-year prospective study of an ADHD sample. *Journal of the American Academy of Child and Adolescent Psychiatry, 40,* 290–298.

Brestan, E. V., & Eyberg, S. M. (1998). Effective psychosocial treatments of conduct-disordered children and adolescents: 29 years, 82 studies, and 5,272 kids. *Journal of Clinical Child Psychology, 27,* 180–189.

Caspi, A., Elder, G., & Herbener, E. (1990). Childhood personality and the prediction of life-course patterns. In L. Robbins & M. Rutter (Eds.), *Straight and devious pathways from childhood to adulthood* (pp. 13–35). New York: Cambridge University Press.

Caspi, A., Henry, B., McGee, R. O., Moffitt, T. E., & Silva, P. A. (1995). Temperamental origins of child and adolescent behavior problems: From age three to age fifteen. *Child Development, 66,* 55–58.

Christian, R. E., Frick, P. J., Hill, N. L., Tyler, L., & Frazer, D. R. (1997). Psychopathy and conduct problems in children: II. Implications for subtyping children with conduct problems. *Journal of the American Academy of Child and Adolescent Psychiatry, 36,* 233–241.

Crick, N. B., & Dodge, K. A. (1996). Social information-processing mechanisms in reactive and proactive aggression. *Child Development, 67,* 993–1002.

Dishion, T. J., Patterson, G. R., Stoolmiller, M., & Skinner, M. L. (1991). Family, school, and behavioral antecedents to early adolescent involvement with antisocial peers. *Developmental Psychology, 27,* 172–180.

Dodge, K. A. (1980). Social cognition and children's aggressive behavior. *Child Development, 51,* 162–170.

Dodge, K. A. (1993). Social cognitive mechanisms in the development of conduct disorder and depression. *Annual Review of Psychology, 44,* 559–584.

Dodge, K. A., & Frame, C. L. (1982). Social cognitive biases and deficits in aggressive boys. *Child Development, 53,* 620–635.

Farrington, D. P., Loeber, R., & Van Kammen, W. B. (1990). Long-term criminal outcomes of hyperactivity-impulsivity-attention deficit and conduct problems in childhood. In L. N. Robins & M. Rutter (Eds.), *Straight and devious pathways from childhood to adulthood* (pp. 62–81). New York: Cambridge University Press.

Fergusson, D. M., & Horwood, L. J. (1996). The role of adolescent peer affiliations in the continuity between childhood behavioral adjustment and juvenile offending. *Journal of Abnormal Child Psychology, 24,* 205–221.

Fergusson, D. M., Lynskey, M. T., & Horwood, L. J. (1996). Factors associated with continuity and change in disruptive behavior patterns between childhood and adolescence. *Journal of Abnormal Child Psychology, 24,* 533–553.

Frick, P. J. (1998a). Conduct disorders. In T. H. Ollendick & M. Hersen (Eds.), *Handbook of child psychopathology* (3rd ed., pp. 213–238). New York: Plenum.

Frick, P. J. (1998b). *Conduct disorders and severe antisocial behavior.* New York: Plenum.

Frick, P. J., O'Brien, B. S., Wootton, J. M., & McBurnett, K. (1994). Psychopathy and conduct problems in children. *Journal of Abnormal Psychology, 103,* 700–707.

Gittleman, R., Mannuzza, S., Shenker, R., & Bonagura, N. (1985). Hyperactive boys almost grown up. *Archives of General Psychiatry, 42,* 937–947.

Gray, J. A. (1970). The psychophysiological basis of introversion–extraversion. *Behavior Research and Therapy, 8,* 249–266.

Greene, R. W., & Doyle, A. E. (1999). Toward a transactional conceptualization of oppositional defiant disorder: Implications for assessment and treatment. *Clinical Child and Family Psychology Review, 2,* 129–148.

Hamalainen, M., & Pulkkinen, L. (1996). Problem behavior as a precursor of male criminality. *Development and Psychopathology, 8,* 443–455.

Hinshaw, S. P. (1992). Externalizing behavior problems and academic underachievement in childhood and adolescence: Causal relationships and underlying mechanisms. *Psychological Bulletin, 111,* 127–155.

Hinshaw, S. P., Lahey, B. B., & Hart, E. L. (1993). Issues of taxonomy and co-morbidity in the development of conduct disorder. *Development and Psychopathology, 5,* 31–50.

Holmes, S. E., Slaughter, J. R., & Kashani, J. (2001). Risk factors in childhood that lead to the development of conduct disorder and antisocial personality disorder. *Child Psychiatry and Human Development, 31,* 183–193.

Keenan, K., Loeber, R., & Green, S. (1999). Conduct disorder in girls: A review of the literature. *Clinical Child and Family Psychology Review, 2,* 3–19.

Keenan, K., Loeber, R., Zhang, Q., Stouthamer-Loeber, M., & Van Kammen, W. B. (1995). The influence of deviant peers on the development of boys' disruptive and delinquent behavior: A temporal analysis. *Development and Psychopathology, 7,* 715–726.

Keenan, K., & Shaw, D. (1997). Developmental and social influences on young girls' early problem behavior. *Psychological Bulletin, 121,* 95–113.

Lahey, B. B., Goodman, S. H., Waldman, I. D., Bird, H., Canino, G., Jensen, P., Regier, D., Leaf, P. J., Gordon, R., & Applegate, B. (1999). Relation of age of onset to the type and severity of child and adolescent conduct problems. *Journal of Abnormal Child Psychology, 27,* 247–260.

Lahey, B. B., Loeber, R., Hart, E. L., Frick, P. J., Applegate, B., Zhang, Q., Green, S. M., & Russo, M. F. (1995). Four-year longitudinal study of conduct disorder in boys: Patterns and predictors of persistence. *Journal of Abnormal Psychology, 104,* 83–93.

Lahey, B. B., Schwab-Stone, M., Goodman, S. H., Waldman, I. D., Canino, G., Rathouz, P. J., Miller, T. L., Dennis, K. D., Bird, H., & Jensen, P. S. (2000). Age and gender differences in oppositional behavior and conduct problems: A cross-sectional household study of middle childhood and adolescence. *Journal of Abnormal Psychology, 109,* 488–503.

Lahey, B. B., Waldman, I. D., & McBurnett, K. (1999). Annotation: The development of antisocial behavior: An integrative causal model. *Journal of Child Psychology and Psychiatry, 40*, 669–682.

Lease, C. A., & Ollendick, T. H. (2000). Development and psychopathology. In M. Hersen & A. S. Bellack (Eds.), *Psychopathology in adulthood* (2nd ed., pp. 131–149). Boston: Allyn & Bacon.

Lerner, R. M., Hess, L. E., & Nitz, K. (1990). A developmental perspective on psychopathology. In M. Hersen & C. G. Last (Eds.), *Handbook of child and adult psychopathology: A longitudinal perspective* (pp. 9–32). New York: Pergamon.

Lewin, L. M., Davis, B., & Hops, H. (1999). Childhood social predictors of adolescent antisocial behavior: Gender differences in predictive accuracy and efficacy. *Journal of Abnormal Child Psychology, 27*, 277–292.

Loeber, R. (1990). Development and risk factors of juvenile antisocial behavior and delinquency. *Clinical Psychology Review, 10*, 1–41.

Loeber, R. (1991). Antisocial behavior: More enduring than changeable? *Journal of the American Academy of Child and Adolescent Psychiatry, 30*, 393–397.

Loeber, R., Green, S. M., Keenan, K., & Lahey, B. B. (1995). Which boys will fare worse? Early predictors of the onset of conduct disorder in a six-year longitudinal study. *Journal of the American Academy of Child and adolescent Psychiatry, 34*, 499–509.

Loeber, R., Green, S. M., Lahey, B. B., Frick, P. J., & McBurnett, K. (2000). Findings on disruptive behavior disorders from the first decade of the Developmental Trends Study. *Clinical Child and Family Psychology Review, 3*, 37–60.

Mandel, H. P. (1997). *Conduct disorder and underachievement: Risk factors, assessment, treatment, and prevention.* New York: Wiley.

McBurnett, K., Lahey, B. B., Frick, P. J., Risch, C., Loeber, R., Hart, E. L., Christ, M., & Hanson, K. S. (1991). Anxiety, inhibition, and conduct disorder in children: II. Relation to salivary cortisol. *Journal of the American Academy of Child and Adolescent Psychiatry, 30*, 192–196.

McBurnett, K., Lahey, B. B., Rathouz, P. J., & Loeber, R. (2000). Low salivary cortisol and persistent aggression in boys referred for disruptive behavior. *Archives of General Psychiatry, 57*, 38–43.

Moffitt, T. E. (1993). Adolescence-limited and life-cycle persistent antisocial behavior: A developmental taxonomy. *Psychology Review, 100*, 674–701.

Moffitt, T. E., & Silva, P. A. (1988). Self-reported delinquency, neuropsychological deficit, and history of attention deficit disorder. *Journal of Abnormal Child Psychology, 16*, 553–569.

O'Brien, B. S., & Frick, P. J. (1996). Reward dominance: Associations with anxiety, conduct problems, and psychopathy in children. *Journal of Abnormal Child Psychology, 24*, 223–240.

O'Brien, B. S., Frick, P. J., & Lyman, R. D. (1994). Reward dominance among children with disruptive behavior disorders. *Journal of Psychopathology and Behavioral Assessment, 16*, 131–145.

Ollendick, D. G., & Ollendick, T. H. (1976). The inter-relationship of measures of locus of control, intelligence, and achievement in juvenile delinquents. *Educational and Psychological Measurement, 36*, 1111–1113.

Ollendick, T. H. (1979). Verbal-performance IQ discrepancies and subtest scatter on the WISC–R in juvenile delinquents. *Psychological Reports, 45*, 563–568.

Ollendick, T. H., Seligman, L. D., & Butcher, T. (1999). Does anxiety mitigate the behavioral expression of severe conduct disorder in delinquent youths? *Journal of Anxiety Disorders, 13*, 565–574.

Ollendick, T. H., Weist, M. D., Borden, M. C., & Greene, R. W. (1992). Sociometric status and academic, behavioral, and psychological adjustment: A five-year longitudinal study. *Journal of Consulting and Clinical Psychology, 60*, 80–87.

Olson, S. L., Bates, J. E., Sandy, J. M., & Lanthier, R. (2000). Early developmental precursors of externalizing behavior in middle childhood and adolescence. *Journal of Abnormal Child Psychology, 28*, 119–133.

Patterson, G. R., DeGarmo, D. S., & Knutson, N. (2000). Hyperactive and antisocial behaviors: Comorbid or two points in the same process? *Development and Psychopathology, 12*, 91–106.

Ruchkin, V. V., Koposov, R. A., Eisemann, M., & Hagglof, B. (2001). Conduct problems in Russian adolescents: The role of personality and parental rearing. *European Child and Adolescent Psychiatry, 10*, 19–27.

Rutter, M., & Casaer, P. (1991). *Biological risk factors for psychosocial disorders.* New York: Cambridge University Press.

Rutter, M., Giller, H., & Hagell, A. (1998). *Antisocial behavior in young people.* Cambridge, England: Cambridge University Press.

Schulz, K. P., Halperin, J. M., Newcorn, J. H., Sharma, V., & Gabriel, S. (1997). Plasma cortisol and aggression in boys with ADHD. *Journal of the American Academy of Child and Adolescent Psychiatry, 36*, 605–610.

Serbin, L. A., Peters, P. L., McAffer, V. J., & Schwartzman, A. E. (1991). Childhood aggression and withdrawal as predictors of adolescent pregnancy, early parenthood, and environmental risk for the next generation. *Canadian Journal of Behavioural Science, 23*, 318–331.

Short, R. J., & Simeonsson, R. J. (1986). Social cognition and aggression in delinquent adolescent males. *Adolescence, 21*, 159–176.

Siegel, A. W., & Scovill, L. C. (2000). Problem behavior: The double symptom of adolescence. *Development and Psychopathology, 12*, 763–793.

Smart, D., Sanson, A., & Prior, M. (1996). Connections between reading disability and behavior problems: Testing temporal and causal hypotheses. *Journal of Abnormal Child Psychology, 24*, 363–383.

Steiner, H., Dunne, J. E., Ayres, W., Arnold, V., Benedek, E., Benson, R. S., Bernstein, G. A., Bernet, W., Bukstein, O., Kinlan, J., Leonard, H., & McClellan, J. (1997). Practice parameters for the assessment and treatment of children and adolescents with conduct disorder. *Journal of the American Academy of Child and Adolescent Psychiatry, 36*, 122–140.

Toth, S. L., & Cicchetti, D. (1999). Developmental psychopathology and child psychotherapy. In S. W. Russ & T. H. Ollendick (Eds.), *Handbook of psychotherapies with children and families* (pp. 15–44). New York: Kluwer Academic/Plenum.

Tremblay, R. E., Pihl, R. O., Vitaro, F., & Dobkin, P. L. (1994). Predicting early onset of male antisocial behavior from preschool behavior. *Archives of General Psychiatry, 51*, 732–739.

Vitaro, F., Gendreau, P. L., Tremblay, R. E., & Oligny, P. (1998). Reactive and proactive aggression differentially predict later conduct problems. *Journal of Child Psychology and Psychiatry, 39*, 377–385.

Vitiello, B., & Stoff, D. M. (1997). Subtypes of aggression and their relevance to child psychiatry. *Journal of the American Academy of Child and Adolescent Psychiatry, 36*, 307–315.

Wootton, J. M., Frick, P. J., Shelton, K. K., & Silverthorn, P. (1997). Ineffective parenting and childhood conduct problems: The moderating role of callous-unemotional traits. *Journal of Consulting and Clinical Psychology, 65*, 301–308.

5

The Social Ecology of Community and Neighborhood and Risk for Antisocial Behavior

Deborah Gorman-Smith
University of Illinois at Chicago

That youth delinquency and antisocial behavior relate to community characteristics such as poverty level, ethnic heterogeneity, and residential mobility, particularly in urban communities, was one of the earliest empirical findings supporting an ecological perspective on the development of delinquency and violence (Shaw & McKay, 1942). Recently, there has been resurgent interest in community effects on youth development, expanding this perspective to show that community economic and social conditions affect not only involvement in delinquent and criminal behavior but also other aspects of child development (Brooks-Gunn, Duncan, Klebenov, & Sealand, 1993; Bursik, 1988; Chase-Lansdale, Gordon, Brooks-Gunn, & Klebanov, 1997; Coulton, Korbin, Su, & Chow, 1995; Ensminger, Lamkin, & Jacobson, 1996; Sampson, 1997; Sampson & Groves, 1989). Much of the recent research has been spurred by the work of William Julius Wilson. In *The Truly Disadvantaged: The Inner City, the Underclass, and Public Policy*, Wilson (1987) argued that the deindustrialization of the U.S. economy, the shift of jobs from cities to suburbs, and the flight of the minority middle class from the inner cities led to increasingly concentrated poverty in urban areas. The number of neighborhoods with poverty rates that exceed 40%, a threshold definition of extreme poverty or underclass neighborhoods, rose precipitously. Wilson argued that as a result, people living in neighborhoods of concentrated poverty had become isolated from job networks, mainstream institutions, and role models and that this isolation was related to a number of problems including school dropout and the proliferation of single-parent families. With this increased focus on the characteristics of inner-city life came interest in understanding what this context meant for children's development (see for example Brooks-Gunn, Duncan, & Aber, 1997; Duncan & Brooks-Gunn, 1997).

Much of the work on community effects on child development has been guided by a developmental-ecological model (Bronfenbrenner, 1979, 1988). A central tenet of developmental-ecological theory is that individual development is influenced by the ongoing qualities of the social settings in which the child lives or participates and the extent and nature of the interaction between these settings (Bronfenbrenner, 1979, 1988; Szapocznik & Coatsworth, 1999; Tolan, Guerra, & Kendall, 1995). Child development is influenced by family functioning, peer relationships, schools, communities, and larger societal influences (e.g., media). There are direct influences of each of these characteristics as well as interactions among them that relate to risk and development. Thus, an important aspect of developmental-ecological theory is the presumption that the impact of major developmental influences such as family functioning depends on the sociological characteristics of the communities in which youth and families reside (Szapocznik & Coatsworth, 1999; Tolan & Gorman-Smith, 1997). How families function or how they parent might differ depending on the neighborhood in which they live, and the same level of family functioning may have different effects on risk depending on neighborhood residence (Gorman-Smith, Tolan, & Henry, 2000; Furstenberg, 1993; Sampson, 1997). In addition to context, a developmental-ecological model incorporates the capacity for change over time. That is, the same factor may have a different impact depending on the age of the child. Thus, it is important to evaluate the impact of multiple risk factors over time.

The purpose of this chapter is to review the literature on community and neighborhood impact on problem behavior. Much of this work has focused more specifically on delinquency and crime. The most influential work has focused on identifying aspects of community characteristics related to increased delinquency or crime occurring within a specific neighborhood or community (Sampson, 2001; Sampson & Raudenbush, 1999; Sampson, Raudenbush, & Earls, 1997). That is, what aspects of community and neighborhood relate to crime occurring within that neighborhood? Although this work is extremely important and is obviously critical to aid intervention and guide policy around crime prevention, those studies are not the focus of this chapter. Rather, the focus of this chapter is on how community context relates to individual development and specifically involvement in delinquent and antisocial behavior. That is, how does where one lives relate both directly and indirectly (through other types of risk and protective factors, e.g., family, peers) to child behavior? In addition, this chapter focuses primarily on youth and families living in economically disadvantaged neighborhoods within inner-city and urban poor communities. This is done both because the majority of the research in this area has focused on this population and because it has become clear that children in these environments are at increased risk for most social and psychological problems (Children's Defense Fund, 1991). Although seeming obvious, the emerging data suggests that poor urban neighborhoods provide a qualitatively different kind of environment in which to grow up, and community characteristics may have their most pronounced effects in the worst neighborhoods.

URBAN NEIGHBORHOODS

As stated previously, urban neighborhoods have undergone a dramatic transformation in the last 30 years. There has been a steady increase in the number of families and young children living in areas of concentrated poverty. Teenage pregnancies, out-of-wedlock childbirths, and female-headed households have all escalated. It is of importance that residents of inner-city neighborhoods are disproportionately members of minority groups (Jargowsky & Bane, 1991; Massey & Eggers, 1990). In 1990, there were 11.2 million people living in inner-city, underclass neighborhoods. More than 50% of the population were African American, 33% were Hispanic, and only 12% were White, despite the fact that Whites comprised 75% of the U.S. population. Thus, minorities disproportionately experience the effects of concentrated poverty and other forms of social disadvantage.

Although data suggests there are risks associated with living in inner-city neighborhoods, there are also differences in level of risk associated within different types of urban poor neighborhoods. The distinctions between ghetto inner-city neighborhoods and otherwise poor urban communities have been clearly described (Crane, 1991; Wilson, 1987). Inner-city neighborhoods are characterized by high concentrations of families living in poverty, higher crime rates, less owner-occupied housing, and more public housing. They also have a higher proportion of single-headed households. Urban poor neighborhoods are distinguished from inner-city neighborhoods by a population with more range of income and greater access to resources. Although less destitute overall than the inner-city communities, the urban poor neighborhoods also have elevated rates of poverty, single-headed households, and face significant economic and social impediments. Although both types of neighborhoods may carry some risk, it is likely that residence in inner-city neighborhoods may have more pronounced effects on children and families (Garbarino, Dubrow, Kostelny, & Pardo, 1992; Garbarino & Sherman, 1980; Wilson, 1987), and it is likely that risk occurs for children living in inner-city neighborhoods irrespective of other risk factors (Brooks-Gunn et al., 1993; Crane, 1991). For example, Tolan et al. (2001), using Wilson's (1987) criteria for the inner city of 40% or more households below poverty level, found that rates for all types of psychopathology among children living in inner-city neighborhoods were elevated above national rates but were not elevated in other urban poor neighborhoods. For example, aggression and delinquency rates were 2.5 and 2.8 times greater, respectively, than the national rate in the inner-city communities. Similarly, Crane (1991) reported a sharp increase in risk of school dropout and teen pregnancy for adolescents living in inner-city neighborhoods. These findings suggest a particularly risky developmental trajectory attributable to inner-city residence, that community characteristics can have a nonlinear effect, and there may be pronounced differences among economically disadvantaged urban neighborhoods.

COMMUNITIES AND RISK FOR BEHAVIOR PROBLEMS

A recent review of neighborhood effects on child and adolescent outcomes suggests that community characteristics are related to behavior problems among children across levels of development (Leventhal & Brooks-Gunn, 2000). The strongest effects appear to be for the adverse effect of low socioeconomic status (SES) neighbors on children's externalizing problems. For example, using data from the Infant Health and Development Project, a nationally based study, Brooks-Gunn et al. (1993) found that among 3-year-olds a low number of managerial and professional workers in the neighborhood was associated with higher amounts of reported problem behaviors. Among children ages 5 to 6, the presence of low-income neighbors (as compared with middle-income neighbors) was associated with increased amounts of externalizing behavior problems (Chase-Lansdale et al., 1997).

Kupersmidt, Griesler, De Rosier, Patterson, and Davis et al. (1995) examined peer-reported aggression and peer rejection in a sample of second through fifth graders. Their findings suggested that African American children in middle-SES neighborhoods displayed less peer-reported aggression than did their peers in low-SES neighborhoods. In this same study, for low-SES Euro-American children from single-parent families, living in a middle-SES neighborhood was associated with greater peer rejection compared with their peers in low-SES neighborhoods.

Using data from the Pittsburgh Youth Study, Loeber and colleagues (Loeber & Wikstrom, 1993; Peeples & Loeber, 1994) found that, among 13- and 16-year-old boys, living in low-SES or underclass neighborhoods was associated with increased delinquent and criminal behavior and was also associated with severity and frequency of delinquency. The effect of neighborhood residence on young adolescents' problem behavior was stronger than that found among older adolescents (Loeber & Wikstrom, 1993).

Data from two experimental studies suggest that neighborhood socioeconomic status is associated with adolescents externalizing behavior problems. The first set of data came from an evaluation of the Yonkers Project, a quasi-experimental study in which some families residing in inner-city public housing projects were moved to low-rise housing projects in mostly Euro-American, middle-income neighborhoods. A comparison group was composed of people who signed up for the program but were not selected. The evaluation found that adolescents who remained in low-income neighborhoods were more likely to have had problems with alcohol and drugs than those who moved to the better neighborhoods (Briggs, 1997). The second set of data came from the Moving to Opportunity project. This project was funded by the U.S. Department of Housing and Urban Development. Families living in housing projects in five of the nations largest cities were randomly assigned to one of three conditions: (a) an experimental or treatment group that received Section 8 housing vouchers and special assistance to move with the requirement that the move be to a low-poverty neighborhood; (b) a control group that received Section 8 housing vouchers but no special assistance and no stipulation as to where to move; or (c) a second control group that did not receive vouchers or special assistance and remained in public housing. Initial findings suggest that boys who moved to low-poverty neighborhoods were less likely to be arrested for violent crimes (assaults, robbery, rape, and other sex crimes) than were their peers who remained in public housing or their peers who moved out of public housing but moved to predominately low- to middle-income neighborhoods (Ludwig, Duncan, & Hirschfield, 1998). Among youth who moved to low- to middle-income neighborhoods, crime rates for nonviolent and non-property crimes were significantly lower than the rates for youth who remained in public housing in poor neighborhoods.

Although all of these studies suggest that neighborhood residence is related to externalizing problem behaviors, including involvement in delinquency and crime, these data provide no understanding of the process through which neighborhood characteristics might be related. Notably, the shared perspective across many of the initial studies was to evaluate community effects from an ecological perspective, considering how variation in community characteristics corresponds to variation in outcome. However, in most cases indicators of community influences were applied without much theoretical explanation of the expected relation among the indicators or their overall relation to outcome. Community-level influences have often been simply considered markers of risk, losing understanding of the process through which these characteristics effect family functioning and child development.

PROCESS OF COMMUNITY EFFECTS
ON DEVELOPMENT

More recent work has suggested that it is not just community structural characteristics (such as poverty, economic investment, heterogeneity, crime rates) that are important to understanding risk but also the social processes or organization within the neighborhood (Sampson et al., 1997; Tolan, Gorman-Smith, & Henry, in press; Wilson, 1987). The social organization of the neighborhood is reflected in processes such as felt social support and cohesion among neighbors, sense of belonging to the community, supervision and control of children and adolescents by other adults in the community, and participation in formal and voluntary organizations. The theory is that within some communities, the structural barriers of the community can impede the development of neighborhood social organization. In turn, lack of neighborhood social organization relates to increased risk among youth (Elliott et al., 1996; Sampson et al., 1997).

This work suggests that communities' influence should be considered as occurring at two levels: the structure of the community (e.g., mobility, political economy, heterogeneity) and the social organization of the neighborhood or network of relations and organization. Theoretically, neighborhood social organization represents a more proximal level of influence of a smaller geographical unit nested within the larger context of community level influences. Perhaps the most influential study among the current literature is the report of Sampson et al. (1997) that applied an elegant multilevel sampling procedure to evaluate these relations. They found that the relation of community structural characteristics to crime was mediated by neighborhood social processes; Sampson et al. (1997) labeled these processes "collective efficacy." *Collective efficacy* refers to the extent of social connection within the neighborhood combined with the degree of informal social control (extent to which residents monitor the behavior of others with the goal of supervising and monitoring children and maintaining public order). Thus, this community-level comparison suggested that characteristics of neighborhood social processes are important in understanding how communities relate to delinquent behavior and should be included in risk studies. However, the Sampson et al. (1997) study did not focus on whether collective efficacy relates to individual involvement in delinquent or criminal behavior (Leventhal & Brooks-Gunn, 2000).

Expanding on the work of Sampson et al. (1997), Gorman-Smith, Tolan, and Henry (1998) tested a model of the relation of the structural characteristics of the community to aspects of neighborhood social organization and their impact on risk for delinquent behavior within urban poor communities. Using data from the Chicago Youth Development Study (CYDS), a longitudinal study of the development of serious delinquent behavior among minority adolescent males living in the inner city and other urban poor communities, Gorman-Smith et al. (1998) evaluated the relation of community structural characteristics and neighborhood social organization to different aspects of individual's delinquent involvement. In those analyses, the structural characteristics of the community related to neighborhood social organization, which in turn related to delinquency level of youth. These results suggest that risk-related neighborhood social processes are affected by structural characteristics of the community. These analyses also suggest some differential relations between aspects of neighborhood social processes and different parameters of delinquent careers. For example, neighborhood social organization had a direct effect on onset of delinquent behavior, as well as an effect through concerns about safety. There was not a direct effect of neighborhood social organization on the final level of involvement in delinquent behavior, although there was an effect through concerns about safety. Thus, in regard to individual behavior these analyses suggested that both community structural characteristics and neighborhood social organization are important, and different aspects of community-level risk might relate to different parameters of delinquent involvement.

Community and Neighborhood Influences on Family

There is emerging evidence that these structural characteristics and the social organization of the neighborhood have an influence on family functioning and its relation to risk (Brooks-Gunn et al., 1997; Gorman-Smith, Tolan, & Henry, 1999; Sampson, 1997). Studies suggest that across communities that are similar in regard to structural dimensions such as poverty and single parenthood, there are significant differences in neighborhood social organization and networks that relate to differences in the ways families function and how parents manage their children (Furstenberg, 1993; Garbarino & Sherman, 1980; Sampson & Laub, 1994; Sullivan, 1989). For example, in a study of parenting among single mothers in poor urban neighborhoods, Furstenberg (1993) found that those residing in the most dangerous neighborhood adapted to this environment by isolating themselves and their families from those around them. Although this served to increase the mother's sense of safety, it also cut her off from potential social supports. Similarly, Jarrett (1997) found that parents in poor neighborhoods often use "bounding" techniques that restrict children to their homes and limit access to neighborhood influences, particularly peers. In the Yonkers Project, parents who moved to middle-income neighborhoods used less restrictive monitoring practices with adolescents than did parents who stayed in low-income neighborhoods (Briggs, 1997). Other research has pointed to the importance of "precision parenting" in poor urban neighborhoods (Gonzales, Cauce, Friedman & Mason, 1996; Mason, Cauce, Gonzales, & Hiraga, 1996).

That is, in some urban neighborhoods, the relation between parental monitoring and involvement is such that both too little and too much is associated with increased behavior problems among youth. This curvilinear relation is not found in studies of families residing in other types of neighborhoods. This relation, dependent on neighborhood type, may reflect a variation by neighborhood in the configuration of family relationship and parenting characteristics relating to delinquency risk.

Gorman-Smith et al. (2000) conducted a set of analyses to evaluate the interaction between community type and family functioning and the relation to types of delinquent involvement. Using data from four waves of the CYDS, they conducted a series of cluster analyses to identify types of urban communities, patterns of delinquent offending, and patterns of family functioning over time. They then evaluated interactions between family and community type and the relation to delinquency pattern.

Community Types. Measures of the structural dimensions of community (i.e., concentrated poverty, ethnic heterogeneity, business investment, and violent crime based on census and archival reports) and neighborhood social organization and concerns for safety (both mother and child report) were included in cluster analyses (Gorman-Smith et al., 2000) to identify different configurations of these variables to identify community types. They derived three types of neighborhoods defined by the cluster patterns. Two groups were characterized by high structural problems (e.g., high levels of poverty and violent crime, low business investment) but were differentiated by levels of neighborhood social organization. The third neighborhood type was differentiated by lower structural problems (e.g., lower levels of poverty and crime and higher levels of business investment). This neighborhood type also evidenced low levels of neighborhood social organization with low concerns about safety. Thus, the three neighborhood types found were

1. Inner-city communities without functioning social processes; those with high rates of crime, high concentrations of poverty, low business investment, high concerns about safety, and low neighborhood social organization (22%).

2. Inner-city neighborhoods with functioning social processes; those that had similar levels of structural problems as the first cluster but low concerns about safety and high levels of neighborhood social organization (39%).

3. Other urban poor; those with lower crime rates, lower concentrations of poverty, higher business investment, low concerns about safety, and low neighborhood social organization (38%).

Patterns of Delinquent Involvement. Data from four waves of mother and son report of delinquent and violent offending were also included in a Gorman-Smith et al. (2000) cluster analysis. Four nonoverlapping groups emerged: 26% of the sample were classified as nonoffenders (those with some aggression and fighting, but no delinquent behaviors); 34% were classified as chronic minor offenders (those consistently involved in minor offenses only over each of the four waves); 12% were classified as escalators (those starting delinquent involvement at a later wave (ages 13 to 15) and quickly (within a year) escalating to more seriousness and violent offending); and 28% were classified as serious chronic offenders (those involved in serious and violent offending at every wave). These patterns were consistent with pathways reported by others (Loeber, Stouthamer-Loeber, Van Kammen, & Farrington, 1991).

Patterns of Family Functioning. Measures of parenting practices and family relationship characteristics gathered over 4 years of early adolescence were also used to empirically identify patterns of family functioning over time (Gorman-Smith et al., 2000). Four types of family functioning were identified. Exceptionally functioning families (27%) were those with high levels of parenting practices and structure over time and were also emotionally enriching, as evidenced by high levels of cohesion with strong beliefs about the importance of family. The second group was task-oriented families (25%), or those with high levels of parenting practices and structure but low levels of emotional warmth and low beliefs about the family. The third group was struggling families (20%), those with consistently low discipline, monitoring, structure, cohesion, and beliefs about the family over time. The fourth group was moderately functioning families (27%) and included those with adequate but not high levels of discipline and monitoring over time. This group also showed a slight improvement in cohesion and beliefs over time. All four groups were fairly equally distributed across the three types of neighborhoods.

Relation of Family and Neighborhood to Risk. To evaluate the relation between family, neighborhood, and delinquency, Gorman-Smith et al. (2000) performed a logistic regression predicting the odds of involvement in each of the three delinquent pathways from the four family patterns and the three neighborhood clusters. These analyses suggested that youth from the struggling families were at increased risk for each type of delinquent offending. Youth from the exceptionally functioning families were less likely to be involved in each pattern of delinquent offending. Of interest was the fact that those from task-oriented families were more likely to be involved in the serious chronic pattern of offending.

With regard to neighborhood effects, youth living in the most plagued neighborhoods (inner city without functioning social processes) were more likely to show all three patterns of offending—chronic minor, escalating, and serious chronic offending—than youth living in "other" urban poor neighborhoods (Gorman-Smith et al., 2000).

Also, and of most interest, several community–family interactions were significant in Gorman-Smith et al. (2000). Across each of the three neighborhoods, youth from exceptionally functioning families were significantly less likely to be involved in each of the three delinquency patterns. This difference was greatest in the other urban poor communities, that is, those with more structural resources. There was a trend for youth from exceptionally functioning families to have a greater probability of chronic minor offending in inner-city neighborhoods. These data suggest that although exceptionally functioning families continue to have a protective effect for youth across neighborhoods, the extent to which they might protect children from all risk may be blunted by the impact of neighborhood characteristics, particularly poverty and crime.

Those youth with task-oriented families were more likely to be involved in serious chronic offending in each of the two neighborhood types that had low neighborhood social organization (Gorman-Smith et al., 2000). However, the association between task-oriented families and the serious chronic pattern was not found for the neighborhoods with high levels of neighborhood social organization. These neighborhood differences were not found for either of the other two delinquency groups (chronic minor or escalating offenders). These data suggest that for families in which emotional needs are not emphasized, neighborhoods with high social organization may provide protection for youth from susceptibility to serious and violent offending.

The effect of struggling families was also limited to the two neighborhoods with low levels of neighborhood social organization in Gorman-Smith et al. (2000). In such neighborhoods, children from families struggling with basic family functions showed elevated risk for the escalating pattern of offending. They were also less likely to be nondelinquent. In the inner-city neighborhoods that evidenced functioning social processes, there was no elevated risk for youth from families with this configuration of characteristics for any of the delinquency patterns. Again, these results suggest that neighborhoods with functioning social processes may provide some protection for youth, even for those coming from families with less than adequate functioning.

The results of Gorman-Smith et al. (2000) suggest that different configurations of family characteristics relate to different patterns of delinquency. The protective role of families that emphasize emotional cohesion and strong family orientation, as well as consistent parenting and clear family roles and responsibilities, can be found in all neighborhoods. Regardless of neighborhood, children from these families were less likely to show any pattern of delinquency and were most protected from serious delinquency. However, the effects varied in magnitude by neighborhood; they were greatest in neighborhoods with greater social organization.

The importance of including this broad set of family relationship characteristics was illustrated in Gorman-Smith et al. (2000) by the elevated risk of task-oriented families. These families had relatively high levels of discipline consistency, parental monitoring, and structure in family roles but low levels of cohesion and beliefs about family importance. Children from these families were the most at risk for serious and chronic (including violent) delinquency. These findings are consistent with previous work suggesting that the lack of an emotional base is related to increased risk for violence (Gorman-Smith, Tolan, Zelli, & Huesmann, 1996). In these stressful neighborhoods, the lack of family emotional closeness and dependability may affect risk substantially. Good parenting may not be enough (Gorman-Smith, Tolan, Loeber, & Henry, 1998; Mason et al., 1996).

However, the relations also depended on neighborhood context. The task-oriented families had no greater probability of serious and chronic delinquency in neighborhoods with functioning processes. It may be that if emotional needs such as a sense of belonging and support are met by the neighborhood, the risk carried by the family is minimized. This may indicate an important consideration for prevention or intervention work with such families; it may be as useful to help them connect to neighborhood support as it is to try to improve family functioning (Gorman-Smith et al., 1996; Sampson, 1997).

Peer Influences, Risk, Neighborhood, and Community

Although there has been some attention given to the interaction of family functioning and community type, there has been very little focus on peer effects despite the widespread evidence that peer groups play an important role in the development of delinquency and violence (Elliott, Huizinga, & Ageton, 1985; Thornberry, Krohn, Lizotte, & Chard-Wierschen, 1993). It appears that deviant peer influence is an important direct influence on risk independent of prior individual tendency. Studies have repeatedly found that involvement with deviant peers is the most proximal influence on delinquency onset and may be the best explanation of escalation to violence (Dishion, Andrews, & Crosby, 1995; Hawkins, Catalano, & Miller, 1992; Henry, Tolan, & Gorman-Smith, 2001). Some studies suggest peer deviancy is the final and full mediator of other less proximal and prior developmental influences on youth delinquency and violence (e.g., Elliott et al., 1985). Others conclude that other factors remain a direct and substantial influence even as peer factors emerge as figural during adolescence (e.g., Dishion, Spracklen, Andrews, & Patterson, 1996; Henry et al., 2001).

That community characteristics and neighborhood social processes relate to peer influence is, in fact, a central tenet of social disorganization theory (Leventhal & Brooks-Gunn, 2000; Sampson, 1997). Studies applying this theory have suggested that there is less informal and formal social control of youth groups in poor urban neighborhoods that relate to increased influence of delinquent peer groups (Elliott et al., 1996; Sampson & Groves, 1989). Other studies have provided evidence that friends of antisocial boys tended to live in the same neighborhood and activities of youth in those neighborhoods were less structured and supervised (Dishion, Andrews, et al., 1995). In the Yonkers study, youth who moved to middle-income neighborhoods and youth with high levels of problem behavior maintained strong ties with peers in the prior, low income neighborhoods even after moving to middle-income neighborhoods (Briggs, 1997).

Youth gangs have long been a peer social group thought to promote deviant behavior, including tendency toward violence (Loeber & Farrington, 1998). Thornberry and colleagues (Thornberry et al., 1993) have shown that youth involvement in violent behavior is dependent on involvement in gangs; youth violence involvement increased markedly with the onset of gang involvement and dropped off if involvement was stopped. This work suggests that gang involvement may play a precipitating role in youth violence, possibly through increasing involvement with violent peers or the support for violence by deviant peers.

Some studies have related peer influences to parenting practices. For example, Dishion and colleagues (Dishion, Capaldi, Spracklin, & Li, 1995) showed that coercive parenting and poor monitoring related to more involvement with deviant peers and greater susceptibility to their influence; parenting practices set the stage for deviant peers' influence. Specific to youth in high-risk urban communities, Zimmerman, Steinman, and Rowe (1998) found that family emotional cohesion buffered the effects of deviant peers on youth delinquency. Henry et al. (2001) found peer violence to partially mediate the relation between types of family organization and parenting practices and individual delinquency and violence of adolescent males in inner-city communities. Family influences remained important into adolescence. Also, the evidence suggested it was peer violence specifically, not general deviance, that related to violence risk. These results are consistent with those reported by Dishion et al. (1996) for another urban sample.

In an attempt to begin to evaluate the relation of family, peer, and community factors to delinquency risk, we again used data from the CYDS. For this set of analyses Tolan et al. (in press) six waves were used to evaluate the impact of all three levels of system (i.e., community, family, and peer) on risk for delinquent and violent behavior.

The results were generally consistent with those found in other analyses (Tolan et al., in press). In general, adolescents and their caretakers residing in inner-city communities were more likely than those in other urban poor communities to perceive higher levels of problems and lower levels of social organization: Bivariate relations and full measurement model analyses suggested that in the poorest and most crime ridden communities there is less felt support among neighbors, lower sense of belonging to the neighborhood, and lower involvement in the community. These results are consistent with those reported by Sampson et al. (1997).

The results also suggest that the impact of community structural characteristics on violence through parenting was due to the mediating impact of both social organization and level of perceived problems. In regard to parenting, once the perceived extent of problems was considered there remained a direct and positive relation between structural characteristics and parenting practices. It appears that in more impoverished and distressed communities parents are more vigilant about parenting, as they probably feel more of a need to act to protect and direct their child away from risky community characteristics (Mason et al., 1996). This interpretation is reinforced by findings that parenting skills did not seem to relate to residence in the inner city versus other poor urban communities (Gorman-Smith et al., 1999) and findings that protective neighborhood social processes in inner-city communities adds to the protection parenting practices might provide (Gorman-Smith et al., 2000). Thus, these results suggest that neighborhood problems and deleterious community structural characteristics do not add to the harm of poor parenting. Rather, the challenges of such a community may demand stronger parenting, but in the inner-city parenting may provide limited protective benefits (Tolan & Gorman-Smith, 1997). If this interpretation is correct, an important approach to reducing youth risk in such neighborhoods may be to build on the environmentally induced requirement of greater parental vigilance to form strong networks for neighborhood monitoring and protection of youth (Jarrett, 1997; Spencer, 2001).

This interpretation is bolstered by the finding that, as expected, parenting practices related negatively to negative peer influences, but this was limited to gang membership. If gang membership was not included then parenting practices would relate to peer violence. It appears that gang involvement is the avenue through which, in these poor urban communities, parenting practices influence tendency towards violence. Perhaps, as has been suggested by others, poor parenting leads to greater interest in and susceptibility to antisocial peer groups such as gangs, which then leads to greater risk for antisocial behaviors such as violence (Dishion et al., 1996). Consistent with the findings of Thornberry et al. (1993), it appears that involvement in youth violence is highly related to gang involvement and not just overall level but increasing involvement over late adolescence. As has been suggested elsewhere, in these poor urban communities gangs are ominous and often ubiquitous social organizations regarding adolescent male social lives, challenging parents' and other adults' authority and efforts to protect their children. They may tip the social ecology of development from one of risk to one of likely poor outcomes (Crane, 1991: Henry et al., 2001). This view is also supported by the relation of involvement to violence and its growth, with these both relating to violence and growth in individuals' violence. The gangs may set a stage for deviancy training that is quite serious and apart from other microsystem influences once engaged. These results suggest that any prevention efforts aimed at adolescents in the inner city may need to work directly on lessening likelihood of recruitment into gangs, perhaps through bolstering parenting skills and informal social processes within neighborhoods that will support strong parenting.

Social Organization Across Communities

These and other analyses suggest that the social organization of communities plays an important role, both directly and through the impact on parenting, on child risk and development. There appears to be wide variation in the extent of social organization within neighborhoods, even within poor urban communities. Even across communities that are similar in regard to structural characteristics of the community (i.e., similar levels of poverty, single-parent households, mobility, crime) differences in levels of social organization are found. What accounts for these differences? What can be done to promote social organization within different types of communities?

Although the answers are likely complex, one piece of the puzzle may be the physical environment of the community. Although the physical deterioration of urban communities has been noted as potentially related to the social organization of the neighborhood and risk for problem behaviors among youth (Sampson, 1997; Wilson, 1987), little empirical work has been conducted to identify what specific aspects of the architectural structure and urban design features might be related to neighborhood social organization and risk. Research in environmental psychology has documented that gross aspects of neighborhood disorder such as graffiti, litter, abandoned buildings, and dilapidated buildings create environments in which people are fearful (Fisher & Nasar, 1992; Nasar & Fisher, 1993; Taylor, Shumaker, & Gottfredson, 1985). In addition to abandoned and neglected areas, this research suggests that certain physical structures such as multifamily units with little foliage induce greater fear than single family housing (Hanyu, 1995). Because people tend to avoid areas that induce fear, there are fewer people to monitor the activities in the common areas of those streets or neighborhoods (Nasar & Fisher, 1993). Crime statistics show a clear relation between physical spaces which are dilapidated or neglected and increased risk for crime activity (Newman, 1972; Taylor, 1989). These findings have been based on relatively gross indicators of the built environment that could be easily identified by social scientists. There are, however, likely other aspects of the built environment that have been identified by practitioners in architecture and town planning that may have important implications for the social organization of the neighborhood or may have a direct relation to risk. However, adequate documentation of the most pertinent features and empirical evaluation of their impact has not yet occurred. Furthermore, those studies that have posited relations between risk or fear and specific aspects of environment have tended to focus on the relation of only one aspect of the physical environment. An area of architecture and urban design that may be able to provide some direction is "new urbanism" (Plater-Zyberk, 1995).

New urbanism is based on the ideals of community design of the early 1900s when residences were typically located closer to each other, providing greater opportunities for support and involvement. A major tenet of the theory guiding new urbanism is that smaller neighborhoods promote a greater connection to others and increased opportunity to interact with other community members. Neighborhoods that are diverse in population and use are hypothesized to enhance neighborhood social processes. Following from this hypothesis, it is suggested that civic, business, residential, and recreational buildings and space should be built in close proximity. One benefit of this approach to planning is that increased shared monitoring and support is likely because residents know one another. Having businesses and residences close to one another creates less dependence on cars so residents can walk within the neighborhood and become familiar with their neighbors, resulting in increased interest in monitoring neighborhood activities. In addition, the construction of town squares and other public gathering places create additional spaces where residents can socialize and provides informal opportunities for social support.

Although no empirical data is yet available, a large study is currently underway and is designed to evaluate the relation of characteristics of the built environment to neighborhood social organization, family functioning, and adolescent problem behavior (specifically delinquency and substance use). Guided by an interdisciplinary team of architects and urban planners, clinical community psychologists, and developmental epidemiologists, data regarding the architectural and physical characteristics (built environment) of East Little Havana in Miami will be gathered and merged with existing archival data regarding adolescent drug use and crime, along with self-report measures of family functioning and adolescent behavior (Szapocznik, Gorman-Smith, Plater-Zyberk, Lombard, Martinez & Mason,

1999). It is hoped that the findings from this investigation may provide some data regarding the extent to which variations in social organization seen between similarly poor urban neighborhoods might be related to the built environment of the community. Although this is not likely to provide the full explanation, this information may be useful in informing urban planning zoning and redevelopment policies with specific attention to reducing risk for children and families living in inner-city neighborhoods.

CONCLUSIONS

The literature reviewed here provides strong support for the perspective that multiple social-ecological factors relate to individual development, and in particular individual antisocial and delinquent behavior (Leventhal & Brooks-Gunn, 2000). These studies suggest that developmental trajectories and the role of risk factors vary across community types. Where one lives matters as it relates to both individual development and other influences on risk (e.g., family and peer). A focus on only one level, although valid, may limit full understanding of the influences on risk. When multiple levels are considered, effects are often independent, sometimes are not direct, and frequently have complex relations to outcomes. Understanding risk, even in high-risk communities, will necessitate consideration of how community and neighborhood characteristics constrain or facilitate aspects of parenting and peer relations related to risk and conversely how these more proximal influences might mitigate community and neighborhood risk and protective factors (Pettit, Bates, & Dodge, 1997).

This body of research also has implications for intervention and prevention. The accumulated findings suggest that for youth living in urban environments, interventions that focus on family factors without consideration of this important aspect of community context may have limited impact on outcome. The task faced by families living in inner-city communities are likely quite different than those faced by families living in other types of communities. Traditional interventions that focus on parenting practices such as discipline and monitoring may not be as effective with families living in the inner city as has been found with families living in other settings. It is not that these characteristics of families are not important. Rather, the task for families living in the inner city may be to maintain these characteristics in the face of stressors associated with living in an urban environment. The basic work for intervention and prevention efforts may be to help families learn to manage and cope with these stressors (Tolan & Gorman-Smith, 1997). In addition, a focus only on increasing family functioning is not likely to be enough to mitigate risk, as risk in these communities is not necessarily related to family functioning. Rather, programs and policies aimed at reducing the amount of stress experienced and building social support and communication among families living in the neighborhood may be more effective in changing behavior in these communities. Increased support and social organization within the neighborhood may provide support to families to help negotiate and manage the demands of community stressors (Furstenberg, 1993; Sampson, 1997). Policies aimed at improving the quality of the neighborhood, those effecting the structural characteristics of the community such as the economic and social resources available, are likely to make the most significant changes for children and families in inner-city communities (Brooks-Gunn et al., 1993).

ACKNOWLEDGMENTS

This work was supported by funding from National Institute of Mental Health (R01 MH48248), National Institute of Child Health and Human Development (R01 HD35415), Centers for Disease Control and Prevention (R49 CCR512739), National Science Foundation (SBR 9601157) and a Faculty Scholar Award from the William T. Grant Foundation.

REFERENCES

Briggs, X. S. (1997). Moving up versus moving out: Neighborhood effects in housing mobility programs. *Housing Policy Debate, 8*, 195–234.

Bronfenbrenner, U. (1979). *The ecology of human development: Experiments by nature and design.* Cambridge, MA: Harvard University Press.

Bronfenbrenner, U. (1988). Interacting systems in human development. Research paradigms: Present and future. In N. Bolger, A. Caspi, G. Downey, & M. Moorehouse (Eds.), *Persons in context: Developmental processes* (pp. 25–49). New York: Cambridge University Press.

Brooks-Gunn, J., Duncan, G. J., & Aber, J. L. (1997). *Neighborhood poverty.* New York: Russell Sage Foundation.

Brooks-Gunn, J., Duncan, G. J., Klebenov, P. K., & Sealand, N. S. (1993). Do neighborhoods influence child and adolescent development? *American Journal of Sociology, 99*, 353–395.

Bursik, R. J. (1988). Social disorganization and theories of crime and delinquency: Problems and prospects. *Criminology, 26*, 519–551.

Bursik, R. J., & Grasmick, H. (1993). *Neighborhoods and crime: The dimensions of effective community control.* New York: Lexington.

Byrne, J., & Sampson, R. J. (1986). Key issues in the social ecology of crime. In J. Byrne & R. J. Sampson (Eds.), *The sociology of crime.* New York: Springer-Verlag.

Chase-Lansdale, P. L., Gordon, R. A., Brooks-Gunn, J., & Klebanov, P. K. (1997). Neighborhood and family influences on the intellectual and behavioral competence of preschool and early school-age children. In J. Brooks-Gunn, G. J. Duncan, & J. L. Aber (Eds.), *Neighborhood poverty: Vol 1. Context and consequences for children* (pp. 79–118). New York: Russell Sage Foundation.

Children's Defense Fund. (1991). *The adolescent and young adult fact book.* Washington, DC.

Coulton, C. J., Korbin, J. E., Su, M., & Chow, J. (1995). Community level factors and child maltreatment rates. *Child Development, 66,* 1262–1276.

Crane, J. (1991). The Epidemic theory of ghettos and neighborhood effects on dropping out and teenage childbearing. *American Journal of Sociology, 96,* 1226–1259.

Dishion, T. J., Andrews, D. W., & Crosby, L. (1995). Antisocial boys and their friends in early adolescence: Relationship characteristics, quality, and interactional process. *Child Development, 66,* 139–151.

Dishion, T. J., Capaldi, D., Spracklen, K. M., & Li, F. (1995). Peer ecology of male adolescent drug use. *Development and Psychopathology, 7,* 803–824.

Dishion, T. J., Spracklen, K. M., Andrews, D. W., & Patterson, G. R. (1996). Deviancy training in male adolescents friendships. *Behavior Therapy, 27,* 373–390.

Duncan, G. J., & Brooks-Gunn, J. (Eds.). (1997). *Consequences of growing up poor.* New York: Russell Sage Foundation.

Elliot, D., Huizinga, D., & Ageton, S. (1985). *Explaining delinquency and drug use.* Beverly Hills, CA: Sage.

Elliot, D., Wilson, W., Huizinga, D., Sampson, R., Elliot, A., & Ranking, D. (1996). The effects of neighborhood disadvantage on adolescent development. *Journal of Research in Crime and Delinquency, 33,* 389–426.

Ensminger, M. E., Lamkin, R. P., & Jacobson, N. (1996). School leaving: A longitudinal perspective including neighborhood effects. *Child Development, 67,* 2400–2416.

Fisher, B. S., & Nasar, J. L. (1992). Fear of crime in relation to three exterior site features: Prospect, refuge, and escape. *Environment and Behavior, 24,* 35–65.

Furstenberg, F. (1993). How families mange risk and opportunity in dangerous neighborhoods. In W. J. Wilson (Ed.), *Sociology and the public agenda* (pp. 231–258). Newbury Park, CA: Sage.

Garbarino, J., Dubrow, N., Kostelny, K., & Pardo, C. (1992). *Children in anger.* Hillsdale, NJ: Lawrence Erlbaum Associates, Inc.

Garbarino, J., & Sherman, D. (1980). High-risk neighborhoods and high-risk families: The human ecology of maltreatment. *Child Development, 51,* 188–198.

Gonzales, N. A., Cauce, A. M., Friedman, R. J., & Mason, C. A. (1996). Family, peer, and neighborhood influences on academic achievement among African-American adolescents: One-year prospective effects. *American Journal of Community Psychology, 24,* 365–387.

Gorman-Smith, D., Tolan, P. H., & Henry, D. (1999). The relation of community and family to risk among urban poor adolescents. In P. Cohen, L. Robins, & C. Slomkowski (Eds.), *Where and when: Influence of historical time and place on aspects of psychopathology* (pp. 349–367). Hillsdale, NJ: Lawrence Erlbaum Associates, Inc.

Gorman-Smith, D., Tolan, P. H., & Henry, D. B. (1998, November). *Community and neighborhood risk for delinquency.* Paper presented at the meeting of the American Society of Criminology, Chicago, IL.

Gorman-Smith, D., Tolan, P. H., & Henry, D. (2000). A developmental-ecological model of the relation of family functioning to patterns of delinquency. *Journal of Quantitative Criminology, 16,* 169–198.

Gorman-Smith, D., Tolan, P. H., Loeber, R., & Henry, D. B. (1998). Relation of family problems to patterns of delinquent involvement among urban youth. *Journal of Abnormal Child Psychology, 26,* 319–333.

Gorman-Smith, D., Tolan, P. H., Zelli, A., & Huesmann, L. R. (1996). The relation of family functioning to violence among inner-city minority youths. *Journal of Family Psychology, 10,* 115–129.

Hanyu, K. (1995). Visual properties and affective appraisals in residential areas after dark. *Journal of Environmental Psychology, 17,* 301–315.

Hawkins, J. D., Catalano, R. F., & Miller, J. Y. (1992). Risk and protective factors for alcohol and other drug problems in adolescence and early adulthood: Implications for substance abuse prevention. *Psychological Bulletin, 112,* 64–105.

Henry, D. B., Tolan, P. H., & Gorman-Smith, D. (2001). Longitudinal family and peer group effects on violent and non-violent delinquency. *Journal of Child Clinical Psychology, 30*, 172–186.

Jargowsky, P. A., & Bane, M. J. (1991). Ghetto poverty in the United States, 1970–1980. In L. E. Lynn, Jr. & M. G. McGeary (Eds.), *Inner city poverty in the United States.* Washington, DC: Brookings Institute.

Jarrett, R. L. (1997). Bringing families back in: Neighborhoods' effects on child development. In J. Brooks-Gunn, G. J. Duncan, & J. L. Aber (Eds.), *Neighborhood poverty: Vol. 2. Policy implications in studying neighborhoods* (pp. 48–64). New York: Russell Sage Foundation.

Kupersmidt, J. B., Griesler, P. C., De Rosier, M. E., Patterson, C. J., & Davis, P. W. (1995). Childhood aggression and peer relations in the context of family and neighborhood factors. *Child Development, 66*, 360–375.

Leventhal, T., & Brooks-Gunn, J. (2000). The neighborhoods they live in: The effects of neighborhood residence on child and adolescent outcomes. *Psychological Bulletin, 126*, 309–337.

Loeber, R., & Farrington, D. P. (1998). *Serious and violent juvenile offenders: Risk factors and successful interventions.* Washington, DC: Office of Juvenile Justice and Delinquency Prevention.

Loeber, R., Stouthamer-Loeber, M., Van Kammen, W. B., & Farrington, D. P. (1991). Initiation, escalation and desistance in juvenile offending and their correlates. *Journal of Criminal Law and Criminology, 82*, 36–82.

Loeber, R., & Wikstrom, P. H. (1993). Individual pathways to crime in different types of neighborhoods. In D. P. Farrington, R. J. Sampson, & P. O. H. Wikstrom (Eds.), *Integrating individual and ecological aspects of crime* (pp. 169–204). Stockholm: National Council for Crime Prevention.

Ludwig, J., Duncan, G., & Hirschfield, P. (2001). Urban poverty and juvenile crime: Evidence from a randomized housing-mobility experiment. *Quarterly Journal of Economics, 116*, 655–680.

Mason, C. A., Cauce, A. M., Gonzales, N., & Hiraga, Y. (1996). Neither too sweet nor too sour: Problem peers, maternal control, and problem behavior in African American adolescents. *Child Development, 67*, 2115–2130.

Massey, D. S., & Eggers, M. L. (1990). The ecology of inequality: Minorities and the concentration of poverty, 1970–1980. *American Journal of Sociology, 95*, 1153–1188.

Nasar, J. L., & Fisher, B. (1993). "Hot spots" of fear and crime: A multi-method investigation. *Journal of Environmental Psychology, 13*, 187–206.

Newman, O. (1972). *Defensible space.* New York: Macmillan.

Peeples, F., & Loeber, R. (1994). Do individual factors and neighborhood context explain ethnic differences in juvenile delinquency? *Journal of Quantitative Criminology, 10*, 141–57.

Plater-Zyberk, E. (1995). *It takes a village to raise a child. Suburbs and cities: Changing patterns in metropolitan living.* Paper presented at the Aspen Institute meeting. Washington, DC.

Sampson, R. J. (1997). The embeddedness of child and adolescent development: A community-level perspective on urban violence. In J. McCord (Ed.), *Violence and childhood in the inner city* (pp. 31–77). Cambridge, England: Cambridge University Press.

Sampson, R. J. (2001). How do communities undergird or undermine human development? Relevant contexts and social mechanisms. In A. Booth & A. C. Crouter (Eds.), *Does it take a village?: Community effects on children, adolescents, and families* (pp. 3–30). Mahwah, NJ: Lawrence Erlbaum Associates, Inc.

Sampson, R. J., & Groves, W. B. (1989). Community structure and crime: Testing social-disorganization theory. *American Journal of Sociology, 94*, 774–780.

Sampson, R. J., & Laub, J. H. (1994). Urban poverty and the family context of delinquency: A new look at the structure and process in a classic study. *Child Development, 65*, 523–539.

Sampson, R. J., & Raudenbush, S. W. (1999). Systematic social observation of public spaces: A new look at disorder in urban neighborhoods. *American Journal of Sociology, 105*, 603–651.

Sampson, R., Raudenbush, S., & Earls, F. (1997). Neighborhood and violent crime: A multilevel study of collective efficacy. *Science, 277*, 918–924.

Shaw, C. R., & McKay, H. D. (1942). *Juvenile delinquency and urban areas.* Chicago: University of Chicago Press.

Spencer, M. B. (2001). Resiliency and fragility factors associated with the contextual experiences of low-resource urban African-American male youth and families. In A. Booth & A. C. Crouter (Eds.), *Does it take a village? Community effects on children, adolescents and families* (pp. 51–77). Mahwah, NJ: Lawrence Erlbaum Associates, Inc.

Sullivan, M. L. (1989). *Getting paid: Youth, crime and work in the inner city.* Ithaca, NY: Cornell University.

Szapocznik, J., & Coatsworth, J. D. (1999). An ecodevelopmental framework for organizing the influences on drug abuse: A developmental model of risk and protection. In M. Glantz & C. R. Hartel (Eds.), *Drug abuse: Origins and interventions.* Washington, DC: American Psychological Corporation.

Szapocznik, J., Gorman-Smith, D., Plater-Zyberk, E., Lombard, J., Martinez, F., & Mason, C. (1999). The role of the built environment in risk for adolescent substance abuse. Grant funded by the Robert Wood Johnson Foundation.

Taylor, R. B. (1989). Towards an environmental psychology of disorder: Delinquency, crime, and fear of crime. In D. Stokols & I. Altman (Eds.), *Handbook of environmental psychology* (Vol. 2, pp. 951–986). New York: Wiley.

Taylor, R. B., Shumaker, S. A., & Gottfredson, S. D. (1985). Neighborhood-level links between physical features and local sentiments: Deterioration, fear of crime, and confidence. *Journal of Architectural & Planning Research, 2,* 261–275.

Thornberry, T. P., Krohn, M. D., Lizotte, A. J., & Chard-Wierschem, D. (1993). The role of juvenile gangs in facilitating delinquent behavior. *Journal of Research in Crime & Delinquency, 30,* 55–87.

Tolan, P. H., & Gorman-Smith, D. (1997). Families and development of urban children. In H. J. Walberg, O. Reyes, & R. P. Weissberg (Eds.), *Urban children and youth: Interdisciplinary perspectives on policies and programs* (Vol. 1). Thousand Oaks, CA: Sage.

Tolan, P. H., Gorman-Smith, D., & Henry, D. (in press). Developmental ecology of urban males youth violence. *Developmental Psychology.*

Tolan, P. H., Guerra, N. G., & Kendall, P. C. (1995). A developmental-ecological perspective on antisocial behavior in children and adolescents: Toward a unified risk and intervention framework. *Journal of Consulting and Clinical Psychology, 63,* 579–584.

Tolan, P. H., Henry, D., Guerra, N. G., Huesmann, L. R., VanAcker, R., & Eron, L. D. (2001). *Patterns of psychopathology among urban poor children: 1. Community, age, ethnicity, and gender effects.* Manuscript submitted for publication.

Wilson, W. J. (1987). *The truly disadvantaged: The inner city, the underclass, and public policy.* Chicago: University of Chicago Press.

Zimmerman, M. A., Steinman, K. J., & Rowe, K. J. (1998). Violence among urban African American adolescents: The protective effects of parental support. In X. B. Arriaga & S. Oskamp (Eds.), *Addressing community problems: Psychological research and interventions. The Clarement Symposium on applied social psychology* (pp. 78–103). Thousand Oaks, CA: Sage.

6

Familial and Genetic Factors

Wendy S. Slutske
Nikole J. Cronk
Rachel E. Nabors-Oberg
University of Missouri–Columbia

An appreciation of the multifactorial etiology of juvenile antisocial behaviors, as well as efforts to determine the relative importance of these multiple causes, dates back to early in the 20th century (e.g., C. L. Burt, 1925; Healy, 1915). Healy, director of the Psychopathic Institute of the Juvenile Court of Chicago, examined the case records of 823 juvenile delinquents to identify the most frequently occurring causative factors. Two of the most common causes identified by Healy were "defective home conditions, including alcoholism," and "defects of heredity" (Healy, 1915, as cited in Reckless & Smith, 1932, p. 199).

The familial factors (defective home conditions) associated with juvenile antisociality have been extensively studied and well characterized over the many decades since Healy's work, and there has also been substantial progress in the last few decades in documenting and explaining the genetic risk factors (defects of heredity). (Although Healy's, 1915, ideas have stood the test of time, the pejorative labels of *defective* and *defect* have not.) Kazdin (1995), in his summary of the risk factors for the development of conduct disorder (CD), lists six categories of familial factors: (a) genetic loading; (b) parental psychopathology; (c) parent–child interaction; (d) parental separation, divorce, and marital discord; (e) birth order and family size; and (f) socioeconomic disadvantage. Because all of these risk factors tend to covary in families of biologically related individuals, the challenge for current investigators has been to parse their independent contribution to CD risk and to specify the causal relations among them. In this chapter, we summarize recent research that has examined the independent contribution and causal significance of some of these familial and genetic factors in the development of juvenile antisociality, with a particular focus on studies of psychiatrically defined juvenile antisociality, that is, CD and oppositional defiant disorder (ODD).

BEHAVIORAL GENETIC STUDIES OF CONDUCT DISORDER

The classical twin study design provides a very powerful starting point for dissecting the genetic and environmental causes of CD and ODD. The classical twin study method capitalizes on the fact that monozygotic (MZ) twins share 100% of their genes and dizygotic (DZ) twins share, on average, just 50% of their polymorphic genes. Thus, when higher concordances between MZ than DZ pairs for (for example) CD are observed, genetic factors are implicated as an important cause.

Earlier reviews (e.g., Cloninger & Gottesman, 1987; DiLalla & Gottesman, 1989) concluded that "genetic factors appear to be unimportant in most cases of juvenile delinquency" (Cloninger & Gottesman, 1987, p. 96). This conclusion was based on a review of six studies conducted between 1937 and 1977 of 144 pairs of mostly court-adjudicated juvenile delinquent twins. The overall weighted MZ and DZ concordances for juvenile delinquency were 87% and 72%, respectively (DiLalla & Gottesman, 1987). These studies suggest a high degree of twin similarity for juvenile delinquency for both MZ and DZ twin pairs, which is more consistent with an environmental than a genetic etiology.

The last decade has seen a substantial improvement in the quality of twin research on juvenile antisociality. In more recent studies, rather than relying on legal detection of antisocial behaviors (which may be biased), investigators have conducted large surveys of antisocial behavior with representative samples of youth (or adults retrospectively reporting about their childhood antisocial behaviors) in the community. In addition, contemporary model-fitting methods that can better partition the genetic and environmental risk for juvenile antisociality have been employed.

In the model fitting of twin data, the relative role of genetic and environmental factors in the development of CD can be inferred from the pattern of resemblance in MZ compared to DZ twins, and environmental factors are further decomposed into shared family environmental and nonshared individual-specific environmental factors. Shared family environmental factors are those risk factors for CD that twins share and that make them similar to each other, such as family socioeconomic status, characteristics of their parents (e.g., parental psychopathology, parental separations, divorce, or marital discord), the influence of shared peer groups, and neighborhood characteristics. When the DZ twin correlation for CD is (significantly) greater than one half of the MZ twin correlation for CD, shared family environmental factors are implicated as an important cause of CD. Nonshared individual-specific environmental factors are those risk factors for CD that are unique to a twin and that do not contribute to their similarity, such as differential treatment from parents (e.g., different types or amounts of discipline or supervision or affection for one twin than the other), the influence of different peers, or traumatic events. When the MZ correlation for CD is less than perfect, nonshared individual-specific environmental factors (after accounting for measurement error, which will also be included in this residual component) are implicated as an important cause of CD.

In Table 6.1 the results of the seven studies of *Diagnostic and Statistical Manual of Mental Disorders* DSM-defined CD, all conducted between 1995 and 2002, are reported. The combined sample size of these seven studies is 13,048 twin pairs. Three of the studies were based on retrospective reports of childhood antisocial behaviors among adults, one study was of preadolescent children, two studies were based on samples of mostly adolescents, and one study included both preadolescent children and adolescents. In five of the studies, both males and females were included. In all seven studies, CD was assessed by structured psychiatric interview (in the Virginia adult study only the male–male twin pairs were interviewed). Five of the studies were based on *DSM–III–R* (American Psychiatric Association, 1987) CD criteria and two were based on *DSM–IV* (American Psychiatric Association, 1994) CD criteria. In most of the studies, counts of CD symptoms were analyzed rather than CD diagnoses. In four of the studies CD symptoms were assessed by self-report, in one study CD symptoms were assessed by mother report, in one study both self-reports and mother reports were obtained and combined, and in one study all three of these approaches were used (as well as reporting results based on father reports).

What is most striking about the results of these seven studies of CD or CD symptoms in Table 6.1 is the wide range of heritability estimates obtained, ranging from 7% to 69%. When the heritability estimates are aggregated across studies, a weighted mean heritability of 37% is obtained. Estimates of the proportion of variation attributable to shared family environmental factors range from 0% to 39%, and the weighted mean estimate across studies is 21%. This suggests that shared familial and genetic factors account for approximately 58% of the variation in CD risk. Assuming a reliability of CD or CD symptoms of about 0.80, we can estimate that approximately 22% of the variation in risk for CD or CD symptoms can be explained by nonshared individual-specific environmental factors (this estimate would be lower if we assume that CD or CD symptoms are less reliable).

TABLE 6.1
Twin Studies of CD

Study	Age	N Pairs	CD Assessment	Male–Male Twins r_{MZ}	Male–Male Twins r_{DZ}	Female–Female Twins r_{MZ}	Female–Female Twins r_{DZ}	Male–Female Twins r_{DZ}	Heritability Estimate (%)
Adult twin studies of retrospectively reported CD									
U.S. Vietnam era									
Lyons et al. (1995)	36–55	3,226	Interview DSM–III–R symptom count						
			Self-report	.39	.33	na	na	na	M: 7
Slutske et al. (2001)	34–54	3,372	Interview DSM–III–R diagnosis						
			Self-report	.49	.38	na	na	na	M: 23
Australia									
Slutske et al. (1997)	27–90	2,682	Interview DSM–III–R diagnosis						
			Self-report	.70	.37	.68	.48	.34	M: 65/F: 43
Virginia									
Jacobson, Prescott, & Kendler (2000)	19–56	1,512	Interview DSM–III–R symptom count						
			Self-report	.48	.32	na	na	na	M: 32
Goldstein, Prescott, & Kendler (2001)	M = 38	558	Questionnaire DSM–III–R symptom count						
			Self-report	na	na	.41	.23	na	F: 36
Jacobson et al. (2002)	M = 37	2,604	Questionnaire DSM–III–R symptom count						
Childhood CD (<15 years)			Self-report	na	na	na	na	na	M: 6/F: 29
Adolescent CD (15–17 years)			Self-report	na	na	na	na	na	M: 41/F: 50

Child and adolescent twin studies of CD

Study	Age	N	Measure						Heritability
Virginia									
Eaves et al. (1997)	8–16	1,355	Interview *DSM–III–R* symptom count						
			Self-report	.36	.13	.24	.19	.10	M: 36/F: 23
			Mother-report	.66	.38	.68	.37	.32	M: 69/F: 69
			Father-report	.62	.49	.64	.26	.44	M: 27/F: 58
Meyer et al. (2000)[a]	8–16	1,350	Interview *DSM–III–R* symptom count						
			Combined report	.54	.32	.50	.30	.31	M + F: 25
Minnesota									
S. A. Burt, Krueger, McGue, & Iacono (2001)	10–12	753	Interview *DSM–III–R* symptom count						
			Combined report	.68	.54	.64	.27	na	M + F: 52
Colorado									
Young, Stallings, Corley, Krauter, & Hewitt (2000)[b]	12–18	334	Interview *DSM–IV* symptom count						
			Self-report	.35	.17	na	na	na	M + F: 35
Missouri									
Cronk et al. (2002)	11–23	1,948	Interview *DSM–IV* symptom count						
			Mother-report	na	na	.88	.66	na	F: 50

Note. CD = conduct disorder; MZ = monozygotic; DZ = dizygotic; M = males; F = females. Heritability estimate is the percentage of variation (or of variation in risk) due to genetic factors. Combined report is self-report and mother-report combined. Unweighted $M = 42$ and weighted $M = 37$ from independent samples with multiple estimates from the same sample averaged.
[a]Parental history of CD was also included in the analyses. [b]Data from males and females were combined in analyses.

The substantial heterogeneity in heritability estimates across twin studies of CD or CD symptoms suggests that there might be important moderators of genetic effects. In particular, investigators have focused on whether genetic effects might differ by gender, age cohort, or for different CD subtypes or dimensions.

Gender Differences in the Familial Causes of CD

One of the most consistent, but as yet unexplained, findings is the marked gender difference in the rates of CD (e.g., Moffitt, Caspi, Rutter, & Silva, 2001), which may (or may not) reflect gender differences in the causes of CD. So far, however, there is not convincing evidence that there are major differences between males versus females in the contribution of genetic, shared family environmental, and nonshared individual-specific environmental factors in the etiology of antisociality (more broadly defined) or for CD. In their quantitative review of 51 twin and adoption studies of (broadly defined) antisocial behavior, Rhee and Waldman (2002) obtained very similar estimates by aggregating results from 17 studies that included both males and females of the contribution of genetic factors (43% vs. 41%), shared family environmental factors (19% vs. 20%), and nonshared individual-specific environmental factors (38% vs. 39%). Five of the seven twin studies of *DSM*-defined CD summarized in Table 6.1 included both male and female twins, and in three of these separate estimates for males and females are reported. The weighted mean heritability estimates for males and females, obtained by aggregating across these three studies, are 40% and 43%, respectively; the weighted mean estimates of the proportion of variation attributable to shared family environmental factors for males and females are 12% and 15%, respectively; and estimates of the contribution of nonshared individual-specific environmental factors and measurement error are 48% for males and 42% for females.

In studies that include male–male, female–female, and male–female twin pairs, the degree to which the familial and genetic risk factors for CD for males versus females are distinct or overlapping can be tested by comparing the similarity of male–female DZ twin pairs to the same-sex DZ pairs. In three recent studies such an analysis was conducted (Jacobson, Prescott, & Kendler, 2002; Meyer et al., 2000; Slutske et al., 1997), and in all three it was concluded that the familial and genetic risk factors for CD are the same for the two sexes. For example, in Slutske et al. (1997), the DZ twin correlations for CD were .37, .48, and .34; in Meyer et al. (2000), the DZ twin correlations for CD were .32, .30, and .31 for male–male, female–female, and male–female pairs, respectively.

It has been suggested that the familial causes of antisocial behavior disorders are largely overlapping in males and females, but that females require more familial risk factors before they will become antisocial (Cloninger, Christianson, Reich, & Gottesman, 1978). Twin studies that include male–male, female–female, and male–female twin pairs enable one to test this hypothesis as well by comparing the risk of CD among the male DZ cotwins of male probands (affected individuals) with the risk to male DZ cotwins of female probands. In the Australian twin study (Slutske et al., 1997), 37% of the male DZ cotwins of male probands had a history of CD compared to 45% of the male DZ cotwins of female probands. Among females, 8% of the DZ cotwins of male probands and 18% of the female DZ cotwins of female probands had a history of childhood CD. These results are consistent with the hypothesis that, on average, girls with CD have more familial and genetic risk factors than boys with CD; therefore, the family members of such affected girls are at greater risk for becoming antisocial than the family members of affected boys. Moffitt et al. (2001) conducted a more direct test of this hypothesis by comparing the differences on 17 parental and family risk factors (e.g., parental conviction, years with a single parent) for 686 children with and without a history of CD identified from a large representative birth cohort. For none of the 17 risk factors were girls with CD more extreme relative to nondisordered girls than boys were relative to nondisordered boys. Overall, the hypothesis that girls require more risk factors or greater risk to develop CD has received mixed support at best (see Moffitt et al., 2001, for a more thorough treatment of this issue).

Cohort Differences in the Familial Causes of CD

Another consistently observed phenomenon is the higher rate of CD among more recently born cohorts (e.g., Robins, 1999). The same factors that have led to the higher rates of CD may also have led to differences in the contribution of genetic and environmental factors. Studies that include participants born at different periods in time allow one to test the extent to which the contribution of familial or genetic factors to the risk for CD have changed with more recently born cohorts. One hypothesis is that genetic factors should become more important because adolescents in more recently born cohorts have more personal freedom and opportunities to engage in antisocial activities. For example, more recently born adolescents may be less likely to be supervised by their parents than adolescents born at earlier points in history. Thus, it should be more likely that the genetic predisposition for developing CD will be actualized in the more recently born than in the earlier born adolescents (Slutske, 2001).

In two recent studies, one of men in the United States born between 1940 and 1974 (Jacobson, Prescott, Neale, & Kendler, 2000), another of men and women in Australia born between 1902 and 1964 (Slutske et al., 1997), cohort differences in the genetic and environmental contributions to the risk for CD were examined. Surprisingly, given the broad age ranges studied, in neither study was there a detectable increase or decrease in the contribution of genetic factors with more recently born cohorts. In the United States study, shared family environmental factors accounted for more variation in CD symptoms among more recently born men (Jacobson et al., 2000).

CD Subtypes or Dimensions

The *DSM–IV* (American Psychiatric Association, 1994) distinguishes between two types of CD based on the age of onset of symptoms. Childhood-onset type CD is diagnosed when symptoms are evident prior to age 10 and adolescent-onset type CD is diagnosed when symptoms are not observed until age 10 or later. It is suggested that these two developmental subtypes of CD may represent the outcomes of distinct etiological mechanisms. A related developmental subtype of antisociality is Moffitt's (1993) adolescence-limited and life-course persistent distinction. Individuals with life-course persistent antisociality commit antisocial acts starting early in life and persist in their antisociality into adulthood; children with a neurological vulnerability in combination with an adverse rearing environment are at risk for developing life-course persistent antisociality (Moffitt, 1993; Moffitt & Caspi, 2001). Adolescence-limited antisociality, in contrast, is described as a normal phase of development that is caused by social modeling of peer antisocial behaviors and positive reinforcement of antisocial acts. DiLalla and Gottesman (1989) described three etiologically distinct patterns of antisocial behavior: continuous, transitory, and late-blooming, based on whether antisocial behaviors occur only during childhood or adolescence, only during the adult years, or during both phases of life. Again, persistent or continuous antisociality is considered to be etiologically distinct from transitory antisociality that is limited to a single phase of life. Transitory antisociality, that is, antisociality that occurs only during adolescence, is hypothesized to be largely environmentally influenced. Genetic factors are hypothesized to play a relatively greater role in the development of late blooming and especially continuous antisociality. Thus, within groups of children diagnosed with CD there may be distinct subgroups that potentially can be separated based on the age of onset of their symptoms or the persistence of their antisociality into adulthood.

Few behavioral genetic investigations of the early onset versus late onset or transitory versus persistent antisocial behavior distinction have been conducted. Taylor, Iacono, and McGue (2000) examined twin similarity for early-onset (onset of antisociality at or before age 12) versus late-onset (onset of antisociality after age 12) delinquency among 63 MZ and 33 DZ pairs selected from the Minnesota twin study (included in Table 6.1; S. A. Burt, Krueger, McGue, & Iacono, 2001). The MZ and DZ twin concordances for early-onset delinquency (55% vs. 29%, respectively) were consistent with a genetic contribution, whereas the MZ and DZ concordances for late-onset delinquency (43% vs. 39%) were not. In the U.S. Vietnam era twin study, continuous or persistent antisocial behavior was operationalized as meeting the criteria for antisocial personality disorder (ASPD; three or more antisocial symptoms occurring prior to age 15 and four or more antisocial symptoms occurring after age 17). ASPD was the most heritable definition of antisocial behavior examined in this twin cohort, with a heritability of 67% (Slutske et al., 2001). Although there already is some modest supporting evidence, theories about etiologically distinct developmental subtypes of CD still await more rigorous testing as new data from prospective behavioral genetic investigations become available.

Another perspective on identifying etiologically distinct aspects of CD has been to focus on more homogeneous dimensions of antisocial behavior. For example, in the Virginia twin study (included in Table 6.1; Eaves et al., 1997; Meyer et al., 2000), symptoms of CD and ODD were combined to form four dimensions that were initially proposed by Frick, Van Horn, et al. (1993): property violations, status violations, oppositional behavior, and aggression (Simonoff, Pickles, Meyer, Silberg, & Maes, 1998). Genetic influences were higher for aggression (58%) and property violations (47%) than for status violations (26%) and oppositional behavior (14%), and shared family environmental influences were higher for oppositional behavior (61%) and status violations (50%) than for property violations (20%) and aggression (18%) when mother reports of behaviors were analyzed (these differences were not observed when self-reports were analyzed). Eley, Lichtenstein, and Stevenson (1999) also obtained higher heritabilities for aggressive than nonaggressive antisocial behavior in two independent samples of 7- to 9-year-old Swedish twins and 8- to 16-year-old British twins. The higher heritability of aggressive versus nonaggressive antisocial behavior was also partially replicated using a sibling adoption design. Deater-Deckard and Plomin (1999) obtained heritabilities of 49% for aggression and 17% for delinquency among 78 adoptive and 94 biologically related sibling pairs when teacher reports were analyzed (these differences were not observed when parent reports were analyzed). Thus, there is some evidence to suggest that the dimension of aggression may be more heritable than other nonaggressive dimensions of antisocial behavior. Aggression (in addition to early age of onset and persistence) may mark a more heritable subtype of CD. However, this conclusion runs counter to earlier findings from the adult criminality literature indicating that property crimes are more heritable than violent crimes or crimes against persons (e.g. Cloninger & Gottesman, 1987; Mednick, Gabrielli, & Hutchings, 1984).

In addition to identifying CD subtypes or dimensions that may be more or less heritable, or for which shared family environmental factors account for more or less of the variation in risk, behavioral genetic research designs have also been utilized to better understand the relation between CD and other disruptive behavior disorders, other forms of child and adult psychopathology, and other correlates such as dimensions of personality or intellectual functioning.

Are CD and ODD Etiologically Distinct?

ODD or ODD symptoms as defined by the *DSM* have been the focus of only three behavioral-genetic investigations (Eaves et al., 1997; S. A. Burt et al., 2001; and Cronk et al., 2002), with a combined sample size of 4,056 twin pairs (see Table 6.2). Heritability estimates from these three studies range from 21% to 79%, and the weighted mean heritability estimate aggregated across the three studies is 60%. Estimates of the proportion of variation attributable to shared family environmental factors range from 0% to 31%, and the weighted mean estimate is 7%. This suggests that shared familial and genetic factors account for approximately 67% of the variation in ODD risk. Assuming a reliability of ODD or ODD symptoms of about 0.80, we can estimate that approximately 13% of the variation in risk for ODD or ODD symptoms can be explained by nonshared individual-specific environmental factors. These results suggest that the contribution of genetic, shared family environmental, and nonshared individual-specific environmental factors are roughly similar for CD and ODD. However, these results do not address the issue of whether or to what extent the same genetic and environmental risk factors are etiologically relevant for the two disorders. The frequent co-occurrence of these syndromes suggests that there may be quite extensive overlap in their risk factors. Genetically informative studies can disentangle whether the co-occurrence of CD and ODD is due to their sharing common genetic, common shared family environmental, or common nonshared individual-specific environmental risk factors and whether there are genetic or environmental risk factors that are unique to CD or to ODD.

When twin data for a single trait are analyzed, the correlation between twins for the trait is compared in MZ and DZ twins. When data are collected for two or more traits, one can make similar inferences about the sources of the correlation between traits by comparing the cross-twin, cross-trait correlations in MZ and DZ twins in relation to the within-twin correlation between the two traits. For example, if the MZ cross-twin correlation between CD and ODD is nearly as large as the within-twin correlation between CD and ODD, this suggests that there are important familial factors (either genetic or environmental) that are causing the correlation between the traits.

TABLE 6.2
Twin Studies of ODD

Study	Age	N Pairs	ODD Assessment	Twin Correlations					Heritability Estimate (%)
				Male–Male Twins		Female–Female Twins		Male–Female Twins	
				r_{MZ}	r_{DZ}	r_{MZ}	r_{DZ}	r_{DZ}	
Virginia Eaves et al. (1997)	8–16	1,355	Interview DSM–III–R symptom count						
			Self-report	.20	.13	.26	.00	.08	M: 21/F: 23
			Mother report	.48	.30	.50	.21	.22	M: 53/F: 51
			Father report	.66	.21	.50	.14	.39	M: 65/F: 49
Minnesota S. A. Burt, Krueger, McGue, & Iacono (2001)	10–12	753	Interview DSM–III–R symptom count						
			Combined report	.69	.47	.69	.53	na	M + F: 39
Missouri Cronk et al. (2002)	11–23	1,948	Interview DSM–IV symptom count						
			Mother report	na	na	.82	.45	na	F: 79

Note. ODD = oppositional defiant disorder; MZ = monozygotic; DZ = dizygotic; M = males; F = females. Heritability estimate is percentage of variation (or of variation in risk) due to genetic factors. Combined report is self-report and mother report combined. Unweighted $M = 51$ and weighted $M = 60$ from independent samples with multiple estimates from the same sample averaged.

The magnitude of the DZ cross-twin, cross-trait correlation determines the relative importance of genetic and shared family environmental factors in explaining the correlation between the traits. If the DZ cross-twin correlation between CD and ODD is lower than the MZ cross-twin correlation, this suggests that genetic influences (at least partially) explain the correlation between CD and ODD. Conversely, if the DZ cross-twin correlation between CD and ODD is nearly as large as the MZ cross-twin correlation, then shared family environmental factors may be important in causing the correlation between CD and ODD. Just as the variation in liability for a single trait can be partitioned into that due to genetic, shared family environmental, and nonshared individual-specific environmental factors in twin model-fitting analyses of a single trait, the correlation between two traits can be similarly decomposed. One can then test whether the genetic (or shared family environmental) correlation between CD and ODD differs significantly from zero (which would indicate that there are overlapping sets of genetic, or shared family environmental, risk factors for CD and ODD) and whether the genetic (or shared family environmental) correlation between CD and ODD differs significantly from unity (which would indicate that there are unique genetic, or shared family environmental, risk factors for CD and for ODD). Thus, various models for the familial or genetic cotransmission of CD and ODD (and between CD/ODD and other associated psychiatric disorders or other correlates) can be tested.

In two twin studies (S. A. Burt et al., 2001; Eaves et al., 2000), the association between CD and ODD was examined, and quite different conclusions were reached. In the Minnesota twin study, S. A. Burt et al. (2001) obtained within-twin correlations between CD and ODD of .50 for boys and .36 for girls, MZ cross-twin correlations between CD and ODD of .39 for boys and .25 for girls, and DZ cross-twin correlations between CD and ODD of .35 for boys and .28 for girls. These results suggest modest overlap in the genetic and nonshared individual-specific environmental risk factors for CD and ODD and substantial overlap in shared family environmental risk factors. The hypothesis that CD and ODD share all of their shared family environmental risk factors could not be rejected. Thus, the results of S. A. Burt et al. (2001) indicate that CD and ODD are etiologically distinct at the genetic and nonshared individual-specific environmental level but not with respect to aspects of the shared family environment.

Eaves et al. (2000) used a more complex multivariate extension of twin model-fitting analysis to combine information about two traits (CD and ODD) assessed by three different informants (child, mother, and father) for each member of a twin pair—essentially a behavioral-genetic extension of the multitrait–multimethod matrix concept (Campbell & Fiske, 1959). Genetic and environmental correlation matrices were estimated based on the information from all possible pairs of variables measured in MZ and DZ twins, and the resulting genetic and environmental correlation matrices were submitted to an exploratory factor analysis. In contrast to the findings of S. A. Burt et al. (2001), shared family environmental factors did not contribute substantially to the etiology of CD or ODD.

If CD and ODD were etiologically distinct at the genetic level (for example), one would expect to find a factor corresponding to CD and a factor corresponding to ODD in the exploratory factor analysis of the genetic correlation matrix. Instead, Eaves et al. (2000) found at both the genetic and the nonshared individual-specific environmental level that the correlation matrices could be summarized by three factors corresponding primarily with the informant. For example, the first genetic factor had high loadings for child self-reports of CD and ODD, the second genetic factor had high loadings for father reports of CD and ODD, and the third genetic factor had high loadings for mother reports of CD and ODD. The method of assessment was more salient in contributing to the pattern of correlations among the variables than were the traits of CD or ODD. Thus, at neither the genetic level nor the environmental level was discriminant validity between CD and ODD demonstrated. The results of the study of Eaves et al. (2000) suggest that CD and ODD are not etiologically distinct and that the risk factors identified for CD are also likely to contribute to the risk for ODD.

Behavioral Genetic Studies of CD Comorbidity

Behavioral genetic studies have also explored the extent to which the familial and genetic factors that increase the risk for CD are distinct or overlapping with those for other associated disorders. The causes of the well-documented co-occurrence of CD/ODD with attention deficit hyperactivity disorder (ADHD) has been the focus of four twin studies (see Table 6.3). In three of these studies (Nadder, Silberg, Eaves, Maes, & Meyer, 1998; Silberg et al., 1996; Young, Stallings, Corley, Krauter, & Hewitt, 2000) shared family environmental factors did not contribute substantially to the risk for CD/ODD or ADHD and therefore also did not contribute substantially to their co-occurrence, whereas the results of a fourth study found evidence for substantial overlap in the shared family environmental risk for CD/ODD and ADHD (S. A. Burt et al., 2001). Similarly, three studies (Nadder et al., 1998; Silberg et al., 1996; Young et al., 2000) found substantial overlap in the genetic risk factors for CD/ODD and ADHD, whereas the fourth study (S. A. Burt et al., 2001) found that the genetic risk for CD/ODD was completely independent of the genetic risk for ADHD. The average within-twin correlation between CD/ODD across these studies is .37 to .44, the average MZ cross-twin correlation between CD/ODD and ADHD is .24 to .33, and the average DZ cross-twin correlation between CD/ODD and ADHD is .11 to .14. Taken together, the results of these four studies suggest that the familial

TABLE 6.3
Twin Studies of the Causes of Comorbidity Between Symptoms of CD/ODD and ADHD

Study	N Pairs	Informant	Male–Male Twins				Female–Female Twins				Male–Female Twins	
			Within-Twin Correlations		Cross-Twin Correlations		Within-Twin Correlations		Cross-Twin Correlations		Within-Twin Correlations	Cross-Twin Correlations
			r_{MZ}	r_{DZ}	r_{MZ}	r_{DZ}	r_{MZ}	r_{DZ}	r_{MZ}	r_{DZ}	r_{DZ}	r_{DZ}
Virginia (1987–1990) Silberg, Rutter, et al. (1996) combined CD/ODD and ADHD	1,197	Mother										
Ages 8–11 years			.51	.35	.43	.16	.56	.39	.51	.31	.41	.16
Ages 12–16 years			.47	.42	.37	.10	.38	.44	.25	.13	.47	.05
Virginia (1992–1993) Nadder, Silberg, Eaves, Maes, & Meyer (1998) combined CD/ODD and ADHD	900	Mother										
Ages 7–13 years			.52	.41	.35	–.02	.41	.42	.19	–.03	na	na
Colorado Young, Stallings, Corley, Krauter, & Hewitt (2000)[a] CD and ADHD	334	Self										
Ages 12–18 years			na	na	.28	.11	na	na	na	na	na	na
Minnesota S. A. Burt, Krueger, McGue, & Iacono (2001)	753	Combined report										
CD and ADHD			.34	.33	.29	.23	.17	.24	.13	.12	na	na
ODD and ADHD Ages 10–12 years			.37	.26	.31	.20	.21	.39	.15	.32	na	na

Note. CD = conduct disorder; ODD = oppositional defiant disorder; ADHD = attention deficit hyperactivity disorder; MZ = monozygotic; DZ = dizygotic. Correlations are the average of those presented in the original publications for first and second twins from twin pairs.

[a]Data from males and females were combined in analyses.

and genetic risk factors for CD/ODD overlap substantially with the familial and genetic risk factors for ADHD and that much of the shared familial risk can be explained by shared genetic risk for CD/ODD and ADHD.

It is important to recognize that there are several alternate explanations for a significant shared genetic risk for CD/ODD and ADHD. These results are equally consistent with there being one or more genetic loci that jointly increase the risk for both CD/ODD and ADHD, causal chains such as gene(s) → ADHD → CD/ODD and gene(s) → CD/ODD → ADHD, and a statistical association between different susceptibility genes for CD/ODD and ADHD, for example, because there is a susceptibility locus for CD/ODD and one for ADHD that are very close to each other on the same chromosome. Combining knowledge gained from other types of study designs can help to refine the interpretation of the results of cross-sectional behavioral genetic investigations by ruling out certain implausible explanations. For example, prospective longitudinal studies documenting that when ADHD and CD/ODD co-occur, the onset of ADHD always precedes the onset of CD/ODD would rule out gene(s) → CD/ODD → ADHD. Prospective longitudinal behavioral genetic studies will be especially valuable in sorting through these alternate causal and noncausal interpretations of significant genetic associations.

In two twin studies (Lyons et al., 1995; Jacobson et al., 2002), the extent to which the familial and genetic risk factors for juvenile versus adult antisocial behaviors are distinct or overlapping was examined. Both Lyons et al. (1995) and Jacobson et al. (in press) found that the genetic influences that contribute to the risk for childhood CD also contribute to the risk for engaging in later antisocial behaviors in adulthood and that additional genetic risk factors come into play in adolescence and adulthood. Both studies also found that the shared family environmental risk factors for antisocial behavior in adolescence and adulthood completely overlapped with those involved in the risk for childhood CD and that there were no distinct family environmental risk factors coming into play after childhood. These results must be interpreted with caution because they are based on retrospective reports of juvenile antisocial behaviors obtained with adults. When results become available from prospective longitudinal behavioral genetic studies, we will be able to draw much firmer conclusions about the interplay of genetic and environmental factors in the development of antisocial behaviors over the life course.

The results of behavioral genetic studies suggest that the genetic risk for juvenile antisociality is also significantly associated with the genetic risk for problems of addiction such as alcohol misuse (Jang, Vernon, & Livesley, 2000) or dependence (Slutske et al., 1998) and pathological gambling (Slutske et al., 2001), as well as symptoms of depression (O'Connor et al., 1998), and that the shared family environmental risk for antisociality is significantly associated with the shared family environmental risk for symptoms of depression (O'Connor, McGuire, Reiss, Hetherington, & Plomin, 1998), alcohol dependence (True et al., 1999), marijuana dependence (True et al., 1999), and drug use (Young et al., 2000).

The results of behavioral genetic studies of CD comorbidity suggest that the search for the familial and genetic risk factors for CD will partially involve the identification of broad underlying behavioral dispositions that contribute to CD as well as to the risk for other forms of psychopathology. The identification of these intermediate traits, or endophenotypes, may provide a more useful target for molecular genetic research than heterogeneous diagnostic categories such as CD or ODD. Young et al. (2000) found that 22% of the variation in CD symptoms could be explained by a higher level latent trait (an unmeasured trait inferred from the pattern of correlations between the measured variables) they termed *behavioral disinhibition*, which was highly heritable (84% of the variation in the trait of behavioral disinhibition was due to genetic factors) and also explained to varying degrees the variation in drug use, ADHD symptoms, and the personality trait of novelty seeking. Slutske et al. (2002) examined in a twin study the extent to which the genetic risk for CD and the common genetic risk for CD and alcohol dependence could be explained by measured dimensions of personality. A broad personality dimension of behavioral undercontrol (i.e., impulsivity, rebelliousness, and social nonconformity) explained 37% of the genetic variation in the risk for CD and 88% of the genetic variation in risk that is common to CD and alcohol dependence. Carey and Goldman (1997) examined in a family study the extent to which the familial transmission for CD/ASPD and the familial cotransmission of CD/ASPD with alcohol and drug abuse could be explained by measured intelligence. They found that 7% of the familial transmission for CD/ASPD, 6% of the familial cotransmission between CD/ASPD and alcohol abuse, and 8% of the familial cotransmission between CD/ASPD and drug abuse could be explained by the familial transmission of intelligence. These results suggest that more basic dimensions of personality but not intellectual functioning are important endophenotypes of CD/ODD.

We estimated earlier that the combined cumulative effect of shared familial and genetic factors account for 58% of the variation in CD risk and 67% of the variation in ODD risk. The cumulative effect of genes account for 37% and 60% of the variation in risk for CD and ODD, respectively, and the cumulative effect of shared family environmental risk factors account for 21% and 7% of the variation in risk for CD and ODD, respectively. Although the approximate contributions of these anonymous unmeasured latent components of risk have been well characterized by the biometrical modeling of twin data, the specific measurable genetic and environmental risk factors involved are still largely speculative. The cumulative effect of these risk factors is relatively easy to detect, but it is much more difficult to detect the influence of a single specific risk factor, in part because any given individual factor may explain only a small part of the variation in risk for CD or ODD (Meyer et al., 2000).

Specific Familial Risk Factors for CD and ODD

Numerous studies have documented differences in the families of children affected with CD or ODD compared to the families of unaffected children. For example, a recent meta-analysis (Amato, 2001) of results obtained from 93 independent samples found a mean difference of about one-fourth *SD* on measures of conduct problems between children from divorced homes and children from intact homes. The existence of such associations between family environmental factors and CD/ODD among children is rarely questioned; rather, the interpretation of such associations has been a matter of debate. Family environmental risk factors are all substantially associated with each other (e.g., Christ et al., 1990; Frick et al., 1992; Lahey, Hartdagen, et al., 1988), are also associated with extrafamilial risk factors (e.g., Harris, 1995), and in nuclear families of biologically related individuals are also associated with genetic risk factors (e.g., Plomin, 1995; Rowe, 1994). Thus, it is very difficult (and impossible in studies of nuclear families) to determine the "active ingredient" that is accounting for the increased risk of CD/ODD in the offspring. For example, higher rates of ASPD, substance use disorders, and major depression are observed among the parents of children with CD/ODD compared to parents of children without CD/ODD (Frick, 1993). However, given what we are beginning to discover about the common genetic underpinnings of CD/ODD and other forms of psychopathology, it is unclear the extent to which this association is due to the ineffective parenting or familial disruption associated with psychopathology in the parents contributing to CD/ODD in the offspring or whether it is better explained by the common genetic risk for adult psychopathology and childhood CD/ODD that is transmitted from parents to offspring. In the following sections, we consider two putative environmental risk factors that have been the focus of recent efforts to target an active ingredient involved in the etiology of CD/ODD: parental separation, divorce, or marital discord, and prenatal environmental exposure to maternal smoking.

Parental Separation, Divorce, or Marital Discord. Traditionally, it has been assumed that adverse outcomes among children, including antisociality, are a direct consequence of divorce (this is inferring a causal connection from correlational data, a mistake that all introductory research methods textbooks warn us against). Emery, Waldron, Kitzmann, and Aaron (1999) highlighted the importance of considering preexisting

characteristics of the parents who divorce (such as antisociality) and outlined three possible alternatives to the traditional interpretation of the association between divorce and the development of antisociality in the
children: (a) divorce completely explains the relation between antisociality in the parents and the development of antisociality among the children (an example of environmental transmission); (b) the relation between divorce and the development of antisociality is spurious and is
completely explained by the antisociality of the parents (possibly by genetic transmission of risk for antisociality from parent to offspring); and
(c) a combined model allowing for both explanations. Emery et al. (1999)
examined the evidence for these alternate explanations in a sample of
1,204 mother–offspring pairs. A unique feature of the study is that antisociality among the mothers was assessed prior to the birth of their children in 1980 when they were 15 to 22 years old, and antisociality among
the offspring was assessed 14 years later in 1994. There was support for
the combined model in which there was a direct effect of maternal antisociality on offspring antisociality and also an indirect effect mediated by
parental divorce; the effect mediated by parental divorce was substantially reduced by taking into account demographic correlates such as
race, sex of the child, the ages of the mother and the child, and the age of
the mother at the birth of her first child. This study established, using a
prospective research design, that preexisting characteristics of the mothers significantly contribute to the well-established association between divorce and the development of antisociality in the offspring.

Several studies have attempted to examine, using behavioral-genetic research designs, whether the link between parental divorce (or marital discord) and antisociality among children is genetically or environmentally
mediated. O'Connor, Caspi, DeFries, and Plomin (2000) examined the association between divorce and externalizing problems among children in 188
adoptive families and 210 biological families. The adoption design is very
useful in separating genetic and environmental influences. If the association
between divorce and children's externalizing problems is due to genetic
transmission, then there should be a stronger association observed among
the biological families than among the adoptive families. If the association
between divorce and children's externalizing problems is due to environmental transmission, then there should be an association observed even
among the adoptive families. Unfortunately, in neither adoptive families nor
biological families was there a significant association between divorce and
externalizing problems of the children; although not significantly different,
there was a stronger association between divorce and externalizing problems (as rated by teachers) for biological families than for adoptive families
(O'Connor et al., 2000). In contrast, Cadoret, Yates, Troughton, Woodworth,
and Stewart (1995) found that an adverse adoptive home environment (in-

cluding divorce or marital instability, psychopathology, or legal problems of the adoptive parents) was significantly associated with the development of CD among 197 adoptees. In addition, the effect of an adverse adoptive home environment was especially potent when an adoptee was already at increased genetic risk for CD because they had a biological parent with a history of ASPD. Unfortunately, the use of a composite measure of the adverse adoptive home environment makes it impossible to determine whether there is a unique effect of divorce or marital instability. Meyer et al. (2000) directly estimated the unique contribution of two measured indexes of family functioning in a study of 1,350 twin pairs and their parents (the Virginia twin study; Eaves et al., 1997). Family maladaptability and marital discord together explained about 17% of the shared family environmental risk and about 4% of the total risk for CD after controlling for genetic factors involved in the parent–offspring transmission of CD.

In sum, the results of a recent meta-analysis (Amato, 2001) suggests that the association between parental divorce and childhood antisociality is modest; the results of a large prospective study (Emery et al., 1999) suggests that a substantial portion of this association is spurious and due to preexisting characteristics of the mother; and the results of an adoption study (Cadoret et al., 1995) and a twin parent study (Meyer et al., 2000) suggests that even after controlling for genetic factors, there is evidence that some of the association might represent true environmental mediation. Therefore, although the effect is likely to be very modest, parental divorce or marital discord may actually be an active ingredient in the development of CD/ODD.

Prenatal Environmental Exposure to Maternal Smoking. At least six published reports in the last decade have documented increased rates of externalizing disorders such as CD/ODD among the offspring of women who smoked cigarettes during their pregnancy compared to the offspring of women who did not smoke during their pregnancy (Fergusson, Horwood, & Lynskey, 1993; Fergusson, Woodward, & Horwood, 1998; Wakschlag et al., 1997; Weissman, Warner, Wickramaratne, & Kandel, 1999; Weitzman, Gortmaker, & Sobol, 1992; Rantakallio, Laara, Isohanni, & Moilanen, 1992). For example, in a cohort of 1,022 children studied since birth, offspring of mothers who smoked an average of 20 cigarettes per day while pregnant had a mean CD symptoms score of about one-half *SD* above the mean CD symptoms score of the offspring of mothers who did not smoke during their pregnancy (Fergusson et al., 1998). This suggests that the physiological effects of nicotine on the developing fetus, such as reduced access to nutrients and fetal hypoxia (Weitzman et al., 1992) or changes to the serotinergic and dopaminergic systems during brain development (Fergusson, 1999), may predict later CD/ODD in the child. However, prenatal exposure to cigarette smoking may not be the active ingredient increasing the risk for CD/ODD because women who smoke while pregnant are also more likely to be socioeconomically disadvantaged, to consume other psychoactive substances while pregnant, to be less nurturing towards their children, to be divorced or separated, and to have a history of alcohol abuse or dependence or criminal offending compared to women who do not smoke while pregnant (Fergusson et al., 1998). In addition, offspring of mothers who smoke during their pregnancy are more likely to be sexually abused and to receive physical forms of discipline than offspring of mothers who do not smoke during their pregnancy (Fergusson et al., 1998).

Although researchers have established that maternal smoking during pregnancy increases the risk for offspring externalizing psychopathology even after controlling for these correlated familial risk factors, Fergusson (1999), in his review of the evidence, suggested that confirmation of a specific etiologic link between prenatal exposure to smoking and CD/ODD would require ruling out potential genetic confounding. Mothers who smoke while pregnant compared to mothers who do not smoke while pregnant, in addition to potentially placing their child at higher risk for developing CD/ODD from the prenatal environmental exposure to cigarettes, may also be more likely to transmit susceptibility genes for CD/ODD to their offspring. These alternate explanations could (at least partially) be disentangled by using within-family controls such as studies of matched pairs of children born to the same parents who are discordant for exposure to maternal smoking in utero (these would need to be siblings from two separate pregnancies, not twins), or offspring of MZ twin pairs who are discordant for smoking while pregnant (from a genetic perspective, cousins who are the offspring of MZ twin mothers effectively have the same mother). Higher rates of CD/ODD among the offspring exposed to maternal smoking in utero compared to the within-family controls not exposed would provide more convincing evidence of a specific effect of prenatal exposure to maternal smoking on subsequent risk for CD/ODD by controlling for potential genetic confounding. Studies such as these have not yet been conducted. Nonetheless, the available evidence suggests that smoking of the mother during the pregnancy of her child may represent another mechanism for the familial transmission of risk for CD/ODD.

Susceptibility Genes for CD and ODD

Many experts characterize the search to identify specific susceptibility genes for psychiatric disorders as disappointing. Typically, the report of an association is published with great fanfare, only to be followed by several studies that fail to replicate the association. For this reason, Sullivan, Eaves,

Kendler, and Neale (2001) recommended that the results of single studies of genetic associations should be interpreted with caution and that the results of multiple studies should be combined using meta-analytic techniques. Even when individual studies fail to detect a significant association, there may be a significant association when they are combined. Thus, meta-analyses of genetic association studies have been recommended as a way to detect genetic effects that are relatively small (Sullivan et al., 2001).

ADHD has been singled out as one example of a psychiatric disorder in which molecular genetic research appears to be making significant progress in identifying potential susceptibility genes (Collier, Curran, & Asherson, 2000; McGuffin et al., 2001). CD/ODD has been the focus of fewer molecular genetic studies than ADHD, and these have not yet produced replicated findings. Given the overlap in the genetic risk factors for CD/ODD and ADHD, it is likely that susceptibility genes for ADHD will also be associated with the genetic liability for CD/ODD. Most of the molecular genetic research with ADHD has focused on genes involved in the dopamine neurotransmitter system, including genes that code for proteins involved in the synthesis of dopamine, dopamine receptors, the reuptake of dopamine, or the metabolism of dopamine. The most robust finding has been with the dopamine D4 receptor gene (DRD4) on chromosome 11 (Collier et al., 2000; McGuffin et al., 2001). In 1996, two studies (Benjamin et al., 1996; Ebstein et al., 1996) reported a significant association between the long form of the DRD4 gene and the personality trait of novelty seeking. Individuals who were high on the dimension of novelty seeking were more likely to have at least one copy of the long form of the DRD4 gene than individuals who were low on novelty seeking. An association of the long form of the DRD4 gene with ADHD was also found in a single study published that same year (LaHoste et al., 1996).

Since the first positive report of an association between the long form of the DRD4 gene and ADHD, 15 more studies have been published (Faraone, Doyle, Mick, & Biederman, 2001). Six of these studies detected an association between the long form of DRD4 and ADHD and 9 studies did not. When the results of all 16 studies were combined with meta-analysis, a small but significant association was obtained (Faraone et al., 2001). Thus, the evidence suggests that DRD4 (or a gene close to it on chromosome 11) may be a susceptibility gene for ADHD. Other genes involved in the dopamine neurotransmitter system, including the dopamine D5 receptor gene on chromosome 4 and the dopamine transporter gene on chromosome 5, have also shown promise in potentially accounting for genetic variation in ADHD risk (Collier et al., 2000; McGuffin et al., 2001). However, the associations of this handful of genes with ADHD will probably only account for a small portion of the genetic variation in ADHD risk (and possibly risk for CD/ODD). Many of the susceptibility genes involved are still unknown.

CONCLUDING COMMENTS

In the spirit of Healy (1915), we attempted to determine the relative importance of familial and genetic factors in recent research on CD by searching
the PsycINFO database. According to the PsycINFO database, there were
2,113 papers with the keywords *conduct disorder* published from 1990 to
2001 (there were 548 papers with the keywords *oppositional defiant disorder*). Of these 2,113 papers related to CD, 561 (27%) contained the keywords
family or *genetic*. In a short chapter such as this, it is impossible to do justice to the large volume of research that has focused on familial and genetic
factors in the development of CD. Instead, we highlighted novel research
approaches and findings that may offer some new insights. In particular, we
preferentially focused our review on studies of large representative population-based samples, longitudinal studies, genetically informative studies (or
studies that combine two or more of these three characteristics), and meta-
analyses of the results from multiple studies. By revisiting old questions
with new and better research methods, we hopefully will develop a more
sophisticated understanding of the familial and genetic causes of CD.

ACKNOWLEDGMENT

Preparation of this chapter was supported in part by National Institutes of
Health Grant AA00264.

REFERENCES

Amato, P. R. (2001). Children of divorce in the 1990s: An update of the Amato and Keith (1991)
    meta-analysis. *Journal of Family Psychology, 15*, 355–370.
American Psychiatric Association. (1987). *Diagnostic and statistical manual of mental disorders*
    (3rd ed., rev.). Washington, DC: Author.
American Psychiatric Association. (1994). *Diagnostic and statistical manual of mental disorders*
    (4th ed.). Washington, DC: Author.
Benjamin, J., Li, L., Patterson, C., Greenberg, B., Murphy, D., & Hamer, D. (1996). Population and
    familial association between the dopamine D4 receptor gene and measures of novelty seek-
    ing. *Nature Genetics, 12*, 81–84.
Burt, C. L. (1925). *The young delinquent.* New York: Appleton.
Burt, S. A., Krueger, R. F., McGue, M., & Iacono, W. G. (2001). Sources of comorbidity among atten-
    tion deficit/hyperactivity disorder, oppositional defiant disorder, and conduct disorder: The
    importance of shared environment. *Journal of Abnormal Psychology, 110*, 516–525.
Cadoret, R. J., Yates, W. R., Troughton, E., Woodworth, G., & Stewart, M. A. (1995). Genetic-
    environmental interaction in the genesis of aggressivity and conduct disorders. *Archives of
    General Psychiatry, 52*, 916–924.
Campbell, D. T., & Fiske, D. W. (1959). Convergent and discriminant validation by the multitrait–
    multimethod matrix. *Psychological Bulletin, 56*, 81–105.

Carey, G., & Goldman, D. (1997). The genetics of antisocial behavior. In D. M. Stoff, J. Breiling, & J. D. Maser (Eds.), *Handbook of antisocial behavior* (pp. 243–254). New York: Wiley.

Christ, M. A. G., Lahey, B. B., Frick, P. J., Russo, M. F., McBurnett, K., Loeber, R., Stouthamer-Loeber, M., & Green, S. (1990). Serious conduct problems in the children of adolescent mothers: Disentangling confounded correlations. *Journal of Consulting and Clinical Psychology, 58*, 840–844.

Cloninger, C. R., Christiansen, K. O., Reich, T., & Gottesman, I. I. (1978). Implications of sex differences in the prevalences of antisocial personality, alcoholism, and criminality for familial transmission. *Archives of General Psychiatry, 35*, 941–951.

Cloninger, C. R., & Gottesman, I. I. (1987). Genetic and environmental factors in antisocial behavior disorders. In S. A. Mednick, T. E. Moffitt, & S. A. Stack (Eds.), *The causes of crime: New biological approaches* (pp. 92–109). Cambridge, England: Cambridge University Press.

Collier, D. A., Curran, S., & Asherson, P. (2000). Mission: Not impossible? Candidate gene studies in child psychiatric disorders. *Molecular Psychiatry, 5*, 457–460.

Cronk, N. J., Slutske, W. S., Madden, P. A. F., Bucholz, K. K., Reich, W., & Heath, A. C. (2002). Emotional and behavioral problems among female twins: An evaluation of the equal environments assumption. *Journal of the American Academy of Child and Adolescent Psychiatry, 41*, 827–837.

Deater-Deckard, K., & Plomin, R. (1999). An adoption study of the etiology of teacher and parent reports of externalizing behavior problems in middle childhood. *Child Development, 70*, 144–154.

DiLalla, L. F., & Gottesman, I. I. (1989). Heterogeneity of causes for delinquency and criminality: Lifespan perspectives. *Development and Psychopathology, 1*, 339–349.

Eaves, L., Rutter, M., Silberg, J. L., Shillady, L., Maes, H., & Pickles, A. (2000). Genetic and environmental causes of covariation in interview assessments of disruptive behavior in child and adolescent twins. *Behavior Genetics, 30*, 321–334.

Eaves, L. J., Silberg, J. L., Meyer, J. M., Maes, H. H., Simonoff, E., Pickles, A., Rutter, M., Neale, M. C., Reynolds, C. A., Erikson, M. T., Heath, A. C., Loeber, R., Truett, K. R., & Hewitt, J. K. (1997). Genetics and developmental psychopathology: 2. The main effects of genes and environment on behavioral problems in the Virginia twin study of adolescent behavioral development. *Journal of Child Psychology and Psychiatry, 38*, 965–980.

Ebstein, R., Novick, O., Umansky, R., Priel, B., Osher, Y., Blaine, D., Bennett, E., Nemanov, L., Katz, M., & Belmaker, R. (1996). Dopamine D4 receptor (D4DR) exon III polymorphism associated with the human personality trait of novelty-seeking. *Nature Genetics, 12*, 78–80.

Eley, T. C., Lichtenstein, P., & Stevenson, J. (1999). Sex differences in the etiology of aggressive and nonaggressive antisocial behavior: Results from two twin studies. *Child Development, 70*, 155–168.

Emery, R. E., Waldron, M., Kitzmann, K. M., & Aaron, J. (1999). Delinquent behavior, future divorce or nonmarital childbearing, and externalizing behavior among offspring: A 14-year prospective study. *Journal of Family Psychology, 13*, 568–579.

Faraone, S. V., Doyle, A. E., Mick, E., & Biederman, J. (2001). Meta-analysis of the association between the 7-repeat allele of the dopamine D4 receptor gene and attention deficit hyperactivity disorder. *American Journal of Psychiatry, 158*, 1052–1057.

Fergusson, D. M. (1999). Prenatal smoking and antisocial behavior. *Archives of General Psychiatry, 56*, 223–224.

Fergusson, D. M., Horwood, L. J., & Lynskey, M. T. (1993). Maternal smoking before and after pregnancy: Effects on behavioral outcomes in middle childhood. *Pediatrics, 92*, 815–822.

Fergusson, D. M., Woodward, L. J., & Horwood, L. J. (1998). Maternal smoking during pregnancy and psychiatric adjustment in late adolescence. *Archives of General Psychiatry, 55*, 721–727.

Frick, P. J. (1993). Child conduct problems in a family context. *School Psychology Review, 22*, 376–385.

Frick, P. J., Lahey, B. B., Loeber, R., Stouthamer-Loeber, M., Christ, M. A. G., & Hanson, K. (1992). Familial risk factors to oppositional defiant disorder and conduct disorder: Parental psychopathology and maternal parenting. *Journal of Consulting and Clinical Psychology, 60,* 49–55.

Frick, P. J., Van Horn, Y., Lahey, B. B., Christ, M. A. G., Loeber, R., Hart, E. A., Tannenbaum, L., & Hanson, K. (1993). Oppositional defiant disorder and conduct disorder: A meta-analytic review of factor analyses and cross-validation in a clinic sample. *Clinical Psychology Review, 13,* 319–340.

Goldstein, R. B., Prescott, C. A., & Kendler, K. S. (2001). Genetic and environmental factors in conduct problems and adult antisocial behavior among adult female twins. *The Journal of Nervous and Mental Disease, 189,* 201–209.

Harris, J. R. (1995). Where is the child's environment? A group socialization theory of development. *Psychological Review, 102,* 458–489.

Healy, W. (1915). *The individual delinquent: A text-book of diagnosis and prognosis for all concerned in understanding offenders.* Boston: Little, Brown.

Jacobson, K. C., Prescott, C. A., & Kendler, K. S. (2000). Genetic and environmental influences on juvenile antisocial behaviour assessed at two occasions. *Psychological Medicine, 30,* 1315–1325.

Jacobson, K. C., Prescott, C. A., & Kendler, K. S. (2002). Sex differences in the genetic and environmental influences on the development of antisocial behavior. *Development and Psychopathology, 14,* 395–416.

Jacobson, K. C., Prescott, C. A., Neale, M. C., & Kendler, K. S. (2000). Cohort differences in genetic and environmental influences on retrospective reports of conduct disorder among male adult twins. *Psychological Medicine, 30,* 775–787.

Jang, K. L., Vernon, P. A., & Livesley, W. J. (2000). Personality disorder traits, family environment, and alcohol misuse: A multivariate behavioural genetic analysis. *Addiction, 95,* 873–888.

Kazdin, A. E. (1995). *Conduct disorders in childhood and adolescence.* New Haven, CT: Sage.

LaHoste, G. J., Swanson, J. M., Wigal, S. B., Glabe, C., Wigal, T., King, N., & Kennedy, J. L. (1996). Dopamine D4 receptor gene polymorphism is associated with attention deficit hyperactivity disorder. *Molecular Psychiatry, 1,* 121–124.

Lahey, B. B., Hartdagen, S. E., Frick, P. J., McBurnett, K., Connor, R., & Hynd, G. W. (1988). Conduct disorder: Parsing the confounded relation to parental divorce and antisocial personality. *Journal of Abnormal Psychology, 97,* 334–337.

Lyons, M. J., True, W. R., Eisen, S. A., Goldberg, J., Meyer, J. M., Faraone, S. V., Eaves, L. J., & Tsuang, M. T. (1995). Differential heritability of adult and juvenile antisocial traits. *Archives of General Psychiatry, 52,* 906–915.

McGuffin, P., Riley, B., & Plomin, R. (2001). Genomics and behavior: Toward behavioral genomics. *Science, 291,* 1232, 1249.

Mednick, S. A., Gabrielli, W. F., & Hutchings, B. (1984). Genetic influences in criminal convictions: Evidence from an adoption cohort. *Science, 224,* 891–894.

Meyer, J. M., Rutter, M., Silberg, J. L., Maes, H. H., Simonoff, E., Shillady, L. L., Pickles, A., Hewitt, J. K., & Eaves, L. J. (2000). Familial aggregation for conduct disorder symptomatology: The role of genes, marital discord and family adaptability. *Psychological Medicine, 30,* 759–774.

Moffitt, T. E. (1993). "Life-course-persistent" and "adolescence-limited" antisocial behavior: A developmental taxonomy. *Psychological Review, 100,* 674–701.

Moffitt, T. E., & Caspi, A. (2001). Childhood predictors differentiate life-course-persistent and adolescence-limited antisocial pathways among males and females. *Development and Psychopathology, 13,* 355–375.

Moffitt, T. E., Caspi, A., Rutter, M., & Silva, P. A. (2001). *Sex differences in antisocial behaviour: Conduct disorder, delinquency, and violence in the Dunedin Longitudinal Study.* Cambridge, England: Cambridge University Press.

Nadder, T. S., Silberg, J. L., Eaves, L. J., Maes, H. H., & Meyer, J. M. (1998). Genetic effects on ADHD symptomatology in 7- to 13-year olds twins: Results from a telephone survey. *Behavior Genetics, 28,* 83–99.

O'Connor, T. G., Caspi, A., DeFries, J. C., & Plomin, R. (2000). Are associations between parental divorce and children's adjustment genetically mediated? An adoption study. *Developmental Psychology, 36*, 429–437.

O'Connor, T. G., McGuire, S., Reiss, D., Hetherington, E. M., & Plomin, R. (1998). Co-occurrence of depressive symptoms and antisocial behavior in adolescence: A common genetic liability. *Journal of Abnormal Psychology, 107*, 27–37.

Plomin, R. (1995). Genetics and children's experiences in the family. *Journal of Child Psychology and Psychiatry, 36*, 33–68.

Rantakallio, P., Laara, E., Isohanni, M., & Moilanen, I. (1992). Maternal smoking during pregnancy and delinquency of the offspring: An association without causation? *International Journal of Epidemiology, 21*, 1106–1113.

Reckless, W. C., & Smith, M. (1932). *Juvenile delinquency.* New York: McGraw-Hill.

Rhee, S. H., & Waldman, I. D. (2002). Genetic and environmental influences on antisocial behavior: A meta-analysis of twin and adoption studies. *Psychological Bulletin, 128*, 490–529.

Robins, L. N. (1999). A 70-year history of conduct disorder: Variations in definition, prevalence, and correlates. In P. Cohen, C. Slomkowski, & L. Robins (Eds.), *Historical and geographical influences on psychopathology* (pp. 37–56). Mahwah, NJ: Lawrence Erlbaum Associates, Inc.

Rowe, D. C. (1994). *The limits of family influence: Genes, experience, and behavior.* New York: Guilford.

Silberg, J., Rutter, M., Meyer, J., Maes, H., Hewitt, J., Simonoff, E., Pickles, A., Loeber, R., & Eaves, L. (1996). Genetic and environmental influences on the covariation between hyperactivity and conduct disturbance in juvenile twins. *Journal of Child Psychology and Psychiatry, 37*, 803–816.

Simonoff, E., Pickles, A., Meyer, J., Silberg, J., & Maes, H. (1998). Genetic and environmental influences on subtypes of conduct disorder behavior in boys. *Journal of Abnormal Child Psychology, 26*, 495–509.

Slutske, W. S. (2001). The genetics of antisocial behavior. *Current Psychiatry Reports, 3*, 158–162.

Slutske, W. S., Eisen, S. A., Xian, H., True, W. R., Lyons, M. J., Goldberg, J., & Tsuang, M. T. (2001). A twin study of the association between pathological gambling and antisocial personality disorder. *Journal of Abnormal Psychology, 110*, 297–308.

Slutske, W. S., Heath, A. C., Dinwiddie, S. H., Madden, P. A. F., Bucholz, K. K., Dunne, M. P., Statham, D. J., & Martin, N. G. (1997). Modeling genetic and environmental influences in the etiology of conduct disorder: A study of 2,682 adult twin pairs. *Journal of Abnormal Psychology, 106*, 266–279.

Slutske, W. S., Heath, A. C., Dinwiddie, S. H., Madden, P. A. F., Bucholz, K. K., Dunne, M. P., Statham, D. J., & Martin, N. G. (1998). Common genetic risk factors for conduct disorder and alcohol dependence. *Journal of Abnormal Psychology, 107*, 363–374.

Slutske, W. S., Heath, A. C., Madden, P. A. F., Bucholz, K. K., Statham, D. J., & Martin, N. G. (2002). Personality and the genetic risk for alcohol dependence. *Journal of Abnormal Psychology, 111*, 124–133.

Sullivan, P. F., Eaves, L. J., Kendler, K. S., & Neale, M. C. (2001). Genetic case-control association studies in neuropsychiatry. *Archives of General Psychiatry, 58*, 1015–1024.

Taylor, J., Iacono, W. G., & McGue, M. (2000). Evidence for a genetic etiology of early-onset delinquency. *Journal of Abnormal Psychology, 109*, 634–643.

True, W. R., Heath, A. C., Scherrer, J. F., Xian, H., Lin, N., Eisen, S. A., Lyons, M. J., Goldberg, J., & Tsuang, M. (1999). Interrelationship of genetic and environmental influences on conduct disorder and alcohol and marijuana dependence symptoms. *American Journal of Medical Genetics (Neuropsychiatric Genetics), 88*, 391–397.

Wakschlag, L. S., Lahey, B. B., Loeber, R., Green, S. M., Gordon, R. A., & Leventhal, B. L. (1997). Maternal smoking during pregnancy and the risk of conduct disorder in boys. *Archives of General Psychiatry, 54*, 670–676.

Weissman, M. M., Warner, V., Wickramaratne, P. J., & Kandel, D. B. (1999). Maternal smoking during pregnancy and psychopathology in offspring followed to adulthood. *Journal of the American Academy of Child and Adolescent Psychiatry, 38,* 892–899.

Weitzman, M., Gortmaker, S., & Sobol, A. (1992). Maternal smoking and behavior problems of children. *Pediatrics, 90,* 342–349.

Young, S. E., Stallings, M. C., Corley, R. P., Krauter, K. S., & Hewitt, J. K. (2000). Genetic and environmental influences on behavioral disinhibition. *American Journal of Medical Genetics (Neuropsychiatric Genetics), 96,* 684–695.

7

Neuropsychological and Neuroendocrine Factors

Robert O. Pihl
Jonathan Vant
Jean-Marc Assaad
McGill University, Quebec, Canada

Our fascination with the brain's involvement in behavior is seemingly as old as humanity. Multiple trepanations, in which holes are gouged or pounded or punctured into the cranium, had one likely intent of altering behavior. Similarly, the various fluids produced by the body were seen by the ancient Greeks as the basis for an early theory of personality. For example, an excess of yellow bile was viewed as producing a pattern of behaviors that today might draw the label of *conduct disorder* (CD) or *oppositional defiant disorder* (ODD). Currently, we are in a period of resurgence of interest in the brain and behavior. This renewed interest is driven in part by the poor predictability of strictly sociological/psychological theories but mostly because of an explosion in new technologies for neuroscientific inquiry. This focus is further abetted by the burgeoning enthusiasm for genetic explanations also borne of paradigm shifting new technologies. In regard to the flood of genetic findings, the quintessential question remains: What are the affected mechanisms or structures that effect behavior? Although the rapid growth of this knowledge gives the impression of drinking from a fire hose and rampant enthusiasm abounds, a quote by Newton (*Oxford Dictionary of Quotations*, 1980) is quite germane. "We are," Newton said, "finding pretty pebbles on the beach while the great ocean of truth lies undiscovered before us" (p. 362). What follows is an attempt to count and order some pebbles. First, however, there are three caveats. We do not simply focus on those strategies that have investigated the psychobiology of CD and ODD. Healthy debate over the definitions of these concepts persists. Though perhaps clinically useful, the dichotomous and multisymptomatic nature of these terms is a bane to replicable scientific inquiry. Thus, what is required are more specific dependent variables. Hence, "physical aggression" is in essence added to the title of this chapter. A second caveat is that we liberally speculate regarding likely mechanisms, as meaning will ultimately be derived from whichever explanation proves to have staying power. The third and most important caveat involves the framework in which one reads and digests the following facts and speculations. The behaviors in question in this text are the result of multifactorial influences that are likely very interactive. Thus, it is imperative that one see the following as a part of a bigger picture and think in terms of contributing interacting factors at many levels of analysis.

NEUROPSYCHOLOGICAL ASPECTS

The Facts

A number of existent reviews are rather unanimous in the conclusion that many diagnosed with CD and aggressive individuals have an increased likelihood of displaying neuropsychological deficits. The clinical literature abounds with case histories of individuals who suffered various amounts of frontal lobe brain damage and then underwent a metamorphosis of behavior. The classical case of Phineas Gage (Harlow, 1868) is frequently quoted. Phineas was a young, friendly, formal, and highly conscientious railroad construction foreman who happened to get too close to an explosion and had a $3\frac{1}{2}$ foot iron rod blown through his left cheek under the eye and into the top of his head. Although seemingly not impaired intellectually (a common finding), the conservative Gage, after a quick recovery, displayed intemperate, irrelevant, profane, and capricious behavior. His physician at the time (Harlow, 1868, as cited in Stuss, Gow, & Hetherington, 1992) perceptively wrote "the equilibrium between his intellectual faculty and animal propensities had been destroyed." The "frontal lobe syndrome" (Mesulam, 1986) that Gage represents has come to define this increased argumentativeness, irritability, impulsivity, loss of social grace, and fundamental disregard for behavioral consequences that frequently follows frontal lobe damage. New enthusiasm in pointing to the frontal lobes and antisocial relationships emanates from neuroimaging and neuropsychological studies.

Neuroimaging

The iron rod that traversed through the brain of Gage has been shown using neuroimaging techniques of his skull (which now is displayed in the Smithsonian Museum) to have involved the ventral medial regions of both frontal lobes (H. Damasio, Grabowski, Frank, Galaburda, & Damasio, 1994). We find it interesting that in a study of Vietnam veterans it was found that subjects with frontal ventral medial lesions demonstrated the highest scores on an aggression/violence scale (Grafman et al., 1996). In one of the earliest imaging studies, Volkow and Tancredi (1987), compared four violent patients to four normal controls using positron emission tomography and found compromised function of frontal areas in the violent patients. In a follow-up study (Volkow et al., 1995) with a larger sample, seven of eight violent patients showed low brain frontal metabolism. This methodology has also revealed more frontal lobe abnormalities in murderers when compared to controls (Raine et al., 1994). Again, in a follow-up study (Raine et al., 1998) with a larger group (which seems endemic to this type of research), these experimenters found specific reduced functioning in the prefrontal cortex, the superior parietal gyrus, the left angular gyrus, and the corpus collosum. Further, they found that individuals who murdered impulsively tended to show more reduced left than right prefrontal functioning than so-called predatory killers (Raine et al., 1998). Using the technique of single photon emission computerized tomography, another study found that individuals who had displayed physically aggressive behavior in the prior 6 months displayed decreased prefrontal cortical activity as well as increased left temporal and limbic activity (Amen, Stubblefield, Carmichael, & Thisted, 1996). A similar finding was reported in pretrial psychiatric patients convicted of impulsive crimes (Sodderstrom, Tullberg, Wikkelso, Ekholm, & Forsman, 2000). Finally, one experimental study (Pietrini, Guazzelli, Basso, Jaffe, & Grafman, 2000) showed regional blood flow reductions in the ventral medial prefrontal cortex when healthy volunteers imagined aggressive scenarios versus control scenarios. In sum, the various neuroimaging techniques clearly point to aspects of the frontal lobes as being involved in aggressive behavior, but they are also notable for their current paucity. The bulk of the evidence supporting the role of frontal lobes and antisocial behavior is derived from neuropsychological studies.

Neuropsychological Findings

Numerous literature reviews of neuropsychological abnormalities in antisocial individuals unanimously conclude that deficits in cognitive functioning are involved in the regulation of aggressive behavior (Buikhuisen, 1988; Kandel & Freed, 1989; Moffit, 1990, 1993; Pennington & Benetto, 1993; Pennington & Ozonoff, 1996). Violent or antisocial individuals compared to controls have been shown to reflect some form of frontal lobe dysfunction on a wide variety of batteries and tests including the Halstead–Ratian Psychological Test Battery (Yeudall & Fromm-Auch, 1979); the Luria Nebraska Neuropsychological Battery (Bryant, Scott, Tori, & Golden, 1984); the Wisconsin

Card Sort Test (Krakowski et al., 1997); the Porteous Maze (Vaillant, Gristey, Pottier, & Kosmyna, 1999); Motor Restraint, Block Design, Vigilance, and Forbidden Toy tests (Giancola, Martin, Tarter, Pelham, & Moss, 1996); the Stroop test (Giancola, Mezzich, & Tarter, 1998); the Continuous Performance Test (Kruesi, Schmidt, Donnelly, Hibbs, & Hamburger, 1989); and the Self-Ordered Pointing and the Condition Association test (Séguin, Pihl, Harden, Tremblay, & Boulerice, 1995).

An illustrative neuropsychological study is that by Séguin et al. (1995) who gave a large battery of tests to a sample of adolescents whose physical aggressivity had been repeatedly assessed since age 6. Three groups were created: stable aggressives who continuously over the years had demonstrated aggressive behavior, unstable aggressives who occasionally had shown aggressive behavior, and nonaggressives. Of the 13 neuropsychological and cognitive measures tested, factor analysis yielded four discreet factors. These four factors were labeled *verbal learning, incidental spatial learning, tactile lateralization,* and *executive functions.* The adjusted means and standard errors for these neuropsychological factors by the aggressive groups are represented in Fig. 7.1. Stable aggressives were distinctive in their low scores on the verbal and the executive factor.

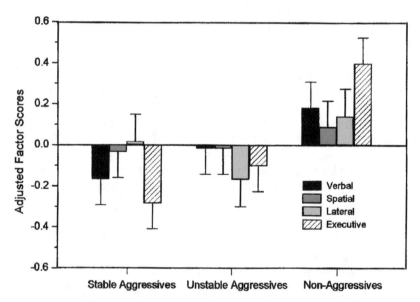

FIG. 7.1. Adjusted means and standard errors for regression factor scores by aggression group. *Note.* From "Cognitive and Neuropsychological Characteristics of Physically Aggressive Boys," by J. R. Séguin, R. O. Pihl, P. W. Harden, R. E. Tremblay, and B. Boulerice, 1995, *Journal of Abnormal Psychology, 104,* pp. 614–625. Copyright © 1995 by the American Psychological Association. Reprinted with permission.

Executive functioning is an abstract, often ill-defined (Zelazo, Carter, Reznick, & Frye, 1997) and multidefined (Robbins, 1998) concept. It is often used to refer to cognitive processes that include abstraction, sequencing, strategy formation, set shifting, and planning, which overall deal with the ability to plan, initiate, and maintain or alter goal-directed behavior. Executive functioning seems to require the utilization of the information held on line in working memory (Goldman-Rakic, 1992), the direction of attentional processes (Shallice, 1982), the inhibition of inappropriate responses (Shallice & Burgess, 1993), and finally the monitoring of behavior from a motivational affective context (A. Damasio, 1994). In spite of this breadth, the concept of executive functioning is highly useful, for it allows for not only the focus on deficits and their ramifications but also on individuals who perform well on these neuropsychological tests and the accrued benefits. For example, recent research has shown that tests of executive functioning successfully predict school performance over and above IQ at grade school, high school, and university level (Higgins, Peterson, Pihl, & Lee, 2001; Peterson, Pihl, Higgins, Séguin, & Tremblay, 2001). In addition, until differential functioning of frontal lobe areas and specificity of testing is available, the generalized term *executive cognitive functioning* (ECF) is a good summary of overall abilities traditionally associated with frontal lobe functioning. The high level of interconnectedness between frontal lobe structures (Pandya & Barnes, 1987) may in fact mean that clear localization and differentiation of function may not occur. Finally, ECF is also implicated in laboratory studies of aggression in which the intensity of administered shock to a presumed opponent under provocation has been related to low scores on various well-defined frontal lobe tests (Giancola & Zeichner, 1994; Hoaken, Assaad, & Pihl, 1998; Lau & Pihl, 1996; Lau, Pihl, & Peterson, 1995).

The other important cognitive factor derived from the Séguin et al. (1995) study was verbal learning. Verbal deficits have been a common finding in aggressive populations. There has been a plethora of research generally demonstrating that participants with CD and conduct disordered and delinquent participants score lower in verbal IQ than performance IQ (Lynam & Henry, 2001; Moffit, 1993; Moffit & Henry, 1991; Pennington & Ozonoff, 1996; Teichner & Golden, 2000). This verbal-performance discrepancy has also been found to be related to a greater hostile attributional bias in social problem solving (Wong & Cornell, 1999). Differences are stronger for those with CD than individuals diagnosed with attention deficit hyperactivity disorder (ADHD; Njiokiktjien & Verschoor, 1998) and are greatest in those with CD who are older and more delinquent (Hogan, 1999). Given this relative verbal deficit, a right hemispheric asymmetry is suspected and often confirmed (Raine & Scerbo, 1991). Even in highly sociable individuals, those with greater right frontal asymmetry have been shown to display more externalizing problems (Fox, Schmidt, Calkins, Rubin, & Coplan, 1996).

Further, girls diagnosed with ODD at $4\frac{1}{2}$ and 8 years of age have been shown to reflect greater right frontal compared to left frontal activation (Baving, Laucht, & Schmidt, 2000).

The general consistency of these verbal deficits and the differentiations that have been reported between individuals with CD and ADHD has drawn the suggestion that other mediating variables—not frontal lobe functioning per se—are involved in aggressive behavior (Pennington & Ozonoff, 1996). However, what is notable about the verbal and executive functioning factors illustrated in Fig. 7.1 are that when socioeconomic status is used as a covariate, the verbal deficits seen in the stable aggressive individuals evaporates. The executive functioning deficit, however, remains constant. In addition, in a further analysis of this data (Séguin, Boulerice, Harden, Tremblay, & Pihl, 1999) the relation between stable aggression and deficit in executive functioning remained after accounting for ADHD, memory, and intelligence.

EXPLANATORY MODELS

Recently, Miller and Cohen (2001) presented an integrated theory of prefrontal cortical functioning. These authors marshaled evidence to argue that the prefrontal cortex operates in top-down processing whenever behavior must be guided by internal states or intentions. The basic assumption of this model is that all brain processing is competitive; that is, pathways carrying different sources of information compete, with the winner expressing the outcome behavior. Thus, the prefrontal cortex, in a top-down fashion, provides bias signals that guide neural activity according to the goals, rules, and task demands perceived by the prefrontal cortex. The system therefore operates to bias the sensory system by directing attention, to effect the motor system by response selection and inhibition, and to facilitate other systems by supporting working memory and retrieval of long-term memory. In a sense, it reroutes or creates new pathways so as to avoid impulsive, inappropriate, and disorganized behavior. In support of the model, Miller and Cohen detailed the rich ascending, descending, and interconnecting pathways involved in the prefrontal cortex as well as how learned associations can come to establish the bases of this goal-directed behavior.

Just as the prefrontal cortex can be viewed as a system to which the metaphor ECF is applicable, other systems with strong relations to aggression and antisociality that the prefrontal cortex modulates also provide some explanatory power. Conceptualized systems that were previously discussed (Pihl & Peterson, 1995a) that have direct applicability to antisocial behavior and are interactional with the prefrontal cortex are the cue for reward system, and the cue for the punishment or threat system and the satiation system.

Cue for Reward System

When stimulated, this system results in psychomotor activity and psychologically in excitement, curiosity, pleasure, and hope. When activated, approach behavior toward biologically relevant stimuli occurs. The evolutionary purpose of this system is to force approach toward that which may be primarily reinforcing and thus potentially life sustaining. It has been well demonstrated that stimulation of this system either electrically or chemically can produce new learning (Fibiger & Phillips, 1988). Specifically implicated in the functioning of this system are dopaminergic pathways with high concentrations particularly in the ventral tegmental-nucleus accumbens brain areas (Koob, 1992; Wise & Bozart, 1987). The various stimulant drugs that activate this system are known to release dopamine and result in the motor behavior, associated learning, and psychological states previously mentioned. It is also notable that the high use and abuse of drugs that stimulate these areas are particularly prevalent in individuals diagnosed with antisocial personality disorders. Alcoholics, for example, are 21 times more likely than nonalcoholics to have been so labeled (Helzer & Pryzbeck, 1988).

There is a wide range of neurochemical individuality regarding the functioning of the dopaminergic system (Cravchik & Goldman, 2000). Pihl et al. (2001) recently, for example, demonstrated that in those individuals who after consuming an intoxicating dose of alcohol show a relatively high increased heart rate response display a selective high release of dopamine in the nucleus accumbens area. Assaad, Leiserson, Pihl, and Tremblay (1999) also recently showed that there is a strong relation between individuals who show this high heart rate response on alcohol challenge and the likelihood of a history of antisocial behavior involving stealing, physical aggression, and destruction of property when compared to low heart rate responders. The high heart rate responders in this study also scored significantly higher than low heart rate responders on the sensation seeking scales of Boredom Susceptibility and Disinhibition, as well as the Big 5 scale of Extraversion. These results are shown in Fig. 7.2. The behavioral characteristics displayed by the high heart rate responders have been related to individuals with CD (Quay, 1993), participants with early onset alcohol abuse (Cloninger, 1987), and individuals with antisocial personality disorder and alcoholics who exhibited antisocial behavior (Howard, Kivlahan, & Walker, 1997; Tremblay, Pihl, Vitaro, & Gagnon, 1994). Activation of this conceptualized system by alcohol in these individuals has been shown to result in increased craving for alcohol (Pihl, Giancola, & Peterson, 1994), high levels of self-reported alcohol consumption (Peter-

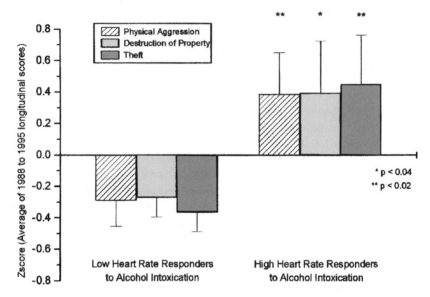

FIG. 7.2a. Heart rate responder group differences in the average of age 10 to 17 Delinquency subscale scores. *Note.* From "High Heart Rate Responders to Alcohol Intoxication: Personality Characteristics and Behavior Patterns," by J.-M. Assaad, V. Leiserson, R. O. Pihl, and R. Tremblay, 1999, Paper presented at the 22nd Annual Meeting of the Research Society on Alcoholism, Santa Barbara, CA.

son, Pihl, Séguin, & Finn, 1993), enhanced mood (Conrod, Peterson, & Pihl, 2001), and facilitated learning (Bruce, Shestowsky, Mayerovitch, & Pihl, 1999). Aggression, one could theorize, is potentiated by stimulation of this system first by increasing psychomotor approach behavior, which increases the likelihood of confrontation, and then by altering the subjective responses of pleasure and elation that accompany the stimulation of this system. The elevation of these affective states can also dampen cues of punishment that inhibit aggression. This effect has already received empirical support in a sample of criminal offenders in which the presentation of punishment cues resulted in response facilitation instead of inhibition when occurring after the establishment of a dominant response set for reward (Arnett & Newman, 2000).

Cue for Punishment System

Also fundamental to survival is the need for a system that evaluates and quickly responds to threat. This theorized system functions to inhibit ongoing behavior or prevent injury and can often take the form of fear and anxiety. These latter cues alert us to current, past, and future danger. Likely

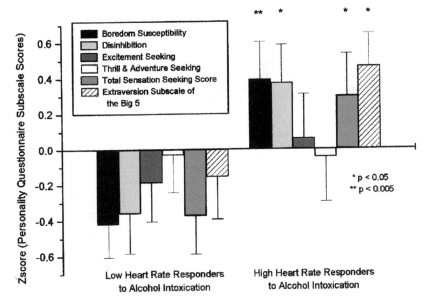

FIG. 7.2b. Heart rate responder group differences in Zucherman's Sensation Seeking subscales of Boredom Susceptibility, Disinhibition, Excitement Seeking, Thrill and Adventure Seeking, and Total Sensation Seeking score, as well as the Extraversion subscale of Goldberg's Adjective Markers of the Big Five. *Note.* From "High Heart Rate Responders to Alcohol Intoxication: Personality Characteristics and Behavior Patterns," by J.-M. Assaad, V. Leiserson, R. O. Pihl, and R. Tremblay, 1999, Paper presented at the 22nd Annual Meeting of the Research Society on Alcoholism, Santa Barbara, CA.

guided by the prefrontal cortex, certain neurotransmitters can stimulate or inhibit the functioning of this threat system. In the case of aggression, its activation typically provides an inhibitory role. The increased propensity for aggressive responding following the inhibition of the threat system can be exemplified through the alcohol–violence relation.

Alcohol and violence readily mix. A survey of crime statistics worldwide (Murdoch, Pihl, & Ross, 1990) found that alcohol was present in approximately half of murders, assaults, and rapes, which is basically double the frequency of nonviolent alcohol-related crimes. These statistics have been replicated in numerous other studies (Roizen, 1997) and cover the gamut of violent behaviors. Notable is the fact that victims of violence also have been found to frequently have been intoxicated. Laboratory studies with challenge procedures further confirm this alcohol–aggression relation (Bushman, 1997; Bushman & Cooper, 1990). Many explanations have been offered for this relation (see Giancola, 2000). Among those is the notion illustrated in Fig. 7.3 of how alcohol inhibits activation of the threat system, thus negating responsivity to possible negative consequences of violent behavior. This is true

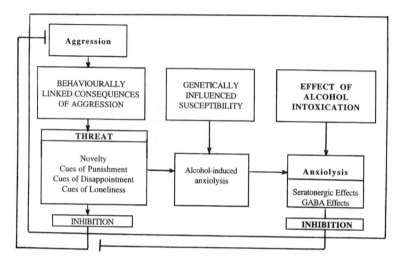

FIG. 7.3. Alcohol's inhibition of the threat system and its potential effect on aggression. *Note.* From "A Biosocial Model of the Alcohol–Aggression Relationship," by R. O. Pihl, J. B. Peterson, and M. A. Lau, 1993. Reprinted with permission from *Journal of Studies on Alcohol*, Supplement No. *11*, pp. 128–139, 1993. Copyright by Alcohol Research Documentation, Inc., Rutgers Center of Alcohol Studies, Piscataway, NJ 08854.

both in the case of a perpetrator and the victim who places oneself in harm's way. Substantial evidence has been marshaled to support this view (Pihl & Peterson, 1995b; Pihl, Peterson, & Lau, 1993) involving both animal and human studies in both laboratory and natural settings. We find it interesting that there is evidence that aggressive individuals remain aware of the consequences of their behavior (Pihl et al., 1993); however, prospective consequences do not seem to guide behavior (Zeichner & Pihl, 1979, 1980). The argument of the illustrated model is that potential aversive consequences of acting aggressively tend to maintain sociability even in the face of provocation. Simply perceived negative consequences of behavior that would activate the threat system are dampened by alcohol and other similar drugs. The importance of the amygdala/hippocampus and the prefrontal cortex in the operation of this threat system has been detailed with sensory experiences being labeled as *threatening* or *promising* via amygdaloid functions (Kling & Brothers, 1992). Pihl and Peterson (1995a) previously speculated that if individuals are appropriately socialized their own potential aggressive behavior is in fact a cue for punishment and should elicit fear and anxiety. This of course is dependent on the level of socialization, and thus, some individuals will be highly inhibited and some not at all. A general lack of socialization training and absence of meaningful external controls particularly during periods of early developmental rebellion would seem to contribute to this latter condition. It is suggested that such socialization is required at a very early age, as the onset of physical aggression is seen in most children by the end of their 2nd year after birth, and most learn to inhibit physical aggression by school entry (Tremblay et al., 1999). As we have stated previously it is not so much that aggression is learned but rather that control of aggression is not learned, and the relevant control systems in this case the threat system is not sufficiently developed (Pihl & Peterson, 1995a).

Satiation System

Rewards for positive reinforcement are consequences that increase the future likelihood of behaviors and are not the same as cues that indicate that such rewards are forthcoming. The receipt of primary rewards result in satiation and a cessation of behaviors, whereas cues for rewards produce approach behavior and accompanying positive affect. Ancient serotonergic systems that guide neural development and organization throughout the brain also operate on basic reward systems (Soubrie, 1986; Spoont, 1992). We analogized the role of this serotonergic system to the maestro of an orchestra who must meld constituent parts into a harmonious unit. The functioning of this system has been implicated in many studies investigating violent behavior. This has been demonstrated in numerous studies with successful suicide victims (Mann, Arango, & Underwood, 1990), in individuals with poor impulse control (Linnoila et al., 1983), violent recidivistic criminals (Virkkunen & Linnoila, 1993), and in children who display cruelty toward animals (Kruesi et al., 1990). It is likely that depleted 5-hydroxytryptamine (5-HT) levels in certain brain areas result in increased saliency of behavior activation induced by cues of either punishment or reward with a decrease in behavioral control. Thus, the individual who is low in serotonergic functioning would often appear irritable, particularly reactive to sensory input, and hyporesponsive to cues of reward and punishment. Because many different motivational systems are affected by 5-HT levels, the depleted individual can simultaneously be behaviorally anxious and impulsive. Thus, with the lack of integration between systems resulting from dysfunctions in the serotonergic system, anxiety would likely be ineffective in controlling behavior.

NEUROENDOCRINE FACTORS

The Facts

Neuroendocrine factors in disruptive behavior disorders have been investigated from primarily two different perspectives. Most of the research in this area has been with regard to gonadal androgens, primarily testosterone, and their possible role in aggressive behavior. The bulk of the remainder of the literature deals with adrenal hormones such as cortisol and the role they may play as a mediator in aggressive behavior.

There is a strong body of evidence that suggests a relation between hormones (usually testosterone) and socially disruptive behaviors such as CD, ODD, and physical aggression. The main hypothesis driving this research is that a person's level of a given hormone can influence directly how aggressive this person will act. The simplistic rationale, particularly with regard to androgens, can be summarized as follows: "Males have both higher concentrations of androgens and higher levels of aggressive behavior than females. Therefore, androgens are suggested to be involved in the etiology of aggressive behavior" (Brain & Susman, 1997, p. 317). However, in one review, Archer (1991) concluded that although evidence exists for the androgen–aggression relation in nonhuman mammals, the human evidence to date is inconclusive. In human adults, comparisons between groups of defined low and high aggression tend to reveal that the more aggressive group has higher testosterone levels. However, correlations are low, particularly for trait measures, although they are somewhat higher when aggressiveness ratings are made by others in the person's environment (Archer, 1994).

Some recent representative studies demonstrating a positive relation between aggression and serum testosterone levels have shown that violent sexual offenders had significantly higher testosterone levels than nonviolent sexual offenders (Brooks & Reddon, 1996), that there is a positive correlation between testosterone and the giving and receiving of aggression in the context of social interactions (Sanchez-Martin et al., 2000), and that judo contestants with higher testosterone levels demonstrated a greater number of offensive behaviors (threats, fights, and attacks) during competition (Salvador, Suay, Martinez-Sanchis, Simon, & Brain, 1999); similar results have been reported by several authors (Aromeki, Lindman, & Eriksson, 1999; Gerra, 1997; Raesaenen et al., 1999; Soler, Vinayak, & Quadagno, 2000; Stalenheim, Eriksson, von Knorring, & Wide, 1998). The effects of testosterone on aggression in females has also been explored. Aggression and testosterone have been correlated in patients with bulimia nervosa but not in normal controls (Cotrufo et al., 2000), and testosterone levels have been related to criminal violence and aggressive dominance among female inmates (Dabbs & Hargrove, 1997), which replicated earlier findings involving male inmates (Dabbs, Carr, Frady, & Riad, 1995).

Also of interest to researchers has been the potential for increased aggression when a person artificially increases the amount of testosterone in their body. Pope and his colleagues have begun to test the effects of supraphysiologic doses of androgens on aggressive behavior; in one study (Pope, Kouri, & Hudson, 2000), these researchers gave participants doses of testosterone rising to 600mg/wk and demonstrated increased aggressive scores on a laboratory aggression task and on a Verbal Hostility scale. These results allowed the researchers to conclude that low doses of testosterone (300mg/wk) had little effect, whereas a high dosage (600mg/wk) can have prominent effects on aggression. Similar results on the same laboratory aggression task have been found using a gradually increasing dose of testosterone cypionate (Kouri, Lukas, Pope, & Oliva, 1995). Finally, in a sample of prisoners, the research team of Pope, Kouri, Powell, Campbell, and Katz (1996) discovered that 2 of 133 cases involved crimes that appeared to be induced by anabolic steroid usage, demonstrating the rare yet potentially significant effects of supraphysiologic androgen usage.

These and related studies seem to lend support to a testosterone–aggression relation. However, there is also considerable contradictory evidence. For example, Schaal, Tremblay, Soussignan, and Susman (1996) found that boys with high physical aggression from age 6 to 12 had lower testosterone levels at age 13 and were less liked and performed less well in school than low-aggressive boys. It appears that the aggression testosterone relation may be unstable in early to middle adolescence, casting doubt on any lifetime consistency for the testosterone–aggression relation. Other studies (Campbell, Muncer, & Odber, 1997; Susman & Ponirakis, 1997) have reported no significant findings for testosterone and antisocial behavior for adolescent boys. The results of research with females are equally inconsistent. Dougherty, Bjork, Moeller, and Swann (1997) found that during the menstrual cycle, despite fluctuations in testosterone levels, aggressive responses to provocation using a laboratory aggression task were unchanged. Using the same methodology (Allen, Dougherty, Rhoades, & Cherek, 1996), no significant relation was found between testosterone and aggressive responding for both men and women.

Whereas most studies involving the role of hormones in disruptive behavior have focused on physical aggression, some studies have considered diagnostic categories. Chance, Brown, Dabbs, and Casey (2000) found elevated levels of testosterone in boys with disruptive behavior disorders (CD, ODD, and ADHD). In this study, testosterone accounted for 16% of the variance in aggressiveness. Relatedly, van Goozen et al. (2000) found that children with ODD had higher levels of the androgen dehydroepiandrosterone sulphate (DHEAS) than psychiatric and normal controls. DHEAS levels proved to be a better differentiator between ADHD and ODD than did the Child Behavior Checklist (Achenbach, 1991). In another recent study (van Goozen, Matthys, Cohen-Kettenis, Thijssen, & van Engeland, 1998), CD boys had higher levels of DHEAS than normal controls, and DHEAS was correlated with the intensity of aggression and teacher and parent ratings of delinquency. An interesting finding in this particular study was that there were no significant results found for testosterone, suggesting the possible importance of adrenal as opposed to gonadal androgens in aggression in young boys.

A large portion of the remaining hormone–aggression literature deals with the relation between adrenal hormones and aggression. The focus of this research is on both the activity of the hypothalamic pituitary adrenal axis and the role of cortisol. Some representative findings are that boys with both CD and anxiety disorder have been shown to display higher cortisol levels than boys with only CD, as well as less police contacts and lower ratings of aggressiveness (McBurnett et al., 1991; McBurnett, Lahey, Rathouz, & Loeber, 2000); furthermore, there is a negative correlation between antisocial behavior and cortisol when ODD boys are compared to normal controls (van Goozen, Matthys, Cohen-Kettenis, Gispen-de Wied, et al., 1998). However, just like the testosterone literature, the findings regarding cortisol are also contradictory. For instance, Gerra (1997) found that cortisol was high in aggressive participants. Such discrepancies may be related to the type of aggressivity (McBurnett, Pfifner, Capasso, Lahey, & Loeber, 1997).

It does appear, however, that both testosterone and cortisol play some role in the manifestation of aggressive behavior (Brain & Susman, 1997). In fact, the research of Dabbs, Jurkovic, and Frady (1991) points to the possible interaction between the two hormones. These researchers demonstrated that a link between testosterone and cortisol may exist in that the effect of testosterone on aggression was most pronounced in offenders who had low salivary cortisol.

Hormones can also affect neurocognitive functions (Erlanger, Kutner, & Jacobs, 1999), and this may be another pathway through which the neuroendocrine factors described previously affect aggressive behaviors. However, much of this research focuses on memory and verbal and spatial cognitive abilities, as well as on an older population. At present it is difficult to draw any clear conclusions concerning how different hormone levels impact on different cognitive abilities (i.e., executive functioning) in a younger population. Nevertheless, Dohnanyiova, Ostatnikova, and Laznibatova (2000) found intellectually gifted boys to have lower mean testosterone levels compared to control boys. In an older population, this relation may be different, as increased total testosterone was associated with increased fluid intelligence in healthy older men (Aleman et al., 2001). In addition, both low and high levels of testosterone are associated with poorer performance on tests of spatial cognition (Sternbach, 1998). Adding to the difficulties in drawing clear conclusions from this body of literature, Sternbach (2000) stated that the complex relation between testosterone levels and cognitive function is influenced by multiple other hormonal and nonhormonal variables.

As for cortisol, results are somewhat more consistent in finding that increased levels are associated with poorer cognitive performance. For example, high levels of cortisol have been linked to memory impairments (Greendale, Kritz-Silverstein, Seeman, & Barrett-Connor, 2000). In older adults, an increased level of cortisol was related to decreased performance gains in fluid ability performance (Kelly & Hayslip, 2000) and predicted worsened category fluency in postmenopausal women (Greendale et al., 2000). At the other end of the age spectrum, results from a study by Dessens et al. (1998) suggest that prenatal exposure to the anticonvulsant drugs phenobarbital and phenytoin, which disturb steroid hormone balances in the fetus, affects holistic spatial processing. As for experimentally induced changes in hormone levels, the chronic administration of hydrocortisone in normal males leads to deficits in selected neuropsychological tests that are sensitive to frontal lobe dysfunction (Young, Sahakian, Robbins, & Cowen, 1999). Finally, a study (Vedhara, Hyde, Gilchrist, Tytherleigh, & Plummer, 2000) investigating the relation between environmentally induced acute changes in cortisol and memory in students found that a reduction in cortisol was associated with enhanced short-term memory, although no significant effects on auditory verbal working memory were found.

Given the inconsistency of results regarding the relation between hormones and aggression, many researchers have begun to look at alternate explanations of the role of increased testosterone and how this may lead to aggressive behavior in certain situations. It has been demonstrated, for example, that in a competitive situation testosterone for winners rose relative to losers, and testosterone continued on this trend leading up to the next match (Booth, Shelley, Mazur, Tharp, & Kittok, 1989; Mazur, Booth, & Dabbs, 1992). These observations have led to the conclusion that testosterone affects social dominance. The argument is that high levels of endogenous testosterone seem to lead to behavior that is intended to dominate or to enhance one's status over other people. This dominant behavior can be aggressive but is often typically expressed nonaggressively (Mazur & Booth, 1998).

Explanatory Models

The findings regarding neuroendocrine factors, although often confusing and contradictory, demonstrate that there is a role played by hormones in disruptive behavior disorders. Exactly why these effects exist and the likely mechanisms remains the subject of discussion. It may be that differential hormone levels are the result of events at the genetic level, or the developmental level, or the social/environmental level. In a recent study (Comings, Chen, Wu, & Muhleman, 1999), the genetics of androgens in ADHD and CD were investigated via the role of the glutamine and glycine alleles at the androgen receptor (AR) gene. It was found that the AR gene accounted for only 2.1% of the variance for ADHD scores, indicating a modest role for genetic variation of the AR gene. Another study (Harris, Vernon, & Boomsma,

1998) looked at the heritability of testosterone by examining adolescent twins and their parents to determine the heritability of total plasma testosterone levels. Correlations of testosterone levels were higher in monozygotic than dizygotic twins; no relation was found between fathers and their children, whereas only moderate correlations existed between mothers and their children. In spite of substantial heritability, Harris et al. suggested that any phenotypic correlations among testosterone and behavior (including aggressive behavior) are likely due to environmental factors or a model of phenotypic causation in which reciprocal interaction applies.

Because hormones play a major role in the development of the human body, it is important to examine how differences in hormone levels at early developmental stages may play a role in altering the organizational effects of these hormones. It is well known that the presence of gonadal steroids during early life effects structural and organizational changes in the brain (Brain & Susman, 1997; Coe & Lubach, 2000; Hiemke et al., 1992). In one illustrated study (Berenbaum & Resnick, 1997), it was demonstrated that participants with congenital adrenal hyperplasia who were exposed to high levels of androgens in prenatal and early postnatal periods had different levels of aggression, suggesting that early androgens may contribute to variability in human aggression. However, in his early review, Archer (1991) noted that clear data was lacking to sufficiently explore the possible role of the neonatal organizing effects of androgens. More recently, Brain and Susman (1997) noted that socialization processes may override or alter the influence of hormones on behavior at several points during development.

Another developmental aspect to explore is how hormone levels can be affected by stressors experienced prenatally. Several studies have explored the effects of prenatal exposure to various stressors on the cortisol levels of infants. Exposure to alcohol, tobacco, and cocaine seem to have differing effects on cortisol levels in infants. Prenatal exposure to alcohol has been related to elevated basal cortisol levels, exposure to cocaine to lower basal cortisol levels, and heavy alcohol exposure to elevated poststress cortisol levels in eighty-three 13-month-old inner city African American infants (Jacobson, Bihun, & Chiodo, 1999). Prenatal psychosocial factors including prenatal stress are significantly associated with plasma levels of adrenocorticotropic hormone, betaE, and cortisol (Wadhwa, Dunkel-Schetter, Chicz-DeMet, & Porto, 1996). Infants prenatally exposed to alcohol and cigarettes have shown higher prestressor cortisol levels at 2 months (Ramsay, Bendersky, & Lewis, 1996), whereas infants exposed to cocaine had lower cortisol responses to both invasive and noninvasive stressful events (Magnano, Gardner, & Karmel, 1992).

In examining possible environmental roles in hormone levels, the question of cause and effect can be turned around. Instead of looking at what hormones cause what behaviors and what environmental stimuli lead to these hormonal fluctuations, it is also possible to examine what environmental stimuli lead to what behaviors and which of these behaviors lead to changes in hormone levels. The reciprocal nature of the hormone–behavior relation in which behavior can lead to hormone change, which can in turn lead to altered behavior, has been the subject of a number of studies. Testosterone, for example, has been shown to rise before a competitive event, as if in anticipation, and to rise in winners relative to losers at the conclusion of the competition (Mazur & Booth, 1998). It would seem that gaining or maintaining high rank boosts testosterone and encourages even more competitive behavior. Losing depresses testosterone and encourages less dominant and thus less competitive behavior.

Several studies have manipulated testosterone levels and social dominance hierarchies in animals. For instance, when male prepubertal lambs are given testosterone, they show an increase in their tendency to establish dominance relations (Ruiz-de-la-Torre & Manteca, 1999). In rats, an increase in dominance behavior due to exogenous testosterone can be reversed by serotonergic agonists (Bonson, Johnson, Fiorella, Rabin, & Winter, 1994; Bonson & Winter, 1992). Castrating male rats leads to a decline in aggressiveness accompanied by a loss of social dominance that can be reversed with subsequent implantation of testosterone (Albert, Walsh, Gorzalka, Siemens, & Louie, 1986).

Studies with olive baboons have shown that when the psychological advantages associated with high social status in a stable environment are lost, endocrine efficiency that was also associated with high social status is also lost. In other words, when in socially stable conditions, high ranking males have high testosterone titers during stress and low basal cortisol. In unstable social conditions, previously high ranking males have elevated basal cortisol and decreased testosterone titers during stress (Sapolsky, 1983). Eberhart, Keverne, and Meller (1980) demonstrated that social status can have an influence on endocrine status. Male talapoin monkeys who became dominant had increases in testosterone, whereas those who became subordinate tended to have decreases in testosterone (Eberhart et al., 1980). Higley et al. (1996) proposed a model in which the mediating factor amongst monkeys with high testosterone who are classified either as dominant or as aggressive may be their serotonin levels. Those high in testosterone but with average serotonin levels may be more assertive in ways that characterize socially dominant males, whereas those who are high in testosterone but with lower than average serotonin functioning may display impaired impulse control. Because testosterone may increase the propensity for aggression, those who have lowered impulse control due to lower serotonin levels may more readily become involved in an aggressive act and would have more trouble stopping an aggressive act. Individuals with normal serotonin levels, able to control their impulses and behave aggressively only when demanded by the situation, would thus maintain dominant status (Higley et al., 1996).

Social dominance theory has received support from experimental results with humans. It has been found that testosterone is significantly positively correlated with peer ratings of dominance for boys, whereas those boys high in physical aggression were perceived as less dominant and had lower testosterone levels (Schaal et al., 1996; Tremblay et al., 1997). In a later study (Tremblay et al., 1998), it was found that testosterone and body mass index predicted social dominance, whereas body mass alone correlated with physical aggression. The finding of lower testosterone levels in 13-year-old participants who had been previously rated as highly aggressive from ages 6 to 12 could be due to social rejection. Another possibility is that androgen levels in these children were depressed because of stable anxiety, which led to chronic adrenal axis activity and the relative suppression of the testicular axis and gonadal androgens (Schaal et al., 1996). Such an explanation would be in agreement with findings presented earlier that demonstrated boys with anxiety disorders to be high in cortisol only when they had comorbid CD (McBurnett et al., 1991). Socialization of another form may be involved in the relation between a hyporesponsive hypothalamic-pituitary-adrenocortical axis activity and CD. Resurrecting the discarded *Diagnostic and Statistical Manual of Mental Disorders* (3rd ed.; American Psychiatric Association, 1980) CD subclassification of undersocialized aggressive CD (characterized by callous behavior, absence of feelings of guilt or remorse, and an absence of empathy or bonding with others), it may be that anxiety level differentiates those with CD who are undersocialized versus those that are socialized. This would help explain the cortisol–aggression relation with individuals without comorbid anxiety disorders. Relatedly, one study (Deutsch & Erickson, 1989) found significantly higher life stressors at age 2 and 4 were the best predictor of whether a child belonged to the undersocialized or socialized CD group.

As previously described, the expression of a violent act can expose a potential aggressor to threat or punishment in the form of interpersonal retaliation or societal revenge. Thus, fear and anxiety produced in response to such a threat can encourage appropriately socialized individuals to avoid harm and thus abstain from aggressive responding. However, individuals who do not display such a response in the face of threat, either due to low levels of physiological arousal (Raine & Liu, 1998) or to substance-induced inhibition of the threat system (Pihl et al., 1993), will be less likely to inhibit their aggressive responding. This would be consistent with such findings as a negative correlation between antisocial behavior and cortisol (van Goozen, Matthys, Cohen-Kettenis, & Gispen-de Wied, et al., 1998).

Conversely, increased physiological arousal can be related to increased aggressive behavior (Rule & Nesdale, 1976; Tannenbaum & Zillman, 1975), conforming to the notion of visceral influences on behavior (Loewenstein, 1996). For example, some perpetrators of domestic violence demonstrate increased experimentally induced, fear-related behavioral responses as compared to controls, confirming their self-reported increases in symptoms of autonomic arousal, sense of fear, and loss of control at the time of the violence (George et al., 2000). On a psychophysiological level, increased heart rate, blood pressure, and skin conductance have also been observed both before and during aggressive behaviors (Dengerink, 1971; Donnerstein, 1980). This would be consistent with such findings as a high cortisol level in aggressive participants (Gerra, 1997).

Taking both of these bodies of literature into consideration, an inverted U-shaped relation between aggression and arousal can be proposed in which intermediate levels of arousal are most adaptive on average, and too low or too high levels increase the propensity for violent responding. Taken within this context, coherence can be found in the otherwise contradictory cortisol–aggression findings previously discussed. This model also resolves the apparent paradox in the literature, implicating both increased and decreased arousal or anxiety in increased aggressive responding.

Supporting this U-shaped relation, a study by Harden, Pihl, Vitaro, Gendreau, and Tremblay (1995) reported that aggressive individuals could be regrouped in terms of anxious and nonanxious. Anxious aggressive boys displayed significant increases in responsivity to a stressor, whereas the nonanxious aggressives did not. Thus, increases in the likelihood of aggressive behaviors would be related to decreased anxiety or sensitivity to cues of punishment (Quay, 1988) in nonanxious aggressive participants and to increased arousal interfering with the cognitive processes that normally inhibit reactive aggression (Tyson, 1998) in anxious aggressive participants.

GENERAL SUMMARY

Both areas of study, especially the studies of testosterone's role in aggression, are replete with contradictory results and are confusing to decipher when attempting to draw conclusions. It is clear that research is still needed in these areas, and preferably research will move forward with increased consistency. Consistent definitions of *aggression, dominance,* and what exactly constitutes the various *behavior disorders* are needed to ensure findings are in relation to the same variables and thus comparable. Measurements of hormones also need to be consistent so that comparison of results can be made accurately and with assurances that what is being compared to each other is consistent in terms of method of sampling and analysis. Nevertheless, it is clear from the previously detailed findings that neuropsychological and neuroendocrine factors play an important role in the antisocial behavior of children and adolescents.

REFERENCES

Achenbach, T. M. (1991). *Manual for the Child Behavior Checklist and 1991 Profile.* Burlington: University of Vermont, Department of Psychiatry.

Albert, D. J., Walsh, M. L., Gorzalka, B. B., Siemens, Y., & Louie, H. (1986). Testosterone removal in rats results in a decrease in social aggression and a loss of social dominance. *Physiology and Behavior, 36*, 401–407.

Aleman, A., de Vries, W. R., Koppeschaar, H. P. F., Osman-Dualeh, M., Verhaar, H. J. J., Samson, M. M., Bol, E., & de Haan, E. H. F. (2001). Relationship between circulating levels of sex hormones and insulin-like growth factor-1 and fluid intelligence in older men. *Experimental Aging Research, 27*, 283–291.

Allen, T. J., Dougherty, D. M., Rhoades, H. M., & Cherek, D. R. (1996). A study of male and female aggressive responding under conditions providing an escape response. *The Psychological Record, 46*, 651–664.

Amen, D. G., Stubblefield, M., Carmichael, B., & Thisted, R. (1996). Brain SPECT findings and aggressiveness. *Annals of Clinical Psychiatry, 8*, 129–137.

American Psychiatric Association. (1980). *Diagnostic and statistical manual of mental disorders* (3rd ed.). Washington, DC: Author.

Archer, J. (1991). The influence of testosterone on human aggression. *British Journal of Psychology, 82*, 1–28.

Archer, J. (1994). Testosterone and aggression. *Journal of Offender Rehabilitation, 21*, 3–25.

Arnett, P. A., & Newman, J. P. (2000). Gray's three-arousal model: An empirical investigation. *Personality & Individual Differences, 28*, 1171–1189.

Aromeki, A. S., Lindman, R. E., & Eriksson, C. J. P. (1999). Testosterone, aggressiveness, and antisocial personality. *Aggressive Behavior, 25*, 113–123.

Assaad, J.-M., Leiserson, V., Pihl, R. O., & Tremblay, R. (1999, June). *High heart rate responders to alcohol intoxication: Personality characteristics and behavior patterns.* Paper presented at the 22nd annual meeting of the Research Society on Alcoholism, Santa Barbara, CA.

Baving, L., Laucht, M., & Schmidt, M. H. (2000). Oppositional children differ from healthy children in frontal brain activation. *Journal of Abnormal Child Psychology, 28*, 267–275.

Berenbaum, S. A., & Resnick, S. M. (1997). Early androgen effects on aggression in children and adults with congenital adrenal hyperplasia. *Psychoneuroendocrinology, 22*, 505–515.

Bonson, K. R., Johnson, R. G., Fiorella, D., Rabin, R. A., & Winter, J. C. (1994). Serotonergic control of androgen-induced dominance. *Pharmacology, Biochemistry and Behavior, 49*, 313–322.

Bonson, K. R., & Winter, J. C. (1992). Reversal of testosterone-induced dominance by the serotonergic agonist quipazine. *Pharmacology, Biochemistry and Behavior, 42*, 809–813.

Booth, A., Shelley, G., Mazur, A., Tharp, G., & Kittok, R. (1989). Testosterone, and winning and losing in human competition. *Hormones and Behavior, 23*, 556–571.

Brain, P. F., & Susman, E. J. (1997). Hormonal aspects of aggression and violence. In D. M. Stoff, J. Breiling, & J. D. Masser (Eds.), *Handbook of antisocial behavior* (pp. 314–323). New York: Wiley.

Brooks, J. H., & Reddon, J. R. (1996). Serum testosterone in violent and non-violent young offenders. *Journal of Clinical Psychology, 52*, 475–483.

Bruce, K. R., Shestowsky, J. S., Mayerovitch, J. I., & Pihl, R. O. (1999). Motivational effects of alcohol on memory consolidation and heart rate in social drinkers. *Alcoholism: Clinical and Experimental Research, 23*, 693–701.

Bryant, E. T., Scott, M. L., Tori, C. D., & Golden, C. J. (1984). Neuropsychological deficits, learning disability, and violent behavior. *Journal of Consulting and Clinical Psychology, 52*, 323–324.

Buikhuisen, W. (1988). Chronic juvenile delinquency: A theory. In W. Buikhuisen & S. A. Mednick (Eds.), *Explaining criminal behaviour: Interdisciplinary approaches* (pp. 27–47). Leiden, The Netherlands: Brill.

Bushman, B. J. (1997). Effects of alcohol on human aggression: Validity of proposed explanations. In M. Galanter (Ed.), *Recent developments in alcoholism. V. 13 Alcohol and violence: Epidemiology, neurobiology, psychology, family issues* (pp. 227–243). New York: Plenum.

Bushman, B. J., & Cooper, H. M. (1990). Effects of alcohol on human aggression: An integrative review. *Psychological Bulletin, 107*, 341–354.

Campbell, A., Muncer, S., & Odber, J. (1997). Aggression and testosterone: Testing a bio-social model. *Aggressive Behavior, 23*, 229–238.

Chance, S. E., Brown, R. T., Dabbs, J. M., Jr., & Casey, R. (2000). Testosterone, intelligence and behavior disorders in young boys. *Personality and Individual Differences, 28*, 437–445.

Cloninger, C. R. (1987). Neurogenetic adaptive mechanisms in alcoholism. *Science, 236*, 410–416.

Coe, C. L., & Lubach, G. R. (2000). Prenatal influences on neuroimmune set points in infancy. In A. Conti & G. J. M. Maestroni (Eds.), *Neuroimmunomodulation: Perspectives at the new millennium. Annals of the New York Academy of Sciences, Vol. 917* (pp. 468–477). New York: New York Academy of Sciences.

Comings, D. E., Chen, C., Wu, S., & Muhleman, D. (1999). Association of the androgen receptor gene (AR) with ADHD and conduct disorder. *NeuroReport, 10*, 1589–1592.

Conrod, P., Peterson, J., & Pihl, R. (2001). Reliability and validity of alcohol-induced heart rate decrease as a measure of sensitivity to the stimulant properties of alcohol. *Psychopharmacology, 157*(1), 20–30.

Cotrufo, P., Monteleone, P., d'Istria, M., Fuschino, A., Serno, I., & Maj, M. (2000). Aggressive behavioral characteristics and endogenous hormones in women with bulimia nervosa. *Neuropsychobiology, 42*, 58–61.

Cravchik, A., & Goldman, D. (2000). Neurochemical individuality: Genetic diversity among human dopamine and serotonin receptors and transporters. *Archives of General Psychiatry, 57*, 1105–1114.

Dabbs, J. M., Jr., Carr, T. S., Frady, R. L., & Riad, J. K. (1995). Testosterone, crime, and misbehavior among 692 male prison inmates. *Personality and Individual Differences, 18*, 627–633.

Dabbs, J. M., Jr., & Hargrove, M. F. (1997). Age, testosterone, and behavior among female prison inmates. *Psychosomatic Medicine, 59*, 477–480.

Dabbs, J. M., Jurkovic, G. J., & Frady, R. L. (1991). Salivary testosterone and cortisol among late adolescent male offenders. *Journal of Abnormal Child Psychology, 19*, 469–478.

Damasio, A. (1994). *Descartes' error: Emotion, reason, and the human brain.* New York: Grosset/Putnam.

Damasio, H., Grabowski, T., Frank, R., Galaburda, A. M., & Damasio, A. R. (1994). The return of Phineas Gage: Clues about the brain from the skull of a famous patient. *Science, 264*, May, 1102–1105.

Dengerink, H. (1971). Anxiety, aggression, and physiological arousal. *Journal of Personality and Social Psychology, 39*, 269–277.

Dessens, A., Cohen-Kettenis, P., Mellenbergh, G., van de Poll, N., Koppe, J., & Boer, K. (1998). Prenatal exposure to anticonvulsant drugs and spatial ability in adulthood. *Acta Neurobiologiae Experimentalis, 58*, 221–225.

Deutsch, L. J., & Erickson, M. T. (1989). Early life events as discriminators of socialized and undersocialized delinquents. *Journal of Abnormal Child Psychology, 17*, 542–551.

Dohnanyiova, M., Ostatnikova, D., & Laznibatova, J. (2000). Physical development of intellectually gifted children. *Homeostasis in Health and Disease, 40*, 123–125.

Donnerstein, E. (1980). Aggressive erotica and violence against women. *Journal of Personality and Social Psychology, 39*, 269–277.

Dougherty, D. M., Bjork, J. M., Moeller, F. G., & Swann, A. C. (1997). The influence of menstrual cycle phase on the relationship between testosterone and aggression. *Physiology and Behavior, 62*, 431–435.

Eberhart, J. A., Keverne, E. B., & Meller, R. E. (1980). Social influences on plasma testosterone levels in male talapoin monkeys. *Hormones and Behavior, 14*, 247–266.

Erlanger, D. M., Kutner, K. C., & Jacobs, A. R. (1999). Hormones and cognition: Current concepts and issues in neuropsychology. *Neuropsychology Review, 9*, 175–207.

Fibiger, H. C., & Phillips, A. G. (1988). Mesocorticolimbic dopamine systems and reward. *Annals of the New York Academy of Sciences, 537*, 206–215.

Fox, N. A., Schmidt, L. A., Calkins, S. D., Rubin, K. H., & Coplan, R. J. (1996). The role of frontal activation in the regulation and dysregulation of social behavior during the preschool years. *Development and Psychopathology, 8*, 89–102.

George, D. T., Hibbeln, J. R., Ragan, P. W., Umhau, J. C., Phillips, M. J., Doty, L., Hommer, D., & Rawlings, R. R. (2000). Lactate-induced rage and panic in a select group of subjects who perpetrate acts of domestic violence. *Biological Psychiatry, 47*, 804–812.

Gerra, G. (1997). Neurotransmitter-neuroendocrine responses to aggression: Personality influences. In A. Raine, P. Brennan, D. Farrington, & S. A. Mednick (Eds.), *Biosocial bases of violence* (pp. 333–335). New York: Plenum.

Giancola, P. R. (2000). Executive cognitive functioning: A conceptual framework for alcohol related aggression. *Experimental and Clinical Pharmacology, 8*, 576–597.

Giancola, P. R., Martin, C. S., Tarter, R. E., Pelham, W. E., & Moss, H. B. (1996). Executive cognitive functioning and aggressive behavior in preadolescent boys at risk for substance abuse/dependence. *Journal of Studies on Alcohol, 57*, 352–359.

Giancola, P. R., Mezzich, A. C., & Tarter, R. E. (1998). Executive cognitive functioning, temperament, and antisocial behavior in conduct-disordered adolescent females. *Journal of Abnormal Psychology, 107*, 629–641.

Giancola, P. R., & Zeichner, A. (1994). Neuropsychological performance on tests of frontal-lobe functioning and aggressive behavior in men. *Journal of Abnormal Psychology, 103*, 832–835.

Goldman-Rakic, P. S. (1992). Working memory and the mind. *Scientific American, 267*, 111–117.

Grafman, J., Schwab, K., Warden, D., Pridigen, A., Brown, H. R., & Salazar, A. M. (1996). Frontal lobe injuries, violence, and aggression: A report of the Vietnam Head Injury Study. *Neurology, 46*, 1231–1238.

Greendale, G. A., Kritz-Silverstein, D., Seeman, T., & Barrett-Connor, E. (2000). Higher basal cortisol predicts verbal memory loss in postmenopausal women: Rancho Bernardo Study. *Journal of the American Geriatrics Society, 48*, 1655–1658.

Harden, P. W., Pihl, R. O., Vitaro, F., Gendreau, P. L., & Tremblay, R. E. (1995). Stress response in anxious and nonanxious disruptive boys. *Journal of Emotional and Behavioral Disorders, 3*, 183–190.

Harlow, J. M. (1868). Recovery after severe injury to the head. *Publication of the Massachusetts Medical Society, 2*, 327–346.

Harris, J. A., Vernon, P. A., & Boomsma, D. I. (1998). The heritability of testosterone: A study of Dutch adolescent twins and their parents. *Behavior Genetics, 28*, 165–171.

Helzer, J. E., & Pryzbeck, T. R. (1988). The co-occurrence of alcoholism with other psychiatric disorders in the general population and its impact on treatment. *Journal of Studies on Alcohol, 49*, 219–224.

Hiemke, C., Banger, M., Koshik, R., Hundt, M., & Ghraf, R. (1992). Actions of sex hormones on the brain. *Progress in Neuro-Psychopharmacology and Biological Psychiatry, 16*, 377–388.

Higgins, D., Peterson, J., Pihl, R. O., & Lee, A. (2001, June). *Computerized neuropsychological and Big 5 Personality performance and academic achievement at Harvard.* Poster session presented at the 15th Annual American Psychological Society Convention, Toronto, Ontario, Canada.

Higley, J. D., Mehlman, P. T., Pol, R. E., Taub, D. M., Vickers, J., Suomi, S. J., & Linnoila, M. (1996). CSF testosterone and 5-HIAA correlate with different types of aggressive behaviors. *Biological Psychiatry, 40*, 1067–1082.

Hoaken, P., Assaad, J. M., & Pihl, R. O. (1998). Cognitive functioning and inhibition of alcohol induced aggression. *Journal of Studies on Alcohol, 59*, 599–607.

Hogan, A. E. (1999). Cognitive functioning in children with oppositional defiant disorder and conduct disorder. In H. C. Quay & A. E. Hogan (Eds.), *Handbook of disruptive behavior disorders* (pp. 317–335). New York: Kluwer Academic/Plenum.

Howard, M. O., Kivlahan, D., & Walker, R. D. (1997). Cloninger's tridimensional theory of personality and psychopathology: Applications to substance use disorders. *Journal of Studies on Alcohol, 58,* 48–66.

Jacobson, S. W., Bihun, J. T., & Chiodo, L. M. (1999). Effects of prenatal alcohol and cocaine exposure on infant cortisol levels. *Development and Psychopathology, 11,* 195–208.

Kandel, E., & Freed, D. (1989). Frontal-lobe dysfunction and anti-social behaviour: A review. *Journal of Clinical Psychology, 45,* 404–413.

Kelly, K. S., & Hayslip, B., Jr. (2000). Gains in fluid ability performance and their relationship to cortisol. *Experimental Aging Research, 26,* 153–157.

Kling, A. S., & Brothers, L. A. (1992). The amygdala and social behavior. In J. P. Aggleton (Ed.), *The amygdala: Neurobiological aspects of emotion, memory, and mental dysfunction* (pp. 353–377). New York: Wiley-Liss.

Koob, G. F. (1992). Neural mechanisms of drug reinforcement. In P. W. Kalivas & H. H. Samson (Eds.), *The neurobiology of drug and alcohol addiction. Annals of the New York Academy of Sciences,* Vol. 654 (pp. 171–191). New York: New York Academy of Sciences.

Kouri, E. M., Lukas, S. E., Pope, H. G., Jr., & Oliva, P. S. (1995). Increased aggressive responding in male volunteers following administration of gradually increased doses of testosterone cypionate. *Drug and Alcohol Dependence, 40,* 73–79.

Krakowski, M., Czobor, P., Carpenter, M. D., Libiger, J., Kunz, M., Papezova, H., Parker, B. B., Schmader, L., & Abad, T. (1997). Community violence and inpatient assaults: Neurobiological deficits. *Journal of Neuropsychiatry and Clinical Neurosciences, 9,* 549–555.

Kruesi, M. J., Rapoport, J. L., Hamburger, S., Hibbs, E. D., Potter, W. Z., Lenane, M., & Brown, G. L. (1990). Cerebrospinal fluid monoamine metabolites, aggression and impulsivity in disruptive behavior disorders of children and adolescence. *Archives of General Psychiatry, 47,* 419–426.

Kruesi, M. J., Schmidt, M. E., Donnelly, M., Hibbs, E. D., & Hamburger, S. D. (1989). Urinary free cortisol output an disruptive behavior in children. *Journal of the American Academy of Child and Adolescent Psychiatry, 28,* 441–443.

Lau, M., & Pihl, R. O. (1996). Cognitive performance, inhibition and aggression. *Aggressive Behavior, 22,* 417–430.

Lau, M. A., Pihl, R. O., & Peterson, J. B. (1995). Provocation, acute alcohol intoxication, cognitive performance, and aggression. *Journal of Abnormal Psychology, 104,* 150–155.

Linnoila, M., Virkkunen, M., Scheinin, M., Nuutila, A., Rimon, R., & Goodwin, F. K. (1983). Low cerebrospinal fluid 5-hydroxyindoleacetic acid concentration differentiates impulsive from non-impulsive violent behavior. *Life Sciences, 33,* 2609–2614.

Loewenstein, G. (1996). Out of control: Visceral influences on behavior. *Organizational Behavior and Human Decision Processes, 65,* 272–292.

Lynam, D. R., & Henry, B. (2001). The role of neuropsychological deficits in conduct disorders. In J. Hill & B. Maughan (Eds.), *Conduct disorders in childhood and adolescence* (pp. 235–263). New York: Cambridge University Press.

Magnano, C. L., Gardner, J. M., & Karmel, B. Z. (1992). Differences in salivary cortisol levels in cocaine exposed and non-cocaine exposed NICU infants. *Developmental Psychobiology, 25,* 93–103.

Mann, J. J., Arango, V., & Underwood, M. D. (1990). Serotonin and suicidal behavior. *Annals of the New York Academy of Science, 600,* 476–485.

Mazur, A., & Booth, A. (1998). Testosterone and dominance in men. *Behavioral and Brain Sciences, 21,* 353–397.

Mazur, A., Booth, A., & Dabbs, J. M. (1992). Testosterone and chess champions. *Social Psychology Quarterly, 55,* 70–77.

McBurnett, K., Lahey, B. B., Frick, P., Risch, C., Loeber, R., Hart, E. L., Christ, M. A. G., & Hanson, K. (1991). Anxiety, inhibition, and conduct disorder in children: II-Relation to salivary cortisol. *Journal of the American Academy of Child and Adolescent Psychiatry, 30*, 192–196.

McBurnett, K., Lahey, B. B., Rathouz, P. J., & Loeber, R. (2000). Low salivary cortisol and persistent aggression in boys referred for disruptive behavior. *Archives of General Psychiatry, 57*, 38–43.

McBurnett, K., Pfifner, L. J., Capasso, L., Lahey, B. B., & Loeber, R. (1997). Children's aggression and DSM–III–R symptoms predicted by parent psychopathology, parenting practices, cortisol and SES. In A. Raine, P. Brennan, D. Farrington, & S. A. Mednick (Eds.), *Biosocial bases of violence* (pp. 345–348). New York: Plenum.

Mesulam, M. M. (1986). Frontal cortex and behaviors. *Annals of Neurology, 19*, 319–323.

Miller, E. K., & Cohen, J. D. (2001). An integrative theory of prefrontal cortex function. *Annual Review of Neuroscience, 24*, 167–202.

Moffitt, T. E. (1990). Juvenile delinquency and attention deficit disorder: Boys' developmental trajectories from age 3 to age 15. *Child Development, 61*, 893–910.

Moffitt, T. E. (1993). The neuropsychology of conduct disorder. *Development and Psychopathology, 5*, 135–151.

Moffitt, T. E., & Henry, B. (1991). Neuropsychological studies of juvenile delinquency and juvenile violence. In J. S. Milner (Ed.), *The neuropsychology of aggression* (pp. 67–92). Boston: Kluwer Academic.

Murdoch, D., Pihl, R. O., & Ross, D. (1990). Alcohol and crimes of violence: Present issues. *The International Journal of the Addictions, 25*, 1059–1075.

Njiokiktjien, C. H., & Verschoor, C. A. (1998). Attention deficits in children with low performance IQ: Arguments for right hemisphere dysfunction. *Human Physiology, 24*, 145–151.

Oxford Dictionary of Quotations. (1980). Third edition. Camp Hill, PA: Oxford University Press.

Pandya, D. N., & Barnes, C. L. (1987). Architecture and connections of the frontal lobe. In E. Perecman (Ed.), *The frontal lobes revisited* (pp. 41–72). New York: Institute for Research in Behavioral Neuroscience.

Pennington, B. F., & Benetto, L. (1993). Main effects of transactions in the neuropsychology of conduct disorder? Commentary on "The neuropsychology of conduct disorder." *Development and Psychopathology, 5*, 153–164.

Pennington, B. F., & Ozonoff, S. (1996). Executive functions and developmental psychopathology. *Journal of Child Psychology and Psychiatry and Allied Disciplines, 37*, 51–87.

Peterson, J. B., Pihl, R. O., Séguin, J. R., & Finn, P. R. (1993). Heart rate reactivity and alcohol consumption among sons of male alcoholics and sons of non-alcoholics. *Journal of Psychiatry and Neuroscience, 18*, 190–198.

Pietrini, P., Guazzelli, M., Basso, G., Jaffe, K., & Grafman, J. (2000). Neural correlates of imaginal aggressive behavior assessed by positron emission tomography in healthy subjects. *American Journal of Psychiatry, 157*, 1772–1781.

Pihl, R. O., Benkelfat, C., Boileau, F., Assaad, J.-M., Leyton, M., Tremblay, R., & Dagher, A. (2001). Acute ethanol consumption increases synaptiv dopamine in vnetral striatum: A PET/11C raclopride study in healthy volunteers. *Alcoholism: Clinical and Experimental Research, 25*, 57.

Pihl, R. O., Giancola, P. R., & Peterson, J. B. (1994). Cardiovascular reactivity as a prediction of alcohol consumption in taste test situation. *Journal of Clinical Psychology, 50*, 280–286.

Pihl, R. O., & Peterson, J. B. (1995a). Alcoholism: The role of different motivational systems. *Journal of Psychiatry and Neuroscience, 20*, 372–396.

Pihl, R. O., & Peterson, J. B. (1995b). Drugs and aggression: Correlations, crime and human manipulative studies and some proposed mechanisms. *Journal of Psychiatry and Neuroscience, 20*, 141–149.

Pihl, R. O., Peterson, J. B., & Lau, M. A. (1993). A biosocial model of the alcohol–aggression relationship. *Journal of Studies on Alcohol, 11*, 128–139.

Pope, H. G., Jr., Kouri, E. M., & Hudson, J. I. (2000). Effects of supraphysiologic doses of testosterone on mood and aggression in normal men: A randomized controlled trial. *Archives of General Psychiatry, 57*, 133–140.

Pope, H. G., Jr., Kouri, E. M., Powell, K. F., Campbell, C., & Katz, D. L. (1996). Anabolic andronergic steroid use among 133 prisoners. *Comprehensive Psychiatry, 37*, 322–327.

Quay, H. C. (1988). The behavioral reward and inhibition system in childhood behavior disorder. In L. M. Bloomingdale (Ed.), *Attention deficit disorder: New research in attention, treatment, and psychopharmacology* (Vol. 3, pp. 176–186). Oxford, England: Pergamon.

Quay, H. C. (1993). The psychobiology of undersocialized aggressive conduct disorder: A theoretical perspective. *Development and Psychopathology, 5*, 165–180.

Raesaenen, P., Hakko, H., Visuri, S., Paanila, J., Kapanen, P., Suomela, T., & Tiihonen, J. (1999). Serum testosterone levels, mental disorders and criminal behavior. *Acta Pschiatrica Scandinavica, 99*, 348–452.

Raine, A., Buschbaum, M. S., Stanley, J., Lottenberg, S., Abel, L., & Stoddard, J. (1994). Selective reductions in prefrontal glucose metabolism in murderers. *Biological Psychiatry, 36*, 365–373.

Raine, A., & Liu, J.-H. (1998). Biological predispositions to violence and their implications for biosocial treatment and prevention. *Psychology, Crime and Law, 4*, 107–125.

Raine, A., Meloy, J. R., Bihrle, S., Stoddard, J., LaCasse, L., & Buschbaum, M. S. (1998). Reduced prefrontal and increased subcortical brain functioning assessed using positron emission tomography in predatory and affective murderers. *Behavioral Sciences and The Law, 16*, 319–332.

Raine, A., & Scerbo, A. (1991). Biological theories of violence. In J. S. Milner (Ed.), *The neuropsychology of aggression* (pp. 1–26). Boston: Kluwer Academic.

Ramsay, D. S., Bendersky, M. I., & Lewis, M. (1996). Effect of prenatal alcohol and cigarette exposure on two and six-month-old infants adrenocorticol reactivity to stress. *Journal of Pediatric Psychology, 21*, 833–840.

Robbins, T. W. (1998). Dissociating executive functions of the prefrontal cortex. In A. C. Roberts, T. W. Robbins, & L. Weiskrantz (Eds.), *The prefrontal cortex: Executive and cognitive functions* (pp. 117–130). New York: Oxford University Press.

Roizen, R. (1997). Whither youthful drinking in the United States, 1980–1992? *Drugs and Society, 11*, 93–115.

Ruiz-de-la-Torre, J. L., & Manteca, X. (1999). Effects of testosterone on aggressive behaviour after social mixing in male lambs. *Physiology and Behavior, 68*, 109–113.

Rule, B. G., & Nesdale, A. R. (1976). Emotional arousal and aggressive behavior. *Psychological Bulletin, 83*, 851–863.

Salvador, A., Suay, F., Martinez-Sanchis, S., Simon, V. M., & Brain, P. F. (1999). Correlating testosterone and fighting in male participants in judo contests. *Physiology and Behavior, 68*, 205–209.

Sanchez-Martin, J. R., Fano, E., Ahedo, L., Cardas, J., Brain, P. F., & Azpiroz, A. (2000). Relating testosterone levels and free play social behavior in male and female pre-school children. *Psychoneuroendocrinology, 25*, 773–783.

Sapolsky, R. M. (1983). Endocrine aspects of social instability in the olive baboon (Papio Anubis). *American Journal of Primatology, 5*, 365–379.

Schaal, B., Tremblay, R. E., Soussignan, R., & Susman, E. J. (1996). Male testosterone linked to high social dominance but low physical aggression in early adolescence. *Journal of the American Academy of Child and Adolescent Psychiatry, 35*, 1322–1330.

Séguin, J. R., Boulerice, B., Harden, P. W., Tremblay, R. E., & Pihl, R. O. (1999). Executive functions and physical aggression after controlling for attention deficit hyperactivity disorder, general memory and IQ. *Journal of Child Psychology and Psychiatry and Allied Disciplines, 40*, 1197–1208.

Séguin, J. R., Pihl, R. O., Harden, P. W., Tremblay, R. E., & Boulerice, B. (1995). Cognitive and neuropsychological characteristics of physically aggressive boys. *Journal of Abnormal Psychology, 104*, 614–624.

Shallice, T. (1982). Specific impairments of planning. *Philosophical Transactions of the Royal Society of London, 298*, 199–209.

Shallice, T., & Burgess, P. (1993). Supervisory control of action and thought selection. In A. D. Baddeley & L. Weiskrantz (Eds.), *Attention: Selection, awareness, and control: A tribute to Donald Broadbent* (pp. 171–187). Oxford, England: Oxford University Press.

Sodderstrom, H., Tullberg, M., Wikkelso, C., Ekholm, S., & Forsman, A. (2000). Reduced regional cerebral blood flow in non-psychotic violent offenders. *Psychiatry Research, 98*, 29–41.

Soler, H., Vinayak, P., & Quadagno, D. (2000). Biosocial aspects of domestic violence. *Psychoneuroendocrinology, 25*, 721–739.

Soubrie, P. (1986). Reconciling the role of central serotonin neurons in human and animal behavior. *Behavioral and Brain Sciences, 9*, 319–335.

Spoont, M. R. (1992). Modulatory role of serotonin in neural information processing: Implications for human psychopathology. *Psychological Bulletin, 112*, 330–350.

Stalenheim, E. G., Eriksson, E., von Knorring, L., & Wide, L. (1998). Testosterone as a biological marker in psychopathy and alcoholism. *Psychiatry Research, 77*, 79–88.

Sternbach, H. (1998). Age-associated testosterone decline in men: Clinical issues for psychiatry. *American Journal of Psychiatry, 155*, 1310–1318.

Sternbach, H. (2000). "Cognitive effects of testosterone supplementation": Reply. *American Journal of Psychiatry, 157*, 308.

Stuss, D. T., Gow, C. A., & Hetherington, C. R. (1992). "No longer Gage": Frontal lobe dysfunction and emotional changes. *Journal of Consulting and Clinical Psychology, 60*, 349–359.

Susman, E. J., & Ponirakis, A. (1997). Hormones-context interactions and antisocial behavior in youth. In A. Raine, P. Brennan, D. Farrington, & S. A. Mednick (Eds.), *Biosocial bases of violence* (pp. 251–269). New York: Plenum.

Tannenbaum, P. H., & Zillman, D. (1975). Emotional arousal in the facilitation of aggression through communication. In L. Berkowitz (Ed.), *Advances in experimental social psychology* (Vol. 8, pp. 149–191). New York: Academic.

Teichner, G., & Golden, C. J. (2000). The relationship of neuropsychological impairment to conduct disorder in adolescence: A conceptual review. *Aggression and Violent Behavior, 5*, 509–528.

Tremblay, R. E., Japel, C., Perusse, D., McDuff, P., Boivin, M., Zoccolillo, M., & Montplaisir, J. (1999). The search for the age of 'onset' of physical aggression: Rousseau and Bandura revisited. *Criminal Behaviour and Mental Health, 9*, 8–23.

Tremblay, R., Pihl, R., Vitaro, F., & Gagnon, C. (1994). Predicting early onset of male antisocial behavior from preschool behavior: A test of two personality theories. *Archives of General Psychiatry, 51*, 732–739.

Tremblay, R. E., Schaal, B., Boulerice, B., Arsenault, L., Soussignan, R., Paquette, D., & Laurent, D. (1998). Testosterone, physical aggression, dominance, and physical development in early adolescence. *International Journal of Behavioral Development, 22*, 753–777.

Tremblay, R. E., Schaal, B., Boulerice, B., Arsenault, L., Soussignan, R., & Perusse, D. (1997). Male physical aggression, social dominance and testosterone levels at puberty: A developmental perspective. In A. Raine, P. Brennan, D. Farrington, & S. A. Mednick (Eds.), *Biosocial bases of violence* (pp. 271–291). New York: Plenum.

Tyson, P. D. (1998). Physiological arousal, reactive aggression, and the induction of an incompatible relaxation response. *Aggression and Violent Behavior, 3*, 143–158.

Valliant, P. M., Gristey, C., Pottier, D., & Kosmyna, R. (1999). Risk factors in violent and nonviolent offenders. *Psychological Reports, 85*, 675–680.

van Goozen, S. H. M., Matthys, W., Cohen-Kettenis, P. T., Gispen-de Wied, C., Wiegant, V. M., & van Engeland, H. (1998). Salivary cortisol and cardiovascular activity during stress in oppositional defiant disorder boys and normal controls. *Biological Psychiatry, 43*, 531–539.

van Goozen, S. H. M., Matthys, W., Cohen-Kettenis, P. T., Thijssen, J. H. H., & van Engeland, H. (1998). Adrenal androgens and aggression in conduct disorder prepubertal boys and normal controls. *Biological Psychiatry, 43*, 156–158.

van Goozen, S. H. M., van den Ban, E., Matthys, W., Cohen-Kettenis, P. T., Thijssen, J. H. H., & van Engeland, H. (2000). Increased adrenal androgen functioning in children with oppositional defiant disorder: A comparison with psychiatric and normal controls. *Journal of the American Academy of Child and Adolescent Psychiatry, 39*, 1446–1451.

Vedhara, K., Hyde, J., Gilchrist, I. D., Tytherleigh, M., & Plummer, S. (2000). Acute stress, memory, attention and cortisol. *Psychoneuroendocrinology, 25*, 535–549.

Virkkunen, M., & Linnoila, M. (1993). Brain serotonin, type II alcoholism and impulsive violence. *Journal of Studies on Alcohol* (Suppl. 11), 163–169.

Volkow, N. D., & Tancredi, L. (1987). Neural substrates of violent behaviour: A preliminary study with positron emission tomography. *British Journal of Psychiatry, 151*, 668–673.

Volkow, N. D., Tancredi, L., Grant, C., Gillespie, H., Valentine, A., Mullani, N., Wang, G., & Hollister, L. (1995). Brain glucose metabolism in violent psychiatric patients: A preliminary study. *Psychiatry Research, 61*, 243–253.

Wadhwa, P. D., Dunkel-Schetter, C., Chicz-DeMet, A., & Porto, M. (1996). Prenatal psychosocial factors and the neuroendocrine axis in human pregnancy. *Psychosomatic Medicine, 58*, 432–446.

Wise, R. A., & Bozart, M. A. (1987). A psychomotor stimulant theory of addiction. *Psychological Review, 94*, 469–492.

Wong, W. K., & Cornell, D. G. (1999). PIQ>VIQ discrepancy as a correlate of social problem solving and aggression in delinquent adolescent males. *Journal of Psychoeducational Assessment, 17*, 104–112.

Yeudall, L. T., & Fromm-Auch, D. (1979). Neuropsychological impairments in various psychopathological populations. In J. Gruzelier & P. Flor-Henry (Eds.), *Hemisphere asymmetries of function and psychopathology* (pp. 5–13). New York: Elsevier/North Holland.

Young, A. H., Sahakian, B. J., Robbins, T. W., & Cowen, P. J. (1999). The effects of chronic administration of hydrocortisone on cognitive function in normal male volunteers. *Psychopharmacology, 145*, 260–266.

Zeichner, A., & Pihl, R. O. (1979). The effects of alcohol and behavior contingencies on human aggression. *Journal of Abnormal Psychology, 88*, 153–160.

Zeichner, A., & Pihl, R. O. (1980). Effects of alcohol and instigator intent on human aggression. *Journal of Studies on Alcohol, 41*, 265–276.

Zelazo, P. D., Carter, A., Reznick, J. S., & Frye, D. (1997). Early development of executive function: A problem solving framework. *Review of General Psychology, 1*, 198–226.

PREVENTION AND INTERVENTION

8

Prevention Programs

Mark R. Dadds
University of New South Wales, Sydney, Australia

Jennifer A. Fraser
Griffith University, Queensland, Australia

Conduct disorder (CD) in children and adolescents has been the subject of a large research effort over the last several decades. More recently, much attention has been paid to determining developmental patterns of the disorder and risk factors for its persistence. Further, several treatments have been developed and evaluated that can minimize the problem during its early stages. However, if it is not effectively treated, it often represents a lifetime of social impairment and distress for the sufferer and his or her social environment. Although treatment remains an important part of comprehensive service delivery, a broader approach is needed. Interventions that take place once a persistent pattern of antisocial behavior has been established are generally expensive to implement and of limited effectiveness. Early intervention and prevention strategies seek to prevent the emergence of CD, and treatments that intervene early in the development of the disorder tend to have more positive outcomes. This chapter reviews progress toward effective prevention and early intervention strategies.

The use of the formal diagnostic category of CD carries certain advantages, allowing clinicians and researchers a common language and facilitating the interpretability and generalizability of clinical studies of children thus diagnosed. However, it has inherent problems that are especially evident when focusing on the issue of prevention. CD incorporates a wide range of behavior problems in children and adolescents that are best viewed dimensionally and developmentally. The extent to which a child has disruptive behavior is a dimensional phenomenon. That is, children vary in the type, frequency, and severity of their behavior that causes problems to parents, teachers, peers, and society in general. Many children are referred for treatment of disruptive behavior problems not meeting the formal diagnostic criteria. The formal term *CD* is used to identify a subset of disruptive children who show severe and persistent behavior problems. The cutoff point between those who attract a formal diagnosis and those for whom behavior problems are subclinical is largely arbitrary. Although research indicates that referred and nonreferred samples are readily distinguishable (e.g., Forehand & Long, 1988), there are few studies documenting differences other than the severity of their problems, between children referred for disruptive behavior problems with and without a formal diagnosis of CD. Although reasonable consensus now exists on the diagnostic features of the disorder, there is still some disagreement as to the central characteristics that are hypothesized to underlie the disorder. Further, if it is assumed that there are one or more central characteristics that underlie the disorder, the behavioral manifestations vary across specific children and their developmental stage (Loeber, 1990). Thus, this chapter focuses on a broad definition of conduct problems, referring to the general population of children who are referred at various developmental stages for disruptive behavior problems that are common in CD.

APPROACHES TO PREVENTION

The term *prevention* is used broadly to indicate any intervention program designed to build resilience and reduce risk and/or suffering prior to the establishment of clear-cut psychological disorders. *Early intervention* is also used broadly but focuses more on strategies that target groups in which some risk or problems are already evident. Prevention programs are frequently grouped according to classifications used in preventive medicine (Caplan, 1964). These are termed *primary, secondary*, and *tertiary* intervention strategies. Primary prevention programs aim to reach the wider community by raising public awareness and using widespread campaigns. Secondary efforts include programs applied to particular populations identified as being at increased risk of experiencing CD. Tertiary prevention involves treatment of parents and their children with the aim of preventing further and recurrent disorders.

Alternatively, prevention efforts can be defined according to their target population (Gordon, 1983; Mrazek & Haggerty, 1994). Using strategies for intervention that operate at a community level offering support to all new families before or soon after the birth of a child is *universal* prevention. An example is a home visiting service provided to all families after the birth of a newborn aiming to enhance parental competence and provide parenting education. Second, families, children, and environments can be screened to identify risk for CD. This strategy for prevention indicates prevention is useful when resources are scarce. High-risk children are identified and given priority for intervention programs. Finally, selected prevention programs target children in which CD is considered to be more likely to occur due to membership of a particular community such as an estate with high rates of criminal activities. Notwithstanding these classifications, the approach is usually to operate at different levels of prevention. This is due to the complexity of personal and social systems factors that predispose children to violence and the scarcity of resources available to service providers.

There are advantages and disadvantages associated with the use of different types of intervention. For example, an advantage of universal programs is that no selection procedures are needed, and thus stigmatization is unlikely to result. However, such programs are likely to be more expensive from both a financial and a human resource perspective and without careful and thoughtful design, risk the possibility of doing harm to healthy people. Shochet and O'Gorman (1995) argued that the first guiding principle of any universal intervention must be to quarantine harm. Especially in initial trials when outcomes of prevention initiatives remain uncertain, it is imperative that above all people are not worse off as a result of participating in the program. For example, concern is often expressed about possible iatrogenic effects of suicide prevention programs when applied universally to young people. Similarly, there is growing evidence that universal programs for preventing eating problems in school children can be associated with increases in eating and body image concerns (O'Dea, 2000).

Selected programs target individuals most likely to be in need of assistance and optimize the use of financial and human resources. Such programs increase the probability of identifying and intervening with individuals who otherwise may have gone unnoticed and progressed to a more severe level of dysfunction. Within some contexts, selected programs are termed *early intervention* especially if some level of dysfunction already exists within the sample. However, the selection procedures associated with selected and indicated programs carry the risk of stigmatizing or labeling individuals.

In terms of programs, this chapter is limited to those that focus primarily on the child and/or family; programs that prevent psychological problems by modifying community and school factors will not be covered. Similarly, the chapter does not cover programs that are entirely universal unless they also assess change in at-risk subgroups.

Prevention is valued not just for the potential to directly avoid psychopathology but also to reduce need for the wide range of services required to address the consequences of conduct problems once they are established. The capacity to plan and implement prevention efforts for CD thus relies on a clear understanding of risk characteristics, how they switch in and out developmentally, and what opportunities exist in the community for influencing these risk and protective factors. As such, risk and protective factors for the development of CD are reviewed first.

RISK FACTORS FOR CONDUCT DISORDER

The idea of causality is very complex when applied to complex phenomena like CD. Specific causes have not been identified and the field of developmental psychopathology has responded by embracing models of etiology that are multifactorial, interactional, idiopathic, and developmental. That is, multiple interacting variables can lead to or protect against CD. The pattern of these factors will vary across individual children and will change according to the stage of life. Thus, for one child CD may result from early experiences of a violent and rejecting family life. For another, it may be associated with a long history of learning problems and social skills problems leading to school failure, peer rejection, and adoption by neighborhood gangs. The following review first considers individual risk factors; however, it should be noted that to consider them in isolation is problematic. The likelihood that problems will be persistent through life is directly proportional to the number of risk factors present in the life of the individual (see Loeber & Farrington, 2000).

Rates of CD and disruptive behavior in general are much higher in boys than girls (Forehand & Long, 1988; Lahey et al., 2000). Accordingly, research has tended to be gender biased. However, in a review of the literature, Keenan, Loeber, and Green (1999) emphasized that CD in girls is not uncommon and is associated with poorer life outcomes and early pregnancy. It is of importance that it appears that research efforts to model different developmental progression for childhood onset and adolescent onset antisocial behavior suggested by Moffitt and her colleagues (Moffitt, 1993; Moffitt, Caspi, Dickson, Silva, & Stanton, 1996) need to be advanced with particular investment into the development of CD in girls. Onset of antisocial behavior appears to be delayed until adolescence in girls such that female adolescent-onset CD is more common. Consequently, the characteristics and course of CD in girls is quite different from that of boys. Adolescent-onset CD in girls shares a similar trajectory toward adult psychopathology and criminal activity to childhood-onset CD but not adolescent-onset CD in boys (Silverthorn & Frick, 1999).

Rates of CD are generally higher in families and geographical areas marked by low socioeconomic status (SES; West, 1982). Low SES is a marker for many possible risk factors including genetics, environmental toxicity, poor educational opportunities, poverty, social isolation, lack of employment, and modeling of violence. Although low SES is a clear risk factor for CD, it has been identified as a risk factor for many other forms of behavioral disturbance and psychopathology as well.

Comorbidity is a critical factor in CD. Kazdin, Siegel, and Bass (1992) found that 70% of youth aged 7 to 13 years referred for CD met criteria for more than one disorder, with the mean number of diagnoses per case at slightly over two. The prevalence of major depressive disorder among imprisoned juvenile delinquents, for example, ranges from 10% to 30% (Wierson, Forehand, & Frame, 1992). This is high compared with the estimated prevalence of 2% of school-age children and 4% of adolescents (Ryan, 2001). Disorders such as depression, personality and psychotic disorders, substance abuse, learning difficulties, and adjustment problems co-occur with CD, but the most common comorbid conditions are oppositional defiant disorder (ODD) and hyperactivity or attention deficit hyperactivity disorder (ADHD; see Wierson et al., 1992, for a comprehensive review). In fact, the degree of overlap between these disorders is so high as to call into question their independence. For example, estimates of co-occurrence of ODD and CD range from 20% to 60% and co-occurrence of CD and ADHD from 60% to 90% (Abikoff & Klein, 1992). The current wisdom is that ODD is probably a milder form of, and in many cases a developmental precursor to, CD, leading many authors to group them together in diagnostic (e.g., Abikoff & Klien, 1992) and treatment (e.g., Dadds, Schwartz, & Sanders, 1987) studies.

The relation between CD and ADHD is more problematic. Hinshaw (1987) concluded that the dimensions of hyperactivity–inattention and conduct problems–aggression are moderately correlated ($r = .56$) even when attempts to remove overlapping assessment items are made. In studies of nonclinic populations using cutoff scores to classify children, between 30% and 90% of children classified in one category of CD or ADHD will also be classified in the other. However, children classified as CD are more likely to be also classified ADHD than vice versa, and this is true for clinic-referred samples as well (Hinshaw, 1987). For example, Reeves, Werry, Elkind, and Zametkin (1987) found that "pure" ADHD children were easy to identify, whereas the vast majority of CD children had co-existing ADHD features.

Adult rating and referral factors as well as the actual nature of the disorders may influence these patterns of comorbidity. One important and replicated finding is that teachers' ratings of hyperactivity in a child will be inflated if the child displays conduct problems, but ratings of conduct problems are not similarly inflated by displays of hyperactivity (Abikoff, Courtney, Pelham, & Koplewicz, 1993; Schachar, Sandberg, & Rutter, 1986). These effects have not been tested in parents as yet, but they indicate that the covariance of CD and ADHD contains a complex mix of actual manifest and adult rating phenomena.

It is important to consider the early presence of ADHD symptoms and other cognitive deficits in the development of CD. When children display ADHD as well as conduct problems, there is an increased risk of persistent CD in adolescence (Loeber, 1990; Loeber & Farrington, 2000). Moffitt and Silva (1988) compared delinquents with and without ADHD. The former scored worse on test of verbal and visual integration, but children with ADHD who did not develop CD were less impaired on measures of verbal memory. Rather than presenting ADHD as one component of a lifetime pattern of antisocial behavior, it is usually considered to be a developmental forerunner for more serious offending in adolescence (Loeber & Farrington, 2000; Patterson, DeGarmo, & Knutson, 2000).

DEVELOPMENTAL PATHWAYS

The seminal work of researchers such as Patterson, Loeber, Moffitt, Farrington, Rutter, and others has provided the cornerstone for more recent work that suggests distinct developmental pathways of CD. CD, in its most severe and persistent forms, takes an identifiable path from childhood to adulthood. Along this path, different causal factors can be seen to emerge. There is now a significant body of published research concerning both the development and persistence of aggressive and antisocial behaviors of children with CD. Severe antisocial behavior is considered to develop through at least two distinct pathways, one that can be observed from childhood and the other that arises with the onset of adolescence (Hinshaw, Lahey, & Hart, 1993; Moffitt, 1993). The age of onset of CD can range from early childhood through to the teenage years, and there is evidence to suggest that early onset is associated with a poorer prognosis (Loeber & Farrington, 2000). Similarly, the extent to which the problem behavior is expressed across multiple settings (i.e., in the home, school, community) is also a predictor of severity and durability of the CD (Kazdin, 1993; Loeber, 1990).

Of course, the prescription of a developmental course refers to a commonality among groups of CD children, and it is easy to think of exceptions to the general pattern: youths who, after years of being well behaved showed the first signs of conduct problems in adolescence, and children who were highly oppositional and difficult as children but "grew out of it" by adolescence. Notwithstanding these individual differences, it is crucial that CD is conceptualized as a developmental sequence and as involving the interplay of multiple causative factors. Thus, the causes are best thought of as a series of risk factors that interact at various critical points or transition phases to produce the more chronic possibilities of this disorder. Given this conceptualization, it is clear that there can be no one cause or treatment of choice for CD. Rather, there exist a number of windows of opportunity corresponding to the developmental progress of the disorder and the settings in which it occurs, at which time different interventions can be used to ameliorate current problems in the child's life or prevent potential problems from developing. Given this developmental perspective on the disorder, the usual distinction between treatment and prevention becomes blurred. That is, the treatment of current problems can and should be seen as a preventive strategy against the next stage or transition in the chronic potential of the disorder (e.g., Conduct Problems Prevention Research Group [CPPRG], 1992). As Loeber (1990) pointed out, given the early detectable signs of the disorder, pure primary prevention efforts are only possible in the earliest stages of child development.

Early Biological Markers and Child Temperament

The first definite signs of disruptive behavior problems can be observed and measured in the toddler years as the child learns to walk and speak and interact with others socially. Child characteristics such as irritability, noncompliance, inattentiveness, and impulsivity measured at as young as 2 and 3 years of age are predictive of later CD (e.g., Campbell, 1991; Loeber & Farrington, 2000). Children vary in their vulnerability to these early signs of behavioral problems. The review by Rutter et al. (1990) indicates that the evidence of genetic vulnerability differs across different disorders, but the evidence with regard to oppositional, conduct, and hyperactivity disorders in children is currently too weak to make any definitive conclusions (although being male is clearly a genetic risk factor for CD). Among other factors that may have a genetic component, numerous authors have pointed to the presence of temperamental difficulties (i.e., high activity level, feeding and sleeping difficulties) as a precursor to disruptive behavior problems (Loeber, 1990; Thomas & Chess, 1977).

As noted earlier, the presence of ADHD and other cognitive deficits significantly contributes to the persistence of CD; therefore, any factors that predict ADHD and other learning problems need to be considered. The presence of neurotoxic chemicals such as lead in the blood of children is significantly associated with ADHD and other cognitive deficits (Needleman & Bellinger, 1981), as are early malnutrition, low birthweight, and substance abuse by the mother during pregnancy (Loeber, 1990). These factors are easily but mistakenly interpretable as genetic factors across generations and are also linked with low SES. Thus, the early biochemical environment may make the child vulnerable to cognitive and behavior problems predictive of ADHD and CD.

On a more controversial note, several authors have invoked the concept of psychopathy to describe a subset of children who may be at risk for persistent and high-level aggressive and antisocial behavior. In the adult literature, *psychopathy* is defined as a combination of impulsive, antisocial behavior and callous, manipulative, and unemotional traits (e.g., Harpur, Hare, & Hakstian, 1989). The behavioral dimension is not controversial; it is well established that severity of conduct problems and impulsivity are predictive of persistence of problems. Measures of the emotional or motivational traits dimension have recently been developed for children (Frick, Bodin, & Barry, 2000; Lynam, 1997), and preliminary data show that conduct problem children high on callous or unemotional traits are more likely to show severe aggressive behavior, are less distressed by their behavior problems, and are less likely to show other risk factors such as poor parenting and neurological or learning problems (see Frick et al., 2000). Thus, this work suggests that there may be distinct yet recognizable pathways to CD. Kochanska (1993) argued that a child temperament characterized by impulsivity and low punishment sensitivity places a child at risk for antisocial behavior. Her work is increasingly providing a conceptual model for these models of early markers of psychopathy in children. That is, children who are insensitive to punishment and guilt (i.e., are not aroused by empathy and guilt) are more difficult to socialize and fail to develop normal moral standards. The co-occurrence of impulsivity adds to the likelihood that aggressive behavior will be enacted.

The extent to which biological and temperament markers can be used to guide early interventions is as yet unknown. Behavioral characteristics such as the early onset of multiple behavioral problems comorbid with learning problems and impulsivity are clearly identifiable factors that can be used to guide early interventions. Traits hypothesized to be early markers of psychopathy are more controversial. Longitudinal studies are needed to validate their predictive power, and if they are important, intervention studies are needed to test whether such traits can be used to inform interventions.

Early Family Influences

The earliest signs of behavioral problems are evident from infancy onward, are clearly related to parental adjustment problems (Zeanah, Keener, Stewart, & Anders, 1985), and mark a pattern of parent–child conflict and use of high-punitive/low-nurturing parental discipline strategies that characterize the early stages of the disruptive behavior problems of childhood (Dadds, 1995; Patterson, 1982). At extremes, the presence of physical abuse and neglect of the young child may also be associated with the development of conduct problems (Cicchetti & Toth, 1995).

Case studies have been fairly consistent in describing the families of these children as aggressive; disorganized and chaotic; economically stressed; marked by parent rejection, harsh discipline, and abuse; and disrupted by divorce and separation (Kazdin, 1987). At the systemic level, there have been a number of case descriptions that describe these families as marked by chaotic, disengaged relationships, and as having power imbalances (e.g., Minuchin, Montalvo, Guerney, Rosman, & Schumer, 1967). Correlational studies have tended to confirm this pattern of aggression and disruption. Group comparison studies have confirmed a pattern in which a range of family risk factors is associated with increased risk for aggression and conduct problems. These include marital distress, parental depression, paternal antisocial problems, socioeconomic stress and social isolation, harsh punishment, insufficient parental monitoring, abuse, and neglect (Dadds, 1995).

Case studies and correlational designs leave little doubt that these associations exist between conduct problems and a range of family factors. Studies demonstrating that experimental manipulations of parent behavior result in concomitant changes in aggressive, noncompliant child behaviors have been common in the child behavior therapy literature (Lochman, 1990). The most important parenting behaviors are use of harsh discipline, lack of modeling and positive attention to prosocial behavior, and deficits in monitoring in the child's activities (Loeber, 1990; Patterson, 1986). Clinical trials have typically involved the modification of parent behavior via parent training programs and behavioral family therapy (Miller & Prinz, 1990) and have provided strong evidence of the dependent relation between oppositional child behavior and interactional patterns with parents. Specifically, these interactional patterns involve the direct contingencies that parents provide to aggressive and oppositional child behavior. It appears that disturbed children tend to come from families who engage in relatively high rates of the disturbed behavior themselves in their day-to-day interactions. The aggressive child is regularly exposed to conflicts among family members, is likely to receive high rates of aversive instructions, and many of his or her behaviors will be followed by aversive consequences regardless of their appropriateness.

There may also be evidence to support the systemic hypothesis that children with conduct problems come from families with deviant or reversed family hierarchies in which the child has more power than parents (Haley, 1976; Minuchin, 1974). Green, Loeber, and Lahey (1992) showed that these structures appear to be specific to families of children with CD (compared to overanxiousness, ODD, depression, and ADHD). However, examination of their longitudinal data revealed that CD in the child predicted a deviant family hierarchy 1 year later, but the reverse was not true. Thus, it appears that the family system organizes itself into this reversed hierarchical form because of the child's aggressive behavior and is not a causal factor.

One of the most productive areas relating the family to the early development of conduct problems focuses on the actual moment-to-moment interactions that the family provides as a learning context for children (e.g.,

Patterson & Reid, 1984). Interactions are conceived of and measured as sequences of discreet but interdependent communicative behaviors. Some very important methodologies and findings have emerged from this approach. For example, observations of families of disruptive and aggressive children in natural environments have shown members of families that contain aggressive and conduct problem children are more likely to initiate and reciprocate aggressive behaviors than members of families of non-problem children (Patterson, 1982; Sanders, Dadds & Bor, 1989). Thus, the families of conduct problem children provide their child with an environment conducive to the learning a repertoire of aggressive behavior.

Patterson (1982) developed a model for understanding these repetitive family interaction patterns in terms of coercion or reinforcement. First, it is very common to find that parents inadvertently reinforce problematic child behaviors because reinforcing the child for problem behavior is, in itself, reinforcing to the parent because the child's problem behavior temporarily ceases. Second, reinforcement traps work by diminishing the contrast between problematic and desirable child behavior. The more a child engages in problem behaviors, the less likely the child will be reinforced for positive behaviors. If parents feel they are spending hours engaged in unpleasant interactions with a child (sorting out fights, arguing over chores, having attention demanded) the less likely the parents will notice and attend to positive behaviors by the child. Thus, a vicious circle entraps the parent and the child in which the parent has a "break" whenever the child is not misbehaving, and the child has to escalate problem behaviors to obtain the parent's attention. The examples considered previously refer to problem interactions between two persons; however, reinforcement traps can occur in considerably more complex forms (see, e.g., Sanders & Dadds, 1993).

Developmentally, the importance of family factors may be concentrated in the early years. Many researchers have pointed to a transitional model in which the learning of aggressive behavior occurs first in the home during infancy and early childhood. This aggressive behavior then generalizes, resulting in poor school performance and problematic peer relationships, which then become risk factors for further progressions in antisocial behavior. Thus, identification and modification of problematic family and parent–child relationships represents a critical ingredient in the prevention of persistent CD that should be focused in the early years of development.

Development of Social Cognition

Other interpersonal models of parent–child interactions have come from attachment theory and the development of social cognition. Bowlby (1973, 1969/1980, 1982), the prominent attachment theorist, integrated the clinical observations of the psychoanalysts with an ethological approach usually used by evolutionists and biologists. He drew on observations of children reared under different degrees of attachment to parental figures such as occurs in orphanages and intact families. He argued that infants are driven to form a small number of stable attachments with other people and that the creation and maintenance of these bonds are necessary for healthy human development. The disruption of these bonds results in displays of ethologically fixed behavior patterns of fear, anger, aggression, and despair.

The idea that loss of attachment bonds are central to the development of psychopathology has met with both theoretical and empirical difficulties (Rutter, 1972). Evidence shows that although loss of significant parental figures does pose a general risk for child behavior problems, it does not appear to be differentially associated with different forms of child psychopathology, and its effect size is generally small compared to other psychosocial factors. However, attachment bonds can vary in many ways other than simply losing them through separation or death of the parent(s). As Brewin (1987) pointed out, Bowlby's model of how attachment leads to the development of self-esteem is highly consistent with current thinking in experimental cognitive psychology. Bowlby (1980) argued that children appraise new situations and develop behavioral plans guided by mental models of themselves and their main attachment figures. In healthy human development, these models are gradually integrated into a stable and confident sense of self. Thus, Bowlby (1982) argued that the disruption of these bonds leads to expectations of self and others based on anger, fear, and despair, which form the basis of many forms of emotional disturbance.

Such mental models or cognitive styles appear to characterize various forms of behavioral disturbance. For example, research has shown that conduct problem adolescents may be less skilled at interpreting social messages, tending to expect and thus overdetect and elicit hostility and rejection in other people (Dodge, 1985). Most research has examined these cognitive styles in the individual, but increasingly attention is being paid to the interpersonal context of these cognitive styles. That is, researchers are increasingly focusing on how individuals learn to interpret social meaning from early family experiences. For example, the study by Barrett, Rapee, Dadds, and Ryan (1996) showed that the plans of conduct problem and anxious children for responding to an ambiguous but potentially threatening social situation were heavily influenced by the way the family discussed the particular problem. Conduct problem children and their parents were more likely to perceive threat in ambiguous social situations and to respond to this perceived threat with aggression. Further, the level of aggression in the child's responses increased when the child was given the opportunity to discuss their responses with their parents.

With regard to prevention, a number of issues are raised by a consideration of cognitive factors in CD. First, hostile attributional biases may not be characteristic of all CD children. Research has indicated that these biases are generally limited to children who show predominantly reactive aggression. That is, their aggression is a reaction to perceived hostility and injustice from others. More severe CD children may also show patterns of proactive aggression in which aggression is deliberately targeted to achieve goals (see Crick & Dodge, 1996). These children may be less likely to benefit from social-cognitive interventions. Second, it is difficult to identify, assess, and intervene with cognitions in children who have not achieved abstract levels of cognitive maturity. In nonproblem children this generally occurs around the 7th or 8th year but can be considerably later in children with learning and neurological problems. Third, the evidence that cognitive changes can produce changes in CD without concurrent changes in the child's social, family, and school environments is limited.

Stressful Environments and Events

The literature on stress and coping and their relation to the development of psychopathology is very complex, in part due to inherent ambiguities about the meaning of the terms. It is very difficult to differentiate between stressful events, the stress effects they produce, and the coping strategies that are thought to mediate the relation between the two. Generally, researchers think about a stressful event as one that produces a stress reaction because the event demands more coping skills than the person has at their disposal (Lazarus & Folkman, 1984). With regard to CD, research has shown that children and the families of children with CD experience a relatively high level of disruptive life events (see Goodyer, 1990). For example, the impact of parental divorce or separation on the child has been relatively well researched, and marital breakdown affects a substantial proportion of families in most developed countries (Emery, 1982). Children from separated households are at greater risk to develop disruptive behavioral and emotional problems than children from intact households (Emery, 1982). Further, recent evidence indicates that reformation of an intact family via the remarriage of the sole parent places even further risk for the behavioral and emotional adjustment of children (Fergusson, Horwood, & Shannon, 1984).

However, there is little evidence that the pressure on the child's behavior comes from the life event so much as a combination of the daily changes the life event incurs and the vulnerability of the child exposed to the event. Thus, the effects of divorce on children are largely mediated by the amount and type of conflict between the parents, the disruption caused to the child's life, and the presence of preexisting behavioral and emotional problems in the child. Literature reviewed by Emery (1982) showed that the likelihood that the child's behavior would deteriorate following divorce was related to observed changes in the custodial parent's discipline practices. After separation, parents tended to show decreases in their use of limit setting, maturity demands, affection, and clear communication. These were accompanied by increases in disturbed child behavior that tended to peak approximately 1 year after the event. Further, boys were exposed to more of this inconsistency than were their sisters and were observed to have the most behavioral adjustment problems. Thus, the effects of divorce as a stressor largely impact on the child via changes in the parental or family processes described in Patterson's (1982) coercive family process model.

There is also evidence that the effects of severe economic hardship on developing children are mediated by changes in the interactional patterns of parents and their children (Elder, Nguyen, & Caspi, 1985). Similarly, the relation between parental psychopathology and child behavior disorders may also be mediated by the impact of the parent's psychopathology on family processes, namely, the marital relationship and related parenting styles (Billings & Moos, 1983; Emery, 1982).

It is clear from the studies cited previously that significant amounts of the variance of the effects of disruptive events on children may be accounted for by changes in the interactions the child has with parents concomitant with the event. In the words of Hetherington and Martin (1979)

> The artificiality of separating social learning experiences in the family from extrafamilial social factors, specific traumatic experiences, and hereditary or constitutional factors must be emphasized. Although any one of these factors may initiate a developmental process, unidirectional causality quickly gives way to an interactive process between the child and other family members. (p. 72)

Thus, although stressful life events may not be directly causal in CD, they may have potential in terms of marker points during or after which the behavior of vulnerable children would be expected to deteriorate. Thus, school transitions, family breakdown, traumatic events, and other life events could possibly provide high risk times for identifying children with escalating behavior problems.

Social Factors

One of most consistently documented risk factors for pathology, whether it be physical or psychological, is low SES. Its effects do not appear to be specific to any specific form of distress; it is a generally noxious factor for ill health. However, one of the most extensively studied relations is that of low SES to conduct problems in children. Major steps toward understanding the development of childhood problems, in particular CDs, have recently been made by clarifying the mechanisms by which low SES impacts on children and families. Although a number of factors—such as urban crowding, poor educational resources, lack of employment opportunities and unemployment, community violence, and social isolation and disempowerment—may be important, the social support available to parents may be one important variable mediating the relation (Lamb & Elster, 1985; Wahler, 1980; Webster-Stratton, 1985).

It appears that factors discussed earlier, such a parent–child interactions, maternal depression, marital discord, and a parent's personal adjustment may need to be seen in the context of the family's interactions within the system and with the local community. The observation that day-to-day social contacts and subjective evaluations of social support are predictive of a range of parent–parent and parent–child interaction patterns is an excellent example of the analysis of interacting hierarchical systems (Wahler & Dumas, 1984) and emphasizes the relation between "molar" (e.g., SES delinquency) and "molecular" (e.g., parent–child interaction) variables (Patterson & Reid, 1984).

School failure, dropping out of school, identification with a deviant peer group, and lack of adult supervision are all potential contributors to the development of CD (Loeber, Burke, Lahey, Winters, & Zera, 2000). Although many of these factors may themselves be driven by the behavior of the child, his or her learning potential, and early family environment, any characteristics of school environments that exacerbate their likelihood must also be seen as potential contributors to the development of CD. Although little research is available to support speculation, it is possible that school environments marked by poor supervision and teaching, lack of educational resources and opportunities, the availability of drugs, weapons of violence, and antisocial gangs, may facilitate a child's transition in to the later and more severe forms of CD.

CONCLUSIONS

The etiology of CD is seen as a set of systems, subsystems, and components of systems interacting at the biological, interpersonal, family, and social levels. Further, the importance of any one factor will vary according to the developmental stage of the child. Authors tend to think of these causes as additive risk factors (e.g., Loeber, 1990; Loeber & Farrington, 2000). Further, the idea of identifiable pathways is useful. Although each child's problems may be associated with a different pattern of risk factors, it is likely that there are common pathways that describe a common sequence of risk and problems in substantial groups of children. In the worst case scenario involving common risk factors, CD can be characterized by the early onset of behavioral problems that escalate due to poor parenting and family disruption. The child's problems generalize to school and other social settings and are complicated by learning and social skills problems, resulting in school failure and engagement with deviant peer groups or social isolation.

Developmentally, the literature indicates clusters of risk that also may be seen as windows of opportunity for guiding the establishment of comprehensive intervention programs. Table 8.1 summarizes the developmental sequence of risk with some potential interventions at each point. In the next section, early intervention (EI) and prevention strategies are reviewed within this developmental framework, highlighting the need to target preventive services and promote intensive EIs.

EI

Spence and Dadds (1996) outlined several prerequisites for the establishment of effective EI programs. These include an empirically tested model of the etiology of the target problem that identifies risk and protective factors, a reliable and valid method of identifying children at risk, effective strategies for reducing risk and enhancing protective factors, and the opportunity to apply these methods in practice. Similarly, Simeonsson (1994) argued that to develop a program one must begin with clear understanding of risk factors, protective factors, and characteristics of the targeted population, which all inform the formulation of the prevention program. Clearly, the selection criteria apply more to EI than universal preventive programs. By targeting the entire group, the need for identifying children at risk is largely overcome. Further, if the goal is to increase resilience in the group, a model of specific problems may not be needed as much as a clear model of protective factors and their relation to health. However, most EI and prevention programs aim to reduce the incidence of specific problems.

Before looking at EI and prevention programs for CD, it is useful to briefly review literature on tertiary treatments for CD, especially its earliest manifestations. As noted previously, the presence of effective strategies for change is critical to the potential effects of prevention strategies. Most evidence for change in CD comes from the tertiary treatments in literature and existing prevention programs are attempts to utilize combinations of these interventions at a larger community level. Thus, it is critical that potential interventions are identified as the first step. For more detail on tertiary treatments, the reader is referred to Prinz and Jones (chap. 11, this volume).

Tertiary Interventions for CD

Considerable work has been done on the development and evaluation of tertiary treatments for CD. The most successful are parent training and family interventions and individual or group social-cognitive work with the

TABLE 8.1

Developmental Risk Factors for Conduct Disorder and Associated Intervention Opportunities

Developmental Phase		Risk Factors	Potential Interventions
Prenatal to infancy	Child	Environmental toxicity	Environmental safety (e.g., lead minimization)
		Temperamental difficulties	Early identification of children at risk through temperamental and behavioral problems
	Family	Poverty, low SES, social isolation	Early identification of children at risk through families at high risk through socioeconomic adversity
		Family violence, conflict, separation	Provision of adequate parental and infant support programs, home visiting programs
		Parental psychopathology	Early identification of children at risk through families at high risk through parental psychopathology
		Poor health, nutrition	Provision of adequate health care; home visiting programs
	Social	Economic hardship, unemployment	Promotion of social equality, support, community connectedness
		Family breakdown, isolation	Provision of family support, education and therapy services, premarital and preparenting education programs
		Cultures of violence	Promotion of nonviolent cultures and communities

Developmental period	Level	Risk factors	Interventions
Toddler to late childhood	Child	Learning and language difficulties	Early remediation of learning and language difficulties
		Comorbid impulsivity and attention deficit hyperactivity disorder	Provision of parent training and broader family interventions; medication
	Family	Callous, manipulative, unemotional traits	Data unavailable
		Coercive family processes, violence	Parent training, family, and marital support programs
		Low care and nurturance	Family support programs
	Social	Inadequate monitoring of child	After-school care and monitoring of children
		Inadequate child care and parental support	Peer social skills programs
		Lack of educational opportunities	Provision of positive school environments and educational opportunities
		Negative parent–school relation	Promotion of quality parent–school relations
Adolescence	Child	School, employment failure	Academic and work transition skills programs
		Cognitive bias to threat, hostility	Cognitive behavioral skills programs for teenagers
		Peer rejection, deviant peer group	Social skills programs
		Substance abuse, depression	Substance abuse prevention programs
	Family	Conflict, individuation problems	Family–adolescent therapy
		Rejection, homelessness	Crisis support for family or youth individuation problems, breakdown, and homelessness
	Social	Culture of violence	Cultures of community respect and connectedness
		Lack of education, employment	

Note. SES = socioeconomic status.

child. Research evaluating treatments for child conduct problems has supported the efficacy of behavioral family interventions in the short term and over follow-up periods of years after the termination of treatment (Miller & Prinz, 1990). The last few decades have witnessed continuous refinement of the behavioral family intervention (BFI) approach. Empirical evidence and clinical experience suggests that not all parents or families benefit to the same extent from treatment (Miller & Prinz, 1990), and difficulties are commonly encountered when there are concurrent family problems, parental psychopathology, and economic hardship. Several authors have made various proposals to improve the outcome of treatment by expanding the focus of treatment to the multiple systems that provide the context for family life (Henggeler, Melton, Brondino, Scherer, & Hanley, 1997; Miller & Prinz, 1990). Of particular interest to EI is the Triple P approach (Sanders, 1999) that offers various levels of intervention intensity, from simple provision of information through to a full multisystemic, individually tailored intervention. Of the different approaches encompassed by BFI, parent training for the treatment of younger ODD children has the most accumulated evidence regarding its therapeutic benefits. There is less evidence to suggest that BFI is effective in altering the course of the more severe end CD children, especially beyond the years of early childhood.

Social-cognitive interventions are based on the finding that CDs are characterized by a tendency to overinterpret threat and hostility in others and poor social problem problem-solving skills. Thus, these interventions aim to help the child to more accurately interpret the behavior of others and formulate nonaggressive, prosocial responses in common social situations that would usually provoke them to aggression. Given this emphasis on abstract cognitive and social analysis, social-cognitive interventions with CD youth are generally limited to older children and youth who can operate at abstract cognitive levels (i.e., approximately 7 to 8 years and older). According to Kazdin (1993), variations on social-cognitive interventions are numerous, but they share some central features such as a focus on the cognitive processes; teaching a step-by-step approach to solving interpersonal problems; using a range of activities to train these skills that are engaging and understandable to the developmental level of the target children; and emphasizing learning of skills via the provision of clear information, modeling of skills, role playing with the provision of feedback, and shaping strategies.

Social-cognitive interventions are a relatively recent development, and less research into therapeutic outcomes and processes has been undertaken in comparison to BFI. Reviews of treatment outcome (e.g., Baer & Nietzel, 1991; Durlak, Furhman, & Lampman, 1991; Kazdin, 1993) are generally positive. However, treatment effect sizes associated with social-cognitive interventions are often not clinically significant, interventions are limited to older children who can benefit from abstract social problem solving, and the putative relation between therapeutic change and the development of cognitive skills has not been clearly established.

There is a range of well-known problems associated with tertiary treatments for CD in the real world. These have been reviewed in depth by Dadds (1995). Many families may not seek help as part of a larger marginalization from traditional health services associated with low SES, low education, poverty, cultural and racial isolation, the lack of services in rural regions and urban areas of poverty, and general disempowerment in society. Thus, the very families that are at highest risk for CD may be ones least likely or able to access the services that can potentially help. With CD, comprehensive assessments and treatments need to take a broader parent training and family focus. Mental health services require the physical structures (e.g., child care facilities, group work consultation rooms, home visit services) and the political structures that allow clinicians to consult with the entire family. Family breakdown is also a major impediment to successful treatment, often associated with frequent geographical moves, disrupted routines, multiple caregivers and schools, and changes of family composition. Dropout from treatment is a common problem for clinicians working with CD; dropout rates can be as high as 50% of initial starters (Kazdin, 1993; Miller & Prinz, 1990).

Due to the fact that CD is associated with multiple problems in families, schools, and society, the delivery of comprehensive interventions presents a major challenge to the skill level of the clinician. Most especially, the provision of a state-of-the-art BFI requires multiple therapist skills involving individual and family assessment, behavior change strategies, family engagement and therapy process skills, and communication and interagency liaison skills (Sanders & Dadds, 1993). It cannot be guaranteed that any particular mental health setting will have clinicians who can provide these interventions. Given that the development and effective treatment of CD can involve the interplay of multiple child, family, school, and societal factors, another common impediment to intervention is lack of communication and coordination between different health and educational agencies.

Family interventions for CD have the strongest research support. With younger children, the evidence for these interventions is strong. However, as children move into the teen years, the evidence for the effectiveness of these interventions becomes weaker. Thus, early detection and intervention is a major factor in the prevention and treatment of CD. Clinical settings in which the most common referral of CD is for teenagers, especially those that are well established into a pattern of antisocial behavior, will have relatively little success with the sole use of these family interventions. The applied problems mentioned previously show that the existence of an effective treatment does not guarantee the child and family receiving it. Tertiary models of treatment, although necessary, are probably not the best way to tackle CD in their early stages. Thus, we now consider programs that attempt to reduce the incidence of CD using an EI approach.

EI for CD

Home visiting programs focus on improving the capacity of at-risk parents to provide a nurturing, healthy environment for their children in the early years of life. Parents are usually selected into such programs via the neonatal health care systems on the basis of multiple risk factors such as poverty, teenage mother, low birth weight child, and history of abuse. Models of intervention generally revolve around the formation of a trusting, empathic relationship with the home visitor (usually a nurse) who promotes parenting efficacy and an ensuing increase in healthy parenting behaviors and secure attachment with the infant. These programs have been implemented throughout the world for many years. However, controlled designs have only recently been used to evaluate their effectiveness. The most comprehensive evaluation of such a program was reported by Olds et al. (1998) who now have data up to 15 years follow-up from their original intervention.

In the original trial (Olds, 1989) 400 women with low income, single-parent status, unmarried, or teenage pregnancy were recruited during pregnancy and randomized to standard well-child infant care or two levels of home visiting by a trained nurse. In the most intense condition, the visiting continued until the child's second birthday. Although a range of positive outcomes have been shown to be associated with the intensive visiting, perhaps the most impressive are the recent data showing reductions in delinquency, substance use, and numbers of sexual partners for the children at 15 years of age (Olds et al., 1998). Olds and Kitzman (1993) reviewed similar well-designed studies and concluded that there is substantial evidence to support the effectiveness of these home visiting EI programs in promoting a range of healthy outcomes for children at risk. Further, sufficient research has been reported in this area to allow for analyses of factors moderating intervention outcomes (e.g., Cole, Kitzman, Olds, & Sidora, 1998).

Given the effects attributable to interventions in most other EI research, it is difficult to understand how a nonspecific intervention in the first 2 years of life can lead to such powerful effects 15 years later. Replications and results from other communities are needed because most of the evidence supporting home visitations comes from the one study. A recent trial of a similar program for at-risk mothers in Australia was also successful in producing immediate gains for mothers and infants (Armstrong, Fraser, Dadds, & Morris, 1999); however the results were not impressive in terms of differences from the control group at 2-year follow-up (Fraser, Armstrong, Morris, & Dadds, 2000).

Overall, these results are generally impressive. They are also consistent with the previous literature reviewed on CD showing that the most impressive findings come from programs that target children early in the first few years of life within a broad ecological framework. Waiting till the school years, and especially adolescence, may be too late to affect delinquency and violence.

There are a number of prevention programs that aim to reduce aggression and promote social skills in children via universal curriculum-based programs in schools. These may have some impact on CD but are outside the scope of this review (see Greenberg, Domitrovich, & Bumbarger, 2001). Greenberg et al. located 10 EI programs that have shown success in reducing CD or its risk factors. Similar to tertiary models, the majority of these utilize child cognitive skills training, parent training, or both. Only the most recent and well evaluated are reviewed here.

As an example of a child-focused program, Lochman, Coie, Underwood, and Terry (1993) evaluated a 26-session social skills training program focusing on peer relations, problem solving, and anger management with a sample ($n = 52$) of 9- to 11-year-old aggressive rejected children. Compared to controls, the program children were rated as significantly less aggressive by teachers and more socially accepted by peers at posttreatment and at 1-year follow-up. By contrast, in Lochman's (1985) program, children who had received an anger coping program were, 3 years after the intervention, not different from controls in terms of parent ratings of aggression and observations of disruptive aggressive behavior, or in terms of self-reported delinquency. Tierney, Grossman, and Resch (1995; Big Brother/Big Sister Program) randomly assigned 959 10- to 16-year-old adolescents to a mentor or a wait list control condition. Those with a mentor reported they engaged in significantly less fighting, were less likely to initiate the use of drugs and alcohol, and perceived their family relationships more positively. However, there were no significant differences between groups in terms of self-reported delinquency. Although encouraging, these data were based solely on self-report.

One problem with the use of group interventions for indicated conduct problem youth is that iatrogenic effects have been found in programs in which antisocial youth were grouped together (Dishion, Andrews, Kavanagh, & Soberman, 1996). In contrast, studies have found that conduct problem youth benefit from being in groups with nonproblem children. For example, Hudley and Graham (1993, 1995) paired aggressive 10- to 12-year-old boys with nonaggressive peers in a 12-lesson, school-based intervention focusing on improving the accuracy of children's perceptions and interpretations of others' actions. Compared to controls, teacher ratings indicated that the program successfully reduced aggressive behavior immediately following the intervention. There has been no follow-up data to date. A similar 22-session integration program by Prinz, Blechman, and Dumas (1994) was evaluated up to 6 months following the intervention. Children in the program were rated by teachers as significantly less aggressive than controls at posttest and follow-up. Significant improvements were also noted in the intervention children's prosocial coping and teacher-rated social skills.

Overall, the evidence is not strong that child-focused EI interventions are effective with CD. In general, their results are modest and not durable, the sample sizes are small, and due to the nature of the interventions they are limited to older children and adolescents. However, child-focused interventions remain a component of more comprehensive programs that are showing more impressive results.

Parent-focused interventions generally have produced more clinically significant outcomes. As noted earlier, there have been numerous demonstrations of the effectiveness of social-learning based parent-training programs for families of children with CD. Numerous independent replications in community settings have produced significant results (Sanders, 1999). Although most of these programs developed as tertiary treatments and have been evaluated on clinical populations, a number of authors have argued they are excellent EI strategies in that they effectively reduce conduct problems in early childhood, and thus diminish risk for later delinquency (e.g., Sanders, 1999). As we saw earlier, however, one limitation of a referral-based approach is that it leaves initiatives for intervention in the hands of parents who, as we saw earlier, may not seek help even in extreme situations.

Parent interventions have also been recently applied in both universal prevention and EI formats. Webster-Stratton and Hammond (1998) recently used a parent training model with young Head Start children. The program can thus be regarded as selected and the entry procedure is not dependent on parent referrals. Parents of Head Start children were randomly assigned to receive the intervention or serve as a control by only receiving the usual services. The 9-week intervention consisted of parent training groups and a teacher-training program. Results at posttest and 12 to 18 months follow-up indicate significant improvements in parent behavior, parental involvement in school, child conduct problems, and school-based behavior.

Recently, a number of EI programs have been evaluated that adopt developmental models of CD and as such, utilize multiple interventions across settings and time. This is consistent with a general view that a more comprehensive approach is necessary to alter the developmental trajectories of children who live in high-risk environments and are showing early signs of CD (CPPRG, 1992; Reid & Eddy, 1997). In the Montreal Prevention Experiment, Tremblay and colleagues (McCord, Tremblay, Vitaro, & Desmarais-Gervais, 1994; Tremblay, Masse, Pagani, & Vitaro, 1996; Tremblay et al., 1992; Vitaro & Tremblay, 1994) combined parent training and child skill training.

Primary-school boys rated high on aggressive and disruptive behavior (n = 166) were randomly assigned to a 2-year intervention or placebo control condition. Children worked with normative peers to develop more pro-social and adaptive social behavior, whereas parents worked with family consultants approximately twice a month for 2 years to learn positive discipline techniques and how to support their child's positive behavior. Initial results did not reveal clear group differences. At the 3-year follow-up when the boys were age 12, the treatment group was significantly less likely than control boys to engage in fighting, be classified as having serious adjustment difficulties, and to engage in aggression or delinquent activity. These results came from a variety of self-, teacher-, peer-, and parent-report measures. Effects of the treatment on other forms of antisocial behavior (e.g., self-reported stealing) and substance use continued into early adolescence. Other EI programs have found durable effects that did not emerge until follow-up assessments (see Dadds et al., 1999; Dadds, Spence, Holland, Barrett, & Laurens, 1997). It should also be noted how intervention effects were reported by multiple informants across multiple domains of adjustment (i.e., behavioral, social, school or academic).

The Linking the Interests of Families and Teachers intervention was a large-scale, population-based intervention designed for first- and fifth-grade students and their families from communities reporting high levels of juvenile delinquency (Reid, Eddy, Fetrow, & Stoolmiller, 1999). Its influence on antecedents of CD in the home, classroom, and playground was tested using a randomized trial with 671 children from 12 schools. The intervention offered three distinct components. The school component was designed to be appropriate for both 1st- and 5th-year levels. Classroom instruction and discussion of social and problem-solving skills was combined with cooperative games and presentation of daily rewards in twenty 1-hr sessions within a 10-week period. A phone and answering machine was installed to increase parental involvement in school activities as part of the school–parent communication component. A weekly newsletter with a description of project activities and suggestions for home activities was distributed. Parent training was conducted in weekly groups, and although content was modified to be appropriate for parents of first- and fifth-grade students, the basic parenting skills were similar. Immediate impact was demonstrated for reducing aggression in the playground, maternal aversive behavior, and difficult classroom behavior.

The First Steps Program (Walker et al., 1998) also intervenes with both parents and children, the latter having been identified at kindergarten for exhibiting elevated levels of antisocial behavior. Families with an at-risk child receive a 6-week, home-based program and children participate in a classroom-based, skill-building, and reinforcement program that lasts 2 months. The program has been evaluated with 42 participants in two cohorts using a randomized-controlled design. Positive treatment effects were found for both adaptive and academic behavior at postintervention and at follow-up into early primary school. Similar positive results have been found for a program for students age 6 to 12 exhibiting aggressive and disruptive behavior that targets the child, the parents, and the classroom (Pepler, King, & Byrd, 1991; Pepler, King, Craig, Byrd, & Bream, 1995). In this program, the parent training is optional and it is important to note that significant group differences were only found on teacher ratings. Parents failed to see significant behavior changes in the intervention children.

The CPPRG (1992) implemented Fast Track, a school-wide program that integrates universal, selective, and indicated models of prevention into a comprehensive longitudinal model for the prevention of CD and associated adolescent problem behaviors. A randomized-control trial of 50 elementary schools in four U.S. urban and rural locations is still underway. The universal intervention includes teacher consultation in the use of a series of grade-level versions of the PATHS Curriculum (Greenberg & Kusche, 1993) throughout the elementary years. The targeted intervention package includes a series of family (e.g., home visiting, parenting skills, case management), child (e.g., academic tutoring, social skills training), school, peer group, and community interventions. Targeted children were identified by multigate screening for externalizing behavior problems during kindergarten and consisted of children with the most extreme behavior problems in schools (10%) in neighborhoods with high crime and poverty rates (selected aspect). At present, evaluations are available for the first 3 years (CPPRG, 1999a, 1999b). There have been significant reductions in special education referrals and aggression both at home and at school for the targeted children. The initial results provide evidence for improved social and academic development, including lower sociometric reports of peer aggression and improved observers' ratings of the classroom atmosphere in the intervention sample. Evaluations will continue through middle school as Fast Track adopts a ecological-developmental model that assumes that, for high-risk groups, prevention of antisocial behavior will be achieved by enhancing and linking protective factors within the child, family, school, and community.

In conclusion, it can be seen that only recently have community trials been conducted that use randomized-controlled designs to evaluate multicomponent programs based on comprehensive ecological and developmental models of CD. There are a number of characteristics that appear to be associated with successful EI for conduct problems in children. These include the following:

1. Early identification and intervention beginning not later than preschool or early primary school years.

2. Incorporation of family-based intervention as a core target for change.
3. Adoption of a comprehensive model that emphasizes a broad ecology (child, family, school, community).
4. Adoption of a longitudinal or developmental approach to risk and protective factors and windows of opportunity for intervention.
5. Use of a comprehensive mix of selected (e.g., poor neighborhoods), indicated (identification of aggressive children), and universal (e.g., classroom program) strategies.

SUMMARY

Many effective tertiary treatments for child psychopathology have been developed in the last few decades. However, many children who need help do not benefit from these because they are not referred to appropriate services. If they are referred, their problems have often become severe, generalized, and difficult to treat. EI programs target individuals at risk of developing a disorder or showing early or mild signs of the problem. They thus have advantages over referral-based interventions by intervening before problems become severe and entrenched and by not being dependent on clinical referral. The best EI programs are based on developmental models of how disorders emerge over time, the changing patterns of risk and protective factors, and windows of opportunity for identification and intervention. Such programs have been successfully used to prevent the development of conduct problems and substance use problems in young people. For conduct problems, the most effective EI programs intervene early in childhood using a broad ecological approach to family and school adjustment. These EI approaches to conduct problems have the potential to reduce the incidence of substance use problems later in adolescence and adulthood. A range of practical and ethical issues associated with the use of these programs has been identified. These include concerns about processes of informed consent and confidentiality, stigmatization, accuracy of identification of at-risk children, recruitment processes and participation rates, and intersectorial overlap between health care jurisdictions.

REFERENCES

Abikoff, H., Courtney, M., Pelham, W. E., & Koplewicz, H. S. (1993). Teachers' ratings of disruptive behaviors: The influence of halo effects. *Journal of Abnormal Child Psychology, 21*, 519–533.

Abikoff, H., & Klein, R. G. (1992). Attention-deficit, hyperactivity and conduct disorder: Comorbidity and implications for treatment. *Journal of Consulting and Clinical Psychology, 60*, 881–892.

Armstrong, K. L., Fraser, J. A., Dadds, M. R., & Morris, J. (1999). A randomised controlled trial of nurse home visiting to vulnerable families with newborns. *Journal of Pediatrics and Child Health, 35,* 237–244.

Baer, R. A., & Nietzel, M. T. (1991). Cognitive and behavior treatment of impulsivity in children: A meta-analytic review of the outcome literature. *Journal of Clinical Child Psychology, 20,* 400–412.

Barrett, P. M., Rapee, R. M., Dadds, M. R., & Ryan, S. M. (1996). Family enhancement of cognitive style in anxious and aggressive children. *Journal of Abnormal Child Psychology, 24,* 187–203.

Billings, A. G., & Moos, R. H. (1983). Comparisons of children of depressed and non-depressed parents: A social environmental perspective. *Journal of Abnormal Child Psychology, 11,* 463–486.

Bowlby, D. (1973). *Attachment and loss II: Separation.* New York: Basic Books.

Bowlby, D. (1980). *Attachment and loss I: Attachment.* New York: Basic Books. (Original work published 1969)

Bowlby, D. (1982). *Attachment and loss III: Loss.* New York: Basic Books.

Brewin, C. R. (1987). *Cognitive foundations of clinical psychology.* London: Lawrence Erlbaum Associates, Inc.

Campbell, S. B. (1991). Longitudinal studies of active and aggressive preschoolers: Individual differences in early behavior and outcome. In D. Cicchetti & S. L. Toth (Eds.), *Rochester Symposium on Developmental Psychopathology, Vol. 2: Internalising and externalising expressions of dysfunction* (pp. 57–90). Hillsdale, NJ: Lawrence Erlbaum Associates, Inc.

Caplan, G. (1964). *Principles of preventative therapy.* New York: Basic Books.

Cicchetti, D., & Toth, S. L. (1995). A developmental psychopathology perspective on child abuse and neglect. *Journal of the American Academy of Child and Adolescent Psychiatry, 34,* 541–565.

Cole, R., Kitzman, H., Olds, D., & Sidora, K. (1998). Family context as a moderator of program effects in prenatal and early childhood home visitation. *Journal of Community Psychology, 26,* 37–48.

Conduct Problems Prevention Research Group. (1992). A developmental and clinical model for the prevention of conduct disorder: The FAST Track Program. *Development and Psychopathology, 4,* 509–527.

Conduct Problems Prevention Research Group. (1999a). Initial impact of the FastTrack Prevention trial for conduct problems: Classroom effects. *Journal of Consulting and Clinical Psychology, 67,* 631–647.

Conduct Problems Prevention Research Group. (1999b). Initial impact of the FastTrack Prevention trial for conduct problems: The high risk sample. *Journal of Consulting and Clinical Psychology, 67,* 648–657.

Crick, N. R., & Dodge, K. A. (1996). Social information-processing mechanisms in reactive and proactive aggression. *Child Development, 67,* 993–1002.

Dadds, M. R. (1995). *Families, children, and the development of dysfunction.* New York: Sage.

Dadds, M. R., Holland, D. E., Laurens, K. R., Mullins, M., Barrett, P. M., & Spence, S. H. (1999). Early Intervention and prevention of anxiety disorders: Results at two year follow-up. *Journal of Consulting and Clinical Psychology, 67,* 145–150.

Dadds, M. R., Schwartz, S., & Sanders, M. R. (1987). Marital discord and treatment outcome in the treatment of childhood conduct disorders. *Journal of Consulting and Clinical Psychology, 55,* 396–403.

Dadds, M. R., Spence, S. H., Holland, D. E., Barrett, P. M., & Laurens, K. R. (1997). Prevention and early intervention for anxiety disorders: A controlled trial. *Journal of Consulting and Clinical Psychology, 65,* 627–635.

Dishion, T. J., Andrews, D. W., Kavanagh, K., & Soberman, L. H. (1996). Preventive interventions for high-risk youth: The adolescent transition project. In R. DeV. Peters & R. J. McMahon (Eds.), *Preventing childhood disorders, substance abuse and delinquency* (pp. 184–214). Thousand Oaks, CA: Sage.

Dodge, K. A. (1985). Attributional bias in aggressive children. In P. C. Kendall (Ed.), *Advances in cognitive-behavioral research and therapy* (Vol. 4, pp. 73–110). Orlando, FL: Academic.

Durlak, J. E., Furhman, T., & Lampman, C. (1991). Effectiveness for cognitive-behavioral therapy for maladapting children: A meta-analysis. *Psychological Bulletin, 110*, 204–214.

Elder, G. H., Nguyen, T. V., & Caspi, A. (1985). Linking family hardship to children's lives. *Developmental Psychology, 56*, 361–375.

Emery, R. E. (1982). Interparental conflict and the children of discord and divorce. *Psychological Bulletin, 9*, 310–330.

Fergusson, D. M., Horwood, L. J., & Shannon, F. T. (1984). A proportional hazards model of family breakdown. *Journal of Marriage and the Family, 46*, 539–549.

Forehand, R. L., & Long, N. (1988). Outpatient treatment of the acting out child: Procedures, long term follow-up data, and clinical problems. *Advances in Behavior Research and Therapy, 10*, 129–177.

Fraser, J. A., Armstrong, K. L., Morris, J., & Dadds, M. R. (2000). Home visiting intervention for vulnerable families with newborns: Follow-up results of a randomised controlled trial. *Child Abuse and Neglect, 24*, 1399–1429.

Frick, P. J., Bodin, S. D., & Barry, C. T. (2000). Psychopathic traits and conduct problems in community and clinic-referred samples of children: Further development of the Psychopathy Screening Devise. *Psychological Assessment, 12*, 382–393.

Goodyer, I. N. (1990). Family relationships, life events and child psychopathology. *Journal of Child Psychology and Psychiatry, 31*, 161–192.

Gordon, R. S. (1983). An operational classification of disease prevention. *Public Health Reports, 98*, 107–109.

Green, S. M., Loeber, R., & Lahey, B. B. (1992). Child psychopathology and deviant family hierarchies. *Journal of Child and Family Studies, 1*, 341–349.

Greenberg, M. T., Domitrovich, C., & Bumbarger, B. (2001). The prevention of mental disorders in school-aged children: Current state of the field. *Prevention and Treatment, 4*, Article 0001a. Retrieved http://journals.apa.org/prevention/volume4/pre0040001a.html

Greenberg, M. T., & Kusche, C. A. (1993). *Promoting social and emotional development in deaf children: The PATHS Curriculum.* Seattle: University of Washington Press.

Haley, J. (1976). *Problem solving therapy.* New York: Harper.

Harpur, T. J., Hare, R. D., & Hakstian, A. R. (1989). Two factor conceptualisation of psychopathy: Construct validity and assessment implications. *Psychological Assessment, 1*, 6–17.

Henggeler, S. W., Melton, G. B., Brondino, M. J., Scherer, D. G., & Hanley, J. H. (1997). Multisystemic therapy with violent and chronic juvenile offenders and their families: The role of treatment fidelity in successful dissemination. *Journal of Consulting and Clinical Psychology, 65*, 821–833.

Hetherington, E. M., & Martin, B. (1979). Family interaction. In H. C. Quay & J. S. Werry (Eds.), *Psychopathological disorders of childhood* (pp. 30–82). New York: Wiley.

Hinshaw, S. P. (1987). On the distinction between attentional deficits/hyperactivity and conduct problems/aggression in children with attentional deficits. *Journal of Clinical Child Psychology, 20*, 301–312.

Hinshaw, S. P., Lahey, B. B., & Hart, E. L. (1993). Issues of taxonomy and co-morbidity in the development of conduct disorder. *Development and Psychopathology, 5*, 31–50.

Hudley, C., & Graham, S. (1993). An attributional intervention to reduce peer-directed aggression among African-American boys. *Child Development, 64*, 124–138.

Hudley, C., & Graham, S. (1995). School-based interventions for aggressive African-American boys. *Applied and Preventive Psychology, 4*, 185–195.

Kazdin, A. E. (1987). *Conduct disorder in childhood and adolescents.* Newbury Park, CA: Sage.

Kazdin, A. E. (1993). Treatment of conduct disorder: Progress and directions in psychotherapy research. *Development and Psychopathology, 5*, 277–310.

Kazdin, A. E., Siegal, T., & Bass, D. (1992). Cognitive problem solving skills and parent manage-ment training in the treatment of antisocial behavior in children. *Journal of Consulting and Clinical Psychology, 60*, 733–747.

Keenan, K., Loeber, R., & Green, S. (1999). Conduct disorder in girls: A review of the literature. *Clinical Child and Family Psychology Review, 2*, 3–19.

Kochanska, G. (1993). Towards a synthesis of parental-socialization and child temperament in early development of conscience. *Child Development, 64*, 325–347.

Lahey, B. B., Schwab-Stone, M., Goodman, S. H., Waldman, I. D., Canino, G., Rathouz, P. J., Miller, T. L., Dennis, K. D., Bird, H., & Jensen, P. S. (2000). Age and gender differences in oppositional behavior and conduct problems: A cross-sectional household study of middle childhood and adolescence. *Journal of Abnormal Psychology, 109*, 488–503.

Lamb, M., & Elster, A. B. (1985). Adolescent mother-infant-father relationships. *Developmental Psychology, 21*, 768–773.

Lazarus, R. S., & Folkman, S. (1984). *Stress, appraisal and coping*. New York: Springer.

Lochman, J. E. (1985). Effects of different length treatments in cognitive-behavioral interventions with aggressive boys. *Child Psychiatry and Human Development, 16*, 45–56.

Lochman, J. E. (1990). Modification of childhood aggression. In M. Hersen, R. M. Eisler, & P. M. Miller (Eds.), *Progress in behavior modification* (Vol. 25, pp. 47–85). New York: Academic.

Lochman, J. E., Coie, J. D., Underwood, M. K., & Terry, R. (1993). Effectiveness of a social relations intervention for aggressive and nonaggressive, rejected children. *Journal of Consulting and Clinical Psychology, 61*, 1053–1058.

Loeber, R. (1990). Development and risk factors of juvenile antisocial behavior and delinquency. *Clinical Psychology Review, 10*, 1–41.

Loeber, R., Burke, J. D., Lahey, B. B., Winters, A., & Zera, M. (2000). Oppositional defiant and con-duct disorder: A review of the past 10 years, part 1. *Journal of the American Academy of Child and Adolescent Psychiatry, 39*, 1468–1484.

Loeber, R., & Farrington, D. P. (2000). Young children who commit crime: Epidemiology, develop-mental origins, risk factors, early interventions, and policy implications. *Development and Psychopathology, 12*, 737–762.

Lynam, D. R. (1997). Childhood psychopathy: Capturing the fledgling psychopath in a nomo-logical net. *Journal of Abnormal Psychology, 106*, 425–438.

McCord, J., Tremblay, R. E., Vitaro, F., & Desmarais-Gervais, L. (1994). Boys' disruptive behavior, school adjustment, and delinquency: The Montreal Prevention Experiment. *International Journal of Behavioral Development, 17*, 739–752.

Miller, G. E., & Prinz, R. J. (1990). Enhancement of social learning family interventions for child-hood conduct disorder. *Psychological Bulletin, 108*, 291–307.

Minuchin, S. (1974). *Families and family therapy*. Cambridge, MA: Harvard University Press.

Minuchin, S., Montalvo, B., Guerney, B., Rosman, B., & Schumer, F. (1967). *Families of the slums*. New York: Basic Books.

Moffitt, T. E. (1993). Adolescence-limited and life-course-persistent antisocial behaviour: A devel-opmental taxonomy. *Psychological Review, 100*, 674–701.

Moffitt, T. E., Caspi, A., Dickson, N., Silva, P., & Stanton, W. (1996). Childhood-onset versus adoles-cent-onset antisocial conduct problems in males: Natural history from ages 3 to 18 years. *De-velopment and Psychopathology, 8*, 399–424.

Moffitt, T. E., & Silva, P. A. (1988). Self-reported delinquency, neuropsychological deficit, and his-tory of attention deficit disorder. *Journal of Abnormal Child Psychology, 16*, 553–569.

Mrazek, P. J., & Haggerty, R. J. (1994). *Reducing risks for mental disorders: Frontiers for preventive intervention research*. Washington, DC: National Academy Press.

Needleman, H. L., & Bellinger, D. C. (1981). The epidemiology of low-level lead exposure in child-hood. *Journal of Child Psychiatry, 20*, 496–512.

O'Dea, J. (2000). School-based interventions to prevent eating problems: First do no harm. *Eating Disorders: The Journal of Treatment and Prevention, 8*, 123–130.

Olds, D. L. (1989). The Prenatal/Early Infancy Project: A strategy for responding to the needs of high risk mothers and their children. *Prevention in Human Services, 7*, 59–87.

Olds, D., & Kitzman, H. (1993). Review of research on home visiting for pregnant women and parents of young children. *Future of Children, 3*, 53–92.

Olds, D., Henderson, C. R., Cole, R., Eckenrode, J., Kitzman, H., Luckey, D., Pettitt, L., Sidora, K., Morris, P., & Powers, J. (1998). Long-term effects of nurse home visitation on children's criminal and antisocial behavior: 15-year follow-up of a randomized controlled trial. *Journal of the American Medical Association, 280*, 1238–1244.

Patterson, G. R. (1982). *Coercive family process*. Eugene, OR: Castalia.

Patterson, G. R. (1986). Performance models for antisocial boys. *American Psychologist, 41*, 432–444.

Patterson, G. R., DeGarmo, D. S., & Knutson, N. (2000). Hyperactive and antisocial behaviours: Comorbid or two points in the same process? *Development and Psychopathology, 12*, 91–106.

Patterson, G. R., & Reid, J. B. (1984). Social interactional processes in the family: The study of the moment by moment family transactions in which human social development is embedded. *Journal of Applied Developmental Psychology, 5*, 237–262.

Pepler, D. J., King, G., & Byrd, W. (1991). A socially cognitive-based social skills training program for aggressive children. In D. J. Pepler & K. Rubin (Eds.), *The development and treatment of childhood aggression* (pp. 361–379). Hillsdale, NJ: Lawrence Erlbaum Associates, Inc.

Pepler, D. J., King, G., Craig, W., Byrd, B., & Bream, L. (1995). The development and evaluation of a multisystem social skills training program for aggressive children. *Child and Youth Care Forum, 24*, 297–313.

Prinz, R. J., Blechman, E. A., & Dumas, J. E. (1994). An evaluation of peer coping-skills training for childhood aggression. *Journal of Clinical Child Psychology, 23*, 193–203.

Reeves, J. C., Werry, J. S., Elkind, G. S., & Zametkin, A. (1987). Attention deficit, conduct and anxiety disorders in children. II. Clinical characteristics. *Journal of the American Academy of Child and Adolescent Psychiatry, 26*, 144–155.

Reid, J. B., & Eddy, J. M. (1997). The prevention of antisocial behavior: Some considerations in the search for effective interventions. In D. Staff, J. Breiling, & J. D. Maser (Eds.), *Handbook of antisocial behavior* (pp. 343–356). New York: Wiley.

Reid, J. B., Eddy, J. M., Fetrow, R. A., & Stoolmiller, M. (1999). Description and immediate impacts of a preventive intervention for conduct problems. *American Journal of Community Psychology, 27*, 483–517.

Rutter, M. (1972). *Maternal deprivation reassessed*. Middlesex, England: Penguin.

Rutter, M., McDonald, H., LeCouteur, A., Harrington, R., Bolton, P., & Bailey, A. (1990). Genetic factors in child psychiatric disorders—II. Empirical findings. *Journal of Child Psychology and Psychiatry, 31*, 39–83.

Ryan, N. D. (2001). Diagnosing pediatric depression. *Society of Biological Psychiatry, 49*, 1050–1054.

Sanders, M. R. (1999). Triple P-Positive Parenting Program: Towards an empirically validated multilevel parenting and family support strategy for the prevention of behavior and emotional problems in children. *Clinical Child and Family Psychology Review, 2*, 71–90.

Sanders, M. R., & Dadds, M. R. (1993). *Behavioral family intervention*. Boston, MA: Allyn & Bacon.

Sanders, M. R., Dadds, M. R., & Bor, W. (1989). A contextual analysis of oppositional child behavior and maternal aversive behavior in families of conduct disordered children. *Journal of Clinical Child Psychology, 18*, 72–83.

Schachar, R., Sandberg, S., & Rutter, M. (1986). Agreement between teachers' ratings and observations of hyperactivity, inattentiveness, and defiance. *Journal of Abnormal Child Psychology, 14*, 331–345.

Shochet, I. M., & O'Gorman, J. (1995). Ethical issues in research on adolescent depression and suicidal behaviour. *Australian Psychologist, 30*, 183–187.

Silverthorn, P., & Frick, P. J. (1999). Developmental pathways to antisocial behaviour: The delayed-onset pathway in girls. *Development and Psychopathology, 11*, 101–126.

Simeonsson, R. J. (1994). Toward an epidemiology of developmental, educational, and social problems of childhood. In R. J. Simeonsson (Ed.), *Risk, resilience and prevention: Promoting the well-being of all children* (pp. 13–32). Baltimore: Brookes.

Spence, S. H., & Dadds, M. R. (1996). Preventing childhood anxiety disorders. *Behaviour Change, 13*, 241–249.

Thomas, A., & Chess, S. (1977). *Temperament and development.* New York: Brunner/Mazel.

Tierney, J. P., Grossman, J. B., & Resch, N. L. (1995). *Making a difference: The impact study of Big Brother/Sister.* Philadelphia: Public/Private Ventures.

Tremblay, R. E., Masse, L. C., Pagani, L., & Vitaro, F. (1996). From childhood aggression to adolescent maladjustment: The Montreal Prevention Experiment. In R. DeV. Peters & R. J. McMahon (Eds.), *Preventing childhood disorders, substance abuse and delinquency* (pp. 268–298). Thousand Oaks, CA: Sage.

Tremblay, R. E., Masse, L. C., Perron, D., LeBlanc, M., Schwartzman, A. E., & Ledingham, J. E. (1992). Early disruptive behavior, poor school achievement, delinquent behavior, and delinquent personality; Longitudinal analyses. *Journal of Consulting and Clinical Psychology, 60*, 64–72.

Vitaro, F., & Tremblay, R. E. (1994). Impact of a prevention program on aggressive children's friendships and social adjustment. *Journal of Abnormal Child Psychology, 22*, 457–475.

Wahler, R. G. (1980). The insular mother: Her problems in parent–child treatment. *Journal of Applied Behavior Analysis, 13*, 207–219.

Wahler, R. G., & Dumas, J. E. (1984). Changing the observational coding style of insular and non-insular mothers: A step toward maintenance. In R. F. Dangel & R. A. Polster (Eds.), *Parent training: Foundations of research and practice* (pp. 379–461). New York: Guilford.

Walker, H. M., Kavanagh, K., Stiller, B., Golly, A., Severson, H. H., & Feil, E. G. (1998). First step to success: An early intervention approach for preventing school antisocial behavior. *Journal of Emotional and Behavioral Disorders, 6*, 66–80.

Webster-Stratton, C. (1985). Predictors of outcome in parent training for conduct disordered children. *Behavior Therapy, 16*, 223–243.

Webster-Stratton, C., & Hammond, M. (1998). Conduct problems and level of social competence in head start children: Prevalence, pervasiveness, and associated risk factors. *Clinical Child and Family Psychology Review, 1*, 101–124.

West, D. J. (1982). *Delinquency: Its roots, careers and prospects.* Cambridge, MA: Harvard University Press.

Wierson, M., Forehand, R. L., & Frame, C. L. (1992). Epidemiology and treatment of mental health problems in juvenile delinquents. *Advances in Behaviour Research and Therapy, 14*, 93–120.

Zeanah, C. H., Keener, M. A., Stewart, L., & Anders, T. F. (1985). Prenatal perception of infant personality. *Journal of the American Academy of Child and Adolescent Psychiatry, 24*, 204–210.

9

Community-Oriented Interventions for Conduct Disorder: Theoretical Progress Needing Empirical Support

Wendy M. Craig
Angela R. Digout
Queen's University
Kingston, Ontario, Canada

Behaviors symptomatic of conduct disorder (CD) are one of the most common reasons for referral to children's mental health services (Kazdin, 1995). CD is a chronic childhood disorder that is highly resistant to treatment and the primary precursor to antisocial behavior in adulthood (Kazdin, 1993). Consequently, over the last 2 decades there has been a surge of etiological and developmental research on CD to facilitate the development of effective prevention and intervention strategies. Children with CD are at risk for developing psychiatric problems, substance abuse, chronic unemployment, divorce, a range of physical disorders, motor vehicle accidents, dependence on welfare systems, and generalized levels of reduced attainment and competence in adulthood (Moffitt, Caspi, Rutter, & Silva, 2001). CD and its associated behavior problems are not only persistent across an individual's life span but are often transmitted across generations (Huesmann, Eron, Lefkowitz, & Walder, 1984; Serbin et al., 1998). In addition, CD often has severe effects on others such as siblings, peers, parents, educators, and strangers who are victims of children's antisocial and aggressive acts. The individual, social, and monetary costs of CD are high: CD children generate life-long costs because they are involved in multiple systems such as the mental health, juvenile justice, special education, and social services. To date, there is a large body of research identifying and reviewing the risk factors associated with CD (see Tremblay, LeMarquand, & Vitaro, 1999, for a review), but effective treatments over the long term remain elusive.

Due to the chronic nature of CD and its resistance to treatment, researchers have recently focused on more systemic based interventions. Historically, the focus was treating the individual child and the family (Patterson, DeBaryshe, & Ramsey, 1989). Currently, researchers and clinicians have taken a more systemic or community approach to the problem and in the 1990s there has been a surge of what is termed *community-based treatment*. Today, this community-oriented approach to preventing antisocial behavior has become entrenched in both public policies and practices in the United States and Canada. The goal of this chapter is to critically examine community-based approaches to CD, the empirical evaluation of these approaches, and to increase our understanding of the challenges associated with this approach.

DEFINING COMMUNITY-BASED TREATMENTS

One difficulty in reviewing community-based treatments for CD, oppositional defiant disorder (ODD) and other problem behaviors is the broad range of definitions used to classify the interventions. Kazdin (1995) described community-wide interventions as those that "focus on activities and community programs to foster competence and peer relations" (p. 77). Key processes "develop prosocial behavior and connections with peers [and] activities are seen to promote prosocial behavior and to be incompatible with antisocial behavior" (Kazdin, 1995, p. 77). However, a large number of programs target prosocial behavior, and not all of these interventions focus on community involvement or systemic aspects. Schoenwald and Henggeler (1999) provided a more practical definition of community-based treatments such that ". . . treatment [is] delivered to youth and their caregivers (generally parents or relatives; in some cases, foster parents) in their indigenous communities, in the home or another service setting likely to be available in most communities" (p. 476). However, interventions delivered within a child's community do not necessitate a systemic approach to treatment, nor do they necessarily target relevant processes.

We propose the following definition that highlights what are, in our opinion, the key components of community-based interventions. First, the intervention should take place within the community or in the setting where the behavior is most likely to occur (i.e., where treatment takes place). As such, the skills learned during treatment will be more likely to generalize to relevant settings. Second, interventions should be implemented not only with the individuals with CD but within the school, within the peer group, and with parents and family (i.e., who is targeted). In other words, CD and related behavior problems do not occur in isolation and therefore interventions with the individual with CD are necessary but not sufficient. Consequently, we need to extend our focus beyond the individual to include peers, school, parents, community, and society. Third, CD and its associated problems need to be addressed from a systemic perspective (i.e., what is targeted). This systemic perspective can take one of two forms: single component interventions occurring within a system that allow for generalizability of skills (e.g., treatment within the peer system where there is an opportunity for children to practice their skills with other peers) or multicomponent interventions in which change between systems is targeted (e.g., family–school change). Given the complexity of CD, multicomponent interventions targeting change both within and between levels are hypothesized to be more effective.

Although defining community-based treatment is a first step, we must also evaluate the programs. Evaluation that demonstrates the empirical validity and utility of community-based treatment needs to occur at all levels of the system if we are to be able to identify both the unique contributions of intervention at each of the levels of the system, as well as the combined, cumulative, and interactive effects of the intervention.

Evaluating Community-Based Treatments

Most community intervention programs are grounded in ecological theory as discussed by Belsky (1981) and Bronfenbrenner (1979). An ecological theory of development asserts that individuals operate within larger systems such as families, peer groups, schools, community, and larger social contexts. It is the interactions between these systems and the interactions between individuals within these systems that contribute to either healthy or unhealthy development. Thus, if we are to intervene successfully in CD, it is important to understand from a theoretical and empirical perspective the factors that are present in each of the systems that may be contributing to the disorder, as well as those factors that may protect individuals from the development of CD. As such, effective interventions should then be designed based on this knowledge. Theoretical assumptions behind community approaches encompass a wide variety of programs and strategies. These programs are primarily based on the involvement of the community and the coordination of individuals, families, peers, and educators through engaging them in a mutually compatible set of strategies. Prevention models have been adapted from the field of medical health (i.e., Mrazek & Haggerty, 1994) in which there has been considerable success in reducing both heart and lung diseases (Schooler, Farquhar, Fortmann, & Flora, 1997). Mental health professionals, as well as researchers, now are applying the same principles from these medical interventions to the prevention and intervention of CD.

Kazdin (1993) proposed criteria that are useful to consider when identifying promising treatments. These include conceptualization, or theory relating mechanisms to dysfunction; basic research supporting that the mechanism is related to dysfunction; outcome evidence of the efficacy of the treatment; and process outcome relation. With respect to community interventions, we argue that the first three of these objectives have to some extent been successfully met. Empirical evaluation, however, of community intervention is limited, primarily due to the fact that to be effective in addressing the comprehensive range of risk factors associated with CD, interventions need to be similarly comprehensive. In addition, evaluations are complex because of the heterogeneity of the intervention, the services involved, the treatment practices, and the coordination of these services and treatments.

More specifically, Tremblay and Craig (1995) summarized the delinquency prevention experiments literature with the following observations:

1. When interventions target more than one risk factor, there are significant differences between treated and untreated groups. Thus, it is important to intervene in multiple contexts where it is likely more effective than intervention in a single context.

2. Successful interventions are implemented long before adolescence. Tremblay et al. (1999) argued that in fact the group to target is adolescent mothers because research suggests that babies born to adolescent mothers with a history of behavior problems are at a very high risk for many developmental problems (Serbin, Peters, & Schwartzman, 1996). Adolescent mothers with behavioral problems tend not to provide adequate care to their developing fetus and furthermore mate with males who also have a long history of behavior problems (Rowe & Farrington, 1997). If we intervene with these parents, the intervention may have a large effect because having a child is a time of dramatic change and having children does elicit caring behavior from parents (Carter, Lederhendler, & Kirkpatrick, 1997). It is important to note, however, that the effect of the intervention will not only change the course of development for the mother but likely will be most effective on the child or the next generation.

3. The intervention needs to last for a relatively long period of time, over 2 years.

4. Implementation of the programs need to address issues of program integrity and consistency to ensure the fidelity of the program.

5. Finally, preventive interventions should be evaluated with long-term follow-ups that utilize experimental designs. These evaluations should be intensive, well designed, and methodological sound.

When reviewing the community based interventions targeting CD and its associated behavior problems, we assessed them relative to these principles.

RESEARCH EVIDENCE FOR COMMUNITY-BASED TREATMENTS

In general, researchers conduct most treatment outcome studies under highly controlled laboratory conditions or efficacy trials. Many meta-analyses support the efficacy of these treatments provided under controlled conditions (e.g., Weisz, Weiss, Han, Granger, & Morton, 1995). However, the characteristics of laboratory-based treatments often differ from the characteristics of treatments provided in mental health clinics and other community-based settings (i.e., effectiveness trials). For example, the population referred to clinics are often more severe, more heterogeneous, and have a broader, multiproblem focus (Weisz, 1998). In addition, clinic-based treatments are often more flexible, longer in duration, and more eclectic in nature than laboratory-based treatments. Often nonbehavioral interventions are selected, and treatment manuals are likely not used. These considerable differences highlight a need for well-designed treatment outcome studies carried out in both clinic and community settings (Weisz, Weiss, & Donenberg, 1992).

According to Brestan and Eyberg (1998), a large proportion of the studies included in their review of empirically supported treatments for CD occurred in community locations. Of the 82 outcome studies with CD children, 43.0% took place in the child or adolescent's school and 11.4% in the child or adolescent's home, whereas 24.7% took place in other, possibly community, locations. However, it is not mentioned if these interventions targeted systemic change, if they took place in multiple domains simultaneously, or if each unique aspect of the intervention was evaluated and the cumulative effect of the intervention was assessed.

An early review by Joffe and Offord (1987) found little support for community-based interventions. They examined 10 community prevention projects targeting antisocial behavior. The programs included components such as friendships with a responsible adult, individual and group counseling, access to existing community services, or the establishment of new community services. Joffe and Offord reported either iatrogenic effects or nonsignificant findings across all 10 studies, even in long-term follow-ups. However, the authors also noted that these early studies used inadequate methodology (e.g., unbalanced method of data collection, potential responder bias) and lacked objective and systematic evaluation. These problems made the overall effectiveness of early community-based programs difficult to determine.

More recently, Zigler, Taussig, and Black (1992) looked at the effects of universal early childhood intervention programs on the prevention of juvenile delinquency. In their review, Zigler et al. suggested programs such as the High/Scope Perry Preschool Project (Schweinhart, Barnes, & Weikart,

1993) and Yale Child Welfare Project (Seitz, Rosenbaum, & Apfel, 1985), initiated to reduce school failure, may help to reduce future delinquency as well. These programs often examined systemic change and are based in such theories as Bronfenbrenner's (1979) ecological systems theory. It is hypothesized that the early prevention programs alleviate some of the risk factors associated with CD. More specifically, successful experiences (e.g., cognitive, socioemotional, improved parenting) early in childhood are hypothesized to "snowball" into further success in school and other contexts. Although these programs do not specifically target delinquency, they do reduce delinquency because they target multiple risk factors or theoretical developmental factors related to delinquency; they are multisystem programs working in multiple domains, and they have high external validity.

We turn to a consideration of more recently developed programs to see how they fare. We review some of the current community-based programs and evaluate them based on the criteria proposed by Tremblay and Craig (1995) and Kazdin (1993). In our review, we have selected intervention and prevention programs that meet the following criteria: (a) they target aggression, delinquency, disruptive behavior, CD, or ODD; in the case of prevention, the program targets high risk families or neighborhoods; (b) they are services provided in the child's naturalistic setting (e.g., school, home, other community locations), thus promoting generalizability of learned skills; and (c) they target systemic change either within or between peer, family, and community systems.

Although individually focused treatments may target community building processes (e.g., prosocial behavior), these interventions are not included unless there is an opportunity to generalize skills (e.g., peer interventions) within the program. Treatments sometimes defined as community based (e.g., wilderness programs and boot camps) do not fulfill the criteria previously listed, as they are not provided in the child's naturalistic setting. Tables 9.1, 9.2, 9.3a, and 9.3b provide summaries of selected community-based intervention and prevention programs by describing a representative study of the program, describing the study setting, who took part, and the processes targeted by the intervention. Using the criteria we have laid out for community-based treatments, the following selected studies represent four broad categories of interventions: peer, parent/family, multicomponent intervention, and multicomponent prevention approaches to community-based treatment.

Community-Based Peer Interventions

There is strong evidence to support the use of skills-based training to reduce aggression in children and adolescents (e.g., Bierman & Furman, 1984; Lochman, 1992), and these interventions are described elsewhere in this

TABLE 9.1
Description of Selected Empirical Papers Ordered Alphabetically

Researchers/Date	Program Title	Treatment Type[a]	Theoretical Approach	Setting/Treatment Context	I/P	Components	Population
Bierman & Furman (1984)	Social Skills Training Peer Involvement	Behavior therapy	Social/developmental ?[b]	School	I	Single	Disliked preadolescents
Borduin et al. (1995)	Missouri Delinquency Project/Multisystemic Therapy	Community-wide intervention	Ecological systems Family systems	Community	I	Multi	Serious juvenile offenders
Chamberlain (1990, 1996a, 1996b)	Treatment Foster Care	Residential treatment	Social learning theory	Residential, home, school	I	Multi	Youth with severe delinquency
CPPRG (1999)	Fast Track	Community-wide intervention	Developmental and systemic theories	School, home	P	Multi	High-risk schools, disruptive children and their parents
Cunningham, Bremner, & Boyle (1995)	Community-Based Parent Training	Parent management training	Behavioral	Community & clinic	I	Single	Parents of preschoolers at risk for disruptive behavior disorders
Dishion & Andrews (1995)	Adolescent Transition Program	Community-wide intervention	Social learning theory	Community ?[b]	P	Multi	High-risk adolescents and their families
Guevremont & Foster (1993)	Social Problem Solving Training	Cognitive based	Cognitive behavioral	School	I	Single	Teacher referred aggressive and disruptive boys
Hawkins et al. (1992)	Seattle Social Development Project	Community-wide intervention	Social development model	School	P	Multi	Risk factors for delinquency in elementary school children
Kamps, Tankersley, & Ellis (2000)	Social Skills Intervention	Community-wide intervention	Social learning ?	School	I	Multi	Children with behavior problems in Head Start
Kellam et al. (1994)	Good Behavior Game	Behavior therapy	Developmental epidemiological	School	P	Single	Epidemiologically defined population
Lochman (1992); Lochman, Burch, Curry, & Lampron (1984)	Anger Coping	Cognitive based	Cognitive behavioral	School	I	Single	Teacher referred aggressive and disruptive boys

(Continued)

TABLE 9.1
(Continued)

Researchers/Date	Program Title	Treatment Type[a]	Theoretical Approach	Setting/Treatment Context	I/P	Components	Population
McDonald & Sayger (1998)	FAST (Families and schools together)	Community-wide intervention	Family stress theory, ecological systems	School	P	Multi	At risk elementary & middle school children & families
McCord (1978)	Cambridge-Somerville Youth Study	Community-wide intervention	?	Family, community	I	Multi	Average and difficult boys
Pepler, King, Craig, Byrd, & Bream (1995)	Earlscourt Social Skills Group Program	Community-wide intervention	Social learning/Social cognitive & Systems theory	School	I	Multi	Aggressive school-age children and their parents
Peters et al. (2000)	Better Beginnings, Better Futures	Community-wide intervention	Ecological systems	Home, school, community	P	Multi	High-risk neighborhoods
Prinz, Blechman, & Dumas (1994)	Peer Coping Skills	Behavior therapy cognitive based	Social learning/Developmental	School	I	Single	Aggressive school-age children
Reid, Eddy, Fetrow, & Stoolmiller (1999)	Linking the Interest of Families and Teachers	Community-wide intervention	Developmental	School	P	Multi	First and fifth graders in at-risk neighborhoods
Thompson, Ruma, Schuchmann, & Burke (1996)	Common Sense Parenting	Parent training	Social learning theory ?	Community	I	Single	Parents of children with behavior problems
Tremblay, Pagani-Kurtz, Masse, Vitaro, & Pihl (1995)	Montreal Longitudinal-Experimental Study	Community-wide intervention	Developmental	School/home	P	Multi	Disruptive boys from low socioeconomic status schools
Webster-Stratton (1998)	PARTNERS	Parent management training	Developmental	Community	I	Single	Parents of Head Start children at risk for conduct problems

Note. I = intervention; P = prevention.
[a]Based on Kazdin's (1995) classes of treatments.
[b]? means it is unclear if set in community.

TABLE 9.2
Results of Community-Based Treatment

Authors	Age (in Years)	Constructs Assessed	No. of Participants	Length of Treatment	Treatment Description	Length of Follow-Up	Results at Posttest or Follow-Up[a]	
							Behavior Problems	Other
Bierman & Furman (1984)	5th and 6th graders	Conversational skills, peer acceptance, peer interactions, child self-perception	56 (28 boys 28 girls)	Ten 30 min sessions over 6 weeks	1. Social skills (coaching); 2. Peer involvement; 3. Combined; 4. Control	6 weeks	Peer acceptance +	1. Social skills + social interaction +; 2. Peer acceptance + self-perception +
Borduin et al. (1995)	12–17	Psychiatric symptomatology; adolescent behavior problems; family functioning, interactions; peer relations; criminal activity	176 (119 boys 57 girls)	MST M = 23 months; IT M = 28 months	1. MST 2. IT	4 years	1. Recidivism +	1. Family correlates of antisocial behavior +; 1. Future criminal behavior +
Chamberlain (1990, 1996a, 1996b)	12–18	Number of problem behaviors institutionalization rates	16 + match	Average 6 months	Individual treatment, family therapy, school consultation, etc.	2 years	Incarcerations +	

(Continued)

231

TABLE 9.2
(Continued)

Authors	Age (in Years)	Constructs Assessed	No. of Participants	Length of Treatment	Treatment Description	Length of Follow-Up	Results at Posttest or Follow-Up[a]		
							Behavior Problems	Other	
CPPRG (1999)	M = 6.5	Child social cognition, peer relations and reading, social competence, parent behavior, social cognition, child aggression, disruptive behavior	891	22 weekly 2-hour sessions + classroom intervention over 1 year	Universal: classroom social skills training; selective: academic tutoring, parent training; home visits	0	Observed disruptive behavior +	Parent- and teacher-rated aggression 0; social, emotional and academic skills +
Cunningham, Bremner, & Boyle (1995)	M = 52.3–54.2 months	Behavior problems at home, problem solving skills, cost analyses, parent–child interactions	150 families	11–12 weeks	1. Community Parent Group 2. Clinic Parent Group 3. Wait list control	6 months	Problem behaviors in home +	1. Had greater behavior improvements, lower cost, & better maintenance
Dishion & Andrews (1995)	10–14	Videotaped family interaction, Family Events Checklist, CBCL/TRF, early adolescent smoking	158	12 weekly 90 min sessions	1. Parent focus 2. Teen focus 3. Combined 4. Self-directed change	1 year	Family conflict +	1. Subsequent tobacco use +; 2. Favorable attitudes toward substance abuse –

Study	Age	Measures	N	Duration	Conditions	Follow-up		
Guevremont & Foster (1993)	11–12	Teacher rated behavior, problem-solving skills	5 boys	18 sessions, 40–45 min over 6 weeks	1. Baseline ratings 2. Problems solving training 3. Generalization	6 months	3. disruptive behavior +	Problem solving abilities +
Hawkins et al. (1992)	1st–4th grade	Delinquency, substance use, family constructs, norms/beliefs	199 (102 boys, 97 girls) + 709 controls	4 years	1. Teacher training, child skills training, parent training; 2. Control group	0	Delinquency initiation +	Family communication +; norms 0
Kamps, Tankersley, & Ellis (2000)	4–7	Observed classroom behavior, teacher-rated behavior, observed peer interactions	31 (13 girls, 18 boys)	Weekly over 3 years	1. Social skills training, peer tutoring, parent training, parent–child activities; 2. Control group	3 years	Aggression +; inappropriate behavior +	Negative verbal statements +; teacher complaints +
Kellam et al. (1994)	5–9	Teacher rated aggressive behavior conduct disorder	590	3 weekly sessions for 2 years	1. Good behavior game; 2. Mastery learning as active control group	6 years	Teacher-rated aggressive behavior +	
Lochman (1992) Lochman, Burch, Curry, & Lampron (1984)	9–12	General behavioral deviance; substance use, self-esteem; social problem solving; behavioral observations	145 boys	4–5 months	1. Anger control; 2. Untreated aggression; 3. Nonaggression	2.5–3.5 years	Self-reported delinquency 0	Self-esteem +; problem solving +; substance use +; class behavior 0

(Continued)

TABLE 9.2
(Continued)

Authors	Age (in Years)	Constructs Assessed	No. of Participants	Length of Treatment	Treatment Description	Length of Follow-Up	Behavior Problems	Other
							Results at Posttest or Follow-Up[a]	
McDonald & Sayger (1998)	4–14	Class/home behavior, family cohesiveness, changes in parent behavior	104 families	8 weekly sessions & then monthly for 2 years	Family therapy, parent-mediated play, parent training	6 months & 2 years	Parent-reported conduct disorder	Family cohesion +
McCord (1978)	5–13	Criminal behavior, adjustment problems	506 boys	Average twice a month for 5.5 years	Flexible, home visits, tutoring, summer camp, mentoring, family counseling	37 years	Court records –	Adjustment problems –; subjective evaluation +
Pepler, King, Craig, Byrd, & Bream (1995)	6–12	Peer-, teacher-, and parent-rated aggressive behavior	74 (11 girls, 63 boys)	Two 75 min sessions a week for 12 to 15 weeks	1. Social skills training & parent groups 2. Wait-list control	3 months, 9 months	Teacher-rated aggression +	Parent ratings 0; peer reputations 0
Peters et al. (2000)	0–4 (younger cohort) & 4–8 (older cohort)	Parent- and teacher-rated behavior problems, prosocial behavior, school readiness	700 children	Site dependent	Site dependent: social skills training, home visits, nutritional, play groups, drop ins, school-based programs, etc.	5 years	Teacher-rated self-controlled behaviors +	Parent-rated co-operative behaviors +; teacher-rated emotional problems +

Study	Population	Measures	N	Dose	Conditions	Follow-up		
Prinz, Blechman, & Dumas (1994)	1st–3rd graders	Teacher ratings of aggression, social skills, communication effectiveness, internalizing, observed communication effectiveness, peer acceptance	196	50 min weekly for 22–24 weeks	1. Peer coping group; 2. No peer coping group	6 months	Teacher-rated aggression +	Social skills +; information exchange +; consumer evaluation +; peer acceptance 0; iatrogenic effects
Reid, Eddy, Fetrow, & Stoolmiller (1999)	1st and 5th graders	Child behavior problems, academic skills, peer relations, family management skills	382 + 289 controls (51% girls)	10 weeks	Child skills training, parent training, school–parent communication	1 year	Physical aggression +	Children's classroom behavior +; mother aversive behavior +
Thompson, Ruma, Schuchmann, & Burke (1996)	2–17, M = 10	Child behavior problems, parent sense of competence, family satisfaction, cost information	39 + 27 control (~2/3 boys)	2 hr per week for 6 weeks	1. Common sense parenting; 2. Wait list control	3 months	Externalizing problems +; clinically significant change 0	Parent efficacy +; family relationship satisfaction +

(Continued)

TABLE 9.2
(Continued)

Authors	Age (in Years)	Constructs Assessed	No. of Participants	Length of Treatment	Treatment Description	Length of Follow-Up	Results at Posttest or Follow-Up[a]	
							Behavior Problems	Other
Tremblay, Pagani-Kurtz, Masse, Vitaro, & Pihl (1995)	7 at start of program	Teacher-rated disruptive behavior, self-reported juvenile delinquency, juvenile court records, school adjustment, perceptions of parenting	166 boys across conditions	2 years	1. Parent training/child social skills; 2. Attention control; 3. Control group	6 years	Self-reported delinquency +	Teacher-rated disruptive behavior 0; juvenile court records 0; age appropriate classes +
Webster-Stratton (1998)	M = 56.53 months	Child social competence, child conduct problems, parent competence, parent–school involvement	426 (224 boys, 202 girls)	2 hr weekly for 8–9 weeks	1. Parent training program; 2. Regular Head Start	12 – 18 months	Observed negative behaviors +; mother-rated behavior problems 0	Teacher-rated social competence +

Note. MST = multisystemic therapy; IT = individual therapy; CBCL = Child Behavior Checklist; TRF = Teacher Report Form; + = positive effects of the intervention; 0 = no intervention effect; – = negative intervention effects.

[a]Numbers in Results at Posttest or Follow-Up column refer to the corresponding treatment component listed in Treatment Description column.

TABLE 9.3a

Components of Community Treatment Programs: Setting and Participants

Reference	Setting (Where)					Participants (Who)				
	Home	School	Community Location	Residential	Hospital/Clinic	Individual	Peer	Parent	Family	School/Community
Peer focused										
Bierman & Furman (1984)		X				X	X			
Guevremont & Foster (1993)		X				X				
Kellam et al. (1994)		X				X	X			
Lochman (1992)		X				X	X			
Lochman, Burch, Curry, & Lampron (1984)										
Prinz, Blechman, & Dumas (1994)		X				X	X			
Parent/family focused										
Cunningham, Bremner, & Boyle (1995)			X		X			X		
Thompson, Ruma, Schuchmann, & Burke (1996)			X					X		
Webster-Stratton (1998)			X					X		
Multicomponent intervention										
Borduin et al. (1995)	X	X	X			X		X	X	X
Chamberlain (1990, 1996a, 1996b)	X	X		X		X		X	X	X
Kamps, Tankersley, & Ellis (2000)		X				X	X	X	X	
McCord (1978)	X		X			X		X		
Pepler, King, Craig, Byrd, & Bream (1995)		X				X	X	X	X	X
Multicomponent prevention										
CPPRG (1999)	X	X				X	X	X	X	X
Dishion & Andrews (1995)		X?				X		X		
Hawkins et al. (1992)		X				X	X	X		X
McDonald & Sayger (1998)		X	X			X	X	X	X	X
Peters et al. (2000)	X	X	X			X	X	X	X	X
Reid, Eddy, Fetrow, & Stoolmiller (1999)		X				X	X	X		X
Tremblay, Pagani-Kurtz, Masse, Vitaro, & Pihl (1995)	X	X				X	X	X		X

Note. CPPRG = Conduct Problems Prevention Research Group.

TABLE 9.3b

Components of Community Treatment Programs: Individual and Systemic Processes

References	Individual Processes					Within and Between Systems Processes				
	Cognitive	Emotional	Social	Behavioral	Academic/ Psychoeducational	Peer	Parent	Family	School/ Community	Between Systems
Peer focused										
Bierman & Furman (1984)		X	X	X		X				
Guevremont & Foster (1993)	X		X	X						
Kellam et al. (1994)				X		X				
Lochman (1992)	X	X	X	X		X				
Lochman, Burch, Curry, & Lampron (1984)										
Prinz, Blechman, & Dumas (1994)	X	X	X	X		X				
Parent/family focused										
Cunningham, Bremner, & Boyle (1995)	X			X			X			
Thompson, Ruma, Schuchmann, & Burke (1996)	X			X			X			
Webster-Stratton (1998)	X			X			X			

Multicomponent intervention									
Borduin et al. (1995)	X	X	X	X	X		X	X	X
Chamberlain (1990, 1996a, 1996b)		X	X	X	X		X	X	
Kamps, Tankersley, & Ellis (2000)	X	X	X	X	X	X	X		X
McCord (1978)		X	X	X	X	X	X	X	
Pepler, King, Craig, Byrd, & Bream (1995)	X	X	X	X	X		X	X	X
Multicomponent prevention									
CPPRG (1999)	X	X	X	X	X		X	X	X
Dishion & Andrews (1995)	X	X	X	X	X		X		
Hawkins et al. (1992)	X	X	X	X	X			X	
McDonald & Sayger (1998)	X	X	X	X	X		X	X	X
Peters et al. (2000)	X	X	X	X	X	X	X	X	X
Reid, Eddy, Fetrow, & Stoolmiller (1999)	X	X	X	X	X		X	X	X
Tremblay, Pagani-Kurtz, Masse, Vitaro, & Pihl (1995)	X	X	X	X	X		X		X

Note. CPPRG = Conduct Problems Prevention Research Group.

239

book (see chap. 10, this volume). However, some individual treatments can be classified as community-based treatments; interventions that occur in a naturalistic setting, target peer processes, and allow for practice of the skills learned within a dyad or group of peers are community oriented under the criteria we have set forth. For example, Bierman and Furman (1984) described an intervention in which children were given an opportunity to practice their new skills with other children. Lochman, Burch, Curry, and Lampron (1984) and Lochman's (1992) anger coping program involved group sessions in which children practiced social problem-solving skills among other related tasks. Kellam, Rebok, Ialongo, and Mayer's (1994) good behavior game; Prinz, Blechman, and Dumas' (1994) peer coping-skills program; and Guevremont and Foster's (1993) social problem-solving training are programs targeting similar processes. These programs typically have strong theoretical rationales and target risk factors relevant to CD. Although shown to be effective, these interventions target only a single domain and are thought to be necessary but not sufficient for comprehensive approach to CDs.

Community-Based Parent/Family Interventions

The evidence to support the efficacy of parenting management training (PMT) interventions for CDs and other behavior problems is impressive (e.g., Kazdin, 1997; Webster-Stratton, 1997; see chap. 11, this volume for more detail). However, few studies have examined the effectiveness of PMT programs in the community context. Exceptions include a study by Cunningham, Bremner, and Boyle (1995) who compared individual parent training in a clinical setting to parent training groups held in the community. Parents of children with severe behavior problems, immigrant families, and those using English as a second language were more likely to enroll in the community groups, and these groups reported greater improvements and better maintenance. Cunningham et al. also highlighted the cost effectiveness of community-based parenting programs; community groups were more than six times as cost effective as the individual programs. Thompson, Ruma, Schuchmann, and Burke (1996) and Webster-Stratton (1998) noted similar findings; community-based parenting programs were as effective, if not more so, than clinic-based interventions.

Based on the criteria we have highlighted, the strengths of the parent/family programs identified previously are their strong theoretical basis to the intervention, targeting of multiple behaviors, and assessment occurring at the level of intervention (i.e., parenting behavior and behaviors in the home). In addition, treatment integrity was monitored in all studies mentioned. From a social policy perspective, a unique and important aspect of both the Thompson et al. (1996) and Cunningham et al. (1995) programs was to address issues of cost effectiveness. Although occurring in naturalistic settings of the community, a weakness of the programs were their targeting of only a single system. Cunningham et al. noted families in both conditions were able to enroll their children in an activities-based social skills program, but no mention is made of the effects of these sessions. Furthermore, all three programs were short in duration and had a relatively limited follow-up period.

Multicomponent Interventions

Although many community-based peer and family interventions have proven effective in treating behavior problems, most researchers have noted limited success in terms of the magnitude of results and generalizability across childhood environments (e.g., Guevremont & Foster, 1993; Lochman, 1992). CD and ODD are complex problems, and evidence suggests that comprehensive interventions targeting multiple domains of functioning provide stronger, more generalizable effects. In the following, we briefly summarize some examples of these types of approaches.

McCord and McCord's (1959) Cambridge-Somerville Youth Study (CSYS) was one of the earliest multicomponent delinquency intervention programs. The CSYS study was based on the knowledge that children at risk of committing crime often lack affectionate guidance (Powers & Witmer, 1951). Over 300 "average" and "difficult" boys between the ages of 5 and 13 years took part in this treatment that continued, on average, twice a month over 5 years. The participants were matched with comparison children on intelligence, age, source of referral, and boys' aggression, among other variables. The intervention itself was individualized, often taking place in the child's home and local community. Over half of the participants were tutored academically, some received medical or psychiatric attention, and some were brought into contact with local community programs such as the YMCA, summer camps, and Boy Scouts. The control group was required only to provide information about themselves (McCord, 1978). A follow-up study (McCord, 1978), almost 30 years later indicated the treatment group showed negative side effects: A higher proportion of these men had committed crimes, had received more serious psychiatric diagnoses, and tended to die at younger ages.

Although the strengths of this intervention include a long treatment duration, 30-year follow-up, and the targeting of multiple domains (individual, family, community), there were some weaknesses. Researchers, including Offord and Bennett (1994), noted the difficulties inherent in interpreting the results of the CSYS; possible confounds and methodological concerns threaten the validity of the follow-up data. Lack of a theoretical rationale for each intervention is also a weakness. Although care was taken to match boys in the intervention to comparisons, treatment intensity varied greatly for each child, and therefore, it is difficult to draw conclusions with respect to individual component effectiveness. In addition, there was no measure of treatment integrity. Dishion, McCord, and Poulin (1999) raised another important concern regarding the role the peer group played in creating iatrogenic effects, as the most damaging effects of the CSYS appeared among boys sent to summer camp more than once. This effect highlights the importance of looking at each component as well as combined or interactive effects. It is possible work done in one domain may have been undone in another domain (i.e., peer processes).

Multisystemic therapy (MST; Henggeler & Borduin, 1990) is an intensive intervention approach repeatedly shown to effectively treat serious juvenile offenders (e.g., Borduin et al., 1995), adolescent sexual offenders (e.g., Borduin, Henggeler, Blaske, & Stein, 1990), and rural samples of serious juvenile offenders (e.g., Scherer, Brondino, Henggeler, Melton, & Hanley, 1994), among other populations. MST is a flexible and time-limited (3–4 months) approach to solving these problematic transactions through present-focused and action-oriented activities. Based on Bronfenbrenner's (1979) social-ecological model, clinicians conceptualize behavior problems as being maintained by problematic transactions within and between systems, such as peer, family, family–school, and family–peer systems. The setting for MST is often the family's home (in keeping with a family preservation model of service delivery) or community locations. Chapter 12 (this volume) provides a more detailed description of MST.

As one example, Borduin et al. (1995) compared MST to individual therapy (IT) in a sample of 176 serious juvenile offenders. Participants were referred by juvenile court personnel and were randomly assigned to either the MST or IT condition. The majority of MST participants received treatment in more than one system (e.g., family and school), whereas in contrast, most of the IT group received treatment in only one system (i.e., the adolescent). MST was more effective than IT in both the short term and in a 4-year follow-up. For instance, the MST group exhibited decreased family conflict at posttest as well as decreased parent reports of problem behavior. More important, the MST participants were significantly less likely to be rearrested at follow-up.

Strengths of the MST intervention include its naturalistic setting, strong theoretical underpinnings for selected components, targeting of multiple risk factors, and dedication to treatment integrity. Of particular note is the large research base supporting the effectiveness of MST at both treatment completion and follow-up and its inclusion as an empirically supported treatment for CD (Brestan & Eyberg, 1998). MST targets multiple individual and systemic processes and is flexible yet well documented. Overall, MST appears to be an effective intervention. However, the impact of each individual treatment component is unclear, as are the interactions between treatment components.

The Oregon Social Learning Center's Treatment Foster Care Program (TFC; Chamberlain, 1990) is a multilevel, multicomponent intervention that has been shown effective with chronic delinquency and conduct problems in adolescence. Although many components of the intervention take place in a residential setting, TFC attempts to target all the important contexts that adolescents interact in (e.g., peer, parent, and teacher relationships). Adolescents are placed in foster treatment homes to minimize their association with deviant peers (Chamberlain, 1996a). Foster parents are seen as critical agents of change. Six service elements are added to daily treatment in the foster home: individual therapy, family therapy for the adolescent's biological or adoptive family, regular school consultations, consultation with parole or probation officers, psychiatric consultation if needed, and case management to coordinate services and consult with foster parents (Chamberlain, 1996b). Chamberlain (1990) examined the feasibility of using the TFC model with severely delinquent adolescents. Sixteen referrals were matched with other adolescents on many family risk factors; the experimental and control groups were shown not to differ on numerous factors such as child risk factors, felonies, or dangerousness to self and others. At 2 years posttreatment, TFC participants had lower incarceration rates than the control group.

Although residential care is not a child's natural environment, TFC targets the child's natural home and school systems as well as helping the individual within the foster home. Other strengths include TFC's strong theoretical basis, flexibility, and the involvement of parents, teachers, and other individuals. However, there are empirical weaknesses to the evaluation of TFC. For example, the few research studies of TFC that have been conducted to date typically have not measured treatment fidelity and have used small sample sizes. Overall, the generalizability of the TFC model appears promising.

Pepler, King, Craig, Byrd, and Bream (1995) described the Earlscourt Social Skills Group Program (ESSGP) as a broad-based skills training program that targets children's aggressive behavior in the peer, family, and school systems. Based on social-learning, social-cognitive, and systems theories, the ESSGP was assessed in a sample of 74 teacher-rated aggressive children. The program was a 12 to 15 week intervention in which groups of 7 participants were taught a series of social skills (e.g., listening, dealing with anger, using self-control, joining a group, following instructions) by two trained child care workers in the school. Parents were invited to parent groups and teachers were also involved. In their evaluation, Pepler et al. noted a clinically significant improvement in teacher-rated aggression in the intervention group as compared to the wait-list control. This improvement was maintained to a lesser extent at 9-month follow-up. Parent ratings indicated improvement, but there were no significant differences between the intervention and control groups. In addition, there were no changes in peer reputation ratings.

Strengths of the ESSGP include a theoretical framework (social-learning theory) for selected interventions and strong research design, including the targeting of more than one risk factor. However, the program clearly puts a focus on social-skills training, and it is unclear how much parent groups contributed to the overall results. There is no mention of the influence of components on each other or the unique contribution of individual components. Although the intervention targeted multiple domains, it did not appear that any positive outcomes generalized to settings other than the classroom. In addition, the intervention was not long, follow-up was done shortly after treatment completion, and program integrity issues were not addressed.

Kamps, Tankersley, and Ellis (2000) noted encouraging results with a multicomponent, social-skills intervention for young children displaying aggressive and antisocial behaviors. Two cohorts of children were identified as having behavioral risks during their Head Start program by teacher report and nomination. Thirty-one children were participants in the experimental group across two cohorts, and a comparison group of 18 participants, also from Head Start programs, was selected using the same procedures. Kamps et al.'s intervention included both school- and family-based components. The experimental group received social-skills instruction with reinforcement (e.g., tokens on a chart), affection activities, as well as peer tutoring programs in the latter years. In addition, parent support training sessions and group parent–child activities were conducted over the course of the study. A 2-year follow-up indicated promising results. When observed directly, children in the experimental group showed fewer inappropriate behaviors in the class (i.e., aggression, negative verbal comments, grabbing, out-of-seat behavior) than the control group. As well, children in the experimental group showed higher levels of positive peer interaction.

Strengths of the program include the targeting of multiple risk factors across multiple systems and the measurement of changes in each domain. In addition, the intervention has a strong research design and a long-term follow-up. However, how each component contributed to the overall results and how they interacted was unclear. It seems the intervention components were selected because they represent risk factors for behavior problems later in life, but there was no apparent theory driving the selection of each component.

Summary. Aside from the CSYS, studies of multicomponent interventions, particularly those targeting both individual and parent/family systems, show promising results with serious juvenile delinquents (Borduin et al., 1995), juvenile delinquents in foster care (Chamberlain, 1990), and young children with behavior problems (Kamps et al., 2000; Pepler et al., 1995). However, each program provides differing theoretical rationales for selected interventions (or none at all), and interactions between individual components often go unexamined.

Multicomponent Prevention Programs

Zigler et al. (1992) described many universal prevention programs that have secondary results including the prevention of conduct problems. The Seattle Social Development Project (SSDP; Hawkins et al., 1992; Hawkins, Von Cleve, & Catalano, 1991) and the Linking the Interests of Family and Teachers (LIFT; Reid, Eddy, Fetrow, & Stoolmiller, 1999) program are examples of current universal interventions. In addition, there are numerous specific multicomponent prevention programs designed to target problem behaviors at a young age. The Montreal Longitudinal-Experimental Study (MLES; Tremblay, Pagani-Kurtz, Masse, Vitaro, & Pihl, 1995), Fast Track Prevention Trial for Conduct Problems (Fast Track; Conduct Problems Prevention Research Group [CPPRG], 1999), Adolescent Transitions Program (ATP; Dishion & Andrews, 1995), and Families and Schools Together Program (FAST; McDonald, 1996) are all prevention programs that have provided promising results over the last decade.

The SSDP is a universal prevention program designed to reduce shared childhood risk factors for delinquency and drug abuse. Based on a social development model, the SSDP attempts to increase young children's bonding to school and family through parent and teacher training. Researchers followed Seattle students through Grade 1 to 4 in eight schools during this 4-year intervention. Teacher training in the experimental condition involved classroom management, interactive teaching, and cooperative learning skills. Teachers also taught cognitive problem-solving skills (based on Shure & Spivack, 1988) to their students. Parents training occurred while children were in Grades 1 and 2, and took place over 7 weekly sessions.

Research results after 2 years of the intervention provided promising results (Hawkins et al., 1991). White boys in the experimental condition were teacher rated as less aggressive than those in the control condition, whereas White girls were rated as less self-destructive than White girls in the control condition (there were no differences among other samples). Data collected in the fall of fifth grade (after 4 years of intervention) indicated the experimental group had significantly less delinquency initiation and alcohol initiation than the control group, as well as the group finding school more rewarding and experiencing greater family communication. A follow-up at 6 years (Hawkins, Catalano, Kosterman, Abbott, & Hill, 1999) supported the enduring effects of intervention; the experimental group reported less school misbehavior, fewer violent delinquent acts, and better academic achievements, among other results.

Strengths of the program include a theoretical rationale for components, a strong research design, and the longitudinal nature of the study, as well as a 6-year follow-up. The treatment took place across multiple domains, was started in early childhood, and was adjusted as required developmentally. Although the overall effect of the intervention was positive, it is unclear how each component contributed to the findings, and the interactions between intervention components were not explored.

LIFT is a developmentally based intervention program designed to prevent conduct problems. Designed for first and fifth grade, LIFT has three main components: (a) a 10-week school component designed to teach children specific social and problem-solving skills in small and large groups; (b) a parent component designed to teach parents effective discipline and supervision, and this component is implemented in groups of 10 to 12 families over 6 weeks; and (c) a school–parent communication component. Six hundred and seventy-one children from 12 randomly assigned schools in at-risk neighborhoods took part in the program (382 in the intervention group and 289 in the control group; approximately equal numbers of boys and girls). The intervention had a positive effect on both first and fifth grade children such that the experimental group showed significantly less aggression on the playground than the control condition.

The LIFT program has a strong theoretical basis; involves parents, teachers, and children; assesses treatment fidelity; and targets multiple systems. Weaknesses of the program, however, include a short length of treatment (10 weeks) and a follow-up of only 1 year. There has been no attempt to replicate the intervention to our knowledge, and the interactive effects of components were not explored.

The MLES has provided an opportunity for numerous experiments to be done within a longitudinal study (e.g., Tremblay et al., 1995). The MLES is based on the theory that both parent and child factors are important in the development of disruptive behavior and that interventions should be designed to intervene at crucial developmental stages (e.g., early childhood) and target both these systems. Teachers rated disruptive boys from inner-city, low socioeconomic status schools in Quebec were invited to participate in the longitudinal study. Boys were randomly assigned to one of three conditions: prevention, attention-control, or control group. The intervention itself included both home- and school-based components, and continued over a 2-year period. At lunchtime in the schools, professionals taught social skills to groups of disruptive boys and their prosocial peers (e.g., groups of 4–7 boys) for nine sessions over the 1st school year. The 2nd year of the intervention involved 10 sessions of cognitive problem-solving skills and self-control. A parent training portion of the intervention (based on the

Oregon Social Learning Center's model of parent training) took place in the parent's home and averaged a mean of 17.4 sessions.

Analyses of the MLES data have provided mixed support for its reduction of disruptive behaviors (Tremblay et al., 1995). Children in the prevention program were followed up for 6 years after the intervention (when the children were 10–15 years old). There were no significant differences between the attention-control and control groups on variables of importance and they were therefore combined for the analyses. The experimental group reported significantly less delinquent behavior than the control group in 1 to 6 years of postinterventions. However, teacher-rated disruptive behaviors and juvenile court records showed no significant group differences. Tremblay et al. (1995) speculated a lack of statistical power given the small number of treated participants may have affected their ability to detect differences in juvenile court records. They also suggest teacher-rated disruptive behavior may not be a good indicator of outcome. Better adjustment in the disruptive boys or teacher's inability to observe their disruptive behavior could explain teacher's progressively lower ratings.

Strengths of the MLES program include a strong theoretical model and the targeting of multiple domains, as well as strong methodology and a long-term follow-up. However, unique and interactive outcomes of the intervention components are not addressed or are dismissed (e.g., teacher ratings). Although the intervention occurred in a school setting, teachers were minimally involved, as professionals ran the program during the lunch hour. In addition, the number of parent training sessions were variable and the intervention was only used with boys.

CPPRG (1999) has recently published the first set of findings from their Fast Track Prevention Trial for Conduct Problems. Fast Track is a developmentally based, long-term, multicomponent prevention project that targets major risk factors in the child, family, and classroom (CPPRG, 1992). High-risk children were identified before Grade 1 through a multistage screening procedure involving both parent and teacher ratings of problem behavior. Those children in the top 10% of the screening measures (or approximately 891 high risk kindergarten students) were invited to participate in the longitudinal study. As part of the intervention was school based, entire schools were randomly assigned to either the intervention or the control conditions. The intervention itself had both universal and selective components. All children received the classroom-based component of the intervention consisting of skills targeting friendship, emotional understanding and communication, self-control, and social problem solving. Over 99% of parents and children also took part in at least one of the selective interventions, which included parent groups, child social skills training groups, and academic tutoring. Results of the initial analyses of the Fast Track program are promising; the experimental group was less likely than the control group to provide aggressive responses to curriculum situations and more often engaged their peers in prosocial activities. Although findings with respect to child aggression were mixed (i.e., parent and teacher reports did not indicate significant differences, but observers did note improvements in disruptive behavior in school), the authors noted one possible explanation is that small changes did occur but were not large enough to change the categorical response parents and teachers selected (CPPRG, 1999).

Although a relatively new program, Fast Track has a strong theoretical rationale, is based on known risk factors for CD, and addresses multiple systems. Additional strengths include a strong research design (e.g., randomized design with no-intervention control), attention to treatment integrity issues, the targeting of young children, and comprehensive assessment of outcomes. There are many strengths to this program, and the outcome data will allow us to determine its effectiveness.

FAST is a prevention program designed for at-risk youth that is grounded in both family systems and Bronfenbrenner's (1979) ecological systems theories. Participants are teacher identified with problem behaviors and therefore considered at risk for future social and academic problems. Trained recruiters visit parents at home to invite them to participate in FAST, and families gather in groups of 8 to 12 for sessions at the child's school. The 8-week curriculum involves parent, parent–child, and multiple family group activities (e.g., structured family communication exercises, family feelings identification exercises, parent support) and is followed up with 2 years of monthly meetings (FASTWORKS). FAST evaluations through nonexperimental designs have shown promise; significant improvements in child's classroom behavior, home behavior, and self-esteem have been noted (McDonald & Sayger, 1998).

The FAST program targets problem behaviors in multiple domains and is a collaborative, family-based approach including parents, children, and teachers as participants. Weaknesses of the program are short treatment and follow-up duration and little mention of treatment integrity. In addition, the FAST program has yet to be evaluated through experimental design, although six U.S. federal government agencies have identified FAST as a program model that works.

The ATP is an indicated prevention program based on an ecological model of antisocial behavior. Participants were identified for this school-based intervention by telephone screening. If parents endorsed 4 or more of 10 possible risk areas, families were invited to participate. The intervention itself had two main components: teen focus and parent focus groups. The teen focus involved groups of eight adolescents learning skills such as developing peer support, setting personal limits, and learning problem-solving skills over 12 weeks. The parent focus group skills-based curriculum was based on the work of the Oregon Social Learning Center (e.g., Patterson, Reid, & Dishion, 1992). Eight families discussed skills as a group and then tried them at home.

A total of 158 families' adolescents between 11 and 14 years old participated in research on the ATP. Of these, 119 families were randomly assigned to one of four groups: teen focus only, parent focus only, teen and parent focus, and self-directed change (where only materials were provided). The additional 39 families were recruited as a quasi-experimental control. Results of the study indicate a reduction in negative engagement for all intervention groups as compared to controls. The parent focus group showed positive effects on adolescent behavior problems. At 1-year follow-up, iatrogenic effects were noted in the teen only group. That is, adolescents in the teen focus group reported significantly higher levels of school problem behavior than adolescents in the control group.

Based on the criteria we have highlighted, strengths of the ATP include a strong theoretical foundation and an approach that targets known risk factors of conduct problems. Data analyses also indicate the contribution of individual components as well as combined effects. Of particular interest are analyses indicating iatrogenic effects in the peer group only condition. However, the ATP does not target young children (participants are adolescents and their parents), does not target change in school or community systems (although they assess change in school behaviors), and is of relatively short treatment duration (12 weeks) and follow-up (1 year). As well, it is unclear if the intervention takes place in a naturalistic or a clinic setting.

The Better Beginnings, Better Futures Project (BBBF; Peters & Russell, 1996) is the first long-term prevention policy research demonstration project of its kind in Canada. BBBF has three primary goals. First, BBBF is designed to prevent serious social, emotional, behavioral, physical, and cognitive problems in young children. Second, the project promotes healthy child development in the aforementioned domains. Third, BBBF aims to enhance the abilities of socioeconomically disadvantaged families and communities to provide for their children. By definition, children in the BBBF project and comparison sites are from socioeconomically disadvantaged neighborhoods (Peters & Russell, 1996). Seven communities in Ontario were selected to implement one of two service models: an infant/preschool integration model (younger cohort) or a preschool/primary school integration model (older cohort), with three additional communities serving as research comparison sites. Each site selected individualized projects designed with the following concepts in mind: focused programming, creating partnerships, empowering resident participation, community development, and building a project organization. For example, although the older cohort sites offered varied programs from site to site, all sites offered playgroups, focused on nutrition, and involved cultural focus. BBBF is unique in their focus on child, family, neighborhood, and school outcomes.

The short-term findings of the BBBF project are encouraging (Peters et al., 2000). The BBBF project employed a quasi-experimental design, using both a baseline-focal design and longitudinal comparison site design. Seven hundred children took part in the program, and data was collected at 3, 18, 33, and 48 months in the younger cohort, and at ages 4, 5, 6, 7, and 8 in the older cohort. General cross-site patterns suggest these broad range of prevention programs improved self-controlled behaviors as rated by teachers and improved cooperative behaviors as rated by parents in the older cohorts. There were also site-specific findings indicating reduced child behavior problems in both younger and older cohorts. A 25-year longitudinal follow-up of the BBBF initiative is also planned.

BBBF is a true community-based intervention; initial programming needs are identified by a board with strong community input, and changes are targeted at multiple systems. Another strength is the program's baseline-focal and longitudinal research designs. Although still in an early evaluation stage, BBBF's mandates include examination of cost, process, and organizational issues. However, the program's site-specific interventions make replication, assessment of treatment integrity, and comparisons across sites (or to other prevention programs) difficult.

Summary. Although some of the prevention programs selected are still in early evaluation stages (e.g., Fast Track and BBBF) or have not been evaluated in clinical trials (e.g., FAST), most have shown encouraging results in the prevention of CD and related behavior problems. As with the multicomponent intervention programs, prevention programs often target multiple systems and include many participants. However, few assess the effect of individual components, and many fail to assess the interactions between these components.

Lessons From Current Community-Based Programs

This review is not meant to be comprehensive in the sense that not all community-based programs have been presented. It does, however, provide a representation of the various types of programs and their evaluations. There are several themes that emerge from this review. Of the programs reviewed, most had a theoretical approach, were based on empirical research identifying risk and protective factors, and targeted more than one risk factor. Nonetheless, there were very few that had a long-term follow-up and none of them looked at cumulative and interactive effects across different contexts. In this chapter we have suggested that community interventions need to take place in community contexts. Furthermore, evaluations are needed at each level of the multisystem interventions, and the interactive and cumulative effects of these interventions require more systematic empirical evaluation. There are many challenges in conducting such an evaluation.

INHERENT CHALLENGES IN COMMUNITY INTERVENTION

Because of the complexity underlying the risk for CD and the causal individual and environmental factors involved, there are many challenges faced when launching community interventions. In the following, we identify some implementation and evaluation issues that need to be addressed. For a more complete review of these factors, see Catalano, Arthur, Hawkins, Berglund, and Olsen (1999).

Implementation

One of the areas identified as critical to success of these programs is creating local ownership over the intervention and prevention efforts. This type of ownership is an integral component of the success of the program because it can serve to maximize the impact of the intervention through a reduction of social disorganization, it promotes strong community norms against antisocial behavior, and it creates community investment in preventing antisocial behavior (Catalano et al., 1999). However, there is a paucity of knowledge regarding the methods of enhancing community mobilization. There is some research to indicate that the community needs to have readiness for change (Price & Lorion, 1989), yet factors associated with readiness to change are not known at this time. None of the interventions discussed previously addressed this issue. It is important to document this issue so that researchers and clinicians can learn about success and unsuccessful attempts at mobilizing a community. More empirical research is needed in this area and such research will enhance implementation efforts.

Once engagement of a community has been established, it is important to assess and then provide the community with the skills needed to strategically select, coordinate, and implement the package of interventions that address both risk factors as well as enhancing protective factors. This is also an area that is poorly documented and infrequently commented on in the literature, yet it is inherent in the success of the program.

Process measures and evaluations that ensure that the intervention is implemented with a high level of fidelity are critical. Though the majority of interventions are now manualized, there is little data or information on how the intervention is monitored or on the coordination of implementation across contexts. Such steps are needed to ensure fidelity and integrity, as well as to enable a replication.

Empirical Evaluation

The theoretical perspective guiding community interventions is systemic. Communities are complex systems and interventions that occur within the community need to recognize the interrelatedness among the systems (e.g., individual, family, peer, community). The goal of the community intervention is to bring both behavioral and attitudinal change in each of these systems. Furthermore, there needs to be an evaluation of the systemic components and their isolated effects. This has proven to be an elusive and difficult goal in community oriented intervention programs.

In addition, within each of the systems, individual's attitudes and behaviors are required to change. This change may be a long process, hence the effect of the intervention may not be realized for many years. Typically, our outcome data on community-oriented programs do not extent over long periods of time.

Change needs to be assessed at each level of the system. Evaluation needs to examine the multilevel constructs and the development of these evaluations is still in its infancy (e.g., what are the best indicators of change at each level and what is the relationship among these indicators).

Analyzing data from these evaluations is also a challenging task. For example, it is difficult to determine the unit of analyses. Typically, individuals are often utilized as the unit of measurement. There needs to be, however, independent units of analyses at each level of the model. Recently, new statistical techniques such as hierarchical modeling have aided in determining both the individual and the group level of analyses (Bryk & Raudenbush, 1992).

Another statistical issue is that there may be differential effects of the intervention on particular groups (i.e., women, races). Thus, it is important to determine for whom the intervention is targeted and what the effect size of the intervention will be. Furthermore, as the McCord study (McCord, 1978; McCord & McCord, 1959) informed us, there may be individuals in the populations for whom there are the potential of negative effects of the intervention. Both types of information are valuable and informative.

One of the challenges in a systemic intervention is the problem of systematic biased attrition. As others have noted, those for whom the intervention is most needed may be the individuals who are most at risk might be the most mobile and the least likely to reside in a neighborhood for the duration of the intervention. Research indicates that those who have the highest level of antisocial behavior at baseline are most likely to be lost at follow-up (Ary et al., 1990). Such attrition biases may undermine the generalizability of the intervention. For example, the results may not be generalized to other communities or in fact may be inflated because the most at risk are unlikely to be present at follow-up evaluations.

CONCLUSION

CD represents a heavy burden in society. Community-based approaches are compelling because of the limited effectiveness achieved to date of clinic approaches and the cost effectiveness of these approaches (Offord & Bennett, 1994). Currently, significant advances have been made in the development and implementation of community interventions. There is still much work, however, to be done. In this chapter, we reviewed the criteria for designing effective community-oriented interventions. We suggest that successful interventions are likely to have a theoretical basis, have multiple components, have a strong empirical evaluation, address individual and systemic processes, and finally, occur in naturalistic settings. Our review suggests that researchers are now in a position to design and implement effective community-wide interventions. There is, however, a significant amount of both empirical and evaluation work that needs to be done before the problem of CD can successfully be reduced through community-oriented interventions.

REFERENCES

Ary, D. V., Biglan, A., Glasgow, R., Zoref, L., Black, C., Ochs, L., Severson, H., Kelly, R., Weissman, W., Lichtenstein, E., Brozovsky, P., Wirt, R., & James, L. E. (1990). The efficacy of social-influence prevention programs versus "standard care": Are new initiatives needed? *Journal of Behavioral Medicine, 13*, 281–296.

Belsky, J. (1981). Early human experience: A family perspective. *Developmental Psychology, 17*, 3–23.

Bierman, K. L., & Furman, W. (1984). The effects of social skills training and peer involvement on the social adjustment of preadolescents. *Child Development, 55*, 151–162.

Borduin, C. M., Henggeler, S. M., Blaske, D. M., & Stein, R. (1990). Multisystemic treatment of adolescent sexual offenders. *International Journal of Offender Therapy and Comparative Criminology, 34*, 105–113.

Borduin, C. M., Mann, B. J., Cone, L. T., Henggeler, S. W., Fucci, B. R., Blaske, D. M., & Williams, R. A. (1995). Multisystemic treatment of serious juvenile offenders: Long-term prevention of criminality and violence. *Journal of Consulting and Clinical Psychology, 63*, 569–578.

Brestan, E. V., & Eyberg, S. M. (1998). Effective psychosocial treatments of conduct-disordered children and adolescents: 29 years, 82 studies, and 5,272 kids. *Journal of Child Clinical Psychology, 27*, 180–189.

Bronfenbrenner, U. (1979). *The ecology of human development: Experiments by nature and design.* Cambridge, MA: Harvard University Press.

Bryk, A. S., & Raudenbush, S. W. (1992). Hierarchical linear models: Applications and data analysis methods. In *Advanced qualitative techniques in the social sciences, Volume 1.* Thousand Oaks, CA: Sage.

Carter, C. S., Lederhendler, I., & Kirkpatrick, B. (1997). *The integrative neurobiology of affiliation: Annals of The New York Academy of Sciences, Vol. 807.* New York: New York Academy of Sciences.

Catalano, R., Arthur, M., Hawkins, D., Berglund, L., & Olsen, J. (1999). Comprehensive community and school based interventions to prevent antisocial behaviour. In R. Loeber & D. P. Fatrrington (Eds.), *Serious and violent juvenile offenders: Risk factors and successful interventions* (pp. 248–281). London: Sage.

Chamberlain, P. (1990). Comparative evaluation of specialized foster care for seriously delinquent youths: A first step. *Community Alternatives: International Journal of Family Care, 2*, 21–36.

Chamberlain, P. (1996a). Community-based residential treatment for adolescents with conduct disorder. In T. H. Ollendick & R. J. Prinz (Eds.), *Advances in child clinical psychology* (Vol. 18, pp. 63–88). New York: Plenum Press.

Chamberlain, P. (1996b). Intensified foster care: Multi-level treatment for adolescents with conduct disorders in out-of-home care. In E. D. Hibbs & P. S. Jensen (Eds.), *Psychosocial treatments for child and adolescent disorders: Empirically based strategies for clinical practice* (pp. 475–495). Washington, DC: American Psychological Association.

Conduct Problems Prevention Research Group. (1992). A developmental and clinical model for the prevention of conduct disorders: The FAST Track Program. *Development and Psychopathology, 4*, 509–527.

Conduct Problems Prevention Research Group. (1999). Initial impact of the Fast Track prevention trial for conduct problems: I. The high-risk sample. *Journal of Consulting and Clinical Psychology, 67*, 631–647.

Cunningham, C. E., Bremner, R., & Boyle, M. (1995). Large group community-based parenting programs for families of preschoolers at risk for disruptive behaviour disorders: Utilization, cost effectiveness, and outcome. *Journal of Child Psychology and Psychiatry, 36*, 1141–1159.

Dishion, T. J., & Andrews, D. W. (1995). Preventing escalation in problem behaviors with high-risk young adolescents: Immediate and 1-year outcomes. *Journal of Consulting and Clinical Psychology, 63*, 538–548.

Dishion, T. J., McCord, J., & Poulin, F. (1999). When interventions harm: Peer groups and problem behavior. *American Psychologist, 54*, 755–764.

Guevremont, D. C., & Foster, S. L. (1993). Impact of social problem-solving training on aggressive boys: Skill acquisition, behavior change, and generalization. *Journal of Abnormal Child Psychology, 21*, 13–27.

Hawkins, J. D., Catalano, R. F., Kosterman, R., Abbott, R., & Hill, K. (1999). Preventing adolescent health risk behaviors by strengthening protection during childhood. *Archives of Pediatric Adolescent Medicine, 153*, 226–234.

Hawkins, J. D., Catalano, R. F., Morrison, D. M., O'Donnell, J., Abbott, R. D., & Day, L. E. (1992). The Seattle Social Development project: Effects of the first four years on protective factors and problem behaviors. In J. McCord & R. Tremblay (Eds.), *The prevention of antisocial behavior in children* (pp. 139–160). New York: Guilford.

Hawkins, J. D., Von Cleve, E., & Catalano, R. F. (1991). Reducing early childhood aggression: Results of a primary prevention program. *Journal of the American Academy of Child and Adolescent Psychiatry, 30*, 208–217.

Henggeler, S. W., & Borduin, C. M. (1990). *Family therapy and beyond: A multisystemic approach to treating the behavior problems of children and adolescents*. Pacific Grove, CA: Brooks/Cole.

Huesmann, L. R., Eron, L. D., Lefkowitz, M. M., & Walder, L. O. (1984). Stability of aggression over time and generations. *Developmental Psychology, 20*, 1120–1134.

Joffe, R. T., & Offord, D. R. (1987). The primary prevention of antisocial behavior. *Journal of Preventative Psychiatry, 3*, 251–259.

Kamps, D. M., Tankersley, M., & Ellis, C. (2000). Social skills interventions for young at-risk students: A 2-year follow-up study. *Behavioral Disorders, 25*, 310–324.

Kazdin, A. E. (1993). Treatment of conduct disorder: Progress and directions in psychotherapy research. *Development and Psychopathology, 5*, 277–310.

Kazdin, A. E. (1995). *Conduct disorders in childhood and adolescence* (2nd ed.). Thousand Oaks, CA: Sage.

Kazdin, A. E. (1997). Parent management training: Evidence, outcomes, and issues. *Journal of the American Academy of Child and Adolescent Psychiatry, 36,* 1349–1356.

Kellam, S. G., Rebok, G. W., Ialongo, N., & Mayer, L. S. (1994). The course and malleability of aggressive behavior from early first grade into middle school: Results of a developmental epidemiologically-based preventive trial. *Journal of Child Psychology and Psychiatry, 35,* 259–282.

Lochman, J. E. (1992). Cognitive-behavioral intervention with aggressive boys: Three-year follow-up and preventative effects. *Journal of Consulting and Clinical Psychology, 60,* 426–432.

Lochman, J. E., Burch, P. R., Curry, J. F., & Lampron, L. B. (1984). Treatment and generalization effects of cognitive-behavioral and goal-setting interventions with aggressive boys. *Journal of Consulting and Clinical Psychology, 52,* 915–916.

McCord, J. (1978). A thirty year follow-up of treatment effects. *American Psychologist, 33,* 284–289.

McCord, J., & McCord, W. (1959). A follow-up report on the Cambridge-Somerville youth study. *Annals of the American Academy of Political and Social Science, 322,* 89–96.

McDonald, L. (1996). Families together with schools (FAST). In R. Talley & G. Waltz (Eds.), *Safe schools, safe students* (pp. 59–63). Washington, DC: NECP, NAPSO, APA, ERIC.

McDonald, L., & Sayger, T. V. (1998). Impact of a family and school based prevention program on protective factors for high risk youth. In J. Valentine, J. A. De Jong, & N. Kennedy (Eds.), *Substance abuse prevention in multicultural communities* (pp. 61–85). Binghamton, NY: Haworth.

Moffitt, T. E., Caspi, A., Rutter, M., & Silva, P. A. (2001). *Sex differences in antisocial behaviour: Conduct disorder, delinquency, and violence in the Dunedin longitudinal study.* Cambridge, England: Cambridge University Press.

Mrazek, P. J., & Haggerty, R. J. (1994). *Reducing Risks for Mental Disorders: Frontiers for Preventive Intervention Research.* Committee on Prevention of Mental Disorders, Institute of Medicine.

Offord, D., & Bennett, K. J. (1994). Conduct Disorder: Long-term outcomes and intervention effectiveness. *Journal of the American Academy of Child and Adolescent Psychiatry, 33,* 1069–1078.

Patterson, G. R., DeBaryshe, B. D., & Ramsey, E. (1989). A developmental perspective on antisocial behavior. *American Psychologist, 44,* 329–335.

Patterson, G. R., Reid, J. B., & Dishion, T. J. (1992). *Antisocial boys.* Eugene, OR: Castalia.

Pepler, D. J., King, G., Craig, W., Byrd, B., & Bream, L. (1995). The development and evaluation of a multisystem social skills group training program for aggressive children. *Child and Youth Care Forum, 24,* 297–313.

Peters, R. DeV., Arnold, R., Petrunka, K., Angus, D. E., Brophy, K., Burke, S. O., Cameron, G., Evers, S., Herry, Y., Levesque, D., Pancer, S. M., Roberts-Fiati, G., Towson, S., & Warren, W. K. (2000). *Developing capacity and competence in the Better Beginning, Better Futures communities: Short-term findings report.* Kingston, ON: Better Beginnings, Better Futures Research Coordination Unit Technical Report.

Peters, R. DeV., & Russell, C. C. (1996). Promoting development and preventing disorder: The better beginnings, better futures project. In R. DeV. Peters & R. J. McMahon (Eds.), *Preventing childhood disorders, substance abuse and delinquency* (pp. 19–47). Thousand Oaks, CA: Sage.

Powers, E., & Witmer, H. (1951). *An experiment in the prevention of delinquency: The Cambridge-Somerville Youth Study.* New York: Columbia University Press.

Price, R. H., & Lorion, R. P. (1989). Prevention programming as organizational reinvention: From research to implementation. In D. Shaffer, I. Phillips, & N. B. Enzer (Eds.), *Prevention of Mental Disorders, Alcohol and other Drug Use in Children and Adolescents.* Rockville, MD: Department of Health and Human Services.

Prinz, R. J., Blechman, E. A., & Dumas, J. E. (1994). An evaluation of peer coping-skills training for childhood aggression. *Journal of Clinical Child Psychology, 23,* 193–203.

Reid, J. B., Eddy, M., Fetrow, R. A., & Stoolmiller, M. (1999). Description and immediate impacts of a prevention intervention for conduct problems. *American Journal of Community Psychology, 27,* 483–517.

Rowe, D. C., & Farrington, D. P. (1997). The familial transmission of criminal convictions. *Criminology, 35,* 177–201.

Scherer, D. G., Brondino, M. J., Henggeler, S. M., Melton, G. B., & Hanley, J. H. (1994). Multisystemic family preservation therapy: Preliminary findings from a study of rural and minority serious adolescent offenders. *Journal of Emotional and Behavioral Disorders, 2,* 198–206.

Schoenwald, S. K., & Henggeler, S. W. (1999). Treatment of oppositional defiant disorder and conduct disorder in home and community settings. In H. C. Quay & A. E. Hogan (Eds.), *Handbook of disruptive behavior disorders* (pp. 475–493). New York: Kluwer Academic/Plenum Publishers.

Schooler, C., Farquhar, J. W., Fortmann, S. P., & Flora, J. (1997). Synthesis of findings and issues from community prevention trials. *Annals of Epidemiology, 7(Supplement),* S54–S68.

Schweinhart, L. J., Barnes, H. V., & Weikart, D. P. (1993). *Significant Benefits: The High/Scope Preschool Study through Age 27.* Monographs of the High/School Education Research Foundation Number 10, Ypsilianti, MI: High/Scope Press.

Seitz, V., Rosenbaum, L. K., & Apfel, N. H. (1985). Effects of family support intervention: A ten-year follow-up. *Child Development, 56,* 376–391.

Serbin, L. A., Cooperman, J. M., Peters, P. L., Lehoux, P. M., Stack, D. M., & Schwartzman, A. E. (1998). Intergenerational transfer of psychosocial risk in women with childhood histories of aggression, withdrawal, or aggression and withdrawal. *Developmental Psychology, 34,* 1246–1262.

Serbin, L. A., Peters, P. L., & Schwartzman, A. E. (1996). Longitudinal study of early childhood injuries and acute illnesses in the offspring of adolescent mothers who were aggressive, withdrawn, or aggressive-withdrawn in childhood. *Journal of Abnormal Psychology, 105,* 500–507.

Shure, M., & Spivack, G. (1988). Interpersonal cognitive problem solving. In R. Price, E. Cowen, R. Lorion, & J. Ramos-McKay (Eds.), *14 ounces of prevention: A casebook for practitioners.* Washington, DC: American Psychological Association.

Thompson, R. W., Ruma, P. R., Schuchmann, L. F., & Burke, R. V. (1996). A cost-effectiveness evaluation of parent training. *Journal of Child and Family Studies, 5,* 415–429.

Tremblay, R. E., & Craig, W. M. (1995). Developmental Juvenile Delinquency Prevention. In M. Tonry & D. P. Farrington (Eds.), *Building a safer society: Strategic approaches to crime prevention* (pp. 151–236). Chicago, IL: The University of Chicago Press.

Tremblay, R. E., LeMarquand, D., & Vitaro, F. (1999). The prevention of oppositional defiant disorder and conduct disorder. In H. C. Quay & A. E. Hogan (Eds.), *Handbook of disruptive behavior disorders* (pp. 525–555). New York: Kluwer Academic/Plenum Publishers.

Tremblay, R. E., Pagani-Kurtz, L., Masse, L. C., Vitaro, F., & Pihl, R. (1995). A bimodal prevention intervention for disruptive kindergarten boys: Its impact through mid-adolescence. *Journal of Consulting and Clinical Psychology, 63,* 560–568.

Webster-Stratton, C. (1997). From parent training to community building. *Families in Society, 78,* 156–171.

Webster-Stratton, C. (1998). Preventing conduct problems in head start children: Strengthening parenting competencies. *Journal of Consulting and Clinical Psychology, 66,* 715–730.

Weisz, J. R. (1998). Empirically supported treatments for children and adolescents: Efficacy, problem and prospects. In K. S. Dobson & K. S. Craig (Eds.), *Empirically supported therapies: Best practice in professional psychology* (pp. 66–92). Thousand Oaks, CA: Sage.

Weisz, J. R., Weiss, B., & Donenberg, G. R. (1992). The lab versus the clinic: Effects of children and adolescent psychotherapy. *American Psychologist, 47,* 1578–1585.

Weisz, J. R., Weiss, B., Han, S. S., Granger, D. A., & Morton, T. (1995). Effects of psychotherapy with children revisited: A meta-analysis of treatment outcome studies. *Psychological Bulletin, 117,* 450–468.

Zigler, E., Taussig, C., & Black, K. (1992). Early childhood intervention: A promising preventative for juvenile delinquency. *American Psychologist, 47,* 997–1006.

10

Child-Focused Cognitive-Behavioral Therapies

Michael A. Southam-Gerow
Virginia Commonwealth University

Cognitive-behavioral therapy (CBT) is one of the most widely researched approaches for childhood psychological problems. CBT has been successfully applied to a wide variety of problems in childhood from phobias and generalized anxiety disorder, to depression, to impulsivity, and to antisocial behavior. In particular, the success of child-focused CBT has been greatest for children with internalizing disorders. Empirical support for CBT has also been accumulated for treatment of antisocial youth, but the data have not been as strong and other treatment approaches appear as, if not more, effective (e.g., parent management training, see, e.g., American Academy of Child and Adolescent Psychiatry, 1997; Brestan & Eyberg, 1998). Still, many clinical researchers continue to see a role for child-focused CBT in a broader treatment plan for antisocial youth. This review provides an overview of the evidence to date on child-focused individual and group CBT for antisocial behavior in childhood and adolescence. I begin by briefly discussing the theoretical framework of CBT and illustrating some of the general techniques used in the typical cognitive-behavioral approach. Then, in a review of the extant literature, I consider the evidence for several child-focused CBT approaches. Finally, I discuss the role that child-focused CBT can and should play in a treatment plan for antisocial children.

THEORETICAL OVERVIEW OF CBT

CBT is an integrative treatment approach combining two distinct schools of psychotherapy: behavior therapy and cognitive therapy. The integration of the two therapeutic approaches was thought to provide a comprehensive treatment model able to address the cognitive and behavioral deficits of clients. In its original form, CBT drew heavily from the work of information-processing and social-learning theorists (e.g., Kendall & Bacon, 1988). However, the approach is by design open to integration of new empirical findings. Hence, there has been increasing attention to other theoretical viewpoints, including a recent emphasis on the role of emotion in the development and treatment of child psychopathology (e.g., Samoilov & Goldfried, 2000; Southam-Gerow & Kendall, 2002).

The cognitive-behavioral model views psychological problems as related to emotional, behavioral, and cognitive antecedents (e.g., Beck, Shaw, Rush, & Emery, 1979; Southam-Gerow & Kendall, 2000). A therapist using CBT pays close attention to emotional factors such as a child's *emotion regulation* (e.g., the purposeful and dynamic ordering and adjusting of emotion; Cole, Michel, & Teti, 1994; see Southam-Gerow & Kendall, 2002, for discussion), including an assessment of the extent to which this set of developmental processes has been detoured. Concerning antisocial children, there is evidence that youth with oppositional defiant disorder exhibit difficulties regulating negative emotion such as anger (e.g., Casey, 1996). In addition, a child's *emotion understanding* (e.g., a child's knowledge of the causes of emotions and ways of coping with feelings; see, e.g., Harris, 1993) is viewed as a key factor in conceptualizing and planning treatment.

Behavioral factors related to child psychological problems are also examined. These factors include a child's familial and extrafamilial (e.g., peer relationships) experiences, which are examined for evidence of limited learning opportunities or potentially pathogenic experiences (e.g., child abuse, marital conflict). In addition, a child's learning history is closely examined, often via a functional assessment of the presenting problems to identify reinforcements related to maintaining problem behaviors. Along these lines, research has indicated that the negative (e.g., aggressive) behavior of antisocial youth has received reinforcement, whereas their prosocial behavior has been largely ignored (e.g., Patterson, 1997; Strand, 2000).

In terms of cognitive factors, cognitive-behavioral theory distinguishes between cognitive distortion and cognitive deficiency (Kendall, Ronan, & Epps, 1991). Some children process information in a distorted fashion (e.g., misinterpretation of the intentionality of others), whereas others evidence deficiencies in their cognitive processing leading to action that does not benefit from forethought (Kendall & MacDonald, 1993). These different cognitive processing difficulties have been associated with various childhood disorders (Kendall & MacDonald, 1993; Vasey, 1993). For example, aggressive and antisocial youth demonstrate both cognitive distortions and cognitive deficiencies. CBT also focuses on social information-processing and problem-solving biases that often lead to maladjustment. For example, some children exhibit problem-solving biases toward agonistic or avoidant solutions (or both), and these patterns appear to increase risk for psychopathology (see, e.g., Barrett, Rapee, Dadds, & Ryan, 1996; Dodge, 1980; Dunn, Lochman, & Colder, 1997).

Given this broad framework, child-focused CBT involves providing an appropriate therapeutic environment, teaching relevant coping skills, and then creating opportunities to practice them with the hope of fostering new learning. From this perspective, child-focused treatment of aggressive youth would involve the teaching of several skills (e.g., emotion regulation, cognitive restructuring, problem solving), provision of opportunities to practice the skills, shaping by the therapist of this practice, and an assessment of the benefits of implementing the skills. In the next section, I outline some of the most common treatment strategies used in CBT approaches for antisocial youth.

COMMON COGNITIVE-BEHAVIORAL TREATMENT STRATEGIES

A central treatment goal of CBT is to help children (and their families) augment their coping repertoire via new skill acquisition and enrichment and refinement of already possessed skills. Relatedly, another objective is that children will develop new—or modify existing—ways of experiencing and understanding the world (e.g., schema modification). An important part of this process involves children practicing new ways of thinking (about themselves, about their emotions) and new ways of acting (including not acting) in the presence of a supportive, encouraging therapist and whenever possible, parent(s). A therapist provides feedback aimed at shaping the new or improved coping behaviors. Realizing these treatment goals requires the use of many different treatment strategies. For the purposes of this chapter, I focus on those strategies with particular relevance to child-focused CBT with antisocial youth: relaxation training, social problem solving, cognitive restructuring/attribution retraining, and contingent reinforcement. For a more detailed examination of CBT techniques, see Southam-Gerow and Kendall (2000).

Teaching relaxation skills is often a part of a child-focused CBT program for antisocial youth, as these skills help children in the self-regulation of their emotions, particularly anger. Progressive, cue-controlled, and covert relaxation techniques are all used with children. In a *progressive* relaxation exercise, major muscle groups are successively relaxed through systematic tension-release exercises (King, Hamilton, & Ollendick, 1988). This helps the child to perceive bodily tension and encourages him or her to use that tension as a cue to relax. *Cue-controlled* relaxation involves associating the relaxed state with a personalized cue word, such as *relax* or *calm*. In practice, the child repeatedly subvocalizes the cue word while in the relaxed state. In session, such relaxation exercises are frequently accompanied by the incorporation of comforting imagery. Finally, *covert* relaxation skills, usually in the form of diaphragmatic breathing exercises, are also often incorporated into the child's relaxation routine, providing an effective alternative for use in public situations. Weisz et al. (1999), for example, describe an approach called "secret calming" that involves breathing exercises designed to be invisible to the observer and hence usable in many settings.

The process of examining ones thinking with an effort to change faulty cognitive functioning and replace it with more adaptive thinking is sometimes called *cognitive restructuring*. The first step involves helping children identify their self-talk. To do so, children may be asked to think of thoughts running through their heads as "thought bubbles," similar to those seen in comic strips (e.g., Kendall et al., 1992). Once the content of their self-talk has been identified, the therapist helps children assess the veracity and helpfulness of the cognitions. If the thoughts are judged inaccurate or unhelpful, the therapist coaches children to consider alternative and more realistic or helpful ones. Attribution retraining is similar in that children can be trained to examine critically the explanations they construct for various events, with an eye to reduce the deleterious impact of exaggerated or inaccurate attributions and entertain alternative attributions for the given circumstances. For example, aggressive children have consistently demonstrated a hostile-attribution bias wherein they view another child's ambiguous behavior (e.g., bumping into someone in a lunch line) as purposefully mean. A child with this bias may use in-session time to practice generating alternative explanations for the ambiguous behaviors of others. Additionally, the therapist will help the child consider alternative responses if the child's interpretation of hostility is accurate. Older children are often taught to identify specific common cognitive "errors" (e.g., Beck, Rush, Shaw, & Emery, 1979) such as *mind-reading*, wherein one attributes negative thoughts to another based on limited or no knowledge of the actual content of the person's thoughts and *all-or-nothing thinking*, wherein one declares an effort a failure if any one aspect of it does not succeed wholly. These various cognitive techniques often require adaptation based on a child's level of cognitive development (see e.g., Durlak, Fuhrman, & Lampman, 1991; Weisz & Weersing, 1999).

Child-focused CBT is viewed as a collaborative problem-solving endeavor and as such, a common treatment strategy with antisocial youth involves teaching a set of problem-solving strategies. The process of problem solving is presented as a multistep process involving (a) description of the problem and the major goals for the solution; (b) generation of alternative solutions; (c) evaluation of these alternatives in terms of how well they will assist in the achievement of the goal; (d) selection and enactment of the best strategy or strategies identified; and finally, (e) evaluation of the degree of success of the outcome, with emphasis on problem-solving effort rather than simply winning. Social problem solving entails the application of this set of steps to problematic or troubling social interactions.

When a successful outcome (e.g., progress toward a goal) is achieved through a newly mastered skill such as problem solving, the therapist assures that the skill is rewarded. Contingent reinforcement, a cornerstone of behavior therapy, allows the therapist to shape adaptive child behavior. Achieving a desired end result (e.g., no fighting) often requires breaking down the larger outcome into incremental steps (e.g., each challenging interaction without a fight, 1 week without a fight) and rewarding each step (i.e., shaping via successive approximations). The eventual goal is to teach children to evaluate their own behavior and provide their own rewards accordingly. Different children experience different problems in learning to self-evaluate; some may be overly critical, whereas others may forget to self-evaluate at all. Rewards may also be useful in encouraging the child to complete homework assignments. In addition, response-cost procedures are often used to penalize off-task and undesirable behavior.

In line with pragmatic nature of CBT, a therapist carefully chooses which of these techniques (and others—see, e.g., Southam-Gerow & Kendall, 2000) to use with a given child, frequently retooling as the situation changes. Indeed, flexibility, long hailed as a critical element of successful implementation of manualized treatments (e.g., Dobson & Shaw, 1988), plays a central role in most CBT approaches (e.g., Kendall, Chu, Gifford, Hayes, & Nauta, 1998). In a sense, the therapist acts as a coach, varying the drills and practice regimens to address each child's specific constellation of problems and strengths, taking into account his or her unique context.

REVIEW OF RESEARCH FINDINGS

Childhood conduct problems and youth violence are a source of tremendous distress for parents, other children, policymakers, and the public in general. As a result, a large body of research has developed studying the ontogenesis, maintenance, and treatment of these behavioral problems. Aggressive behaviors in children are common and not of themselves a cause for great concern. However, aggressive behavior becomes a matter of diagnostic significance if it is severe and frequent or if it occurs across multiple settings. Epidemiological evidence has suggested that between 5% to 10% of children display clinically significant problems of aggression or conduct or both (Offord, Boyle, & Racine, 1991; Rutter, Tizard, & Whitmore, 1970), with boys outnumbering girls by approximately 4 to 1 (see, e.g., Zoccolillo, Tremblay, & Vitaro, 1996, for discussion of the gender disparity). In the short term, early childhood aggression is correlated with several poor outcomes including peer rejection (Coie, Dodge, & Coppotelli, 1982; Newcomb, Bukowski, & Pattee, 1993; but see Rodkin, Farmer, Van Acker, & Van Acker, 2000) and academic problems (e.g., Hinshaw & Anderson, 1996). In addition, behavior problems in childhood are responsible for one third to one half of all child treatment referrals by parents or teachers (e.g., Patterson, Reid, Jones, & Conger, 1975). The stability of aggression over time and its relation to later antisocial behaviors has prompted much clinical and public policy concern (e.g., Huesmann, Lefkowitz, Eron, & Walder, 1984; Olweus, 1980). Despite the influence of situational factors on the expression of aggression, the stability coefficient for aggression in males is estimated to be .68 (Olweus, 1980).

There is evidence that biological (Bates, Bayles, Bennett, Ridge, & Brown, 1991; Brennan, Mednick, & Kandel, 1991; Raine, Brennan, & Mednick, 1994; Tremblay, Pihl, Vitaro, & Dobkin, 1994) and family (e.g., Patterson, 1982; Strand, 2000) factors play an important role in understanding aggressive behavior in childhood and other chapters in this volume discuss this evidence and their relation to treatments (e.g., see chaps. 6, 7, 11, 12, & 13, this volume). An approach integrating cognitive and behavioral facets of aggression has proven useful in both the conceptualization and treatment of childhood aggression. Several child-focused CBT approaches have been developed to treat antisocial behavior in youth and three of these were identified by Brestan and Eyberg (1998) as "probably efficacious" using criteria established by the American Psychological Association's Division 12 Task Force on Empirically Supported Treatments (e.g., Chambless et al., 1996). I review the evidence supporting these three programs. I also identified three additional CBT approaches with some empirical support (though not enough to meet the Task Force criteria). Table 10.1 summarizes some key aspects of each treatment.

Kazdin and his colleagues (Kazdin, Bass, Siegel, & Thomas, 1989; Kazdin, Esveldt-Dawson, French, & Unis, 1987; Kazdin, Siegel, & Bass, 1992) have developed a treatment package called *social problem-solving skills training* (PSST) by integrating Kendall and Braswell's (1985, 1993) approach to treating impulsivity with earlier problem-solving work by Spivack and Shure (1974). The 20- to 25-session individually administered CBT program emphasizes the acquisition and mastery of problem-solving and interpersonal social skills. Sessions focus on the teaching and practice of these skills, gradually increasing the difficulty of the in-session practice (e.g., from application in simple games and academic exercises to their use in real social situations). Within sessions, social reinforcement and response-cost procedures are used to encourage appropriate use of the skills. There is also an emphasis on extrasession application of the skills via role playing and homework assignments.

TABLE 10.1

Characteristics of Child-Focused CBT Programs

Treatment Program	Format	Setting(s)	Ages (Years)	Minorities?	Superior to?
PSST (e.g., Kazdin, Esveldt-Dawson, French, & Unis, 1987)	Individual	Inpatient/Outpatient	7–13	AA (23–45)	RT, WL, PMT[a]
AC (e.g., Lochman, Burch, Curry, & Lampron, 1984)	Group	Outpatient	9–12	AA (53)	NO, AT
Feindler, Marriott, & Iwata (1984)	Group	Inpatient	12–18	AA (31), L (3)	NO
Webster-Stratton & Hammond (1994)	Group	Outpatient	4–8	UN (<20)	WL
Kendall, Reber, McLeer, Epps, & Ronan (1990)	Individual	Day treatment	6–13	AA (96), L (4)	AT
Kolko, Loar, & Sturnick (1990)	Group	Inpatient	10	Not reported	AT

Note. Under the "Minorities?" heading, each number reflects the percentage of non-Euro-American children in the sample. When a range is presented, it reflects the range across more than one study. Under the "Superior to?" heading, each code refers to any control or comparison treatment group to which the treatment program was superior. CBT = cognitive-behavioral therapy; PSST = problem-solving skills training; AA = African American; L = Latino; UN = unspecified minority group(s); RT = relationship therapy; WL = wait list; PMT = parent management training; NO = no treatment; AT = other active therapy.
[a]Superior on a minority of the measures. On most measures, outcomes for the two treatments were not different.

Kazdin and his colleagues (Kazdin et al., 1989, 1987, 1992) have conducted several empirical examinations of the program in inpatient and outpatient settings. In a randomized clinical trial, Kazdin et al. (1987) compared PSST to a relationship therapy program and a wait-list control in an inpatient setting with 56 youth (11 girls and 45 boys) ages 7 to 13. The sample was 77% White and 23% African American. PSST was superior to both control conditions across several indexes, including aggressive behaviors, prosocial behavior, and externalizing behavior problems. Youth in the PSST condition also evidenced more improvement into the normative range compared to the other two conditions. It is notable, though, that despite the positive findings, the majority of youth in all three groups remained in the nonnormative range of behavior posttreatment.

In a second study, Kazdin et al. (1989) compared two variants of PSST (with and without applied homework assignments) to a relationship therapy condition in a study involving one hundred and twelve 7- to 13-year-old youth (55% White and 45% African American; 25 girls and 87 boys) in inpatient and outpatient treatment for antisocial behavior. Although few differences emerged between the two PSST programs, they were both superior to the relationship therapy condition across multiple domains (e.g., antisocial and prosocial behavior) and multiple reporters (e.g., teacher, parent), at posttreatment and 1-year follow-up. Still, the majority of treated children remained outside of the normal range on most measures indicating continued dysfunction.

Another study (Kazdin et al., 1992) compared the PSST program to a parent management training (PMT) intervention and to a combined PSST/PMT package with a sample of ninety-seven 7- to 13-year-old children (69% White and 31% African American; 21 girls and 76 boys) with antisocial behavior problems seen in an outpatient clinic. The PMT program was a basic parent training intervention. Such programs, and the empirical evidence supporting their use, are described in detail by Prinz and Jones (chap. 11, this volume) and others (e.g., Brestan & Eyberg, 1998; Kazdin, 1996; Southam-Gerow & Kendall, 1997). All three treatments led to significant improvements on most measures. However, the combined treatment was superior to the PSST and PMT programs on several indexes, including parental stress, family functioning, and child aggressive and antisocial behavior. In addition, the combined treatment moved significantly more children into the normative range. On most measures, no differences were found between PSST and PMT; what few significant differences were detected favored PSST.

Lochman and colleagues (Lochman, Burch, Curry, & Lampron, 1984; Lochman & Lenhart, 1993) developed the second of the three probably efficacious treatment programs. Their program teaches children to identify physiological and affective cues and environmental precipitants of anger arousal in a group format. Children are aided in the recognition and labeling of their emotional experiences and are instructed in self-monitoring and self-control strategies such as self-talk. In addition, problem-solving skills and conflict-resolution skills are emphasized. The group-administered intervention also uses videotaped modeling of the application of skills taught in session. Lochman et al. (1984) compared the Anger Coping (AC) program to a goal-setting intervention, a combination of AC and goal setting, and a no-treatment control group in a sample of seventy-six boys ages 9 to 12 (53% African American and 47% Euro-American). Their findings supported the efficacy of the AC and combined treatments on some (but not all) measures. Specifically, children receiving AC or the combined treatment were on task more often, were less disruptive and aggressive in the classroom, and scored lower on the maternal-report Child Behavior Checklist Aggressive Behavior scale (Achenbach, 1991) compared to children receiving no treatment or the goal-setting intervention. At a 3-year follow-up (Lochman, 1992), youth who received the AC intervention had better outcomes than a group of untreated aggressive children on several important indexes, including alcohol and drug use and self-esteem and problem-solving measures. Furthermore, youth receiving the AC program did not differ from nonaggressive youth on these same variables, suggesting that they were within normative levels. Effects of the AC program on classroom behavior at the follow-up, however, were not significant.

Feindler and her colleagues (e.g., Feindler, Ecton, Dubey, & Kingsley, 1986) amassed empirical support for their group CBT program. The program involves teaching youth to self-monitor (e.g., know their anger "triggers"), self-instruct (e.g., use self-statements to manage anger), plan ahead (e.g., use problem-solving skills), use relaxation skills, and implement assertiveness skills appropriately. Youth are encouraged to practice these strategies in group to assist in generalization to difficult interpersonal situations.

Controlled studies have supported the efficacy of the intervention (e.g., Feindler, Ecton, Dubey, & Kingsley, 1986; Feindler, Marriot, & Iwata, 1984). In the first of these studies, Feindler et al. (1984) compared the treatment to a no-treatment control group with 36 multiply suspended children ages 12 to 15 (no gender or ethnicity information was provided in the report) in an outpatient, school-based setting. Their findings supported the efficacy of the treatment program across child-report (e.g., problem-solving ability) and teacher-report (e.g., self-control, severe aggressive incidents) measures. A second trial (Feindler et al., 1986) compared the intervention to no-treatment in an inpatient setting with 29 male youth, ages 13 to 18 (66% White, 31% African American, and 3% Hispanic/Latino). Results indicate that the intervention was efficacious in reducing negative consequences on the inpatient unit for treated youth (e.g., fewer fines). In addition, staff viewed youth treated with the CBT program as possessing greater self-control posttreatment.

Webster-Stratton and Hammond (1997) developed a child-focused group intervention (referred to as *child training* or CT hereafter) for preschool and early elementary school-age children with antisocial behavior problems. The CT program involved children watching videotaped vignettes designed to teach a wide array of interpersonal (e.g., conflict-resolution, social, problem-solving, and anger management skills) and cognitive skills (e.g., attribution retraining). Therapists facilitated discussion about the videos and used fantasy play with dinosaur puppets to teach and practice the skills introduced in the video. The program involved twenty-two 2-hour sessions, led by two therapists. Time out and rewards were used during the sessions to enhance acquisition of the skills.

Webster-Stratton and Hammond (1997) compared the CT program to a videotape-based parent training (PT) package, a combination of the two treatments, and a wait-list control group. Ninety-seven youth ages 4 to 8 years (more than 80% were White; 25 girls and 72 boys) participated in the trial. Results indicate that all three treatments showed strong improvements over the wait-list group. Furthermore, the CT program reduced child symptoms compared to the wait-list control group and was even superior to the PT program on a measure of conflict management. However, the PT and combined interventions were generally better than CT at reducing child symptoms and at improving parenting behavior. For example, 81% of youth in the PT were in the normal range on the Child Behavior Checklist posttreatment compared to 70% in the combined treatment, 37% in the CT program, and 27% in the wait-list control group. Webster-Stratton and Hammond (1997) concluded that the combined treatment demonstrated the most significant "improvements across a broader range of outcome variables" (p. 107). It is notable that group differences were attenuated at the 1-year follow-up.

A child-focused individual CBT intervention developed by Kendall, Reber, McLeer, Epps, and Ronan (1990) has received empirical support. Based in part on Kendall and Braswell's (1985) program for impulsive children, the 20-session treatment was developed for use in a day-treatment setting. The program involved teaching youth self-instruction and problem-solving skills via a five-step process: problem definition, problem approach, focusing of attention, selecting a course of action, and self-reinforcement for accurate or appropriate performance. Coping modeling, in which the therapist presents a model of desired coping behavior involving real trial-and-error efforts to handle tough situations instead of instant mastery, was also employed. Reinforcement principles were also applied in the treatment program in the form of social and self-reward skills and response-cost procedures.

A crossover design study (Kendall et al., 1990) was conducted to compare the efficacy of the CBT approach to a supportive/dynamic approach.

Twenty-nine 6- to 13-year-olds (96% African American, 4% Latino/Hispanic; 3 girls, 26 boys) diagnosed with conduct disorder were randomly assigned to receive the CBT approach first, followed by the supportive/dynamic approach or the reverse. Results indicated that gains were largely evident in response to the CBT and not the supportive/dynamic treatment program.

Finally, a social-cognitive skills training (SCST) program was described and tested by Kolko, Loar, & Sturnick (1990). The group program, developed for use in an inpatient setting, focused on training children to proficiency on a set of social and cognitive skills. These skills included appropriate eye contact, appropriate physical space in interpersonal situations, appropriate vocal volume and inflection, appropriate verbal content (e.g., compliments, acknowledgment), use of conversational openers, assertiveness skills, responses to provocation, and appropriate play and sharing skills. Taught across 15 sessions, these skills were adapted for the specific identified problem areas of treated children. A clinical trial comparing the SCST program with a social activity treatment (SAT) program was conducted with 56 youth (18 girls and 38 boys, *M* age 10.4 years, no ethnicity information provided). The SAT program consisted of semistructured sessions designed to provide opportunities for children to socialize during group activities with themes relevant to peer relations. Similar to the SCST program, the SAT program was conducted in a group format and lasted about 15 sessions for each child. Results of the trial indicated that the SCST program was superior to the SAT program across several (but not all) measures, including indexes of child loneliness, child social competence, and incidence of social problems with staff. In addition, SCST produced observed improvements of social skills over the SAT.

SUMMARY AND DISCUSSION

The evidence for child-focused CBT for antisocial youth is quite promising if somewhat modest. These treatment programs all evidenced positive treatment effects. However, when the entire research literature is considered, child-focused CBT is not the ideal solution by itself. In their recent review applying American Psychological Association Division 12 Task Force criteria to treatments for children with antisocial behavior problems, Brestan and Eyberg (1998) concluded that only parent-focused interventions (i.e., Webster-Stratton, 1984, 1990, 1994) have thus far met criteria for well-established status (see also Southam-Gerow & Kendall, 1997, for review). By focusing on the child, CBT may lack sufficient attention to the familial variables that have been implicated in the development and maintenance of antisocial behavior in children (Patterson, 1982, 1997; Snyder, Schrepferman, & St. Peter, 1997; Strand, 2000). Additionally, in child-focused treatment there is risk that the clinician will neglect a consideration of the larger societal context in the expression of disorder (Henggeler, Schoenwald, Borduin, Rowland, & Cunningham, 1998; LeClair & Innes, 1997; Staub, 1996). Because of these shortcomings, in the concluding section of the chapter I discuss what role child-focused (individual, group or both) CBT can play in the optimal treatment plan for youth. First, though, I briefly highlight several issues related to the body of research just reviewed.

One issue concerns the extent to which each treatment program dealt with development. Developmental psychopathology research and the efforts of many clinical researchers have increased attention on the importance of constructing developmentally sensitive treatments (e.g., Silverman & Ollendick, 1999; Southam-Gerow & Kendall, 2002; Vernberg, 1998). One solution used by the treatment developers reviewed in the chapter was to restrict the ages to which the treatment was applied. Hence, several of the programs were used with preteens (Kazdin et al., 1992; Kendall et al., 1990; Kolko et al., 1990; Lochman et al., 1984), whereas Feindler et al.'s (e.g., 1984) program was designed for teenagers and Webster-Stratton and Hammond's (1997) program was designed for children age 4 to 8. The treatments varied in the extent to which they discussed developmental adaptations to the treatment program. The best example is that of Webster-Stratton and Hammond. Because of the importance of fantasy play in the daily lives of young children, their program included the use of play with dinosaur puppets to illustrate key concepts. This explicit matching of treatment technique to developmental level is an important model for future treatment development.

Adapting treatments for different ethnic groups has also become a guiding principle in treatment development. However, none of the treatment programs explicitly made adaptations based on the ethnic groups represented in their trials, despite there being considerable ethnic diversity in most of the samples. Because the findings were generally positive, one can surmise that child-focused CBT has applicability for ethnically diverse populations (particularly for African American youth). However, more consideration of how culture and ethnicity was considered in the development of treatment programs is warranted. Ignoring the actual content of the treatment programs for a moment, one issue is the matching of client and therapist ethnicity. The literature has shown that client perseverance in treatment may be related to this match; data on treatment outcomes has been more inconclusive (e.g., Takeuchi, Sue, & Yeh, 1995; Gray-Little & Kaplan, 2000). Given the growing literature on adapting treatments for specific ethnic groups (e.g., Bernal, Bonilla, & Bellido, 1995; Gray-Little & Kaplan, 2000), treatment developers should discuss how the culture of the clients was considered in treatment development and implementation.

Finally, as noted in the review, a number of the programs were group interventions and these demonstrated solid efficacy. However, recent concern has been raised about the possible iatrogenic effects of group interventions for antisocial youth (Dishion, McCord, & Poulin, 1999). The development of antisocial behavior has been linked to both early coercive training by parents (e.g., Patterson, 1997; Strand, 2000) and to peer deviancy training (e.g., Dishion, Spracklen, Andrews, & Patterson, 1996). The deviancy training literature essentially demonstrates that deviant peers aggregate and selectively reinforce deviant acts, thereby increasing each other's deviancy. Given these data, the appropriateness of group therapy for antisocial youth is not clear. On one hand, the group interventions reviewed in this chapter demonstrated largely positive, though modest, effects. However, Dishion et al.'s (1999) review of the literature and their own research suggest that group treatments of antisocial youth sometimes increase antisocial behaviors (e.g., increased tobacco use, increased delinquent behavior as reported by the teacher). Older youth seem particularly prone to this effect. In addition, and perhaps even more concerning, the deviancy training effect is not immediately evident, meaning that a treatment leading to good outcomes at posttreatment may actually have iatrogenic effects that only show up later. Given the infrequency of long-term follow-ups in the child outcome literature (e.g., Kendall & Southam-Gerow, 1996; Lochman, 1992), the possibility of a "sleeper effect" is unsettling. Overall, the work of Dishion et al. (1999) raises important concerns about the advisability of child-focused group CBT, at least those approaches that only include antisocial peers in the group. Although more research is needed to clarify these preliminary findings, caution is urged in using group treatments with this population.[1]

WHAT IS THE ROLE FOR CHILD-FOCUSED CBT?

As reviewed, child-focused CBT produces reliable change in antisocial children behavior. However, extant evidence indicates that there is a better treatment available (i.e., parent training), and the change produced, though statistically significant, lacks clinical significance for many treated youth. Adopting a broader based treatment strategy—integrating social-cognitive training interventions within a family or context-based framework—would seem to be a better approach to maximize treatment effect. The child-focused CBT approach does not directly address several factors that have been demonstrated as critical in the development and maintenance of child antisocial behavior. In this concluding section, I briefly review the evidence

---

[1]It is worth noting that Dishion et al. (1999) discussed how careful they were in creating groups in which deviancy was not rewarded. Despite their best efforts, they were unable to keep peer reinforcement of deviancy from deleteriously impacting outcomes.

on the factors poorly addressed in child-focused CBT approaches to treating childhood antisocial behavior. Next, I discuss how child-focused CBT fits into a comprehensive treatment package. Finally, I consider circumstances that sometimes make a child-focused CBT approach the only feasible one.

First, there is ample evidence that parent–child relational processes play a pivotal role in the development of antisocial behavior in children. As one example, the coercion theory proposed by Patterson (1982) has garnered considerable empirical support. In brief, the theory proposes that for antisocial children the relationship between child and parent is characterized by escalating coercive interactions. In addition, Patterson and his colleagues (e.g., Patterson, 1997; Patterson et al., 1975) have outlined a macromodel of parenting that contains two factors, discipline and monitoring, that explain considerable variance in child antisocial behavior (see Patterson, 1997, for discussion). Others have pointed to importance of other factors within the parent–child relationship such as affect dysregulation (see, e.g., Snyder et al., 1997). Thus, a treatment plan that does not attempt to assess or address familial factors that influence the maintenance and escalation of child antisocial behavior is unlikely to achieve optimal success. Most recent treatment research in the area recognizes this fact by including both child-focused and parent-focused treatments simultaneously (e.g., Prinz & Jones, chap. 11, this volume; Kazdin, 1996; Webster-Stratton & Hammond, 1997).

Second, many contextual factors appear to influence child antisocial behavior. Using the seminal work of Bronfenbrenner (e.g., 1979) as a foundation, Henggeler et al. (1998) described how the broader social ecology affects youth and families and how to use a multimodal treatment package to remedy this. In a related study, LeClair and Innes (1997) found that child referral to a mental health center for behavior problems was nonrandomly distributed in terms of geography: Knowing the ecological structure of a child's neighborhood greatly increased one's ability to predict if a child would be referred. Specifically, they found that living in areas characterized by higher population density and older, predominantly rental housing greatly increased the likelihood of referral. Henggeler et al. (1998) identified several factors likely to serve as protective factors, including proximity to and support from extended family, access to prosocial peers, supportive school environment with adequate resources to assist a struggling youth, and safe neighborhood with limited exposure to criminal subculture. Thus, therapies that address relevant contextual variables will likely enhance treatment effectiveness. Borduin et al. (chap. 12, this volume) describes one such approach, multisystemic therapy (MST). Child-focused treatment is often one component within the overall MST treatment plan.

Third, children with conduct disorder or oppositional defiant disorders (or both) commonly experience multiple co-occurring problems (e.g., academic problems, learning disorders) and multiple comorbid psychological disorders (e.g., attention deficit hyperactivity disorder, depressive disorders, anxiety disorders; Angold, Costello, & Erkanli, 1999; Caron & Rutter, 1991; Russo & Beidel, 1994). Most child-focused CBT approaches designed for antisocial children address problems related to aggression and dysregulated anger. As such, problems related to poor attention, depressed mood, and academic failure—all sources of great stress for the child and parent— may be ignored. This dilemma is not unique to treatments for childhood antisocial behavior (or other problems in childhood; see, e.g., Southam-Gerow & Kendall, 2000). The therapeutic reach of all disorder-focused, manual-based treatments is limited by the spotlighted disorder. However, the secondary and tertiary problems of children with antisocial behavior problems may receive less focus because of the dramatic and other-impairing nature of antisocial symptoms.

Overall, a multifaceted treatment approach combining child-focused CBT with other interventions, such as PMT, or a school-based program, or a broadly focused approach like MST, may represent the optimal treatment package. More and more studies are beginning to systematically evaluate such integrative treatment approaches and promising findings are emerging (e.g., Borduin et al., 1995; Henggeler, Melton, & Smith, 1992; Horne & Sayger, 1990; Kazdin et al., 1992; Webster-Stratton, 1994). Thus, child-focused CBT represents one of several tools that a clinician would use to make the necessary repairs.[2]

However, some circumstances may make child-focused approaches the best and perhaps only choice as the method of treatment. These circumstances can be categorized as parent factors and clinician and service agency factors. Regarding the former, parent-focused treatment programs require a parent to be regularly involved in treatment and willing to make changes in her or his behaviors. To the extent that parents view the child as the owner of the problem and the person needing to make changes, they may be unwilling to attend parenting classes. Even those parents that attend therapy sessions find parent-training approaches challenging (e.g., to their self-esteem, to their financial and time resources). Related to the challenges facing parents in these treatment programs, Patterson and colleagues (Patterson & Chamberlain, 1994; Stoolmiller, Duncan, Bank, & Patterson, 1993) have studied parental resistance to treatment. Their careful study has indicated that some parents simply do not engage in or work through that resistance; such parents experienced the poorest outcomes. Finally, some children do not have a stable or available parent figure who could be the client in a parent training intervention. In some instances, the

---

[2]This discussion does not even touch on the potentially important role that medications may play in the treatment of these youth. Bukstein (chap. 13, this volume) reviews this literature.

child may be a foster child in a temporary placement, be a ward or dependent of the state, or have his or her primary caregiver in prison at the time of the referral for treatment. Thus, if parents are unwilling or unable to attend treatment, a child-focused approach may represent the only option.

Other obstacles to the implementation of broad-based treatment are related to clinicians and service agencies. For example, the expertise required to master the diversity of the techniques involved in broader treatments is considerable. Many clinicians in community mental health centers have 2 years of advanced training and may have mastered only one or two of the several techniques that the research literature suggests for a particular case. Compounding this obstacle, agencies may be unable to staff their centers with the full breadth of expertise in the empirically supported treatments, even across clinicians (i.e., including the full knowledge of the entire staff). Thus, although there is solid empirical evidence that there are long-term cost benefits to using broader based treatments, in the short run they appear more expensive (e.g., need to provide training for many staff).

Finally, some of the procedures in broader treatment packages are not easily assimilated into the routine of the typical practitioner or the typical agency. For instance, treatment goals in a broad approach may include regular meetings with a community organization to assist an antisocial boy in acquiring an appropriate part-time job or frequent home visits to assist a parent in applying newly acquired parenting skills. These interventions require ample time investments on the part of the therapist, a good deal of which would occur outside of the office. To the extent that such time reduces the therapist's productivity as measured in billable hours, these treatments operate counter to the extant contingencies in the agency. In addition, most service agencies are oriented toward providing service on site and the infrastructure is organized around this premise (e.g., liability insurance, billing, productivity requirements). If sessions occur outside of the agency and if session length varies according to the needs of the client, there will be a need for agencies to have processes in place to recognize these interventions. Furthermore, third-party payors will need to agree to pay for these services. In all likelihood such changes within the agencies (and their associated payors) are likely to be slow in coming.

As this discussion illustrates, limited resources and insufficient training sometimes make it impractical (or prohibitively difficult) to provide the ideal treatment package for a particular case. Obviously, if these broad-based treatments are significantly better than other approaches (and extant evidence suggests that they probably are), changes will be needed across various systems (e.g., training of mental health workers, agency infrastructures, third-party payors) to accommodate these forms of treatment. Some progress in this direction is occurring, as many agencies are moving toward broader, systems-of-care models. Still, in most agencies, a child-focused (or clinic-based parent-training) program is likely to be an initial line of treatment. Thus, more broadly disseminated knowledge about, and continued study of, these interventions (especially in real-world settings (see, e.g., Southam-Gerow & Kendall, 2000; Weisz, 2000; Weisz, Southam-Gerow, Gordis, & Connor-Smith, in press) will best serve the diverse and compelling needs of antisocial youth and their families.

REFERENCES

Achenbach, T. M. (1991). *Manual for the child behavior checklists/4-18 and 1991 profile*. Burlington, VT: University of Vermont.

American Academy of Child and Adolescent Psychiatry. (1997). Summary of practice parameters for the assessment and treatment of children and adolescents with conduct disorder. *Journal of the American Academy of Child and Adolescent Psychiatry, 36*, 1482–1485.

Angold, A., Costello, E. J., & Erkanli, A. (1999). Comorbidity. *Journal of Child Psychology and Psychiatry, 40*, 57–87.

Barrett, P. M., Rapee, R. M., Dadds, M. M., & Ryan, S. M. (1996). Family enhancement of cognitive style in anxious and aggressive children. *Journal of Abnormal Child Psychology, 24*, 187–203.

Bates, J. E., Bayles, K., Bennett, D. S., Ridge, B., & Brown, M. M. (1991). Origins of externalizing behavior problems at eight years of age. In D. J. Pepler & K. H. Rubin (Eds.), *The development and treatment of childhood aggression* (pp. 93–120). Hillsdale, NJ: Lawrence Erlbaum Associates, Inc.

Beck, A. T., Rush, A. J., Shaw, B. F., & Emery, G. (1979). *Cognitive therapy of depression*. New York: Guilford.

Bernal, G., Bonilla, J., & Bellido, C. (1995). Ecological validity and cultural sensitivity for outcome research: Issues for the cultural adaptation and development of psychosocial treatments with Hispanics. *Journal of Abnormal Child Psychology, 23*, 67–82.

Borduin, C. M., Mann, B. J., Cone, L. T., Henggeler, S. W., Fucci, B. R., Blaske, D. M., & Williams, R. A. (1995). Multisystemic treatment of serious juvenile offenders: Long-term prevention of criminality and violence. *Journal of Consulting and Clinical Psychology, 63*, 569–578.

Brennan, P., Mednick, S., & Kandel, E. (1991). Congenital determinants of violent and property offending. In D. J. Pepler & K. H. Rubin (Eds.), *The development and treatment of childhood aggression* (pp. 81–92). Hillsdale, NJ: Lawrence Erlbaum Associates, Inc.

Brestan, E. V., & Eyberg, S. M. (1998). Effective psychosocial treatments of conduct-disordered children and adolescents: 29 years, 82 studies, and 5,272 kids. *Journal of Clinical Child Psychology, 27*, 180–189.

Bronfenbrenner, U. (1979). *The ecology of human development: Experiments by nature and design*. Cambridge, MA: Harvard University Press.

Caron, C., & Rutter, M. (1991). Comorbidity in child psychopathology: Concepts, issues and research strategies. *Journal of Child Psychology and Psychiatry and Allied Disciplines, 32*, 1063–1080.

Casey, R. J. (1996). Emotional competence in children with externalizing and internalizing disorders. In M. Lewis & M. W. Sullivan (Eds.), *Emotional development in atypical children* (pp. 161–183). Mahwah, NJ: Lawrence Erlbaum Associates, Inc.

Chambless, D. L., Sanderson, W. C., Shoham, V., Johnson, S. B., Pope, K. S., Crits-Christoph, P., Baker, M., Johnson, B., Woods, S. R., Sue, S., Beutler, L., Williams, D. A., & McCurry, S. (1996). An update on empirically validated therapies. *The Clinical Psychologist, 49*, 5–18.

Coie, J. D., Dodge, K. A., & Coppotelli, H. (1982). Dimensions and types of social status: A cross-age perspective. *Developmental Psychology, 18*, 557–570.

Cole, P. M., Michel, M. K., & Teti, L. O. (1994). The development of emotion regulation and dysregulation: A clinical perspective. *Monographs of the Society for Research in Child Development, 59* (2–3, Serial No. 240).

Dishion, T. J., McCord, J., & Poulin, F. (1999). When interventions harm: Peer groups and problem behavior. *American Psychologist, 54*, 755–764.

Dishion, T. J., Spracklen, K. M., Andrews, D. W., & Patterson, G. R. (1996). Deviancy training in male adolescents friendships. *Behavior Therapy, 27*, 373–390.

Dobson, K. S., & Shaw, B. F. (1988). The use of treatment manuals in cognitive therapy: Experience and issues. *Journal of Consulting and Clinical Psychology, 56*, 673–680.

Dodge, K. A. (1980). Social cognition and children's aggressive behavior. *Child Development, 51*, 162–170.

Dunn, S. E., Lochman, J. E., & Colder, C. R. (1997). Social problem-solving skills in boys with conduct and oppositional defiant disorders. *Aggressive Behavior, 23*, 457–469.

Durlak, J. A., Fuhrman, T., & Lampman, C. (1991). Effectiveness of cognitive-behavior therapy for maladapting children: A meta-analysis. *Psychological Bulletin, 110*, 204–214.

Feindler, E. L., Ecton, R. B., Dubey, D., & Kingsley, D. (1986). Group anger-control training for institutionalized psychiatric male adolescents. *Behavior Therapy, 17*, 109–123.

Feindler, E. L., Marriott, S. A., & Iwata, M. (1984). Group anger control training for junior high school delinquents. *Cognitive Therapy and Research, 8*, 299–311.

Gray-Little, B., & Kaplan, D. (2000). Race and ethnicity in psychotherapy research. In C. R. Snyder & R. E. Ingram (Eds.), *Handbook of psychological change: Psychotherapy processes & practices for the 21st century* (pp. 591–613). New York: Wiley.

Harris, P. L. (1993). Understanding emotion. In M. Lewis & J. M. Haviland (Eds.), *Handbook of emotions* (pp. 237–246). New York: Guilford Press.

Henggeler, S. W., Melton, G. B., & Smith, L. A. (1992). Family preservation using multisystemic therapy: An effective alternative to incarceration. *Journal of Consulting and Clinical Psychology, 60*, 953–961.

Henggeler, S. W., Schoenwald, S. K., Borduin, C. M., Rowland, M. D., & Cunningham, P. B. (1998). *Multisystemic treatment of antisocial behavior in youth.* New York: Guilford.

Hinshaw, S. P., & Anderson, C. A. (1996). Conduct and oppositional defiant disorders. In E. J. Mash & R. A. Barkley (Eds.), *Child psychopathology* (pp. 113–149). New York: Guilford.

Horne, A. M., & Sayger, T. V. (1990). *Treating conduct and oppositional defiant disorders in children.* New York: Pergamon.

Huesmann, L. R., Lefkowitz, M. M., Eron, L. D., & Walder, L. O. (1984). Stability of aggression over time and generations. *Developmental Psychology, 20*, 1120–1134.

Kazdin, A. E. (1996). Problem-solving and parent management in treating aggressive and antisocial behavior. In E. D. Hibbs & P. S. Jensen (Eds.), *Psychosocial treatments for child and adolescents disorders: Empirically based strategies for clinical practice* (pp. 377–408). Washington, DC: American Psychological Association.

Kazdin, A. E., Bass, D., Siegel, T., & Thomas, C. (1989). Cognitive-behavioral therapy and relationship therapy in the treatment of children referred for antisocial behavior. *Journal of Consulting and Clinical Psychology, 57*, 522–535.

Kazdin, A. E., Esveldt-Dawson, K., French, N. H., & Unis, A. S. (1987). Problem-solving skills training and relationship therapy in the treatment of antisocial child behavior. *Journal of Consulting and Clinical Psychology, 55*, 76–85.

Kazdin, A. E., Siegel, T. C., & Bass, D. (1992). Cognitive problem-solving skills training and parent management training in the treatment of antisocial behavior in children. *Journal of Consulting and Clinical Psychology, 60*, 733–740.

Kendall, P. C., & Bacon, S. F. (1988). Cognitive behavior therapy. In D. B. Fishman, F. Rotgers, & C. M. Franks (Eds.), *Paradigms in behavior therapy: Present and promise* (pp. 141–167). New York: Springer.

Kendall, P. C., & Braswell, L. (1985). *Cognitive-behavioral therapy with impulsive children*. New York: Guilford.

Kendall, P. C., & Braswell, L. (1993). *Cognitive-behavioral therapy with impulsive children* (2nd ed.). New York: Guilford.

Kendall, P. C., Chansky, T. E., Kane, M. T., Kim, R. S., Kortlander, E., Ronan, K. R., Sessa, F. M., & Siqueland, L. (1992). *Anxiety disorders in youth: Cognitive-behavioral interventions*. Needham Heights, MA: Allyn & Bacon.

Kendall, P. C., Chu, B., Gifford, A., Hayes, C., & Nauta, M. (1998). Breathing life into a manual. *Cognitive and Behavioral Practice, 5*, 177–198.

Kendall, P. C., & MacDonald, J. P. (1993). Cognition in the psychopathology of youth and implications for treatment. In K. S. Dobson & P. C. Kendall (Eds.), *Psychopathology and cognition* (pp. 387–432). San Diego, CA: Academic.

Kendall, P. C., Reber, M., McLeer, S., Epps, J., & Ronan, K. R. (1990). Cognitive-behavioral treatment of conduct-disordered children. *Cognitive Therapy and Research, 14*, 279–297.

Kendall, P. C., Ronan, K. R., & Epps, J. (1991). Aggression in children/adolescents: Cognitive-behavioral treatment perspectives. In D. J. Pepler & K. H. Rubin (Eds.), *The development and treatment of childhood aggression* (pp. 341–360). Hillsdale, NJ: Lawrence Erlbaum Associates, Inc.

Kendall, P. C., & Southam-Gerow, M. A. (1996). Long-term follow-up of a cognitive-behavioral therapy for anxiety-disordered youth. *Journal of Consulting and Clinical Psychology, 64*, 724–730.

King, N., Hamilton, D., & Ollendick, T. (1988). *Children's phobias: A behavioral perspective*. Chichester, England: Wiley.

Kolko, D. J., Loar, L. L., & Sturnick, D. (1990). Inpatient social-cognitive skills training groups with conduct-disordered and attention deficit disordered children. *Journal of Child Psychology and Psychiatry, 31*, 737–748.

LeClair, J. A., & Innes, F. C. (1997). Urban ecological structure and perceived child and adolescent psychological disorder. *Social Science Medicine, 44*, 1649–1659.

Lochman, J. E. (1992). Cognitive-behavioral interventions with aggressive boys: Three-year follow-up and preventive effects. *Journal of Consulting and Clinical Psychology, 60*, 426–432.

Lochman, J. E., Burch, P. R., Curry, J. F., & Lampron, L. B. (1984). Treatment and generalization effects of cognitive-behavioral and goal-setting interventions with aggressive boys. *Journal of Consulting and Clinical Psychology, 52*, 915–916.

Lochman, J. E., & Lenhart, L. A. (1993). Anger coping intervention for aggressive children: Conceptual models and outcome effects. *Clinical Psychology Review, 13*, 785–805.

Newcomb, A. F., Bukowski, W. M., & Pattee, L. (1993). Children's peer relations: A meta-analytic review of popular, rejected, neglected, controversial, and average sociometric status. *Psychological Bulletin, 113*, 99–128.

Offord, D. R., Boyle, M. H., & Racine, Y. A. (1991). The epidemiology of antisocial behavior in childhood and adolescence. In D. J. Pepler & K. H. Rubin (Eds.), *The development and treatment of childhood aggression* (pp. 31–54). Hillsdale, NJ: Lawrence Erlbaum Associates, Inc.

Olweus, D. (1980). Stability of aggressive reaction patterns in males: A review. *Psychological Bulletin, 86*, 852–875.

Patterson, G. R. (1982). *A social learning approach to family intervention: 3. Coercive family process*. Eugene, OR: Castalia.

Patterson, G. R. (1997). Performance models for parenting: A social interactional perspective. In J. E. Grusec & L. Kuczynski (Eds.), *Parenting and children's internalization of values: A handbook of contemporary theory* (pp. 193–226). New York: Wiley.

Patterson, G. R., & Chamberlain, P. (1994). A functional analysis of resistance during parent training therapy. *Clinical Psychology: Science & Practice, 1*, 53–70.

Patterson, G. R., Reid, J. B., Jones, R. R., & Conger, R. E. (1975). *A social learning approach to family intervention. 1. Families with aggressive children*. Eugene, OR: Castalia.

Raine, A., Brennan, P., & Mednick, S. A. (1994). Birth complications combined with early maternal rejection at age 1 year predispose to violent crime at age 18 years. *Archives of General Psychiatry, 51,* 984–988.

Rodkin, P. C., Farmer, T. W., Van Acker, R. P., & Van Acker, R. (2000). Heterogeneity of popular boys: Antisocial and prosocial configurations. *Developmental Psychology, 36,* 14–24.

Russo, M. F., & Beidel, D. C. (1994). Comorbidity of childhood anxiety and externalizing disorders: Prevalence, associated characteristics, and validation issues. *Clinical Psychology Review, 14,* 199–211.

Rutter, M. R., Tizard, J., & Whitmore, K. (1970). *Education, health, and behavior.* London: Longman.

Samoilov, A., & Goldfried, M. R. (2000). Role of emotion in cognitive-behavior therapy. *Clinical Psychology: Science & Practice, 7,* 373–385.

Silverman, W. K., & Ollendick, T. H. (Eds.). (1999). *Developmental issues in the clinical treatment of children.* Boston, MA: Allyn & Bacon.

Snyder, J., Schrepferman, L., & St. Peter, C. (1997). Origins of antisocial behavior: Negative reinforcement and affect dysregulation as socialization mechanisms in family interaction. *Behavior Modification, 21,* 187–215.

Southam-Gerow, M. A., & Kendall, P. C. (1997). Parent-focused and cognitive-behavioral treatments of antisocial youth. In D. Stoff, J. Breiling, & J. D. Maser (Eds.), *Handbook of antisocial behavior* (pp. 384–394). New York: Wiley.

Southam-Gerow, M. A., & Kendall, P. C. (2000). Cognitive-behavior therapy with youth: Advances, challenges, and future directions. *Clinical Psychology and Psychotherapy, 7,* 343–366.

Southam-Gerow, M. A., & Kendall, P. C. (2002). Emotion regulation and understanding: Implications for child psychopathology and therapy. *Clinical Psychology Review, 22,* 189–222.

Spivack, G., & Shure, M. B. (1974). *Social adjustment of young children: A cognitive approach to solving real-life problems.* San Francisco: Jossey-Bass.

Staub, E. (1996). Cultural-societal roots of violence—The example of genocidal violence and of contemporary youth violence in the United States. *American Psychologist, 51,* 117–132.

Stoolmiller, M., Duncan, T., Bank, L., & Patterson, G. R. (1993). Some problems and solutions in the study of change: Significant patterns in client resistance. *Journal of Consulting and Clinical Psychology, 61,* 920–928.

Strand, P. S. (2000). A modern behavioral perspective on child conduct disorder: Integrating behavioral momentum and matching theory. *Clinical Psychology Review, 20,* 593–615.

Takeuchi, D. T., Sue, S., & Yeh, M. (1995). Return rates and outcomes from ethnicity-specific mental health programs in Los Angeles. *American Journal of Public Health, 85,* 638–643.

Tremblay, R. E., Pihl, R. O., Vitaro, F., & Dobkin, P. L. (1994). Predicting early onset of male antisocial behavior from preschool behavior. *Archives of General Psychiatry, 51,* 732–739.

Vasey, M. W. (1993). Development and cognition in childhood anxiety: The example of worry. In T. H. Ollendick & R. Prinz (Eds.), *Advances in clinical child psychology* (Vol. 15, pp. 1–39). New York: Plenum.

Vernberg, E. M. (1998). Developmentally based psychotherapies: Comments and observations. *Journal of Clinical Child Psychology, 27,* 46–48.

Webster-Stratton, C. (1984). Randomized trial of two parent-training programs for families with conduct-disordered children. *Journal of Consulting and Clinical Psychology, 52,* 666–678.

Webster-Stratton, C. (1990). Long-term follow-up of families with young conduct problem children: From preschool to grade school. *Journal of Clinical Child Psychology, 19,* 144–149.

Webster-Stratton, C. (1994). Advancing videotape parent training: A comparison study. *Journal of Consulting and Clinical Psychology, 62,* 583–593.

Webster-Stratton, C., & Hammond, M. (1997). Treating children with early-onset conduct problems: A comparison of child and parent training interventions. *Journal of Consulting and Clinical Psychology, 65,* 93–109.

Weisz, J. R. (2000). Lab-clinic differences and what we can do about them: I. The clinic-based treatment development model. *Clinical Child Psychology Newsletter, 15*, 1–3, 10.

Weisz, J. R., Moore, P. S., Southam-Gerow, M. A., Weersing, V. R., Valeri, S. M., & McCarty, C. A. (1999). *Therapist manual: Primary and secondary control enhancement training program.* (Available from J. R. Weisz, UCLA Dept. of Psychology, Franz Hall, Los Angeles, CA 90095).

Weisz, J. R., Southam-Gerow, M. A., Gordis, E. B., & Connor-Smith, J. K. (in press). Primary and Secondary Control Enhancement Training for youth depression: Applying the Deployment-Focused Model of treatment development and testing. In A. E. Kazdin & J. R. Weisz (Eds.), *Evidence-based treatments for children and adolescents.* New York: Guilford.

Weisz, J. R., & Weersing, V. R. (1999). Developmental outcome research. In W. K. Silverman & T. H. Ollendick (Eds.), *Developmental issues in the clinical treatment of children* (pp. 457–469). Boston, MA: Allyn & Bacon.

Zoccolillo, M., Tremblay, R., & Vitaro, F. (1996). DSM–III–R and DSM–III criteria for conduct disorder in preadolescent girls: Specific but insensitive. *Journal of the American Academy of Child and Adolescent Psychiatry, 35*, 461–470.

CHAPTER

11

Family-Based Interventions

Ronald J. Prinz
Tracy L. Jones
University of South Carolina, Columbia

Family-based treatments for childhood and adolescent conduct problems divide roughly into two categories based on targeted age groups. For preadolescents including preschool and elementary school ages, evidence-based family treatments concentrate on parenting and the parent or caregiver role as a socialization agent. For the adolescent age group, the evidence-based family treatments for conduct disorder (CD) and delinquency mainly involve therapy with the whole family, focusing on a broad array of social-ecological factors.

TREATMENT WITH PRESCHOOL AND ELEMENTARY SCHOOL CHILDREN

Although there are some subtle differences in application, conduct-problem treatment programs for preschool children are quite similar to those used with elementary school children. The focus for both age groups is on parenting, parent–child interaction, enhancement of family relations, and skill acquisition.

Assumptions About Etiology of Conduct Problems

Essentially, the family-based treatment approaches assume that features of children's social environment account for conduct problems in terms of propogation or at least maintenance of problematic behavior. For young children, the family is a key environment. Parenting practices in particular are thought to play a central role in child conduct problems.

During the preschool years, parenting difficulties taking the form of poor discipline (Farrington & West, 1981; McCord, 1988; Patterson, Reid, & Dishion, 1992), coercive family processes (Patterson, 1982), and low levels of positive teaching or nurturant interactions (Loeber & Stouthamer-Loeber, 1986; Wadsworth, 1980), which contribute to the development of early conduct problems. Parenting difficulties are not always the sole contributing factor in the development of either oppositional defiant disorder (ODD) or early-onset CD. Early temperament problems in children can heighten risk for conduct problems (Campbell, 1990). However, even in those instances parenting difficulties may adversely affect such children in a transactional manner that escalates conduct problems and associated functioning (Bates, Bayles, Bennett, Ridge, & Brown, 1991; Campbell, Breaux, Ewing, & Szumowski, 1986; Offord, Boyle, & Racine, 1991).

During the elementary school years, conduct problems may escalate as children who are already undersocialized encounter classroom challenges and distressed peer relations (Bierman, 1986; Cantrell & Prinz, 1985; Dodge, 1989; Parker & Asher, 1987). As children experience increased problems at school, this places greater strain on parents and home–school relations (Campbell, 1991; Patterson et al., 1992). Parenting difficulties already present may become more apparent as child behavior problems increase.

Family-Based Approaches and Delivery Formats

The family-based treatment approaches to conduct problems with preschool and elementary school children focus for the most part on parents. Much of the evidence-based treatment with this age group emphasizes Parent Management Training (PMT) which generally means intervening through the parents rather than working directly with the entire family. Ten such programs with some evidence of outcome via at least one controlled study were identified. These are prototypes and this is not intended to be an exhaustive list. Some of the parent-oriented treatments are delivered using an individual-family format: Helping the Noncompliant Child (Forehand & McMahon, 1981), Oregon Social Learning Program (Patterson, Dishion, & Chamberlain, 1993; Patterson, Reid, Jones, & Conger, 1975), Parent–Child Interaction Therapy (PCIT; Eyberg, 1988; Eyberg, Boggs, & Algina, 1995), PMT (Barkley, 1997), and Synthesis Training (Wahler, Cartor, Fleischman, & Lambert, 1993; Wahler & Dumas, 1989). Other programs are delivered in a group format (i.e., with parents from several families participating): The Incredible Years Basic Program (Webster-Stratton, 1984a; Webster-Stratton & Hancock, 1998), Exploring Together (Hemphill & Littlefield, 2001), Reciprocal Skills Training (Barrett, Turner, Rombouts, & Duffy, 2000), Coping Skills Parenting Program (Cunningham, 1990; Cunningham, Bremner, & Boyle, 1995). The Triple P Positive Parenting Program has both individual-family and group programs (Sanders, 1999; Sanders & Markie-Dadds, 1996; Sanders, Markie-Dadds, & Turner, 2001; Turner, Markie-Dadds, & Sanders, 2000).

In all of these treatments emphasizing PMT, a key assumption is that parents will operate as the primary treatment or socialization agents to help children overcome negative behavior patterns. Typically, parents receive instruction in parenting and behavior management skills, collaborate in designing treatment plans, and then carry out programming at home. Some of the treatments rely on parents as reporters, whereas other treatments involve observation of in vivo parent–child interaction to supplement parent report.

Process and Engagement Issues

Process and engagement issues with this population are important but complicated. Parental dropout rates for group parent training programs and to some extent for therapy programs with individual families are higher than optimum (Armbruster & Fallon, 1994; Armbruster & Kazdin, 1994; Gould, Shaffer, & Kaplan, 1985; Pekarik & Stephenson, 1988; Weisz, Weiss, & Langmeyer, 1987). Families with children exhibiting conduct problems experience disproportionately higher rates of adversity associated with socioeconomic disadvantage, family conflict and divorce, and parental psychopathology or substance abuse. These sources of adversity place parents and families under considerable duress, which in turn undermines parenting effectiveness and confidence but also contributes to attrition in therapy (Armbruster & Kazdin, 1994; Miller & Prinz, 1990; Prinz & Miller, 1994, 1996; Weisz et al., 1987).

Parental cognitions and attributions play a role in how fully therapists are able to engage parents in treatment (Morrissey-Kane & Prinz, 1999). Parents bring to therapy specific beliefs about what they think causes children to have behavior problems and how they think treatment should proceed. Parental attributions are relevant as well. Parents who attribute their child's problems to factors outside the family may be harder to engage in a parenting-focused treatment than parents who take responsibility for their contributions to the situation.

Methods and Strategies of Treatment

Operational Facets. As reflected in Table 11.1, the family-based treatment programs draw on a wide variety of operations. Most of the programs focus on direct acquisition or strengthening of parenting skills via behavioral rehearsal or practice, modeling (live or from videotape), feedback, and coaching. Programs commonly involve didactic presentations, discus-

TABLE 11.1

Operational Facets of Family-Based Treatment Programs for Children's Conduct Problems

Operations	Family-Based Treatment Program									
	1	2	3	4	5	6	7	8	9	10
Behavioral rehearsal or practice	X	X	X	X	X	X	X	X	X	
Modeling	X	X	X	X	X	X	X	X		X
Feedback and coaching	X	X		X	X	X		X		
Didactic presentations	X	X	X	X	X	X			X	
Homework assignments	X	X	X		X	X	X	X		
Readings or other handout materials	X	X		X	X	X		X		
Discussion or group discussion		X	X	X	X		X	X	X	X
Parental monitoring of child behavior	X	X		X	X					X
Additional program modules available (e.g., classroom, partner conflict resolution, parent coping skills, child social skills)	X	X	X	X	X		X		X	
Live coaching by therapist during or directly after parent–child play session	X			X	X	X			X	X
Child involved in some sessions	X				X					
Parent–therapist problem solving			X	X			X			
Videotape demonstration		X	X				X			
Goal setting		X					X	X		
Booster sessions						X	X	X		
Telephone follow-ups			X	X		X				
Home observation	X			X						
Home visits for programming		X	X							
Synthesis teaching			X							
Weekly evaluation of session										X

Note. 1 = Helping the Noncompliant Child (ages 3–8); 2 = Triple P: Positive Parenting Program (ages 2–12); 3 = The Incredible Years: BASIC (ages 2–8); 4 = Oregon Social Learning Program (ages 3–14); 5 = Parent–Child Interaction Therapy (ages 2–7); 6 = Barkley Parent Management Training (ages 2–11); 7 = Coping Skills

sion between parent and therapist or with a larger group, and use of readings or other written materials. Live coaching after parent–child interaction is also a common strategy. Most programs assign homework tasks to parents, which typically involve trying out parenting strategies at home and then reporting back to the therapist (or the group) what occurred. Few programs though actually conduct therapist observations or programming visits in the home, with a few exceptions (e.g., Triple P). Content of treatment programs is described in Table 11.2.

Treatment Strategies for Managing Problematic Behavior. All of the treatment programs have some components focused on management of problematic child behavior. The most common strategies for managing problematic behavior include time out or quiet time, planned ignoring, and effective use of antecedents (e.g., clear instructions or requests, ground rules). Some programs teach the use of logical consequences (e.g., turning the television off when children are fighting over what to watch). Token systems, directed discussion, and other various strategies are used to a limited extent.

Strategies for Building Up Positive Behaviors. The most prevalent strategies for building up positive child behaviors include positive reinforcement in terms of praise, contingent positive attention, and use of tangible rewards or incentives, and to a lesser extent the use of behavior charts. A few programs focused on more specific strategies to improve parental teaching via incidental teaching, ways to promote independence and self-regulation, modeling, and ways to teach prosocial behaviors. Similarly, the rare program focused explicitly on ways to restructure the environment by showing parents how to provide engaging activities and environments for children and by using a planned activities approach that anticipates high-risk situations and explicitly promotes positive behaviors.

Strengthening Family Relations. An indirect benefit or goal from building up positive child behavior is the strengthening of the parent–child relationship. Some of the treatment programs include elements or components that more explicitly target family relations. Some of the identified operations and goals focus on relationship building skills, how to promote cooperation, enhancing family conversations and communication, increasing physical affection and quality time, and promoting shared problem solving between parent and child.

Treatment Outcomes. A large research base has accumulated in support of family-based treatments for conduct problems in young children (Biglan, 1992, 1995; Dumas, 1989; Eyberg & Boggs, 1998; Harachi, Catalano, & Hawkins, 1997; Hawkins & Lishner, 1987; Kazdin, 1995, 1997; McMahon, 2000;

TABLE 11.2

Content of Family-Based Treatment Programs for Children's Conduct Problems

Types of Content	Family-Based Treatment Program									
	1	2	3	4	5	6	7	8	9	10
Strategies for managing misbehavior										
Using time out or quiet time	X	X	X	X	X		X	X	X	X
Using planned ignoring	X	X	X		X		X	X	X	
Giving clear instructions and making effective requests or commands	X		X		X			X		X
Using logical consequences	X						X		X	
Ground rules or house rules	X		X							
Managing noncompliance in public places	X									
Teach parents to anticipate and plan for potential future behavior problems				X						
Prompting child to plan in advance of difficult situations				X						
Limit setting or helping children learn to accept limits					X					
Using a token system for problem behaviors							X			
Maintaining a predictable routine									X	
Anger management for both parents and children		X								
Using directed discussion		X								
Disengaging from coercive interaction	X									
Teaching parents to use immediate, specific, and consistent consequences					X					
Teaching responsibility to children in terms of short- and long-term consequences of their actions				X						
Establishing incentive system before using punishment		X								
Differential attention				X						
Transitional strategies			X							
Problem-solving skills					X					
Behavior management principles and techniques, unspecified						X				

Strategies for building positive behaviors

Strategy								
Giving clear instructions and making effective requests or commands	X		X		X		X	
Praise	X	X	X				X	
Providing social reinforcement for positive behaviors including physical, nonverbal, and verbal positive attention	X			X	X		X	X
Attending to prosocial behaviors by describing child's appropriate behavior (i.e., play), answering questions, using reflective listening, showing interest in child's activities		X	X	X			X	X
Tangible rewards or incentives	X		X	X				
The importance of play, how to play, independent play	X		X	X		X		
Helping children learn	X					X		
Increasing compliance to commands and requests			X		X			
Avoiding commands, questions, and criticism in child-directed play			X	X				
Teaching children prosocial behaviors			X	X				
Providing engaging activities and environment for child (i.e., toys, materials, persons)	X							
Planned activities (apply strategies for promoting positive behaviors and managing misbehaviors to high-risk situations in home and community)	X							
Using incidental teaching	X							
Encourage independence and teach children self-care skills through "Ask, say, do"	X							
Parental modeling of desirable behaviors	X							
Using behavior charts	X							
Encourage positive interaction					X			

(Continued)

TABLE 11.2
(Continued)

Types of Content	Family-Based Treatment Program									
	1	2	3	4	5	6	7	8	9	10
Strengthening family relations										
Parent–child relationship building skills	X					X				
Enhance parent–child communication and effective conversation in the family	X	X	X			X				
Cooperation and working together		X				X				
Having realistic expectations	X	X								
Teach parents about reciprocity of interaction patterns in families and uselessness of fault finding				X						
Providing a nonjudgmental setting for positive interaction	X					X				
Giving physical affection to child	X									
Spending quality time with child	X									
Conversing with child about an activity or interest of the child	X									
Promoting empathy		X								
Shared problem solving between parent and child						X				
Individual family members focus attention on own behavior		X								
Caregiver-focused strategies										
Educating parents about causes of child behavior problems and challenge negative perceptions	X			X		X				
Taking care of oneself as a parent, self-care, and stress management	X	X								
Exploring and attempting to resolve parent's personal difficulties and parenting, marital, family of origin issues						X				
Assisting parents to recognize their feelings, strengths, and resources						X				

Note. 1 = Triple P- Positive Parenting Program (ages 2–12); 2 = Reciprocal Skills Training (ages 2–12); 3 = Parent–Child Interaction Therapy (ages 2–7); 4 = Barkley Parent Management Training (ages 2–11); 5 = Coping Skills Parenting Program (ages 2–8); 6 = Exploring Together (ages 6–11); 7 = The Incredible Years: BASIC (ages 2–8); 8 = Helping the Noncompliant Child (ages 3–8); 9 = Oregon Social Learning Program (ages 3–14); 10 = Synthesis Training (ages 5–9).

Miller & Prinz, 1990; Patterson, 1982; Patterson et al., 1992; Prinz, 1992, 1995; Prinz & Connell, 1997; Prinz & Miller, 1994; Reid, 1991; Reid & Eddy, 1997; Sanders & Dadds, 1993; Sanders & Glynn, 1981; Sanders & Plant, 1989a; Spoth, Redmond, & Shin, 1998; Webster-Stratton, 1985, 1997, 1998; Webster-Stratton & Hammond, 1997; Webster-Stratton & Hancock, 1998; Webster-Stratton & Herbert, 1994; Webster-Stratton & Taylor, 1998).

The Incredible Years Basic Program developed by Webster-Stratton and colleagues (Webster-Stratton, 1984a; Webster-Stratton & Hancock, 1998) has been well supported in a series of studies that employed randomization and controls, primarily involving 4- to 8-year-old children with CD or ODD. The parenting program produced reductions in aggressive and destructive behavior in several outcome studies (Webster-Stratton, 1981, 1982a, 1982b, 1984b; Webster-Stratton, Hollinsworth, & Kolpacoff, 1989; Webster-Stratton, Kolpacoff, & Hollinsworth, 1988). Other researchers have replicated this work and also found positive impact of the program (Scott, Spender, Doolan, Jacobs, & Aspland, 2001; Spaccarelli, Cotler, & Penman, 1992; Taylor, Schmidt, Pepler, & Hodgins, 1998).

PCIT, developed by Eyberg and colleagues (Eyberg & Boggs, 1998), has shown treatment efficacy. Controlled studies have demonstrated that PCIT can significantly reduce child conduct and oppositional problems, move substantial proportions of children diagnosed with ODD into the nonclinical range, strengthen parent–child interactions for mothers and fathers, enhance child cooperativeness and family relations, and produce some generalization across settings and over time (Eisenstadt, Eyberg, McNeil, Newcomb, & Funderburk, 1993; Eyberg, 1988; Eyberg & Boggs, 1989; Eyberg et al., 1995; Eyberg & Robinson, 1982; Schuhmann, Foote, Eyberg, Boggs, & Algina, 1998)

The Triple P-Positive Parenting Program, developed by Sanders and colleagues (Sanders, 1999), has shown consistent treatment effects in reducing child conduct problems and strengthening parent skills for both the group and individual delivery formats. The Triple P approach is well supported by an impressive collection of efficacy and effectiveness trials (Connell, Sanders, & Markie-Dadds, 1997; Dadds, Schwartz, & Sanders, 1987; Lawton & Sanders, 1994; Markie-Dadds & Sanders, under review; Markie-Dadds, Sanders, & Smith, 1997; Nicholson & Sanders, 1999; Sanders, 1992, 1996, 1998, 1999; Sanders, Bor, & Dadds, 1984; Sanders & Christensen, 1985; Sanders & Dadds, 1982, 1993; Sanders & Duncan, 1995; Sanders & Glynn, 1981; Sanders & Markie-Dadds, 1992, 1996, 1997; Sanders, Markie-Dadds, Tully, & Bor, 2000; Sanders & McFarland, 2000; Sanders & Plant, 1989; Williams, Zubrick, Silburn, & Sanders, 1997).

Other family-based treatment programs have also shown efficacy in reducing child conduct problems. For example, evidence of positive impact has been reported for the Oregon Social Learning Program (Arnold, Levine,

& Patterson, 1975; Patterson, 1974; Patterson & Reid, 1973; Wiltz & Patterson, 1974), Helping the Noncompliant Child (Forehand & Long, 1988; Long, Forehand, Wierson, & Morgan, 1994; McMahon & Forehand, 1984; Wells, Forehand, & Griest, 1980), Coping Skills Parenting Program (Cunningham et al., 1995; Cunningham, Davis, Bremner, Dunn, & Rzasa, 1993), Synthesis Training (Wahler et al., 1993), Reciprocal Skills Training (Barrett et al., 2000), and Exploring Together (Hemphill & Littlefield, 2001).

For a more detailed examination of outcome studies, the reader is referred to several recent reviews that focus on family-based treatment programs (Barlow & Stewart-Brown, 2000; Corcoran, 2000; Frick, 2000; Kazdin, 2001; Serketich & Dumas, 1996).

TREATMENT WITH ADOLESCENTS

The evidence-based family treatments for adolescent CD and delinquency generally work with the whole family, incorporate ecological systems into the conceptualizations and actual operations, and target family functioning in addition to amelioration of youth problem behavior.

Assumptions About Etiology of Conduct Problems

Parenting difficulties persisting throughout childhood can contribute to the development or escalation of conduct problems in adolescence. Two major family-related problems often contribute to youth antisocial behavior. The first is insufficient monitoring and supervision by parents, which makes it easier for youth to be influenced by deviant peers and then get into trouble in the community (Dishion, Patterson, Stoolmiller, & Skinner, 1991; Patterson et al., 1992; Snyder, Dishion, & Patterson, 1986). The second is aversive family interaction associated with elevated family conflict (Prinz, Foster, Kent, & O'Leary, 1979) or coercive parenting practices (Dishion et al., 1991).

Family-Based Approaches and Delivery Formats

The family-based treatments with younger children work primarily through the parents. In contrast, most of the family treatments with adolescents involve the youth much more in the treatment process. Four such treatment programs are considered. All four of the programs described following focus on adolescents with problems of delinquency, CD, or substance abuse.

Functional Family Therapy (FFT; Alexander & Parsons, 1982; Alexander, Pugh, Parsons, & Sexton, 2000) focuses primarily on understanding how the adolescent's family relational system promotes or maintains maladaptive behavior. Utilizing a multisystemic perspective, FFT targets both adolescent and family functioning. The emphasis is on how various problematic behaviors have functionality with the context of the family. FFT moves through three phases of treatment: engagement and motivation, behavior change, and generalization. Each phase includes both assessment and treatment facets. During the engagement and motivation phase, the goals are to develop an alliance, reduce negative communication, and enhance engagement and optimism. During the behavior change phase, the goals are to implement individualized change plans, alter delinquent behavior, and build relational skills. The third phase focuses on generalization of changes, relapse prevention, and utilizing community support. All family members attend the sessions together. Treatment typically consists of 8 to 12 hr and can extend to 26 to 30 hr for particular cases. FFT can be flexibly delivered in home, clinic, and school settings.

Multisystemic Therapy (MST; Henggeler, 1998; Henggeler, Schoenwald, Borduin, Rowland, & Cunningham, 2000) seeks to intervene using a social-ecological approach that takes into account the network of interconnected systems that encompass adolescent, family, and extrafamilial (peer, school, neighborhood) factors. MST is a highly individualized and comprehensive treatment that seeks to build on identified adolescent and family strengths to protect against operating risk factors. There is a focus on parental and youth empowerment. The main goals are to reduce youth delinquent activity, reduce other types of antisocial behavior such as substance abuse, and decrease rates of incarceration and out-of-home placements. Service is provided in the home so as to reduce barriers to treatment, prevent dropout, allow the therapist to provide intensive services, and maintain treatment gains. Typically, MST lasts for 60 hr over a 4-month period, although youth and family needs dictate frequency and duration of sessions.

Brief Strategic Family Therapy (BSFT; Coatsworth, Szapocznik, Kurtines, & Santisteban, 1997; Szapocznik & Williams, 2000) grew out of a need for a culturally appropriate and acceptable treatment for Hispanic youth exhibiting antisocial behavior problems such as CD and substance abuse. BSFT draws from the structural and strategic approaches to traditional family therapy. The approach assumes that the behaviors of individual family members affect each other greatly and interact to organize the family system, and that treatments that fail to take this into account are doomed to limited success.

BSFT therapists are particularly interested in the repetitive interaction patterns that characterize the family. A key assumption is that a maladaptive family structure can help to maintain problematic behaviors. BSFT attempts to change the repetitive interactions within or between systems in the family social ecology, particularly ones that are unsuccessful at achieving the goals of the family or its members. BSFT operates by (a) emphasizing practicality, for example by focusing on the family's reality using positive or negative reframing; (b) staying problem focused, for example by targeting family interaction patterns that relate most directly to the identified problem behaviors; and (c) acting in a deliberate manner, for example by having the therapist determine which maladaptive interaction patterns need to be changed to achieve adaptive behavior. Several variations and extensions of BSFT have been developed, such as Bicultural Effectiveness Training, which addresses stressors related to acculturation across generations; Strategic Structural Systems Engagement, which is a set of procedures developed to better engage adolescents and families; and, Structural Ecosystems Therapy, which places a major emphasis on cultural issues in applying BSFT principles related for example to joining, diagnosing, and restructuring. Although heavily focused on adolescents, BSFT has also been conducted with 6- to 11-year-old youth (Szapocznik et al., 1989). BSFT typically involves 12 to 24 hr involving weekly sessions over 4 to 6 months.

Multidimensional Family Therapy (Liddle, Rowe, Dakof, & Lyke, 1998; Liddle et al., 2000; Schmidt, Liddle, & Dakof, 1996) is a multicomponent family intervention designed to treat adolescent substance abuse and problem behaviors. Multidimensional Family Therapy targets four main areas for intervention: the intrapersonal and interpersonal functioning of the adolescent, the intrapersonal and interpersonal functioning of the parent, parent–adolescent interactions, and interactions between family members and influences outside the family system. Individual symptoms are addressed in context, and changes in the individual such as decreasing maladaptive behaviors and increasing prosocial functioning are assumed to result from changes in the family system. Treatment tends to last between 14 to 16 sessions over 6 months.

Process and Engagement Issues

Therapists conducting family-based treatment with adolescents face the dual problem of engaging both the parent(s) and the youth. Some parents who have struggled with long-standing problems in their children may have given up in defeat (Patterson et al., 1992). Other parents may simply not see their role in either contributing to, or addressing, the youth's problems and instead might attribute to external and non-familial (Morrissey-Kane & Prinz, 1999). Youth engagement has its own problems. Youth who are operating within a permissive family environment may perceive therapy as undermining their power and might be reluctant to cooperate with the treatment process. Youth who have experienced harsh or coercive parenting might be less trusting of other adults or may fear retribution at home for speaking up in therapy.

How the various family-based treatment approaches navigate these issues is not well documented but nonetheless of major concern to investigators and program implementers. With adolescents and their families, the emphasis across several of the treatment programs seems to be on using reframing, joining, paradox, and other family-therapy techniques to enhance engagement (Henggeler et al., 2000; Kazdin, 2001; Szapocznik & Williams, 2000).

Treatment Strategies

A number of strategic similarities are apparent in the evidence-based family treatments for adolescent conduct problems.

1. Goal setting is a consistent component. Therapists assist families in identifying youth-related and family-related treatment goals that are realistic and achievable.

2. In various ways, all of the treatments address family communication. Family sessions provide a working laboratory for promoting clear, direct, and nonprovocative ways for family members to talk to one another. Therapists use reframing to diffuse problematic interactions and then feedback and coaching to help families develop more effective and less aversive styles of communication.

3. Adopting an ecological perspective, therapists analyze how adolescents' problem behaviors fit into patterns of family functioning and relate to other systems (e.g., neighborhood, peer group, school). The treatment programs employ various strategies to help families recognize and then alter the patterns rather than only focusing on the youth's behavior.

4. There is an emphasis on developing action plans and then formalizing them as agreements or contracts. This approach addresses the past criticism that nonevidenced-based treatment tended to involve a lot of talking without much in the way of behavior change or real-world action.

5. The programs attempt to build on existing family strengths rather than focusing mainly or exclusively on psychopathology. This stance is intended to empower family members to act instead of putting them on the defensive.

Treatment Outcomes

FFT has shown promising outcomes with delinquent youth. Fourteen studies evaluating FFT are summarized in the Blueprints for Violence Prevention series (Alexander, Pugh, et al., 2000). Several randomized, controlled studies have demonstrated that FFT can improve family functioning and reduce recidivism in adolescents with delinquent histories and improve functioning of adolescents with conduct and substance-abuse problems (Alexander & Barton, 1976, 1980; Alexander, Pugh, et al., 2000; Alexander, Robbins, & Sexton, 2000; Friedman, 1989; Klein, Alexander, & Parsons, 1977; Parsons & Alexander, 1973).

Treatment outcomes for MST are discussed in Chapter 12 in this volume with regard to delinquent, substance-abusing, and clinical populations.

BSFT and its variants have shown success particularly with Hispanic youth who have substance abuse and concomitant conduct problems. A review of the BSFT studies can be found in Szapocznik and Williams (2000). For example, BSFT proved effective in reducing conduct problems in adolescents and in producing greater family engagement than usual-care community treatment (Coatsworth, Santisteban, McBride, & Szapocznik, 2001).

CONCLUSIONS

Family-based treatment for conduct problems in children and adolescents is both a promising and challenging endeavor. With younger children, there is a large research base of parenting-focused treatment that continues to progress. For adolescents, the research base is smaller but growing with the more recent advances of ecologically oriented family treatments. Future research will clarify under what conditions and with which families and youth certain programming facets are more effective. Treatment researchers need to better understand the parameters of successful and unsuccessful engagement and to find ways to more efficiently match treatment intensity to family need.

REFERENCES

Alexander, J. F., & Barton, C. (1976). Behavioral systems therapy with families. In D. H. Olson (Ed.), *Treating relationships* (pp. 167–188). Lake Mills, IA: Graphic Publishing.

Alexander, J. F., & Barton, C. (1980). Functional family therapy. In F. Kaslow (Ed.), *Voices in family psychology* (pp. 167–188). Carmel, CA: Sage.

Alexander, J., & Parsons, B. V. (1982). *Functional family therapy*. Monterey, CA: Brooks/Cole.

Alexander, J., Pugh, C., Parsons, B., & Sexton, T. (2000). *Functional family therapy*. Boulder, CO: Center for the Study and Prevention of Violence.

Alexander, J. F., Robbins, M. S., & Sexton, T. L. (2000). Family-based interventions with older, at-risk youth: From promise to proof to practice. *The Journal of Primary Prevention, 21*, 185–205.

Armbruster, P., & Fallon, T. (1994). Clinical, sociodemographic, and systems risk factors for attrition in a children's mental health clinic. *American Journal of Orthopsychiatry, 64*, 577–585.

Armbruster, P., & Kazdin, A. E. (1994). Attrition in child psychotherapy. In T. H. Ollendick & R. J. Prinz (Eds.), *Advances in clinical child psychology* (Vol. 16, pp. 81–108). New York: Plenum.

Arnold, J. E., Levine, A. G., & Patterson, G. R. (1975). Changes in sibling behavior following family intervention. *Journal of Consulting and Clinical Child Psychology, 43*, 683–688.

Barkley, R. A. (1997). *Defiant children: A clinician's manual for assessment and parent training* (2nd ed.). New York: Guilford.

Barlow, J., & Stewart-Brown, S. (2000). Behavior problems and group-based parent education programs. *Developmental and Behavioral Pediatrics, 21,* 356–370.

Barrett, P., Turner, C., Rombouts, S., & Duffy, A. (2000). Reciprocal skills training in the treatment of externalising behaviour disorders in childhood: A preliminary investigation. *Behaviour Change, 17,* 221–234.

Bates, J. E., Bayles, K., Bennett, D. S., Ridge, B., & Brown, M. M. (1991). Origins of externalizing behavior problems at eight years of age. In D. J. Pepler & K. H. Rubin (Eds.), *The development and treatment of childhood aggression* (pp. 93–119). Hillsdale, NJ: Lawrence Erlbaum Associates, Inc.

Bierman, K. (1986). The relationship of social aggression and peer rejection in middle childhood. In R. J. Prinz (Ed.), *Advances in behavioral assessment of children/families* (pp. 151–178). Greenwich, CT: JAI.

Biglan, A. (1992). Family practices and the larger social context. *New Zealand Journal of Psychology, 21,* 37–43.

Biglan, A. (1995). Translating what we know about the context of antisocial behavior into a lower prevalence of such behavior. *Journal of Applied Behavior Analysis, 28,* 479–492.

Campbell, S. B. (1990). *Behavior problems in preschool children. Clinical and developmental issues.* New York: Guilford.

Campbell, S. B. (1991). Longitudinal studies of active and aggressive preschoolers: Individual differences in early behavior and outcome. In S. L. T. D. Cicchetti (Ed.), *Rochester Symposium on Developmental Psychopathology, Vol. 2: Internalizing and externalizing expressions of dysfunction* (Vol. 2, pp. 57–90). Hillsdale, NJ: Lawrence Erlbaum Associates, Inc.

Campbell, S. B., Breaux, A. M., Ewing, L. J., & Szumowski, E. K. (1986). Correlates and predictors of hyperactivity and aggression: A longitudinal study of parent-referred problem preschoolers. *Journal of Abnormal Child Psychology, 14,* 217–234.

Cantrell, V. L., & Prinz, R. J. (1985). Multiple perspectives of rejected, neglected, and accepted children: Relationship between sociometric status and behavioral characteristics. *Journal of Consulting and Clinical Psychology, 53,* 884–889.

Coatsworth, J. D., Santisteban, D. A., McBride, C. K., & Szapocznik, J. (2001). Brief strategic family therapy versus community control: Engagement, retention, and an exploration of the moderating role of adolescent symptom severity. *Family Process, 40,* 313–332.

Coatsworth, J. D., Szapocznik, J., Kurtines, W., & Santisteban, D. A. (1997). Culturally competent psychosocial interventions with antisocial problem behavior in hispanic youths. In D. M. Stoff & J. Breiling, (Eds.), *Handbook of antisocial behavior.* New York: Wiley.

Connell, S., Sanders, M. R., & Markie-Dadds, C. (1997). Self-directed behavioral family intervention for parents of oppositional children in rural and remote areas. *Behavior Modification, 21,* 379–408.

Corcoran, J. (2000). Family treatment of preschool behavior problems. *Research on Social Work Practice, 10,* 547–588.

Cunningham, C. E. (1990). A family systems approach to parent training. In R. A. Barkley (Ed.), *Attention deficit hyperactivity disorder: A handbook for diagnosis and treatment* (pp. 432–461). New York: Guilford.

Cunningham, C. E., Bremner, R., & Boyle, M. (1995). Large group community-based parenting programs for families of preschoolers at risk for disruptive behaviour disorders: Utilization, cost effectiveness, and outcome. *Journal of Child Psychology and Psychiatry, 36,* 1141–1159.

Cunningham, C. E., Davis, J. R., Bremner, R., Dunn, K. W., & Rzasa, T. (1993). Coping modeling problem solving versus mastery modeling: Effects on adherence, in-session process, and skill acquisition in a residential parent-training program. *Journal of Consulting and Clinical Child Psychology, 61,* 871–877.

Dadds, M. R., Schwartz, S., & Sanders, M. R. (1987). Marital discord and treatment outcome in the treatment of childhood conduct disorders. *Journal of Consulting and Clinical Psychology, 55,* 396–403.

Dishion, T. J., Patterson, G. R., Stoolmiller, M., & Skinner, M. L. (1991). Family, school, and behavioral antecedents to early adolescent involvement with antisocial peers. *Developmental Psychology, 27*, 172–180.

Dodge, K. A. (1989). Enhancing social relationships. In E. J. Mash & R. J. Barkley (Eds.), *Behavioral treatment of childhood disorders* (pp. 222–244). New York: Guilford.

Dumas, J. E. (1989). Treating antisocial behavior in children: Child and family approaches. *Clinical Psychology Review, 9*, 197–222.

Eisenstadt, T. H., Eyberg, S., McNeil, C. B., Newcomb, K., & Funderburk, B. (1993). Parent–child interaction therapy with behavior problem children: Relative effectiveness of 2 stages and overall treatment outcome. *Journal of Clinical Child Psychology, 22*, 42–51.

Eyberg, S. (1988). Parent–Child interaction therapy: Integration of traditional and behavioral concerns. *Child and Family Behavior Therapy, 10*, 33–46.

Eyberg, S., & Boggs, S. R. (1989). Parent training for oppositional-defiant preschoolers. In C. E. Schaefer & J. M. Briesmeister (Eds.), *Handbook of parent training: Parents as co-therapists for children's behavior problems* (pp. 105–132). New York: Wiley.

Eyberg, S. M., & Boggs, S. R. (1998). Parent–child interaction therapy: A psychosocial intervention for the treatment of young conduct-disordered children. In J. M. Briesmeister & C. E. Schaefer (Eds.), *Handbook of parent training: Parents as co-therapists for children's behavior problems* (2nd ed., pp. 61–97). New York: Wiley.

Eyberg, S. M., Boggs, S. R., & Algina, J. (1995). Parent–child interaction therapy—A psychosocial model for the treatment of young children with conduct problem behavior and their families. *Psychopharmacology Bulletin, 31*, 83–91.

Eyberg, S. M., & Robinson, E. A. (1982). Parent–child interaction training: Effects on family functioning. *Journal of Clinical Child Psychology, 11*, 130–137.

Farrington, D. P., & West, D. J. (1981). The Cambridge study in delinquent development (United Kingdom). In S. A. Mednick & A. E. Baert (Eds.), *Prospective longitudinal research: An empirical basis for the primary prevention of psychosocial disorders* (pp. 137–145). New York: Oxford University Press.

Forehand, R. L., & Long, N. (1988). Outpatient treatment of the acting out child: Procedures, long term follow-up data, and clinical problems. *Advances in Behaviour Research and Therapy, 10*, 129–177.

Forehand, R. L., & McMahon, R. J. (1981). *Helping the noncompliant child: A clinician's guide to parent training*. New York: Guilford.

Frick, P. J. (2000). A comprehensive and individualized treatment approach for children and adolescents with conduct disorders. *Cognitive and Behavioral Practice, 7*, 30–37.

Friedman, A. S. (1989). Family therapy vs. parent groups: Effects on adolescent drug abusers. *American Journal of Family Therapy, 17*, 335–347.

Gould, M. S., Shaffer, D., & Kaplan, D. (1985). The characteristics of dropouts from a child psychiatry clinic. *Journal of the American Academy of Child and Adolescent Psychiatry, 24*, 316–328.

Harachi, T. W., Catalano, R. F., & Hawkins, J. D. (1997). Effective recruitment for parenting programs within ethnic minority communities. *Child and Adolescent Social Work Journal, 14*, 23–39.

Hawkins, J. D., & Lishner, D. (1987). Etiology and prevention of antisocial behavior in children and adolescents. In D. H. Crowell, I. M. Evans, & C. R. O'Donnell (Eds.), *Childhood aggression and violence: Sources of influence, prevention, and control* (pp. 263–282). New York: Plenum.

Hemphill, S. A., & Littlefield, L. (2001). Evaluation of a short-term group therapy program for children with behavior problems and their parents. *Behaviour Research and Therapy, 39*, 823–841.

Henggeler, S. W. (1998). *Multisystemic therapy*. Boulder, CO: Center for the Study and Prevention of Violence.

Henggeler, S. W., Schoenwald, S. K., Borduin, C. M., Rowland, M. D., & Cunningham, P. B. (2000). *Multisystemic treatment of antisocial behavior in youth*. New York: Guilford.

Kazdin, A. E. (1995). *Conduct disorders in childhood and adolescence* (2nd ed.). Thousand Oaks, CA: Sage.

Kazdin, A. E. (1997). Parent management training: Evidence, outcomes, and issues. *Journal of the American Academy of Child and Adolescent Psychiatry, 36,* 1349–1356.

Kazdin, A. E. (2001). Treatment of conduct disorders. In J. Hill & B. Maughan (Eds.), *Conduct disorders in childhood and adolescence* (pp. 408–448). New York: Cambridge University Press.

Klein, N. C., Alexander, J. F., & Parsons, B. V. (1977). Impact of family systems intervention on recidivism and sibling delinquency: A model of primary prevention and program evaluation. *Journal of Consulting and Clinical Child Psychology, 45,* 469–474.

Lawton, J. M., & Sanders, M. R. (1994). Designing effective behavioral family interventions for stepfamilies. *Clinical Psychology Review, 14,* 463–496.

Liddle, H. A., Rowe, C., Dakof, G. A., & Lyke, J. (1998). Translating parenting research into clinical interventions for families of adolescents. *Clinical Child Psychology and Psychiatry, 3,* 419–443.

Liddle, H. A., Rowe, C., Diamond, G. M., Sessa, F., Schmidt, S., & Ettinger, D. (2000). Towards a developmental family therapy: The clinical utility of adolescent development research. *Journal of Marital and Family Therapy, 26,* 491–506.

Loeber, R., & Stouthamer-Loeber, M. (1986). Family factors as correlates and predictors of juvenile conduct problems and delinquency. In N. Morris & M. Tonry (Eds.), *Crime and justice: An annual review of research* (Vol. 7, pp. 29–149). Chicago: University of Chicago Press.

Long, P., Forehand, R., Wierson, M., & Morgan, A. (1994). Does parent training with young noncompliant children have long-term effects? *Behaviour Research and Therapy, 32,* 101–107.

Markie-Dadds, C., & Sanders, M. R. (under review). Effectiveness of a self-directed program for parents of children at high and low risk of developing conduct disorder.

Markie-Dadds, C., Sanders, M. R., & Smith, J. I. (1997, June). *Self-directed behavioural family intervention for parents of oppositional children in rural and remote areas.* Paper presented at the 20th National Conference of the Australian Association for Cognitive and Behavior Therapy, Brisbane, Queensland, Australia.

McCord, J. (1988). Parental behavior in the cycle of aggression. *Psychiatry, 51,* 14–23.

McMahon, R. J. (2000). Parent training. In S. W. Russ & T. Ollendick (Eds.), *Handbook of psychotherapies with children and families* (pp. 153–180). New York: Plenum.

McMahon, R. J., & Forehand, R. L. (1984). Parent training for the noncompliant child: Treatment outcome, generalization, and adjunctive therapy procedures. In R. F. Dangel & R. A. Polster (Eds.), *Parent training: Foundations of research and practice* (pp. 298–328). New York: Guilford.

Miller, G. E., & Prinz, R. J. (1990). The enhancement of social learning family interventions for childhood conduct disorder. *Psychological Bulletin, 108,* 291–307.

Morrissey-Kane, E., & Prinz, R. J. (1999). Engagement in child and adolescent treatment: The role of parental cognitions and attributions. *Clinical Child and Family Psychology Review, 2,* 183–198.

Nicholson, J. M., & Sanders, M. R. (1999). Behavioural family intervention with children living in step families. *Journal of Marriage and Divorce, 30,* 1–23.

Offord, D. R., Boyle, M. C., & Racine, Y. A. (1991). The epidemiology of antisocial behavior in childhood and adolescence. In D. J. Pepler & K. H. Rubin (Eds.), *The development and treatment of childhood aggression* (pp. 31–54). Hillsdale, NJ: Lawrence Erlbaum Associates, Inc.

Parker, J. G., & Asher, S. R. (1987). Peer relations and later personal adjustment: Are low accepted children at risk? *Psychological Bulletin, 102,* 357–389.

Parsons, B. V., & Alexander, J. F. (1973). Short term family intervention: A therapy outcome study. *Journal of Consulting and Clinical Child Psychology, 41,* 195–201.

Patterson, G. R. (1974). Interventions for boys with conduct problems: Multiple settings, treatments, and criteria. *Journal of Consulting and Clinical Child Psychology, 42,* 471–481.

Patterson, G. R. (1982). *Coercive family process.* Eugene, OR: Castalia.

Patterson, G. R., Dishion, T. J., & Chamberlain, P. (1993). Outcomes and methodological issues relating to treatment of antisocial children. In T. R. Giles (Ed.), *Handbook of effective psychotherapy* (pp. 43–87). New York: Plenum.

Patterson, G. R., & Reid, J. B. (1973). Intervention for families of aggressive boys: A replication study. *Behaviour Research and Therapy, 11*, 383–394.

Patterson, G. R., Reid, J. B., & Dishion, T. J. (1992). *Antisocial boys.* Eugene, OR: Castalia.

Patterson, G. R., Reid, J. B., Jones, R. R., & Conger, R. E. (1975). *A social learning approach to family intervention: Volume 1. Families with aggressive children.* Eugene, OR: Castalia.

Pekarik, G., & Stephenson, L. (1988). Adult and child client differences in therapy dropout research. *Journal of Clinical Child Psychology, 17*, 316–321.

Prinz, R. J. (1992). Overview of behavioural family interventions with children: Achievements, limitations, and challenges. *Behaviour Change, 9*, 1–6.

Prinz, R. J. (1995). Prevention. In G. P. Sholevar (Ed.), *Conduct disorders in children and adolescents* (pp. 341–350). Washington, DC: American Psychiatric Press.

Prinz, R. J., & Connell, C. (1997). Prevention of conduct disorders and antisocial behavior. In R. T. Ammerman & M. Hersen (Eds.), *Handbook of prevention and treatment with children and adolescents: Intervention in the real world context* (pp. 238–258). New York: Wiley.

Prinz, R. J., Foster, S., Kent, R. N., & O'Leary, K. D. (1979). Multivariate assessment of conflict in distressed and nondistressed mother–adolescent dyads. *Journal of Applied Behavior Analysis, 12*, 116–125.

Prinz, R. J., & Miller, G. E. (1994). Family-based treatment for childhood antisocial behavior: Experimental influences on dropout and engagement. *Journal of Consulting and Clinical Psychology, 62*, 645–650.

Prinz, R. J., & Miller, G. E. (1996). Parental engagement in interventions for children at risk for conduct disorder. In R. D. Peters & R. J. McMahon (Eds.), *Prevention and early intervention: Childhood disorders, substance abuse, and delinquency* (pp. 161–183). Newbury Park, CA: Sage.

Reid, J. B. (1991). Involving parents in the prevention of conduct disorder: Rationale, problems, and tactics. *The Community Psychologist, 24*, 28–30.

Reid, J. B., & Eddy, J. M. (1997). The prevention of antisocial behavior: Some considerations in the search for effective interventions. In D. M. Stoff, J. Breiling, & J. D. Maser (Eds.), *The handbook of antisocial behavior* (pp. 343–356). New York: Wiley.

Sanders, M. R. (1992). Enhancing the impact of behavioural family intervention with children: Emerging perspectives. *Behaviour Change, 9*, 115–119.

Sanders, M. R. (1996). New directions in behavioral family intervention with children. In T. H. Ollendick & R. J. Prinz (Eds.), *Advances in clinical child psychology* (Vol. 18, pp. 283–330). New York: Plenum.

Sanders, M. R. (1998). The empirical status of psychological interventions with families of children and adolescents. In L. L'Abate (Ed.), *Family psychopathology: The relational roots of dysfunctional behavior* (pp. 427–465). New York: Guilford.

Sanders, M. R. (1999). Triple P–Positive Parenting Program: Towards an empirically validated multilevel parenting and family support strategy for the prevention of behavior and emotional problems in children. *Clinical Child and Family Psychology Review, 2*, 71–90.

Sanders, M. R., Bor, B., & Dadds, M. R. (1984). Modifying bedtime disruptions in children using stimulus control and contingency management procedures. *Behavioural Psychotherapy, 12*, 130–141.

Sanders, M. R., & Christensen, A. P. (1985). A comparison of the effects of child management and planned activities training across five parenting environments. *Journal of Abnormal Child Psychology, 13*, 101–117.

Sanders, M. R., & Dadds, M. R. (1982). The effects of planned activities and child-management training: An analysis of setting generality. *Behavior Therapy, 13*, 452–461.

Sanders, M. R., & Dadds, M. R. (1993). *Behavioral family intervention.* Boston: Allyn & Bacon.

Sanders, M. R., & Duncan, S. B. (1995). Empowering families: Policy, training, and research issues in promoting family mental health in Australia. *Behaviour Change, 12*, 109–121.

Sanders, M. R., & Glynn, T. (1981). Training parents in behavioural self-management: An analysis of generalisation and maintenance. *Journal of Applied Behaviour Analysis, 14*, 223–237.

Sanders, M. R., & Markie-Dadds, C. (1992). Toward a technology of prevention of disruptive behaviour disorders: The role of behavioural family intervention. *Behaviour Change, 9*, 186–200.

Sanders, M. R., & Markie-Dadds, C. (1996). Triple P: A multilevel family intervention program for children with disruptive behavior disorders. In P. Cotton & H. Jackson (Eds.), *Early intervention and prevention in mental health* (pp. 59–85). Melbourne, Victoria, Australia: Australian Psychological Society.

Sanders, M. R., & Markie-Dadds, C. (1997). Managing common child behaviour problems. In M. R. Sanders, C. Mitchell, & G. J. A. Byrne (Eds.), *Medical consultation skills: Behavioural and interpersonal dimensions of health care*. Melbourne, Victoria, Australia: Addison Wesley Longman.

Sanders, M. R., Markie-Dadds, C., Tully, L., & Bor, B. (2000). The Triple P Positive Parenting Program: A comparison of enhanced, standard, and self-directed behavioral family intervention for parents of children with early onset conduct problems. *Journal of Consulting and Clinical Psychology, 68*, 624–640.

Sanders, M. R., Markie-Dadds, C., & Turner, M. T. (2001). *Practitioner's manual for Standard Triple P*. Brisbane, Queensland, Australia: Families International.

Sanders, M. R., & McFarland, M. L. (2000). The treatment of depressed mothers with disruptive children: A controlled evaluation of cognitive behavioural family intervention. *Behavior Therapy, 31*, 89–112.

Sanders, M. R., & Plant, K. (1989). Generalization effects of behavioral parent training to high and low risk parenting environments. *Behavior Modification, 13*, 283–305.

Schmidt, S. E., Liddle, H. A., & Dakof, G. A. (1996). Changes in parenting practices and adolescent drug abuse during multidimensional family therapy. *Journal of Family Psychology, 10*, 12–27.

Schuhmann, E. M., Foote, R. C., Eyberg, S. M., Boggs, S. R., & Algina, J. (1998). Efficacy of parent–child interaction therapy: Interim report of a randomized trial with short-term maintenance. *Journal of Clinical Child Psychology, 27*, 34–45.

Scott, S., Spender, Q., Doolan, M., Jacobs, B., & Aspland, H. (2001). Multicentre controlled trial of parenting groups for childhood antisocial behaviour in clinical practice. *British Medical Journal, 323*, 1–6.

Serketich, W. J., & Dumas, J. E. (1996). The effectiveness of behavioral parent training to modify antisocial behavior in children: A meta-analysis. *Behavior Therapy, 27*, 171–186.

Snyder, J., Dishion, T. J., & Patterson, G. R. (1986). Determinants and consequences of associating with deviant peers. *Journal of Early Adolescence, 6*, 29–43.

Spaccarelli, S., Cotler, S., & Penman, D. (1992). Problem-solving skills training as a supplement to behavioral parent training. *Cognitive Therapy and Research, 16*, 1–18.

Spoth, R., Redmond, C., & Shin, C. (1998). Direct and indirect latent-variable parenting outcomes of two universal family-focused preventive interventions: Extending a public health-oriented research base. *Journal of Consulting and Clinical Psychology, 66*, 385–399.

Szapocznik, J., Murray, E., Scopetta, M., Hervis, O., Rio, A., Cohen, R., Rivas-Vazquez, A., Posada, B., & Kurtines, W. (1989). Structural family versus psychodynamic child therapy for problematic Hispanic boys. *Journal of Consulting and Clinical Child Psychology, 57*, 571–578.

Szapocznik, J., & Williams, R. A. (2000). Brief Strategic Family Therapy: Twenty-five years of interplay among theory, research and practice in adolescent behavior problems and drug abuse. *Clinical Child and Family Psychology Review, 3*, 117–134.

Taylor, T. K., Schmidt, S., Pepler, D., & Hodgins, H. (1998). A comparison of eclectic treatment with Webster-Stratton's Parents and Children Series in a children's mental health center: A randomized control trial. *Behavior Therapy, 29*, 221–240.

Turner, M. T., Markie-Dadds, C., & Sanders, M. R. (2000). *Facilitator's manual for Group Triple P*. Brisbane, Queensland, Australia: Families International.

Wadsworth, M. E. J. (1980). Early life events and later behavioral outcomes in a British longitudinal study. In S. B. Sells, K. Crandell, M. Roff, J. S. Strauss, & W. Pollin (Eds.), *Human functioning in longitudinal perspective* (pp. 168–180). Baltimore: Williams & Wilkins.

Wahler, R. G., Cartor, P. G., Fleischman, J., & Lambert, W. (1993). The impact of synthesis teaching and parent training with mothers of conduct-disordered children. *Journal of Abnormal Child Psychology, 21*, 425–440.

Wahler, R. G., & Dumas, J. E. (1989). Attentional problems in dysfunctional mother–child interactions: An interbehavioral model. *Psychological Bulletin, 105*, 116–130.

Webster-Stratton, C. (1981). Modification of mothers' behaviors and attitudes through videotape modeling group discussion program. *Behavior Therapy, 12*, 634–642.

Webster-Stratton, C. (1982a). The long-term effects of a videotape modeling parent training program: Comparison of immediate and one-year followup results. *Behavior Therapy, 13*, 702–714.

Webster-Stratton, C. (1982b). Teaching mothers through videotape modeling to change their children's behaviors. *Journal of Pediatric Psychology, 7*, 279–294.

Webster-Stratton, C. (1984a). *The Incredible Years training manual: BASIC program.* Seattle: University of Washington.

Webster-Stratton, C. (1984b). Randomized trial of two parent-training programs for families with conduct-disordered children. *Journal of Consulting and Clinical Child Psychology, 52*, 666–678.

Webster-Stratton, C. (1985). Predictors of treatment outcome in parent training for conduct-disordered children. *Behavior Therapy, 16*, 223–243.

Webster-Stratton, C. (1997). From parent training to community building. *Families in Society, 78*, 156–171.

Webster-Stratton, C. (1998). Preventing conduct problems in Head Start children: Strengthening parenting competencies. *Journal of Consulting and Clinical Psychology, 66*, 715–730.

Webster-Stratton, C., & Hammond, M. (1997). Treating children with early-onset conduct problems: A comparison of child and parent training interventions. *Journal of Consulting and Clinical Psychology, 65*, 93–109.

Webster-Stratton, C., & Hancock, L. (1998). Training for parents of young children with conduct problems: Content, methods, and therapeutic processes. In J. M. Briesmeister & C. E. Schaefer (Eds.), *Handbook of parent training: Parents as co-therapists for children's behavior problems* (2nd ed., pp. 98–152). New York: Wiley.

Webster-Stratton, C., & Herbert, M. (1994). Strategies for helping parents of children with conduct disorders. In M. Hersen & R. M. Eisler (Eds.), *Progress in behavior modification* (Vol. 29, pp. 121–142). Pacific Grove, CA: Brooks/Cole.

Webster-Stratton, C., Hollinsworth, T., & Kolpacoff, M. (1989). The long-term effectiveness and clinical significance of three cost-effectiveness training programs for families with conduct-problem children. *Journal of Consulting and Clinical Child Psychology, 57*, 550–553.

Webster-Stratton, C., Kolpacoff, M., & Hollinsworth, T. (1988). Self-administered videotape therapy for families with conduct-problem children: Comparison with two cost-effective treatments and a control group. *Journal of Consulting and Clinical Child Psychology, 56*, 558–566.

Webster-Stratton, C., & Taylor, T. K. (1998). Adopting and implementing empirically supported interventions: A recipe for success. In A. Buchanan & B. L. Hudson (Eds.), *Parenting, schooling, and children's behavior: Interdisciplinary approaches* (pp. 127–160). London: Ashgate.

Weisz, J. R., Weiss, B., & Langmeyer, D. B. (1987). Giving up on child psychotherapy: Who drops out? *Journal of Consulting and Clinical Psychology, 55*, 916–918.

Wells, K. C., Forehand, R., & Griest, D. L. (1980). Generality of treatment effects from treated to untreated behaviors resulting from a parent training program. *Journal of Clinical Child Psychology, 9*, 217–219.

Williams, A., Zubrick, S., Silburn, S., & Sanders, M. (1997, May). *A population based intervention to prevent childhood conduct disorder: The Perth Positive Parenting Program demonstration project.* Paper presented at the 9th National Health Promotion Conference, Darwin, Northern Territory, Australia.

Wiltz, N. A., & Patterson, G. R. (1974). An evaluation of parent training procedures designed to alter inappropriate aggressive behavior of boys. *Behavior Therapy, 5*, 215–221.

12

Multisystemic Treatment of Serious Antisocial Behavior in Adolescents

Charles M. Borduin
University of Missouri–Columbia

Cindy M. Schaeffer
University of Maryland, Baltimore County

Scott T. Ronis
University of Missouri–Columbia

Serious antisocial behavior in adolescents presents significant problems at several levels of analysis, and these problems argue for the development of effective treatment approaches. On a personal level, adolescents who engage in serious antisocial behavior experience numerous psychosocial problems as well as reduced educational and occupational opportunities (Lyons, Baerger, Quigley, Erlich, & Griffin, 2001; Melton & Pagliocca, 1992). Moreover, serious antisocial behavior in adolescents has extremely detrimental emotional, physical, and economic effects on victims, their families, and the larger community (Britt, 2000; Cohen & Miller, 1998; Gottfredson, 1989; Robinson & Keithley, 2000). Therefore, effective treatment may not only benefit the adolescent and his or her family but may also save many persons from victimization.

On an epidemiological level, adolescents commit higher rates of serious antisocial acts than any other age group. Indeed, youths under the age of 18 years account for approximately 29% of all arrests for index offenses, including 17% of violent crimes and 33% of property crimes (Federal Bureau of Investigation, 1999), and such arrests greatly underestimate the prevalence of adolescent criminal activity (Elliott, Dunford, & Huizinga, 1987; Loeber, Farrington, & Waschbusch, 1998). In addition, although only about one fourth of adolescents arrested for delinquent acts could be characterized as serious offenders and even fewer (approximately 15%) could be characterized as chronic offenders, adolescent serious and chronic offenders account for more than one half of the total volume of youth crime in a community (Farrington, Ohlin, & Wilson, 1986; Loeber et al., 1998; Moffitt, 1993). Thus, if one purpose of treating antisocial behavior in adolescents is to decrease crime, then adolescents who are involved in serious and chronic antisocial behavior are a logical target for intervention efforts.

On a social services level, delinquent adolescents, especially those who are violent, consume much of the resources of the child mental health, juvenile justice, and special education systems and are overrepresented in the "deep end" of these systems (Cocozza, 1992; Melton, Lyons, & Spaulding, 1998) with considerable cost to the public treasury and intrusion on family integrity and youth autonomy. Moreover, adolescents who engage in violence and other serious forms of antisocial behavior often have continued contact with the mental health and criminal justice systems well into adulthood (Borduin & Schaeffer, 1998; Moffitt, 1993; Pajer, 1998). Therefore, the development of effective treatments for serious antisocial behavior in adolescents may help to free resources to address other important problems of children and their families.

Unfortunately, as numerous reviewers have concluded (e.g., Kazdin, 2000; Melton & Pagliocca, 1992; Tate, Reppucci, & Mulvey, 1995), the development of effective treatments for serious antisocial behavior in adolescents has been an extremely difficult task. In part, this difficulty is due to the fact that serious antisocial behaviors, especially those involving aggression, tend to be highly stable in individuals (Loeber & Hay, 1996; Moffitt, 1993) and across generations (Hawkins et al., 1998; Huesmann, Lefkowitz, Eron, & Walder, 1984). However, an even more important reason for the general lack of effective treatments for adolescents who commit serious antisocial acts is that most extant treatments do not address the multiple and changing mental health needs of these youth. Clearly, there is a pressing need to develop effective alternatives to the narrowly focused treatments that are commonly used with adolescents involved in serious antisocial behavior.

Multisystemic therapy (MST; Borduin & Henggeler, 1990; Henggeler & Borduin, 1990) was developed to address major limitations of existing mental health services for adolescents who evidence serious antisocial behavior and has been viewed as a promising treatment for violence and criminality in adolescents (see, e.g., Kazdin, 2000; Levesque, 1996; Tate et al., 1995). The primary purpose of this chapter is to address the empirical rationale for the application of MST, as well as the features of MST that make it well-suited for treating serious antisocial behavior in adolescents. More specifically, this chapter begins with a brief review of empirical findings regarding the correlates and causes of violent and other serious antisocial behaviors in adolescents. Next, the theoretical and clinical foundations of MST are described, followed by a brief description of key administrative elements of MST programs. Findings from controlled evaluations that demonstrate the efficacy of MST with adolescent serious offenders are then summarized. Finally, important aspects of MST that contribute to its success and that distinguish MST from commonly available treatments and service programs for serious antisocial behavior in adolescents are discussed.

EMPIRICAL FOUNDATIONS OF MST

Correlates and Causes of Antisocial Behavior

A large number of studies have evaluated correlates of clinically severe antisocial behavior in adolescents. These studies indicate that serious antisocial behavior is linked with multiple characteristics of the individual adolescent and of the key social systems (family, peers, school, neighborhood) in which the adolescent is embedded. In general, the factors linked with antisocial behavior are relatively constant whether the examined antisocial behavior is conduct disorder (Kazdin, 1995; McMahon & Estes, 1997), delinquency (Borduin & Schaeffer, 1998; Farrington & Loeber, 2000; Hawkins et al., 1998; Thornberry, Huizinga, & Loeber, 1995), or substance abuse (Hawkins, Catalano, & Miller, 1992; Office of Technology Assessment, 1991). Table 12.1 lists the correlates of antisocial behavior that have consistently emerged in the literature.

In light of the numerous correlates of serious antisocial behavior in adolescents, an ever increasing number of research groups have developed empirically based multidimensional causal models of delinquent behavior. These research groups have used path analysis or structural equation modeling to examine the interrelations among variables from several of the psychosocial domains (i.e., individual, family, peers, school, neighborhood) that have been linked with antisocial behavior. Such causal modeling studies allow a determination of which variables have direct versus indirect effects on antisocial behavior and which variables are no longer linked with antisocial behavior when the effects of other correlates are controlled. Findings from the fields of delinquency (Henggeler, 1991; Henry, Tolan, & Gorman-Smith, 2001; Herrenkohl et al., 2001; LeBlanc & Kaspy, 1998; Paschall & Hubbard, 1998) and substance abuse (Ary et al., 1999; Henggeler, 1997; Wills, Sandy, Yaeger, & Shinar, 2001) are relatively clear and consistent:

- Involvement with deviant peers is virtually always a powerful direct predictor of antisocial behavior.
- Family relations predict antisocial behavior either directly (contributing unique variance) or indirectly by predicting involvement with deviant peers.
- School difficulties predict involvement with deviant peers.

TABLE 12.1
Correlates of Antisocial Behavior

Individual adolescent characteristics
- Low verbal skills
- Favorable attitudes toward antisocial behavior
- Immature moral reasoning
- Cognitive bias to attribute hostile intentions to others

Family characteristics
- Lax and ineffective parental discipline
- Lack of parental monitoring
- Low affection and cohesion
- High conflict and hostility
- Parental difficulties, such as substance abuse, psychiatric conditions, and criminality

Peer relations
- High involvement with deviant peers
- Poor social skills
- Low involvement with prosocial peers

School factors
- Low commitment to education
- Poor academic performance
- Dropout
- Poor academic quality and weak structure of school

Neighborhood and community characteristics
- Low organizational participation among residents
- High mobility
- Low social support available from church, neighbors, and the like
- Criminal subculture (e.g., drug dealing, prostitution)

- Neighborhood and community support characteristics add small portions of unique variance or indirectly predict antisocial behavior by, for example, affecting family, peer, or school behavior.

Thus, across studies and in spite of substantial variation in research methods and measurement, investigators have shown that adolescent antisocial behavior is linked directly or indirectly with key characteristics of adolescents and of their social systems.

Clinical Implications of Findings

If the primary goal of treatment is to optimize the probability of decreasing rates of antisocial behavior, then treatment approaches must have the flexibility to address the multiple known determinants of such behavior. Indeed, there is a growing consensus among reviewers that the major limitation of most treatments for serious antisocial behavior is their failure to account for the multidetermined nature of such behavior and that effective treatments must have the capacity to intervene comprehensively at individual, family, peer, school, and possibly even neighborhood levels (Borduin, 1994; Kashani, Jones, Bumby, & Thomas, 1999; Kazdin, 2000; Levesque, 1996; Melton & Pagliocca, 1992; Mulvey, Arthur, & Reppucci, 1993). A critical feature of MST is its capacity to address the multiple determinants of serious antisocial behavior in a comprehensive, intense, and individualized fashion.

THEORETICAL FOUNDATIONS OF MST

Family systems theory (Bateson, 1972; Hoffman, 1981; Minuchin, 1985) and the theory of social ecology (Bronfenbrenner, 1979) fit closely with research findings on the correlates and causes of serious antisocial behavior in adolescents and serve as a basis for case conceptualization and treatment planning in MST. Family systems theory views the family as a rule-governed system and an organized whole that transcends the sum of its separate parts. From this perspective, it is assumed that problematic individual behaviors and symptoms are intimately related to patterns of interaction between family members and must always be understood within the context of those interaction patterns. Although there are differences in how various schools of family therapy interpret systems theory, most attempt to understand how emotional and behavioral problems fit within the context of the individual's family relations and emphasize the reciprocal and circular nature of such relations. Thus, a therapist working from a family systems conceptual framework would consider not only how parental discipline strategies influence child behavior but also how the behavior of the child shapes and guides the behavior of the parents and what function the misbehavior might serve in the family.

The theory of social ecology (Bronfenbrenner, 1979) shares some of the basic tenets of family systems theory but encompasses broader and more numerous contextual influences within a child's life. The child is viewed as being nested within a complex of interconnected systems that include the individual child, the child's family, and various extrafamilial (peer, school, neighborhood, community) contexts (see Figure 12.1). The child's behavior is seen as the product of the reciprocal interplay between the child and these systems and of the relations of the systems with each other. Thus, although the interactions between the child and family or peers are seen as important, the connections between the systems are viewed as equally important. It is assumed, then, that child behavior problems can be maintained by problematic transactions within any given system or between some combination of pertinent systems. Importantly, social-ecological theory emphasizes the significance of ecological validity in understanding behavior, that is, the basic assumption that behavior can be fully understood only when viewed within its naturally occurring context.

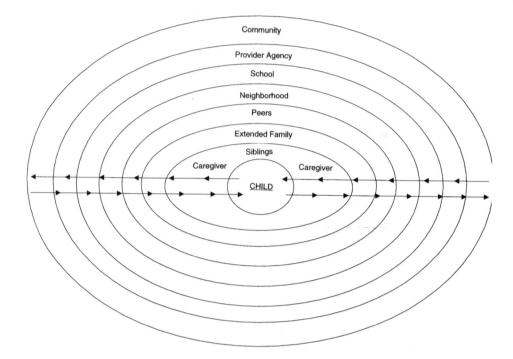

FIG. 12.1. Social-ecological environment. The child and family are embedded in multiple systems with dynamic and reciprocal influences (represented by arrows) on the behavior of family members. Problem behavior can be maintained by problematic transactions within and/or between any one or combination of these systems. From S. W. Henggeler, S. K. Schoenwald, C. M. Borduin, M. D. Rowland, and P. B. Cunningham (1998), *Multisystemic treatment of Antisocial Behavior in Children and Adolescents.* New York: Guilford Press.

CLINICAL FOUNDATIONS OF MST

Interventions in MST

Consistent with both the empirically established correlates and causes of adolescent antisocial behavior and with systemic and social-ecological theories, MST interventions target identified youth and family problems within and between the multiple systems in which family members are embedded, and such interventions are delivered in the family's natural environment (home, school, neighborhood) to optimize ecological validity. Delivering interventions in the natural environment also greatly decreases barriers to service access in a population (i.e., families of adolescents presenting serious antisocial behavior) that has very high no-show and dropout rates from traditional institution-based services. Indeed, working with families on their own turf sends a message of therapist commitment and respect that can greatly facilitate family engagement and the development of a therapeutic alliance—prerequisites for achieving desired outcomes.

The overriding goals of MST are to empower parents with the skills and resources needed to independently address the inevitable difficulties that arise in raising adolescents and to empower adolescents to cope with familial and extrafamilial problems. Using well-validated treatment strategies derived from strategic family therapy, structural family therapy, behavioral parent training, and cognitive-behavioral therapy, MST directly addresses intrapersonal (e.g., cognitive), familial, and extrafamilial (i.e., peer, school, neighborhood) factors that are known to contribute to adolescent serious and violent antisocial behavior. Biological contributors to identified problems (e.g., major depression, attention deficit hyperactivity disorder) in family members are also identified, and, when appropriate, psychopharmacological treatment is integrated with psychosocial treatment. Because different contributing factors are relevant for different adolescents and families, MST interventions are individualized and highly flexible.

Although the exact nature and sequence of interventions in MST can vary widely from family to family, several types of interventions are commonly used with antisocial adolescents and their parents. At the family level, MST interventions generally aim to remove barriers to effective parenting (e.g., parental substance abuse, parental psychopathology, low social support, high stress, marital conflict), to enhance parenting knowledge, and to promote affection and communication among family members. At the peer level, interventions frequently are designed to decrease affiliation with delinquent and drug using peers and to increase affiliation with prosocial peers (e.g., through church youth groups, organized athletics, afterschool activities). Such interventions are optimally conducted by the adolescent's parents, with the guidance of the therapist, and often consist of active support and encouragement of associations with nonproblem peers (e.g., providing transportation, increased privileges) and substantive discouragement of associations with deviant peers (e.g., applying significant sanctions). Likewise, under the guidance of the therapist, the parents often develop strategies to monitor and promote the adolescent's school performance or vocational functioning (or both); interventions in this domain typically focus on establishing positive communication lines between parents and teachers and on restructuring after-school hours to promote academic efforts. Finally, in some cases individual interventions are used with an adolescent or parent to modify the individual's social perspective-taking skills, problem-solving skills (e.g., learning to deal assertively with negative peer pressure), belief system, or motivational system.

MST is usually delivered by a master's level therapist with a caseload of four to eight families. The MST therapist is a generalist who directly provides most mental health services and coordinates access to other important services (e.g., medical, educational, recreational), always monitoring quality control. Although the therapist is available to the family 24 hr a day, 7 days a week, therapeutic intensity is titrated to clinical need; thus, the range of direct contact hours per family can vary considerably. In general, therapists spend more time with families in the initial weeks of therapy (daily, if indicated) and gradually taper off (as infrequently as once a week) during a 3- to 5-month course of treatment.

MST Treatment Principles

MST does not follow a rigid protocol in which therapists conduct sets of predetermined tasks in an invariant sequence. Indeed, because MST is typically used with complex cases that present serious and diverse problems and that also evidence a wide variety of possible strengths, fully detailing treatment parameters for each possible combination of situations would be an impossible task. Nevertheless, in the absence of strong specification, the value of MST would be greatly diminished. Thus, rather than providing session-by-session breakdowns of recommended clinical procedures, we have developed treatment principles to guide therapists' case conceptualizations, prioritization of interventions, and implementation of intervention strategies in MST.

The nine treatment principles enumerated next serve as general guidelines for designing multisystemic interventions. Detailed descriptions of these principles and examples that illustrate the translation of these principles into specific intervention strategies are provided in a clinical volume (Henggeler & Borduin, 1990) and a treatment manual (Henggeler, Schoenwald, Borduin, Rowland, & Cunningham, 1998). MST therapists and supervisors often refer to the principles while planning interventions, and treatment fidelity can be evaluated by measuring therapist adherence to the principles.

1. The primary purpose of assessment is to understand the fit between the identified problems and their broader systemic context.
2. Therapeutic contacts emphasize the positive and use systemic strengths as levers for change.
3. Interventions are designed to promote responsible behavior and decrease irresponsible behavior among family members.
4. Interventions are present focused and action oriented, targeting specific and well-defined problems.
5. Interventions target sequences of behavior within and between multiple systems that maintain the identified problems.
6. Interventions are developmentally appropriate and fit the developmental needs of the youth.

7. Interventions are designed to require daily or weekly effort by family members.
8. Intervention effectiveness is evaluated continuously from multiple perspectives with providers assuming accountability for overcoming barriers to successful outcomes.
9. Interventions are designed to promote treatment generalization and long-term maintenance of therapeutic change by empowering caregivers to address family members' needs across multiple systemic contexts.

Findings from several studies indicate that therapists' adherence to the MST treatment principles is directly related to clinical outcomes with adolescents. For example, in an MST clinical trial with adolescent violent and chronic offenders, Henggeler, Melton, Brondino, Scherer, and Hanley (1997) found that parent, adolescent, and therapist reports of high treatment fidelity (assessed with a 26-item measure of MST adherence; Henggeler & Borduin, 1992) were associated with low rates of rearrest and incarceration for adolescents at a 1.7-year follow-up. Similarly, in a study of substance abusing or dependent adolescent offenders, Henggeler, Pickrel, and Brondino (1999) found that high ratings of treatment fidelity (on the MST adherence measure) were associated with decreased criminal activity and out-of-home placement for adolescents during the first year following referral. Other, related studies (Huey, Henggeler, Brondino, & Pickrel, 2000; Schoenwald, Henggeler, Brondino, & Rowland, 2000) have supported the view that therapist adherence to the MST principles influences those processes (e.g., family relations, association with deviant peers) that sustain adolescent antisocial behavior. Thus, significant empirical support is emerging for the association between treatment adherence and adolescent outcomes in MST.

Clinical Supervision in MST

Treatment fidelity in MST is maintained by weekly group supervision meetings involving three to four therapists and a doctoral level clinical supervisor (usually a child psychologist or child psychiatrist). During these meetings, the treatment team (i.e., therapists, supervisor, and, as needed, a consulting psychiatrist) review the goals and progress of each case to ensure the multisystemic focus of therapists' intervention strategies and to identify obstacles to success. Importantly, the treatment team accepts responsibility for engaging families in treatment and for effecting therapeutic change. Thus, when obstacles to successful engagement or to therapeutic change are identified, the team develops strategies to address those obstacles and to promote success.

The clinical supervisor plays a critical role in the MST treatment process. The primary focus of the MST clinical supervisor is on the therapist's thinking, behavior, and interactions with the family and with the systems in which the family is embedded. Clinical supervisors ensure that therapists adhere to the nine principles of MST in all aspects of treatment (i.e., engagement and alignment, conceptualization of the causes of referral problems, design and implementation of interventions, overcoming barriers to intervention effectiveness, and assessment of outcomes). In addition, supervisors must be able to assess and promote the development of therapists' MST-like conceptualization and intervention skills across cases (generalization). To facilitate therapists' implementation of MST and the attainment of favorable family outcomes, supervisors reinforce critical thinking about all aspects of treatment. Figure 12.2 depicts the various aspects of treatment, the relations among them, and the analytical process used to identify and execute them.

ISSUES RELATED TO SUCCESSFUL IMPLEMENTATION OF MST PROGRAMS

MST programs for adolescents who commit serious offenses are typically implemented by public (mental health, juvenile justice, social welfare) or private service organizations to provide a community-based alternative to incarceration and other out-of-home placements. Although the preceding clinical elements are believed to be fundamental to the successful implementation of MST programs with adolescent serious offenders (see the following section on effectiveness), an MST program cannot be successful without several key administrative elements as well. As discussed elsewhere (Schoenwald & Henggeler, 2002), a service organization (including key administrators, supervisors, and therapists) must be fully committed to the philosophical (e.g., definition of the mental health professional's role) and empirical (e.g., accountability for clinical outcomes) framework of the MST approach and should receive intensive training and ongoing consultation in the MST model. The MST program should have distinct, dedicated staff (i.e., full-time MST therapists) and include a clinical supervisor who has credible authority regarding clinical decisions. Substantial changes in agency policies and in staff members' work routines are often required to successfully implement the clinical approach of MST, and concrete support should be evident from the administration of the service organization (e.g., implementing flex time and comp time policies for staff, scheduling supervision and consultation times, providing highly competitive salaries and incentives).

Successful implementation of an MST program also requires initiative in developing and maintaining collaborative relations with other agencies in

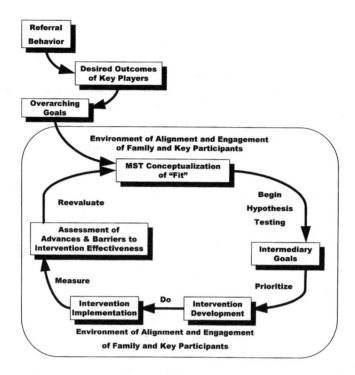

FIG. 12.2. The multisystemic therapy (MST) analytical process. MST supervisors ensure that therapists are able to (a) develop and refine a multisystemic conceptualization of the causes of identified problems, (b) identify barriers to the successful engagement of key participants (family members, school personnel, sources of parental social support) and implement strategies to overcome these barriers, (c) logically and clearly connect intermediary goals to overarching goals, (d) design and effectively implement intervention strategies to meet intermediary and overarching goals, and (e) identify barriers to the successful implementation of interventions and implement strategies to overcome them. From S. W. Henggeler, S. K. Schoenwald, C. M. Borduin, M. D. Rowland, and P. B. Cunningham (1998), *Multisystemic treatment of Antisocial Behavior in Children and Adolescents.* New York: Guilford Press.

the community (i.e., schools, juvenile justice, social welfare, mental health, and substance abuse) that are involved in the lives of adolescent serious offenders (Schoenwald & Henggeler, 2002). Indeed, a strength of the MST approach is that it assumes accountability as the single point of responsibility for ensuring that the broad needs of adolescent serious offenders and their families are met. Thus, the main purpose of coordinating MST activities with those of other agencies is to produce favorable long-term clinical outcomes. Moreover, given that the funding mechanisms in many communities include disincentives for public agencies to use community-based services in lieu of out-of-home placements, an MST program is unlikely to attain a sufficient referral base and concomitant funding without first seeking the support and cooperation of key agencies and stakeholders in the community. One mechanism for funding used in MST programs at different sites across the United States has involved shifting local or state children's services monies allocated for residential treatment or other out-of-home placements (e.g., foster care) to the MST program.

EFFECTIVENESS OF MST WITH ADOLESCENT SERIOUS OFFENDERS

Clearly, for both ethical and pragmatic reasons, it is important that mental health services for adolescents who engage in serious antisocial behavior be evaluated rigorously. Rigorous evaluation of outcomes produced by MST has been a high priority since the initial development of this treatment model in the late 1970s.

General Delinquency

The first MST outcome study (Henggeler et al., 1986) was conducted with inner-city adolescent offenders ($N = 80$) with arrest histories that included relatively serious violent and nonviolent crimes ($M = 2.1$ arrests). Findings showed that MST was more effective than usual services in decreasing adolescent behavior problems, decreasing adolescent association with deviant peers, and improving family relations, especially family communication and affect. The favorable effects of MST in improving key correlates of antisocial behavior supported the viability of conducting further evaluations of MST with adolescent serious offenders.

Violent and Chronic Offenses

Two different randomized clinical trials have been conducted to evaluate the efficacy of MST with adolescent violent and chronic offenders. In the first study, Henggeler, Melton, and Smith (1992) compared MST and usual services (provided by a state agency) in the treatment of 84 adolescent serious offenders (54% violent offenders), who averaged 3.5 previous arrests and 9.5 weeks of prior incarceration. Findings at posttreatment showed that MST improved family and peer relations of the adolescents and their families. In addition, at a 59-week postreferral follow-up, adolescents who received MST had significantly fewer rearrests ($Ms = 0.87$ vs. 1.52) and weeks incarcerated ($Ms = 5.8$ vs. 16.2) than did adolescents who received usual services; the cost per adolescent for treatment in the MST group was also substantially lower than the average cost in the usual services group ($2,800 vs. $16,300, respectively). Results from a 2.4-year follow-up (Henggeler, Melton, Smith, Schoenwald, & Hanley, 1993) showed importantly that MST doubled the survival rate (i.e., percentage of adolescents not rearrested) of these violent and chronic offenders when compared with usual services.

In the most comprehensive and extensive evaluation of MST to date, Borduin et al. (1995) examined the long-term effects of MST versus individual therapy (IT) on violent offending and other criminal offending in 200 adolescent serious offenders who averaged 4.2 previous arrests. Results from multi-agent, multimethod assessment batteries conducted before and after treatment showed that MST was more effective than IT in improving key family correlates of antisocial behavior and in ameliorating adjustment problems in individual family members. Moreover, results from a 4-year follow-up of rearrest data showed that adolescents treated with MST were significantly less likely to be rearrested than adolescents treated with IT (26.1 % vs. 71.4%). In addition, an examination of recidivists from each group revealed that MST adolescents arrested during follow-up were less likely to be arrested for violent (i.e., rape, attempted rape, sexual assault, aggravated assault, assault/battery) and other serious crimes (i.e., burglary, larceny, auto theft, arson) than were comparison counterparts. More recently, in a 13.7-year follow-up of the adolescents (now in their 20s and early 30s) who participated in this clinical trial, results showed that participants treated with MST evidenced 50% fewer rearrests (Ms = 0.14 vs. 0.28 arrests per year) and 60% fewer days incarcerated (Ms = 40.20 vs. 102.54 days incarcerated per year) than did participants treated with IT (Borduin & Schaeffer, 2002).

Substance Use and Abuse

Prior to the completion of the two MST trials with adolescent violent and chronic offenders (Borduin et al., 1995; Henggeler et al., 1992), Henggeler et al. (1991) examined the effects of MST on reductions in substance use and abuse in the offenders participating in these studies. Analyses of arrest data from the Borduin et al. (1995) sample indicated that adolescents who participated in MST had a significantly lower rate of substance-related arrests 4 years following treatment than did adolescents who participated in IT (i.e., 4% vs. 16%, respectively). Similarly, analyses of self-report data from the Henggeler et al. (1992) sample showed that adolescent offenders in the MST condition reported significantly less soft drug use (i.e., alcohol, marijuana) at posttreatment than did offenders who received usual services.

In a more recent study of substance abusing or dependent adolescent offenders (N = 118), Henggeler, Pickrel, et al. (1999) found that in comparison to youths who received usual community services, youths who participated in MST reported less alcohol and marijuana and other drug use at posttreatment and had 26% fewer rearrests and 50% fewer days in out-of-home placements (i.e., incarceration, residential treatment, inpatient treatment) at a 6-month follow-up. Other results with the same sample of substance abusing or dependent offenders (Brown, Henggeler, Schoenwald, Brondino, & Pickrel, 1999) indicated that MST (but not usual services) significantly increased adolescents' school attendance at posttreatment and 6-month follow-up. In a related study, Schoenwald, Ward, Henggeler, Pickrel, and Patel (1996) found that the incremental costs of MST (i.e., costs that were above and beyond the usual costs of services for substance abusing or dependent adolescent offenders) were nearly offset by the savings incurred as a result of reductions in days of out-of-home placement during the 1st year following referral.

Sexual Offenses

Though modest in scope and size ($N = 16$), Borduin, Henggeler, Blaske, and Stein (1990) was the first published randomized trial with adolescent sexual offenders. Adolescents and their families were randomly assigned to treatment conditions: home-based MST delivered by doctoral students in clinical psychology versus outpatient IT (i.e., an eclectic blend of psychodynamic, humanistic, and behavioral approaches) delivered by community-based mental health professionals. Recidivism results at a 3-year follow-up revealed that MST was more effective than IT in reducing rates of rearrest for sexual crimes (12.5% vs. 75.0%, respectively) and in reducing the mean frequency of rearrests for both sexual crimes (0.12 vs. 1.62, respectively) and nonsexual crimes (0.62 vs. 2.25, respectively). The favorable effects of MST supported the viability of conducting a second evaluation of MST with adolescent sexual offenders.

In a recently completed clinical trial, Borduin, Schaeffer, and Heiblum (2002) used a multiagent, multimethod assessment battery to evaluate instrumental (i.e., theory driven) and ultimate (i.e., common to all treatments of adolescent sexual offenders) outcomes in aggressive (i.e., sexual assault, rape) and nonaggressive (i.e., molestation of younger children) adolescent sexual offenders ($N = 48$) who were randomly assigned to MST or usual services. Compared to adolescents who received usual services, adolescents who received MST showed improvements on a range of instrumental outcomes including fewer behavior problems, less criminal offending (self-reported), improved peer relations (i.e., more emotional bonding with peers, less involvement with deviant peers), improved family relations (i.e., more warmth, less conflict), and better grades in school, and their parents showed decreased symptomatology. In addition, adolescents in the MST condition spent an average of 75 fewer days in out-of-home (i.e., Division of Youth Services) placements during the 1st year following referral to treatment than did adolescents in the usual services condition. Most important, an 8-year follow-up of ultimate outcomes revealed that adolescents who participated in MST were less likely than their usual services counterparts to be arrested for sexual (12.5% vs. 41.7%, respectively) and nonsexual (29.2% vs. 62.5%, respectively) crimes and spent one third as many days incarcerated as adults.

CURRENT AND FUTURE EVALUATIONS

The refinement of MST with adolescent serious offenders is a continuous, ongoing, and dynamic process (see Henggeler et al., 1998). Current projects are examining treatment processes and potential moderators of MST effectiveness in families of adolescent serious offenders (Schaeffer & Borduin, 2002), the integration of MST into juvenile drug courts (Randall, Halliday-Boykins, Cunningham, & Henggeler, 2002), and the integration of MST with empirically based drug and violence prevention programs in urban middle school settings (Cunningham & Henggeler, 2001). Another current project is evaluating the transportability and dissemination of MST to various community settings serving adolescent violent and chronic offenders (see Schoenwald & Hoagwood, 2001); a major task in our dissemination research is to evaluate those factors (e.g., therapist characteristics, supervisory behaviors, agency policies) that are linked with treatment adherence and with clinical outcomes. We are also planning to conduct another (i.e., larger) randomized trial with adolescent sexual offenders as well as a 15-year follow-up of the adolescent violent and chronic offenders who participated in the Henggeler et al. (1992) and Borduin et al. (1995) randomized trials; a major component of the follow-up is an assessment of each participant's service utilization (mental health, juvenile justice, social welfare, education) during the follow-up period and a delineation of the costs of such services to evaluate the cost effectiveness of MST.

Additional evaluations of MST are currently under way in an effort to adapt and extend the treatment model to other populations with serious clinical problems. Recent work has been evaluating the clinical and cost effectiveness of MST as an alternative to inpatient psychiatric hospitalization for adolescents presenting mental health emergencies (e.g., suicidal behavior, psychosis). To date, the findings from this work (see, e.g., Henggeler, Rowland, et al., 1999; Schoenwald, Ward, Henggeler, & Rowland, 2000) have been very promising and suggest that an intensive, well-specified, and empirically supported treatment model such as MST can effectively serve as a family- and community-based alternative to the emergency psychiatric hospitalization of adolescents. Another project, in collaboration with the Annie E. Casey Foundation, is currently under way in Philadelphia, Pennsylvania to evaluate the clinical and cost effectiveness of an MST-based continuum of care for adolescents with serious emotional disturbances. This project will allow us to better understand which components of treatment are most essential for maintaining such adolescents safely in the community.

IMPLICATIONS FOR DEVELOPING EFFECTIVE TREATMENTS FOR SERIOUS ANTISOCIAL BEHAVIOR IN ADOLESCENTS

The effectiveness of MST in reducing criminality and violence in serious adolescent offenders has important implications that can help guide the development of potentially more effective interventions for such youths. If, as suggested earlier, a major shortcoming of most interventions for treating serious antisocial behavior has been their neglect of the multiple determinants of such behavior, then the success of MST may be linked with its comprehensive and flexible nature; that is, the results of MST may be due to its explicit focus on ameliorating key social-ecological factors associated with serious antisocial behavior including behavior problems, parental disturbance, problematic family relations, association with deviant peers, and poor school performance. In light of the multidetermined nature of adolescent serious antisocial behavior, it is unrealistic to expect even the best conceived office-based treatments to be effective due to their relatively narrow focus.

A second implication of findings from our randomized clinical trials pertains to the accessibility and ecological validity of services. Traditionally, as Melton and Pagliocca (1992) emphasized, mental health services for adolescent offenders either have been inaccessible (i.e., office based) or have provided interventions (e.g., residential treatment centers, wilderness programs, boot camps, incarceration) that have little bearing on the real-world environmental conditions that led to the adolescent's criminal behavior and to which the adolescent will eventually return. In contrast, MST is provided in natural community contexts (e.g., home, school, recreation center). The delivery of services in adolescents' natural environments enhances family cooperation, permits more accurate assessment of identified problems and of intervention results, and promotes long-term maintenance of therapeutic changes (Henggeler & Borduin, 1990). Likewise, other aspects of MST (e.g., intensive training and supervision of therapists, development of collaborative interagency relations) may also contribute to the positive clinical outcomes that have been obtained with many adolescents and their families.

In conclusion, our work indicates that a comprehensive intervention, intensively addressing the multiple determinants of antisocial behavior in adolescents' naturally occurring systems, can successfully reduce criminal activity and violent offending in adolescent serious offenders. Of course, extensive validation and replication are needed for even the most promising treatment approaches. Nevertheless, given the significant problems that adolescent serious offenders present for our society, as well as the questionable ethics of providing these adolescents with treatments that do not produce durable changes, it is time that priority be placed on the evaluation of promising treatment models such as MST.

REFERENCES

Ary, D. V., Duncan, T. E., Biglan, A., Metzler, C. W., Noell, J. W., & Smolkowski, K. (1999). Development of adolescent problem behavior. *Journal of Abnormal Child Psychology, 27*, 141–150.

Bateson, G. (1972). *Steps to an ecology of the mind.* New York: Ballantine.

Borduin, C. M. (1994). Innovative models of treatment and service delivery in the juvenile justice system. *Journal of Clinical Child Psychology, 23*(Suppl.), 19–25.

Borduin, C. M., & Henggeler, S. W. (1990). A multisystemic approach to the treatment of serious delinquent behavior. In R. J. McMahon & R. DeV. Peters (Eds.), *Behavior disorders of adolescence: Research, intervention, and policy in clinical and school settings* (pp. 62–80). New York: Plenum.

Borduin, C. M., Henggeler, S. W., Blaske, D. M., & Stein, R. (1990). Multisystemic treatment of adolescent sexual offenders. *International Journal of Offender Therapy and Comparative Criminology, 34*, 105–113.

Borduin, C. M., Mann, B. J., Cone, L. T., Henggeler, S. W., Fucci, B. R., Blaske, D. M., & Williams, R. A. (1995). Multisystemic treatment of serious juvenile offenders: Long-term prevention of criminality and violence. *Journal of Consulting and Clinical Psychology, 63*, 569–578.

Borduin, C. M., & Schaeffer, C. M. (1998). Violent offending in adolescence: Epidemiology, correlates, outcomes, and treatment. In T. P. Gullotta, G. R. Adams, & R. Montemayor (Eds.), *Delinquent violent youth: Theory and interventions* (pp. 144–174). Newbury Park, CA: Sage.

Borduin, C. M., & Schaeffer, C. M. (2002). *Long-term outcomes in multisystemic treatment of serious juvenile offenders.* Manuscript submitted for publication.

Borduin, C. M., Schaeffer, C. M., & Heiblum, N. (2002). *Multisystemic treatment of juvenile sexual offenders: Instrumental and ultimate outcomes.* Manuscript submitted for publication.

Britt, C. L. (2000). Health consequences of criminal victimization. *International Review of Victimology, 8*, 63–73.

Bronfenbrenner, U. (1979). *The ecology of human development: Experiments by nature and design.* Cambridge, MA: Harvard University Press.

Brown, T. L., Henggeler, S. W., Schoenwald, S. K., Brondino, M. J., & Pickrel, S. G. (1999). Multisystemic treatment of substance abusing and dependent juvenile delinquents: Effects on school attendance at posttreatment and 6-month follow-up. *Children's Services: Social Policy, Research, and Practice, 2*, 81–93.

Cocozza, J. J. (Ed.). (1992). *Responding to the mental health needs of youth in the juvenile justice system.* Seattle, WA: National Coalition for the Mentally Ill in the Criminal Justice System.

Cohen, M. A., & Miller, T. R. (1998). The cost of mental health care for victims of crime. *Journal of Interpersonal Violence, 13*, 93–110.

Cunningham, P. B., & Henggeler, S. W. (2001). Implementation of an empirically based drug and violence prevention and intervention program in public school settings. *Journal of Clinical Child Psychology, 30*, 221–232.

Elliott, D. S., Dunford, F. W., & Huizinga, D. (1987). The identification and prediction of career offenders utilizing self-reported and official data. In J. D. Burchard & S. N. Burchard (Eds.), *Prevention of delinquent behavior* (pp. 90–121). Newbury Park, CA: Sage.

Farrington, D. P., & Loeber, R. (2000). Epidemiology of juvenile violence. *Child and Adolescent Psychiatric Clinics of North America, 9*, 733–748.

Farrington, D. P., Ohlin, L., & Wilson, J. Q. (1986). *Understanding and controlling crime.* New York: Springer-Verlag.

Federal Bureau of Investigation, U. S. Department of Justice. (1999). *Uniform crime reports.* Washington, DC: Author.

Gottfredson, G. D. (1989). The experiences of violent and serious victimization. In N. A. Weiner & M. E. Wolfgang (Eds.), *Pathways to criminal violence* (pp. 202–234). Newbury Park, CA: Sage.

Hawkins, J. D., Catalano, R. F., & Miller, J. Y. (1992). Risk and protective factors for alcohol and other drug problems in adolescence and early adulthood: Implications for substance abuse prevention. *Psychological Bulletin, 112*, 64–105.

Hawkins, J. D., Herrenkohl, T., Farrington, D. P., Brewer, D., Catalano, R. F., & Harachi, T. W. (1998). A review of predictors of youth violence. In R. Loeber & D. P. Farrington (Eds.), *Serious and violent juvenile offenders: Risk factors and successful interventions* (pp. 106–146). Thousand Oaks, CA: Sage.

Henggeler, S. W. (1991). Multidimensional causal models of delinquent behavior and their implications for treatment. In R. Cohen & A. W. Siegel (Eds.), *Context and development* (pp. 211–231). Hillsdale, NJ: Lawrence Erlbaum Associates.

Henggeler, S. W. (1997). The development of effective drug abuse services for youth. In J. A. Egertson, D. M. Fox, & A. I. Leshner (Eds.), *Treating drug abusers effectively* (pp. 253–279). New York: Blackwell.

Henggeler, S. W., & Borduin, C. M. (1990). *Family therapy and beyond: A multisystemic approach to treating the behavior problems of children and adolescents.* Pacific Grove, CA: Brooks/Cole.

Henggeler, S. W., & Borduin, C. M. (1992). *Multisystemic therapy adherence scales.* Unpublished manuscript, Department of Psychiatry and Behavioral Sciences, Medical University of South Carolina, Charleston.

Henggeler, S. W., Borduin, C. M., Melton, G. B., Mann, B. J., Smith, L. A., Hall, J. A., Cone, L., & Fucci, B. R. (1991). Effects of multisystemic therapy on drug use and abuse in serious juvenile offenders: A progress report from two outcome studies. *Family Dynamics of Addiction Quarterly, 1*, 40–51.

Henggeler, S. W., Melton, G. B., Brondino, M. J., Scherer, D. G., & Hanley, J. H. (1997). Multisystemic therapy with violent and chronic juvenile offenders and their families: The role of treatment fidelity in successful dissemination. *Journal of Consulting and Clinical Psychology, 65*, 821–833.

Henggeler, S. W., Melton, G. B., & Smith, L. A. (1992). Family preservation using multisystemic therapy: An effective alternative to incarcerating serious juvenile offenders. *Journal of Consulting and Clinical Psychology, 60*, 953–961.

Henggeler, S. W., Melton, G. B., Smith, L. A., Schoenwald, S. K., & Hanley, J. H. (1993). Family preservation using multisystemic treatment: Long-term follow-up to a clinical trial with serious juvenile offenders. *Journal of Child and Family Studies, 2*, 283–293.

Henggeler, S. W., Pickrel, S. G., & Brondino, M. J. (1999). Multisystemic treatment of substance abusing and dependent delinquents: Outcomes, treatment fidelity, and transportability. *Mental Health Services Research, 1*, 171–184.

Henggeler, S. W., Rodick, J. D., Borduin, C. M., Hanson, C. L., Watson, S. M., & Urey, J. R. (1986). Multisystemic treatment of juvenile offenders: Effects on adolescent behavior and family interaction. *Developmental Psychology, 22*, 132–141.

Henggeler, S. W., Rowland, M. D., Randall, J., Ward, D., Pickrel, S. G., Cunningham, P. B., Miller, S., Edwards, J., Zealberg, J., Hand, L., & Santos, A. (1999). Home-based multisystemic therapy as an alternative to the hospitalization of youths in psychiatric crisis: Clinical outcomes. *Journal of the American Academy of Child and Adolescent Psychiatry, 38*, 1331–1339.

Henggeler, S. W., Schoenwald, S. K., Borduin, C. M., Rowland, M. D., & Cunningham, P. B. (1998). *Multisystemic treatment of antisocial behavior in children and adolescents.* New York: Guilford.

Henry, D. B., Tolan, P. H., & Gorman-Smith, D. (2001). Longitudinal family and peer group effects on violence and nonviolent delinquency. *Journal of Clinical Child Psychology, 30*, 172–186.

Herrenkohl, T. I., Huang, B., Kosterman, R., Hawkins, J. D., Catalano, R. F., & Smith, B. H. (2001). A comparison of social development processes leading to violent behavior in late adolescence for childhood initiators and adolescent initiators of violence. *Journal of Research in Crime and Delinquency, 38*, 45–63.

Hoffman, L. (1981). *Foundations of family therapy*. New York: Basic Books.

Huesmann, L. R., Lefkowitz, M. M., Eron, L. D., & Walder, L. O. (1984). Stability of aggression over time and generations. *Developmental Psychology, 20*, 1120–1134.

Huey, S. J., Henggeler, S. W., Brondino, M. J., & Pickrel, S. (2000). Mechanisms of change in multisystemic therapy: Reducing delinquent behavior through therapist adherence and improved family and peer functioning. *Journal of Consulting and Clinical Psychology, 68*, 451–467.

Kashani, J. H., Jones, M. R., Bumby, K. M., & Thomas, L. A. (1999). Youth violence: Psychosocial risk factors, treatment, prevention, and recommendations. *Journal of Emotional and Behavioral Disorders, 7*, 200–210.

Kazdin, A. E. (1995). *Conduct disorders in childhood and adolescence* (2nd ed.). Thousand Oaks, CA: Sage.

Kazdin, A. E. (2000). Treatments for aggressive and antisocial children. *Child and Adolescent Psychiatric Clinics of North America, 9*, 841–858.

LeBlanc, M., & Kaspy, N. (1998). Trajectories of delinquent and problem behavior: Comparison of social and personal control characteristics of adjudicated boys on synchronous and nonsynchronous paths. *Journal of Quantitative Criminology, 14*, 181–214.

Levesque, R. J. R. (1996). Is there still a place for violent youth in juvenile justice? *Aggression and Violent Behavior, 1*, 69–79.

Loeber, R., Farrington, D. P., & Waschbusch, D. A. (1998). Serious and violent juvenile offenders. In R. Loeber & D. P. Farrington (Eds.), *Serious and violent juvenile offenders: Risk factors and successful interventions* (pp. 13–29). Thousand Oaks, CA: Sage.

Loeber, R., & Hay, D. F. (1996). Key issues in the development of aggression and violence from childhood to early adulthood. *Annual Review of Psychology, 48*, 371–410.

Lyons, J. S., Baerger, D. R., Quigley, P., Erlich, J., & Griffin, E. (2001). Mental health service needs of juvenile offenders: A comparison of detention, incarceration, and treatment settings. *Children's Services: Social Policy, Research, and Practice, 4*, 69–85.

McMahon, R. J., & Estes, A. M. (1997). Conduct problems. In E. J. Mash & L. G. Terdal (Eds.), *Assessment of childhood disorders* (3rd ed., pp. 130–193). New York: Guilford.

Melton, G. B., Lyons, P. M., & Spaulding, W. J. (1998). *No place to go: The civil commitment of minors*. Lincoln: University of Nebraska Press.

Melton, G. B., & Pagliocca, P. M. (1992). Treatment in the juvenile justice system: Directions for policy and practice. In J. J. Cocozza (Ed.), *Responding to the mental health needs of youth in the juvenile justice system* (pp. 107–139). Seattle, WA: National Coalition for the Mentally Ill in the Criminal Justice System.

Minuchin, P. P. (1985). Families and individual development: Provocations from the field of family therapy. *Child Development, 56*, 289–302.

Moffitt, T. E. (1993). Adolescence-limited and life-course-persistent antisocial behavior: A developmental taxonomy. *Psychological Review, 100*, 674–701.

Mulvey, E. P., Arthur, M. A., & Reppucci, N. D. (1993). The prevention and treatment of juvenile delinquency: A review of the research. *Clinical Psychology Review, 13*, 133–167.

Office of Technology Assessment. (1991). *Adolescent health: Vol. II. Background and the effectiveness of selected prevention and treatment services* (GPO Stock No. 052-003-01235-9). Washington, DC: U.S. Government Printing Office.

Pajer, K. A. (1998). What happens to "bad" girls? A review of the adult outcomes of antisocial adolescent girls. *American Journal of Psychiatry, 155*, 862–870.

Paschall, M. J., & Hubbard, M. L. (1998). Effects of neighborhood and family stressors on African American male adolescents' self-worth and propensity for violent behavior. *Journal of Consulting and Clinical Psychology, 66,* 825–831.

Randall, J., Halliday-Boykins, C. A., Cunningham, P. B., & Henggeler, S. W. (2002). *Integrating evidence-based substance abuse treatment into juvenile drug courts: Implications for outcomes.* Manuscript submitted for publication.

Robinson, F., & Keithley, J. (2000). The impacts of crime on health and health services: A literature review. *Health, Risk, and Society, 2,* 253–266.

Schaeffer, C. M., & Borduin, C. M. (2002). *Moderators and mediators of therapeutic change in multisystemic treatment of serious juvenile offenders.* Manuscript submitted for publication.

Schoenwald, S. K., & Henggeler, S. W. (2002). Mental health services research and family-based treatment: Bridging the gap. In H. Liddle, G. Diamond, R. Levant, J. Bray, & D. Santisteban (Eds.), *Family psychology intervention science* (pp. 259–282). Washington, DC: American Psychological Association.

Schoenwald, S. K., Henggeler, S. W., Brondino, M. J., & Rowland, M. (2000). Multisystemic therapy: Monitoring treatment fidelity. *Family Process, 39,* 83–103.

Schoenwald, S. K., & Hoagwood, K. (2001). Effectiveness, transportability, and dissemination of interventions: What matters when? *Psychiatric Services, 52,* 1190–1197.

Schoenwald, S. K., Ward, D. M., Henggeler, S. W., Pickrel, S. G., & Patel, H. (1996). Multisystemic therapy treatment of substance abusing or dependent adolescent offenders: Costs of reducing incarceration, inpatient, and residential treatment. *Journal of Child and Family Studies, 5,* 431–444.

Schoenwald, S. K., Ward, D. M., Henggeler, S. W., & Rowland, M. D. (2000). MST vs. hospitalization for crisis stabilization of youth: Placement outcomes 4 months post-referral. *Mental Health Services Research, 2,* 3–12.

Tate, D. C., Reppucci, N. D., & Mulvey, E. P. (1995). Violent juvenile delinquents: Treatment effectiveness and implications for future action. *American Psychologist, 50,* 777–781.

Thornberry, T. P., Huizinga, D., & Loeber, R. (1995). The prevention of serious delinquency and violence: Implications from the program of research on the causes and correlates of delinquency. In J. C. Howell, B. Krisberg, J. D. Hawkins, & J. J. Wilson (Eds.), *A sourcebook: Serious, violent, and chronic juvenile offenders* (pp. 213–237). Newbury Park, CA: Sage.

Wills, T. A., Sandy, J. M., Yaeger, A., & Shinar, O. (2001). Family risk factors and adolescent substance use: Moderation effects for temperament dimensions. *Developmental Psychology, 37,* 283–297.

13

Psychopharmacology of Disruptive Behavior Disorders

Oscar G. Bukstein
University of Pittsburgh School of Medicine

Disruptive behavior disorders (DBDs; e.g., conduct disorder [CD], oppositional defiant disorder [ODD], and attention deficit hyperactivity disorder [ADHD]) are among the most common behavioral and emotional problems for children and adolescents to present to clinical settings. Prevalence data from population-based studies show rates of DBDs ranging from 2.1% to 14.2% in children and 4.5% to 15.8% in adolescents (Loeber, Burke, Lahey, Winters, & Zera, 2000). Consensus among delinquency studies show an increase from childhood through adolescence in the prevalence of nonaggressive CD behaviors such as serious theft and fraud (Loeber & Farrington, 1998; Loeber, Farrington, & Waschbusch, 1998) and covert behaviors (Loeber & Stouthamer-Loeber, 1998). Although many forms of aggression decrease into adolescence, the prevalence of more serious forms of aggression such as rape, robbery, and attempted or completed homicide tend to increase during adolescence (Loeber & Farrington, 1998). DBDs have a high level of comorbidity not only with other DBDs but with other psychiatric disorders such as anxiety and depressive disorders and substance use disorders (Jensen et al., 1999; Loeber et al., 2000). Overall, 30% to 80% of diagnosed hyperactive children continue to have features of ADHD persisting into adolescence and up to 65% into adulthood (Barkley, Murphy, & Kwasnik, 1996; Weiss & Hechtman, 1993). In one recent study (Barkley, Murphy, & Kwasnik, 1996), over 70% of hyperactive children continued to meet criteria for ADHD as adolescents. A family history of ADHD, psychosocial adversity, and comorbidity with conduct, mood, and anxiety disorders increase the risk of persistence of ADHD symptoms (Biederman et al., 1996). As suggested by these potential adverse outcomes, DBDs in children and adolescents carry an increased risk for a heavy burden of suffering in terms of its relatively high prevalence and high societal costs (Offord, Boyle, & Racine, 1989).

Interventions for DBDs must address a potentially wide array of problems including the direct targeting of the symptom behaviors, comorbid diagnoses or other concurrent problems, and environmental factors such as parenting. Depending on the severity of the problems, a range of intervention levels and intensities may be needed. Because of the contribution of a multitude of risk factors such as family, community, individual, and peer characteristics, interventions often involve multiple components and strategies. The use of multiple interventions is commonly termed *multimodal* and is clearly the rule rather than the exception in more severe cases of DBDs. As described elsewhere in this volume, psychosocial interventions for DBDs are effective (American Academy of Child and Adolescent Psychiatry [AACAP], 1997). Increasingly, psychopharmacology or medication treatment is recognized as a valuable intervention, usually as an adjunct to psychosocial treatments. This chapter reviews the biological basis for the pharmacologic treatment of DBDs, the research literature, and practical considerations in evaluation for medication treatment.

BIOLOGICAL CONTRIBUTION FOR DBDs

Although research has implicated a variety of psychosocial or environmental risk factors in the etiology of DBDs, the recent literature has expanded our knowledge of the potential contribution of genetic and neurobiological factors in the development and persistence of DBDs. Twin studies (Lyons et al., 1995) and adoptions studies (Cadoret, Yates, Troughton, Woodworth, & Stewart, 1995) both suggest a significant hereditability of CD and antisocial behavior. Certain psychophysiological abnormalities have repeatedly been reported as risk factors for CD (Raine, 1993; Lahey, McBurnett, Lober, & Hart, 1995), supporting the possibility of at least partial genetic control. For ADHD, neurochemical studies, especially of serotonergic metabolites, suggest abnormalities in neurotransmitter systems have been found with regularity, although compared to the psychophysiological literature the findings are less consistent. Of particular interest are the compounds reflecting the activity of sympathetic arousal, especially in light of Raine and associates' (Raine, 1993; Raine, Venables, & Williams, 1995) findings and the fact that many regulatory hormones for this neurotransmitter system are under genetic control.

Various theories of the pathophysiology of ADHD have evolved, most depicting problems in brain frontal lobe function. Recent theories of dysfunction in ADHD focus on the prefrontal cortex, which controls many executive functions (e.g., planning, impulse control) that are impaired in ADHD. Stimulants used for treatment of children with ADHD have putative effects on central dopamine (DA) and norepinephrine (NE) pathways that are crucial in frontal lobe function. Stimulants act in the striatum by binding to the DA transporter, with a resulting increase in synaptic DA. This may enhance the functioning of executive control processes in the prefrontal cortex, ameliorating the deficits in inhibitory control and working memory reported in children with ADHD (Barkley, 1997).

Studies using positron emission tomography (PET) scanning have demonstrated that untreated adults with a past and current history of ADHD showed 8.1% lower levels of cerebral glucose metabolism than controls (e.g., Zametkin et al., 1990), with the greatest differences in the superior prefrontal cortex and premotor areas. Methylphenidate (MPH) and dextroamphetamine (DEX) elevate glucose metabolism in the brains of rats, although patients with schizophrenia given DEX show decreased glucose metabolism. No consistent changes in cerebral glucose metabolism were found in PET scans done before and on medication for 19 MPH-treated and 18 DEX-treated adults with ADHD, even though the adults showed significant improvements in behavior (Matochik et al., 1993).

PET scans of adult volunteers have added useful data. When given orally, [^{11}C]-MPH occupies a high proportion of DA transporter sites in the striatum, but is not associated with euphoria, which is found after intravenous administration (Swanson & Volkow, 2000; Volkow et al., 1998). Acute administration of stimulant medications increases NE and DA in the synaptic cleft, but whether compensatory mechanisms occur after slower oral absorption is not known (Grace, 2000).

Targets and Rationale for the Use of Medications in Children With DBDs

Medications for disruptive behavior disorders, especially stimulants, are the most prescribed agents in the United States (Jensen et al., 1999). Although the use of stimulants has increased dramatically in the past decade (Zito et al., 1998, 2000), evaluation of prevalence rate and various forms of treatment indicate that a minority of children diagnosed with ADHD actually receive stimulant medications (Jensen et al., 1999).

In recognition of the importance of pediatric psychopharmacology, both government and private industry have in recent years supplied a substantial investment in promoting this area of psychopharmacologic research. The National Institute of Mental Health (NIMH) has funded a new research network, the Research Units of Pediatric Psychopharmacology. The NIMH has also funded multisite, multimodal studies such as the Multimodal Treatment Study of Attention Deficit Hyperactivity Disorder (MTA) and current studies for obsessive compulsive disorder and major depressive disorder (MDD).

Prompted by governmental and public concern about the safety of medication for children and the previous widespread exclusion of children and adolescents from clinical drug trials, the Food and Drug Administration (FDA; 1997) encouraged industry and government organizations to initiate pharmacologic studies involving children and adolescents. Although many of these trials have consisted of Phase IV or postmarketing trials of medications previously approved for adults, many studies and medications in various stages of the FDA approval process are currently being developed or marketed for the treatment of ADHD. Although many of these medications consist of novel or improved formulations of currently approved medications such as MPH or Adderall®, several new, nonstimulant medications such as Atomoxetine have shown promise in clinical trials (Kratochvil et al., 2002).

Despite overall progress in research into pediatric psychopharmacology, particularly for DBDs, there remain substantial concerns about the applicability of efficacy or well-controlled trials to real-world clinical settings. There is a paucity of long-term (greater than 3 months) studies of medications, adverse event (side effect) monitoring in studies and in clinical practice, and the need for valid and reliable assessment instruments (Riddle, Kastelic, & Frosch, 2001).

In general, there are several areas for the use of medications in children and adolescents with DBDs. Diagnostic specific uses consist of the treatment of ADHD and the treatment of specific psychiatric disorders frequently comorbid with DBDs (e.g., mood and anxiety disorders). An emerging clinical practice is the treatment of target symptoms or behaviors such as aggression, impulsivity, and mood dysregulation. Comorbid conditions and their specific symptoms, such as aggression, mood lability, or impulsivity, may be targets for psychopharmacological intervention (Marriage, Fine, Moretti, & Haley, 1986).

ADHD

Stimulants. The behavioral effects of stimulants were first described over 60 years ago (Bradley, 1937). D, l-amphetamine produced a dramatic calming effect while increasing compliance and academic performance. Subsequent studies showed that psychostimulants decreased oppositional behavior of boys with CD (Eisenberg et al., 1961) and reliably improved the target symptoms of ADHD on standardized rating forms filled out by parents and teachers (Conners, Eisenberg, & Barcai, 1967).

In subsequent years, many short-term controlled treatment studies revealed that psychostimulants were effective, with most protocols lasting between 1 and 3 months. Between 1962 and 1993 there were over 250 reviews and over 3,000 articles on stimulant effects (Swanson, 1993). Reviews of controlled studies (AACAP, 1997, 2001; Barkley, 1977, 1982; DuPaul & Barkley, 1990; Schmidt, Solanto, & Sanchez, 1984; Gittelman-Klein, 1980, 1987) have demonstrated beneficial stimulant effects for children with ADHD.

The therapeutic effects of stimulants on both the core symptoms of ADHD as well as associated functional abilities is now well established. In the classroom stimulants decrease interrupting, fidgetiness, and finger tapping, and increase on-task behavior (Abikoff & Gittelman, 1985), whereas at home stimulants improve parent–child interactions, on-task behaviors, and compliance; in social settings, stimulants improve peer nomination rankings of social standing and increase attention while playing baseball (Richters et al., 1995). Stimulant drugs have been shown to affect children's behavior cross-situationally (classroom, lunchroom, playground, and home) when these drugs are repeatedly administered throughout the day. However, time-response studies of stimulant effects show a different pattern of improvement for behavioral and for attentional symptoms, with behavior affected more than attention.

Short-term trials of stimulants—most often 3 months or less in duration—have reported robust efficacy of MPH, DEX, and Pemoline (PEM), with equal efficacy among stimulants (McMaster University Evidence-Based Practice Center, 1998). More than 160 controlled studies involving more than 5,000 school-age children—only 22 lasting more than 3 months (Schachar & Tannock, 1993)—demonstrated a 70% response rate when a single stimulant was tried (Spencer, Biederman, Harding, Faraone, & Wilens, 1996). Short-term trials have reported improvements in the most salient and impairing behavioral symptoms of ADHD, including overt aggression, as long as medication is taken. Individual children show different responses and improvements with stimulants, with fewer than half of the children showing normalization. Therefore, children with ADHD taking stimulant medication continue to have more behavior problems than the average child without a history of problems. Although many recent studies have shown distinct improvements in short-term academic performance, there have been no long-term, controlled prospective studies of the academic achievement and social skills of children with ADHD treated with stimulants in a consistent manner.

Stimulant treatment leads to improvements in both ADHD symptoms and associated problems when compared with placebo, other drug classes, or nonpharmacological treatments (Greenhill, 1998; Jacobvitz, Srouge, Stewart, & Leffert, 1990; Spencer et al., 1996; Swanson, 1993). Effect sizes for changes in behavior or attention in short-term trials range from 0.8 to 1.0 SDs on teacher reports (Elia, Borcherding, Rapoport, & Keysor, 1991; Thurber & Walker, 1983) for both MPH and DEX.

Prospective, longer duration stimulant treatment trials use innovative control conditions such as community standard care (Arnold et al., 1997), double-blind placebo discontinuation (Gillberg et al., 1997), or putting all children on stimulants and then comparing additional treatments (Abikoff & Hechtman, 1996). These studies have shown maintenance of stimulant medication effects over periods ranging from 12 months (Gillberg et al., 1997) to 24 months (Abikoff & Hechtman, 1996).

The NIMH MTA study compared treatment with stimulants alone, stimulants used in combination with intensive behavioral therapy (multimodal therapy), intensive behavioral therapy alone, and treatment as usual in the community for 579 children with ADHD, ages 7 to 9 years, treated over a 14-month period. Details of the MTA medication treatment protocol, which uses a strategy to enhance treatment response, are published elsewhere (Greenhill et al., 1996). The results at the end of the 14-month treatment period showed that optimally titrated MPH was more effective than intensive behavioral therapy, combined treatment was more effective than behavioral treatment, and all three MTA treatments were better than routine care in the community (MTA Cooperative Group, 1999a). Baseline characteristics, such as patient's gender or presence of an anxiety disorder, did not affect the response to stimulant medications.

In addition to the MTA study (MTA Cooperative Group, 1999a, 1999b), there have been three other stimulant medication randomized clinical trials (RCTs) that have lasted 12 months or longer (Abikoff & Hechtman, 1996; Gillberg et al., 1997; Schachar, Tannock, Cunningham, & Corkum, 1997). The Gillberg et al. (1997) study examined children comorbid for ADHD and pervasive developmental disorder and showed good response to DEX, although the small number in the study ($N = 62$) prevented conclusive proof that PDD does not affect response to stimulants. These studies show a persistence of medication effects over a more sustained period of time. Over 24 months of treatment, children with ADHD continued to respond well to MPH treatment, with no sign of a diminution of the drug's efficacy. Domains of greatest improvement differ, with one study (Gillberg et al., 1997) showing greater effects at home and another (Schachar et al., 1997) showing bigger improvements at school.

Stimulant-related side effects reported for children with ADHD appear to be mild, short lived, and responsive to dose or timing adjustments. Adverse drug reactions usually occur early in treatment and often decrease with dose adjustment. Double-blind, placebo-controlled studies report moderate side effects in 4% to 10% of children treated. Delay of sleep onset, reduced appetite, stomachache, headache, and jitteriness are the most frequently cited (Barkley, McMurray, Edelbroch, & Robbins, 1990).

Long-acting stimulant preparations are appealing for children for whom the standard formulations act briefly (2–3 hr), who experience severe rebound, or for whom administering medication every 4 hr is inconvenient, stigmatizing, or impossible. Long-acting stimulants may also be the preferred preparations for adolescents who may be more resistant to having to take medication at school. The most commonly used and systematically studied long-acting stimulants are MPH extended Release (ER), Dexedrine Spansule®, and PEM. (Others include Adderall® and Desoxyn Gradumet®.) In the past 2 years, a number of new long-acting formulations or novel administration devices of MPH (Concerta®, Metadate®, Methylin®, and Ritalin LA®) and Adderall (Adderall XR®) have been approved and several others are in various stages of development (Beiderman et al., 2001; Chandler, Lopez, & Boellner, 2001; Greenhill, 2001). Although initial titration with immediate release stimulant preparations is recommended, particularly for stimulant-naïve children or adolescents, conversion to one of the rapidly increasing choices of effective long-acting preparations is strongly suggested for optimal control of ADHD symptoms.

PEM may be given only once a day, although absorption and metabolism vary widely, and some children need two daily doses. Although it was previously believed that pemoline action was delayed, more recent research shows effects within the first 1 to 2 hr after a dose, lasting for 7 to 8 hr after ingestion (Pelham et al., 1995; Sallee, Stiller, & Perel, 1992). The half-life increases with chronic administration (Sallee, Stiller, Perel, & Bates, 1985). The frequency of choreoathetoid movements (Sallee, Stiller, Perel, & Everett, 1989), insomnia, hepatitis (Nehra, Mullick, Ishak, & Zimmerman, 1990), and even (very rare) fulminant liver failure (Berkovitch, Pope, Phillips, & Koren, 1995; Safer, Zito, & Gardner, 2001), as well as the increasing availability of other long-acting stimulants make pemoline a tertiary option at best. Liver enzymes should be assessed prior to treatment. Because the onset of hepatitis is unpredictable and unrelated to the duration of treatment, routine laboratory follow-up studies may not be useful and parents need to be alert if nausea, vomiting, lethargy, malaise, or jaundice appear, or if abdominal discomfort persists for more than 2 weeks. Pemoline appears to have the least abuse potential of the stimulants.

Buproprion. Buprorion may decrease hyperactivity and aggression and perhaps improve cognitive performance of children with ADHD and CD (Conners et al., 1996; Simeon, Ferguson, & Fleet, 1986). One blind controlled crossover study found efficacy of bupropion to be statistically equal to MPH (Barrickman et al., 1995), although, similar to other nonstimulant medications, the behavioral effects may be greater than the cognitive effects (AACAP, 1997). Bupropion is administered in two or three (in the case of regular bupropion) daily doses, beginning with a low dose (37.5 or 50 mg) twice a day, with titration over 2 weeks to a usual maximum of 250 mg/day (300–400 mg/day in adolescents). The most serious potential side effect is a decrease in the seizure threshold, seen most frequently in patients with eating disorders or at doses greater than 450 mg/day. The use of the SR preparation and divided doses are recommended to reduce the risk of seizure. Bupropion may exacerbate tics (Spencer, Biederman, Wilens, et al., 1993).

Tricyclic Antidepressants (TCAs). Controlled trials of TCAs in both children and adolescents demonstrate efficacy in the treatment of ADHD (Spencer, Biederman, Wilens, et al., 1996). Despite their narrower margin of safety, they may be indicated as second- or third-line drugs for those patients who do not respond to stimulants, or who develop significant depression or other side effects on stimulants, or for the treatment of ADHD symptoms in patients with tics or Tourette's disorder (Riddle et al., 1988; Spencer, Biederman, Harding, et al., 1993; Spencer, Biederman, Kerman, & Steingard, 1993). There are over 30 studies of TCAs of more than 1,000 children, adolescents and adults, with ADHD. The majority of these studies (over 85%) reported substantial improvement in comparison with placebo. Controlled trials include imipramine, desipramine, and nortriptyline. Although some early studies indicated a superiority of TCAs over stimulants (Werry, 1980), more recent studies have reported that stimulants were superior or equal to TCAs (Rapport, Carlson, Kelly, & Pataki, 1993). TCAs may be nearly as efficacious in controlling behavioral abnormalities such as impulsivity and hyperactivity in ADHD but are less effective in improving cognitive symptoms such as inattention (Rapoport, Quinn, Bradbard, Riddle, & Brooks, 1974; Gualtieri & Evans, 1988). Biederman, Baldessarini, Wright, Knee, and Harmatz (1989) reported that desipramine-treated ADHD patients showed a substantial reduction in depressive symptoms compared with patients who received placebo. The use of TCAs in the treatment of ADHD may pose several limitations including reports of tolerance after initial improvement (Quinn & Rapoport, 1975; Waizer, Hoffman, Polizos, & Engelhardt, 1974), the danger of accidental or intentional overdose, troublesome sedating anticholinergic side effects, and potential cardiovascular side effects (Riddle, Geller, & Ryan, 1993; Varley & McClellan, 1997).

Desipramine has fewer anticholinergic side effects than imipramine and well-documented immediate and sustained efficacy in both children and adolescents (Biederman et al., 1989; Donnelly et al., 1986), although less than MPH (Garfinkel, Wender, & Sloman, 1983). In two open trials with children and adolescents, many of whom had a poor response to stimulants, nortriptyline produced improved attitude, increase in attention span, and a decrease in impulsivity (Saul, 1985; Wilens et al., 1993).

Pharmacokinetics for TCAs are different in children than in adolescents or adults. Prepubertal children are prone to rapid dramatic swings in blood levels from toxic to ineffective and should have divided doses to produce more stable levels (Ryan, 1992). The short half-life of TCAs in prepubertal children can produce daily withdrawal symptoms if medication is given only once a day. TCAs should be tapered over a 2- to 3-week period. These symptoms may also indicate that poor compliance is resulting in missed doses. Parents must be reminded to supervise administration of medication and to keep pills in a safe place. Five cases of unexplained sudden death have occurred during desipramine treatment, three of which were following exercise, in three prepubertal children (Popper & Zimnitzky, 1995; Riddle et al., 1991). A causal relationship between the medication and the deaths has not been established. The evidence appears to suggest that treatment with desipramine in usual doses is associated with only slightly added risk of sudden death beyond that occurring naturally (Biederman et al., 1995). In any case, TCAs should be used only for clear indications and with careful monitoring of therapeutic efficacy and of baseline and subsequent vital signs and electrocardiogram (EKG). Revised parameters have recently been published (Wilens et al., 1996). Patient history of cardiac disease or arrhythmia or a family history of sudden death, unexplained fainting, cardiomyopathy, or early cardiac disease may be a contraindication to TCA use. The clinician should be alert to the risk of intentional overdose or accidental poisoning, not only by the patient but also by other family members, especially young children.

Other Antidepressants. Although there has been considerable clinical interest in the use of the selective serotonin reuptake inhibitors (SSRIs) in the treatment of ADHD, the only published data are from one open trial of fluoxetine alone (Barrickman, Noyes, Kuperman, Schumacher, & Verda, 1991), an open case series in which fluoxetine was added to MPH because of inadequate response (Gammon & Brown, 1993), and one single case study of the combination of fluoxetine and methamphetamine (Bussing & Levin, 1993). Anecdotal reports do not support efficacy of the SSRIs for the core symptoms of ADHD. Venlafaxine has been studied for the treatment of ADHD in several open trials (Findling, Schwartz, Flannery, & Manos, 1996; Hedges, Reimherr, Rogers, Strong, & Wender, 1995; Popper, 2000). No RCTs are yet available to more definitively establish the efficacy of venlafaxine for ADHD. Tranylcypromine, a monoamine oxidase inhibitor (MAOI), was shown in one study to be as effective as DEX (Zametkin et al., 1985), but the risk of severe reactions due to dietary indiscretions or drug interaction make its use impractical for potentially impulsive children and adolescents.

Alpha-adrenergic Agonists. Clonidine is an alpha-noradrenergic agonist. Clonidine may be useful in modulating mood and activity level and improving cooperation and frustration tolerance in a subgroup of children with ADHD, especially those who are very highly aroused, hyperactive, impulsive, defiant, and labile (Hunt, Capper, & O'Connell, 1990). Although clonidine may not be effective in treating inattention per se, it may be used alone to treat behavioral symptoms of ADHD in children with tics (Steingard, Biederman, Spencer, Wilens, & Gonzalez, 1993) or those who are non-responders or negative responders to stimulants. Open trials suggest that it may be most useful in combination with a stimulant, when stimulant response is only partial, or stimulant dose is limited by side effects (Hunt, Lau, & Ryu, 1991). The combination may allow a lower dose of stimulant medication (Hunt et al., 1991). Questions have been raised about the safety of combining MPH and clonidine (see section following on medication combinations). Clonidine often improves ability to fall asleep, whether insomnia is due to ADHD overarousal, oppositional refusal, or stimulant effect or rebound (Wilens, Biederman, & Spencer, 1994).

For clondine, a thorough cardiovascular history to include recent clinical cardiac examination, measurement of pulse and blood pressure, and EKG is necessary (AACAP, 1997). Pulse and blood pressure should be monitored for bradycardia or hypotension. The skin patch or transdermal form may be useful to improve compliance and reduce variability in blood levels (Hunt, 1987). Erratic compliance with medication increases the risk of adverse cardiovascular events. Families should be cautioned about this, and clonidine should not be prescribed if it cannot be administered reliably. The most common side effect of clonidine is sedation, although it tends to decrease after several weeks (Hunt, Minderaa, & Cohen, 1985). Dry mouth, nausea, and photophobia have been reported, with hypotension and dizziness possible at high doses. The skin patch often causes local pruritic dermatitis and may cause a toxic reaction if eaten or chewed.

Guanfacine hydrochloride, a long-acting alpha-2 noradrenergic agonist with a longer half-life and a more favorable side effect profile than clonidine, has recently begun to be used alone for children with ADHD and Tourette's disorder whose tics worsen on a stimulant, or in combination with a stimulant in the treatment of children with ADHD who cannot tolerate the sedative side effects of clonidine or in whom clonidine has too short a duration of action, leading to rebound effects. As yet, only open trials have been published (Chappell, Leckman, & Riddle, 1995; Horrigan & Barnhill, 1995; Hunt, Arnsten, & Asbell, 1995).

Although not related to clondine or guafacine, atomoxetine is a potent inhibitor of the presynaptic norepinephrine transporter while having minimal affinity for other noradrenergic receptors or other neurotransmitter systems. RCT and comparison studies with MPH suggest that Atomoxetine is efficacious for the treatment of ADHD, is well tolerated, and is comparable with MPH (Kratochvil et al., 2001).

Medication Combinations.   The most common combination used currently for ADHD is probably a stimulant and clonidine, although there are no published controlled trials of safety or efficacy of this combination. Anecdotal clinical experience supports the usefulness of these two drugs, especially in children with severe ADHD who are not able to be managed satisfactorily on a stimulant alone. There have been four deaths reported to the FDA of children who at one time had been taking both MPH and clonidine, but the evidence linking the drugs to the deaths is tenuous at best (Fenichel, 1995; Popper, 1995; Swanson, Lerner, & Williams, 1995). Pending additional data, caution is advised when treating children with cardiac or cardiovascular disease, when combining clonidine with additional medications, or if dosing of medication is inconsistent (Swanson et al., 1995). An alternative strategy might be to substitute DEX or Adderall for MPH or guanfacine for clonidine.

Although used safely in some settings (Pataki, Carlson, Kelly, Rapport, & Biancaniello, 1993), the combination of imipramine and MPH has been associated with a syndrome of confusion, affective lability, marked aggression, and severe agitation (Grob & Coyle, 1986). MPH may interfere with hepatic metabolism of imipramine, resulting in a longer half-life and elevated blood levels. One study found that the combination of desipramine and MPH had more side effects than either drug alone, but they were not more serious than with desipramine alone (Pataki et al., 1993). Carlson, Rapport, Kelly, and Pataki (1995) have evaluated the use of the combination of desipramine and MPH in a blind controlled crossover study of 16 psychiatrically hospitalized children with ADHD, mood disorder, or both, and either CD or ODD. The efficacy of the combination was statistically significantly better than either drug alone, but clinically the improvements were modest.

Neuroleptics. Early studies suggested some usefulness of thioridazine or other major tranquilizers in the treatment of ADHD (Green, 2001), but they should be used only in the most extreme circumstances (i.e., extreme levels of aggressive or disruptive behavior; see chap. 2, this volume) because of lesser effectiveness relative to stimulants as well as adverse effects, which include excess sedation and potential cognitive dulling and risk of tardive dyskinesia or neuroleptic malignant syndrome.

Other Drugs. There is little data to support the use of fenfluramine, benzodiazepines, or lithium in ADHD (AACAP, 1997; Green, 1995).

Comorbid Psychiatric Disorders

Comorbidity is present in up to two thirds of clinically referred children with ADHD, including up to 50% for ODD, 30% to 50% for CD, 15% to 20% for mood disorders, and 20% to 25% for anxiety disorders (Biederman, Newcorn, & Sprich, 1991; Newcorn & Halperin, 1994). A large community epidemiologic study in New Zealand found that of children with hyperactivity, 47% also had ODD or CD and 26% anxiety or phobic disorder. As many as 18% had two or more comorbid conditions (Anderson, Williams, McGee, & Silva, 1987). The Ontario Child Health Study (Szatmari, Offord, & Boyle, 1989) found that in children ages 4 to 11 years, 53% of boys and 42% of girls who had attention deficit disorder with hyperactivity (ADDH; *Diagnostic and Statistical Manual of Mental Disorders*, 3rd ed.; American Psychiatric Association, 1980) had at least one other Axis I diagnosis. For children ages 12 to 16 years, the prevalence of ADDH participants with at least one other diagnosis was 48% for boys and 76% for girls (Szatmari et al., 1989). Referral bias and clinical experience suggest that children referred to specialized psychiatric health settings are more likely to have comorbid disorders than those treated by pediatricians.

Although the pharmacologic treatment of other psychiatric disorders such as mood, anxiety, and psychotic disorders is beyond the scope of this chapter, the clinician should be aware of the considerable psychiatric comorbidity within the population of children and adolescents with DBDs. If the onset of disruptive symptoms appear to follow or be concurrent with mood, anxiety, or psychotic symptoms, treating the primary psychiatric disorder should be the first concern, followed by specific attention to the seeming secondary disruptive symptoms, if necessary. However, more commonly the DBD clearly predates the comorbid disorder and treating the comorbidity involved adding an intervention or medication or choosing a medication that could treat the comorbid disorders concurrently. Unfortunately, comprehensive treatment of comorbid disorders often involves polypharmacy and careful clinical considerations.

One common comorbid problem is that of ADHD and depressive disorders. Among the therapeutic options are using antidepressants that have shown efficacy in the treatment of ADHD. Although effective in the treatment of ADHD, TCAs have not been found to be superior to placebo in RCT of depression in children and adolescents. In an open trial of bupropion SR with 24 adolescents (ages 11–16) with ADHD and either comorbid MDD or dysthymic disorder (DD), Daviss and associates (2001) reported that adolescent and parent rating of depressive symptoms and parent rating of ADHD symptoms were significantly improved after the over 8-week trial. However, teacher ratings of ADHD did not significantly improve. Gammon and Brown (1993) reported increased responsivity of ADHD with the addition of fluoxetine to MPH in a group of 32 youth with comorbid ADHD and depression (78% with DD and 18% with MDD) noting significant improvements in measures of mood, behavior, and global status.

Because a majority of adolescents with substance use disorders (SUDs) also have DBDs (Bukstein, Brent, & Kaminer, 1989), DBD comorbidity with SUD represents an important area for clinical and research efforts. Common pharmacotherapeutic strategies consist of treating withdrawal symptoms, substitution therapy (e.g., replacing heroin with methadone), craving reduction along with blocking strategies (i.e., using naltrexone for treatment of alcoholism), and aversive therapy (i.e., using disulfiram to maintain alcohol abstinence; Kranzler, Amin, Modesto-Lowe, & Oncken, 1999; Solhkhah & Wilens, 1998). This list can be further expanded to include comorbid psychiatric conditions that lead to early use or contribute to continued use. The limited research literature on the use of pharmacotherapies with adolescents necessitates the guidance of the adult literature on the use of pharmacologic agents to assist the clinician in the most supported approaches for adolescents. Although some pharmacological therapies have empirical support for their use in adolescents, the use of medications should always be part of a multimodal treatment approach.

To date, only two published studies have evaluated the efficacy of fluoxetine or any other SSRI antidepressant in adolescents with substance dependence. Riggs, Mikulich, Coffman, and Crowley (1997) conducted an open-label trial involving 8 male adolescent participants who were treated with a 20 mg dose of fluoxetine for 7 weeks. These participants displayed either cannabis abuse or cannabis dependence and CD in addition to an alcohol use disorder (AUD) and MDD. Of the 8 adolescents, 7 demonstrated marked improvement in depressive symptoms and wished to continue on fluoxetine after the trial. Significant within-group improvement in depression was noted on the Clinical Global Impression (CGI) scale (Guy, 1976), as well as on observer-rated and self-rated measures of depressive symptoms. As the study was conducted in the controlled environment of a residential treatment center, the efficacy of fluoxetine for treating alcohol or substance use could not be assessed. No serious side effects were noted during the trial, and no patient was discontinued from the medication because of side effects. Cornelius et al. (2000) conducted a 12-week open-label study of fluoxetine in an outpatient setting with 13 adolescents diagnosed with comorbid AUD and MDD. The study found a significant within-group decrease (improvement) for both depressive symptoms and drinking. The fluoxetine was well tolerated.

Given the absence of evidence establishing the effectiveness of TCAs in adolescents and the potential of adverse events and interactions with substances of abuse (Wilens, Spencer, & Biederman, 1997), the use of TCAs in adolescents with SUDs should be avoided whenever possible. Similarly, the use of MAOIs presents problems due to adolescent impulsivity and potential interactions with various foods and medications or substances of abuse (e.g., opiates or stimulants). In perhaps the only published double-blind, placebo-controlled trial in adolescents with SUD, Geller et al. (1998) conducted a 6-week study of 25 adolescents, ages 12 to 18, who were randomly assigned to receive either placebo or lithium carbonate. Using both intent-to-treat and completer analyses, there were significant differences on continuous and categorical measures between the lithium and the placebo groups for both psychopathology measures and weekly random urine drug screens.

Psychostimulants such as MPH and DEX, although among the most studied and effective of medications in youth with ADHD, present a number of potential problems for use in populations of adolescents with SUDs. Despite their potential for effectively treating ADHD, there are several limitations to the use of stimulants. Stimulants cannot be easily used late in the day or evening, and they may have adverse effects on mood (Barkley et al., 1990). MPH and DEX are classified as Schedule II by the Drug Enforcement Administration, thus indicating a high potential for abuse (Jaffe, 1991; Riggs, 1998). Despite their efficacy in the treatment of ADHD, MPH and DEX have not been studied in the treatment of adolescents with SUDs and ADHD. Although the use of stimulant medication for ADHD symptoms in adolescents is empirically supported (Smith, Pelham, Gnagy, & Yudell, 1998), and for children with ADHD in general (MTA Cooperative Group, 1999b), controversy remains regarding their use among adolescents with substance use-related problems.

Pemoline, another central nervous system stimulant and a Schedule IV medication, has a lower abuse potential as supported by animal and human studies (Langer, Sweeney, Bartenbach, Davis, & Menander, 1986; Riggs et al., 1996). Riggs et al. (1996) conducted a 1-month open trial of pemoline in 13 adolescents, ages 14 to 18, with SUD, ADHD, and CD who were being treated in a residential drug and alcohol treatment center. After 1 month of pemoline treatment, scores of mean ADHD symptom and physical activity decreased from baseline. Concerns about hepatic toxicity raise concerns about its use as a first-line drug (FDA, 1997).

Given the potential risks (as described previously) of prescribing stimulant medications to substance-abusing youth, alternatives to stimulants need to be studied for this population of adolescents with ADHD. A number of antidepressants such as TCAs and bupropion have shown efficacy in the treatment of ADHD. The use of TCAs in the treatment of ADHD may pose several limitations including reports of tolerance after initial improvement and potential cardiovascular system toxicity and reactions. The similarity between some tricyclic and heterocyclic antidepressants and bupropion in their effects on MAOIs has prompted several investigations into the efficacy of bupropion for ADHD. Bupropion is a noradrenergic and dopamine reuptake blocker that is in current use as an antidepressant (Davidson & Connor, 1998). It has a low side effect profile with low cardiotoxicity. A newer preparation, bupropion SR, is an attractive candidate agent for the treatment of comorbid ADHD and AUD/SUDs for several reasons. First, its status as an indirect dopamine agonist and enhancer of norepinephrine bioavailability (Pliska, McCracken, & Maas, 1996) makes it a possible agent for ADHD, in which both noradrenergic and dopaminergic mechanisms are involved (Spencer, Biederman, Wilens, et al., 1996; Pliska et al., 1996). Second, dopaminergic mechanisms in the nucleus acumbens have been implicated in the development of SUDs. Bupropion may also have an effect on aggression in youth with ADHD (Conners et al., 1996). Bupropion appears to have low abuse potential on physiological measures compared with DEX (Griffith, Carranza, Griffith, & Miller, 1983). Bupropion also has few adverse effects (Settle, 1998).

The approval by the FDA for the use of bupropion for smoking cessation and its efficacy in controlled clinical trials (Goldstein, 1998; Hurt et al., 1997) suggests the potential value of this agent for addictive disorders. The only study that has examined the use of bupropion in participants with both ADHD and SUDs is Riggs, Thompson, Mikulich, Whitmore, and Crowley (1998) 5-week open trial of bupropion in 13 nondepressed adolescent boys, ages 14 to 17 ($M = 15.5$) in a residential treatment facility. These adolescents had comorbid diagnoses of SUD, ADHD, and CD. The investigators titrated immediate release bupropion to a maximum of 300 mg/day in three doses. By the 5th week, the participants' mean scores on ADHD symptoms and Clinical Global Impressions (CGI) Scale showed significant improvement over baseline. As the study was conducted in the controlled environment of a residential treatment center, the efficacy of bupropion for treating alcohol or substance use could not be assessed.

The clinical management of the adolescent with comorbid SUD and ADHD is a challenging task, as the results will help determine the ultimate success in controlling the range of academic and social dysfunction that often accompanies ADHD. Emerging evidence suggests that for stimulants, adolescents who are treated with stimulants as adolescents have a lower risk for the development of SUDs than adolescents with ADHD who do not take stimulant medications (Beiderman, Wilens, Mick, Spencer, & Farone, 1999; Molina, Pelham, & Roth, 1999). My clinical experience is that compliance with medication regimens is a bigger problem than abuse or diversion of medication treatments among adolescents.

Psychosocial interventions such as family therapy, targeting parenting practices, and cognitive-behavioral approaches are an essential background to medication decisions. Nonstimulant options should be thoroughly considered. If a stimulant is necessary to produce clinically significant results, close supervision of administration by responsible adults is critical. The choice of a long-acting stimulant is preferred. Newer agents such as OROS® methylphenidate (Concerta®) or Adderall XR® may have lower abuse potential owing to their long duration of action and novel delivery system that does not promote crushing (and nasal ingestion).

Aggression and Mood Dysregulation

Aggression and mood dysregulation appear to be related targets in view of the large overlap in their appearance in youth with DBDs. Manifestations of these problems include verbal and physical aggression, and/or problems with anger control or frequent, severe temper tantrums. Although aggression and mood dysregulation may be part of a larger syndrome consistent with a diagnosis of a specific psychiatric disorder such as a mood disorder, the presence of pathological levels of these dimensions with a specific mood or other psychiatric diagnosis is also quite common.

To date, relatively few studies have addressed the issue of subtyping comorbid aggression into clinically meaningful categories (e.g., Vitiello, Behar, Hunt, Stoff, & Ricciuti, 1990). Some evidence suggests that there may be discrete subtypes of aggression that respond differentially to treatment. For example, lithium may be more efficacious in treating youngsters with CD with explosive aggression (Campbell, Gonzalez, & Silva, 1992; Malone & Simpson, 1998), whereas predatory aggression (Vitiello et al., 1990) may be less responsive to pharmacotherapy.

Mood Stabilizers. Not surprisingly, the most commonly used and studied medications for aggression and mood dysregulation are those used for specific mood disorders such as antidepressants and mood stabilizers. Lithium, carbamazepine, and valproate have all been studied in children and adolescents with DBDs. Lithium has long been known to have antiaggressive properties, especially when a strong mood component is present (Campbell, 1992; Campbell, Kafantaris, & Cueva, 1995). In a double-blind, placebo-controlled trial of lithium carbonate study of 50 hospitalized prepubertal children with severe explosive, aggressive behavior, Campbell et al. (1995) found lithium to be more efficacious than placebo in reducing aggression. In other studies, the effectiveness of lithium appeared limited, although these studies were limited by brief duration and comparison with stimulants (Klein, 1991). Side effects that may be associated with lithium include enuresis, fatigue, ataxia, increased thirst, nausea, vomiting, urinary frequency, and weight gain (Silva et al., 1992). Donovan et al. (2000), in a double-blind, placebo-controlled crossover study of valproate in 20 adolescents with DBDs in addition to explosiveness or mood lability (or both) reported that 12 out of 15 participants who completed the study showed improvements in aggression. However, when administered in doses 400 to 800 mg/day in a small placebo-controlled, double-blind study of 22 prepubertal children, carbamazepine was not found to be more efficacious than placebo in reducing aggression in children with CD (Cueva et al., 1996). A small pilot study (Kafantaris et al., 1992) of carbamazepine showed effectiveness in reducing aggressive target symptoms in 10 hospitalized youth with CD and explosive aggression.

Typical Antipsychotics. Prior to the recent increase in the use of atypical antipsychotics to treat aggression, typical antipsychotics, especially haloperidol, were a primary pharmacologic treatment for aggression in children and adults (Whitaker & Rao, 1992). The empirical evidence for the use of these medications in youth is relatively small (for reviews, see Gillberg, 2000; Whitaker & Rao, 1992). Although mostly prescribed for adults for psychotic symptoms, children and adolescents are given neuroleptics for a wide variety of symptoms and diagnoses (Campbell et al., 1993). The effect may be nonspecific and secondary to sedation rather than any direct antiaggression effects (Miczek & Winslow, 1987). In a double-blind, placebo-controlled trial with a hospitalized sample of children, ages 5 to 12 years, with CD, Campbell, Small, and Green (1984) reported that the group receiving haloperidol were less hyperactive, aggressive, and hostile than the placebo group. In a similar study, Campbell, Cohen, and Small (1982) found chlorpromazine reduced aggressive and explosive behavior. In another controlled-placebo study, molidine and thiroidazine were compared with placebo in 31 children, ages 6 to 11, with aggressive CD. Children on the active medications showed similar improvements beyond placebo in aggression, hyperactivity, hostility, and social responsiveness (Greenhill, Solomon, Pleak, & Ambrosini, 1986). Antipsychotics are commonly used clinically on an as needed basis for acute aggressive, destructive, or self-injurious behavior, especially when the behavior is not responsive to behavioral or other nonmedication interventions despite the absence of controlled trials (Vitiello, Ricciuti, & Behar, 1987). In addition, older neuroleptics may be limited by their short-term sedative effects (Campbell et al., 1984), as well as long term effects such as the risk of tardive or withdrawal dyskinesias (Campbell et al., 1997; Richardson, Haugland, & Craig, 1991). The primary safety concerns about the use of typical antipsychotics in children stem from associations between these medications and tardive and withdrawal dyskinesias in long-term treatment (Richardson et al., 1991; Campbell et al., 1997). Although usually reversible with dose reductions or drug withdrawal, serious tardive dyskinesias have occurred in approximately one in three children treated with typical antipsychotics in some samples (Gillberg, 2000). Gillberg (2000) reported 40 children in the literature who suffered malignant neuroleptic syndromes, 15% of which resulted in the child's death. Although typical antipsychotics appear to be effective for treating aggressive target symptoms in various disorders, the risk of serious and potentially fatal side effects, including dyskinesias and malignant neuroleptic syndromes, raises concern for their use in children and adolescents.

Atypical Antipsychotics. The atypical antipsychotics, which include risperidone, clozapine, olanzapine, quetiapine, and ziprasidone, are distinguished from typicals by their reduced incidence of extrapyramidal symptoms (EPS). Despite the increasingly common use of atypical antipsychotics to treat symptoms of aggression in youth (Pappadopulos & MacIntyre, 2001), a paucity of controlled evidence has accumulated regarding the efficacy and safety of these medications.

Double-blind, placebo-controlled studies of risperadone in aggressive children and adolescents with subnormal intelligence have shown significant reductions in aggressive behavior (Aman, Findling, Derivan, & Merriman, 1999; Buitelaar, Van der Gaag, Cohen-Kettenis, & Melman, 2001). Similarly open-label trials (Buitelaar, 2000), chart reviews (Frazier et al., 1999), and case reports (Schreier, 1998) have reported reduced aggression in youth with normal intelligence and those with complex, comorbid disorders.

Chart reviews of inpatients with schizophrenia and bipolar disorder (Kowatch et al., 1995; Rabinowitz, Avnon, & Rosenberg, 1996) found significant reduction in physical and verbal aggression with clozapine. An open-label trial of olanazapine in children, adolescents, and adults found olanzapine associated with reductions in self-injurious behavior and aggression (Potenza, Holmes, Kanes, & McDougle, 1999). To date, there are no published studies of the efficacy of quetrapine or ziprasidone for aggression.

Perhaps the most common adverse effect of atypical antipsychotics is weight gain, which is common with risperadone (Findling, Aman, & Derivan, 2000; Lombroso et al., 1995; Sikich, 2001), clozapine (Campbell, Rapoport, & Simpson, 1999), olanazapine (Potenza et al., 1999), and quetiapine (Kumra et al., 1998). Increased prolactin levels have been noted with respirdone (Aman et al., 1999; Findling et al., 2000; Sikich, 2001) and olanzapine (Sikich, 2001). Sedation is also quite common in almost all studies of atypicals. The risk of EPS appears to be low with most studies' reports of little, if any, EPS. A risk of aganulocytosis is associated with clozapine use in adults (Alvir, Lieberman, Safferman, Schwimmer, & Schaaf, 1993; Remschmidt et al., 2000) with a possibly higher risk among patients younger than 21 (Alvir et al., 1993). In adults, ziprasidone has been associated with cardiac QTc interval prolongation on EKG with potentially fatal ventricular arrhythmias when used with other mediations that prolong the QTc interval (Gury, Conceil, & Iaria, 2000).

Stimulants. Aggression is a common symptom among children with ADHD. Furthermore, ODD/CD and ADHD commonly co-occur among children and adolescents (MTA Cooperative Group, 1999a, 1999b). Several small sample studies suggest that stimulants are effective in decreasing aggressive behavior in patients with ADHD with or without CD (Gadow, Nolan, Sverd, Sprafkin, & Paolicelli, 1990; Hinshaw, 1991; Murphy, Pelham, & Lang, 1986). A double-blind, placebo-controlled trial of MPH in 18 urban children with ADHD found that participants on this medication showed improvements in ADHD symptoms and had fewer incidents of physical aggression, time-out for deviant behavior, and negative peer interactions, with no reports of serious side effects (Bukstein & Kolko, 1998). When 74 children with CD with or without ADHD were given either MPH or placebo, results showed that behaviors specific to CD were significantly reduced for those given MPH (Klein et al., 1997).

Other Medications. Given the connection between aggression and various mood states, clinicians and researchers have used SSRIs to target aggressive behavior. A placebo-controlled study found statistically significant reductions in impulsive aggressive behavior among 40 nondepressed personality disordered adults (Coccaro & Kavoussi, 1997). Case reports indicate that SSRIs were effective in reducing aggression in male youth with various aggressive disorders (Ghaziuddin & Alessi, 1992; Poyurovsky et al., 1995).

á$_2$ Agonists. In a meta-analysis of 11 double-blind, controlled, and randomized studies from 1980 and 1999, the á$_2$ agonist clonidine demonstrated a moderate effect size of 0.58 to 0.16 on symptoms of ADHD alone and with comorbid CD, developmental delay, and tic disorders (Connor, Fletcher, & Swanson, 1999). Results from an open pilot study of clonidine (maximum optimal dose = 0.4 mg/day) in aggressive children indicate that this medication may be associated with reductions in aggression and only mild side effects (Kemph, DeVane, Levin, Jarecke, & Miller, 1993).

A literature review conducted in 1993 (Connor, 1993) on the use of beta blockers to treat aggression in youth found that 145 (83%) of 175 patients in 31 reports of studies of adults and children showed improvements, although no double-blind studies were found. Beta blockers may also be an effective adjunctive treatment in reducing aggression among a variety of populations. Maoz et al. (2000) conducted an open trial of combined haloperidol and propanolol in 34 adults with schizophrenia who received 7 days of haloperidol, with some receiving subsequent haloperidol-propanolol treatment for 8 weeks. After 4 weeks of combination treatment and on a variety of doses, participants showed significant declines on several dimensions of aggression. In a 5-month, open-label study of nadolol as an adjunctive treatment for aggression or inattention/overactivity (or both) in developmentally delayed children, adolescents, and young adults (M = 109 mg/day), 10 participants (83%) showed improvements on ratings of aggression and experienced few side effects (Connor, Ozbayrak, Benjamin, Ma, & Fletcher, 1997). Beta blockers' capacity to reduce aggression in youth is also suggested by case reports (e.g., Lang & Remington, 1994). Although beta blockers may offer promise in reducing aggression, Connor (1993) noted that beta blockers should always be one part of a multidisciplinary treatment of aggression in youth.

PRACTICAL CONSIDERATIONS
IN THE PHARMACOLOGIC TREATMENT
OF DISRUPTIVE BEHAVIOR DISORDERS

The decision to medicate is based on the presence of a diagnosis of ADHD and persistent target symptoms that are sufficiently severe to cause functional impairment at school and usually also at home and with peers. Although medication is the most powerful and best documented intervention, each of the symptoms may not respond. Some parents and patients (especially adolescents) are resistant to the use of medication, and some patients experience unacceptable side effects or limited efficacy. The careful clinician balances the risks of medication, the risks of the untreated disorder, and the expected benefits of medication relative to other treatments. A baseline for target symptoms is useful before starting medication.

Medication should not be used as a substitute for appropriate educational curricula, student-to-teacher ratios, or other environmental accommodations (Rapport, 1995). At times, the most appropriate response to a behavioral problem is behavior modification, a change in classroom placement, or modification of the teacher's classroom management style. This is particularly the case when there is evidence that the disturbance is localized to one classroom situation, when it seems to be a reaction to a change in teachers or to a particular teacher's approach with the patient, or when the patient has a learning disability. In mild cases, parent education and appropriate school placement or resources are often initiated before medication, although, on the other hand, a decision about special education may best be deferred until the degree of improvement due to medication can be assessed. When severe impulsivity, noncompliance, or aggression are present, initiation of medication may need to be more urgent.

Even children who respond positively to medication continue to show deficits in many areas. Specific learning disabilities, gaps in academic knowledge and skills due to inattention, and impaired organizational abilities may require educational remediation. Parent education and training in techniques of behavior management are often indicated. Social skills deficits and family pathology may need specific treatment.

Administration of Medications

Faithful adherence to a prescribed regimen requires the cooperation of the parents, the patient, school personnel, and often additional caretakers. Medications may be incorrectly used or not given at all because of parental factors such as lack of perceived need for the drug, carelessness, inability to afford medication, misunderstanding of instructions, complex schedules of administration (Briant, 1978), and family dynamics. Both developmental and psychopathological factors may impede the patient's cooperation. Even in intensively monitored protocols, missed doses and unilateral discontinuation by a parent (even when the child responds positively) are common (Brown, Borden, Wynne, Spunt, & Clingerman, 1987; Firestone, 1982). Recent media attention to alleged inappropriate use of Ritalin has increased the resistance of some families and teachers to pharmacotherapy.

Children and adolescents should not be responsible for administering their medication because they are impulsive and disorganized at best and usually dislike the idea of taking medication. They will often avoid, "forget," or outright refuse medication. However, as an adolescent approaches adulthood, an effort should be made to assist the patient to assume responsibility for administering his or her own medication. Many children cannot or will not swallow pills. If necessary, a behavior modification program may be implemented to shape pill-swallowing behavior (Pelco, Kissel, Parrish, & Miltenberger, 1987). Apparent tolerance or decreased drug effect may also be due to a reaction to a change at home or school or the attenuation of a placebo response. Lower efficacy of a generic preparation is another possibility, although supporting data for this effect are only anecdotal.

Attention is required to avoid possible negative emanative effects of medication, that is, indirect and inadvertent cognitive and social consequences such as lower self esteem and self efficacy; attribution by child, parents, and teachers of both success and failure to external causes rather than the child's effort; stigmatization by peers; and dependence by parents and teachers on medication rather than making needed changes in the environment (Whalen & Henker, 1991). On the other hand, self-efficacy can increase as a result of environmental reinforcement of medication-related improvement in behavior.

Monitoring Medication Efficacy

Multiple outcome measures are essential, using more than one source, setting, and method of gathering data. Premedication baseline school data on behavior and academic performance should be available (Fischer & Newby, 1991; Klein et al., 1994; Pelham & Hoza, 1987; Rapport, DuPaul, Stoner, & Jones, 1986). The clinician should work closely with parents on dose adjustments and obtain annual academic testing and frequent reports from teachers. A brief checklist such as the Child Attention Problems profile (Barkley, 1990) or the Iowa Conners Teacher Rating Form (Loney & Milich, 1982) is invaluable in obtaining teacher reports of medication efficacy. A practical schedule includes weekly ratings from teachers and two ratings per week from parents: one for Monday through Friday and one for weekends. Curriculum-based measures and academic performance ratings are useful for monitoring progress in academic subjects (DuPaul, Rapport, & Perriello,

1991; Stoner, Carey, Ikeda, & Shinn, 1994). Measures of academic productivity and accuracy administered in the clinician's office (Pelham, 1985), such as timed brief reading and math tests, may be especially useful in assessing drug effect because of their similarity to tasks expected of the child at school. Protocols have been developed for determining optimal dose in ADHD children of normal IQ and those with mental retardation using direct observation and other measures in the school setting (Gadow, Nolan, Paolicelli, & Sprafkin, 1991; Gadow et al., 1992). A structured side effects checklist can be used, such as the Stimulant Side Effects Checklist (Gadow et al., 1991).

If symptoms are not severe outside of the school setting, a medication-free trial may be arranged for all or part of the summer. The purposes are to assess continuing efficacy of and need for medication, as well as to minimize side effects. If school behavior and academic performance are stable, a carefully monitored trial off medication during the school year (but not at the beginning) will provide data on whether medication is still needed. The duration of medication treatment is individually determined by whether drug-responsive target symptoms are still present. Treatment may be required through adolescence and into adulthood.

Detailed discussion of the use of every medication that can be used in the treatment of ADHD is beyond the scope of this chapter.

Diagnosis and Assessment

First and foremost, the determination of the existence of a significant clinical problem and the nature of this problem forms the basis for pharmacological treatment of DBDs. Diagnostic and symptomatic assessment are a part of a larger comprehensive assessment of the child or adolescent and his or her family and psychosocial circumstances. Information should be obtained not only from the youth and his or her family but also from other relevant informants, especially teachers. Although diagnosis is important, symptomatic assessment and determination of impairment are critical in determining the severity of the behaviors and the potential of these symptoms to respond to pharmacotherapy. Although the use of diagnostic and other assessment instruments, which are valid and reliable, is not a substitute for clinical skill and acumen, the use of such instruments allows a more quantitative assessment that allows for ongoing assessment of the response of target symptoms to interventions such as pharmacotherapy. Many of these assessment instruments are specifically reviewed elsewhere in this volume. Measurement of change should be applied at appropriate points in time, frequent enough to detect change and assist in any necessary modifications in medications and dosages but not too frequent to be perceived as a burden to parents and/or teachers. In addition to targeting symptom-specific measurements, the clinician should assess the baseline and ongoing level of global functioning overall and in such major areas as school and family functioning. For example, the CGI Scale is commonly used as a major variable in controlled pharmacological studies of pharmacotherapy in children.

Decision Process and Informed Consent

Given the multidetermined nature of DBDs and associated target symptoms, the use of nonmedication psychosocial treatments that are empirically proven are the first-line treatment. Obviously, decisions of when to use pharmacotherapy in children and adolescents are determined by such factors as severity and compliance with other interventions. Following assessment, the clinician should identify the specific targets for pharmacological intervention. These symptom targets should cause clinically significant dysfunction or distress, be amenable to pharmacological intervention (according to supporting research literature), and should be able to be measured by using quantifiable data at specific points in time (Kutcher, 2000; Walkup, 1995). Most often, the decision to use pharmacotherapy for DBDs takes the form of a risk–benefit analysis in which the clinician, parent, and youth review the potential for risk (adverse effects) and benefit (alleviation of dysfunction) and come to a decision of whether to use medication and what medication(s) to use. For families to make these deacons, informed consent procedures should include (a) a description of the problem, including target symptoms; (b) all intervention options, including the pros and cons of each option; (c) the option(s) recommended by the clinician and why; (d) a review of the expected benefits and the potential adverse effects of the agent(s), including the probability of each potential adverse event; and (f) the planned treatment course, including any needed medical or laboratory studies, the frequency of visits or follow-ups, the methods of ongoing assessment, and endpoints for treatment in the event of success or failure to control target symptoms.

Psychoeducation

To assist in the making of informed decisions, clinicians need to assist families in obtaining and reviewing information about the disorder and medications and important issues associated with the use of these and other medications. The clinician must tailor psychoeducational information to parent and child needs. The clinician should be honest about what is known and what is not known about the disorder and the effects of medication. The clinicians should address the specific and general beliefs and attitudes of families and youth toward medications, including the perceived addictiveness of an agent, what medication is really changing, and the responsibility of the youth for his or her behavior.

Adverse Effects

The potential adverse effects of pharmacotherapy must be evaluated. The clinician should determine the presence of the level of somatic symptoms prior to the onset of the medication, as many possible medication-induced effects may be already present in the youth. Without a baseline assessment of these somatic symptoms, the clinician and family may mistakenly attribute these symptoms to the medication treatment. Similarly, a comprehensive assessment should include any medical evaluation that may uncover a medical condition responsible for the target symptoms. Prior to the onset of pharmacotherapy, specific procedures such as EKG or laboratory tests such as liver or renal functions may be indicated to uncover the existence of a medical condition that may be adversely effected by a specific medication. In the case of adolescents with a history of psychoactive substance use or suspected abuse, urine toxicology for the presence of drugs may be obtained to determine the presence of such drug use both at baseline or through the course of medication treatment. The clinician should review common adverse effects and rare, but serious effects prior to the onset of medication administration and can supply the family with written information about the medication or allow a guided review of the package insert.

Ongoing evaluation of potential adverse effects should proceeded in a routine but systematic fashion. After an open-ended solicitation of possible complaints form both youth and parent, the clinician can use a medication-specific side effect scale or a verbal review of common and serious potential adverse effects by body system. The clinician must address each significant complaint and facilitate the development of a plan to deal with these effects.

Compliance

Medication therapy rarely works if the agent is not taken as directed or taken at all. Even before the onset of administration, the clinician should review administration procedures with the parent or other responsible adult, as well as the youth. Although responsible adolescents may self-administer medications each day, adults should be responsible for maintaining and monitoring the supply of medication and administering it to younger and less responsible adolescents. Prior to the onset of a mediation trial, the clinician should review his or her expectation that the medication be taken as directed or report why it is not. Procedures for reporting emergent adverse effects or problems and contacting the clinicians or others "on-call" should be reviewed with parents and the child or adolescent. At each visit, the clinician should specifically review compliance during the interval. An adolescent may be seen alone so as to elicit truthful but potentially embarrassing reports of poor or noncompliance.

In the event of an inadequate response, the clinician should attempt to review potential causes for the lack of response including subtherapeutic dose, inadequate duration of the trial, compliance with recommended regimen, and deterioration from baseline status due to the course of the illness or unidentified comorbidities, including substance use or abuse.

Polypharmacy

The frequent presence of psychiatric comorbidity and multiple symptoms targets in children and adolescents with DBDs suggests the possible use of multiple concurrent medication or polypharmacy. An optimal evaluation, psychoeducation and informed consent to allow for reasonable parental expectations, as well as patience, the use of an appropriate level of psychosocial treatments, attempts to avoid the use of medications to treat iatrogenic symptoms, use of adequate ongoing medication assessment procedures including the use of instruments, and frequent visits to review progress should minimize the need for and number of multiple medications. The clinician should always review these issues before considering the addition of medications. Polypharmacy is often the result of desperation in the presence of poorly or uncontrolled behavior or the reinforcement from previous rapid efficacious results in using various drug combinations. Unfortunately, there are few published controlled trials of multiple, concurrent medications for DBDs. The use of polypharmacy requires careful justification, discussion with families, and frequent monitoring. The clinician should determine an interval for assessing the medication combination and consider discontinuation of one or more of the agents if poor or inadequate positive results are observed.

To avoid the worst pitfalls of using polypharmacy in treating severe aggressive behavior in the context of other comorbid disorders, the clinician is advised to follow several guidelines:

1. Begin treatment with psychoeducation and psychosocial treatments.
2. Treat primary disorders before prescribing antipsychotic agents.
3. Preferentially use atypical antipsychotic agents first before typical neuroleptic agents.
4. Use a conservative dosing strategy of single changes at each visit, starting with low doses and proceeding as slowly as possible.
5. Emphasize behavioral crisis management rather than as needed pharmacological treatment.

6. Assess both effectiveness and adverse effects routinely and often.
7. Considering tapering an ineffective medication before adding a new medication.

SUMMARY

The use of pharmacotherapy in the treatment of children and adolescents with DBDs can be a standard, empirically proven intervention, one based on clinical consensus or one based on desperation and gross trial and error. The use of medications for some problems such as ADHD and impulsivity is supported by a massive literature, whereas the use of pharmacotherapy for other problems associated with DBDs is less well-established and requires further research and careful clinical judgment and practice. In almost all cases, pharmacotherapy is seen as an adjunct to empirically established psychosocial treatments.

REFERENCES

Abikoff, H., & Gittelman, R. (1985). Hyperactive children treated with stimulants: Is cognitive training a useful adjunct? *Archives of General Psychiatry, 42,* 953–961.

Abikoff, H., & Hechtman, L. (1996). Multimodal therapy and stimulants in the treatment of children with ADHD. In P. Jensen, & E. D. Hibbs (Eds.), *Psychosocial treatments for child and adolescent disorders: Empirically based approaches* (pp. 341–369). Washington, DC: American Psychological Association.

Alvir, J., Lieberman, J. A., Safferman, A. Z., Schwimmer, J. L., & Schaaf, J. A. (1993). Clozapine-induced agranulocytosis: Incidence and risk factors in the United States. *New England Journal of Medicine, 329,* 62–167.

Aman, M. G., Findling, R. L., Derivan, A., & Merriman, U. (1999, October). Risperidone versus placebo for severe conduct disorder in children with mental retardation. *Scientific Proceedings of the Annual Meeting of the American Academy of Child and Adolescent Psychiatry and the Canadian Academy of Child Psychiatry,* Toronto. 205.

American Academy of Child and Adolescent Psychiatry. (1997). Practice parameters for the assessment and treatment of attention-deficit/hyperactivity disorder. *Journal of the American Academy of Child and Adolescent Psychiatry, 36,* 85s–121s.

American Academy of Child and Adolescent Psychiatry. (2001). Summary of the practice parameter for the use of stimulant medication in the treatment of children, adolescents and adults. *Journal of the American Academy of Child and Adolescent Psychiatry, 40,* 1352–1355.

American Psychiatric Association. (1980). *Diagnostic and statistical manual of mental disorders* (3rd ed.). Washington, DC: Author.

Anderson, J. C., Williams, S., McGee, R., & Silva, P. A. (1987). DSM–III disorders in preadolescent children, prevalence in a large sample from the general population. *Archives of General Psychiatry, 44,* 69–76.

Arnold, L., Abikoff, H., Cantwell, D., Conners, C., Elliott, G., Greenhill, L., Hechtman, L., Hinshaw, S., Hoza, B., Jensen, P., Kraemer, H., March, J., Newcorn, J., Pelham, W., Richters, J., Schiller, E., Severe, J., Swanson, J., Vereen, D., & Wells, K. (1997). NIMH Collaborative multimodal treatment study of children with ADHD (MTA): Design, methodology, and protocol evolution. *Journal of Attention Disorders, 2*, 141–158.

Barkley, R. A. (1977). A review of stimulant drug research with hyperactive children. *Journal of Child Psychology and Psychiatry, 18*, 137–165.

Barkley, R. A. (1982). *Hyperactive children: A handbook for diagnosis and treatment*. New York: Guilford Press.

Barkley, R. A. (1990). *Attention-deficit hyperactivity disorder: A handbook for diagnosis and treatment*. New York: Guilford Press.

Barkley, R. A. (1997). *ADHD and the nature of self-control*. New York: Guilford.

Barkley, R., McMurray, M., Edelbroch, C., & Robbins, K. (1990). Side effects of MPH in children with attention deficit hyperactivity disorder: A systematic placebo-controlled evaluation. *Pediatrics, 86*, 184–192.

Barkley, R. A., Murphy, K., & Kwasnik, D. (1996). Psychological adjustment and adaptive impairments in young adults with ADHD. *Journal of Attention Disorders, 1*, 41–54.

Barrickman, L., Noyes, R., Kuperman, S., Schumacher, E., & Verda, M. (1991). Treatment of ADHD with fluoxetine: A preliminary trial. *Journal of the American Academy of Child and Adolescent Psychiatry, 30*, 762–767.

Barrickman, L., Perry, P. J., Allen, A. J., Kuperman, S., Arndt, S., Herrmann, K. J., & Schumacher, E. (1995). Bupropion versus methylphenidate in the treatment of attention-deficit hyperactivity disorder. *Journal of the American Academy of Child and Adolescent Psychiatry, 34*, 649–657.

Berkovitch, M., Pope, E., Phillips, J., & Koren, G. (1995). Pemoline-associated fulminant liver failure: Testing the evidence for causation. *Clinical Pharmacology Therapeutics, 57*, 696–698.

Biederman, J., Baldessarini, R. J., Wright, V., Knee, D., & Harmatz, J. S. (1989). A double-blind placebo controlled study of desipramine in the treatment of ADD: I. Efficacy. *Journal of the American Academy of Child and Adolescent Psychiatry, 28*, 777–784.

Biederman, J., Faraone, S. V., Milberger, S., Jetton, J. G., Chen, L., Mick, E., Greene, R. W., & Russell, R. L. (1996). Is childhood oppositional defiant disorder a precursor to adolescent conduct disorder? Findings from a four-year follow-up of children with ADHD. *Journal of the American Academy of Child and Adolescent Psychiatry, 35*, 1193–1204.

Biederman, J., Newcorn, J., & Sprich, S. (1991). Comorbidity of attention deficit hyperactivity disorder with conduct, depressive, anxiety, and other disorders. *American Psychiatry, 148*, 564–577.

Biederman, J., Quinn, D., Weiss, M., Wigel, S., Markabi, S., Weidennan, M., Edson, K., Karlsson, G., & Pohlmann, H. (2001, October). *Methylphenidate HCL extended release capsules (Ritalin LA): A new once-daily therapy for ADHD*. Poster session presented at annual meeting of American Academy of Child and Adolescent Psychiatry, Honolulu, HI.

Biederman, J., Thisted, R. A., Greenhill, L. L., & Ryan, N. D. (1995). Estimation of the association between desipramine and the risk for sudden death in 5- to 14-year-old children. *Journal of Clinical Psychiatry, 56*, 87–93.

Biederman, J., Wilens, T., Mick, E., Spencer, T., & Farone, S. V. (1999). Pharmacotherapy of Attention-deficit hyperactivity disorder reduces risk for substance use disorder. *Pediatrics, 104*, e20.

Bradley, C. (1937). The behavior of children receiving benzedrine. *American Journal of Psychiatry, 94*, 577–585.

Briant, R. H. (1978). An introduction to clinical pharmacology. In J. S. Werry (Ed.), *Pediatric psychopharmacology: The use of behavior modifying drugs in children* (pp. 3–28). New York: Brunner/Mazel.

Brown, R. T., Borden, K. A., Wynne, M. E., Spunt, A. L., & Clingerman, S. R. (1987). Compliance with pharmacological and cognitive treatments for attention deficit disorder. *Journal of the American Academy of Child and Adolescent Psychiatry, 26*, 521–526.

Buitelaar, J. K. (2000). Open-label treatment with risperidone of 26 psychiatrically-hospitalized children and adolescents with mixed diagnoses and aggressive behavior. *Journal of Child and Adolescent Psychopharmacology, 10*, 19–26.

Buitelaar, J. K., van der Gaag, R. J., Cohen-Kettenis, P., & Melman, C. T. M. (2001). A randomized controlled trial of risperidone in the treatment of aggression in hospitalized adolescents with subaverage cognitive abilities. *Journal of Clinical Psychiatry, 62*, 239–248.

Bukstein, O. G., Brent, D. A., & Kaminer, Y. (1989). Comorbidity of substance abuse and other psychiatric disorders in adolescents. *American Journal of Psychiatry, 146*, 1131–1141.

Bukstein, O. G., & Kolko, D. J. (1998). Effects of methylphenidate on aggressive urban children with attention deficit hyperactivity disorder. *Journal of Clinical Child Psychology, 27*, 340–351.

Bussing, R., & Levin, G. M. (1993). Methamphetamine and fluoxetine treatment of a child with attention-deficit hyperactivity disorder and obsessive-compulsive disorder. *Journal of Child & Adolescent Psychopharmacology, 3*, 53–58.

Cadoret, R. J., Yates, W. R., Troughton, E., Woodworth, G., & Stewart, M. A. (1995). Genetic-environmental interaction in the genesis of aggressivity and conduct disorders. *Archives of General Psychiatry, 52*, 916–924.

Campbell, M., Adams, P. B., Small, A. M., Kafantaris, V., Silva, R. R., Shell, J., Perry, R., Overall, J. E., Campbell, M., Armenteros, J. L., Malone, R. P., Adams, P. B., Eisenberg, Z. A., & Overall, J. E. (1997). Lithium in hospitalized aggressive children with conduct disorder. *Journal of the American Academy of Child and Adolescent Psychiatry, 34*, 445–453.

Campbell, M., Armenteros, J. L., Malone, R. P., Adams, P. B., Eisenberg, Z. W., & Overall, J. E. (1997). Neuroleptic-related dyskinesias in autistic children: A prospective, longitudinal study. *Journal of the American Academy of Child and Adolescent Psychiatry, 36*, 835–843.

Campbell, M., Cohen, I. L., & Small, A. M. (1982). Drugs in aggressive behavior. *Journal of the American Academy of Child Psychiatry, 21*, 107–117.

Campbell, M., Gonzalez, N. M., Ernst, M., Silva, R. R., & Werry, J. S. (1993). Antipsychotics (neuroleptics). In J. S. Werry & M. G. Aman (Eds.), *Practitioner's guide to psychoactive drugs for children and adolescents* (pp. 269–296). New York: Plenum.

Campbell, M., Gonzalez, N. M., & Silva, R. R. (1992). The pharmacologic treatment of conduct disorders and rage outbursts. *Psychiatric Clinics of North America, 15*, 69–85.

Campbell, M., Kafantaris, V., & Cueva, J. E. (1995). An update on the use of lithium carbonate in aggressive children and adolescents with conduct disorder. *Psychopharmacology Bulletin, 31*, 93–102.

Campbell, M., Rapoport, J. L., & Simpson, G. M. (1999). Antipsychotics in children and adolescents. *Journal of the American Academy of Child and Adolescent Psychiatry, 38*, 537–545.

Campbell, M., Small, A. M., Green, W. H., Jennings, S. J., Perry, R., Bennett, W. G., & Anderson, L. (1984). Behavioral efficacy of haloperidol and lithium carbonate: A comparison of hospitalized aggressive children with conduct disorder. *Archives of General Psychiatry, 41*, 650–656.

Carlson, G. A., Rapport, M. D., Kelly, K. L., & Pataki, C. S. (1995). Methylphenidate and desipramine in hospitalized children with comorbid behavior and mood disorders: Separate and combined effects on behavior and mood. *Journal of Child and Adolescent Psychopharmacology, 5*, 191–204.

Chandler, M. C., Lopez, F. A., & Boellner, S. W. (2001, October). *Long-term safety of SLI1381 in children with ADHD.* Poster session presented at annual meeting of American Academy of Child and Adolescent Psychiatry, Honolulu, HI.

Chappell, P. B., Leckman, J. F., & Riddle, M. A. (1995). The pharmacologic treatment of tic disorders. *Child & Adolescent Psychiatric Clinics of North America, 4*, 197–216.

Coccaro, E. F., & Kavoussi, R. J. (1997). Fluoxetine and impulsive aggressive behavior in personality-disordered subjects. *Archives of General Psychiatry, 54*, 1081–1088.

Conners, C. K., Cast, C. D., Guiltieri, C. T., Welder, E., Mark, R., Reissue, A., Welder, R. A., Khayrallah, M., & Ascher, J. (1996). Bupropion hydrochloride in attention deficit hyperactivity disorder. *Journal of the American Academy of Child and Adolescent Psychiatry, 35*, 1314–1321.

Conners, C. K., Eisenberg, L., & Barcai, A. (1967). Effect of dextroamphetamine on children: Studies on subjects with learning disabilities and school behavior problems. *Archives of General Psychiatry, 17*, 478–485.

Connor, D. F. (1993). Beta blockers for aggression: A review of the pediatric experience. *Journal of Child and Adolescent Psychopharmacology, 3,* 99–114.

Connor, D. F., Fletcher, K. E., & Swanson, J. (1999). A meta-analysis of clonidine for symptoms of attention-deficit hyperactivity disorder. *Journal of the American Academy of Child and Adolescent Psychiatry, 38,* 1551–1559.

Connor, D. F., Ozbayrak, K. R., Benjamin, S., Ma, Y., & Fletcher, K. E. (1997). A pilot study of nadolol for overt aggression in developmentally delayed individuals. *Journal of the American Academy of Child and Adolescent Psychiatry, 36,* 826–834.

Cornelius, J. R., Bukstein, O. G., Birmaher, B., Salloum, I. M., Lynch, K., Pollack, N. K., Gershon, S., & Clark, D. (2000). Fluoxetine in adolescents with major depression and an alcohol use disorder: An open label trial. *Addictive Behaviors, 25,* 1–6.

Cueva, J. E., Overall, J. E., Small, A. M., Armenteros, J. L., Perry, R., & Campbell, M. (1996). Carbamazepine in aggressive children with conduct disorder: A double-blind and placebo-controlled study. *Journal of the American Academy of Child and Adolescent Psychiatry, 35,* 480–490.

Davidson, J. T., & Connor, K. M. (1998). Bupropion sustained release: A therapeutic overview. *Journal of Clinical Psychiatry, 58,* 25–31.

Daviss, W. B., Bentivoglio, P., Racusin, R., Brown, K. M., Bostic, J. Q., & Wiley, L. (2001). Bupropion sustained release in adolescents with comorbid attention-deficit/hyperactivity disorder and depression. *Journal of the American Academy of Child and Adolescent Psychiatry, 40,* 307–314.

Donnelly, M., Zametkin, A. J., Rapoport, J. L., Ismond, D. R., Weingartner, H., Lane, E., Oliver, J., Linnoila, M., & Potter, W. Z. (1986). Treatment of childhood hyperactivity with desipramine: Plasma drug concentration, cardiovascular effects, plasma and urinary catecholamine levels, and clinical response. *Clinical Pharmacology & Therapeutics, 39,* 72–81.

Donovan, S. J., Stewart, J. W., Nunes, E. V., Quitkin, F. M., Parides, M., Daniel, W., Susser, E., & Klein, D. F. (2000). Divalproex treatment for youth with explosive temper and mood liability: A double-blind, placebo-controlled crossover design. *American Journal of Psychiatry, 157,* 818–820.

DuPaul, G. J., & Barkley, R. A. (1990). Medication therapy. In R. A. Barkley (Ed.), Attention deficit hyperactivity disorder: A handbook for diagnosis and treatment (pp. 573–612). New York: Guilford.

DuPaul, G. J., Rapport, M. D., & Perriello, L. M. (1991). Teacher ratings of academic skills: The development of the Academic Performance Rating Scale. *School Psychology Review, 20,* 284–300.

Eisenberg, L., Lachman, R., Molling, P., Lockner, A., Mizelle, J., & Conners, C. (1961). A psychopharmacologic experiment in a training school for delinquent boys: Methods, problems and findings. *American Journal of Orthopsychiatry, 33,* 431–447.

Elia, J., Borcherding, B., Rapoport, J., & Keysor, C. (1991). Methylphenidate and dextroamphetamine treatments of hyperactivity: Are there true non-responders? *Psychiatry Research, 36,* 141–155.

Fenichel, R. R. (1995). Combining methylphenidate and clonidine: The role of post-marketing surveillance. *Journal of Child and Adolescent Psychopharmacology, 5,* 155–156.

Findling, R. L., Aman, M., & Derivan, A. (2000). Long-term safety and efficacy of risperidone in children with significant conduct problems and borderline IQ or mental retardation. *Scientific Proceedings of the 39th Annual Meeting of the American College of Neuropsychopharmacology,* 224.

Findling, R. L., Schwartz, M. A., Flannery, D. J., & Manos, M. J. (1996). Venlafaxine in adults with attention-deficit hyperactivity disorder: An open clinical trial. *Journal of Clinical Psychiatry, 57,* 184–189.

Firestone, P. (1982). Factors associated with children's adherence to stimulant medication. *American Journal of Orthopsychiatry, 52,* 447–457.

Fischer, M., & Newby, R. F. (1991). Assessment of stimulant response in ADHD children using a refined multimethod clinical protocol. *Journal of Clinical Child Psychology, 20,* 232–244.

Food and Drug Administration, U.S. Department of Health and Human Services. (1997). Pemoline and hepatic failure. *Food and Drug Administration Bulletin, 27*, 3.

Frazier, J. A., Meyer, M. C., Biederman, J., Wozniak, J., Wilens, T. E., Spencer, T. J., Kim, G. S., & Shapiro, S. (1999). Risperidone treatment for juvenile bipolar disorder: A retrospective chart review. *Journal of the American Academy of Child and Adolescent Psychiatry, 38*, 960–965.

Gadow, K. D., Nolan, E. E., Paolicelli, L. M., & Sprafkin, J. (1991). A procedure for assessing the effects of methylphenidate on hyperactive children in public school settings. *Journal of Clinical Child Psychology, 20*, 268–276.

Gadow, K. D., Nolan, E. E., Sverd, J., Sprafkin, J., & Paolicelli, L. (1990). Methylphenidate in aggressive-hyperactive boys: I. Effects on peer aggression in public school settings. *Journal of the American Academy of Child and Adolescent Psychiatry, 29*, 710–718.

Gadow, K. D., Pomeroy, J. C., & Nolan, E. E. (1992). A procedure for monitoring stimulant medication in hyperactive mentally retarded school children. *Journal of Child & Adolescent Psychopharmacology, 2*, 131–143.

Gammon, G. D., & Brown, T. E. (1993). Fluoxetine and methylphenidate in combination for treatment of attention deficit disorder and comorbid depressive disorder. *Journal of Child & Adolescent Psychopharmacology, 3*, 1–10.

Garfinkel, B. D., Wender, P. H., & Sloman, L. (1983). Tricyclic antidepressant and methylphenidate treatment of attention deficit disorder in children. *Journal of the American Academy of Child Psychiatry, 22*, 343–348.

Geller, B., Cooper, T. B., Kai, S., Zimmerman, B., Franzier, J., Williams, M., & Heath, J. (1998). Double-blind and placebo-controlled study of lithium for adolescent bipolar disorders with secondary substance dependency. *Journal of the American Academy of Child and Adolescent Psychiatry, 37*, 171–178.

Ghaziuddin, N., & Alessi, N. E. (1992). An open clinical trial of trazodone in aggressive children. *Journal of the American Academy of Child and Adolescent Psychiatry, 2*, 291–297.

Gillberg, C. (2000). Typical neuroleptics in child and adolescent psychiatry. *European Child and Adolescent Psychiatry, 9*, I/2–I/8.

Gillberg, C., Melander, H., von Knorring, A., Janols, L., Thernlund, G., Heggel, B., Edievall-Walin, L., Gustafsson, P., & Kopp, S. (1997). Long-term central stimulant treatment of children with attention-deficit hyperactivity disorder: A randomized double-blind placebo-controlled trial. *Archives of General Psychiatry, 54*, 857–864.

Gittelman-Klein, R. (1980). Diagnosis and drug treatment of childhood disorders: Attention deficit disorder with hyperactivity. In D. F. Klein, R. Gittelman-Klein, F. Quitkin, & A. Rifkin (Eds.), *Diagnosis and drug treatment of psychiatric disorders, adults and children* (pp. 590–695). Baltimore: Williams & Wilkins.

Gittelman-Klein, R. (1987). Pharmacotherapy of childhood hyperactivity: An update. In H. Y. Meltzer (Ed.), *Psychopharmacology: The third generation of progress*. New York: Raven.

Goldstein, M. G. (1998). Bupropion sustained release and smoking cessation. *Journal of Clinical Psychiatry, 59*, 66–72.

Grace, T. (2000). Cellular and molecular neurochemistry of psychostimulant effects on dopamine. In M. Solanto & X. Castellanos (Eds.), *The neuropharmacology of psychostimulant drugs: Implications for ADHD* (pp. 85–100). New York: Oxford University Press.

Green, W. H. (2001). *Child and Adolescent Clinical psychopharmacology* (3rd ed.). Hagerstown, MD: Lippicott, Williams & Wilkins.

Greenhill, L. (1998). Childhood attention deficit hyperactivity disorder, pharmacological treatments. In P. E. Nathan & J. Gorman (Eds.), *Treatments that work* (pp. 42–64). Philadelphia: Saunders.

Greenhill, L. (2001, October). *Once-daily methylphenidate treatment for children with ADHD*. Poster session presented at annual meeting of American Academy of Child and Adolescent Psychiatry, Honolulu, HI.

Greenhill, L., Abikoff, H., Conners, C. K., Elliott, G., Hechtman, L., Hinshaw, S., Hoza, B., Jensen, P., Kraemer, H., March, J., Newcorn, J., Pelham, W., Richters, J., Schiller, E., Severe, J., Swanson, J., Vereen, D., & Wells, K. (1996). Medication treatment strategies in the MTA: Relevance to clinicians and researchers. *Journal of the American Academy of Child and Adolescent Psychiatry, 35*, 444–454.

Greenhill, L., Pliszka, S., & Dulcan, M. K. (2001). Summary of the practice parameter for the use of stimulant medications in the treatment of children, adolescents, and adults. *Journal of the American Academy of Child and Adolescent Psychiatry, 40*, 1352–1355.

Greenhill, L. L., Solomon, M., Pleak, R., & Ambrosini, P. (1986). Molindine hydrochloride of hospitalized children with conduct disorder. *Journal of Clinical Psychiatry, 46*, 20–25.

Griffith, J. D., Carranza, J., Griffith, C., & Miller, L. I. (1983). Bupropion, clinical assay for amphetamine-like potential. *Journal of Clinical Psychiatry, 44*, 206–208.

Grob, C. S., & Coyle, J. T. (1986). Suspected adverse methylphenidate-imipramine interactions in children. *Journal of Developmental & Behavioral Pediatrics, 7*, 265–267.

Gualtieri, C. T., & Evans, R. W. (1988). Motor performance in hyperactive children treated with imipramine. *Perceptual & Motor Skills, 66*, 763–769.

Gury, C., Canceil, O., & Iaria, P. (2000). Antipsychotic drugs and cardiovascular safety: Current studies of prolonged QT interval and risk of ventricular arrhythmia. *Encephale, 26*, 62–72.

Guy, W. (1976). *ECDEU Assessment Manual for Psychopharmacology*, Revised. US Department of Health, Education, and Welfare Publication (ADM) 76-338. Rockville, MD: National Institute of Mental Health.

Hedges, D., Reimherr, F. W., Rogers, A., Strong, R., & Wender, P. H. (1995). An open trial of venlafaxine in adult patients with attention deficit hyperactivity disorder. *Psychopharmacology Bulletin, 31*, 779–783.

Hinshaw, S. P. (1991). Stimulant medication in the treatment of aggression in children with attentional deficits. *Journal of Clinical Child Psychology, 12*, 301–312.

Horrigan, J. P., & Barnhill, L. J. (1995). Guanfacine for treatment of attention-deficit hyperactivity disorder in boys. *Journal of Child and Adolescent Psychopharmacology, 5*, 215–223.

Hunt, R. D. (1987). Treatment effects of oral and transdermal clonidine in relationship to methylphenidate: A one pilot study in ADD-H. *Psychopharmacology Bulletin, 23*, 111–114.

Hunt, R. D., Arnsten, A. F. T., & Asbell, M. D. (1995). An open trial of guanfacine in the treatment of attention-deficit hyperactivity disorder. *Journal of the American Academy of Child and Adolescent Psychiatry, 34*, 50–54.

Hunt, R. D., Capper, S., & O'Connell, P. (1990). Clonidine in child and adolescent psychiatry. *Journal of Child and Adolescent Psychopharmacology, 1*, 87–102.

Hunt, R. D., Lau, S., & Ryu, J. (1991). Alternative therapies for ADHD. In L. L. Greenhill & B. B. Osman (Eds.), *Ritalin: Theory and patient management* (pp. 75–95). New York: Mary Ann Liebert, Inc.

Hunt, R. D., Minderaa, R. B., & Cohen, D. J. (1985). Clonidine benefits children with attention deficit disorder and hyperactivity: Report of a doubleblind placebo-crossover therapeutic trial. *Journal of the American Academy of Child and Adolescent Psychiatry, 24*, 617–629.

Hurt, R. D., Sachs, D. P. L., Glover, E. D., Offord, K. P., Johnston, J. A., Dale, L. C., Khayrallah, M. A., Schroeder, D. R., Glover, P. N., Sullivan, C. R., Croghan, I. T., & Sullivan, P. M. (1997). A comparison of sustained-release bupropion and placebo for smoking cessation. *New England Journal of Medicine, 337*, 1195–1202.

Jacobvitz, D., Srouge, L. A., Stewart, M., & Leffert, N. (1990). Treatment of attentional and hyperactivity problems in children with sympathomimetic drugs: A comprehensive review. *Journal of the American Academy of Child and Adolescent Psychiatry, 29*, 677–688.

Jaffe, S. L. (1991). Intranasal abuse of prescribed methylphenidate by an alcohol and drug abusing adolescent with ADHD. *Journal of the American Academy of Child and Adolescent Psychiatry, 30*, 773–775.

Jensen, P., Kettle, L., Roper, M., Sloan, M., Dulcan, M., Hoven, C., Bird, H., Bauermeister, J., & Payne, J. (1999). Are stimulants overprescribed? Treatment of ADHD in four U.S. Communities. *Journal of the American Academy of Child and Adolescent Psychiatry, 38,* 797–804.

Kafantaris, V., Campbell, M., Padron-Gayol, M. V., Small, A. M., Locascio, J. J., & Rosenberg, C. R. (1992). Carbamazepine in hospitalized aggressive conduct disorder children: An open pilot study. *Psychopharmacology Bulletin, 28,* 193–199.

Kemph, J. P., DeVane, C. L., Levin, G. M., Jarecke, R., & Miller, R. L. (1993). Treatment of aggressive children with clonidine: Results of an open pilot study. *Journal of the American Academy of Child and Adolescent Psychiatry, 32,* 577–581.

Klein, R. G. (1991). Thioridazine effects on the cognitive performance of children with attention-deficit hyperactivity disorder. *Journal of Child & Adolescent Psychopharmacology, 1,* 263–270.

Klein, R. G., Abikoff, H., Barkley, R. A., Campbell, M., Leckman, J. F., Ryan, N. D., Solanto, M. V., & Whalen, C. K. (1994). Clinical trials in children and adolescents. In R. F. Prien & D. S. Robinson (Eds.), *Clinical evaluation of psychotropic drugs: Principles and guidelines* (pp. 501–546). New York: Raven.

Klein, R., Abikoff, H., Klass, E., Ganales, D., Seese, L., & Pollack, S. (1997). Clinical efficacy of methylphenidate in conduct disorder with and without attention deficit hyperactivity disorder. *Archives of General Psychiatry, 54,* 1073–1080.

Kowatch, R. A., Suppes, T., Gilfillan, S. K., Fuentes, R. M., Grannemann, B. D., & Emslie, G. J. (1995). Clozapine treatment of children and adolescents with bipolar disorder and schizophrenia: A clinical case series. *Journal of Child & Adolescent Psychopharmacology, 5,* 241–253.

Kranzler, H. R., Amin, H., Modesto-Lowe, V., & Oncken, C. (1999). Pharmacologic treatments for drug and alcohol dependence. *Psychiatric Clinics of North America, 22,* 401–423.

Kratochvil, C., Heiligenstein, J. H., Dittmann, R., Spencer, T., Biederman, J., Werncke, J., Newcorn, J., Casat, C., Milton, D., & Michelson, D. (2002). *Atomoxetine and methyphenidate treatment in ADHD children: A randomized, open-label trial.* Poster session presented at annual meeting of AAACAP, Honolulu, HI.

Kumra, S., Jacobsen, L. K., Lenane, M., Karp, B. I., Frazier, J. A., Smith, A. K., Bedwell, J., Lee, P., Malanga, C. G., Hamburger, S., & Rapoport, J. L. (1998). Childhood-onset schizophrenia: An open-label study of olanzapine in adolescents. *Journal of the American Academy of Child and Adolescent Psychiatry, 37,* 377–385.

Kutcher, S. (2000). Practical clinical issues regarding child and adolescent psychopharmacology. *Child and Adolescent Psychiatric Clinics of North America, 9,* 245–260.

Lahey, B. B., McBurnett, K., Lober, R., & Hart, E. L. (1995). Psychobiology of conduct disorder. In G. P. Scholevar (Ed.), *Conduct disorder in children and adolescents: Assessments and Interventions* (pp. 27–44). Washington, DC: American Psychiatric Press.

Lang, C., & Remington, D. (1994). Treatment with propranolol of severe self-injurious behavior in a blind, deaf, and retarded adolescent. *Journal of the American Academy of Child and Adolescent Psychiatry, 33,* 265–269.

Langer, D. H., Sweeney, K. P., Bartenbach, D. E., Davis, P. M., & Menander, K. B. (1986). Evidence of lack of abuse or dependence following pemoline treatment: Results of a retrospective survey. *Drug and Alcohol Dependence, 17,* 213–227.

Loeber, R., Burke, J. D., Lahey, B. B., Winters, A., & Zera, M. (2000). Oppositional defiant and conduct disorder: A review of the past 10 years: Part I. *Journal of the American Academy of Child Psychiatry, 39,* 1468–1484.

Loeber, R., & Farrington, D. P. (Eds.). (1998). *Serious and violent juvenile offenders: Risk factors and successful interventions.* Thousand Oaks, CA: Sage.

Loeber, R., Farrington, D. P., & Waschbusch, D. A. (1998). Serious and violent juvenile offenders. In R. Loeber & D. P. Farrington (Eds.), *Serious and violent juvenile offenders: Risk factors and successful interventions* (pp. 13–29). Thousand Oaks, CA: Sage.

Loeber, R., & Stouthamer-Loeber, M. (1998). Development of juvenile aggression and violence: Some common misconceptions and controversies. *American Psychologist, 53,* 242–259.

Lombroso, P. J., Scahill, L., King, R. A., Lynch, K. A., Cappell, P. B., Peterson, B. S., McDougle, C. J., & Leckman, J. F. (1995). Risperidone treatment of children and adolescents with chronic tic disorders: A preliminary report. *Journal of the American Academy of Child and Adolescent Psychiatry, 34*, 1147–1152.

Loney, J., & Milich, R. (1982). Hyperactivity, inattention, and aggression in clinical practice. *Advances in Developmental and Behavioral Pediatrics, 3*, 113–147.

Lyons, M. J., True, W. R., Eisen, S. A., Goldberg, J., Meyer, J. M., Farone, S. V., Eaves, L. J., & Tsuang, M. T. (1995). Differential heriditability of adult and juvenile trait. *Archives of General Psychiatry, 52*, 906–915.

Malone, R. P., & Simpson, G. M. (1998). Use of placebos in clinical trials involving children and adolescents. *Psychiatric Service, 49*, 1413–1414.

Maoz, G., Stein, D., Meged, S., Kurzman, L., Levine, J., Valevski, A., Aviv, A., Sirota, P., Kraus, R., Weizman, A., & Berger, B. D. (2000). The antiaggressive action of combined haloperidol-propranolol treatment in schizophrenia. *European Psychologist, 5*, 312–325.

Marriage, K., Fine, S., Moretti, M., & Haley, G. (1986). Relationship between depression and conduct disorder in children and adolescents. *Journal of the American Academy of Child Psychiatry, 25*, 687–691.

Matochik, J., Nordahl, T., Gross, M., Semple, M., King, A., Cohen, R., & Zametkin, A. (1993). Effects of acute stimulant medication on cerebral metabolism in adults with hyperactivity. *Neuropsychopharmacology, 8*, 377–386.

McMaster University Evidence-Based Practice Center. (1998). The treatment of attention-deficit/hyperactivity disorder: An evidence report (Contract 290–97–0017). Washington, DC: Agency for Health Care Policy and Research.

Miczek, K. A., & Winslow, J. T. (1987). Psychopharmacological research on aggressive behavior. In A. J. Greenshaw & C. T. Dourish (Eds.), *Experimental psychopharmacology: Contemporary neuroscience* (pp. 27–114). Clifton, NJ: Humana Press.

Molina, B., Pelham, W. E., & Roth, J. (1999, June). *Stimulant medication and substance use by adolescents with a childhood history of ADHD.* Poster session presented at the biennial meeting of the International Society for Research on Child and Adolescent Psychopathology, Barcelona, Spain.

MTA Cooperative Group. (1999a). 14-month randomized clinical trial of treatment strategies for attention deficit hyperactivity disorder. *Archives of General Psychiatry, 56*, 1073–1086.

MTA Cooperative Group. (1999b). Moderators and mediators of treatment response for children with ADHD: The MTA Study. *Archives of General Psychiatry, 56*, 1088–1096.

Murphy, D. A., Pelham, W. E., & Lang, A. R. (1986, August). *Methylphenidate effects on aggressiveness in ADD and ADD/CD children.* Paper presented at the annual meeting of the American Psychological Association, Washington, DC.

Neuroleptic-related dyskinesias in autistic children: A prospective, longitudinal study. *Journal of the American Academy of Child and Adolescent Psychiatry, 36*, 835–843.

Newcorn, J. H., & Halperin, J. M. (1994). Comorbidity among disruptive behavior disorders: Impact on severity, impairment, and response to treatment. *Child and Adolescent Psychiatry Clinics of North America 3*, 227–252.

Offord, D. R., Boyle, M. H., & Racine, Y. (1989). Ontario Child Health Study: Correlates of disorder. *Journal of the American Academy of Child Psychiatry, 28*, 856–860.

Pappadopulos, E., & MacIntyre, J. (2001, June). *Developing best practice medication guidelines for child and adolescent psychiatric inpatients.* New York State Office of Mental Health: Best Practices Conference, New York.

Pataki, C. S., Carlson, G. A., Kelly, K. L., Rapport, M. D., & Biancaniello, T. M. (1993). Side effects of methylphenidate and desipramine alone and in combination in children. *Journal of the American Academy of Child and Adolescent Psychiatry 32*, 1065–1072.

Pelco, L. E., Kissel, R. C., Parrish, J. M., & Miltenberger, R. G. (1987). Behavioral management of oral medication administration difficulties among children: A review of literature with case illustrations. *Developmental and Behavioral Pediatrics, 8*, 90–96.

Pelham, W. E. (1985). The effects of stimulant drugs on learning and achievement in hyperactive and learning disabled children. In J. K. Torgesen & B. Wong (Eds.), *Psychological and educational perspectives on learning disabilities* (pp. 259–295). New York: Academic.

Pelham, W. E., & Hoza, J. (1987). Behavioral assessment of psychostimulant effects on ADD children in a summer day treatment program. *Advances in Behavioral Assessment of Children and Families, 3,* 3–34.

Pelham, W. E., Swanson, J., Furman, M., & Schwindt, H. (1995). Pemoline effects of Children with ADHD: A time-response by dose-response analysis on classroom measures. *Journal of the American Academy of Child and Adolescent Psychiatry, 34,* 1504–1513.

Pliska, S. R., McCracken, J. T., & Maas, J. W. (1996). Catecholamines in attention-deficit hyperactivity disorder: Current perspectives. *Journal of the American Academy of Child and Adolescent Psychiatry, 35,* 264–272.

Popper, C. W. (1995). Combining methylphenidate and clonidine: Pharmacologic questions and news reports about sudden death. *Journal of Child & Adolescent Psychopharmacology, 5,* 157–166.

Popper, C. W. (2000). Pharmacologic alternatives to psychostimulants for the treatment of attention-deficit/hyperactivity disorder. *Child and Adolescent Psychiatric Clinics of North America, 9,* 605–646.

Popper, C. W., & Zimnitzky, B. (1995). Sudden death putatively related to desipramine treatment in youth: A fifth case and a review of speculative mechanisms. *Journal of Child and Adolescent Psychopharmacology, 5,* 283–300.

Potenza, M. N., Holmes, J. P., Kanes, S. J., & McDougle, C. J. (1999). Olanzapine treatment of children, adolescents, and adults with pervasive developmental disorders: An open-label pilot study. *Journal of Clinical Psychopharmacology, 19,* 37–44.

Poyurovsky, M., Halperin, E., Enoch, D., Schneidman, M., & Weizman, A. (1995). Fluvoxamine treatment of compulsivity, impulsivity, and aggression. *American Journal of Psychiatry, 152,* 1688–1689.

Quinn, P. O., & Rapoport, J. L. (1975). One-year follow-up of hyperactive boys treated with imipramine or methylphenidate. *American Journal of Psychiatry, 132,* 241–245.

Rabinowitz, J., Avnon, M., & Rosenberg, V. (1996). Effect of clozapine on physical and verbal aggression. *Schizophrenia Research, 22,* 249–255.

Raine, A. (1993). *The psychopathology of crime, criminal behavior as a clinical disorder.* San Diego, CA: Academic.

Raine, A., Venables, P. H., & Williams, M. (1995). High autonomic arousal and electrodermal orienting at age 15 years as protective factors against criminal behavior at age 29 years. *American Journal of Psychiatry, 152,* 1595–1600.

Rapoport, J. L., Quinn, P. O., Bradbard, G., Riddle, K. D., & Brooks, E. (1974). Imipramine and methylphenidate treatments of hyperactive boys. A double-blind comparison. *Archives of General Psychiatry, 30,* 789–793.

Rapport, M. (1995). Attention-deficit hyperactivity disorder. In M. Hersen & R. T. Ammerman (Eds.), *Advanced abnormal child psychology* (pp. 353–373). Hillsdale, NJ: Lawrence Erlbaum Associates, Inc.

Rapport, M., Carlson, G., Kelly, K., & Pataki, C. (1993). Methylphenidate and desipramine in hospitalized children. I. Separate and combined effects on cognitive function. *Journal of the American Academy of Child and Adolescent Psychiatry, 32,* 333–342.

Rapport, M. D., DuPaul, G. J., Stoner, G., & Jones, J. T. (1986). Comparing classroom and clinic measures of attention deficit disorder: Differential, idiosyncratic, and dose-response effects of methylphenidate. *Journal of Consulting and Clinical Psychology, 54,* 334–341.

Remschmidt, H., Hennighausen, K., Clement, H. W., Heiser, P., & Schulz, E. (2000). Atypical neuroleptics in child and adolescent psychiatry. *European Child and Adolescent Psychiatry, 9*(suppl 1), I/1–I/19.

Richardson, M. A., Haugland, G., & Craig, T. J. (1991). Neuroleptic use, parkinsonian symptoms, tardive dyskinesia, and associated factors in child and adolescent psychiatric patients. *American Journal of Psychiatry, 148,* 1322–1328.

Richters, J. E., Arnold, L. E., Jensen, P. S., Abikoff, H., Conners, C. K., Greenhill, L. L., Hechtman, L., Hinshaw, S. P., Pelham, W. E., & Swanson, J. M. (1995). NIMH Collaborative Multisite Multi-modal Treatment Study of Children with ADHD: I. Background and rationale. *Journal of the American Academy of Child and Adolescent Psychiatry, 34,* 987–1000.

Riddle, M. A., Geller, B., & Ryan, N. (1993). Another sudden death treated with desipramine. *Journal of the American Academy of Child and Adolescent Psychiatry, 32,* 792–797.

Riddle, M. A., Hardin, M. T., Soo, C. C., Woolston, J. L., et al. (1988). Desipramine treatment of boys with attention-deficit hyperactivity disorder and tics: Preliminary clinical experience. *Journal of the American Academy of Child and Adolescent Psychiatry, 27,* 811–814.

Riddle, M. A., Kastelic, E. A., & Frosch, E. (2001). Pediatric psychopharmacology. *Journal of Child Psychology & Psychiatry & Allied Disciplines, 42,* 73–90.

Riddle, M. A., Nelson, J. C., Kleinman, C. S., Rasmusson, A., et al. (1991). Sudden death in children receiving Norpramin(R): A review of three reported cases and commentary. *Journal of the American Academy of Child and Adolescent Psychiatry, 30,* 104–108.

Riggs, P. D. (1998). Clinical approach to treatment of ADHD in adolescents with substance use disorders and conduct disorder. *Journal of the American Academy of Child and Adolescent Psychiatry, 37,* 331–332.

Riggs, P. D., Mikulich, S. K., Coffman, L. M., & Crowley, T. J. (1997). Fluoxetine in drug-dependent delinquents with major depression: An open trial. *Journal of Child and Adolescent Psychopharmacology, 7,* 87–95.

Riggs, P. D., Thompson, L. L., Mikulich, S. K., Whitmore, E. A., & Crowley, T. J. (1996). An open trial of pemoline in drug dependent delinquents with attention-deficit hyperactivity disorder. *Journal of the American Academy of Child and Adolescent Psychiatry, 35,* 1018–1024.

Ryan, N. D. (1992). The pharmacologic treatment of child and adolescent depression. *Psychiatric Clinics of North America, 15,* 29–40.

Safer, D. J., Zito, J. M., & Gardner, J. F. (2001). Pemoline hepatotoxicity and postmarketing surveillance. *Journal of the American Academy of Child Psychiatry, 40,* 622–629.

Sallee, F., Stiller, R., & Perel, J. (1992). Pharmacodynamics of pemoline in attention deficit disorder with hyperactivity. *Journal of the American Academy of Child and Adolescent Psychiatry, 31,* 244–251.

Sallee, F. R., Stiller, R. L., & Perel, M. M., et al. (1989). Pemoline-induced abnormal involuntary movements. *Journal of Clinical Psychopharmacology, 9,* 125–129.

Sallee, F. R., Stiller, R., Perel, J., & Bates, T. (1985). Oral pemoline kinetics in hyperactive children. *Clinical Pharmacological Therapy, 37,* 606–609.

Saul, R. C. (1985). Nortriptyline in attention deficit disorder. *Clinical Neuropharmacology, 8,* 382–384.

Schachar, R., & Tannock, R. (1993). Childhood hyperactivity and psychostimulants: A review of extended treatment studies. *Journal of Child and Adolescent Psychopharmacology, 3,* 81–97.

Schachar, R., Tannock, R., Cunningham, C., & Corkum, P. (1997). Behavioral, situational, and temporal effects of treatment of ADHD with methylphenidate. *Journal of the American Academy of Child and Adolescent Psychiatry, 36,* 754–763.

Schmidt, K., Solanto, M. V., & Sanchez, M. (1984). The effect of stimulant medication of academic performance, in the context of multimodal treatment, in attention deficit disorders with hyperactivity. *Journal of Clinical Psychopharmacology, 4,* 100–103.

Schreier, H. A. (1998). Risperidone for young children with mood disorders and aggressive behavior. *Journal of Child & Adolescent Psychopharmacology, 8,* 49–59.

Settle, E. C. (1998). Bupropion sustained release, side effect profile. *Journal of Clinical Psychiatry, 59,* 32–36.

Sikich, L. (2001, May). Comparative use of olanzapine and risperidone in psychotic youth. *154th Annual Meeting of the American Psychiatric Association, 326.*

Silva, R. R., Campbell, M., Golden, R. R., Small, A. M., Pataki, C. S., & Rosenberg, C. R. (1992). Side effects associated with lithium and placebo administration in aggressive children. *Psychopharmacological Bulletin, 28,* 319–326.

Simeon, J. G., Ferguson, H. B., & Fleet, J. V. W. (1986). Bupropion effects in attention deficit and conduct disorders. *Canadian Journal of Psychiatry, 31,* 581–585.

Smith, B. H., Pelham, W. E., Gnagy, E., & Yudell, R. S. (1998). Equivalent effects of stimulant treatment for attention-deficit hyperactivity disorder during childhood and adolescence. *Journal of the American Academy of Child and Adolescent Psychiatry, 37,* 314–321.

Solhkhah, R., & Wilens, T. E. (1998). Pharmacotherapy of adolescent AOD use disorders. *Alcohol Health & Research World, 22,* 122–126.

Spencer, T., Biederman, J., Harding, M., Faraone, S., & Wilens, T. (1996). Growth deficits in ADHD children revisited: Evidence for disorder related growth delays. *Journal of the American Academy of Child and Adolescent Psychiatry, 35,* 1460–1467.

Spencer, T., Biederman, J., Wilens, T., Harding, M., O'Donnell, D., & Griffin, S. (1996). Pharmacotherapy of attention-deficit hyperactivity disorder across the life cycle. *Journal of the American Academy of Child and Adolescent Psychiatry, 35,* 409–432.

Spencer, T., Biederman, J., Kerman, K., Steingard, R., et al. (1993). Desipramine treatment of children with attention-deficit hyperactivity disorder and tic disorder or Tourette's syndrome. *Journal of the American Academy of Child and Adolescent Psychiatry, 32,* 354–360.

Spencer, T., Biederman, J., Wilens, T., Steingard, R., et al. (1993). Nortriptyline treatment of children with attention-deficit hyperactivity disorder and tic disorder or Tourette's syndrome. *Journal of the American Academy of Child and Adolescent Psychiatry, 32,* 205–210.

Steingard, R., Biederman, J., Spencer, T., Wilens, T., & Gonzalez, A. (1993). Comparison of clonidine response in the treatment of attention-deficit hyperactivity disorder with and without comorbid tic disorders. *Journal of the American Academy of Child and Adolescent Psychiatry, 32,* 350–353.

Stoner, G., Carey, S. P., Ikeda, M. J., & Shinn, M. R. (1994). The utility of curriculum-based measurement for evaluating the effects of methylphenidate on academic performance. *Journal of Applied Behavioral Analysis, 27,* 101–113.

Swanson, J. (1993). Effect of stimulant medication on hyperactive children: A review of reviews. *Exceptional Child, 60,* 154–162.

Swanson, J., Lerner, M., & Williams, L. (1995). More frequent diagnosis of attention deficit-hyperactivity disorder. *New England Journal of Medicine, 333,* 944–944.

Swanson, J., & Volkow, N. (2000). Pharmacodynamics and pharmacokinetics of stimulants in AD/HD. In M. Solanto & X. Castellanos (Eds.), *The neuropharmacology of psychostimulant drugs: Implications for AD/HD* (pp. 101–125). New York: Oxford University Press.

Szatmari, P., Offord, D. R., & Boyle, M. H. (1989). Ontario Child Health Study: Prevalence of attention deficit disorder with hyperactivity. *Journal of Child Psychology and Psychiatry, 30,* 219–230.

Thurber, S., & Walker, C. (1983). Medication and hyperactivity: A meta-analysis. *Journal of General Psychiatry, 108,* 79–86.

Varley, C. K., & McClellan, J. (1997). Case study: Two additional sudden deaths with tricyclic antidepressants. *Journal of the American Academy of Child and Adolescent Psychiatry, 36,* 390–394.

Vitiello, B., Behar, D., Hunt, J., Stoff, D., & Ricciuti, A. J. (1990). Subtyping aggression in children and adolescents. *Journal of Neuropsychiatry and Clinical Neurosciences, 2,* 189–192.

Vitiello, B., Ricciuti, A. J., & Behar, D. (1987). P.R.N. medications in child state hospital inpatients. *Journal of Clinical Psychiatry, 48,* 351–354.

Volkow, N., Wang, G., Fowler, J., Gatley, S., Logan, J., Ding, Y., Hitzemann, R., & Pappas, N. (1998). Dopamine transporter occupancies in the human brain induced by therapeutic doses of oral methylphenidate. *American Journal of Psychiatry, 155,* 1325–1331.

Waizer, J., Hoffman, S. P., Polizos, P., & Engelhardt, D. M. (1974). Outpatient treatment of hyperactive school children with imipramine. *American Journal of Psychiatry, 131,* 587–591.

Walkup, J. T. (1995). Clinical decision making in child and adolescent psychopharmacology. *Child & Adolescent Psychiatric Clinics of North America, 4,* 23–40.

Weiss, G., & Hechtman, L. T. (1993). *Hyperactive children grown up: ADHD in children, adolescents, and adults* (2nd ed.). New York: Guilford Press.

Werry, J. S., Aman, M. G., & Diamond, E. (1980). Imipramine and methylphenidate in hyperactive children. *Journal of Child Psychology & Psychiatry & Allied Disciplines, 21,* 27–35.

Whalen, C. K., & Henker, B. (1991). Social impact of stimulant treatment for hyperactive children. *Journal of Learning Disabilities, 24,* 231–241.

Whitaker, A., & Rao, U. (1992). Neuroleptics in pediatric psychiatry. *Psychiatric Clinics of North America, 15,* 243–277.

Wilens, T. E., Biederman, J., Baldessarini, R. J., Geller, B., et al. (1996). Cardiovascular effects of therapeutic doses of tricyclic antidepressants in children and adolescents. *Journal of the American Academy of Child and Adolescent Psychiatry, 35,* 1491–1501.

Wilens, T. E., Biederman, J., Geist, D. E., Steingard, R., et al. (1993). Nortriptyline in the treatment of ADHD: A chart review of 58 cases. *Journal of the American Academy of Child and Adolescent Psychiatry, 32,* 343–349.

Wilens, T. E., Biederman, J., & Spencer, T. J. (1994). Clonidine for sleep disturbances associated with attention-deficit hyperactivity disorder. *Journal of the American Academy of Child and Adolescent Psychiatry, 33,* 424–426.

Wilens, T. E., Spencer, T. J., & Biederman, J. (1997). Sudden (un)explained death. *Journal of the American Academy of Child and Adolescent Psychiatry, 36,* 1487–1488.

Zametkin, A. et al. (1985). Treatment of hyperactive children with monoamine oxidase inhibitors: I. Clinical efficacy. *Archives of General Psychiatry, 42,* 962–966.

Zametkin, A. J., Nordahl, T. E., Gross, M., King, A. C., Semple, W. E., Rumsey, J., Hamburger, S., & Cohen, R. M. (1990). Cerebral glucose metabolism in adults with hyperactivity of childhood onset. *New England Journal of Medicine, 323,* 1361–1366.

Zito, J. M., Safer, D. J., dosReis, S., Gardner, J. F., Boles, M., & Lynch, F. (2000). Trends in the prescribing of psychotropic medications to preschoolers. *Journal of the American Medical Association, 283,* 1025–1030.

Zito, J. M., Safer, D. J., Riddle, M. A., Johnson, R. E., Speedie, S. M., & Fox, M. (1998). Prevalence variations in psychotropic treatment of children. *Journal of Child & Adolescent Psychopharmacology, 8,* 99–105.

OUTSTANDING ISSUES

Epilogue

Cecilia A. Essau

Westfälische Wilhelms-Universität, Münster, Germany

This volume has brought together the state-of-the-art knowledge on the nature and the associated features (e.g., course, comorbidity, risk factors) of conduct disorder (CD) and oppositional defiant disorder (ODD). The introduction of advanced research strategies in epidemiological, psychosocial, family-genetic, biological, and treatment studies has led to our increasing knowledge about the nature of CD and ODD. Despite these progresses, there are numerous unresolved issues and challenges that need attention in future studies. In this chapter, progress and unresolved issues related to CD and ODD in children and adolescents are discussed. I focus my discussion on major aspects of CD and ODD: classification and assessment, the epidemiology, comorbidity and course, risk factors, and prevention and intervention. In discussing some of the unresolved issues, some recommendations for further research are also presented.

CLASSIFICATION ISSUES

As discussed in chapter 1 (this volume), two classification systems commonly used to study CD and ODD are the *Diagnostic and Statistical Manual of Mental Disorders (DSM)* and the *International Classification of Diseases (ICD)*. Although both the *DSM–IV* (American Psychiatric Association, 1994) and *ICD–10* (World Health Organization, 1992) represent major advances than their previous versions, their use is not without critics. The *DSM* and *ICD* represent a categorical system in which the children either meet or do not meet the criteria for CD or ODD or other disorders. However, knowing that the children have CD or ODD may not necessarily tell the whole story about these children and their problems. Although assigning the child with a CD/ODD or other diagnoses would ease communication among clinicians or other health professionals, such labeling practice may lead to stigmatization.

The thresholds of symptomatology in the *DSM–IV* used to differentiate between the presence or absence of CD and ODD have been done arbitrarily, as highlighted by changes made from *DSM–III* (American Psychiatric Association, 1980) to *DSM–IV*. For example, to meet the criteria for ODD, *DSM–III* lists five criteria for which two are required, *DSM–III–R* (American Psychiatric Association, 1987) lists nine criteria for which five are required, and in *DSM–IV*, eight criteria for which four are needed. Furthermore, the criterion at which the behavior (i.e., frequency, severity, or intensity) is sufficient to be considered as a symptom remain unclear. This lack of clarity makes it difficult to justify the criteria for delineating CD or ODD. Further complexity is caused by the fact that some children and adolescents fail to meet diagnostic criteria for CD or ODD, but they still may have some impairments in their daily functioning and are at risk for negative outcomes in adulthood. As shown by Angold, Costello, Farmer, Burns, and Erkanli (1999), some children who are below threshold for CD also have serious problems in need of treatment. Such finding raised the question to which of our diagnostic categories or assessments evaluate the clinical significance of CD. Thus, instead of having information whether or not CD is present or absent, it may be more useful to identify children with a specific number of symptoms and to examine the cutoff point that may best predict a certain course (e.g., antisocial personality disorder) or impairment (e.g., frequent job loss; Kazdin, 1994).

DSM–IV only lists symptoms of CD and ODD that are needed to make the diagnosis and does not specify the sources of information (e.g., direct observation, interviewing the child or parents or teachers) to be used for judging whether a child meets the criteria. All symptoms are given equal weight in making a diagnosis and based on a simple count, a child may be classified as having a CD or ODD. To a certain extent this notion of unidimensionality and symptom equivalency can defy common sense. For example, why should "often stays out at night despite parental prohibitions" and "has deliberately engaged in fire setting with the intention of causing serious damage" be given the same weight in a diagnosis of CD? To make the diagnosis, some symptoms must have caused impairment; however, which symptoms are not specified, nor are criteria of impairment defined. In addition, there are grounds for concern regarding the fundamental nature of conduct problems, namely, whether they should best be defined as social problems or psychiatric disorders (Jensen et al., 1993).

The developmental guidelines given in our classification systems, especially with respect to CD and ODD, are vague. To be considered a symptom, a behavior has to occur more often than is typical in children of the same age. Because many children go through a period of noncompliance and defiant behavior, our classification systems provide little guideline on how to distinguish between ODD and hard to manage but age-appropriate defiance (Campbell, 1990). A related issue is whether there are specific subclusters of CD symptoms for different age groups. Because CD and ODD symptoms may be manifested differently by children in different developmental stages (see chap. 1, this volume), it may be useful to vary the symptoms required to meet the diagnosis by age and gender. As argued by Greenberg, Speltz, DeKlyen, and Jones (2001), meaningful subtypes of ODD may be discernible on the basis of symptom clusters. For example, symptoms related to affective reactivity (e.g., touchy or easily annoyed, resentful, spiteful/vindictive) are less common among preschoolers with ODD than disruptive ODD symptoms (tantrums, noncompliance), but the former are more predictive of diagnostic continuity (Speltz, McClellan, DeKlyen, & Jones, 1999).

Our classification systems stress the importance of an age-of-onset specifier to the CD diagnosis. For example, the *DSM–IV* CD contains a childhood-onset subtype and an adolescent-onset subtype, which are hypothesized to have different developmental pathways and prognosis (Moffitt, 1993). Although previous studies have shown the onset data to be important in predicting the course and outcome of CD (chap. 3, this volume), future studies need to examine the usefulness of such subtyping, especially in the area of intervention. Another concern is the findings that parents and their children are equally unreliable in their reporting of age-of-onset information (Angold, Erkanli, & Rutter, 1996). Therefore, in the absence of a memory aid that could ease recall of past symptoms, the information on the age of onset should be interpreted with caution.

Little attempt has been made to define criteria for CD and ODD in children from different cultural backgrounds. This is surprising because children in different cultures (e.g., in most Asian countries) are expected to submit and conform to parental and teacher authority at a very early age (Essau, 1992); such practice may have implications for deciding on a threshold for ODD. Therefore, an area of future research would be to examine cultural differences in the definition of CD and ODD using culturally sensitive instruments or procedures. This would involve the incorporation of community norms and contexts and adult expectation for the child's behavior (Cummings, Davies, & Campbell, 2000).

ASSESSMENT ISSUES

Among the main aims of assessment are to specify the presence or absence and the severity of symptoms and to monitor the impact of treatment for CD and ODD. However, to fulfill these functions, the instruments used to assess CD and ODD need to be reliable and valid. Although the issues related to unreliability have greatly been reduced by using highly structured diagnostic interview schedules, some important information may be lost, especially in interview schedules in which the items are "gated" (i.e., if the essential symptoms are answered negatively, none of the subsequent symptoms will be asked and the interview will skip to the next diagnostic category). Highly structured diagnostic interviews generally take longer to administer compared to unstructured interviews or the use of self-report questionnaires. For example, the average administration time for most diagnostic interviews (e.g., Diagnostic Interview Schedule for Children; Piacentini, Shaffer, & Fischer, 1993) is about 90 min. Given children's restricted attention span, the degree to which the children can concentrate on the questions being asked and consequently the reliability of the answer given is questionable. Additionally, less than 30% of the 9- to 11-year-old children understood questions related to the time frame, length of symptoms, and frequency of behavior and emotion (Piacentini et al., 1993).

To have a comprehensive picture of the children's problem, data needs to be gathered using multiple methods (e.g., behavioral rating scales, observation) completed by multiple informants (e.g., parents, teachers, and children) about the child's behavior in different settings (e.g., home, school; Kamphaus & Frick, 1996). However, the different sources of information usually show low to moderate correlations with each other (Kazdin, 1995). The challenge is how best to interpret this low level of agreement and consequently decide on which information from which informants to rely on (see chaps. 1 and 2, this volume). Authors differ in their view as to which information should be used. Angold et al. (1987), for example, recommended that the children's report be used to judge the accuracy of the adult's report. By contrast, Puig-Antich and Gittelmann (1982) recommended the use of the adult's report. Therefore, one of the major task of future studies is to define the optimal procedures for dealing with the discrepancies between informants and to determine how to best weigh various informants and data sources according to the child's age, gender, and behavior (Jensen et al., 1993). The value of different informants and data sources in the prediction of long-term outcome of CD and ODD also need to be explored.

Some symptoms of CD such as lying, destroying property, and fighting tend to wax and wave over the course of childhood (Kazdin, 1995). This implies that the evaluation of similar symptoms across the age groups may require different measures or changes of the same measures. However, any changes of assessment procedures may influence the results and conclusions because the same items may be interpreted differently by youths at different developmental stages. Also in assessing age appropriateness versus clinical relevance of children's behavior, we need to know age appropriateness of the behavior. Yet what are age-appropriate behaviors, and how do we operationalize them? In this respect, a strong knowledge on the milestones of normal development may be useful. At the same time, however, we need to recognize the heterogeneity of the child's development.

Given the presence of high comorbid disorders in children with CD and ODD (see chap. 2, this volume), our assessment needs to deal with the comorbidity issues to enable us to obtain information on the different patterns of comorbid disorders, their temporal sequence, and their impact. Such information is not only useful for designing treatment plans but may give hints about the progression of one disorder to the next.

EPIDEMIOLOGICAL ISSUES

Despite the cost and the difficulty of conducting well-designed epidemiological studies in the general population, such studies are important because they provide data on the prevalence and correlates of disorders, which help to generate hypotheses about etiology. Recent years have witnessed much progress in child epidemiology (Essau, Feehan, & Üstun, 1997; Essau, Petermann, & Feehan, 1997). To a large extent, this progress has been connected with the introduction of *DSM–III* with its specific diagnostic criteria, leading to the development of reliable diagnostic assessment instruments.

Although the widespread use of *DSM* or *ICD* in interview-based studies is often thought to solve the problem of diagnostic certainty or caseness, this is far from reality. Even if comparative criteria have been used in many recent studies, the threshold for defining a case varied widely across studies. Some have based their decision on the number of symptoms (McGee, Williams, Anderson, McKenzie-Parnell, & Silva, 1990), need for treatment (Kashani et al., 1987), and social impairment (Bird et al., 1990). Studies also differ in the way in which they combine information from different sources and in the time frame covered (i.e., lifetime, 6 months). Thus, when different rates of CD and ODD are obtained in different studies, it remains an unresolved issue whether these findings reflected true differences or if they simply reflect difference in the methodology used.

The kind of sampling method used to study the target populations is another issue that deserves further attention. For example, sampling from schools may underestimate the rate of CD and ODD because school dropouts and nonattenders will be omitted. Studies that use only one randomly selected child per household (e.g., Bird et al., 1988) may also underestimate the prevalence of these disorders because they generally run in siblings (see chap. 6, this volume). Because sampling issues in child and adolescent epidemiology has rarely been tackled, we know little about the impact in the way participants are identified, enlisted, or maintained in the sample on the prevalence of CD and ODD.

Comorbidity

The findings that CD and ODD co-occur significantly with various types of disorders (chap. 2, this volume) raises the question about the distinctness of the disorders as defined in our classification systems (Nottelmann & Jensen, 1999). Nevertheless, the frequent co-occurrence of CD and ODD with other disorders may have important consequences both from a clinical and research perspective. Clinically, the presence of comorbid disorders may make it difficult to specify which disorder needs to be treated first, and from a research point of view, the co-occurrence of disorder may lead to the misinterpretation of findings.

Despite this high comorbidity rate, its meaning for etiological and classification issues remains unclear. However, the negative impact of comorbid disorders in the clinical picture of CD and ODD is clear. To have a better understanding of comorbidity, future studies need to agree on the definition of comorbidity and the conceptual framework in studying this concept. The former would include the level of comorbidity, that is, whether comorbidity occurs at the symptom, syndrome, and diagnostic level. Another approach to enhance our understanding of comorbid disorders in CD and ODD is by examining the timing (age at onset) and the temporal sequencing of the disorders. Large prospective studies are needed to enable us to study the pattern of comorbid disorders (temporal sequencing of disorders, duration between the onset and offset of disorders) and the factors related to the onset and the duration of each disorder.

COURSE AND OUTCOME

One way to clarify the course and outcome of CD and ODD is to use longitudinal research designs in which children with these disorders are examined on multiple occasions over a period of time. By having repeated measurements over time, it is possible to track the pattern of continuity or change in CD and ODD and on how children change or remain the same over that period. Longitudinal data are also imperative for the identification of the processes that underlie the development of CD and ODD. Given these advantages, numerous longitudinal studies have been conducted in recent years, which has constituted a major methodological progress in this field (e.g., Pittsburgh Youth Study; see chap. 3, this volume). However, longitudinal studies also have some disadvantages, including their cost, logistical difficulty, and attrition problem. The attrition problem is of importance because it may potentially affect the representativeness of the longitudinal data. As reported by Boyle, Offord, Racine, and Catlin (1991), 20% to 30% of the probands who participated in longitudinal studies of childhood psychopathology are no longer available at a follow-up investigation. In this respect, we need to develop a strategy to motivate participants (e.g., sending of cards to the children during a particular event such as at Christmas or birthday) to stay in the longitudinal studies.

One of the major challenges of longitudinal research is to determine the interval of conducting the follow-up investigation. In the absence of some specific guideline, studies vary tremendously in this respect—ranging from 6 months to 18 years. Additionally, there is a lack of agreement on the type of indexes of course and outcome for CD and ODD. All of these together with the frequent changes in the diagnostic criteria for CD and ODD have made it difficult to compare findings across studies. In accordance to the *DSM–IV* general definition for psychiatric disorders, the indicators of course and outcome of CD/ODD should include the presence of CD/ODD symptoms or the presence of other disorders, psychosocial impairment, and health services utilization.

Some authors (e.g., Frick, in press) have argued that the developmental psychopathology approach may be the best method to study the course of CD because children can develop CD through different developmental pathways. This approach should shape the way future studies are conducted to enhance our knowledge of the causal processes related to CD (Richters, 1997) and implications for intervention because it suggests that the same intervention may not be appropriate for all children with CD (Frick, 1998, in press). Such effort may help us discover subgroups of children whose CD seems to have developed through different causal trajectories (Frick, in press).

CORRELATES AND RISK FACTORS

As shown in chapters 4 to 6 (this volume), several factors have been identified as risk factors for CD and ODD. Some of these factors include those that are intrinsic to the child and some that are present in the child's immediate and broad psychosocial context. The knowledge about risk factors is the critical point of departure for generating hypotheses about possible mechanisms. This knowledge is also needed to identify those at elevated risk so they can be targeted for prevention and intervention.

The problem with most studies is their cross-sectional design, which makes it difficult to determine causal link. Thus, the extent to which the association reflects cause or consequences of CD/ODD is inconclusive. Furthermore, no single factor seems sufficient to account for the development of CD/ODD. For example, in testing the effects of 13 risk factors on children's behavior problems, Liaw and Brooks-Gunn (1994) found that as the number of risk factors increased so did the incidence of behavior problems.

In the Rochester Longitudinal Study (Sameroff, Seifer, Barocas, Zax, & Greenspan, 1987), a multiple-risk index that comprised 10 risk factors (e.g., mother's psychological functioning, family socioeconomic status and minority status, family support, life events, and family size) significantly predicted children's social-emotional competence better than any single risk factor alone. Thus, future studies should develop multifactorial models to explain the etiology of CD.

Another unresolved issue is related to the fact that the selection of risk factors examined are generally without a strong theoretical basis (Greenberg et al., 2001). Most studies have focused on demographic and family status data such as the quality of parenting, nature of the parent–child relationship (Patterson, DeBaryshe, & Ramsey, 1989), and the child's temperament or cognitive ability. In most studies, equal weight has been given to risk factors and little attempt has been given to the relative contribution or overlap in these factors. Furthermore, given the heterogeneity in the etiology and form of CD (Richters, 1997), future research needs to develop a strategy to pinpoint the specificity of risk factors, the interactions between them, and their change over time (Jensen et al., 1993). This would involve simultaneous testing of competing models—for example, the use of twin studies to separate genetic from environmental factors (Jensen et al., 1993). Family epidemiologic studies can solve some of the problems of combining genetic and environmental factors (Jensen et al., 1993).

In addition to methodological problems associated with each risk factor examined, one needs to be cautious in interpreting and generalizing the existing results. There is a need to identify risk factors because factors tend to aggregate over time and contribute to CD and ODD (Kazdin & Kagan, 1994). However, the same risk factors do not necessary lead to CD and ODD in most people. It could be possible that a risk factor may interact with the person's characteristics such as age and gender. A challenge would be to identify the contribution of each factors as to how they may co-occur to produce CD. Additionally, some factors may produce their effects differently. For example, marital discord may influence the child directly through exposure of an adverse situation at home, or indirectly through interference in the parent's ability to provide the child with a consistent discipline. A future research direction should be to answer how and why risk factors work that lead to CD or ODD or other disorders. That is, we need to delineate the processes involve in the association between risk factor and CD/ODD.

Another issue is related to the impact of risk factors on treatment. Specifically, would certain combinations of risk domains be better treated by one means, whereas other sets of etiologic factors are treated with alternative interventions? The search for best treatments may depend on particular risk domain combinations; however, best treatments have generally been conceptualized in relation to individuals with specific disorders (i.e., without taking comorbid disorders into account) who are therefore assumed to share similar treatment needs (Greenberg et al., 2001). For example, behaviorally oriented parent training has been regarded as the treatment of choice for most children with conduct problems (Kazdin, 1997). Yet, as reported by Greenberg et al. (2001), 31% of the clinic-referred boys were not classified as high risk in the parenting practices domain; about half of these boys were found to have vulnerable child characteristics and family adversity. In such cases, interventions that aim more selectively at child deficits may be more effective than parent training. Studies testing the interventions that more closely match treatments to a particular risk or risk combination in children with conduct problems are needed.

Exposure to risk does not necessarily predict the occurrence of CD and ODD. In fact, there are many children, despite formidable risk, who are able to overcome adversity and do not meet the diagnosis of CD/ODD. In this respect, we need information on factors that protect the children who overcome adversity.

PREVENTION AND INTERVENTION

Despite progress made in the area of prevention (see chaps. 8 and 9, this volume), there are several challenges in the implementation and evaluation of prevention programs. The first issue is to determine in which developmental stage of the children to start with the program. Some authors have proposed the necessity of prevention before age 12 (Loeber & Farrington, 1995; Reid, 1993); however, the optimal period for prevention within this preadolescence period is unclear. The second issue is related to the strategies needed to prevent CD/ODD, given numerous risk factors of CD/ODD. This makes it difficult to pinpoint the specific risk factors that need to be the focus of prevention. In selected prevention programs, there is a need to be clear about how the at-risk children are defined. Another issue is related to putting the prevention program into practice. Whereas most programs have been conducted in schools, schools are often overburdened with academic curriculum demands. Adding a separate, multisession curriculum to prevent CD/ODD, in addition to the program to prevent, for example, substance abuse, would swamp the schools. Finally, little is known about the cost of running a prevention program. Therefore, an area of future research would be to provide cost–benefit analyses, specifically in terms of the cost of providing prevention compared to the reduction in cost of treatment for CD/ODD. It may also be worth investigating in future studies the role of health promotion strategies such as physical health promotion, the presence of high-quality day care and after-school care, positive parenting, and positive coping in the reduction of CD/ODD (Table E.1).

TABLE E.1
Strategies for the Promotion of Mental Health

Strategies	Specific Aims
Physical health promotion	Improve physical health in order to be resistant to fatigue and stress; participation in sport help to enhance self-esteem, develop skills, and foster relationship between youth and adults; self-discipline, a sense of responsibility and leadership
Day care and After-school care	Prevent children of working mothers from being alone in the afternoon after school; influence positive social, emotional, and intellectual outcomes
	Government contribution
	Subsidize high-quality day care that is widely available for all citizens from all social backgrounds at a modest fee; introduce longer paid maternal leaves for working mothers
Positive parenting	Focus on relationship building skills, enhancing family conversations and communication, increasing physical affection and quality time, and promoting shared problem solving between parent and child
Schoolwide programs and positive coping	Introduce age-appropriate activities that promote competence in athletic skills, academic skills, behavioral self-control, and social skills; introduce program to promote positive coping skills.

Recent years have also seen the development of several intervention programs for the treatment of CD/ODD (see chaps. 10–12, this volume). Most of these programs used cognitive-behavioral therapy that is either child-focused individual and group therapy or family-focused. Studies that have examined the effectiveness of these interventions have generally evidenced positive treatment effects, although little information is known why they work for some children but not for others. However, only a few treatments have met the criteria for empirically supported treatments as outlined by the clinical science divisions of the American Psychological Association. Furthermore, most treatment outcome studies have major limitations, including small samples, use of a waiting-list control instead of comparing the test intervention with alternative or placebo treatment, and the wide range of the children's age. Both the generalization of treatment across settings and the maintenance over time on ending the treatment have rarely been demonstrated. Additionally, most studies did not consider presence of comorbid disorders or the co-occurring family problems.

In addition to these methodological problems, almost all the outcome treatment studies have been conducted within the so-called research therapy, which was conducted in volunteers with some predetermined inclusion and exclusion criteria in psychology department clinics (Table E.2). Given differences between the real world of the clinic and the laboratory (Weisz, Donenberg, Han, & Weiss, 1995), we must be cautious in interpret-

TABLE E.2
Differences Between Research Therapy and Clinical Therapy

Research Therapy	Clinical Therapy
Diagnostic Status/Selection Criteria	
Have predetermined inclusion and exclusion criteria	Little, if any, predetermined inclusion and exclusion criteria
Less severe, rarely with comorbid disorders	More severe, mostly with comorbid disorders
Homogeneous groups	Heterogeneous groups
Treatment Setting/Therapist	
Treatment in school settings or in psychology department clinic or laboratory in university	Treatment in clinics or hospitals
Therapy is usually done by research assistant	Treated by clinicians
Mode of Treatment	
Highly structured being guided by treatment manual	Flexible, generally without treatment manual
Group therapy	Individual therapy
Brief and time limited, with predefined number of sessions	Longer duration
Single, focused treatment method	Eclectic, psychodynamic, general counseling

Note. Slightly modified from Weisz, Donenberg, Han, and Weiss (1995).

ing the findings of the research therapy. Differences in the approach used, and the severity and chronicity of CD/ODD seen in research and clinical therapy, make it difficult to compare findings obtained in these two types of studies. Therefore, treatments that are found effective for motivated parents and children may not prove to show the same effect when offered to families in community clinical settings.

With the introduction of managed care, which mandates time-limited therapies with proven effectiveness, we are expected to develop empirically supported treatments. Unfortunately, the criteria to determine whether the treatment is well-enough established to be considered as efficacious do not seen to match the reality of the world of the clinics.

Another challenge is how to reach those who need the help the most. A large proportion of children and adolescents with psychiatric disorders in the community do not receive the professional help they need (Essau, 2000). Even if the children start taking part in treatment, between 40% and 60% of families terminate the treatment prematurely (Kazdin, 1997). An important fact is that it is usually not the children themselves who decide that the behavior needs attention and consequently make the decision about referral, but an adult. Parent's likelihood to seek help for their children may be influenced by the extent to which the child's behavior is noticeable and bothersome, as well as by parents' mental health status and treatment history, family stress, and perceived benefits of treatment (Mash & Krahn, 1995). Other determinants of mental health services utilization include the severity and chronicity of CD/ODD, presence of comorbid disorders, psychosocial impairment, sociodemographic characteristics, and the availability of services, as well as the cost and mechanism of financing.

SUMMARY

Although much progress has been achieved in research in CD and ODD in children and adolescents, there are several issues that need to be resolved in the future. Some of the unresolved issues discussed in this chapter include the validity and reliability of criteria for CD and ODD among youths and the problem of little agreement in the information from different informants. How to deal with these disagreements remains unresolved. Other problems associated with assessment issues are those related to designing age-related questionnaires or interview schedules given the rapid and heterogeneous nature of development, and the unspecific influence of risk factors for CD, in that the risk factors usually found for CD (e.g., life events, parental psychopathology) have also been found for other disorders. Finally, the ultimate goal of research should ideally be the ability to cure or at least reduce the severity of the disorders and the associated impairment. In line with this mission, numerous prevention and intervention programs have been developed and empirically tested. Throughout this chapter I have raised numerous questions related to each of these unresolved issues with the hope of stimulating future research in CD and ODD among children and adolescents.

REFERENCES

American Psychiatric Association. (1980). *Diagnostic and statistical manual of mental disorders* (3rd ed.). Washington, DC: Author.

American Psychiatric Association. (1987). *Diagnostic and statistical manual of mental disorders* (3rd ed., rev.). Washington, DC: Author.

American Psychiatric Association. (1994). *Diagnostic and statistical manual of mental disorders* (4th ed.). Washington, DC: Author.

Angold, A., Costello, E., Farmer, E. M., Burns, B. J., & Erkanli, A. (1999). Impaired but undiagnosed. *Journal of the American Academy of Child and Adolescent Psychiatry, 38*, 129–137.

Angold, A., Erkanli, A., & Rutter, M. (1996). Precision, reliability and accuracy in the dating of symptom onsets in child and adolescent psychopathology. *Journal of Child Psychology and Psychiatry, 37*, 657–664.

Angold, A., Weissman, M. M., John, K., Merikangas, K. R., Prusoff, B. A., Wickramaratne, P., Gammon, G. D., & Warner, V. (1987). Parent and child reports of depressive symptoms in children at low and high risk of depression. *Journal of Child Psychology and Psychiatry, 28,* 901–915.

Bird, H. R., Canino, G., Rubio-Stipec, M., Gould, M. S., Ribera, J., Sesman, M., Woodbury, M., Huertas-Goldman, S., Pagan, A., Sanchez-Lacay, A., & Moscoso, M. (1988). Estimates of the prevalence of childhood maladjustment in a community survey in Puerto Rico: The use of combined measures. *Archives of General Psychiatry, 45,* 1120–1126.

Bird, H. R., Yager, T., Staghezza, B., Gould, M., Canino, G., & Rubio-Stipec, M. (1990). Impairment in the epidemiological measurement of childhood psychopathology in the community. *Journal of the American Academy of Child and Adolescent Psychiatry, 29,* 796–803.

Boyle, M. H., Offord, D. R., Racine, Y. A., & Catlin, G. (1991). Ontario Child Health Study follow-up: Evaluation of sample loss. *Journal of the American Academy of Child and Adolescent Psychiatry, 30,* 449–456.

Campbell, S. B. (1990). *Behavior problems in preschool children: Clinical and developmental issues.* New York: Guilford.

Cummings, E. M., Davies, P. T., & Campbell, S. B. (2000). *Developmental psychopathology and family process: Theory, research, and clinical implications.* New York: Guilford.

Essau, C. A. (1992). *Primary-secondary control and coping: A cross-cultural comparison.* Regensburg, Germany: S. Roderer Verlag.

Essau, C. A. (2000). *Angst und Depression bei Jugendlichen* [Anxiety and depression in adolescents. Post-doctoral thesis]. Habilitationschrift. Bremen, Germany: University of Bremen.

Essau, C. A., Feehan, M., & Üstun, B. (1997). Classification and assessment strategies. In C. A. Essau & F. Petermann (Eds.), *Developmental psychopathology: Epidemiology, diagnostics, and treatment* (pp. 19–62). London: Harwood Academic.

Essau, C. A., Petermann, F., & Feehan, M. (1997). Research methods and designs. In C. A. Essau & F. Petermann (Eds.), *Developmental psychopathology: Epidemiology, diagnostics, and treatment* (pp. 63–95). London: Harwood Academic.

Frick, P. J. (1998). *Conduct disorders and severe antisocial behavior.* New York: Plenum.

Frick, P. J. (in press). Effective interventions for children and adolescents with conduct disorder. *The Canadian Journal of Psychiatry.*

Greenberg, M., Speltz, M., DeKlyen, M., & Jones, K. (2001). Correlates of clinic referral for early conduct problems: Variable vs. person-oriented analyses.

Jensen, P. S., Koretz, D., Locke, B. Z., Schneider, S., Radke-Yarrow, M., Richters, J. E., & Rumsey, J. M. (1993). Child and adolescent psychopathology research: Problems and prospects for the 1990s. *Journal of Abnormal Child Psychology, 21,* 551–580.

Kamphaus, R. W., & Frick, P. J. (1996). *Clinical assessment of child and adolescent personality and behavior* Boston: Allyn & Bacon.

Kashani, J. H., Carlson, G. A., Beck, N. C., Hoeper, E. W., Corcoran, C. M., McAllister, J. A., Fallahi, C., Rosenberg, T. K., & Reid, J. C. (1987). Depression, depressive symptoms, and depressed mood among a community sample of adolescents. *American Journal of Psychiatry, 144,* 931–934.

Kazdin, A. E. (1994). Informant variability in the assessment of childhood depression. In W. M. Reynolds & H. F. Johnston (Eds.), *Handbook of depression in children and adolescents* (pp. 249–271). New York: Plenum.

Kazdin, A. E. (1995). Conduct disorder. In F. C. Verhulst & H. M. Koot (Eds.), *The epidemiology of child and adolescent psychopathology* (pp. 258–291). Oxford, England: Oxford University Press.

Kazdin, A. E. (1997). A model for developing effective treatments: Progression and interplay of theory, research, and practice. *Journal of Clinical Child Psychology, 26,* 114–129.

Kazdin, A. E., & Kagan, J. (1994). Models of dysfunction in developmental psychopathology. *Clinical Psychology: Science and Practice, 1,* 35–52.

Liaw, F., & Brooks-Gunn, J. (1994). Cumulative familial risks and low birth weight on children's cognitive and behavioral development. *Journal of Clinical Child Psychology, 23,* 360–372.

Loeber, R., & Farrington, D. P. (1995). Longitudinal approaches in epidemiological research of conduct problems. In F. C. Verhulst & H. M. Koot (Eds.), *The epidemiology of child and adolescent psychopathology* (pp. 307–336). Oxford, England: Oxford University Press.

Mash, E. J., & Krahn, G. L. (1995). Research strategies in child psychopathology. In M. Hersen & R. T. Hammerman (Eds.), *Advanced abnormal child psychology* (pp. 105–133). Hillsdale, NJ: Lawrence Erlbaum Associates, Inc.

McGee, R., Williams, S., Anderson, J., McKenzie-Parnell, J. M., & Silva, P. A. (1990). Hyperactivity and serum and hair zinc levels in 11 year old children from the general population. *Biological Psychiatry, 28*, 165–168.

Moffitt, T. E. (1993). Adolescence-limited and life-cycle-persistent antisocial behavior: A developmental taxonomy. *Psychology Review, 100*, 674–701.

Nottelmann, E. D., & Jensen, P. S. (1999). Comorbidity of depressive disorders in children and adolescents: Rates, temporal sequencing, course and outcome. In C. A. Essau & F. Petermann (Eds.), *Depressive disorders in children and adolescents: Epidemiology, risk factors, and treatment* (pp. 137–191). Northvale, NJ: Aronson.

Patterson, G. R., DeBaryshe, B. D., & Ramsey, E. (1989). A developmental perspective on antisocial behavior. *American Psychologist, 44*, 329–335.

Piacentini, J., Shaffer, D., & Fischer, P. W. (1993). The Diagnostic Interview Schedule for Children–Revised version (DISC–R): II. Concurrent criterion validity. *Journal of the American Academy of Child and Adolescent Psychiatry, 32*, 658–665.

Puig-Antich, J., & Gittelman, R. (1982). Depression in childhood and adolescence. In E. S. Paykel (Ed.), *Handbook of affective disorders* (pp. 379–392). New York. Guilford.

Reid, J. B. (1993). Prevention of conduct disorder before and after school entry: Relating interventions to developmental findings. *Development and Psychopathology, 5*, 243–262.

Richters, J. E. (1997). The Hubble hypothesis and the developmentalist's dilemma. *Development and Psychopathology, 9*, 193–229.

Sameroff, A. J., Seifer, R., Barocas, R., Zax, M., & Greenspan, S. (1987). Intelligence quotient scores of 4-year-old children: Social-environmental risk factors. *Pediatrics, 79*, 343–350.

Speltz, M. L., McClellan, J., DeKlyen, M., & Jones, K. (1999). Preschool boys with ODD: Clinical presentation and diagnostic change. *Journal of the American Academy of Child and Adolescent Psychiatry, 38*, 838–845.

Weisz, J. R., Donenberg, G. R., Han, S. S., & Weiss, B. (1995). Bridging the gap between laboratory and clinic in child and adolescent psychotherapy. *Journal of Consulting and Clinical Psychology, 63*, 688–701.

World Health Organization. (1992). *International classification of diseases* (10th ed.). Geneva, Switzerland: Author.

Author Index

Subject Index